AF663157

# Terror, Insurgency and the State

## Ending Protracted Conflicts

# *Attention Authors*

Manas Publications is fighting a war to tell the world that India can win the battle not only by the bullet but also by the pen. We are converting fighters into writers. There is no dearth of intellectuals in our country, however, their knowledge is confined to them only. No sincere effort has been made by any other publisher to give the right direction to their knowledge and the talent of every intellectual is lying hidden. An author always presents the raw material in the shape of a manuscript and it is the job of the publisher to convert it to a finished product. Manas has been continually motivating intellectuals and publishing their manuscripts for more than two decades and would like to publish your manuscript too. If you or your colleagues have a manuscript ready for publication or are working on it, contact us with a detailed synopsis and list of contents. Manas will also suggest you a suitable title for writing related to your area of expertise. Manas is known for its publishing quality. We take utmost care in publishing and also give wide publicity to the book and its author through our national and international distribution network.

# *Terror, Insurgency and the State*

**Ending Protracted Conflicts**

Marianne Heiberg,
Brendan O'Leary &
John Tirman

*Published in Collaboration with*
**University of Pennsylvania Press**

**Manas Publications**
New Delhi - 110 002 (India)

**Manas Publications**
(Publishers for Defence, IAS, IPS, IFS, IRS, Press, Judges etc.)
4402/ 5A, Ansari Road (Opp. HDFC Bank),
Darya Ganj, New Delhi - 110 002 (INDIA)
**Ph.: 23260783, 23265523; Fax: 011-23272766**
E-mail: manaspublications@vsnl.com
www.manaspublications.in

© University of Pennsylvania Press, Inc.

2009

ISBN 978-81-7049-354-9
Rs. **995/-**

Only for Sale in: India, Pakistan, Nepal, Bhutan, Afghanistan, Bangladesh, Srilanka, Maldieves, Mauritius, Singapore, Malaysia, Tibet, Burma

All rights reserved. Published by arrangement with the University of Pennsylvania Press. No part of this book can be reproduced or transmitted in any form or by any means, electronic or mechanical, including photocopying, or by any information storage and retrieval system, without written permission from the University of Pennsylvania Press and Manas Publications.

The views expressed in this book are those of the author/editor and not at all of the publishers. The publishers are not responsible for the views of the author/editor and authenticity of the data, in any way whatsoever.

**All Disputes are subject to Delhi Jurisdiction only**

*Typeset at*
Manas Publications

*Printed in India at*
Jaico Printers, Delhi
and Published by Mrs Suman Lata for
**Manas Publications**, 4402/ 5A, Ansari Road,
(Opp. HDFC Bank), Darya Ganj, New Delhi - 110 002 (INDIA)

# Contents

# Preface

JOHN TIRMAN

This volume is the result of a multiyear project involving more than a dozen scholars from around the world—all set in motion and guided by Marianne Heiberg. It was her idea to undertake an in-depth, comparative, and problem-solving analysis of longstanding insurgencies, using scholars who had conducted extensive field research with rebel groups over a number of years. She asked me to join her in organizing this effort from my post at the Social Science Research Council, and I gladly did so. I knew Marianne from our having served as trustees of International Alert, a London-based conflict resolution NGO. I also knew her by reputation, as she had been involved in many peace missions, particularly in the Middle East, and most closely identified with the Oslo peace process in her native Norway. We set out in early 2002, mindful of how terrorism was then being reassessed, and assembled a first rate group of scholars in a workshop in Amsterdam, later convening again in Spoleto, Italy, and Cuenca, Spain.

As we neared the completion of this volume, we were pleased with the emerging results. We had asked our group of scholars to return to the field to ask new questions and refresh their knowledge. The workshops where we examined drafts, formulated challenging queries, and revisited old assumptions were exceptionally stimulating, and a new epistemic community was being created as well. We were poised to complete these studies, with actionable policy recommendations, and to take the results beyond the academy to the policy centers of Brussels, London, Washington, New Delhi, and Oslo, among others. It was conceived from the start as relevant social science research, enriching the gradually developing discourse on conflict and, more importantly, informing the men and women in power who might benefit from these insights.

On 26 December 2004, Marianne Heiberg suddenly died of complications from heart problems. To all of us in this project, and to those many hundreds of friends and colleagues of Marianne's throughout the world, her death was shocking and saddening, and a loss for all people of good will who are dedicated to the non-violent resolution and prevention of armed conflict. Her work as a scholar at the Norwegian Institute of International Affairs (NUPI), one of the world's leading research organizations, reflected that commitment. Naturally, we were quite determined to complete and continue the project as Marianne had first intended.

Among the people she brought into the project from the beginning was Brendan O'Leary, the distinguished international relations scholar who had recently moved from the London School of Economics to the University of Pennsylvania. Upon learning of Marianne's death, Brendan immediately offered to substitute for her in the completion of the volume and the project, and this I gratefully accepted.

The scholars who have written the chapters of this volume deserve the most thanks for their hard work and collegiality. They have brought to this volume an exceptional set of experiences and perspectives, and, we believe, an advance in knowledge based on the field work they have conducted with the rebel groups. Several others contributed in various ways, including Carolyn Nordstrom, Theodor Hanf, and Carla Tamango. We are grateful to Sverre Lodgaard, director of NUPI, for his leadership and confidence. We have been fortunate to have throughout the project the skillful help of Veronica Raffo, program coordinator at the Social Science Research Council, who has been a particularly important contributor, and her colleague, Petra Ticha, who helped organize the early phases of the project.

The Amsterdam workshop in June 2002, where the framework for the project was built, was made possible with support from the William and Flora Hewlett Foundation. The principal work of the project was enabled by generous support from Norway's Ministry of Foreign Affairs. We are particularly grateful to the ministry's Tore Hattrem, who participated in the Spoleto and Cuenca workshops as well.

Edited volumes can be sterile and disconnected affairs. We hope and trust that the exceptional vision and diligence with which Marianne Heiberg galvanized this project, which will go on in several ways during and after publication, are apparent in the lively, in-depth, and prescriptive qualities of these chapters. We are confident that this book, built on new and practical knowledge, can contribute to the peaceful resolution of conflict—a fitting legacy for Marianne to the people she cared about the world over.

*Introduction*

# Thinking About Durable Political Violence

BRENDAN O'LEARY AND JOHN TIRMAN

> *When today's social science has become intellectual history, one question will certainly be asked about it: why did social science, which has produced so many studies of so many subjects, produce so few on violent political disorder—internal war? . . . [B]y any common-sense reckoning the contemporary literature should be brimming over with such studies.*
>
> —*Harry Eckstein,* Internal War

Conflicts may last a very long time. Throughout world history, examples abound of conflicts lasting decades, and there has certainly been more than one Thirty Years' War and, indeed, more than one Hundred Years War. Even after apparently decisive conquests or battlefield victories, many years later brutal engagements may burst out again among the successors of the original contestants. National, ethnic, religious, ideological, and communal antagonists often measure out their time in centuries. Ancestors and descendants, real and imagined, typically figure prominently in their arguments and funeral orations. Yet certain facile assumptions of our time inhibit us from reflecting on these frank truths. It has become too conventional in some circles to reject "ancient hatreds" as having any causal importance, anywhere—or at least in our lifetimes. But this programmatic amnesia is as foolish as the rival vision it rejects, the claim that all conflicts are rooted in primordial animosities recurrently expressed in ancestral voices. Common sense tells us some conflicts may be old, others new, some both, and that others may change their colors and content.

The rash of civil wars, insurgencies, and terrorism that have damaged many peoples and parts of our planet in the last half-century have prompted certain stylized wordings among their reporters and analysts. We have learned to speak of long-lasting conflicts as "protracted," "enduring," "stalemated," or "chronic." These phrasings evince the unsettling conviction that the conflicts in question cannot be terminated short of a complete military victory by one of the protagonists: Israelis or Palestinians, Irish nationalists or British unionists, Basques or Spaniards, Tamils or Sinhalese, Muslim Kashmiris or the Indian state, Acehnese or Indonesians. These polarized dyads, among many others, have become codes for "intractable."

Even such dyadic conflicts end, however, and not always in a unilateral victory. Many of the cases reported here have ended or appear about to end. There may be partial victories. One "warring faction," another of our modern idioms, may emphasize that it was not defeated. There may be shared losses: in not winning many combatants will feel they have been defeated. There may be mutual ruin of the contending parties and their peoples. But there are also negotiated settlements. One critical question for diplomats, practitioners of conflict-resolution, and scholars is how such conflicts can be brought to an end early, before more blood is shed, money squandered, or creative opportunities lost. Perhaps we can learn from the organized political violence of the *longue durée.* Perhaps we might extract and devise policies and practices that optimize the chances for concluding hostilities equitably. Each conflict may have distinctive traits, but each possesses characteristics and tendencies that are universal and that can be turned toward reducing violence and, in the best cases, terminating hostilities with some sense that justice has not been sidelined.

This volume flows from these questions. It is part of the wider political and scholarly challenge to promote better conflict prevention, termination, regulation, and resolution by and within democratic states. Our contributors were asked by the Norwegian Institute of International Affairs (NUPI) and the Social Science Research Council (SSRC) in New York to report afresh from long-standing conflicts. They were to concentrate on insurgent groups that have sustained a violent assault on a state for more than a decade, groups that are not prima facie criminal in nature. The insurgents in question have political programs, legitimacy among a significant portion of the populace, and objectives that may include the overthrow or reshaping of the existing regime or outright secession. Scholars who have undertaken extensive field research into the relevant rebel groups—and the state officials, and sometimes the pro-regime paramilitaries, with whom they have been in combat—write the cases that follow and contributed to the comparisons and conclusions derived from them. Conducting fresh research with objectives and questions forged collectively by our scholars in advance, reanalyzing their data and previous work comparatively, they have generated numerous insights, problem-solving proposals, and critical appraisals of existing governmental and international policies.

The twelve insurgent organizations investigated here, in alphabetical order of their English language acronyms, which also decided our chapter order, are

| | |
|---|---|
| ETA | Euskadi 'ta Askatasuna (Basque Country and Liberty) |
| FARC | Fuerzas Armadas Revolucinarias de Colombia (Revolutionary Armed Forces of Colombia) |
| GAM | Gerakan Aceh Merdeka (Free Aceh Movement) |
| Hamas | Harakat al-Muqawamah al-Islamiyyah (Islamic Resistance Movement) |
| Hizballah | Party of God |
| IRA | Irish Republican Army |
| JKHM | Jammu and Kashmir Hizb-ul Mujahideen |
| JKLF | Jammu and Kashmir Liberation Front |
| LTTE | Liberation Tigers of Tamil Eelam |
| PCP-SL | Partido Comunista de Perú-Sendero Luminoso (Communist Party of Peru-Shining Path) |
| PKK | Partiya Karkerên Kurdistan (Kurdistan Workers' Party) |
| PLA-CPN (M) | People's Liberation Army of the Communist Party of Nepal (Maoist) |

These organizations reflect several different kinds of insurgency.

- Eight have primarily been in combat to win national liberation or national territory. They have either been secessionists, contending with a central government they regard as foreign or hostile to the natives they fight to lead (GAM, JKLF, LTTE, and PKK), or secessionists *and* irredentists who seek to re-unify a partitioned homeland (ETA, Hamas, IRA, and JKHM). As our researchers confirm, many of these organizations may settle—or be about to settle—for less than the immediate secession or re-unification of their national territory. Indeed, in our group discussions only GAM, as reported by Kirsten Schulze, appeared to be insisting that it would accept nothing less than independence for Aceh, but even its leaders suggested otherwise in "negotiations about negotiations" and, as Schulze reports here, finally agreed an autonomy settlement just before we went to press. The social recruitment base and constituency of support of these eight insurgent organizations is nationally, ethnically, linguistically, or religiously defined—although, as Marianne Heiberg reported, ETA had to widen its conception of the Basque nation because of the demographic and linguistic transformations of its homelands in Spain and France, and in no case are the insurgents wholly supported by their constituency of belonging.
- Three of the organizations have been explicitly Marxist. Two are explicitly Maoist (PLA-CPN (M) and PCP-SL), and one is often

regarded as Maoist but in its heyday was officially Marxist-Leninist (PKK). These three organizations, not surprisingly, have rural and peasant bases. Three other organizations have been influenced by Marxism (ETA, FARC, and LTTE), and one has had a Marxist minority among its modern volunteers (IRA). The three Marxist, and the four Marxist-influenced, organizations have all emphasized economic inequalities, class struggle, and socialism. Nevertheless, it is widely agreed that four of these organizations have primarily mobilized on the grievances of a distinct ethnic or national group (ETA, IRA, LTTE, PKK). The same has been suggested of Peru's Shining Path's relations with indigenous peoples, although Marc Chernick reports to the contrary in Chapter 9. The other overt Maoist organization in our collection, the PLA-CPN (M), is commonly associated with the Magar ethnic group in Nepal, but whether this case demonstrates reciprocal support between Maoists and Magars or of one group using the other is not settled, even among Magar intellectuals.[1] Harald Skar, who reports on the PLA-CPN (M) here, considers the Maoists' strength to be largely rooted in low-caste, ex-slave, and underclass grievances—but with a higher status leadership that has experienced blocked social mobility.

- Three of the organizations are explicitly Islamist (Hamas, Hizballah, and JKHM), and one is nationalist and technically Islamist within a state with an Islamic majority (GAM). Of the explicitly Islamist, two are primarily Sunni (Hamas and JKHM), while Hizballah is the party, movement, and paramilitary organization of Lebanese Shi'a. As reported here, by Sumantra Bose and Jeroen Gunning, the JKHM and Hamas developed from the previous defeats of secular nationalist or leftist organizations within the same ethnic base. Hizballah, the most explicitly Islamist organization in formation, emerged within the cosmopolitan religious agenda of the Iranian revolution, but it has, as Gunning reports, reconciled itself to being a stakeholder in Lebanon, and to a distinct variety of Lebanese nationalism. GAM's Islamist character has been highly tactical, Schulze suggests. It argued for the restoration of Aceh's historic sultanate when that seemed propitious, and then for a democratic Aceh when Indonesia and world opinion made that option more likely to garner support. Islam is subordinate to its nationalist agenda.
- Two of the organizations contain secularized Muslims in their ranks and their leadership (GAM and PKK); and two contain secularized and believing Catholics (ETA and IRA). Nepal's Maoists appear to derive at least some of their strength from their programmatic opposition to Hindu caste religiosity and culture (the state is officially a Hindu kingdom). These cases enable our authors to examine the real and alleged relations between religiosity (and its antithesis) in the recruitment and motivation of the insurgents.

- In four of our cases the insurgent organization analyzed monopolizes the armed struggle within its constituency against the incumbent regime (notably LTTE, PKK, PLA-CPN (M), and PCP-SL—although Sendero Luminoso competed with the smaller Tupac Amaru Revolutionary Movement). In three of them the insurgent organization investigated has been the vanguard insurgent organization (ETA, FARC, and IRA).[2] In the remaining cases two or more contenders (e.g., JKLF and JKHM) have been engaged against the regime.

As the foregoing suggests, our initial selection of cases was intended to display considerable variety across national, ethnic, religious, ideological, and class conflicts, and in the organizational environment of the insurgents. Readers will see that we have selected cases where the insurgents are operating within states that, for at least some of the time, were formally democratic regimes, or at least were opening up to become so—as in Nepal's democratization, which preceded the proclamation, or rather reproclamation, of a royalist absolutism. This decision was deliberate. We did not expect the policy repertoire of strongly authoritarian or totalitarian regimes toward insurgents to be surprising or enlightening. We decided to accept the scarcely disputed evidence that such regimes are often able to defeat insurgents with fearsome repression, as may be the outcome, for example, of the Algerian regime's crackdown on the AIG (Armed Islamic Group).[3]

Many other significant conflicts and significant insurgent organizations could have been chosen for our purposes. Our situation was analogous to the story that is told of CIA director George Tenet. He is said to have advised President George W. Bush that if he really wanted to take on all the states that harbored or supported terrorists he'd have "a sixty country problem." Bush's alleged reply, "we'll pick them off one at a time," is not one that we could afford to consider.[4] We could have headed toward sixty cases by treating the insurgency against the Russia Federation in Chechnya,[5] the hybrid Chiapas movement in Mexico, and the numerous organizations engaged in conflict in West Africa, the Great Lakes of Africa, and the Sudan. We did try to obtain African scholars or scholars of Africa with the time and resources to fulfill the project's requirements, but these efforts were regrettably unsuccessful, and that limited the ambitions with which we started. This was not, however, a choice. We were limited by resource constraints and by the desire to work with a viably sized group of researchers that could meet three times as well as communicate through correspondence.

We did make one critical, explicit methodological, normative, and policy decision in case selection. In the interests of an efficient division of labor in research and evaluation we decided not to support a study of al-Qaeda, or of its affiliated network of Wahhabist and Salafi jihadists,[6] even though several of these organizations met the durability criterion. We made this decision to omit for four reasons. First, this field is being well covered and better funded by others, both publicly and in intelligence studies. Second, we believed that thinking about organizations that are not al-Qaeda or al-Qaeda affiliated might be fruitful for comparative explanation, perhaps enabling our results later to be profitably compared with research on al-Qaeda and its affiliates. Third, prescription shaped this omission. We were interested in knowing whether the U.S.-led "global war on terror," launched in reaction to al-Qaeda's massacres of September 11, 2001, has had benign or adverse (or mixed) consequences for the possible settlement of other conflicts, ones in which al-Qaeda's agenda is not directly salient.[7] Conversely, we were interested in exploring whether there may be policy lessons from research on organizations that are not al-Qaeda, of both domestic and international policy value. Lastly, the personal security of our researchers mattered. In the case of al-Qaeda, we did not want to ask a researcher "to go back into the field," as we felt this would be too dangerous.

Overall, given the project's budgetary, logistical, and human limitations, we think the cases initially chosen—and the reduced number that were successfully delivered—provide richness and complexity, and facilitate comparative analyses and arguments that are at least worth debating. Each of our cases met several criteria: the insurgent organizations have been militarily active for at least a decade; the conflicts were ongoing, or at least not resolved, and, as we went to press, we had two cases of successful negotiations (IRA and GAM) and one of apparently decisive defeat (Shining Path). Hundreds if not thousands of people have been killed in fighting, bombings, or assassinations; none of the organizations began as, or transformed into, predominantly criminal enterprises (though certain organizations, particularly the FARC in Colombia, have become deeply involved in criminal activities primarily to raise resources to sustain and expand military and political capacities); and each has been characterized by a significant amount of political violence against civilians—in a word, terrorism.

We need to be clear how we use the term "terrorism" in this book. For us, terrorism is a method, namely, politically motivated violence that deliberately targets civilians, or to be more precise, noncombatants. The insurgents analyzed here have all targeted civilians, at least at certain junctures, and engaged in political violence in which "collateral damage" and intentional damage to civilians have been so high as plainly to breach humanitarian law criteria of just conduct in war. As they have often violently attacked wholly innocent people, not part of the target regime's coercive or policing agencies, and noncombatants, then, by our definition, they have engaged in terrorism. Intentionally striking fear among defenseless populations has been part of their repertoire of methods. They have acted in accordance with the legal definitions of terrorism in the two most powerful English-speaking states, exercising the "calculated use or threat of violence to inculcate fear, intended to coerce governments or societies" (United States), and "the use or threat, for the purpose of advancing a political, religious or ideological course of action, of serious violence against any person or property" (United Kingdom).[8] They have enacted what Thomas Thornton calls "enforcement" and "agitational" terror.[9] Enforcement terror describes the insurgent organization's security system, the disciplining of its members, and the execution or punishment of alleged or real informers to deter them from cooperating with the regime. Agitational terror, by contrast, advances the organization's public agenda. But, the concepts of terrorism, terrorist, or terror, do not exhaustively describe the organizations investigated here, either in their methods, or their goals. These are partly true and therefore partial characterizations. And, as some of our researchers insist, labeling the insurgent organization on which they report simply as "terrorist" blocks understanding and intelligent policy.

Terrorism has often been a tactic justified by the alleged culpability of some section of the civilian population that has affronted the aggrieved group. For example, Turkish teachers were targeted by the PKK in historic Kurdistan precisely because they were deemed to be instruments of the state's coercively assimilationist goal to "Turkify" the Kurds of southeastern Turkey. The IRA widened its definition of "legitimate targets" to include those providing any kind of commercial services to the UK security forces in Northern Ireland because they were deemed to be collaborating with the British war machine.[10] In several of our cases the insurgents' civilian constituencies were targeted in terrorist attacks either by government forces or by pro-regime paramilitaries, and the insurgent organizations sometimes responded in kind—in acts of revenge and deterrence. But the attacks of some of our insurgent organizations examined here have sometimes been more unrestrained, and at times almost random. It is, we agree, a characteristic of "internal wars,"[11] or "new wars,"[12] as current terminology puts it, that a very high percentage of casualties are civilians, rather than soldiers, reversing the proportions that prevailed during the First World War.[13] But terrorism may be finely tuned, deliberately directed at civilians in often spectacular displays of violence. Suicide bombers are now widely known. We have come almost to expect the use of bombs or guns in schools or school buses, or in entertainment venues. These are not collateral killings of civilians but wholly direct and intentional. These resorts to terrorist methods, so socially alienating for their targets and outsiders, are often evident in long-lasting insurgencies.

But we are not, in general, biased toward states and regimes. It is quite wrong to suggest that terrorism is exclusively the weapon of the weak. Our contributors recognize that governments have been the greatest killers of our times,[14] and that state-terrorism—the killing of innocent civilians by governmental forces or government-sponsored proxies—took far more lives in the bloody twentieth century than the terrorism of insurgents. Even putting to one side the horrors of Nazi Germany and the Stalinist Soviet Union, since 1955 major genocides and politicides have been committed by regimes in Afghanistan, Algeria, Angola, Argentina, Burma, Burundi, Cambodia, Chile, China, the Congo, El Salvador, Ethiopia, Guatemala, Indonesia, Iran, Iraq, Pakistan, the Philippines, Rwanda, Serbia, Somalia, Sri Lanka, Sudan, Syria, Uganda and Vietnam.[15] The scope of our project, however, does not include these enormous matters and their attendant moral enormities—although where state terrorism is relevant to our case histories, it is discussed. It is just that our focus is on insurgent organizations and policy responses to these insurgencies.

None of the organizations studied here have generally conformed to what has been called "the Western way of war." Coined by classicist Victor Hansen, the latter idea encapsulates how typical western states and their supporters think war has been and should be fought, namely through open, decisive engagements in battlefields, where the object is the destruction of the foe, and the combatants are disciplined and technologically well-endowed infantry and, ideally, citizens of constitutional polities with embedded traditions of civic militarism.[16] Even though that ideal has, we suggest, often been mythical,[17] it helps us understand something important. The extent to which our organizations depart from the Western way of war partially accounts for the very widespread normative blockages in understanding them. The IRA in its past (in 1916, and during part of the Irish Civil War) approximated the Western way of war, but lost when it did so. The FARC, which emerged from an earlier period of violence, organized itself as a regular army and operated as a conventional force in certain regions and specific historical junctures. Throughout its long history, however, it has primarily operated in ways similar to most of the insurgent organizations treated here. For most of the time, these insurgent groups have avoided formal battles (but not encounters) and have practiced guerrilla warfare, both urban and rural, and, as noted, terrorism. Equally the regimes they have fought have not fought conventional wars, because they could not, and instead have waged "counterinsurgency" or "counterterrorism" operations.

This project, then, had four main objectives:

- To provide detailed analysis of a wide range of groups that practice political violence, the social base from which these groups derive support and recruits, their political economy, the nature of the grievances that motivate and legitimize them, and how these elements have evolved over time in shifting political environments.

- To examine the military, political, legal, and economic policies that governments have used in dealing with armed militants operating on their territories. In particular, to examine which combination of policies have been effective, which have been successful and the political and social costs of policy failure.
- To analyze how governments have responded to the "global war on terror" with regard to its impact on their domestic policies and to assess the effectiveness of these responses in relation to locally based militant groups.
- To propose improved and more effective domestic policies as well as to develop broad international policy guidelines with general applicability to help generate the conditions required to move militants toward nonviolent strategies.

By focusing on the organizations chosen, examining their structure, ideology, support base, and strategies comparatively, we hoped to uncover a number of useful insights for policy makers and academics alike. The long durability of conflict, especially civil wars, is one of the most vexing problems of international relations and peacemaking. By exploring the dynamics from the bottom up—starting in the insurgents' camps—perhaps new knowledge and practical instruments might be forged.

## Current Thinking on Durability of Conflict

Why some insurgencies last longer than others has only recently attracted significant scholarship, and the results helpfully provided frames within which to assess the conflicts we selected. Interestingly, intellectual accounts often follow on real-world events. For example, the conflicts in Northern Ireland, the Basque country, the Balkans, the Middle East, and Central Africa between the 1970s and the 1990s refocused attention on the resiliency of national, ethnic, and religious categories and stereotypes and the burdens of antagonistic histories. Some analysts read these conflicts primordially, others as wholly modern novelties. Some read them as instrumentally manipulated by elites in failing states, others as the legacies and byproducts of recent colonialism or imperialism or globalization. Still others insisted on seeing the hands of sponsored power plays by the major powers. These interpretations were in turn counterchallenged by those who saw such conflicts as the harbingers of religious and ethnic revivals, or of a generalized world anarchy that the end of the Cold War had produced. At least one large-scale analytical undertaking of the mid-1990s essentially claimed that such deadly conflicts could be prevented or resolved by a more energetic application of "political will" by the major powers, one reflection of a post-Cold War optimism.[18] The tendency of many conflicts to resist such political readings and overtures, however, and the recognition of greater complexity in many of the insurgencies of long duration, compelled scholars and policymakers to dig deeper. As Elizabeth Woods summarized matters:

> The marketing of "war commodities" such as diamonds and cocaine by parties to the conflict and by their regional allies contributes to the intractability of conflict. Third party intervention sometimes contributes to a cessation of hostilities. Ethnic polarization where the parties perceive the stakes of war to be strictly indivisible renders negotiated settlements exceedingly difficult. Ethnic violence (particularly in the form of ethnic cleansing), rhetorical manipulation of ethnic fears by political entrepreneurs, the ease of arms and cash flows in the increasingly globalized world economy particularly where states are weak and transfers electronic, and the all-too-often insufficient response of international and regional actors to initial violence—all of these factors also contribute to civil conflict and render peacebuilding difficult.[19]

This summary highlights what we should have known already, namely, conflicts are not so simple, either in causation, regulation, or resolution.

There is, however, one discipline that prizes simplicity, elegant modeling and reductionism, that seeks to cut though knots of rhetorics of identity and history, to focus on the interplay of interests and strategy, namely, economics. The most provocative recent analyses of enduring conflicts have mainly come from econometric research, employing statistical methods to analyze and correlate quantitative data on certain variables (or their proxies). Underpinning the statistics is an old question, *cui bono?* Who benefits? Professor Paul Collier and his colleagues have carried out the most prominent of these econometric studies for the World Bank.[20] In a 2004 summary report, they noted, in keeping with Collier's emphasis on the pecuniary gains that may motivate many insurgencies, that "rebellions have gradually changed their character, becoming less political and more commercial."[21] This alleged fact it is suggested, in the post-Cold War period, is made possible by the globalized economy, the ease of arms purchases, and the like. Poorer countries may suffer longer wars, because the costs of waging them are less, and their states tend to be weaker. "Violence entrepreneurs," they write, "whether primarily political or primarily commercial, may gain from war to such an extent that they cannot be credibly compensated enough to accept peace."[22] They highlight "greed" above "grievance." The economic incentives to sustain war, "lootable resources," are at the center of this analysis—the suggestion is often made that it is also at the heart of the outbreak or origins of such conflicts. One point about illicitness is worth emphasizing, as some of the Collier school do. Many insurgent activities, including looting, but also including rapid attainment of social status, may be possible only during conflicts, and may have few ready substitutes in peacetime. There may be material incentives, in short, which work against conflict reduction. Such estimations, of course, may be just as applicable to the regime's political and military leaders (and their supporters) as they may be to rebels and their constituents. The question of benefits and costs, central to any calculus about prolonging war, is foregrounded by this work. Our researchers were asked to evaluate whether the Collier-style hypotheses held across their cases. We report their generally critical results in the conclusion.

Political scientist James Fearon has also compiled data to draw conclusions on the origins of long insurgencies. He finds three: what he calls "peripheral" insurgencies, near the state's borders, of which "'sons of the soil' dynamics—land or natural-resource conflicts between a peripheral ethnic minority and state-supported migrants of a dominant ethnic group—are on average quite long-lived."[23] Insurgents with access to easily lootable contraband also tend to stay at war. In the case of the "sons of the soil" rebellions, he argues of autonomous regional agreements, the most logical way to settle these disputes, that they tend to fail because the central government must give up so much that it is tempted to renege once the fighting has stopped, or so is the prevailing perception, and it will come under pressure from the migrants they sent in the first place. For those with field experience in studying conflicts it is not news to learn that borderlands or that settler-native disputes over land and resources are likely to be sites of enduring conflicts, but we asked our contributors to evaluate the salience of these matters in their cases.

In subsequent and similar joint work James Fearon and David D. Laitin maintain that the current prevalence of internal wars is mainly the result of a steady accumulation of protracted conflicts since the 1950s and 1960s, rather than a sudden change in the international system associated with the end of the Cold War.[24] They also claim that, "controlling for per capita income," more ethnically or religiously divided states have been no more likely to experience internal wars since 1945. They emphasize instead factors that "favor insurgency," including "poverty" (which marks financially and bureaucratically weak states and favors rebel recruitment), "political instability," "rough terrain" (which favors guerrilla warfare), and "large" populations. Poverty, they think, is important largely because it makes states weak and creates incentives for guerrilla recruitment. They define insurgency narrowly to be "a technology of military conflict characterized by small, lightly armed bands practicing guerilla warfare from rural base areas."[25] In consequence, their treatment may be of little explanatory value in accounting for the duration of ETA, IRA, or even Hamas, while of obvious pertinence for our Maoist insurgencies. All of our regimes versus insurgent conflicts figure in the Fearon and Laitin data set of 127 states (except that of ETA versus Spain—the death toll does not meet their threshold—and, more remarkably, that of Hamas versus Israel, for the same reason). So our case studies may act as checks on their arguments. Whether they are randomized checks as certain methodological protocols might require is another matter. They are random insofar as they were not initially chosen to test Fearon and Laitin's arguments, but our contributors were asked to consider their propositions in their fieldwork.

The approaches of Paul Collier and the World Bank team and Fearon and Laitin are methodologically interesting and technically impressive, and of undoubted heuristic and theoretical value, but we are very surprised that they are so confident about their results. One concern is with their data—what is measurable may have been accorded more attention than that which is not, and they may be too uncritical of their data sources.[26] Another concern has to do with "mechanisms," or "causality." Essentially these results, in both cases, reveal correlations; they demonstrate no causal mechanisms, although, prima facie, they appear to falsify some. The value of our case studies for their work may be that our field specialists can find mechanisms (e.g., explaining who is recruited) consistent with these approaches—or, as is mostly the case, to the contrary. Their perspective also produces a third concern, demonstrated by our contributors. Essentially they treat insurgency exclusively through a "supply-side" prism: insurgents supply revolts, more durably and successfully in certain kinds of niches. Their explicit rejection of "demand-side" explanations may be intellectually controversial, but it is empirically unconvincing (why do the suppliers of insurgency emphasize political, ideological, constitutional, or economic grievances?) and analytically one-sided (why are states—rather than just insurgents—not modeled as suppliers of violent exploitation or predation, a perspective that would seem more consistent with the genre of economic theorizing from which their work flows?). It is one thing to reject grievances as a sufficient explanation of conflict; it is quite another to prove them to be unnecessary in causal explanations across a very wide range of conflicts.

The end and the endgame matter. Numerous analysts have pointed out that peace processes are fraught with uncertainties and the possibilities of strategic deception by either the government or the insurgents. Unlike an interstate war, as Barbara Walter notes, ending civil wars does not allow all contenders to retain armies.[27] As a result, negotiated settlements are difficult, not, perhaps, because grievances or the key issues are irreconcilable or zero-sum, but rather because of the lack of credible commitments to compliance with the respective obligations of the contenders. Such circumstances naturally reduce the willingness to disarm and demobilize insurgents; while without prior disarmament governments are usually unwilling to allow insurgents into negotiation or political institutions. Spoilers are likely to exist. Spoilers can come from any side, and can have sizable institutional power to block peace talks, disrupt cease-fires, hem in political leaders, and otherwise play maximalist cards. Spoilers can be imagined as well as real: agency may be attributed to inactions or actions that were not intended. There may be rogue or dissident elements from the rebel organization, dissatisfied with the compromise of the leaders, and the same may be true within the incumbent regime. The defectors from a settlement may be the insurgents' leaders themselves, spoiling an agreement once made (as with Jonas Savimbi in Angola in 1992).[28] Leaders of both insurgents and regimes may worry deeply about their prospective post-peace roles and treatment.

The role of international agents' benign goodwill is sometimes helpful, not only to correct for the problem of security guarantees, but to overcome potential spoilers or to pacify them. But what gets the "international community" involved in a conflict? In what ways are neighboring states particularly significant? Does the level of integration of a state or region in the global economy indicate the likelihood of international intervention? It was an article of faith among many commentators that the presence of war on the continent of Europe was intolerable, hence the international efforts to bring an end to the wars of Yugoslav succession (albeit with long delays). By contrast, civil wars in Afghanistan, Rwanda, Sudan and other less economically important places were allowed to fester, sometimes to genocidal levels. Economics is not decisive. Although it was said that the United States intervened in Kuwait but delayed in Bosnia because the former has oil and the latter does not, it was not true: the U.S. and NATO eventually intervened in Bosnia. It would seem to matter whether a civil war is occurring in the sphere of influence or interest of a major power, or where norms appear to be more attuned to conflict resolution, but the comparative evidence for this thesis is either thin or, indeed, contradictory. There were military or diplomatic interventions in places that self-styled realists would not have expected, for example, Haiti, Sierra Leone, and Cambodia.

One notable lacuna in the literature on the duration of conflicts is the role of social forces in duration or resolution. We avoid the loaded term "civil society" since there may be more than one civil society in any state and their relations may not be civil. There has perhaps been too much focus on political leaders and political organizations as agents, for example, or on economic growth or topography or demography as structural factors in explaining the duration of conflicts. Are there social forces that tie, and ones that repel? Social forces of varying configurations generally support insurgent groups, others the regime. A social base (and not simply suitably rough or mountainous terrain) is almost certainly a necessary condition of long-standing rebellions. Social forces may be critical in conveying exhaustion with war, demanding peace, and promoting the social and political "space" for compromise and negotiations. Conversely, social organizations may be the carriers of nationalist narratives, ethnic chauvinism, racism, religious bigotry, linguistic prejudice and other mobilized and militant sentiments that block the pathways to a negotiated settlement. Current scholarship has addressed these matters in bits and pieces (as with "spoilers"), or through "how-to" repertories of action for conflict resolution specialists, but the main thrust of those exploring the duration of conflicts has been either a highly strategic or a highly mechanistic treatment that leaves out such seemingly pivotal elements.

The number of studies of rebel insurgents, by contrast, is large, although uneven. A significant literature has grown on the IRA, and, since the September 11, 2001, attacks, on jihadists generally. The ETA, LTTE, and PKK have earned attention for specific aspects of their activity and of course pervasive news coverage and commentary in the countries and regions in which they operate. Many of these works, including extant scholarship, are cited in the chapters of this volume. But many such treatments have tended to be second-hand accounts. The difficulty of doing work with politically violent groups makes field research a rarity, and policy frameworks for problem solving tend to be an afterthought. Comparative analysis is equally scarce. Recognition of this remarkable absence of a full treatment of a large sample of insurgents and the policy implications of how they have been managed or mismanaged prompted this project.

This project is an example of qualitative research. It has, however, numerous observations, many more than the number of cases of insurgent organizations reported here, so it is not in any straightforward sense an example of "small n research." To what extent, however, does it conform to the methodological desiderata of rigorous social science, as set forward in such texts as *Designing Social Inquiry: Scientific Inference in Qualitative Research,* written by Gary King, Robert Keohane, and Sidney Verba? It may (wrongly) be supposed that we have selected on our dependent variable, on the reading that "long-run insurgencies" is that variable. It is true that we selected long-run insurgencies for study (and therefore that no wholly valid causal inferences can be drawn just from our observations on why insurgencies endure, peter out rapidly, or do not occur at all). But that was not our causal purpose.

What our study aimed to assess qualitatively was the impact on long-run insurgencies of governmental policies on political violence, insurgency, and non-state terrorism. Our study is methodologically robust in two respects. First, we sought and obtained variation on our dependent variable, namely the outcome of government policy on long-run insurgencies. We have observations of:

- practically defeated insurgencies (e.g., Shining Path, JKLF);
- defeated insurgency campaigns in which the organization persists, perhaps to return again (e.g., IRA in 1921, 1945, 1962, and perhaps PKK);
- temporary pauses (including multiple ceasefires by many of our insurgent organizations, e.g., LTTE, FARC, ETA); and
- what are likely to be final terminations accompanied by military disbandings (the IRA of today and GAM).

We have multiple observations in which insurgencies have been temporarily demoralized, as well as observations of stalemated persistence of regime versus insurgency conflicts (e.g., JKHM, ETA, FARC, LTTE, Hamas, Hizballah, and the Nepalese Maoists). This variation in our dependent variable enables us to discuss the impact of policy on outcomes with some confidence of reasonable inferences and to establish more observable implications of our hypotheses that are spelled out in our propositional inventory in the conclusion. Second, our qualitative research was rendered essential by the fact that we could not examine the independent (or treatment) variable, namely government policy, with any quantitative confidence, because there are no publicly available reliable databases (domestic or cross-national) on government responses to insurgencies, political violence or terrorism—that is, that systematically code military, police, legal, economic, and other policies. Analysts are obliged, for now, to do what we have done, namely qualitative evaluations of the impact of policy on durable insurgencies, and that represents the formal scientific scope of what is reported here. The reports of our authors can, however, be used to qualify, or falsify some standard theories of causation of insurgencies, which they do, but we make no more claims on the general question of the causation of long-run insurgencies than that.

## The Comparative Framework for Durable Conflict

The value of comparisons is plain and compelling, if not a sufficient point of departure for policy advice—in some respect, each insurgent organization and conflict is unique. But comparisons help both scholars and policy analysts see beyond the most vivid characteristics of a particular case, to reexamine relationships, structures, and histories and possibilities in a new light. In this volume, all the contributors helped to create the research questions and then returned to the field to answer them. All were tasked with seven basic questions, but all were free to add others and neglect ones that seemed irrelevant to their case:

1. What is the nature of the political goals of the insurgent organizations, and how have they evolved over time?
2. What is the nature of the group's leadership and social organization? This query included a subset of further interrogations about the group's internal politics, its degree of internal openness and capacity for compromise.
3. What is the character of the popular base? We assumed that it mattered who supported the rebels, under what circumstances and why in understanding durability, but were prepared to believe otherwise.
4. What is the impact on the larger society of armed militants and internal war? Does war become a way of life?
5. What is the political economy of insurgency? Insurgent organizations need resources and often resort to crime to get them. Diasporas may

affect conflicts most often through financing. What conclusions about the salience of "greed" versus grievance can be drawn from the cases?
6. For the insurgents, what is the role and function of violence?
7. What are the relations between the insurgents and the state? What, most importantly, has been the state's response to the demands and violence of the insurgents? Which policies have worked, and which have not, and why?

Thinking about these questions comparatively yields useful emphases for policymakers. For example, anti-leadership strategies ("decapitation") tend to be most effective if the cohesion of the militant organization is linked to or symbolized by a charismatic leader, such as in the cases of the Sendero Luminoso or the PKK. Regimes may hope that the capture or assassination of such leaders will shatter the insurgents. In organizations such as ETA or Hamas, in which the leaders are not crucial for group solidarity and mobilization, anti-leadership tactics will rarely have the desired impact—and indeed may radicalize militancy through the creation of "martyrs," or through persuading others that it is impossible to negotiate with the regime. Another insight we suggest may be linked to the nature of demands. Ethnic or nationally inspired violence is, interestingly, usually amenable to policy and negotiation, through autonomy, federation or power-sharing; religiously motivated violence, by contrast, may be much less negotiable, and religious cosmopolitan millenarians of the al-Qaeda type are the most problematic of all.

These comparisons, and the problem-solving lessons they suggest, lead to the policy arena. Four main areas of policy were identified and considered appropriately in each case. The first is the *security* realm, the most typical state response. Military strategies as the sole basis for countering insurgency and alternative strategies, such as policing, or mixed strategies (including the use of "third forces") are assessed. The second is *political.* Negotiation, consensus building, constitutional transformations, the capacity of parties to deliver on agreements, isolation of organizations through strategies that work on public opinion within their social base, third party intervention, among other instruments, were considered. The third is *legal.* Repression of insurgencies can include emergency powers, with implications for human rights; censorship of the news media; specialized prison and interrogation policies for the militant groups; constitutional changes that constrain the space needed for compromise, and so on. Again our researchers were tasked to reflect on these. The fourth area is *economic.* Did policies address insurgencies said to be or claimed to be driven by poverty or regional inequality? Were new initiatives promoted to address such grievances?

In the chapters that follow, consideration of these many questions are woven together in analytical accounts of the insurgent organizations, their social bases, the state policies and responses, and the policies that may reduce or end further violence. But we did not ask authors to write their accounts mechanically. Instead, in the conclusion, based on our collective seminars, we will bring together which generalizations seem to hold, and which do not. The concluding chapter attempts to extract our collective comparative lessons for policymakers. This was an ambitious agenda. Undertaken by a collective group with long knowledge of the insurgent organizations and the states in which they operate we hope it will prove to be of wider value. In our collective judgment, this knowledge is a necessary antecedent to wise and plausible international policy on political violence. We have taken care to examine most reasonable perspectives on responding to violence. We are not impressed by the style of response attributed to President George W. Bush, "I don't care what international lawyers say, we are going to kick some ass,"[29] but we are also not persuaded that all the answers lie in international law. We have, as readers of the cases and the conclusion will see, a message, one buttressed by evidence. Grievances matter in explaining violence, and addressing and redressing grievances is not the same thing as surrendering to terrorism. One must be tough on violence and the causes of violence.

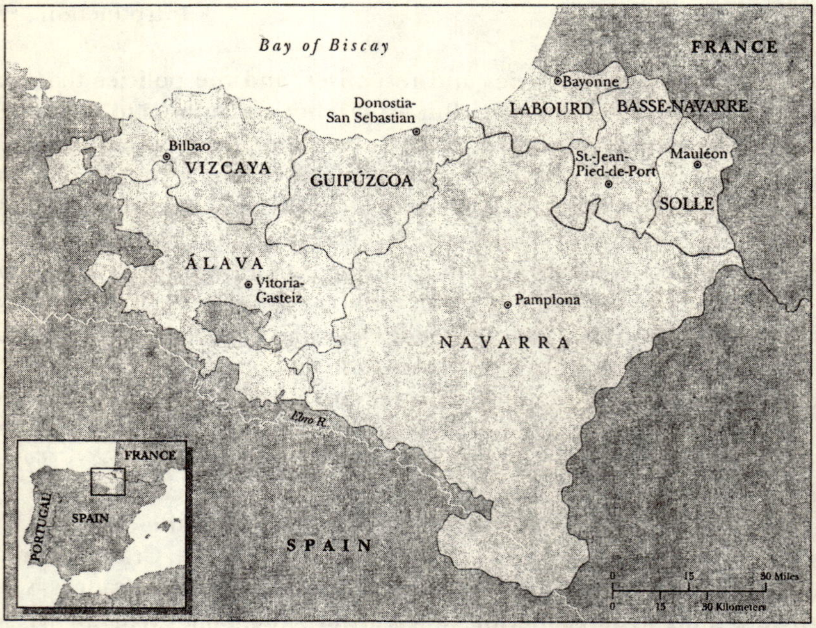


Map 1.1. Basque homeland.

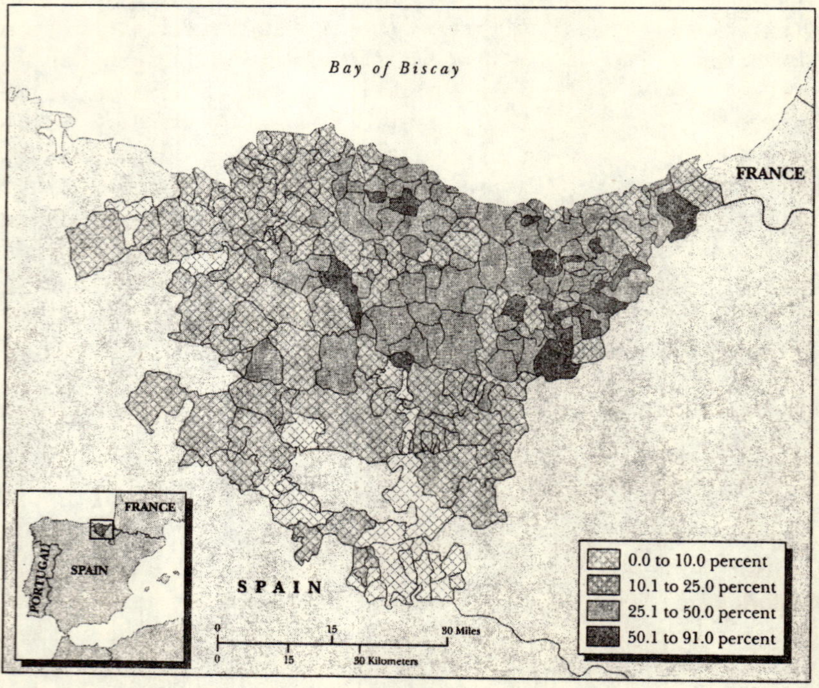


Map 1.2. Distribution by municipality of electoral support for Euskal Herritarrok (formerly Herri Batasuna) 1998 Autonomous Basque Community Parliamentary elections.

*Chapter 1*

# ETA: Redeeming an Arcadia Lost

MARIANNE HEIBERG

## Introduction

If the IRA disbands in Northern Ireland, Euskadi 'ta Askatasuna will be the last major indigenous group in Western Europe waging a continuing campaign of political violence against an incumbent regime. Its violence is currently directed toward those local officials, politicians, journalists, academics, policemen, and judges whom ETA perceives to be its enemies and the enemies of the Basque nation. ETA's violence is particularly difficult to understand for a range of reasons. Over the last thirty years Spain has been transformed into a modern democracy that permits full participation for political parties that advocate independence, provided they do so peacefully. Moreover, the Spanish Basque country is one of the most prosperous regions in Spain and enjoys a remarkable level of regional autonomy, unmatched by almost all regions in Europe. The powers devolved to the autonomous community of Euskadi include authority over matters relating to the Basque electoral regime, public administration, administration of social security, financial institutions, transport, education, culture, the public economic sector, sanitation, public works, and agriculture. In several functions, such as fiscal policy, education and culture, the autonomous region of Euskadi has authorities almost similar to an independent state. Finally, the Basque government and its parliament have been dominated by a constitutional nationalist party, the Partido Nacionalista Vasco (PNV), since the first regional elections in 1980.

The reasons that ETA continues to kill lie in the nature of ETA and its ideology; in the vested interests of organizations that move in the orbit of ETA in its continued existence; in the indirect legitimacy it often receives from moderate Basque nationalists; and, very importantly, the legacy of injudicious central government policy during the transition to democracy.

*Editors' Note:* Dr. Heiberg died suddenly in December 2004 as described in the Preface. This chapter is the draft she had ready in the Fall of 2004. The timeline is not hers; the glossary is.

The conflict in the Basque country is often perceived as an ethnic conflict with ethnic Basques in opposition to ethnic Spaniards. This is only partly true. To be an ethnic Basque, signified by language and/or surname, is not the equivalent of being a Basque nationalist, moderate or radical. The critical cleavages separating the residents of the Basque country are various and often overlapping. The three most important social cleavages separate the rural population from urbanites, those of Basque descent from those who have immigrated from other areas of Spain and, finally, *euskaldunak* (Basque speakers) from Spanish speakers. However, the essential political divide separates a political community—the nationalist *abertzales* (patriots) from the rest of the resident population, nonnationalist *españolistas.* Both of these groups contain urban as well as rural dwellers, those of Basque as well as Spanish descent and Basque and Spanish speakers—although rural *euskaldunak* are more predominant among nationalists. One of Basque nationalism's most revered martyrs, Juan Parades Manot, who allegedly cried, "Gora Euskadi Askatuta" (Long live free Euskadi) as Franco's police executed him, was an immigrant who spoke no Euskera. Conversely, the general secretary of the communist trade unions in the Basque country (CCOO de Euskadi), Josu Onaindi, is a Basque speaker from the Basque rural area. In general each of these two groups has very roughly about 50 percent of the popular vote with a small majority for the nationalists. For political purposes a person is not born Basque. It is a political option, corresponding to an exclusive political loyalty. While all nonnationalists favor regional autonomy, nationalists vary from supporting an even looser association with Spain than currently enjoyed to full independence. However, inside the nationalist community there is another community—that of the radical nationalists, the *abertzales de izquierda* (the left-wing nationalists), at whose core resides ETA. Although active support of ETA is difficult to gauge, the political party close to ETA, Herri Batasuna (HB, Popular Unity),[1] or Batasuna, currently prohibited, has regularly received electoral support ranging from 8 to 20 percent of the vote. HB has never publicly criticized any action of ETA. In broad terms, ideologically this community supports the independence of a unified Spanish and French Basque country, and accepts, at least by its silence, violence as a means of achieving this goal. In short, the conflict in the Basque country does not only involve ethnicity, strictly defined. Instead it centers on a clash between differing political identities and loyalties and the conflicting political projects to which these identities and loyalties have given rise.

## The Origins of Basque Nationalism

The origins of ETA stem from the initial emergence of Basque nationalism. During the last two decades of the nineteenth century, the Basque country, centered on Bilbao in the province of Vizcaya, was subject to two powerful integrative forces that radically changed the political, economic, and social landscape of the region. The first was state centralization. In 1876 Madrid abolished the Basque *fueros*.[2] The *fueros* established custom lines inside the Basque country, rather than along the coast, and constituted a system of political and economic self-government that assured the influence of traditional Basque agrarian elites. The second force was Basque industrialization that took off in earnest at about the same time. Industrialization rapidly transformed the Basque economy from one based on commerce and agriculture to one based on mining, heavy industry, shipbuilding, and banking. Propelled by the massive export of iron ore from the mines surrounding Bilbao, by the end of the century Basque ore comprised around 20 percent of the world's annual output. By 1900, 45 percent of Spain's merchant fleet, nearly all its production of iron and steel, and some 30 percent of its investment capital were in Basque hands.

Basque industrialization created two new social classes—the Basque industrial elite and the non-Basque urban proletariat. The intense rhythm of industrialization demanded an ever-growing pool of cheap, unskilled labor far in excess of that which could be provided by Bilbao or even the Basque country as a whole. Hence, a vast inflow of non-Basque immigrants from the impoverished, rural regions of Spain was pulled into Bilbao. From 1876 to 1900, the population of Bilbao tripled. This demographic crush placed intolerable strains on the social fabric of Bilbao. For the Basque middle classes the whole nature of social life deteriorated rapidly. They experienced a sharp economic decline as many of their traditional businesses went bankrupt. The problems of inflation, urban congestion, crime and a long series of lethal epidemics, due largely to Bilbao's fetid water supply, shattered what had previously been a relatively harmonious and stable community.[3] Although heavily bedecked with the symbols of Basque rural culture and language, Basque nationalism was an urban product designed to deal with the social and economic developments inside the industrializing Basque country. It emerged as an ultraconservative, deeply Catholic and racially exclusive doctrine advocated by Bilbao's preindustrial middle classes. These classes had become marginal with the thrust of industrialization. They felt themselves economically and politically trapped between and threatened by the two main protagonists of industrialization: the Spanish immigrant proletariat and the Basque financial oligarchy.

While social and economic grievances were accumulating among the Basques, simultaneously resentment and rancor were increasing among the immigrant workers in the mines. Lack of basic hygiene, widespread malnutrition, and overwork combined with Bilbao's damp climate made disease among the miners reach alarming proportions. Moreover, after deductions for rent, canteen bills, and time lost to rain or disease, many miners ended the month with little or no pay and often in debt. From about 1890 to 1910, organized by Spanish socialist political parties and trade unions, industrial Bilbao was subject to some 30 partial strikes and 5 general ones, most of which became violent. Indeed, Bilbao—"this Mecca of Socialism"—became the first center of militant socialism in Spain.

In 1893, *La Lucha de Clases* (The Class Struggle), the socialists' newspaper, and *Bizkaitarra* (The Vizcayan), the magazine of an embryonic group of Vizcayan nationalists, appeared for sale on the streets of Bilbao almost simultaneously. Basque nationalism evolved out of Vizcayan nationalism as industrialization, along with Spanish immigrants and socialism, spread to other parts of the Basque country.

Basque nationalism was profoundly backward looking. It was based on a glorification of traditional, religious, Basque rural society and claimed a visceral dislike of capitalist industrialization and all things Spanish, the source of all that was corruptive, immoral and impious. Its ideological aim was complete independence from Spain. Its main supporters were urbanites who had little knowledge of rural society or its language, Euskera. The early Basque nationalists regarded Basque society to be in an advanced state of political and ethnic decay. They viewed the world as morally cleavaged. On the one side were the true Basques who represented tradition, pre-capitalist society, egalitarianism and democracy, peace and social order. On the other were the anti-Basques, consisting of Spanish immigrants, called *maketos*, and the Basque financial elite, who represented modernization, industrial society, hierarchies and authoritarianism, violence and disruption, anticlericalism and spiritual corruption.

The blame for this state of affairs was laid on "that weak and miserable nation, Spain," which the nationalists claimed had humiliated, trampled and debased the formerly independent Basque territories. The solution was clear. The Basque country had to be cleansed of all that was Spanish or Hispanicized. A new and independent Basque country, based on racial purity and traditional Catholic values had to be resurrected. For the nationalists, Spain was not just anti-Basque; it was anti-Christ. Although everything connected to Spain was rejected, for Sabino de Arana, the ideological founder of Basque nationalism, a core target was the struggle against the immigrant, *maketo* invasion. The following passage from his collected works is representative of his views:

> to favoritize the inroads of the *maketos* is to ferment immorality in our land: because it is clear that the customs of our *Pueblo* have notably degenerated in this period, doubtless as a result of the dreadful invasions of *maketos* who bring blasphemy and immorality with them.[4]

Transformed, redecorated and retooled, this intransigent, exclusive nationalist ideology continues to structure how ETA stills perceives its mission. For ETA the main external enemy remains Spain. The internal enemy remains the nonnationalist community resident in the Basque country.

## The Birth of ETA

Until the Spanish Civil War in 1936, socialism and Basque nationalism grew in parallel, each feeding off the other. By the time of the Civil War, El Partido Nacionalista Vasco (PNV) was the dominant political force in the region with the Partido Socialista Obrero de España (PSOE) a close second. Both parties suffered defeat at the hands General Francisco Franco and were forced underground until Franco's death in 1975.

During the Franco period the Basque country was politically repressed—although the scale of repression was not as great as that in other parts of Spain, such as Andalusia. Regarding Basque culture as both symbol and excuse for separatism, the Franco regime issued a range of arbitrary, but often ineffective, regulations prohibiting many overt manifestations of Basque culture. But although the Basques suffered politically and culturally under Franco, economically they thrived. The Basque country became the most industrialized and richest area of Spain. Its inhabitants enjoyed a per capita income close to double the Spanish average. After the much-awaited Allied invasion of Spain following World War II failed to materialize, the PNV became largely passive as its members nurtured nationalist ideology but directed their energies to a new upsurge of industrial growth. This second wave of industrial prosperity pulled a second wave of Spanish immigration into the Basque country.

By 1959, the year ETA was founded, the Basque country was a relatively peaceful, albeit boring place. There was little cultural life or artistic experimentation. Devotedly religious, Basque society was weighted down by factories, bars, and the Catholic Church. The nationalist message had become a family affair transmitted from one generation to the next through "the mother's milk." But there was another carrier of the nationalist message, which was to be of critical importance for the formation of ETA. This was a growing minority of disaffected young Basque priests and seminarists within the Catholic Church.[5] Within the protected sanctuary unwittingly provided by the Church, these priests began to rekindle nationalist activism among small groups of Basque youth. The message was that of early nationalism, the cultural, ethnic, and moral repression of the Basques stemming from an illegitimate Spanish domination. Basque independence was seen as a moral necessity required for cultural, political and spiritual salvation.

There were two groups in particular who took up the message. One group consisted of a dozen or so students in Bilbao, generally from nationalist families. These intellectuals came from well-off professional or industrial families and were, as a whole, Spanish speakers. Many had been seminarists and several were in fact priests. Initially, their main activities were limited to reading articles by the early nationalist writers. These people became organized around a journal called *EKIN*, meaning "to do." This group was to form ETA's initial political leadership.

The second group consisted of youth recruited from the more rural, less industrialized areas of the Basque country. In general priests had recruited them to nationalism. Many of them belonged to the illegal youth organization of the PNV, Euzko Gastedi (Basque Youth). They were usually Basque speakers, had a vocational rather than academic training, were anti-intellectual, and had little patience for theorizing or political nuance of any sort. During the late 1950s these individuals covered the walls and streets of the Basque country with political slogans and propaganda sheets. They were to become the militant, operative base of ETA, a base over which ETA's political leadership rarely managed to gain full control.

In 1959 the two groups merged and ETA was established. It was motivated by resentment at the passivity of the PNV, by protest at the Franco regime, and once again by the "cultural genocide" represented by Spanish immigrants. Unlike the earlier nationalists, ETA abandoned race as the defining concept of Basqueness. Instead it was replaced by Euskera, the Basque language, despite the fact that only about 25 percent of the resident population, and few of ETA's early leaders, spoke the language. Initially, ETA was open to a wide range of political orientations. Although all shared one version or other of nationalism, ETA contained social democrats, Marxists, advocates of producer cooperatives, Catholic humanitarians, Maoists, and so forth.

## ETA, a Third World Movement for National Liberation?

Out of this political pluralism, one factor above all others was instrumental in pushing ETA to the extreme left—the model of national liberation as exemplified in, among others, Cuba, Algeria and Vietnam. ETA argued that Basque nationalism belonged to the revolutionary nationalisms of the Third World. The relevance of this model to the Basque case was most clearly stated in the book, *Vasconia*, published in 1962 by Fredrico Krutwig. Krutwig, a self-taught Basque speaker of Spanish-German descent, first gained public attention when he declared to an astonished audience during the Basque World Congress in 1956 that guerrilla warfare was the only means of liberating Euskadi. Like Sabino de Arana, Krutwig saw a fundamental opposition between Spain and the Basque country; but the terms of the opposition differed. According to Krutwig, Vasconia, which straddled both sides of the Pyrenees, arose as an independent Basque state with the fall of the Roman Empire. The defining element of this state lay in its language, Euskera. The important feature of the language was that it molded thought. Euskera was the motor that forced the Basque speaker to conserve his sense of brotherhood and egalitarianism. Krutwig rejected Arana's argument that the abolition of the *foral* regime marked the beginning of the Basques' existence as a Spanish colony. Instead he argued that the transformation had begun much earlier with the gradual penetration of

Spanish and French capitalism that had drained Vasconia of her resources, introduced a regime of exploitation and produced the struggle between the oppressed and the oppressors. In short, the social and national oppression of the Basques stemmed from the same reality—colonial subjugation. This reality meant that Basque nationalism belonged to the revolutionary nationalism of the Third World. The "colonialist model" gave ETA its ideological framework, military justification and social program. Independence, armed struggle, and socialism were adopted as a package deal.

One addendum filled out this framework. This was the spiral of action-repression-action, which by 1968 formed the justification for ETA's military actions. The aim was to attack the Franco regime in a manner that would encourage the full force of state repression to fall randomly over the Basque people igniting, according to theory, a popular reaction that would become massive and revolutionary. The structure of ETA would be protected from the repression and the organization would prepare militarily for a coup d'état and politically for a takeover of power.

However, the combination of nationalism and socialism in ETA's ideology did not fit comfortably with the economic conditions of Basque life, where capital was largely in Basque hands, and the vast majority of the urban working class of Spanish immigrant origin. In fact the two creeds intersected disastrously. Indeed, popular grievances against immigrants were given renewed vigor during the mid-1960s when the second wave of immigration was at its height. For many young radical nationalists the immigrants were part of a conscious plan by Madrid to wreck Basque society. One of the most ardent advocates of this view was Txillardegi, a founder of ETA and himself of immigrant origins:

> Deprived of Basque political and cultural institutions, the Basque people as such are condemned to disappear submerged by this enormous mass of 20,000 foreigners a year who objectively are at the service of cultural genocide. . . . most immigrants do not realize that they have come to a FOREIGN, OCCUPIED country.[6]

Over the years the contradiction between socialism and nationalism as well as the role of armed struggle would be one of the main factors behind the endless fragmentation of ETA as its more politically minded, open leaders and members were successively hived off the organization. During the 1970s the successive divisions inside ETA filled the Basque political scene with a potpourri of political initials: ETA 6, MCE, ESB, LAIA, HASI, ETA p-m, LAB, and so forth, each of which possessed its own special mixture of socialism and nationalism. In all these splits ETA's military wing managed to retain the ETA name as well as legitimacy. The nature of today's ETA can in part be explained by this process of fragmentation, which functioned to cleanse the organization of all individuals who questioned the absolute primacy of independence achieved through guerrilla warfare over more class-based political action. Currently, uncompromising adherents of radical nationalism dedicated to armed struggle control ETA. Its left-wing pretensions have in general been limited to one of its slogans, "Gora Euskalherria sozialista" (Long live the socialist Basque country), which, in the priorities given to ETA's various slogans, is usually placed last. For many, if not most, of today's militants socialism receives no priority at all.

## The Onset of Armed Struggle

From the beginning ETA decided to open a military front, and in 1959 it planted bombs in Bilbao, Vitoria, and in front of a newspaper office in Santander, causing no casualities. ETA's next military adventure occurred in 1962 when a group of militants attempted unsuccessfully to derail a train taking civil war veterans to San Sebastian. Gradually its activities extended to bank raids and attacks on war memorials, railroad lines, radio transmitters, all viewed as symbols of the Franco regime. The police responded with an accelerating operation of constant road controls, arrests, house searches, and widespread use of torture. In 1968 the first ETA militant was killed. In revenge ETA assassinated the head of the political police in the Basque country, Melitón Manzanas. The government responded by imposing a state of emergency. In the subsequent wave of repression hundreds of alleged ETA militants were arrested, put on trial and given long sentences and at times the death sentence. Sixteen of those implicated in the death of Manzanas, among them two priests, were brought to trial before a military tribunal in Burgos in 1970. Many of the defendants clearly showed signs of torture. The trial sparked an avalanche of national and international protest. The army was placed on full alert for fear of a popular insurrection in the Basque country.

The Burgos trials erased much of the political apathy that had settled over the Basque country since the Civil War. ETA became a symbol of popular resistance to the Franco regime for nationalists and nonnationalists alike, both in the Basque country and in Spain as a whole. Open criticism of ETA was judged as open support for the regime. In the early 1970s ETA's activities expanded to include the imposition of "revolutionary taxation," kidnappings, and ever-increasing attacks on the police and alleged police informers. Under the Franco regime, ETA's spiral of violence culminated with the assassination in 1973 of Spain's prime minister, Admiral Luis Carrero Blanco, Franco's heir apparent. To most of the Spanish democratic opposition, ETA was lauded as heroic. Despite a bomb ETA placed in a cafeteria in Madrid in 1974, killing 12 civilians, at the time few opposition groups recognized the intensely antidemocratic nature of the organization's ideology. Then as now, ETA viewed all those in the Basque country who did not share its goal of Basque independence as the enemies, repressors, and traitors of the true Basque people. Then as now, ETA defined true Basque identity neither in terms of linguistic capabilities, a speaker of Euskera, or by descent, as recognizable by surname. Political loyalty to the cause of Basque independence was and remains for ETA the only marker of acceptable Basque identity. In today's Basque country only those individuals who share this political aspiration can feel secure from potential attack by ETA and its supporters.

## ETA Under Spanish democracy

General Franco died in 1975, and by 1979 Spain had a democratic constitution, full civil liberties and devolution of powers to regional governments. During the transition, the territorial organization of the state was a fundamental issue in drafting the new constitution. On the one hand, demands for ample regional autonomy were strong in both the Basque country and Catalonia and could not be ignored. In the Basque country the PNV insisted that the constitution explicitly recognize Euskadi as a nation endowed with "original sovereignty." On the other hand, the armed forces were antagonistic to any form of autonomy and their potential role as spoiler of the new democratic order was uncertain. Article 2 of the constitution states, "The Constitution is founded in the indissoluble unity of the Spanish nation, the shared and indivisible *patria* of all Spaniards, and recognizes and guarantees the right to autonomy of all its constituent nationalities and regions and the solidarity between them." The Basque country in particular received the most far-reaching self-rule provisions while other regions received more restricted authorities. In the 1978 constitutional referendum, the moderate and radical nationalists joined in insisting on abstention, arguing the clause concerning the "unity of the Spanish nation" denied the Basque country its sovereign historical rights. In conjunction with the referendum ETA unleashed a major offensive that cost the lives of 66 people. One of its more spectacular attacks involved the bombing of the construction site for a nuclear plant in the Basque town of Lemoiz in which 2 died and another 14 were injured. When the results of the referendum were counted, the nationalists combined the 25 percent of the vote opposed to the constitution with the 55 percent who did not vote at all to conclude that the Basque people had not accepted the constitution.

With regard to autonomy, the three Basque provinces of Guipúzcoa, Vizcaya, and Alava became the autonomous region of Euskadi, while Navarre[7] chose to have a separate autonomy statute, which infuriated Basque nationalists in general and radical nationalists most of all. In the 1979 referendum on the Statute of Guernica, the Basque autonomy statute, the moderate nationalists of the PNV campaigned for a "yes" vote, while the radicals, spearheaded by ETA, argued again for abstention largely because the right to self-determination was denied. Once more ETA went on the offensive killing 76 people. The statue was approved by 94 percent of the voters, but the abstention rate was over 40 percent. The following year produced the highest fatality rate in ETA's history: 92 individuals fell victim to ETA's bullets and bombs.[8]

The attempted military coup in February 1981 was partly the result of the frustration felt by discontented elements inside the armed forces with ETA's ongoing violence. In recognition of the fragility of Spain's new democracy, the coup sparked off an intense debate inside ETA concerning the wisdom of further violence. Again ETA split. Its largest faction, which also contained many of ETA's more experienced members, ETA p-m (politico-militar), decided to lay down arms, accept an amnesty from the Spanish government, and in essence dissolve itself. This left ETA confined to its hard-core advocates of armed struggle.

Spain's transition to democracy seemed complete when Felipe González and the Spanish socialists (PSOE) won an absolute majority in the elections of 1982. ETA's most visible response to the consolidation of Spain's democracy was to carry on the killings. The organization argued that unless the constitutional changes it deemed necessary were made, unarmed bystanders would pay the price. ETA began a trend to ever more indiscriminate forms of violence. By 1979 ETA had begun planting bombs in tourist areas as well as train stations. No one was killed in the "beach war," because ETA gave prior notice of the bomb's location before detonation. However, 10 people were killed and over 100 injured in explosions in train stations. In addition to ETA's customary practice of "revolutionary taxation" and kidnapping of those who resisted payment, from 1984 onward ETA began with car bombs killing passersby as well as the intended victims. In 1986 a car bomb in Madrid killed 12 Civil Guards. The following year another car bomb killed 21 and injured 45 people in a commercial center in Barcelona. Assassinations, kidnappings and car bombs have continued until recently, although between 1990 and 2004 fatalities rarely exceeded more than 20 per annum. ETA has also assassinated moderate nationalists whom it felt collaborated too closely with the Spanish government. Placing bombs in Spain's resort areas has become a summer routine.

But perhaps most significantly, from around 1994 ETA adopted a new strategy under the slogan, "Socialize the Suffering." Instead of confining its victims mainly to the security forces and military, ETA began targeting an ever-widening circle of civilians: journalists, local politicians, lawyers, judges, and academics. Although ETA had killed local politicians previously, in 2002 ETA announced that the offices and organized meetings of the governing party, Partido Popular, as well as PSOE would be viewed as "military targets" and threatened the lives of all party activists. The campaign against journalists has been typical of the methods used by ETA. Called "Basque traitors" or "Spanish invaders" or in one case "terrorists of the pen,"[9] several journalists have been killed, many have been injured by failed assassination attempts, letter bombs, and Molotov cocktails, and an untold number have fled the Basque country for the relative safety of Madrid. The family members of journalists have often been threatened. The offices of eight newspapers have been bombed. An estimated 100 journalists currently require bodyguards, including several who work from Madrid. In 2003 when the campaign was at its height, Spain was ranked 43rd among 166 countries in terms of press freedom by Reporters Without Borders, because of the difficulties journalists face in the Basque country.

"Socialize the Suffering" also sparked a new phenomenon in the Basque country called *kale borroka,* "street struggle." In what was once almost a daily ritual, gangs of hooded youth, sympathizers of radical nationalism, terrorize the streets while vandalizing the property of "anti-Basque traitors" using firebombs or any other means of destruction available. *Kale borroka* together with ETA succeeded in paralyzing the democratic process in the Basque country. Their targets were the pillars of democracy. The Basque country became divided into two—those under threat and those who shared ETA's goals and received immunity. *Kale borroka* created an intense climate of fear. A significant majority of non-nationalists as well as about one-third of nationalists say they are afraid to participate actively in political life.[10] These hooded teenagers also provide ETA with a recruiting ground. In fact, many view participation in the "street struggle" as an obligatory *rite de passage* for potential ETA membership.

Open public reaction against ETA grew slowly. Demonstrations started in 1987 after the signing of two antiterrorist pacts, to be discussed, and increased in size with each new assassination. However, the turning point in public attitudes came in 1997 when ETA kidnapped a young councillor from the Partido Popular, Miguel Angel Blanco, killing him some two days later. Massive demonstrations in all of Spain as well as the Basque country mobilized six million to the streets in protest. In the wake of these demonstrations a series of civil society organizations were established in the Basque country, which were not only opposed to ETA, but also critical of nationalism in general. One function of these new organizations was to integrate nonnationalists behind the demand for peace as well as equal social and political legitimacy.

Currently more than 1000 people in the Basque country require 24-hour security protection because of ETA's threats. Many more have received threats, including all members of the Basque national police, the Ertzaintza. In all ETA has killed over 800 people, approximately half of whom have been civilians, the remainder members of the security forces. The armed forces have lost 20 generals in the battle with ETA, more than Spain has ever lost in a single military campaign. Additionally, ETA has kidnapped 77 individuals, one of whom was held for 532 days and several of whom were assassinated. The costs of property damages and extra security expenses incurred because of ETA activities until 1997 is estimated at some €6 billion.[11] Various studies have estimated that without ETA the GDP of the Basque country would have been some 10 to 25 percent higher. Of the ten to fifteen thousand militants ETA claims to have had over the years, some 180 have also been killed, 36 by the premature detonation of their own bombs. Currently some 700 ETA militants are in prisons dispersed throughout Spain and France and another 600 live in exile, mainly in Latin America.

## Inside ETA

In part because of the polarization of the Basque country and in part because of their clandestine status, ETA sympathizers spend most of their time confined to the political, cultural, and social environment created by radical nationalism. This isolation enables them to perceive the wider, surrounding environment one-dimensionally, immune to realities and opinions that do not fit their views. Combined with their intense concern with security, this isolation also induces highly binding in-group solidarity.

ETA's adherents claim with great passion that nothing actually has changed in the Basque country since the days of Franco. Indeed they view Spanish democracy with derision and dismiss it as fraudulent. While the authoritarian Franco regime, they argue, repressed the Basque people heavy-handedly, the new regime does the same thing, but with more subtlety and skill. It is "reformed Francoism." The Spanish constitution with its clause asserting the "unity of the Spanish nation" continues to deny the Basque people their inherent historical right to self-determination, a key ETA demand. The fact that the Statute of Guernica separated Navarre from the rest of the Spanish Basque country is used as just one indication of Madrid's "genocidal strategy against our *Pueblo.*"[12] In its many communiqués ETA states that all political opinions present in the Basque country need to be respected and consulted to reach a resolution of the conflict. However, this alleged broadmindedness collides with its frequent threats, often with a deadly outcome, against all those who do not support ETA's political project. In reality, ETA conceives Basque plural society as distorting and deforming true Basque cultural identity. Until independence, ETA contends, Euskalherria (the Basque country consisting of the 4 Spanish Basque provinces and the 3 French ones) will remain exploited, imprisoned colonies of Spain and France, denied its historic personality and political rights.

ETA's insistence on the right of self-determination is not the same as insistence on a referendum on independence. ETA is well aware that support for independence is weak in Navarre, and majority support is unlikely in any of the other three Spanish provinces with the possible exception of Guipúzcoa. Opinion polls indicate that only about one third of the resident population favor independence.[13] In the French Basque country, Basque nationalism is marginal. Instead the right to self-determination is a basic right of the Basque nation because of its status, according to ETA, as a colony repressed by Spain and France. ETA sympathizers frequently use organic imagery to describe the devastation brought upon the Basque people because of their colonization. One person described it as being born and living without arms in a country where people thought this was a normal state of affairs. When asked why ETA could claim to represent the entire Basque people when only an average 16 percent voted for Herri Batasuna, an ETA sympathizer expressed a commonly held view.

> Many of our people do not vote for us because they are afraid. But that's not the point. Because our historic personality has been denied to us, many Basques simply do not know who they are. If you asked 100 women to cast their ballots on the issue of whether they are men or women and you found that 80 of these women said they were men, what would you think? Issues of identity, of national gender are not decided by the ballot box.[14]

ETA tends to recruit from the towns and villages of Vizcaya and Guipúzcoa. Few come from Álava and even fewer from Navarre. These are localities in which high levels of social control and repression of dissent can be exercised by small social and cultural networks, often developed in childhood, which in the Basque country are called *cuadrillos.* ETA militants tend to be young, between eighteen and twenty-six, male, unmarried and mostly possess a secondary or vocational education. Some are employed as workers in middle level white-collar jobs, but the majority work as unskilled laborers, or, in particular, skilled laborers in the industrial or commercial sectors. Some 16 percent are students. Almost none come from the established upper or urban middle classes. However, there seems to be no correlation between ETA militancy and relative deprivation, and ETA support is not related to high levels of unemployment or other economic indicators. Notably ETA has also managed to recruit many youth with immigrant backgrounds. Some 53 percent of ETA militants have two Basque surnames, indicating Basque descent through both the maternal and paternal lines, 23 percent only one and, very notably, 23 percent have no Basque surnames at all.[15]

ETA has some 100–200 active members with different degrees of affiliation with possibly another 200–300 individuals in subordinated roles.[16] However, those who provide ETA with implicit or explicit support, as measured by the percent of votes given to Herri Batasuna, is significant. On average the party, before illegalization, received roughly 16 percent of votes cast in the Basque country during the post-Franco period.[17] ETA exerts critical influence on the HB leadership, but it would be misleading to conclude that all supporters of HB are also supporters of ETA. Although the vast majority of individuals supportive of HB share ETA's ultimate political goal of incorporating both the French and Spanish Basque country into an independent state, not all them approve of ETA's violent methods. However, public criticism tends to be muted, infrequent, and never official and direct criticism expressed mainly in private.

HB supporters, *abertzales de izquierda,* come from almost every sector of Basque society, although young people from the more recently industrialized areas of the Basque country predominate. ETA views the *abertzales de izquierda* as its loyal political base. These radical nationalists also constitute a parallel community articulated by a dense network of civil society organizations. It has its own youth organizations, mountaineering clubs, cultural societies of all sorts, women's associations, newspapers, publishing houses, musical groups, pro-amnesty groups, trade unions, festivals, and cafes, the *herriko tabernak.* They play a leading role in the *ikastola* movement (schools in which Euskera is the language of instruction) through which they can transmit the nationalist message to younger generations. They can be counted to mobilize in large numbers in raucous demonstrations protesting most government policies dealing with the Basque country. It's this sense of solidarity of purpose, strong sense of identity and ability to mobilize its social infrastructure that gives the nationalist community in general and the radical nationalist in particular a political power far in excess of its electoral support. The hard core of the radical nationalists, mainly underage young men, forms the backbone of *kale borroka* attacks.

Death and martyrdom are constant themes in conversations with ETA. At times it seems that ETA sympathizers view the world mainly through the prism of death and violence. In the bars frequented by ardent ETA sympathizers, heroic pictures of ETA martyrs usually grace the walls. Outsiders are inevitably given detailed accounts of the circumstances under which these individuals made the supreme sacrifice of their lives for the sake of defending the rights of the Basque nation. Previously in meetings with HB officials, thick volumes containing pictures of ETA martyrs and those mistreated or tortured under police interrogation were often produced. The viewer was expected to linger with deference over each photograph, like fine art. These are rituals with thick religious, sacramental overtones, which arguably make ETA similar to more overtly religiously defined movements. For those committed to the armed struggle ETA involves the full person in all his or her roles and offers an absolute vision of a moral, political mission and requires absolute loyalty to that mission. Former ETA members who have refuted armed struggle for government amnesty are viewed as traitors as well as "liquidationists" (ETA's term) and have been frequently threatened, on occasion killed. They have trivialized and betrayed the martyrs and the suffering endured. ETA hardliners have little tolerance for ambiguity, doubt, compromise, or change.

I once asked an ETA member why he was so fond of guns. After a few seconds, he simply answered, "Power." In many ways ETA's violence is not only a means to an end. It has become an end itself. ETA is an organization dedicated to armed struggle. It sees itself at war with a militarily superior, but a morally inferior enemy. Asked about the deaths of civilians, ETA tends to reply that very regrettably in wartime innocent civilians often get caught in the cross fire. But its definition of innocence is a narrow one. As the few attempts to negotiate with ETA have confirmed, its political agenda is absolutist, rigid, and uncompromising. Without the armed struggle, ETA would simply cease to exist. Violence produces the group dynamics that enables ETA not only to survive as a tight, socially integrated organization, but also to reproduce. It is a means by which the sacrifices of the past can be vindicated and the martyrs of tomorrow created. Violence gives meaning, total identity, cause, and solidarity. In many ways ETA is like a closely bonded primitive kinship group with a cherished history and ancestors, its own enclosed belief system, values, and rigorous requirements for group defense. ETA members live in a clandestine mindset that views the world as severely polarized between Basques and anti-Basques. Violence reinforces this polarity and makes it absolute.

## ETA—A Complex of Organizations

Initially ETA *militar* was a somewhat diffuse, loosely organized, nonhierarchical organization.[18] Its central leaders often had only tenuous linkages to the small, semi-autonomous cells in which its militants operated. After every wave of arrests ETA would reorganize to give the political leadership closer control over the militants in order that their activities better conform to a single, understood and agreed upon strategy. Today's ETA is strictly hierarchical with ETA leaders, usually resident in France, in total control over the various commando units which generally consist of three people. Although most commando units operate inside the Basque country, units have also operated throughout Spain, especially in Madrid. Communication between commando units is difficult, if not impossible. All communication concerning, for instance, money, weaponry, bombs, logistics, targets, and so forth, goes through vertical links to the central leadership. Although this form of organization has been necessary for central control over ETA's militants, it has also seriously undermined ETA as a clandestine organization. When an ETA leader is arrested the entire chain of command downward also tends to fall. Conversely, when a militant is detained, the chain of command upward tends to be dismantled.

Although ETA is vertically organized, it does not possess one chief leader nor is it dependent on any specific leader. The various sectors in ETA, information, logistics, international relations, and so forth, each have their own leaders. Each leader coopts his collaborators. When the leader is arrested, the person next in command takes over and is in turn free to choose his own collaborators. The various sectoral leaders of ETA are viewed as equal and together they comprise ETA's executive.

ETA does not have any clear, formalized recruitment procedures. Instead, individuals tend to be brought into the organization through prior, close social relations, often going back to childhood, with existing members. Many, if not most, have belonged to the various youth groups associated with radical nationalism or participated in *kale borroka.* Many post-Franco ETA militants have also been recruited through the parental generation who belonged to ETA under Franco and whose stories of ETA's heroism provided inspiration.

Economically ETA has been dependent on three main sources of financing. The first was bank robbing, which since the 1980s has largely ceased because of better security at banks. The second has been kidnapping, which was a highly lucrative source of revenue but has now stopped, possibly because ETA no longer possesses organizational capacity for such complicated operations. The third, and by far the most important, continues to be "revolutionary taxation." This comes in two forms. The major form of extortion consists of letters sent by ETA to Basque businessmen demanding a fixed sum, usually significant. The second form consists of envelopes distributed by radical youth to the bars and small businesses throughout the Basque country. The owners of these establishments are well aware that a contribution is obligatory or serious consequences could ensue. ETA's annual income is impossible to estimate with any accuracy, but the Spanish Ministry of the Interior believes it to be in the order of some €15 million per year.

For ETA, 1991–1992 were defining years. It was planning a campaign of massive, high publicity attacks on the International Expo in Seville, the Olympics in Barcelona, as well as the 500th Anniversary of the Discovery of America. In the belief that international opinion was supportive of Basque independence, the aim was to foster international pressure on the Spanish government to negotiate with ETA. Although ETA did not manage to carry through any spectacular attacks, smaller actions caused around fifty fatalities. ETA believed international help was at hand, but in fact international governments, particularly France, were helping Spain. In March 1992, in the town of Bidart in southern France the entire ETA leadership and the majority of its commandos in Spain were arrested in one day. Some two months later the entire substitute leadership was also detained. In the wake of these arrests more ETA commando units fell. ETA as well as most of the *abertzales de izquierda* feared that the entire organization could be dismantled. Certainly its ability to carry out military actions had been severely curtailed. With ETA's leadership disseminated, individuals connected to ETA, but not part of its military structure, took over and instituted a new strategy, "Socialize the Suffering" accompanied by street struggle, *kale borroka,* discussed previously. From 1993 to 1998 there were some 6,000 acts of political violence on the streets of the Basque country, injuring some 400 people and costing an estimated € 90 million in property damage.[19] More than 650 attacks occurred in 2000 alone. It was during this period that ETA starting killing politicians as well. However, lacking neither potential recruits nor economic recourses, ETA managed to regroup, albeit under less experienced leaders.

ETA is more than just an armed organization. It is the backbone of a constellation of interlinked organizations. Initially ETA was organized into four fronts: military, cultural, political, and workers, with the military front in explicit or implicit control. The weakness of this front organization was quickly revealed when arrests in ETA's nonmilitary fronts led to arrests of ETA's military commandos. A constant challenge for ETA has been how to protect its military wing while simultaneously conducting a wide range of public activities aimed at mobilizing and expanding radical nationalism as well as making its violence more politically effective. In 1974 ETA created what it called the Movimiento de Liberación Nacional Vasco (MLNV), consisting of the civil society infrastructure of radical nationalism. In the same year ETA founded the Koordinadora Abertzale Sozialista (KAS), designed as the central coordinator of the many activities of the MLNV. KAS consisted of labor organizations, cultural organizations, youth organizations, and a political party (HASI) as well as ETA *militar.* HASI acted as ETA's political front. Although KAS consisted of various organizations, ETA retained ultimate decision-making control. In 1978 HASI and ETA created Herri Batasuna, (HB) as an electoral coalition to contest the general elections of 1979 in which HB received 15 percent of the popular vote.

HB and ETA have had an instrumental relation with the former subordinated to the latter. The electoral lists of HB have frequently contained the names of ETA prisoners. ETA has had the final word on important HB parliamentary votes and decisions, for instance, whether or not to take up its seats. Businessmen who wish to pay their "revolutionary taxes" often go to the local offices of HB in order to arrange transfer of funds to ETA. HB has the same political goals as ETA and has never criticized any act of violence. Until it became illegal, HB had participated in all elections held in the Basque country and enjoyed the immunities, public subsidies, and privileges that came with elected office. However, even when all nonnationalist candidates and representatives were under threat of death from ETA, HB remained resolutely silent. The full weight of evidence concerning the linkage between ETA and HB was presented in a lengthy, detailed report of Judge Baltasar Garzón, written in 2002 suspending the activities of HB. Judge Garzón argued that ETA and HB were in essence the same, and their combined activities made democracy in the Basque country impossible. His findings were confirmed by both the Spanish Constitutional Court and Supreme Court, which prohibited HB permanently in 2003. Needless to say, the leaders of HB staunchly deny any relation to ETA whatsoever. However, even in the small, nationalist villages and towns of the rural areas, the illegalization of HB came as a relief.

In a sense the evidence Judge Garzón presented merely confirmed what many, if not most, people in the Basque country—nationalist and nonnationalist—already knew. Not only did ETA control the leadership of HB, but also ETA was like an octopus, with controlling tentacles penetrating into many of the organizations articulating the radical nationalist community. In addition to HB, seven other organizations as well as a range of commercial enterprises were also made illegal.[20] These include organizations charged with making the Basque cause known abroad, mass media outlets, an organization involved in teaching the Basque language, pro-amnesty organizations, youth organizations, as well as the entire network of *herriko tabernak* (bars of the people, some 120 in all).[21] Garzón's report traces the multiple memberships between these groups as well as their ties to ETA. He also documents how money raised by, for example extortions, finds its way to Latin America in order to support ETA exiles or to finance the newspaper, *EKIN*, also banned. The *herriko tabernak*, for instance, are not just radical nationalist bars, they are also the property of the local HB committees and operate as the local centers for radical nationalist youth groups, such as HAIKA, widely regarded as the youth organization of ETA, and are often used to prepare *kale borroka* attacks. These are the same youth who locally enforce the boycotts of establishments that have failed to "to contribute to the national reconstruction of *euskal herria*"—that is, refused to pay "revolutionary taxes"—or, hooded, firebomb them.

When ETA began its campaign of political murder, local reaction was shock and incomprehension. In traditional Basque society, unlike Andalucian society for instance, personal violence was abhorred. The appropriate manner to deal with conflict and disputes was through avoidance. Under pressure of ETA's campaign, violence has to some extent become normalized in Basque society, especially among the younger generations. In schools and universities, in the workplace and on the street people resort to violence with an ease that would have been unthinkable and definitely censured two generations ago—and indeed did not exist. This generalization of violence has produced a marked deterioration in many spheres of Basque social life. Many people view the outside world as uncertain and unsafe. Increasingly people confine their social activities to family and small networks of friends. Social life has become much more privatized, trust extended hesitantly. Conversations on sensitive issues in public places are conducted guardedly.

## Moderate and Radical Nationalists—An Implicit Collusion

Almost since its inception at the end of the nineteenth century, the Basque nationalist community has had two political expressions, the moderate, centered on the PNV,[22] and the radical, today with ETA at its core.

In the first general elections of the new Spanish democracy in 1977, it was assumed that the PNV, resurrected from its former passivity, would be the absolute victor. Hence, it came as a staggering surprise that Partido Socialista de Euskadi (PSE, PSOE's Basque branch) emerged as the single largest party in the Basque country. However, inside the Basque country the election results had little effect. The PSE may have gained the votes, but the PNV, embedded in its tightly knit nationalist community, retained real social power. The PSE was unable to capitalize on its electoral position, and by the next general election some two years later the PNV regained its position as the largest political party in the Basque country, a position it has held—at times with only a very slim margin—to date.

Although frequently bedecked by separatist rhetoric, most loudly proclaimed by many of its grass-roots members, the moderate nationalist leadership has mainly sought to gain the most favorable autonomy possible for the Basque country in relation to Madrid. Opinion polls indicate that only about one half of PNV members share the radical nationalists' insistence on full independence.[23] However, both moderates and radicals have been allied in striving to endow the nationalist community with exclusive political legitimacy both inside the Basque country with regard to nonnationalist opponents and in relation to Madrid with regard to negotiating autonomy. As a result, on vital issues that concern the balance of power in the Basque country or critical relations with Madrid nonnationalists have often been forced to validate their "Basque" credentials and, thereby, have been placed on the defensive regardless of electoral support.

Many ETA members had been recruited from the PNV's youth branch, and bonds of kinship and friendship unite individuals in the two organizations. Although many in the PNV feel an intense anguish with ETA's increasingly violent methods, there remains an emotional sympathy with ETA's struggle to revindicate sovereign Basque rights. Throughout the post-Franco period, the PNV's attitude to ETA has been marked by ambivalence and oscillation. In part this ambivalence was necessary to appease many of the PNV's grass-roots supporters who shared ETA's separatist goal. Regardless, the PNV and ETA have explicitly or tacitly cooperated to achieve mutually beneficial aims. During the constitutional referendum, both organizations called for abstention and argued afterward that the results meant that the constitution lacked legitimacy in the Basque country. In its negotiations with Madrid concerning the autonomy statute, the PNV frequently linked the cessation of ETA's attacks to the government's acceptance of nationalist demands and successfully forced the government to grant more concessions than initially intended.

Although the PNV has often used ETA's violence to strengthen its bargaining position vis-à-vis Madrid, the relation has also provided ETA with an asset that has legitimized, in the eyes of its supporters, its transition into the democratic period. The PNV's arguments against the constitution and against the autonomy statute reinforced ETA's belief that nothing really had changed and the revindication of Basque rights could never occur within the institutional framework of Spanish democracy, which ETA dismisses in any case.

Despite ETA's violence in the early 1980s, the PNV was hesitant in issuing condemnation. The condemnation that was offered was always conditional and linked to Madrid's alleged failure to respect Basque rights. According to the PNV, ETA's violence was lamentable, but understandable in light of the government's misplaced policies. The first unequivocal condemnation came in 1985 when ETA assassinated a member of the autonomous Basque police force, the Ertzaintza.

A shift in the PNV's attitude seemed to occur in the late 1980s when the party together with all other parties in the Basque country, except those representing radical nationalism, signed two important antiterrorist agreements, the Madrid Agreement of 1987 and the Ajuria Enea Pact.[24] The combined effect of the two agreements, among other things, denied ETA legitimacy in dealing with the political problems of the Basque country, recognized the importance of the autonomy statute, insisted that the incorporation of Navarre into Euskadi was a decision reserved for the Navarrese themselves, and, very important, rejected any dialogue or negotiations with ETA or HB until violence had been abandoned.

However, this shift was more apparent than real. For a range of reasons, some relating to Basque domestic politics, the consensus established by the Madrid Agreement and the Ajuria Enea Pact began to unravel along its nationalist/nonnationalist fault lines. On several occasions, such as a dispute concerning the route of a highway connecting Guipúzcoa and Navarre, the PNV agreed to negotiate with Herri Batasuna and, thereby, with ETA. ETA exploited the concessions offered to reinforce its self-declared position that its violence was effective in defense of the rights of the Basque people.

The consensus concerning Basque violence grew progressively thinner. It ended in 1998 when the PNV *lehendakari*, or president of the Basque government, put on the table a peace plan. The plan proposed that negotiations should be initiated between all the Basque "democratic" parties as well as HB in order to arrive at a settlement of the Basque conflict. It also proposed that the Madrid government and parliament should automatically respect all agreements reached. The nonnationalists immediately dismissed the proposal as unconstitutional since the autonomy statute could not be altered unilaterally. Moreover, for both the Basque socialists and conservatives of the Partido Popular negotiations with HB was an anathema. In reply the PNV argued that it no longer felt bound by its obligations under the Ajuria Enea Pact to isolate HB and started negotiations anyway.[25] These negotiations aimed at exploring the possibility of forming a nationalist front in order to reclaim *soberanismo* and *territorialidad,* nationalist shorthand for independence and the unification of the Spanish and French

Basque country. The negotiations led directly to the Lizarra Pact of September 1998 and ETA's first and only ceasefire, to be discussed below.

Several factors lie behind the PNV's rapprochement with radical nationalism. From the middle of the 1990s onward, most of the provisions of the Statute of Guernica had been implemented and, therefore, the PNV's frequent denouncements of the lack of goodwill on the part of Madrid began to ring hollow.[26] Moreover, the conservatives of the governing Partido Popular were slowly encroaching into the PNV's political support and were overtaking the Basque socialists as the largest nonnationalist party in the Basque country. By 1998 the Partido Popular placed second in the elections to the Basque parliament. Finally, ETA and *kale borroka* had started attacking PNV offices and officials in what ETA termed the *pedagogía de la violencía* in order to force the moderates to realign their position. Specifically ETA wanted the PNV to break with all Spanish parties and abandon support for the Statute of Guernica. The PNV faced a critical choice if it wished to gain more autonomy than the Statute of Guernica allowed and to cement its position as the central coordinator of Basque political life. On one side, the constitutionalist, *españolista* parties regarded the statute as a permanent arrangement and were not interested in a renegotiation. Moreover, the combined electoral support given the PP and the PSE surpassed that of the PNV. The PNV believed further collaboration would lead to a dead end and possible stagnation of the party itself. On the other, despite ETA's continuing violence and the key role of ETA in the leadership of HB, the electoral support for the radicals was large and loyal and the political projects of the moderates and radicals, if not exactly the same, at least overlapped. Although secret discussions had been conducted for some time, in August 1998 the PNV, together with Eusko Alkartasuna (EA), another nationalist party, signed a secret agreement with ETA. The following month the Lizarra Pact was signed and ETA declared an indefinite ceasefire.

The Lizarra Pact takes as its starting point the Northern Ireland Good Friday Agreement and applies it to the Basque conflict. It defines the Basque problem as a "historical political conflict in which the Spanish and French States are involved." It states that "after guns are silent and the conflict caused no violent expression," "a political solution can only be found through an open process of dialogue and negotiation or inclusive talks, that is, talks that include all the parties involved and respect participation of the Basque people as a whole." It goes on to state that this process would further "democracy by providing the Basques with a voice and by making the States in question respect their decision. The Basque country must have a say and power to make decisions." The implication of this last sentence is that these are qualities hitherto denied the Basque population. The document was signed by 9 Basque nationalist political parties,[27] 8 nationalist trade unions, and 21 nationalist civil society organizations. In short it represented the consensus of the Basque nationalist community.

On the surface the Lizarra Pact proposed a nonviolent, all-inclusive, unconditional process of negotiation. However, the 8-point communiqué ETA issued announcing its ceasefire gave a very different interpretation of the meaning and purpose of the Lizarra Pact. It stated that after two decades, "we again have the opportunity to take decisive steps towards independence." It urged "the breaking of pacts and bonds with Madrid and Paris and the creation of a single, sovereign institution for the whole of the Basque country." It ended ominously by stating, "ETA has taken its step. Now it is time for others to move into the space we have created. And it is up to everyone to confront those who continue to be the enemies of this project."

Although ETA's car bombs and guns were silenced, *kale borroka* violence increased. PNV offices, however, were no longer a target. Instead its destructive energies were directed toward French and Spanish economic interests as well as toward the nonnationalists. Some 14 months later, in November 1999, ETA declared the end of its ceasefire and shortly thereafter assassinated a member of the security forces in Madrid.

The main reason ETA resumed its violence can be found in the secret agreement ETA and the PNV signed the previous year. It consisted of four main points: (1) the signatories are to work actively for the creation of an unitary and sovereign body that would encompass the seven Basque provinces; (2) the signatories are to collaborate as much as possible to in order to attain that objective; (3) both the PNV and EA pledge themselves to break all contacts with the parties "whose objective is the construction of Spain and the destruction of Euskal Herria (PP and PSOE)"; (4) ETA would announce a ceasefire.[28] In its communiqué announcing the resumption of armed struggle, ETA placed the burden of blame on the PNV's noncompliance with this secret agreement. The PNV had failed to break all ties to the nonnationalists and, moreover, it had not pursued to ETA's satisfaction the building of an institutional framework joining the French and Spanish Basque provinces. ETA had insisted that parallel elections be held in the entire Basque country in order to create a unitary parliament parallel to those in Madrid and Paris. The PNV refused and termed the proposal surrealistic. The PNV defended its agreement with ETA as an attempt to build peace. However, ETA made it clear that its aim had never been peace, but nation-building. It expected the PNV to pursue the same radical agenda in its entirety. Its threat to resume violence would act, in ETA's view, as a guarantor of the process. Although Lizarra did not produce an end to violence, nonetheless the PNV adopted the radical agenda of *soberanismo* and *territorialidad*. PNV was well aware, however, that the constraints imposed by a democracy precluded it from implementing that the agenda directly.

In 2003 the Basque government, headed by the PNV, published a highly elaborated proposal for a new autonomy statute for the Basque country, called "Propuesta de Estatuto Político de la Commúnidad de Euskadi," normally referred as the Ibarretxe Plan after the current PNV president. Once again the PNV defended this plan as another attempt to force ETA to abandon violence. It establishes the Basque country as freely associated with Spain. The powers extended to Euskadi are far reaching and include, among other things, the right to create a formal Basque nationality that can also be extended, along with citizenship rights, to the Basque diaspora as well as their descendants. Although Euskera and Spanish would be co-official, only the Basque flag, the *ikurriña,* would fly on public buildings. The Basque parliament would be inviolable and a separate Basque supreme court established. Moreover, Euskadi would have its own representation in the organs of the European Union as well as separate representation in international organizations. The list is extensive. The nonnationalists have condemned the project as anticonstitutional, among other reasons, because it was presented unilaterally without negotiation either with Madrid or the nonnationalist Basque parties and establishes a parallel Basque sovereignty. ETA is ambivalent. It approves of the preamble, which reaffirms territorial unity and the right to self-determination, but rejects the remainder because it implies a new pact with Madrid. However, there is a certain level of satisfaction in that ETA believes that even this small and inadequate step toward independence was made possible because of the effectiveness of violence.

## Spain's Campaign Against ETA

Although ETA initially emerged under Francoism, the organization has clearly shown its ability to mobilize public support, recruit and operate within a modern democratic state. The final factor that has permitted ETA to reproduce into the age of Spanish democracy involves state policy especially during the critical period of the transition to democracy.

In the early 1970s, states of emergency, described as "one step short of martial law,"[29] were frequently imposed in response to ETA's violence and general social unrest. During 1975 alone, the year of Franco's death, some 5,000 Basque residents were detained on terrorist related charges. Those arrested were frequently held incommunicado and subjected to interrogation methods that included torture, denied proper legal representation, and, if tried, placed before military courts. Although the use of military tribunals declined, the years immediately following the dictator's demise did not see a marked improvement in Spain's human rights record. Security forces often responded to peaceful demonstrations with tear gas, rubber bullets, and live ammunition, as well as mass arrests, causing frequent injuries and the occasional death. More important, however, the government of the new democracy started to fund paramilitary units, which contained off-duty police officers, the occasional mercenary, and plain thugs. During the period from 1975 to 1981, the most famous of these death squads was the Batallón Vasco-Español, which was responsible for fourteen assassinations, most of which targeted ETA.

The election of the socialist government in 1982 marked a new and the most deadly phase in Spain's *guerra sucia* against ETA. A range of factors helps explain the appearance of the Grupos Antiterroristas de Liberación (GAL). First, to the intense irritation of the Spanish socialists, the French government insisted on continuing its policy of offering ETA a safe haven in southern France, viewing the militants as freedom fighters and political refugees. This safe haven offered ETA the opportunity to train its recruits, plan its operations, headquarter its leadership, and maintain its weapon supplies. After operations in Spain ETA militants would withdraw to the impunity of France. Second, the new Spanish socialist minister of the interior, José Barrionuevo, later to be imprisoned because of his role in GAL, failed to undertake much needed reforms of Spain's security forces which, therefore, remained unchanged both in terms of personnel, policy, and attitude. Third, ETA augmented its assault against the security forces generating a backlash of impotent rage within the Spanish police and military. It is widely believed that the kidnapping and assassination of Captain Martín Barrios in October 1983 triggered the onslaught of GAL.

From 1983 to 1987 GAL killed some 27 people and injured considerably more.[30] One-third of its victims were ordinary citizens. Most operations were conducted in France, creating an atmosphere of acute fear within the Basque refugee community. However, GAL also acted in Spain, assassinating, among others, a leader of HB in his medical dispensary in Bilbao and another HB leader in a hotel in Madrid. Although GAL may have slowed ETA down, probably no other single factor contributed more to the reproduction of ETA into the 1990s. GAL forced the radical nationalists to close ranks and gave ample credibility to ETA's assertion that Spanish democracy was a sham.[31]

Partly because of GAL's campaign on French soil, French authorities came to realize that ETA refugees were beginning to constitute a real problem and not only for bilateral relations with Spain. Islamist violence was on the upsurge in France and French public opinion was growing increasingly hostile to all political violence including that of the Basque militants in their midst. From about 1985 French authorities began to crack down on ETA. Critically in the campaign against ETA cooperation between French and Spanish security forces became increasingly closer and more coordinated over the years. ETA militants were denied mobility, safe houses were monitored and extradition was facilitated. In the wake of the Global War on Terror, cooperation between the two countries has become more or less seamless and has contributed to a serious weakening of ETA's capacity to organize.

Spain's socialist government also instituted two new policies with regard to ETA. The first affected ETA prisoners. Until 1988 ETA prisoners had been concentrated in prisons inside the Basque country. In many ways these prisons operated as universities for ETA members as well as coordination centers for ETA activities. They also imposed a strict discipline on militants to remain faithful to the organization. In 1988 the socialist government dispersed prisoners throughout Spain. The aim was to rupture ETA's organization inside the prisons as well as to encourage those who wished to leave ETA by granting them amnesty, shorter prison sentences, or more favorable conditions. As a result more than 100 ETA members have defected. The relocalization of ETA prisoners to the Basque country has been a subject of constant demonstrations and campaigns mobilizing radical nationalists in particular. As usual ETA responded by killing and kidnapping prison officers. In turn the Madrid government has tried to use this inflamed issue on several occasions as a negotiation card in return for concessions from ETA, such as a ceasefire, inevitably without success.

The second policy change was to open secret negotiations at a time when ETA was considered militarily weak. From the late 1970s a major strategic goal for ETA was negotiating a solution to the conflict initially with the Spanish military—according to ETA, still the real power in Spain—and eventually with the Spanish government. The first set of meetings took place in Algeria in 1988–1989. The meetings proved disastrous. ETA demanded to negotiate its version of a solution, which it presented as non-negotiable. The government wished to explore the possibilities for a permanent ceasefire. The first session has been described as political psychoanalysis in which a wide array of unrelated themes, such as the death of Franco, NATO, and the environment, were discussed. The Spanish negotiators felt that the purpose of the exercise was to extend recognition to ETA's historical purpose and legitimacy as well as provide immunity in relation to violence.[32] The second attempt occurred after the entire ETA leadership had been captured in 1992. The results were equally pointless. ETA continued to insist that it would lay down arms only after its goals had been achieved. Many nationalists assert that Madrid should negotiate with ETA and back-channel communication links are open. However, most observers have concluded that negotiations have only served to legitimate and revitalize the organization.

After the election of the Partido Popular government of José María Aznar in 1996, the fight against ETA was made a prime domestic priority. The year before his election as prime minister, Aznar had been the target of an ETA assassination attempt in which he survived thanks to his armored car, but one woman was killed. However, Aznar's inclinations for a frontal attack were somewhat curbed by the fact that his minority government was dependent on support from, among others, the Basque nationalists of the PNV. This changed in 2000 when elections provided Prime Minister Aznar with an absolute majority. One of his first acts was to broaden Spain's antiterrorist legislation. The reforms made it an offense to praise or publicly justify terrorist acts, redefined terrorism to include damage to state or government facilities and certain acts of arson, and allowed youth accused of terrorist acts to be tried in adult courts. The new laws also allowed for incommunicado detentions and, thereby, reopened the way for abusive interrogation techniques, which have been criticized by Amnesty International, the Committee for the Prevention of Torture and the UN Commission on Human Rights. In the context of the Global War on Terror, Spain's antiterrorist legislation was again broadened in 2002, and Spain played a critical role in formulating the EU's definition of terrorism as well as its legislation.

The impact on Basque violence of these legal changes has been extensive. At the time *kale borroka* violence, usually conducted by minors, was as its height. Legislation introduced enabled these ruffians to be prosecuted under antiterrorism laws resulting in heavy fines and stiff prison sentences for those over eighteen found guilty. Additionally, families were made economically responsible for the damages perpetrated by their children and police procedures improved by, among other things, conducting DNA tests on the discarded hoods used for disguise. The result has been a dramatic decrease of street violence. The new antiterrorist laws also paved the way for the illegalization of HB as well the organizations linked to it. HB has also been placed on the EU's list of terrorist groups. As a result none of these groups can organize public events, bank accounts have been frozen, premises have been closed, and the flows of funds between these organizations and to ETA have been severely curtailed. In addition, more than 200 individuals have been charged with ETA membership, although so far they have been neither arrested nor tried. These changes, together with close police cooperation between Spain and France, have been credited with a notable decrease in ETA activities. Since 2002 only eight individuals have been killed and by the time of this writing no one has died. However, ETA was planning four car bomb attacks, an operation that was canceled after the horrendous Islamist attacks in Madrid of March 11, 2004. During the summer of 2004 ETA continued placing bombs, but they were small, advance warning was given and no damage caused. Street violence continues, but much less frequently. Currently ETA appears unable to train its militants, prepare operations, or indeed assemble in any significant number. The organization is convinced that it is infiltrated by the police and this is most likely the case. If security cooperation remains effective and is not diverted by the increasing concerns over Islamic violence, it is possible that ETA can be contained, although no one expects it to disappear.

Have the policies of the Aznar government, therefore, been successful in dealing with ETA? Currently, the results would appear to be positive, but only on one level. Although for the present unable to absorb them into the organization, ETA does not lack potential recruits. Moreover, until fear vanishes, ETA remains well funded. Although smaller than in previous years, the social base supportive of ETA remains intact. More important, however, the Aznar government launched a frontal attack on the entire Basque nationalist community and succeeded in radicalizing even moderate nationalists, notably the PNV. Support for Basque independence is probably increasing. Many moderates argue that Aznar attempted to discredit all nationalists with ETA. One nationalist leader termed Aznar's government as "a legal GAL."[33] Many contend that the antiterrorist legislation introduced was so broad as to constitute an attack on basic individual liberties and feel that the illegalization of HB was not justified. They argue that if certain individuals had direct links to ETA, they should be arrested and tried, but that such individual links do not warrant the illegalization of the entire party. In addition, they point to a new clause in the Spanish Penal Code, introduced in 2003 in response to the Ibarretxe Plan. If approved by the Basque parliament, but refused by the Spanish government, the PNV wants to submit the Plan to a referendum. In response the government has made such referendums illegal, punishable by a three- to five-year prison term.[34]

## A Short Concluding Observation

More than ever Euskadi has become two separated communities. Relations are uncomfortable, lives are lived apart. Although ETA at least for the moment has been constrained, the political conflict inside the Basque country has deepened. The presence of ETA will continue—at least to some degree—to condition Basque political life as long as this conflict is not managed in an appropriate manner. Nationalists, radical and moderate, argue for the right to self-determination. They claim the right to decide on their future relation to Spain. Successive Spanish governments have rejected as anticonstitutional any demand to renegotiate the Basque autonomy statute in order to include this right. Such a right would violate the clause concerning the "unity of the Spanish nation." However, more to the point, it is entirely unsuitable to the circumstances that obtain. The concept of self-determination belongs to the process of decolonialization. It is not a right that international law automatically extends to all peoples who conceive themselves as a nation. Granting this right to the Basque country would establish it as a de facto colony of Spain, which historically has never been the case. It would also reaffirm in the view of Basque nationalists the anti-Basque nature of the majority of the resident population who combine Basque with Spanish identity. However, ultimately democratic values are more fundamental to the Spanish constitution than Spanish territorial unity. In regions with conflicting national identities, democracy also means that people should be given the option of expressing the type of relation they wish to have with the central state. The prime question should be if the residents of Euskadi wish independence, yes or no. Great Britain and Canada have both used referendums on independence as a means of dealing with separatist movements. In the Basque country the answer in all probability would be no. In any case such a referendum would clear the way for dealing with the core conflict that afflicts the region. This is the lack of an agreed framework through which the various political projects and identities inside the Basque country can be peacefully mediated.

## Glossary

*abertzales de izquierda*: Left-wing nationalists; HB supporters and ETA's political base.

Ajuria Enea Pact: Formally Agreement on the Normalization and Pacification of Euskadi, stated, among other clauses, that no dialogue with ETA was possible until violence had been abandoned.

CCOO de Euskadi: Communist trade unions in the Basque country.

*cuadrillos*: In the Basque region, refers to small social and cultural networks, often developed in childhood.

EA: Euzko Alkartasuna, a Basque nationalist party.

*EKIN*: ETA newspaper.

Ertzaintza: The Basque national police.

ETA: Euskadi 'ta Askatasuna (Basque Fatherland and Liberty, or Basque Homeland and Freedom). Founded in 1959, ETA intends to establish an independent state in the northern Spanish regions of Vizcaya, Guipúzcoa, Álava, and Navarre and the southwestern French regions of Labourd, Basse-Navarre, and Soule.

ETA *militar*: Military wing of ETA.

Euskalherria: Name given to the Basque country consisting of the four Spanish and three French Basque provinces.

Euzko Gastedi: Basque youth organization of the PNV.

GAL: Grupos Antiterroristas de Liberación, antiterrorist paramilitary groups.

*guerra sucia*: Dirty war.

Haika: Basque radical nationalist youth groups.

Hasi: A political party witnin the MLNV-KAS.

HB: Herri Batasuna, political party close to ETA.

*ikurriña*: The Basque flag.

Izquierda Unida: United Left, formerly part of the Communist Party.

KAS: Koordinadora Abertzale Sozialista. Founded in 1974 by ETA, this organ was designed as the central coordinator of the many activities of the MLNV. KAS consisted of labor, cultural, and youth organizations, a political party (Hasi), as well as ETA *militar*.

MLNV: Movimiento de Liberacion Nacional Vasco. Created by ETA in 1974, the Movement for Basque National Liberation is the civil society infrastructure of radical nationalism.

PNV: Partido Nacionalista Vasco (Basque Nationalist Party). The Basque government and parliament have been dominated by the PNV since the first regional elections in 1980.

PP: Partido Popular (Popular Party).

PSOE: Partido Socialista Obrero de España (Spanish Socialist Workers Party).

PSE: Partido Socialista de Euskadi, PSOE's Basque branch. In the first general elections of the new Spanish democracy in 1977, the PSE emerged as the single largest party in the Basque country and beat the PNV.

*soberanismo*: Sovereignty.

*territorialidad*: Territoriality.

## Timeline

Pre-twentieth century: The Basques, a linguistically and culturally distinct group, inhabit the northern mountainous region that straddles the border between modern-day Spain and France. They enjoyed varying degrees of self-government under Spanish and French rulers. Modern Basque nationalism dates to the late nineteenth century: embraces a linguistic and ethnic revival, partly in reaction to immigration of non-Basques.

1936–1939: Spanish civil war; General Franco establishes dictatorship and occupies the Basque country. The autonomy promised under the republic is denied.

1959: ETA, "Basque Fatherland and Liberty," is founded to create an independent homeland.

1961: ETA opts for violent insurgency and attempts to derail a train carrying politicians.

1968: ETA kills Meliton Manzanas, a leading secret police officer in San Sebastian.

1973: ETA assassinates Franco's prime minister Admiral Luis Carrero Blanco in Madrid after the government's execution of Basque militants.

1975: Franco dies; Juan Carlos becomes king. Over the next few years, Spain democratizes, with a new constitution, and becomes a constitutional monarchy and a decentralized unitary state, with special autonomy provisions for the Basque country, Catalonia, and Galicia.

1978: Herri Batasuna is founded.

1979: The Basque Regional Parliament is formed on 25 October, as a consequence of the Statute of Guernica, the Basque autonomy statute. EPA begins planting bombs in tourist areas as well as train stations.

1980: The Basque Regional Parliament convenes its first session on 31 March. (In elections from 1980 to 2005, constitutional Basque nationalists would form the leading party of government. Electoral support for HB, by contrast, has varied between 8 and 20 percent of the regional poll.) Both moderate and insurgent Basques argue that the Spanish constitution does not recognize the Basque people's right to self-determination. More than 90 people are killed in ETA's most violent year of insurgency.

1981: Attempted military coup sparks ETA debate, splitting the group.

1983–1987: "Antiterrorist Liberation Groups" (EIAL), with the covert support of leading members of Socialist Prime Minister Gonzales's government, kill 27 suspected ETA militants. ETA begins using car bombs in addition to kidnappings and assassinations, in campaigns of violence.

1987: Twenty-one shoppers are killed in an attack at a Barcelona commercial center; ETA apologizes for "mistake."

1995: ETA attempts to assassinate the leader of the opposition PP (later prime minister), José María Aznar.

1996 : Conservative PP wins parliamentary majority in Madrid.

1997: ETA campaign against local PP politicians begins; it kidnaps and kills Basque councillor Miguel Angel Blanco, sparking widespread outrage and bringing millions of Spaniards onto the streets. More than 20 leaders of Herri Batasuna are sentenced to seven years in prison for collaborating with ETA.

1998: Herri Batasuna elects new provisional leadership. Spain's main political parties engage in talks to end violence in the Basque region. The Madrid government is not involved. In April the Northern Ireland Good Friday Agreement is signed. ETA and Herri Batasuna are said to be influenced by Irish Republicans. ETA announces its first indefinite ceasefire, effective 18 September.

1999: The first meeting to date between ETA and the Spanish government occurs in Zurich, Switzerland in May. Three months later Spanish prime minister José María Aznar calls on ETA to renew its commitment to peace. ETA states that contact with the Madrid government has been severed, and in November announces an end to its 14-month ceasefire, blaming lack of progress in talks with the Spanish government.

2000: Violence resumes in January and February, with car bombings in Vitoria and Madrid. The film *Yoyes*, based on an ETA member, Dolores González Catarian, is released, providing the first treatment of the group in Spanish cinema. In May, King Juan Carlos leads thousands of Spaniards in a silent protest against the killing of a journalist. In August, thousands demonstrate in support of ETA in Bilbao after four of its members are killed in a blast caused by explosives in a car they are driving. King Juan Carlos condemns ETA in November on the 25th anniversary of his accession to the throne, just after a former government minister is killed in Barcelona.

2001: Socialist politician Froilan Elexpe is shot dead near San Sebastian in March. PP politician Manuel Jiménez Abad is assassinated in Zaragoza in May, just before elections to the Basque parliament. Judge José María Lidon, who had sentenced six ETA sympathizers to long jail terms in 1987, is shot and killed in November. The following month, at the request of the Spanish government, the European Union declares ETA a terrorist organization. A Spanish judge outlaws Gestoras pro Amnistia, an organization supporting families of jailed ETA members.

2002: July and August: Judge Baltasar Garzón orders the seizure of 18 million Euros in assets belonging to Herri Batasuna. Garzón suspends Batasuna for three years for affiliation with ETA, which he declares "guilty of crimes against humanity." The Madrid Parliament seeks an indefinite ban on HB. In September, French police arrest a man and woman suspected of being top leaders of ETA following a joint operation with Spanish police (Juan Antonio Olarra Guribi is believed to be ETA's military head). ETA's Ibon Fernández Iradi escapes from police custody in southern France in December, three days after being captured near the Spanish border.

2003: The Spanish government shuts down Basque newspaper *Euskaldunon Egunkaria* in February; a new newspaper, *Egunero*, is published immediately afterward. In March, Spain's Supreme Court bans HB permanently in response to a government request. The U.S. classifies HB as terrorist in May; the European Union does so in June. In May ETA kills two policemen and seriously injures two civilians in a car bomb attack in Sanguesa, Navarre. Bombs explode in the Spanish resorts of Alicante and Benidorm on 22 July. Five days later another bomb explodes at Santander airport. In November, Spanish police arrest a dozen suspected ETA leaders. Ibon Fernández Iradi is recaptured in the French town of Mont-de-Marsan in December, a year after his escape.

2004: ETA is initially and falsely accused of organizing the 11 March Madrid bombings, which take place just before Spain's parliamentary elections. The incumbent government loses offices after there is a widespread perception that it had manipulated information. The new Socialist government announces it will withdraw from Spain's participation from the U.S.-led coalition in Iraq.

2005: ETA announced a partial and conditional ceasefire on 19 June. It says it will "cease armed activities" against elected politicians in Spain in apparent response to Spanish Prime Minister Zapatero's offer to open talks, provided ETA agrees to abandon violence. The Spanish government says ETA's statement is not sufficient; a spokeswoman for the Basque regional government welcomes the statement but also says it does not go far enough, "businesspeople, university professors, security forces, police and journalists continue to live under threat." ETA has not carried out a fatal attack in over two years.

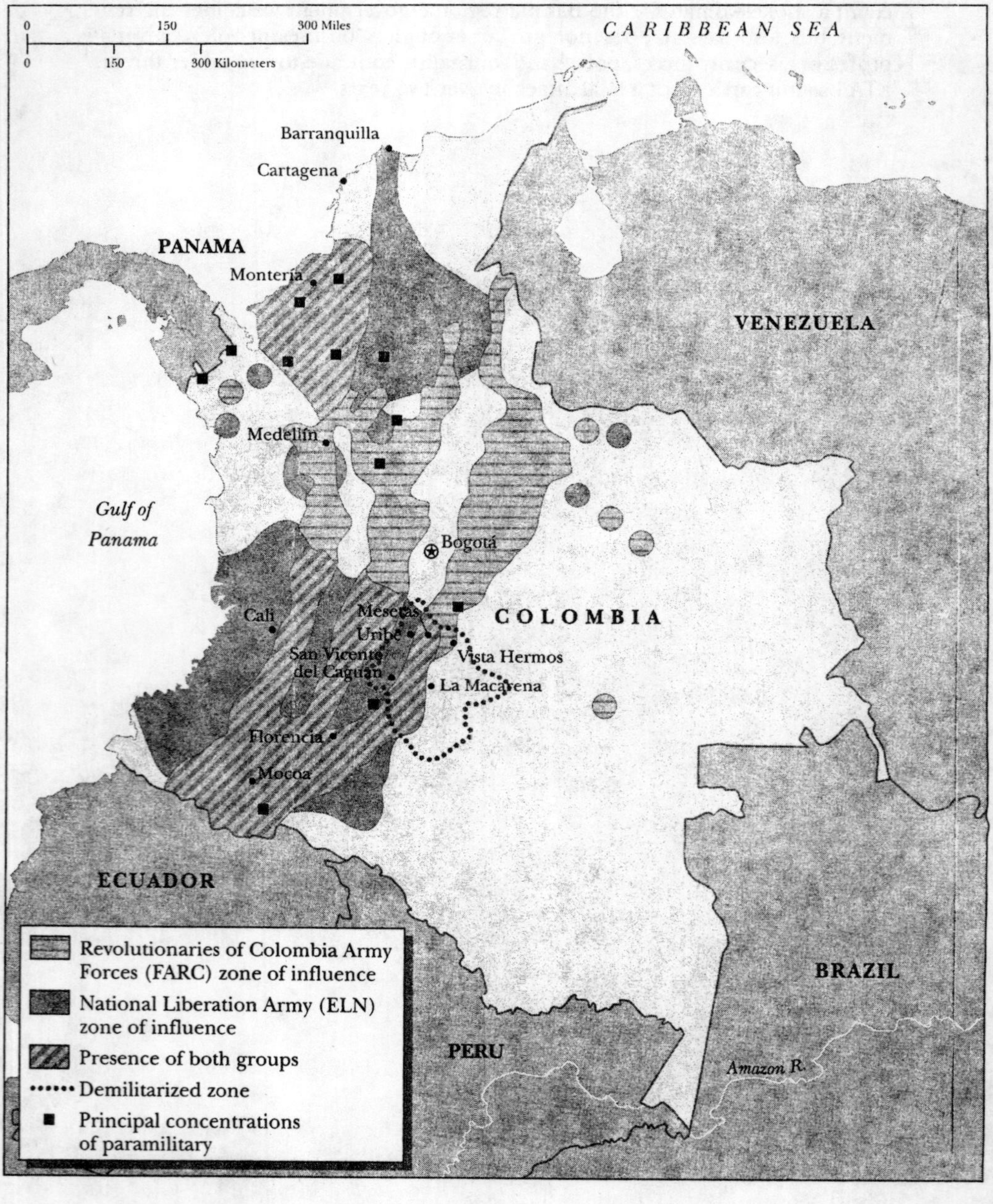


Map 2.1. Principal concentrations of paramilitary groups in Colombia.

*Chapter 2*

# FARC-EP: From Liberal Guerrillas to Marxist Rebels to Post-Cold War Insurgents

MARC CHERNICK

Colombia's internal war is a deep-rooted conflict with multiple armed contenders. Over the last six decades, the conflict has been transformed from a partisan civil war in the 1940s and 1950s between Colombia's two traditional parties, to a low-intensity guerrilla insurgency against the state in the 1960s and 1970s, to a multipolar civil war among left-wing guerrillas, right-wing paramilitaries, and the state beginning in the mid-1980s and continuing into the present.

Several facts make Colombia's conflict distinctive. First, unlike many internal armed conflicts, Colombia's multidimensional insurgency is not shaped or caused by ethnic, national, or religious differences. There are several ethnic groups in Colombia, particularly Afro-Colombian and Indigenous; however, the armed conflict is not waged along these lines. The principal divisions are more closely related to class, rather than ethnicity, nation, or race. To a remarkable degree, the insurgency has represented a prolonged rural rebellion in a rapidly modernizing and urbanizing society. Second, to an unusual degree, Colombia's conflict has become intertwined with the international narcotics trade. The overlay of national and transnational organized crime obfuscates the political dimension of the conflict leaving policymakers from both the United States and Colombia to tilt at the windmills of narcotics production while downplaying the social and political dimensions of the conflict. This dynamic prevailed—particularly from the perspective of U.S. foreign policy—from the mid-1980s until 11 September 2001. Third, after the terrorist attacks on New York and Washington, the dominant narrative of the Colombian conflict was altered and reified once again by both Colombian and U.S. policymakers. The policy of both governments to the war changed dramatically and the conflict itself was again transformed. The United States lifted its formal restrictions that confined all military aid exclusively to counternarcotics operations, and redirected the focus to include counterterrorism. At the same time, Colombian president Alvaro Uribe began to deny that a war even exists; he insisted that the conflict has been caused by a group of terrorists who have taken up arms against society.[1] The objective now was to defeat the terrorists or force them to the negotiating table. The evolution of the protracted war together with the shifting nature of official interpretations and policy responses has meant that each phase of the sixty-year conflict has been viewed as distinct and only superficially related to each other. Thus the violence of the 1940s and 1950s is buried in the distant past while the rise of the drug trade and the terrorist war are currently analyzed in an ahistorical and even apolitical vacuum.

This chapter rejects this ahistorical analysis. There has existed extensive continuity from the first phases of partisan warfare to the current multipolar conflict. Many of the agents, particularly the FARC and its leadership, have traversed each of the phases. A map of the incidence of violence of the 1940s and 1950s is remarkably similar to a map of the sites in the current conflict. The war is still primarily a rural conflict and its epicenter is in approximately 100 municipalities—about one-tenth of the total—that expand outward to cover about half of the country, much of it rural and sparsely populated. These areas have experienced over fifty years of a war that ebbs and flows but has never ended, and the state's nonmilitary presence has been minimal or nonexistent. They are also areas of great inequality and social exclusion. In the 1940s and 1950s, the war was centered in cattle- and coffee-producing zones. By the 1990s, coffee and cattle lands were still at the center of the conflict, particularly as the world price of coffee collapsed in the 1990s and drug traffickers invested a large percentage of their newly acquired wealth into large-scale cattle ranching. The conflict had also spread into new zones, especially areas that produce coca leaves,[2] opium poppies,[3] petroleum, and bananas. Moreover, despite the extraordinary change in the dynamics of the internal war and the profound changes in the geopolitical context—from cold war to drug war to war on terror—the grievances and demands of the guerrillas, particularly the Revolutionary Armed Forces of Colombia (Fuerzas Armadas Revolucionarias de Colombia, FARC), have been remarkably consistent. The FARC's leaders view the war as a prolonged insurrection against an oligarchic state that has denied participation to the rural peasantry, choked off rural development, and assassinated labor and campesino leaders who have mobilized against the regime.[4]

This chapter reviews this history, focusing on the causes and characteristics of the long duration of Colombia's internal war, looking at key processes and events with social science lenses and also from the perspective of the FARC. Several failed peace initiatives that were attempted with the FARC from 1982 to 2002 are then analyzed, identifying key weaknesses and missed opportunities. The FARC's organizational structures, its recruitment bases, and its sources of financing are interrogated. Lastly, the chapter appraises the impact of the drug trade, the drug war, and the global war on terror on shaping the most recent phase of the armed conflict.

## A Short History of the Conflict

The contemporary violence dates to the presidential election of 1946 when the Conservative Party returned to power after an interval of 16 years. The nascent conflict sharply escalated following the assassination of the Liberal Party populist leader, Jorge Eliécer Gaitán on 9 April 1948. Gaitan's murder sparked days of rioting in Bogotá—the Bogotazo—which then mutated into a decade of unrestrained social warfare throughout the nation's rural areas between the followers of the two parties. The English historian Eric Hobsbawm described *la Violencia,* as this early phase of the conflict came to be known, as one of the greatest mobilizations of peasants in the history of the western hemisphere. Over 200,000 people were killed in this period. For Hobsbawm, *la Violencia* was an abortive social revolution, a popular uprising without leadership or ideology.[5]

In 1958, the elite leadership of the two traditional parties, fearing that the violence could lead to a more profound social revolution, negotiated a power-sharing agreement known as "the National Front" that effectively put an end to the partisan civil war. The pact excluded all third parties, such as socialists or communists, from holding office, and consequently helped sow the seeds of further aggression. Reacting to the reassertion of the traditional political elite from both parties, a core group of Liberal guerrillas and communist self-defense militants refused to hand in their arms or accept an amnesty. The National Front agreements ended the partisan civil war between the historic parties, but were unable to impose a lasting peace.

The transformation of the partisan war into a rural, class-based, more ideological peasant insurgency challenged the reassertion of power by the nation's traditional elites. The origins of this second phase of the conflict can be traced not only to the exclusionary National Front pact but also to the unresolved peasant struggles of the mid-twentieth century over land, markets, and political rights that were reheated by the outbreak of revolutionary student movements that appeared in Colombia and throughout the region following the Cuban Revolution in 1959. The FARC was born during this second phase of the conflict, though its leaders and organizational structures were drawn from the preceding phase of the violence. A "low intensity" conflict endured from the 1960s to the early 1980s. During this time, annual deaths caused by the conflict rarely rose above a thousand—in some definitions the threshold for a civil war[6]—and the political violence was largely confined to rural areas. In contrast, from the mid-1980s until 2000, political killings including deaths in combat, extrajudicial killings, and massacres rose to an average of 3,000 per year, while the overall homicide rate soared to over 25,000, making Colombia among the most violent societies in the world. Since 2000, politically motivated homicides have increased to 4000 a year.[7]

The leader of the FARC, Manuel Marulanda Vélez,[8] first took up arms as a Liberal guerrilla in 1948. Following the inauguration of the National Front in 1958, Marulanda and a group of Liberal and Communist guerrillas remained armed and organized in self-defense groups in control of a broad swath of territory in the remote Andean coffee regions in the central and eastern cordilleras.[9] They built on decades of political organization by the pro-Soviet Colombian Communist Party[10] and developed an agrarian movement that came to have great influence in the region. Marulanda made various efforts to reach out and negotiate with the National Front leadership but was rebuffed. From 1962 to 1965, the government declared that these armed communities constituted illegal, communist "independent republics."

The very existence of the "independent republics" represented a challenge to the National Front's leaders, key allies with Washington in the war on communism that was firmly transplanted to the western hemisphere following the Cuban Revolution. Colombia became a "showcase" for the U.S. Alliance for Progress, the principal U.S. military and assistance strategy to Latin America designed to prevent "another Cuba." With the assistance of the United States, the Colombian armed forces initiated a series of aerial bombing campaigns against these communities. The events of those days and the names of those communities—Marquetalia, El Pato, Río Chiquito and others—later became part of the iconography of the FARC. Internal guerrilla lore tells of 48 men in Marquetalia (in the department of Tolima) holding out against 16,000 soldiers armed, trained, and directed by the United States.[11]

The military operation did not, however, lead to the defeat of the armed holdouts. Rather, the offensive turned the armed self-defense communities into a new mobile guerrilla force. Following the second assault on Marquetalia in 1964, the community organized a "General Assembly of Guerrillas" and formed what they called the "Southern Division" (Bloque Sur). On 20 July 1964, Colombia's independence day, the nascent guerrilla movement proclaimed its "National Agrarian Program," a set of demands that has served as the foundation of its struggle for more than forty years:

> We fight for an Agrarian Policy that hands over land taken from the large landed estates to the peasants. Accordingly, as of today, July 20, 1964, we are a guerrilla army struggling for the following agrarian program: ONE: As an alternative to the Oligarchy's Deceitful Agrarian Policy, we propose an effective Revolutionary Agrarian Policy that radically changes the Colombian rural social structure by giving free

land to the peasants that are laboring it or those willing to do so; this will be achieved by confiscating large landed estates for the working people.[12]

On 27 May 1966, the second anniversary of the assault on Marquetalia, the guerrillas announced the formation of the Revolutionary Armed Forces of Colombia, or FARC. Following the bombing of Marquetalia, entire communities were placed completely outside of the institutionalized regime of the National Front. In the resulting political vacuum, the Communist Party and the FARC consolidated many of the functions of local decision-making and state authority, including the provision of education, medical services, physical infrastructure, protection, administration of justice, and civil ceremonies such as marriage and divorce. In fact, the FARC and the Communist Party were better able to mobilize such resources *after* the violent confrontations between the local communities and the National Front regime in 1964–1965. By then they were able to mobilize sufficient resources and "routinely and successfully lay claims on government" at least at the local level.[13] After the dislodgements from Marquetalia in 1964 once again there occurred a rural-rural migration of peasants accustomed to living within areas of communist influence. Marulanda, today the commander of the General Secretariat of the Governing Council of the FARC, described the change in an interview:

After Marquetalia, we were forced to become more mobile. When we left Marquetalia, we entered Cauca and first settled in Río Chiquito. And despite the military confrontations, there we stayed until we created the Bloque Sur. From there we moved on to Natagaima, and later to eastern Tolima in the municipality of Dolores. And then, when we founded the FARC, and adopted the strategy of deploying mobile guerrillas mostly with the personnel from El Pato and Guayabero. These are the men and women who formed the movement. We chose this area because it was a strategic cordillera for us and difficult to control because it is situated among five departments. With the founding of the FARC, a detachment was also sent to Caldas, near Armenia, and another deployed in Libano [Tolima]. Initially it was like that. But although they were mobile guerrillas, they had instructions to maintain contact and to operate according to the changing situation. There was a continual exchange of ideas and opinions among the leadership of each unit, those from Santa Isabel, Pato, Guayabero, and the Central Cordillera principally. And when it was necessary to convene a meeting to examine the military situation, or any other situation, then a site was agreed upon and the commanders used every means possible to arrive at the place of the meeting.[14]

As the FARC guerrillas fanned out into newer areas, they were often accompanied by communities of peasants, in a process that the sociologist W. Ramírez Tobón called "armed colonization." This Colombian sociologist states that the ideology of these peasants was a "blend of radical democratic and conservative components," mixing the new communitarian and social structures of the Communist Party with profound support for an agrarian reform that would give access to the land and entrance into the market.[15] Such a program was not "anti-capitalist, [but] anti-monopolist." Ramírez Tobón accurately describes the FARC in its early stages of development: "The FARC, despite its organizational structure of greater mobility and offensive capability or the greater national extension of its military units, and despite the revolutionary innovations with which it expressed many of its public pronouncements of its relationship with the Communist Party, is actually little more than the advance guard of a colonizing peasantry whose organizational base and political project is resisting the crushing expropriations of large capital and whose objective is the establishment of a democratic statute concerning the agrarian question."[16] He goes on to say that the guerrillas interact with local social organizations, and that

> Such existing organizations remain covered by the military power of the guerrilla, and at the same time they are concerned with maintaining the legal ties with state entities. They participate in the organizational ideas that the guerrilla proposes and seeks to develop. To the extent that the flow [of] migrants [increases] . . . the guerrillas take great pains to propagate their ideology, they are disposed to intense political work with the population, that begins with a recognition of their immediate needs. As one of the necessary experiences of a military organization, the guerrilla finds it indispensable to exercise a degree of necessary authority that exceeds tasks which are purely military. Politics are linked to regional needs. . . . The minimal ordering presumes police functions that the guerrillas assume, if only transitorily.[17]

The FARC has maintained these basic patterns even as it expanded from a small regional organization into a national guerrilla army with operations in every department of the country. In 1966, the FARC was a force of about 200 fighters supported by an equal number of families and a support base throughout the region. Over the decades, the organization steadily increased its numbers and geographic mobility. In 1982, in its Seventh Conference, it formally changed its name to FARC-EP, adding Ejército del Pueblo (Army of the People) to its original name. By 2005 the FARC had built an army of over 18,000 regular fighters. It is the most autochthonous of Colombia's several guerrilla movements. Unusually for Latin American guerrilla groups, its leaders were not intellectuals but peasants who emerged from decades of agrarian and partisan struggles, and who had been forged in the *Violencia.* A decade before Fidel Castro entered Havana, the founders of the FARC were fighting in the mountains of Colombia. At its foundation, the FARC was basically an armed peasant movement in search of an ideology.[18] Liberals such as Marulanda found allies in the communist self-defense communities and the Communist Party of Colombia, but the relationship was not primarily rooted in ideological affinities. The alliance was based on the Communist Party's decades of political organization, but most important, on the fact that dissident Liberals, Communists, self-defense communities, and independent peasant organizations were all excluded from the National Front.

The moment was also propitious for the founding of a rural revolutionary movement in Colombia. The 1960s was a time of great revolutionary ferment in Latin America following the Cuban Revolution. Several other guerrilla movements were formed in Colombia during this same period. These were more directly linked to external ideologies, revolutionary models, and funding sources. One of these other guerrilla movements, the National Liberation Army, ELN, founded by Colombian students in Havana, has also endured into the present. It initially recruited from the growing student movements on the country's large public university campuses, particularly in Bogotá and in the department of Santander in the mid-1960s. Unlike similar pro-Castro guerrilla movements that were formed throughout Latin America in the 1960s and were then quickly defeated, the ELN successfully inserted itself into isolated regions of the country that had already spent much of the previous two decades in rebellion against the state. Yet it too suffered a string of crushing military defeats and internal purges in the early 1970s. In the 1980s, the ELN rebuilt itself around the idea of liberation theology that wedded Marxism with the post-Vatican II Catholic "preferential option for the poor." Its new leaders were revolutionary priests.

Other smaller guerrilla organizations also emerged in the 1960s and 1970s. Most notable was the EPL (Popular Liberation Army), a Maoist group, and the April 19th Movement (M-19), which was founded initially as an urban military-political organization following fraudulent presidential elections in 1970 and modeled after the urban Argentine guerrilla movement, the Montoneros. Until the founding of the M-19, the insurrectionary violence had been largely confined to rural areas. The M-19 broke the mold and brought the conflict directly to Colombia's cities, triggering an increase in repression of many urban labor and student movements, in the late 1970s and early 1980s.

The conflict was transformed once again in the early 1980s with the rise of the drug-export boom and the emergence of a third armed actor, namely, right-wing paramilitaries, known as *paras.* The drug trade led to a worsening of agrarian conflicts in the countryside as narco-investors purchased large estates in traditional cattle and agricultural areas as a way to launder money, and to gain social prestige, and proceeded to expel peasants believed to be sympathetic to the guerrillas. By the 1990s, the drug trade had become a principal source of financing for both the guerrillas and the paramilitaries. The FARC came to control much of the areas where coca was cultivated, largely in the southern and eastern parts of the country in the colonization zones of Guaviare, Caquetá and Putumayo. The *paras* became more directly involved in cocaine production and trafficking. For both groups, the drug trade represented a significant percentage of the financial resources necessary to sustain what quickly became large irregular military forces.

The paramilitaries were initially organized legally by the armed forces, although they developed considerable autonomy as drug traffickers and local powerholders began to provide additional resources and assert control. The law giving the armed forces the right to arm civilians was struck down in 1989. Nevertheless the paramilitaries were not dismantled, and the armed forces did not sever ties to them. By the late 1990s, hundreds of these groups had united to form the United Self-Defense Forces of Colombia (AUC). By 2000, the AUC had more than 8,000 men under arms and had proven itself to be quite effective as a counterinsurgency force, clearing entire regions of guerrilla influence through systematic and relentless assassinations and massacres of the guerrillas' civilian supporters. By 2002, its numbers had grown to about 14,000 and it was increasingly developing a political message and a political following among urban middle classes and large business interests. From the late 1990s through 2004, the paramilitaries were responsible for more than 75 percent of massacres and extrajudicial killings of civilians.[19]

Each of the armed combatants has roots in certain geographic regions and ties to distinct social sectors. By the late 1990s, however, as the conflict spread, many of the initial links between a particular armed organization and its original social and geographic base had been weakened or come under severe attack. Still, the FARC maintains a national presence with prime bases of support in the peasant colonization zones east of the Andes and parts of the old communist peasant zones and coffee-growing regions of the central Andes. The ELN has roots in the central department of Santander, where the nation's primary oil refinery is based, as well as in the oil-producing regions near the Venezuelan border and throughout the mid-Magdalena Valley. It has long-standing ties to oil workers and marginalized peasants in these zones. The AUC's principal base is in the northern cattle and banana-growing areas along the northern Atlantic coast and it is supported by large landowners and business and political elites. By 2000, it too had expanded into a national presence, penetrating parts of the coca colonization zones that had long served as areas of guerrilla operations. In each of these areas, the state has only a limited presence and little effective control.[20]

Fueling this war across the decades has been a struggle over land and rural development. Since it first took up arms, the FARC has insisted on a program favoring small farmers, state investment and easy credit. The AUC has defended the interests of large landowners and has used force to displace peasants and consolidate larger estates, a phenomenon against the regional trend toward the decline and disappearance of rural oligarchies. War and particularly the rapid rise of right-wing paramilitarism since the 1980s has strengthened elite, rural landed, and business sectors. This fact alone separates Colombia from most of its neighbors, though there are some parallels with parts of rural Brazil, particularly in the northeast. Though all sides have been influenced by ideology and sustained through access to economic resources—from illegal narcotics to voluntary and extorted payments from oil companies and other businesses—conflict over land and rural development has been the primary motor of the sixty-year war. The struggle for land and control over territory has also been the source of the greatest humanitarian crisis related to the war: two to three million internally displaced persons (IDPs) have been driven from their homes, either because of combat operations or the use of displacement as a weapon of war by one of the armed agents.[21] In 2005 the United Nations undersecretary for humanitarian affairs called the Colombian situation one of the greatest humanitarian crises in the world, surpassed only by Sudan and Congo.

In 2002, the Colombian government under President Alvaro Uribe inverted previous peace strategies that had been centered on negotiations with the guerrillas and opened up negotiations with the AUC. Simultaneously the armed forces stepped up combat operations against the FARC. This is a novel formula for a "peace process" since the AUC does not represent an insurgency that has taken up arms against the state; it is a *pro-state* counterinsurgency force. Once protected by laws giving the armed forces the legal right to arm civilians, the paramilitary groups were declared illegal when those laws were struck down in 1989. By 2005, they had acquired a large degree of autonomy and were deeply involved in criminal activities and drug trafficking. Nevertheless they continued to operate as an essential ally of the government in the counterinsurgency war. Even as their actions undermined institutional authority and legitimacy, their military prowess was key to keeping the FARC in check and in reversing many of its gains.

From 2002 to 2005, the government reached a series of agreements with the AUC that, if fully implemented, could lead to the demobilization of a significant percentage of AUC fighters and leaders.[22] A negotiated demobilization of paramilitaries, if successful—a big if—would realign the war. Success would substantially reduce human rights violations, and enhance the authority and legitimacy of the state. In the short term, however, it would create a vacuum that would have to be filled by the state or else leave large parts of the country exposed to the FARC. Either way, the result would be a sharpening of the polar struggle between the FARC and the state.

With or without the AUC, the war with the FARC represents the central axis of the conflict. In 2002, the Colombian Armed Forces, with the assistance of the United States, implemented a major new military strategy against the FARC through a program called Plan Patriota, which was designed to project substantial force deep into FARC territory. The strategy represented a substantial gamble that a more robust military strategy can either defeat the insurgents or force a negotiated settlement on terms dictated primarily by the state.

After three years of Plan Patriota, there is no evidence that the FARC has been weakened. During the first two years, the FARC pursued a strategic retreat and reverted to more classical guerrilla tactics of deconcentrated forces, limited engagements, and ambushes. The tactic seemed to lull government forces and officials into boasts and complacency. In early 2005, the FARC unleashed a string of larger attacks that inflicted substantial losses and casualties and publicly declared its own major offensive to combat Plan Patriota.

## Grievances and Demands of the FARC

The FARC has been consistent in its demands throughout the course of the war. From the declaration of its "National Agrarian Program" in 1964 to its positions during several periods of negotiations with the government between 1982 and 2002, it has called for greater access to land, rural development, political participation, and an end to extrajudicial killings of its followers. Even before the formation of the FARC, Manuel Marulanda articulated similar demands and grievances as a leader of the self-defense communities and the Liberal guerrillas of the era. Although Marulanda and his followers did not hand in their arms, a tacit truce endured between the communities and the National Front government in the early years. One analyst familiar with the armed self-defense communities at the time points out how organized these communities were and how extensive were the contacts with the government in the post-*Violencia* and pre-guerrilla war phase of the conflict.

> Marquetalia (as well as the sister communities of El Pato, Guayabero, and Río Chiquito) was founded at the time of government pacification programs and during a time of conversations with the central government. The movement was converted into an intermediary as well as a guarantor that some of the money available through the rehabilitation program be given to the combatants who now were small landholders. That is to say that [the rehabilitation program] opened the possibility of trade and commerce. And these zones became relatively affluent. For example, in Marquetalia during 1962 and '63, the men who lived there, including Marulanda and the others, were relatively wealthy campesinos because it was a large zone that was very productive. In the south of Tolima, the zones of earlier influence remained in the hands of either the communists or the Liberal guerrillas. One of the ways in which the rehabilitation program proposed by the [first National Front] government of Lleras Camargo worked was that the mayorships [which then were appointed positions] and other public positions were given to former guerrillas, but always Liberal guerrillas, and they maintained the old zones of influence. That is to say, there also was a political redistribution based on the earlier zones of influence. This was respected in the accords with the government.[23]

This coexistence between armed self-defense communities and the newly inaugurated National Front government did not last. It fell victim to the anticommunist ideology that reshaped the region following the Cuban Revolution. After Marquetalia, official contact with the FARC was cut off for eighteen years. It was not until the early 1980s that Colombian politicians from both parties sought to move beyond the legacy of the National Front and to open the political system. In the 1982 presidential campaign, both candidates called for a democratic opening and negotiations with the country's guerrilla groups. The Conservative, Belisario Betancur, won and launched the first of what was to be twenty years of intermittent peace negotiations. In total, five successive presidents attempted to negotiate directly with the FARC. Formal face-to-face negotiations occurred from 1984 to 1986, from 1991 to 1992, and finally from 1998 to 2002. Each of these peace processes ended in failure. In 2002, after the breakdown of the final peace process, the election turned not on the issue of peace, as it had done during the five previous presidential campaigns. This time the election was decided on the question of which candidate could implement a more effective security policy. All polls showed that large sections of the Colombian public were exhausted by the endless violence and had turned against the fruitless negotiations.[24] Twenty years of failed peacemaking had left a legacy of higher levels of violence, greater distrust and a more intractable conflict.

The failed negotiations represented missed opportunities and permit us to understand more clearly the question of grievances and demands. In each period of talks, the FARC brought essentially the same set of demands to the negotiating table. Two issues predominated: (1) land reform and state investment in rural development, and (2) political reforms leading to greater political participation, particularly at the local level. Marulanda essentially continued to assert the basic agenda that he first articulated as a Liberal guerrilla within the self-defense communities, or "independent republics" of the 1950s. Let us review some of the past negotiation failures.

## Negotiating Peace 1984–1987

In 1984, the FARC and the government signed a ceasefire agreement, the only time this was achieved in the long history of negotiations. The FARC called for political reforms such as the direct election of mayors and greater guarantees for the exercise of political opposition. The demands were modest and within the realm of democratic political reforms. Their negotiating positions fall closer to a reformist, modernization agenda attuned to center and left parties throughout Latin America in the mid-twentieth century. Despite its long association with the Communist Party of Colombia, the FARC's positions at the negotiating table have not been especially revolutionary or socialist.

In 1985, a year after signing the ceasefire agreement, the FARC announced that it was forming a political party, the Patriotic Union (UP). In national elections in 1986, the UP elected 6 senators and 9 representatives in congressional elections and 350 city councilmen throughout the country. In the presidential election, it received about 4 percent of the total vote, the highest ever achieved by any leftist party in Colombia at that point. In 1988, in the first direct elections ever for mayors in Colombia that partly emerged out of the peace process, the UP won scores of mayorships out of almost a thousand that were contested. At the national level, the UP achieved a modest but significant voice. Two FARC *comandantes* left the mountains, won election, and took up seats as members of congress. Most of the UP's other candidates were not recruited from the FARC, but from other sectors of the left or the Communist Party. At the local level, the UP's gains were more significant. Entire areas of the sparsely populated regions east of the Andes comprising almost half of the national territory came under its electoral influence.

The FARC ran candidates without handing in arms and the UP continued to contest elections even after the peace process collapsed. Party, government, and civil society leaders accused the FARC of exercising "armed proselytism" or electioneering at the point of a gun. Some saw the strategy as simply an updated version of a policy long advocated by the Communist Party of Colombia: *combinación de todas las formas de lucha*, or "combining all forms of struggle."[25] The FARC was combining ballots with bullets. The result was that UP candidates and UP elected officials became military and paramilitary targets. In the first year—even while the ceasefire was still in effect—more than 80 UP candidates for public office were murdered. Following the 1986 election, two UP senators and one UP congressman were assassinated. The 1986 UP presidential candidate was gunned down shortly after the elections. Its 1990 presidential candidate was assassinated while campaigning. Today, the UP barely exists though people affiliated with it continue to be assassinated. By 2002, more than 2,000 of its members had been assassinated. Almost all of these murders were committed with absolute impunity.

The killings worked. They undermined the peace process. This is the objective of "spoilers" during peace processes.[26] In Colombia, the spoilers were comprised of a murky nexus of paramilitaries, members of the armed forces, and others. Killing of unarmed candidates and elected officials—even if these candidates and officials have ties to an illegal armed group—is a violation of the laws of war. Yet this experience still has not been repudiated in Colombia. The killings of the UP's members has become part of the FARC's lists of grievances. Guarantees for political participation are part of their current demands as they have been since 1958. It will be difficult to reach a negotiated settlement with the FARC without Colombian governments and society first recognizing—and later addressing as part of a larger truth and reconciliation process—this brutal and tragic episode in the history of the conflict. It has loomed over all subsequent negotiations.

## Negotiating Peace, 1990–1991

In 1990, the government successfully negotiated the disarmament and reincorporation of several smaller guerrilla groups, including the M-19, the

EPL, and Quintín Lame. The agenda of negotiations was purposely narrow. The government insisted the guerrillas unilaterally call a ceasefire and negotiate the terms of their disarmament and demobilization. One incentive that was offered was participation in a Constituent Assembly to write a new constitution. The M-19 demobilized without even this incentive. It believed that the time was propitious to transform itself into a successful political party.[27] Its gamble yielded contradictory dividends: its leader, Carlos Pizarro, was assassinated while campaigning for president in 1990, but six months later, the M-19 won 27 percent of the vote in a special election for the Constituent Assembly. There was hope that the FARC could also be persuaded to enter negotiations and participate in the Constituent Assembly. Expectations for a new dynamic were augmented by the seismic global events of 1989 and 1990 that forced political groups, parties, and insurgencies everywhere to rethink their positions. Closer to home, the beginning of peace processes in Central America suggested that that peaceful resolution of internal conflicts would be one of the dividends of a post-Cold War world. Yet the FARC refused to negotiate under the terms offered by the government. It insisted on a broader negotiating agenda that included substantive issues such as agrarian and economic reforms, and refused to discuss the issue of arms until after accords had been reached.

Compounding the FARC's recalcitrance, the government overplayed its historic opportunity. Having successfully demobilized several guerrilla groups and having laid the foundation for their participation in a Constituent Assembly, the administration of Colombian president Cesar Gaviria made the decision to bomb Casa Verde in La Uribe (Meta), the principal camp and home to the leadership of the FARC in the region of the old "independent republics." Casa Verde had been the site of negotiations from 1984 to 1986. The aerial assault took place on the same day as the elections for the Constituent Assembly. The dual policies underscored the government's central argument: The world has changed; insurgents can adapt by disarming and participating in elections; those who keep their arms are illegitimate and are on the losing side of history—and will be defeated militarily.

The FARC thought otherwise. Once again its demands had been met by military force. For the FARC leadership, the bombing of Casa Verde echoed back to Marquetalia.[28] As the Constituent Assembly deliberated during the first six months of 1991, the FARC unleashed one of the largest offensives of the war striking the military throughout the country. By August 1991, the government had agreed to return to the negotiating table, this time with fewer conditions. From August 1991 to March 1992, the government met with the FARC in Caracas, Venezuela and in Tlaxcala, Mexico. The FARC negotiated together with the ELN as part of the Simón Bolívar Guerrilla Coordinating Body (Coordinadora Guerrillera Simón Bolívar, CGSB).[29] The FARC and ELN agreed to negotiate a ceasefire but demanded formal control over 150 municipalities in which to locate their fighters during the negotiations, asserting that these areas reflected municipalities where it already was the predominant authority. The government originally recognized 9 such areas; but the ceasefire talks ended without an agreement. In Tlaxcala, the two sides moved on to the broader policy issues. The CGSB called for broad economic and political reforms, but these negotiations never got off the ground. The short-lived peace process definitively collapsed after a series of kidnappings and clashes between government and guerrilla forces, despite the fact that no ceasefire agreement had yet been reached. The government's response to the breakdown of the negotiations was to expand its counterinsurgency strategy while the FARC in particular and the ELN to a less extent accelerated their military buildups. Reflecting the mood of the early post-cold war order, President Gaviria declared: the guerrillas have "lost their Marxist ideals and were now little more than drug traffickers and criminals and uninterested in political or social change."

## Negotiating Peace 1998–2002

Following the collapse of Tlaxcala talks, the CGSB broke down and the FARC and ELN returned to their separate strategies. Political violence continued to escalate and the government of Ernesto Samper (1994–1998) became stalled in a scandal over drug financing of his presidential campaign. From 1992 to 1998, negotiations with the FARC did not resume. Only following the election of Conservative Andrés Pastrana did the climate change and one final attempt at a negotiated settlement to the decade's long conflict was pursued. In the absence of the CGSB, Pastrana was forced to reach out separately to each guerrilla group. At the insistence of the FARC, the Colombian president privileged the relationship with the FARC and, to the great dismay and wrath of the ELN, the Pastrana Administration marginalized the separate talks with the ELN.[30]

Nevertheless, the peace process with the FARC had several innovative components that appeared to address directly some of the flaws and weaknesses of earlier experiences. Yet this initiative, too, ultimately ended in failure and had the unintended consequence of profoundly diminishing public support for a negotiated settlement. The core components and "rules of the game" that both the Pastrana government and the FARC agreed to were:

*No ceasefire.* Both sides agreed to negotiate amid the hostilities without a ceasefire. This policy reflected both the FARC's rejection of the unilateral ceasefire method employed during the negotiations with the M-19 and other groups, and the armed forces rejection of the bilateral ceasefire imposed by Betancur during his government. There also existed a strong international precedent: in El Salvador, the two sides agreed to negotiate during the war and only to discuss a ceasefire after substantive agreements had been reached.

*Political recognition.* The government passed a law that explicitly recognized the FARC as a political group. Based on this law, the government opened up negotiations with the FARC while ruling out negotiations with criminal organizations and drug traffickers.

*Creation of a demilitarized zone.* To facilitate negotiations, the government ceded a 42,000-square-kilometer territory—an area the size of Switzerland—to the FARC. The area was known as the *despeje*, or withdrawal zone. This controversial policy had antecedents in the FARC's insistence on negotiating in Colombia, instead of at a location outside the country as had occurred in the early 1990s. This position reflected the FARC's preoccupation with internal security caused by the dirty war and the tragic experience of the UP. It also demonstrated the FARC's great concern with establishing stable bases of local power.

*Return to the broad negotiating agenda.* The two sides developed a common negotiating agenda largely based on the draft negotiating agenda developed by the FARC, which in turn was based on its Strategic Plan approved in its Eighth Conference, held in April 1993.[31] The agenda represented the articulation of the FARC's demands that had accumulated during more than forty years of guerrilla struggle. Entitled "A Common Agenda for Change Toward a New Colombia," signed 6 May 1999 in the La Machaca (in the *despeje* zone), it was divided into 12-points, whose headings were as follows: Negotiated Political Solution, Protection of Human Rights Is a Responsibility of the State, Integral Agrarian Policies, Exploitation and Conservation of Natural Resources, Economic and Social Structure, Justice Reforms, the Fight Against Corruption and Drug-Trafficking, Political Reform and the Expansion of Democracy, Reform of the State, Agreements on International Humanitarian Law, Armed Forces, International Relations and Formalizing Agreements.[32] (The negotiations stalled almost immediately after defining this agenda. Both sides had agreed to begin with point 5: economic and social structure. Three years were then spent discussing economic reforms and unemployment, without agreement. During February and March 2000, government and FARC leaders jointly toured several European countries studying suitable economic models for Colombia.)[33]

*No discussion of arms or disarmament.* Disarmament would be the byproduct of a successful peace process, not its central objective. Disarmament was not mentioned in the negotiating agenda.

*International participation in the process.* Although no concrete accord was reached at the outset, both sides agreed to a vaguely worded statement that opened the door to international involvement. Eventually, both the FARC and the government accepted the naming of a special advisor of the secretary general of the United Nations and a 10-member "Group of Friends" consisting of four American nations (Venezuela, Mexico, Cuba, and Canada) and six European nations (Norway, Germany, Sweden, Switzerland, France, and Spain).

*Public forums for the participation of civil society.* These forums represented a recognition that peace would require a broad participation of civil society. They were organized around specific themes relating to the negotiating agenda, such as illicit crops or economic reform. They were held both in the *despeje* zone and in other parts of the country.[34]

The FARC also proposed certain conditions for the talks. It insisted that the government must confront the paramilitaries and sever all relations between the armed forces and these groups. Second, the government must agree to a prisoner exchange that would entail releasing the FARC's political prisoners being held by the government in exchange for the more than 400 police and soldiers then held captive by the FARC. These conditions were only partially met. The government removed a few generals accused of having links with the paramilitaries, and in 2001—in the only concrete achievement of the process—several hundred soldiers and police were released by the FARC in exchange for a small number of the FARC's prisoners who were gravely ill.

What went wrong? Both sides accused the other of not having sufficient political will or desire to end the war. In the absence of a ceasefire, each stepped up military activities and capabilities. The FARC denounced the exponential expansion of the AUC from 4,000 to over 8,000 fighters during the first three years of the Pastrana government and accused the armed forces of complicity. It also denounced the sharp rise in paramilitary violence against NGOs, journalists, labor leaders, and leftist activists. Again, the spoilers moved to the center of the process. The FARC also repeatedly condemned the U.S.-sponsored antinarcotics assistance program, Plan Colombia, which greatly increased U.S. military aid to the government and strengthened the military capabilities of the Colombian armed forces. The government, for its part, condemned the FARC's escalation of military activities in all areas of the country and the use of the *despeje* as a military safe haven. The government also accused the FARC of holding kidnapped victims in the *despeje* and denounced its increased involvement in kidnapping and other criminal activities.

The peace process, as structured, was inadequate to address the concerns of both sides and eventually overwhelmed the issues at the negotiating table. The international community had no authority to mediate or resolve impasses and disputes. In the final weeks of the process, the UN special advisor, James Lemoyne, and the representative of the Group of Friends, French ambassador Daniel Parfait, made a courageous attempt to avert the inevitable breakdown. But by then it was much too late. When both sides are engaged in a military buildup trying to gain leverage on the battlefield and at the negotiating table, it is difficult for grievances and demands to get a hearing—even in a sparsely populated demilitarized zone deep in the Colombian jungle.

## Organizational Capacity

The FARC has grown from a small band of guerrilla fighters in 1964 with a support base of a few remote mountainous communities to a national army of 18,000 fighters and roughly 12,000 urban militia fighters with a presence in all areas of the national territory. Over the years, the organization has developed a tightly focused, centralized military hierarchy.

Since 1973, it has been headed by a seven-member National Secretariat of the Central Governing Council (Secretariado General del Estado Mayor Central) that oversees a 25-member Governing Council (Estado Mayor).[35] These in turn oversee seven regional divisions (*bloques*) formed in 1993, that cover all areas of the national territory. The *bloques* oversee the basic military unit of the FARC, the military front or *frente,* first created in 1968. Each *frente* has between 200 and 300 guerrillas. In 2003, the FARC had 72 *frentes* under the command of the regional divisions: Eastern Division (22 *frentes*), Southern (10), Magdalena Medio (8), Northwestern known as the Bloque José María Cordoba (8), Central (5), Caribbean (5), and Western (4).[36] There are some *frentes* that operate independently of the regional divisions. Beneath the *frentes,* military units are organized into "columns" of 110 fighters, "companies" of 54 fighters, "guerrillas" of 26 fighters, "squads" of 12 fighters, and "tactical combat units" of 6 fighters. This military organization allows the FARC to assemble large forces for major assaults such as overrunning a military base or taking over a town, or to disaggregate their forces into classical guerrilla ambush or hit-and-run operations. Each regional division is also overseen politically by a governing council and led by a military-political commander (*comandante*) and a "replacement commander." The *frentes* are similarly organized. The chain of command goes from commander in chief, commander of the governing council, commander of the division, commander of the *frente,* commander of the guerrilla, and commander of the squad.

Politically, all guerrillas are organized into cells, a model adopted from the Communist Party of Colombia and other communist parties in Latin America and elsewhere that were often forced to organize underground. For the FARC, whose members are primarily guerrilla soldiers, cells are basically used as tools of indoctrination, study, and political actions. All members of the FARC, from the general secretariat to basic guerrilla soldiers, belong to a cell.

The general orientation of the FARC is set by the National Conference, a process that began with the First Conference of the Bloque Sur held in Riochiquito in 1964 immediately after the attack on Marquetalia. There, a governing council of the Bloque Sur was established bringing together the leaders of the various "independent republics." This conference was followed by the Constituent Conference of the Revolutionary Armed Forces of Colombia in 1966. There the FARC first established the general political-military objectives of the organization, codes of conduct within the organization, and plans for territorial control and expansion objectives. Since its founding over forty years ago, the FARC has held eight national conferences. At the national conferences, each *frente* sends delegates. The conferences have the authority to re-structure the military, organize new types of combat units, enlarge the composition of the secretariat (in 1993 it was expanded from five to seven), and set political and military strategies and goals for the next period. Following the Uribe bombings in 1990, the members of the secretariat were geographically dispersed. Many became commanders of regional divisions following the formation of these units in 1993.

In 2003, the principal members of the national secretariat were Manuel Marulanda Vélez, commander-in chief; Alfonso Cano, chief political strategist and leader of the FARC clandestine political movement Bolivarian Movement for a New Colombia (Movimiento Bolivariano por la Nueva Colombia) (founded as a clandestine political movement in the 1990s to avoid the fate of the UP)—he is also the commander of the Western Division and was chief negotiator at Caracas and Tlaxcala; Raúl Reyes, commander of the FARC international operations and commander of the Southern Division, chief negotiator during talks with the government in 1998–2002; Iván Márquez, commander of the Northwestern José María Cordoba Division and ex-congressman for the UP representing the Department of Caquetá; and Jorge Briceño (Mono Jojoy), commander of the largest division, the Eastern Division, that covers the Eastern Cordillera and the Eastern Plains and concentrates many fronts in the mountains around Bogotá.

Historically, Manuel Marulanda served as the overall leader as well as chief military leader and strategist. In his years as a guerrilla fighter, he became a formidable military strategist of guerrilla warfare who was able to use the terrain of Colombia's mountains and jungles to the advantage of the FARC. He also was, without question, the *symbolic* leader of the FARC. His person and his life as an agrarian organizer and leader of a forty-year insurrection are viewed with great respect and pride within the movement. Throughout the decades, Marulanda became the subject of legend and myth. The press or army reported his death regularly.[37] Marulanda had little formal education. He is naturally reticent and has the simple directness and humility of a 1950s peasant leader. He is unworldly and it is said that he has never been to Bogotá. He should not be compared to other guerrilla leaders who have completely dominated their forces with their personality, intellect, and authoritarian leadership, such as Abimael Guzmán, leader of Sendero Luminoso in Peru (see Chapter 9), and Abdullah Öcalan, leader of the Kurdistan Workers' Party PKK in Turkey (see Chapter 10). He has led with a collegial style of leadership since the first national conference and the creation of the governing council. His capture or death would have far fewer consequences for the FARC than was the case when guerrilla leaders were captured in Peru and Turkey.

The FARC does not formally distinguish between military and political leaders and does not have the position of political commissar as some other guerrilla movements do, particularly the ELN. Yet for decades, Marulanda assumed the functions of military strategist while the traditional political and ideological leader was Jacobo Arenas, a former Communist labor organizer in the petroleum unions in the 1950s, who was a founding member of the FARC. Arenas died of "old age" in the mountains in 1992. He was succeeded as chief political strategist by Alfonso Cano, member of the *estado mayor*, an anthropologist educated at the National University who came of age during the revolutionary student movements of the 1960s. Since the mid-1990s, Marulanda has handed the military leadership over to Jorge Briceño (Mono Jojoy) a younger disciple who basically grew up within the guerrilla movement. Marulanda is ill and in 2005 he began to transfer the overall leadership to Alfonso Cano.[38] The passing of the leadership mantle from Marulanda to Cano not only represents a generational shift; it also represents the emergence of a more astute political leader who would likely be more receptive to negotiations.

The FARC also has formed about 12,000 urban militias in the country's major and medium-size cities. These are considered "civilian" militias armed by the FARC. They do not pertain to the military chain of command and they live and work in the community. There are two types of militias: the "Bolivarian militias," linked to the FARC's clandestine Bolivarian political movement, and the "popular militias." In reality, the popular militias often resemble armed youth gangs. The FARC uses them but does not fully control them. Their activities span both political and criminal activities with little direct supervision.

## Recruitment

The FARC's historical leadership comes from Liberal and Communist guerrillas of the 1940s and 1950s, from the revolutionary ferment of the student movements of the 1960s, and from the many rural communities that have coexisted with the FARC for decades. The FARC recruits most of its soldiers from the rural areas in which it operates. It accepts boy and girls at sixteen years of age, and has been denounced by the United Nations for recruiting children who are younger. In many rural areas, the FARC represents one of the only effective sources of employment, providing some direction, meaning, or opportunity to a young person's life. Even as its political support has declined at the national level, the FARC has a large source of recruits from rural areas where the numbers living at or below the official poverty line stood at 82 percent in 2000 and where job and educational opportunities are practically nonexistent. Since 1985, women have been recruited as regular fighters and not just in support roles. Today, the composition is roughly 60 percent men and 40 percent women, with some *frentes* approaching 50–50 percent.[39]

## Social Base

Over time, the social base of the FARC has changed and diminished. It has deep roots in certain rebellious communities where the Liberal and Communist guerrillas operated during *la Violencia*. These were rural communities in coffee-growing areas and colonization zones on the agricultural frontier, the Colombian designation for regions where mountains and jungles have been cleared to establish new settlements. The agricultural frontier has been expanding in Colombia for the last two hundred years, first as coffee opened up settlements throughout the Andean region, and then as coca and petroleum opened up the plains and jungles east of the Andes. The FARC has had fairly stable social bases in these communities for decades.

In the 1960s and 1970s, it could count on a significant number of students, intellectuals and cultural elites in the nation's major cities, as well as a cadre of supporters associated with the Communist Party in both rural and urban areas. Since the 1980s, the FARC has gradually lost much of its middle-class urban support network. Moreover, as it has rapidly expanded into all regions of the country beyond its traditional bases, it has had difficulty in generating large reserves of support from the population. Since the 1990s, many of these same zones have been contested by paramilitary forces. The result is that civilians are increasingly caught in the cross-fire or have become victims of the conflict as both sides target individuals linked in any way to its enemy.

As one side expands or loses influence over a given territory, recruitment patterns shift accordingly. Historically, joining the guerrillas for many poor young people in rural areas represented stability, satisfaction of basic needs such as food and shelter, direction, and even education and advancement. Ideological formation came after they became guerrillas, not before. Until 2005 many of these same youths were entering the AUC and dissident paramilitaries. The shift underscores the weak relationship the FARC has with the populations in some areas of the country and also the structural conditions of unemployment where entrance into illegal groups provides one of the few employment opportunities available. The situation is even more unstable in the urban areas where the FARC and paramilitary groups compete with each other to recruit poor urban youth into militias.

## Financing: Drugs, Kidnapping, and Cattle-Rustling

The subject of finances is perhaps the most controversial. In the 1960s and 1970s, the FARC received some support, training, and logistical and military assistance from the Colombian Communist Party and the Soviet Union. It also raised money locally by imposing "revolutionary taxes." The drug export boom reshaped the conflict and the armed actors in multiple ways. The scope and intensity of the war widened and increased. By the 1990s, as the U.S. drug war in the Andean region had repressed production in Peru and Bolivia, Colombia emerged as the center of both coca and cocaine production.

The FARC, though founded decades before the coca/cocaine export boom, now had access to new and higher levels of financial resources. It also found new bases of social support centered around the peasant coca farmers and the large community of itinerant laborers who, by definition, were outside the jurisdiction of the state. The overwhelming majority of these activities were concentrated in areas where the state's presence was minimal or nonexistent and where the FARC had long exercised authority in the vacuum left by the state. By the 1990s, the FARC had turned completely to internal sources for funding. In the process, it emerged as an archetypal post-cold war insurgency in which the lines between war and crimes have been blurred. As can be seen in Table 2.1, the FARC raises the majority of its funds from three sources: kidnapping, cattle rustling, and control or taxation of the lower parts of the drug trade: coca cultivation, coca harvests, coca paste, airstrips, and some cocaine exports. The study summarized in the table was conducted by an elite investigative unit in Colombia's finance ministry. Even allowing for inevitable inaccuracies resulting from any attempt to analyze a clandestine enterprise, the study represents the most serious and exhaustive analysis of the FARC's finances to date and provides a general framework to understand this aspect of the organization.[40] In 2003, FARC's total income was put at more than $83 million. Of this, the two largest sources of annual revenues came from kidnapping, more than $40 million, and stealing cattle, almost $24 million. The drug trade, primarily through the taxing of coca and cocaine processing, earned the FARC about $18 million. What is notable about these figures is how much they differ from those commonly reported in the international press, which often identifies the FARC as a major drug cartel with an income ranging from $600 million to $1 billion.[41] The FARC is primarily involved in the least profitable end of the trade, the cultivation of illicit crops and the first phases of production and commercialization of coca paste. The FARC's direct cocaine sales revenue of just over $3 million was less than the drug revenues of an average street gang in Los Angeles.

More important, the FARC does not operate like a drug cartel or an organized criminal syndicate. It operates as a hierarchically organized guerrilla

TABLE 2.1. FARC INCOMES AND EXPENDITURES 2003, SUMMARY TABLE

| *Income source* | *Amount, U.S.$* | *Expenditures* | *Amount, U.S.$* |
|---|---|---|---|
| Security tax coca cultivation | 245,909 | Outfitting and equipping guerrilla soldiers | 6,425,909 |
| Coca harvest tax | 433,181 | Transport | 685,909 |
| Coca paste tax | 402,727 | Gasoline | 4,740,545 |
| "Gramaje," tax on sale of coca paste | 9,207,272 | Healthcare, medicines, mobile clinics | 657,727 |
| Tax on cocaine HCl production | 1,191,363 | "Solidarity Fund" payments to FARC political prisoners | 1,074,545 |
| Cocaine sales | 3,251,818 | | |
| Tax on use of clandestine airstrips | 2,344,090 | "Solidarity Fund" payments to families of FARC political prisoners | 322,272 |
| Subtotal, drug production | 17,076,360 | Military/political training programs | 2,322,727 |
| Kidnapping | 40,254,545 | | |
| Cattle rustling | 23,940,000 | Operating international front | 216,363 |
| Bank robberies | 1,263,636 | | |
| Extortion | 681,818 | Explosives | 1,934,545 |
| | | Armaments* | 18,784,000 |
| | | Maintaining internet sites | 9,090 |
| | | Losses due to arms seized by public forces | 3,575,000 |
| | | Propaganda | 365,000 |
| | | Food for guerrillas | 14,620,000 |
| | | Food for kidnapped victims | 1,082,272 |
| | | Clandestine radios | 195,909 |
| | | Communications | 3,777,727 |
| **Total** | **83,216,359** | **Total** | **60,789,630** |

Source: "Las cuentas de las FARC," *Semana* 1187, 28 January 2005, based on a study by the Unidad de Información y Análisis Financiero del Ministerio de Hacienda.

*Armaments figure from Junta de Inteligencia Conjunta, "Estimación de ingresos y egresos de las FARC," Bogotá, February 2005.

Exchange rate: $U.S.1 = 2200 pesos, calculations by author based on army of 16,672 guerrilla fighters.

army, and pursues a political-military strategy designed to weaken the state and make parts of the country ungovernable. Yet it also dedicates substantial manpower and resources to kidnapping, guarding illegal crops, taxing coca harvests, the sale of coca paste, and producing cocaine for export. How should these different sides of the same organization be understood?

There has been much discussion by scholars concerning the causes of civil wars and armed insurrections. Paul Collier, an Oxford professor of economics seconded to the World Bank, introduced a controversial but much discussed thesis that internal armed conflict is not caused by political grievances as many social scientists have long maintained. Rather, he argued, internal wars can be explained almost exclusively by access to financial resources, which Collier succinctly and provocatively characterized as "greed." He thus framed his argument as "greed versus grievance."[42] Without entering too far into this debate, the Colombian case[43] merits a brief discussion because there is a common belief that the Colombian conflict was caused and is sustained by the drug trade and that the guerrillas have been transformed into narco-guerrillas and narco-terrorists.

The evidence suggests that the drug trade has fueled much of the expansion of the war and has transformed Colombian society and the armed conflict in the process. However the impact is multicausal and multidimensional. The prime impacts have been: the weakening and corruption of the state and general breakdown of social order, reflected in high crime and homicide rates; the investment of narco-dollars by drug traffickers into rural landholdings which has further aggravated the nation's festering agrarian problem and has helped fuel the expansion of the right-wing paramilitaries; the large increase in U.S. military assistance and U.S. military presence in the country to fight the narcotics trade; territorial struggles between guerrillas, paramilitaries, and organized crime groups to control territory for the growing of illicit crops or to open up strategic territories to support an underground economy; increased resources for guerrilla and right-wing paramilitary armies.

As the Colombian conflict has been transformed, the FARC's original grievances have not disappeared. Indeed, the situation of rural lands and the repression of political alternatives are, by most measures worse than when the FARC was founded. In the absence of external sources of support, as existed during the cold war, the FARC has turned to internal sources of funding, as many other post-cold war guerrillas have. (This was also the case with regard to insurgents and diamonds and timber in Angola or oil and other minerals in Indonesia). But in Colombia, as in many other cases, access to resources is not determinative; it is facilitative. Greed did not cause these wars. Nevertheless, insurrectionary movements—whatever their ideology or legitimacy—require resources. The FARC relies on kidnapping, the drug trade, and other criminal activities to raise finances to maintain and expand an army. There is no evidence that leaders or fighters in the FARC are accumulating individual wealth. No secret bank accounts have ever been exposed or confiscated. FARC guerrillas do not receive salaries, unless they are taken political prisoners. Then they and their families are given small monthly sums. The FARC's statutes expressly prohibit individual property.[44]

Since 1985, all funds have been managed by the central governing council. Each *frente* is assigned a quota, which must be raised by kidnapping, extortion, cattle stealing, or revolutionary taxes. The centralization of finances has meant a more equitable distribution of funds throughout the different regions and much greater control by the governing council. Known cases of commanders of *frentes* who have misappropriated funds or have been involved in corruption have been severely punished by the FARC, generally with the death penalty if caught. Table 2.1 suggests that the FARC spends approximately $52 million arming, outfitting, feeding, and maintaining a guerrilla army. The table also shows a gap between income and expenditures of about $30 million. Not listed in the expenditures column are capital goods that are part of the war-fighting infrastructure: cars, trucks, riverboats, warehouses, buildings, munitions factories. Also absent are capital and earnings in legal investments that are believed to have been made by and for the FARC.[45]

The FARC is known to have exchanged cocaine for weapons. There is a well-known case of a Brazilian arms dealer, Fernando da Costa, also known as Fernandinho Neira Mar, who has been accused of supplying weapons in exchange for FARC cocaine. Similar accusations and arrests have been made against traffickers with FARC connections in Suriname and Mexico.[46]

A final observation on financing in the post-cold war world is worth making. In some cases, insurgent groups are able to draw on support from an international diaspora, as has the IRA, Hamas, or the PKK from large overseas communities of Irish, Palestinians and Kurds. This has not been the case with the FARC. Colombians have settled in large numbers in the United States, Venezuela, Ecuador and increasingly in parts of Western Europe, but there is no substantive movement to support the FARC among Colombians abroad. The FARC's inability to speak to Colombia's exile community is similar to its increased alienation from the predominantly urban and increasingly middle-class areas at home. The FARC still speaks the language of rural Colombia; its grievances, at bottom, are based on a reality that most Colombians no longer directly experience in a country that today is 70 percent urban and 30 percent rural. When Marulanda first took up arms, Colombia was 70 percent rural.

## Global War on Terror and FARC

The FARC is listed on the U.S. State Department list of terrorist groups. Since 2002, over the objections by Sweden and France, the European

Union listed the FARC as a terrorist organization. These designations have specific legal repercussions in the United States and throughout the European Union. Moreover, U.S. policy on Colombia is quickly moving beyond the template of antinarcotics assistance that was codified in the $600 million annual assistance program from 2000 to 2005 known as Plan Colombia. In 2002, the U.S. Congress authorized the use of counternarcotics assistance programs to be redirected if necessary to antiterrorism activities, thereby lifting a long-existing restriction on counterinsurgency activities in Colombia. The Bush administration has indicated that it will continue to provide military assistance to Colombia at the same levels for the foreseeable future. Today, drug trafficking is viewed as a subset of terrorism and Colombia has been placed squarely inside the Global War on Terror[47] as one of the few non-Islamic conflicts fronts in the U.S. global war. The terrorist lens, however, is not helpful.

If terrorism means the violations of international humanitarian law (IHL) and the deliberate harming of noncombatants, then the FARC is a terrorist group. The FARC is bound by Protocol II of the Geneva Conventions. In recent years, it has flagrantly and openly refused to enter into a discussion with human rights groups on such violations as kidnappings, extrajudicial homicides, and the use of inaccurate homemade weapons such as gas cylinders which have caused countless civilian deaths.[48] Yet the terrorist label is not necessary to hold the FARC or any other group accountable for violations of IHL. In Colombia, the term was rarely used before the election of Alvaro Uribe in 2002. Yet since then the label has been used to dehumanize the FARC's leaders, dehistoricize its past, and depoliticize the content of its grievances. In this sense, calling the FARC terrorists has widened the chasm between the guerrillas and the state and has made the possibility of bridging it that much more difficult.

The FARC in the twenty-first century has a dilemma. It is still formed by the ethos of the peasant insurgency it started over forty years ago. Yet today the country is predominantly urban. To remedy this, the FARC has made a concerted effort during the last ten years to expand its urban presence. The large flow of internal refugees fleeing the rural violence has aided this mission as shantytowns in the country's medium and large cities burst with new migrants fleeing the rural violence. The FARC has found these areas to be fertile ground for recruitment and expansion. However, the FARC's urban militias have been difficult to control and it is quite evident that the FARC is not accustomed to acting in an urban setting.

Furthermore, the FARC in recent years has engaged in acts of terrorism, placing bombs in commercial establishments to randomly kill civilians. Under any definition this is terrorism. Yet this is not the signature method of operation of the FARC, and is still relatively rare. It is basically safe to walk the streets of Bogotá or Medellín without fear of being caught in a terrorist incident. There are also no cases of suicide bombings in Colombia.

## Military Strategies Versus Negotiations

The Colombian state has significantly increased its defense spending, from 3.2 percent of GDP in 2000 to 4.19 percent of GDP in 2005, and it is projected to reach 6 percent of GDP in 2006. With the assistance of the United States, it has increased the effectiveness of the armed forces in counterinsurgency and counterterrorism operations. President Uribe has augmented the number of professional soldiers to 70,000, created a new category of 20,000 "peasant soldiers," and added over 20,000 police.[49] At the same time that Uribe initiated this military build-up, he also began a process of separate negotiations with the AUC. The stated aim of these talks is to demobilize and disarm the country's paramilitary forces. If this could be achieved, the strategic balance of power on the ground and the nature of the conflict between the FARC and the state would be transformed significantly. It would make the conflict sharper and less ambiguous.

Since the *paras* primarily fought a dirty war and were (and in 2005 continued to be) responsible for 75 percent of IHL violations, the AUC demobilization could make the war less "dirty" and less terroristic by anyone's definition. It also would permit international organizations and human rights NGOs to better pressure the remaining combatants to respect IHL. However, most important, demobilization could potentially make peace negotiations with the FARC and the ELN more viable by eliminating a force that has been an inveterate spoiler of peace accords for over twenty years.

Yet the negotiations with the AUC are fraught with difficulties. It may not be possible for the state to fully remove one actor from the conflict while at the same time escalating the war with the other. The *paras* will be reluctant to create a vacuum that the FARC could fill. One result could be the demobilization of individuals and even the dismantling of the AUC as a national organization but the continuation of decentralized paramilitary armies at the local level.

At some point, however, the government and the FARC will need to return to the negotiating table. Despite the steady increase of the state's military capacity, the state is still not capable of defeating the guerrillas today or in the foreseeable future. Three years after the launch of Plan Patriota, the FARC is as strong militarily as ever and no member of the FARC's seven-member National Secretariat has ever been captured, though several have died of old age or illness in the course of an insurrection that in 2005 celebrated its 41st anniversary. Its involvement in criminal activities, kidnapping, and the drug trade has diminished its moral authority, and its political projection is far weaker than it once was, particularly in urban Colombia and among the nation's intelligentsia. However, even with its diminished political stature, its organizational structure, recruitment base, and ability to wage guerrilla warfare in all areas of the national territory remain undiminished.

Basic issues that need to a be part of a future negotiating agenda with the FARC minimally include: (1) agrarian reform and equitable rural development, the historic cause of the FARC; (2) an end to the dirty war; (3) reorienting the strategic mission of the armed forces and police away from counterinsurgency in a post-conflict society; and (4) incorporating the FARC into the local and national structures of state and elective politics. As in the agenda approved in May 1999, the issue of illicit crops can and should be on the table and should be part of a broader discussion of rural development.

It is unlikely that peace can achieved without international assistance. The repeated breakdowns and interruptions of the peace process during six presidential administrations convincingly demonstrate that peace is too important to be left to the combatants or the parties in conflict. Outside observers, mediators and facilitators will need to be brought into the peace process. The government, regardless of its popular legitimacy and sovereign authority, cannot be judge, mediator, and party to the conflict at the same time.

One of the strongest arguments for internationalizing a future peace process is that the Colombian conflict has already become internationalized. The drug trade, the U.S. antinarcotics war and now the Global War on Terror have placed Colombian political violence at the center of global security concerns. The U.S. military has forged new ties with its Colombian counterparts, and U.S. diplomats increasingly operate as pro-consular officials, demanding that Colombia eradicate crops and adjust the political system to better attack terrorism and organized crime. At the same time, the human rights tragedy brought the European Union into Colombia's domestic politics and has led to the establishment of a United Nation's human rights office, one of only two field offices in the world.

The choices, then, are stark: escalate the war in search of a military solution or an imposed negotiation, or escalate national and international initiatives that will help create the conditions for a viable peace process. Sixty years of armed conflict is reason enough for the international community to get involved and assist in ending one of the world's most intractable and enduring armed conflicts.

## Glossary

ADO: Autodefensa Obrera (Worker Self-Defense Group). A small urban guerrilla movement that appeared in the 1970s and negotiated a ceasefire agreement with the government in 1984.

AUC: Autodefensas Unidas de Colombia (United Self-Defense Forces of Colombia). Coalition of regional paramilitary forces founded by Carlos Castaño in 1997 that entered into negotiations with the Uribe Administration in 2002 and signed agreements to demobilize by 2006.

Bogotazo: The three-day urban uprising that followed the assassination of Liberal leader Jorge Eliécer Gaitán on 9 April 1948 and sparked a decade of civil war, known as *la Violencia.*

Bloque Sur: The name of the FARC from 1964 to 1966 before establishing the current name.

Casa Verde: A region in the municipality of La Uribe (Meta) that served as home to the FARC national secretariat from 1984 to 1990 and as the site of negotiations during the first peace process from 1984 to 1986. It was bombed in December 1990 on the same day that Colombians went to the polls to elect delegates to a Constituent Assembly.

CGSB: Coordinadora Guerrillera Simón Bolívar, Simón Bolívar Guerrilla Coordinating Body. A short-lived coalition of Colombian guerrilla forces consisting of seven guerrilla groups, including FARC, ELN, EPL, M-19, Quintin Lame, Patria Libre, and ERP. It gradually disintegrated as several members chose to negotiate individually with the government and others chose to wage separate military campaigns.

CNG: Coordinadora Nacional Guerrillera, the forerunner to the CGSB and the first attempt by Colombian guerrilla movements to coordinate their operations.

ELN: Ejéricto de Liberación Nacional (National Liberation Army), Colombian guerrilla movement founded by Colombian students in Havana as a pro-Cuban movement. Reemerged in the 1980s as a Christian-Marxist guerrilla movement based on the "theology of liberation." Changed its name to ELN-UC, adding Unión Camilista (Camilist) Union in honor of slain revolutionary priest Camilo Torres.

EPL: Ejército Popular de Liberación (Popular Liberation Army). Founded in the 1960s as a pro-Maoist insurgency after the Colombian Communist Party divided into pro-Soviet and pro-Chinese camps. Negotiated a separate peace in 1990 and changed its name to Esperanza, Paz y Libertad (Hope, Peace, and Liberty).

FARC: Fuerzas Armadas Revolucionarias de Colombia (Revolutionary Armed Forces of Colombia). Colombia's oldest guerrilla movement, founded as the Bloque Sur in 1964 by former Liberal guerrillas and communist self-defense groups. In 1966, the Bloque Sur became the FARC.

*frentes* or front: the basic military unit of the FARC consisting of 200–300 combatants.

Independent Republic: Following the end of first phase of violence, *la Violencia,* several Liberal and Communist guerrillas organized self-defense communities in former conflict regions that were dubbed "independent republics" by the government. These were displaced by force in 1964 and 1965.

*liberales comunes*: Liberal guerrillas during *la Violencia* willing to cooperate with the communist self-defense groups, peasant organizations and party activists.

liberales officiales: Liberal guerrillas who refused to work with the communists and followed the official leadership of the party.

Marquetalia: The principal independent republic that was bombed in 1964. The assault helped convert the armed self-defense communities into mobile guerrilla groups that became the FARC in 1966.

M-19: Movimiento 19 de abril (April 19th Movement), urban guerrilla movement that took its name from a fraudulent presidential election in 1970. In 1990, negotiated its disarmament and demobilization and initially experienced substantial electoral success. By 1994, its electoral fortunes faded and it disappeared as a political organization though several of its leaders became prominent politicians representing new leftist coalitions.

MRQL: *Movimiento Revolucionario Quintín Lame,* Quintin Lame Revolutionary Movement, an ndigenous guerrilla movement that took up arms in the early 1980s to defend indigenous rights. Demobilized and participated in the Constituent Assembly in 1990 and 1991.

Narional Front: The constitutional agreement between the Liberal and Conservative Parties that brought a definitive end to the partisan civil war of the 1940s and 1950s and established power-sharing and alternation for a 16-year period beginning in 1958.

Plan Colombia: Originally a comprehensive program prepared by Colombia's government to address the nation's multiple crises, the term has come to refer to the $4 billion, five-year U.S. assistance program approved in 2000 to support the military and antinarcotics aspects of that program.

Plan Patriota: A military strategy developed by the U.S. and Colombia implemented in 2002 to penetrate the rear areas of the FARC and target FARC leaders.

UP: Unión Patriótica (Patriotic Union), founded by FARC in 1985, subjected to extermination campaigns over the next ten years.

*la Violencia*: The civil war between Liberal and Conservatives that began in 1946, lasted until 1958, and left 200,000 dead.

*zona de despeje*: A 42,000-square-kilometer area equal to the size of Switzerland created in the southern departments of Meta and Caquetá, where the Colombian government withdrew its security forces and handed over security functions to the FARC in an effort to facilitate negotiations between 1998 and 2002.

ZDU: *Zona de ubicación*, or "location zone," 370-square-kilometer zone in the northern department of Córdoba created in July 2003 to facilitate negotiations with the AUC. All arrest warrants were suspended in the ZDU and paramilitary leaders could maintain their arms inside the zone.

## Timeline

1946: Conservatives win presidential elections ending a 16-year period of Liberal hegemony in the nation's politics. Violence begins as Conservatives begin to recolonize political and bureaucratic positions throughout the country

1946–1958: Rural violence known as *la Violencia*.

1948: Assassination of Liberal leader and presidential candidate Jorge Eliécer Gaitán on 9 April, sparking a three-day urban riot, the Bogotazo, and decade-long rural civil war between the traditional Liberal and Conservative Parties.

1962: First bombing of the independent republic Marquetalia.

1964: Second bombing of Marquetalia, which, according to the FARC, pitted 45 men against 16,000 troops of the Colombian Army; the Bloque Sur is founded by displaced leaders of the armed self-defense communities; the pro-Cuban ELN is founded.

1966: Manuel Marulanda and leaders of the Bloque Sur announce the formation of the FARC, on 28 May, the second anniversary of the bombing of Marquetalia, and declare plans to wage guerrilla war against the oligarchic National Front regime.

1967: Founding of the pro-Maoist EPL.

1970: Suspected fraud in the presidential election on 19 April denies victory to the populist candidate, former military leader Gustavo Rojas Pinilla.

1974: A group of Rojas Pinilla's followers, together with a dissident group from the FARC, found the April 19th Movement, M-19, and announce their struggle by stealing the sword of Simón Bolívar from a museum in downtown Bogotá.

1980: M-19 takes over the Dominican Embassy, holding 15 ambassadors hostages for 61 days, including the U.S. ambassador, leading to first talks between government forces and a guerrilla movement.

1982: General pardon and amnesty granted to guerrilla leaders. Government opens up direct but separate talks with M-19, FARC, EPL, and a small group ADO. ELN refuses to participate but calls for the government to sign international human rights and international humanitarian law agreements in order to "humanize the war."

1983: The first of the contemporary paramilitary groups, MAS (Muerte a Secuestradores, Death to Kidnappers), is founded after the kidnapping of the daughter of a prominent drug kingpin by the M-19.

1984: Separate ceasefire agreements are signed between the government and FARC, EPL, M-19, ADO. M-19 takes over Palace of Justice in the center of Bogotá, taking justices from the Supreme Court and Council of State hostage, and declares its intent to put President Betancur on trial for breaking the ceasefire agreement. The army recaptures the building, killing all but one of the guerrillas, scores of civilians, and 11 justices.

1985: The Patriotic Union Party (UP) is founded by the FARC.

1986: The UP participates in the 1986 presidential and parliamentary elections.

1987: The Simón Bolívar Guerrilla Coordinating Body (CGSB) is founded.

1989: Liberal presidential candidate, Luís Carlos Galán is assassinated.

1990: M-19 breaks away from CGSB and signs a separate peace agreement leading to its disarmament. M-19 leader and presidential candidate Carlos Pizarro is assassinated while campaigning. UP presidential candidate Bernardo Jaramillo Ossa is also assassinated. Special elections are held for a Constituent Assembly. FARC headquarters in Casa Verde are bombed on the day of the special elections.

1991: Constituent Assembly meets from January to June and presents a new constitution; M-19 serves as one of three cochairs of the Assembly. FARC and ELN unleash major military offensive during the period of the Constituent Assembly and rebuff overtures to participate.

1991–1992: The government meets with FARC and ELN in Caracas, Venezuela, and Tlaxcala, Mexico, for peace negotiations.

1992: President Gaviria declares an "integral war" after breakdown of talks in Tlaxcala.

1992–1998: War intensifies; FARC overruns several military and police bases.

1997: Paramilitary leader Carlos Castaño announces the formation of the AUC.

1998: President-elect Andrés Pastrana meets with FARC leader Manuel Marulanda in the jungle and declares intent to restart peace talks. Pastrana withdraws security forces from five municipalities and establishes the *zona de despeje* to facilitate negotiations.

1999: The government and the FARC agree on a common 12-point negotiating agenda..

2000: U.S. Congress approves funding for Plan Colombia, initially a $1.7 billion package of military and antinarcotics assistance for Colombia.

2002: President Pastrana order troops to retake the *zona de despeje* on 20 February, after the FARC hijacks an airplane and kidnaps a congressman. Hardliner Alvaro Uribe is elected. The U.S. and Colombia implement Plan Patriota, designed to penetrate FARC zones and capture FARC leaders. The Uribe government initiates talks with the AUC; AUC declares a unilateral ceasefire.

2003: President Uribe establishes a "location zone" (*zona de ubicación*) in Córdoba to facilitate negotiations on demobilization with leaders of AUC and the Central Bolivar Bloc.

2004: Paramilitaries begin a gradual program of demobilization. AUC leader Carlos Castaño disappears in mysterious circumstances and is believed to have been murdered by his comrades because of positions taken at the negotiation table opening up the possibility of jail time and accountability. The government captures and extradites to United States, a former FARC negotiator Simón Trinidad.

2005: Colombian Congress passes a peace and justice bill with minimal requirements for accountability, truth-telling, or punishment, designed to facilitate demobilization and reincorporation of paramilitary leaders. Human rights groups, civil society and victim's rights organizations, as well as international organizations and some governments, denounce the bill as sanctioning impunity for war criminals and drug traffickers. FARC unleashes offensives in different regions of the country to counter Plan Patriota.

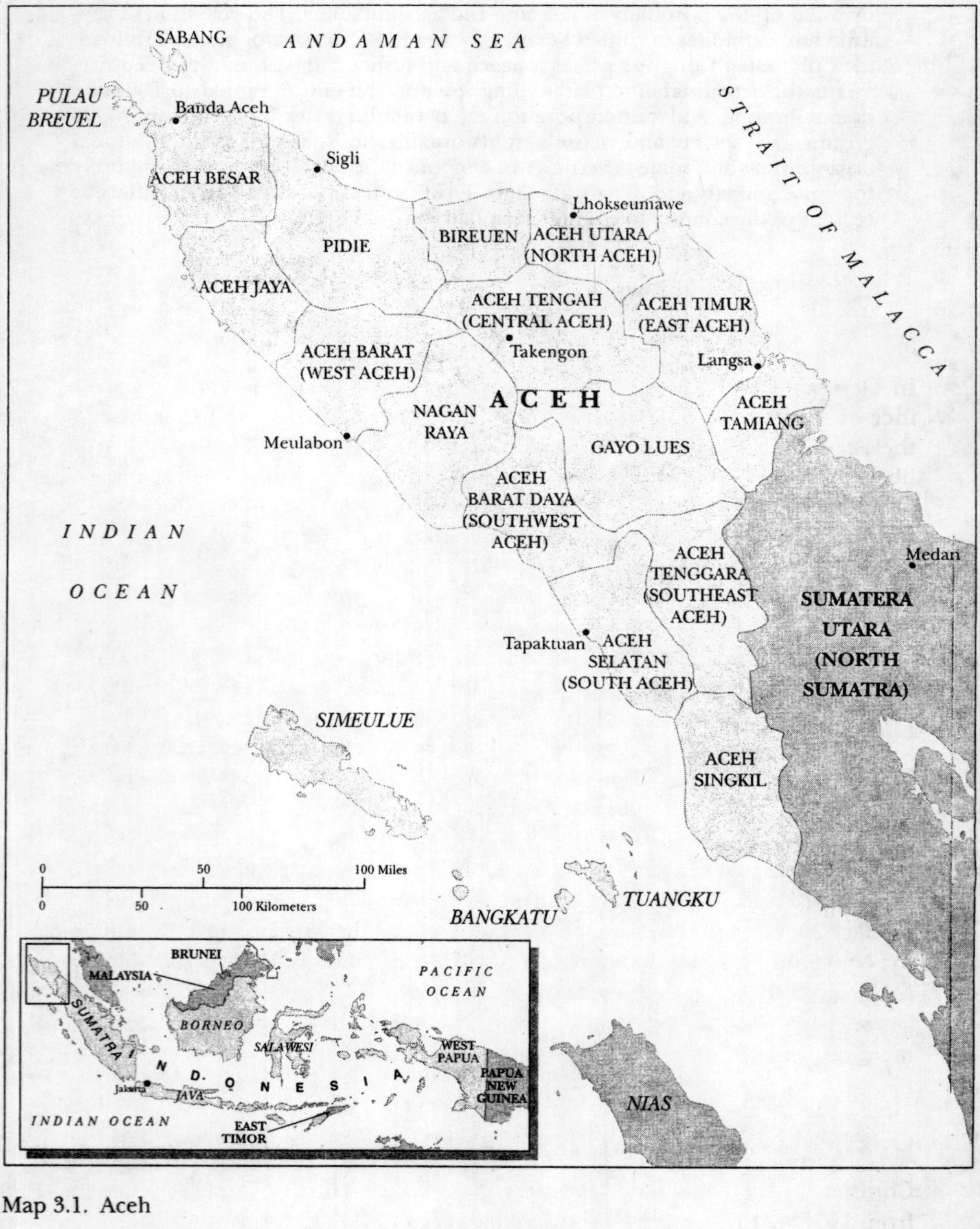

ANDAMAN SEA
SABANG
PULAU BREUEL
Banda Aceh
Sigli
ACEH BESAR
STRAIT OF MALACCA
Lhokseumawe
PIDIE
BIREUEN
ACEH UTARA (NORTH ACEH)
ACEH JAYA
ACEH TENGAH (CENTRAL ACEH)
ACEH TIMUR (EAST ACEH)
Takengon
ACEH BARAT (WEST ACEH)
Langsa
ACEH
NAGAN RAYA
ACEH TAMIANG
Meulabon
GAYO LUES
ACEH BARAT DAYA (SOUTHWEST ACEH)
INDIAN OCEAN
ACEH TENGGARA (SOUTHEAST ACEH)
Medan
SUMATERA UTARA (NORTH SUMATRA)
Tapaktuan
ACEH SELATAN (SOUTH ACEH)
SIMEULUE
ACEH SINGKIL
0 50 100 Miles
0 50 100 Kilometers
TUANGKU
BANGKATU
NIAS
MALAYSIA
BRUNEI
PACIFIC OCEAN
SUMATRA
BORNEO
SALAWESI
WEST PAPUA
PAPUA NEW GUINEA
INDONESIA
Jakarta
JAVA
INDIAN OCEAN
EAST TIMOR


Map 3.1. Aceh

*Chapter 3*

# GAM: Indonesia, GAM, and the Acehnese Population in a Zero-Sum Trap

KIRSTEN E. SCHULZE

In October 1976, a low-level insurgency erupted in the Indonesian province of Aceh, located on the northern tip of the island of Sumatra. Led by the Free Aceh Movement or Gerakan Aceh Merdeka (GAM), it sought to liberate Aceh from what it saw as an illegal Javanese neocolonial occupation and to reestablish an independent Acehnese state. The Indonesian state's response to the separatist challenge was characterized by the so-called "security" approach, which relied heavily on military operations. Only after the fall of the authoritarian New Order regime under President Suharto in May 1998 did Indonesia shift to a more comprehensive strategy, including special autonomy for Aceh and negotiations with GAM. This did not, however, change the zero-sum nature of the conflict. The 2000–2003 Geneva dialogue process was purely bilateral and not surprisingly was quickly deadlocked. Following two failed ceasefires it collapsed in May 2003. This was partially the result of GAM's failure to store its weapons as well as ceasefire violations by both the separatists and the Indonesian military or Tentara Nasional Indonesia (TNI). Above all, it was the result of the inability to bridge the gap between GAM's position of "*nothing* but independence" and Indonesia's position of "*anything* but independence." In January 2005, the devastation of parts of Aceh by the tsunami gave urgency for convening a new peace process, the Helsinki dialogue. In this process GAM shifted tactically to accepting autonomy. An agreement between Indonesia and GAM was thus possible. But GAM has not dropped its ultimate goal of Acehnese independence.

## Overview

Conflict in Aceh has seen three distinct phases. During the first phase, from 1976 to 1979, it was of very low intensity. GAM was a tiny, tightly knit, ideologically driven organization of only 70 men. The movement's support base was limited to the district of its founders—Pidie—and particularly the village of Tiro. The Indonesian response came in the form of a series of intelligence operations, which were successful in reducing the challenge from GAM. By the end of 1979, Indonesian counterinsurgency operations had killed, imprisoned, or driven into exile (Sweden) the GAM leadership; its followers were dispersed and pushed underground.

The second phase, from 1989 to 1998, marked the reemergence of the conflict. The exiled GAM leadership had been searching for international support and found a receptive ear in Libyan president Muammar al-Qadhafi. From 1986 until 1989, GAM guerrillas received paramilitary training in Libya. The return of these guerrillas reignited the insurgency. The renewed separatist challenge was met by large-scale Indonesian counterinsurgency operations. GAM's operational command relocated to neighboring Malaysia. This left the organization's lower ranks and the civilian population to bear the brunt of the Indonesian military campaign.

During the third phase, from 1998 until today, both GAM and the Indonesian government developed properly political strategies. In January 2000, they embarked upon a negotiation process that resulted in the May 2000 Humanitarian Pause and the December 2002 Cessation of Hostilities Agreement (COHA). GAM welcomed the talks as they provided the organization with domestic and international legitimacy. It was not, however, interested in any form of compromise. On 18 May 2003, the COHA collapsed. The next day, 19 May, Indonesia placed Aceh under martial law. In May 2004, martial law was downgraded to civil emergency. In May 2005, civil emergency was lifted; counterinsurgency operations, however, continued.

## Popular Grievances

While the conflict erupted in 1976 with GAM's establishment, GAM is a symptom rather than the cause of the conflict. At the heart of Acehnese popular discontent, upon which GAM draws, are antagonistic center-periphery relations that gave rise to political and economic grievances. The first set of grievances relates to repeatedly broken promises of autonomy by the central government. In 1949, Indonesia's first president, Sukarno, awarded Aceh provincial autonomy in recognition of the Acehnese contribution to the Indonesian war of independence. Yet just over a year later, in early 1951 this status was revoked and Aceh was amalgamated with the neighbouring province of North Sumatra. Aceh's strongly Muslim identity was subordinated to the "secular" state philosophy of *pancasila* ("the five principles"), a religiously neutral nationalism comprising belief in God, nationalism, humanitarianism, social justice, and democracy.

Aceh's first insurgency started in 1953, when former governor Daud Beureueh denounced *pancasila* and joined the Darul Islam rebellions, which sought to transform Indonesia into an Islamic state. This conflict was eventually resolved through a combination of security measures and negotiations, ending in an agreement in May 1959. This agreement conferred special status upon Aceh, or *daerah istimewa*—autonomy in matters of religion, *adat* (customary) law, and education. This special status did not last long. When Indonesia's Old Order under Sukarno was superseded by President Suharto's New Order in 1967, Jakarta embarked upon political and economic centralization. Centralization was promoted to protect the unity and integrity of the state and as an integral part of nation-building. National Indonesian identity was emphasized over regional, tribal, or religious loyalties. The impact of Suharto's centralization policy on Aceh cannot be overstated. In all but name, it reversed the special autonomy status.

The New Order's centralization policy and ideology of developmentalism created fresh economic grievances. In 1971, natural gas was discovered in North Aceh. The Acehnese, however, saw very little of this wealth. From 1980 onward Aceh contributed between $2 and $3 billion annually to Indonesian exports,[1] but the revenue flowed to Jakarta and from there to the rest of Indonesia. Only a small amount of Aceh's export surplus was "recycled" in the form of central government expenditure in the province. Further grievances resulted from the byproducts of the discovery of gas—namely dislocation, industrialization, pollution, foreign corporations, urban-rural migration, the influx of non-Acehnese workers, and enclave development in North Aceh. Farmers were dispossessed and fishermen were forced from their traditional occupations, without provision of alternative employment. Prices rose and urban poverty increased, placing considerable strains on Aceh's social fabric. The emergence of prostitution, gambling, alcohol, drugs, and crime further challenged Aceh's Muslim values. Most Acehnese believed that "outsiders" had "gained a disproportionate share of the benefits of industrial growth."[2]

The final set of popular grievances relates to Indonesia's counterinsurgency operations from 1976 onward, in particular the period from 1989 to 1998 when Aceh was popularly known as the *daerah operasi militer* (DOM) or "military operations area." During this period Indonesian security forces in pursuit of GAM perpetrated large-scale and systematic human rights abuses against the Acehnese population. By the end of 1998 between 1,258[3] and 2,000[4] had been killed and 3,439 tortured.[5] Human Rights Watch put the number of disappeared at 500, while the Aceh regional assembly estimated it at 1,000–5,000. The NGO Forum Aceh believed the number to be as high as 39,000. Some 625 cases of rape and torture of women were recorded.[6] An estimated 16,375 children were orphaned[7] and 3,000 women widowed. After DOM, 7,000 cases of human rights violations were documented[8] and at least 12 mass graves were investigated.[9] The fall of the New Order and the transition to democracy raised Acehnese hopes that at least some of the major incidents during DOM would be investigated and that the perpetrators would be brought to justice. Yet, despite the formation of a special commission, only five cases were ever investigated, of which only one made it to court. Since then, two more counterinsurgency operations have been launched, resulting in further civilian casualties, adding to the Acehnese quest for justice while dashing hopes that it would be obtained.

## The Birth of the Free Aceh Movement

The Aceh Sumatra National Liberation Front (ASNLF), which became locally known first as Aceh Merdeka (AM) and later as Gerakan Aceh Merdeka (GAM), was established in October 1976. Its founding father was Hasan di Tiro, grandson of Teungku Chik di Tiro, hero of the anticolonial struggle against the Dutch. Di Tiro was born in Aceh on 4 September 1930. At the age of twenty he left Aceh to study in the United States, where he also worked at the Indonesian Mission to the United Nations. In 1953 he resigned his post in support of the Darul Islam rebellion. Thereafter he continued as a businessman until his return to Aceh on 30 October 1976. Di Tiro attributes his decision to return to two events in particular: the death of his brother in a hospital in 1974, "murdered by Javanese military intelligence 'doctors'";[10] and an almost fatal plane accident in 1975 that reminded him of his yet unfulfilled obligation as a member of the di Tiro family—to fight for Acehnese independence.[11] Arguably, a third reason should be added: in 1974, di Tiro lost out to the American construction company Bechtel on a bid to build one of the Aceh pipelines for Mobil Oil Indonesia (MOI).[12]

## GAM's Ideology and Political Goals

GAM's ideology has been one of national liberation aimed at freeing Aceh from "all political control of the foreign regime of Jakarta." Its struggle is seen as the continuation of the anticolonial uprising that erupted in response to the 1873 Dutch invasion and subsequent occupation of the sovereign Sultanate of Aceh. GAM maintains that Aceh did not voluntarily join the Republic of Indonesia in 1945, but was illegally incorporated. Its stated objectives are "the survival of the people of Aceh Sumatra as a nation; the survival of their political, social, cultural, and religious heritage which are being destroyed by the Javanese colonialists," and to reopen "the question of decolonization of the Dutch East Indies alias 'Indonesia'."[13]

GAM's version of Acehnese nationalism is ethnic, defined through blood ties, history, religion, and *suku* (ethnic group). It originates from *suku* Aceh, which has its own language and customs and is based along the east coast of the province. The province of Aceh is home to nine *suku*—Aceh,

Alas, Gayo, Singkil, Tamiang, Kluet, Anek Jamee, Bulolehee, and Simeuleue. Yet GAM's nationalism is only based on *suku* Aceh.

As Aceh is 98 percent Muslim, Islam has always been an integral part of GAM's ideology, but mainly as a reflection of Acehnese identity and culture rather than of Islamist political aspirations. But GAM has allowed for different emphases on Islam within its ranks. For instance, the leadership in Sweden made few if any references to Islam throughout the whole period, while at village level, in particular, GAM has relied heavily on the mosque network and has often presented its struggle in Islamist terms, "involving the condemnation of the impious behavior of the rulers, promises of restitution of Shari'a law, and an Islamic base to an independent Aceh."[14] At the same time, in the 1970s, 1980s, and to a lesser extent the 1990s, its vision of an independent Aceh was articulated as the revival of the Sultanate of Aceh, "reestablishing the historic Islamic State,"[15] but in July 2002 this was changed to the establishment of a democratic system.[16]

## GAM's Leadership and Organizational Structure

GAM's top leadership has been in exile. Its president Hasan di Tiro, prime minister and defense minister (operational) Malik Mahmud, foreign minister and health minister Zaini Abdullah, and information minister Bakhtiar Abdullah resided in the Stockholm suburb of Norsborg. The organization's education minister, Musanna Abdul Wahab, was based in the United States and its defense minister (procurement and intelligence), Zakaria Zaman, operated out of Thailand. In July 2002, at a meeting in Stavanger, Norway, GAM's leadership in Sweden became the State of Aceh's government in exile.

By contrast, its mid-level leadership, troops, and members were in Aceh. Modeling itself on the historical governance structures of the independent sultanate, GAM divided Aceh into 17 administrative regions, or *wilayah.* Each *wilayah* is "governed" by a governor. GAM's civilian functions include "tax collecting" as well as issuing birth and marriage certificates.

GAM's civilian structure was shadowed by the parallel structure of the "Forces of the Free Aceh Movement" or Angkatan Gerakan Aceh Merdeka (AGAM), now renamed "The Army of the State of Aceh" or Tentara Negara Aceh (TNA), with the Stavanger Declaration. It was the locus of power within Aceh because most decisions on the ground were dictated by the realities of the conflict and thus military imperatives. The TNA was headed by the commander, or *panglima* TNA, a position last held by Muzakkir Manaf. Under his command were 17 *panglima wilayah* at the regional level, who in turn were responsible for four *panglima daerah* at the district level. Below the *panglima daerah* were the *panglima sagoë* at the subdistrict level. The troops under the latter's command were believed to be organized in a cell structure. It was at this level where the TNA command structure was highly factionalized and the troops were the most undisciplined. It was not uncommon for actions carried out for hard-line ideological reasons or personal economic gain to be at odds with directives of the top leadership.

Contact between the exiled leadership and GAM guerrillas in Aceh was maintained by telephone. According to Peureulak (East Aceh) operational commander Ishak Daud, GAM in the field regularly reported to GAM leaders in Sweden: "Every day our commander, Muzakkir Manaf, makes contact with GAM's political wing in Sweden. And the instruction is clear."[17] While the TNA chain of command appeared to be linear from Sweden to the *panglima* TNA to the troops in the field, the fact that GAM had an exiled leadership, which was in overall command of the operations on the ground, allowed for the emergence of a bypass mechanism, creating a somewhat triangular relationship. This meant that the leadership in Sweden, mainly in the form of Malik Mahmud, was communicating not only with the *panglima* TNA, but at the same time with the 17 *panglima wilayah* and vice versa.[18] This direct contact with the field not only kept Sweden up to date with the situation on the ground, but also ensured that a strike against the *panglima* TNA does not cut Sweden off from Aceh. This mechanism proved its usefulness with the killing of *panglima* AGAM Abdullah Syafi'i on 22 January 2002.

This structure, however, has also blurred the chain of command, with a negative impact upon coordination, discipline, and control. This has been further complicated by the fact that the leadership in Sweden only issues general directives or parameters to the *panglima* AGAM/TNA. According to Tiro field commander Amri bin Abdul Wahab, the actual decisions on strategy and tactics are made at the field commander level.[19]

## GAM's Support Base

As GAM did not have a political party and had never participated in elections it was impossible to say how much popular support GAM really had. The organization's leaders claimed to represent all of the people, but this was not backed up by evidence on the ground across Aceh. To assess the extent of its popular support it is useful to look at four areas: background, motivation, territory, and education.

Support for GAM was initially restricted to the district of Pidie and particularly from the village of Tiro: GAM members and supporters had a shared background that was rural and from *suku* Aceh. They were motivated by loyalty to the di Tiro family and disillusionment with Jakarta. The effect of rapid urbanization and industrialization in the 1970s and 1980s and the impact of Indonesian counterinsurgency operations in the 1990s increased its support base. The new supporters came from North and East Aceh and were motivated by inequality and poverty as well as by revenge. In 1999, after the full revelation of the scale of human rights abuses by the military, another generation fueled by vengeance joined GAM. They too came from Pidie, and North and East Aceh (see Map 3.1). In those "traditional" areas GAM is a genuinely popular movement.

Following the 1998 withdrawal of the Indonesian security forces, the independence movement pushed into the remaining districts of Aceh, some of which had never even heard of GAM. These districts differed ethnically and were untouched by either industrialization or the security forces' brutality. When GAM started to recruit, it was mainly local thugs and petty criminals who joined because they saw the label as a useful tool in their quest for easy money.[20] There is anecdotal evidence that GAM in these "new" territories forcibly recruited by ordering villages to provide one or two volunteers.[21] It certainly had to rely far more on intimidation in order to maintain its position there. Indeed, in Central and South Aceh considerable violence was inflicted upon the local population to silence them, including the shooting of village heads, the burning of houses and schools, and the destruction of businesses. The population in these areas does not genuinely support GAM but cooperates with the movement because it lives in fear of the guerrillas.

The support base is not only differentiated by "traditional" and "new" territories but also by an urban-rural division. Genuine support tends to come from rural areas, especially those that have become the victims of industrialization or a drop in cash crop prices. These villagers are the backbone of GAM's logistics. Urban areas even in GAM's "traditional" territory—such as the cities of Lhokseumawe and Langsa—tend to be pro-Jakarta. But since 1999 GAM has made some inroads into the student population in Banda Aceh. In 2003, teaching staff at Syiah Kuala and Ar-Raniry universities complained bitterly about GAM recruitment on campus.

Level of education matters. While GAM in the 1970s comprised doctors, engineers, and businessmen, since the 1990s it has been largely a movement of the less educated and the unemployed. These members are less able to evaluate GAM claims and thus more susceptible to its propaganda. They also have nothing to lose. In fact, through the guerrilla struggle they have been able to obtain a social status and power otherwise unavailable to them. Data on GAM members who surrendered during martial law in 2003–2004 and were undergoing rehabilitation in Meulaboh showed that the majority of them had not finished primary education; some could neither read nor write.

All four categories of background, motivation, territory, and education were mutually reinforcing. The picture that emerges is that GAM was genuinely supported among the less educated, poor, rural population, particularly in Pidie, Bireuen, and North and East Aceh, but was not generally supported by the better educated, urban population, Acehnese political and commercial elites, and the wider, ethnically different, population in

TABLE 3.1. ESTIMATED GAM MEMBERS, APRIL 2003

| *District* | *Members* |
|---|---|
| Pidie | 2,365 |
| North Aceh | 1,331 |
| East Aceh | 826 |
| West Aceh | 472 |
| Greater Aceh | 323 |
| South Aceh | 89 |
| Central Aceh | 86 |
| Southeast Aceh | 25 |

TABLE 3.2. ESTIMATED GAM WEAPONRY, APRIL 2003

| *District* | *Weapons* |
|---|---|
| North Aceh | 889 |
| Pidie | 420 |
| East Aceh | 346 |
| West Aceh | 113 |
| Central Aceh | 79 |
| South Aceh | 74 |
| Southeast Aceh | 4 |

West, South, Southeast, and Central Aceh, including the newly formed regencies of Nagan Raya, Aceh Barat Daya, and Gayo Lues.

## GAM's Strength and Capacity

When GAM was established in 1976 it comprised only 70 guerrilla fighters. In February 2002, Malik Mahmud claimed that GAM had an active guerrilla army of 30,000 and a reserve of almost the whole population of Aceh.[22] Of these 30,000, according to di Tiro, an estimated 5,000 GAM guerrillas were trained in Libya between 1986 and 1989.[23] The number offered by Malik Mahmud is somewhat lower, at around 1,500 Acehnese.[24] Observers believe that 700–800 had gone to Libya.[25] Indonesian military intelligence estimates set the number of GAM in April 2003 at an estimated 5,500 with 583 being "Libyan graduates," distributed across Aceh as shown in Table 3.1.[26]

The fighting capacity of GAM, however, was a lot smaller than its membership suggests. In 2001, most observers estimated that AGAM had between "1,000 and 1,500 modern firearms, a few grenade launchers, even fewer rocket-propelled grenade launchers, and perhaps one or two 60mm mortars."[27] These weapons, moreover, were unevenly spread over GAM's territory, showing the heaviest arms concentration in the "traditional" GAM areas of Pidie, North Aceh, and East Aceh. Indonesian intelligence in April 2003 provided the estimates in Table 3.2.

GAM's weapons were a mixture of home-made *rakitan* and standard firearms. Standard firearms were obtained both from domestic and foreign sources. Domestically, arms were captured, stolen or purchased from the TNI and the police. Internationally, weapons were widely available from Cambodia as one of the primary sources of illegal small arms in South-East Asia using Thailand as the main conduit or transfer area.

## Financing the Independence Struggle

In November 2003, Malik Mahmud claimed that GAM had spent more than $10 million on weapons for the struggle,[28] raising the question of where it got its money. GAM had three main sources of revenue: "taxation," foreign donations, and criminal activity.

### "Taxation"

GAM levied an Aceh state tax or *pajak nanggroë* on all elements of society. According to senior GAM negotiator Sofyan Ibrahim Tiba, *pajak nanggroë* had been collected since the organization was established and it was based on religion. "In Islam if there is a struggle there is *infaq*. But now that Aceh is no longer struggling for an Islamic state it is called *pajak nanggroë*."[29] In March 2000, GAM was believed to be skimming an estimated 20 percent off the development funds allocated by Jakarta from most of Aceh's villages.[30] It has been claimed that during the early period of the Humanitarian Pause in 2000 it was able to siphon off 50–75 percent from some humanitarian assistance programs.[31] The targeting of humanitarian aid funds repeated itself during the COHA in December 2002. Local partners of international NGOs were presented with tax demands of 15–30 percent. Pressure increased to such an extent that the United Nations Office for the Coordination of Humanitarian Aid (OCHA) felt compelled to complain to the dialogue facilitator, the Henry Dunant Center (HDC).

GAM believed it had the right to tax all parts of Acehnese society and that the population did not mind. According to Pasè (North Aceh) commander Sofyan Dawod "the Acehnese do not object to our taxes . . . because that money [is used] to defend them."[32] The level of taxation depended on the project or the salary. There were two bases for taxation, taxation of the profit, which Dawod claimed as around 2.5 percent, and of the value of the project. Additional contributions were sought for holidays, which Dawod says are used for Acehnese orphans. For instance, ExxonMobil was asked for a special Idul Adha "holiday allowance" of Rp 250 million. (7,500 rupiahs = U.S. $1). Farmers and teachers did not pay taxes, "but we do ask for a voluntary contribution of one day's earning per month. We also ask for donations from Aceh's wealthy to help society, to cover state functions and expenses, and also to buy weapons."[33]

GAM particularly targeted merchants in Greater Aceh (many of whom are ethnic Chinese), contractors in the Lhokseumawe industrial area,

Javanese migrants in the coffee plantations of Central Aceh, and civil servants. The Chinese were seen as "soft targets" because they are comparatively wealthy and will go to lengths to stay out of the conflict, while contractors, civil servants, and the Javanese were seen as "legitimate targets" since they worked for the Indonesian regional government or were seen as potential collaborators with the security forces.

The hardest hit area by far has been the Lhokseumawe industrial complex in North Aceh, which is home to Indonesian and foreign businesses such as PT Arun, ExxonMobil, PT Asean Aceh Fertilizer, and Iskandar Muda Fertilizer as well as a large number of local and some foreign contractors. From mid-1999, ExxonMobil Oil Indonesia (EMOI) experienced an increase in extortion attempts by people claiming to be GAM.[34] According to foreign contractors, GAM regularly demanded 5 percent of the profits, while local third party contractors were issued with demands of up to 20 percent. One such local contractor explained that GAM had asked him several times for 12 percent of the contract value and told him that if "you don't give it, you will be shot a day later."[35] Villages in the vicinity of the Lhokseumawe industrial complex have also been harder hit by GAM's "village tax"—presumably under the assumption that they benefit through either employment or developmental assistance. After the signing of the COHA every village was asked for Rp 35 million to buy weapons.[36] In contrast, other villages in GAM's "traditional" area were asked for Rp 10 million and those in "new" areas for Rp 9 million.[37]

Indonesian military intelligence estimates from April 2003 claimed that GAM received a monthly "tax revenue" of Rp 230 million from Banda Aceh, Greater Aceh, and Sabang, Rp 10 million from Pidie, Rp 36 million from East Aceh and Tamiang, Rp 682 million from Central Aceh, Rp 77 million from West Aceh, and Rp 70 million from South Aceh and Aceh Singkil.[38]

The second important source of funding for GAM was foreign donations, which had come primarily from Acehnese expatriates. The largest amount of this money probably originated from Malaysia. It is estimated that in Kuala Lumpur alone at least 5,000 Acehnese provided GAM with regular donations.[39]

The third source of funding was criminal activity, mainly drug trafficking and kidnapping for ransom. GAM has been actively involved in the cultivation and trade of *ganja*, or marijuana. An estimated 30 percent of Southeast Asia's marijuana is believed to originate from Aceh. GAM's involvement in drug trafficking was directly linked to the arms-drugs nexus, both regionally and domestically. *Ganja* was sold to obtain weapons from Cambodia and Thailand but also from individuals in the Indonesian security forces, Indonesia's arms manufacturer Pindad, Jakarta's black market, and even as far away as West and East Timor, where arms from former pro-Jakarta militias are still widely available.[40]

Kidnapping had been another means for raising funds although this was been officially denied by GAM. While some of the kidnappings were ideologically motivated, such as the detention of students believed to be informers for the TNI, young women dating Indonesian soldiers,[41] or journalists for "biased reporting" and village heads in need of "reeducation"; other kidnappings were for ransom with the targets being local legislators, businessmen, or oil workers.[42] For instance, in early 2001, GAM kidnapped a senior executive of PT Arun and demanded $500,000 to release him. In late August 2001 six Indonesian crew members from the "Ocean Silver" were abducted and U.S.$33,000 demanded for their release.[43] In April 2002, three oil workers contracted to Pertamina were kidnapped. One was released the following day; for the other two GAM demanded a ransom of Rp. 200 million.[44] On 2 July 2002, it was reported that nine crewmen servicing the offshore oil industry were kidnapped from their ship, the *Pelangi Frontier.*[45] During martial law, GAM went on a kidnapping spree, taking some 300 people hostage. The hostages included two RCTI television crew members, the wives of two Indonesian air force officers, 39 village heads, and numerous teachers and civil servants.

### Greed or Grievance?

Paul Collier and Anke Hoeffler in their analysis of greed and grievance in civil war concluded that "rebellion is not explained by motive, but by the atypical circumstances that generate profitable opportunities."[46] In another study for the World Bank, Collier argues that "civil wars occur where rebel organizations are financially viable" and that rebellion is "more like a form of organized crime."[47] In many ways GAM's story fits this picture. GAM's ability to obtain funds for its struggle through kidnapping, extortion, and "taxation" certainly made rebellion viable. Moreover, the fact that from 1999 onward criminal elements flocked toward GAM further suggests that rebellion was not only viable, but profitable. And this had clear implications for the Geneva peace process where "economic" GAM in search of personal gain reinforced "ideological" GAM, which was not capable of compromise. There is no doubt that the two ceasefires collapsed partially because of GAM's greed. And not surprisingly most of the GAM members denounced by the Acehnese to the Indonesian security forces during the martial law period were "tax collectors."

## The Impact of GAM Violence on Aceh's Infrastructure and Economy

The impact of GAM violence on Aceh was particularly pronounced in three areas: local government structures, the education system, and the economy. Since 1976 GAM has targeted Indonesian political structures in Aceh with the aim of loosening Indonesia's control. This was achieved through attacks on public buildings,[48] the intimidation of civil servants at all levels, and the recruitment of as many as possible into GAM's parallel civilian government. Civil servants, judges, members of the regional parliaments, and village heads were intimidated, kidnapped, or shot. In 2000–2001, GAM virtually collapsed Aceh's legal system. In several districts courthouses were destroyed by GAM and judges, prosecutors, and lawyers were subject to repeated intimidation.[49] Many judges fled.[50] When martial law was declared in May 2003, 99 out of 228 districts and 4,750 out of 5,947 villages did not have a functioning local government.[51] Local legislators, especially those who criticized GAM,[52] as well as the governor and deputy governor, were targeted because they were all seen as lackeys of Jakarta.

GAM also systematically destroyed Indonesia's state education system. This included the burning of schools as well as the intimidation and killing of teachers. Between 1998 and 2002 some 60 teachers were killed[53] and 200 others physically assaulted.[54] Some 170 were seriously injured or tortured.[55] Many were kidnapped. Between the beginning of 1989 and June 2002, 527 schools, 89 official houses for teachers, and 33 official houses for principals were burned down.[56] In May–June 2002, 27 schools were destroyed. In the two weeks of the military emergency in May 2003, over 600 schools went up in flames.

The underlying motivations for the destruction of the Indonesian education system in Aceh were primarily ideological. According to GAM, the Indonesian education system actively destroys Acehnese history and culture while promoting "the glorification of Javanese history."[57] Already in the late 1970s, di Tiro recorded in his diary that "for the last 35 years they have used our schools and the mass media to destroy every aspect of our nationality, culture, polity and national consciousness."[58] The destruction of state schools was seen as a direct attack on the curriculum which taught that Aceh joined the Republic of Indonesia voluntarily and has been an integral part of the state ever since. One way of countering this was the tailoring of school curricula in GAM strongholds to include a local view of history.[59] Another way was to burn schools so "that they were not used to turn Acehnese children into Indonesians."[60]

The burning of schools also had more "practical" aspects. During martial law in particular it prevented schools "from being used as billets for troops" and "from housing the displaced so that the humanitarian problem got more international attention."[61] And finally, according to the TNI, GAM also torched the schools to try to divert troops away from offensive operations to guard duties.[62]

The third sector particularly affected by GAM's insurgency was the economy, especially the Acehnese energy infrastructure. This has had two main components: electricity and natural gas. Since 1999, GAM repeatedly targeted electricity pylons. This, of course, caused blackouts in Aceh's urban areas. This slowed down the local economy, made life more difficult for the Indonesian security forces, and instilled a general feeling of fear among the population. During the recent martial law period three electricity pylons were taken down by GAM,[63] and two electricity relay stations in East Aceh were damaged by arson attack. Indonesia's national electricity company, PLN, blamed it on GAM.[64] Blackouts also occurred in some villages. According to a resident of Lhok Jok, GAM cut electricity to the village for security reasons.[65] The oil industry in the Greater Lhokseumawe area has been even harder hit. Employees of both domestic and foreign companies have lived under the threat of intimidation, kidnapping, or death since the early days of GAM. GAM actions, according to di Tiro's diary, aimed at closing "down foreign oil companies . . . to prevent them from further stealing our oil and gas."[66] In early December 1977, three foreign contractors for Bechtel, an American and two Koreans involved in the construction of the Arun Field Cluster III, came under attack. The American was killed by what di Tiro in his diary described as "stray bullets"[67] and Bechtel's doctor at the time recalls as an armed attack on the unarmed foreign contractors. The GAM leadership clearly "viewed the plant and its personnel as symbols of what was wrong in Aceh, and calculated that assaults on the new facilities would draw the maximum possible attention to their cause."[68]

GAM's resentment toward foreign companies like Bechtel, MOI, and later EMOI remained. In fact, in 1999 it stepped up attacks on the vulnerable oil and gas production facilities and pipelines operated by EMOI in Aceh. In March 2001, EMOI was forced to close production from the four onshore gas fields it operates and to evacuate workers. GAM was also believed to have been responsible for firing at aircraft transporting ExxonMobil workers, hijacking the company's vehicles, as well as stopping and burning buses and planting landmines along roads to blow them up.[69] GAM's resentment at the oil industry was twofold: it was seen first as exploiting Aceh's resources, and second as collaborating with the Indonesian military—because the latter was securing premises and receiving funds for this service from state oil company Pertamina. So GAM regarded these corporations as legitimate targets. As its spokesman Isnander al-Pasè explained in April 2003: "ExxonMobil is a legitimate target in war. Why? Because it helps the opponent's military and now Exxon is housing a military base within its complex. And the people living next to Exxon tell us that they do not get anything from Exxon while Exxon takes our oil'.[70]

## Indonesia's New Order "Security Approach"

During the New Order under President Suharto Indonesian counterinsurgency efforts were primarily of a military and intelligence nature. While some attempts were made to deal with the economic grievances of the

Acehnese population, political negotiations or talking to separatists or rebels was unthinkable. Efforts to address the economic and political grievances ran up against the centralized economy, wide-spread corruption, and the conviction that any form of regional autonomy was a threat to the unity of the state.

## Nanggala Intelligence Operations, 1977–1979

The first counterinsurgency operations started in October 1977, almost a year after GAM's establishment and ten months after di Tiro declared Aceh's independence. The Nanggala intelligence operations as a whole were a response to the separatist threat. However, in a more immediate sense they were a direct reaction to GAM leaflets appearing in the Lhokseumawe area calling on Mobil Oil Indonesia and Bechtel foreign personnel to leave,[71] and the subsequent shooting dead of an American contractor. The main objective was "to neutralize the situation, restore security, to enhance the construction of the LNG project, and to destroy Aceh Merdeka."[72] The operations were concluded in 1979 when security was restored and the GAM leadership had fled into exile.

## Kolakops Jaring Merah, *1989–1998*

The second attempt to crush the insurgency started in mid-1990 with Kolakops Jaring Merah, or Red Net Operations, more conventionally referred to as DOM. In response to the reemergence of GAM, some 6,000 nonorganic (centrally recruited and trained) troops were sent into Aceh, including the Kopassus special forces, to join the 6,000 organic (locally recruited territorial) troops already there.[73] Launched with the object of crushing the rebels in six months, DOM lasted until 1998 and was only lifted after the fall of Suharto.

The main challenge for the Indonesian security forces in this operation as in subsequent ones was to separate the insurgents from the population. This was pursued through heavy-handed military reprisals against villages believed to provide logistical help or sanctuary to the insurgents.[74] The Indonesian security forces raised local defense organizations in line with standard counterinsurgency operations, as well as Indonesia's "Total People's Defense and Security System" or *sistem pertahanan keamanan rakyat semesta* (*sishankamrata*).[75] According to Aceh governor Ibrahim Hassan, an estimated 60,000 people were mobilized to assist the security forces in intelligence and security operations,[76] including "fence of legs" operations or *operasi pagar betis,* in which "ordinary villagers were compelled to sweep through an area ahead of armed troops."[77]

Villagers were placed under tight control and some were relocated. During the first four years of the operation scores of guerrillas and civilians were killed, tortured and disappeared. Kidnap victims spoke of being forced to bury people shot by the military; women related accounts of sexual assault and rape. By the end of 1991, many GAM field commanders had been captured or killed.[78] GAM had been virtually crushed, its remnants driven underground or into exile to Malaysia.[79] Operation Jaring Merah I was then superseded by ***Jaring Merah*** II, which aimed at security recovery and stabilizing the situation sufficiently to allow civilian government to function. However, over the next six years the Acehnese saw little change. The civilian administration claimed that development could not proceed because the security situation was not conducive. The military charged the civilians with incompetence and not carrying out their duty.

## Post-Suharto Counterinsurgency Operations

After the fall of Suharto in 1998 and the loss of East Timor in 1999 amid international condemnation over human rights abuses, the Indonesian government changed its approach toward counterinsurgency in two important ways. First, it added a distinctly political dimension, offering both regional autonomy and negotiations with GAM. Second, the Indonesian military made concerted efforts at professionalization as reflected in the special Aceh training (including human rights from the International Committee of the Red Cross (ICRC) and UN High Commissioner for Refugees (UNHCR) for the Rajawali troops during the first operation and the Raider battalions during the second operation under martial law.

### Operasi Pemulihan Keamanan dan Penegakan Hukum, 2001–2003

On 11 April 2001, President Abdurrahman Wahid issued presidential instruction 4, launching a new Operation for the Restoration of Security and Upholding the Law or Operasi Pemulihan Keamanan dan Penegakan Hukum (OKPH). This operation, begun a year after the start of the peace process and concurrent with intermittent negotiations, was a response to the forced shutdown of ExxonMobil's onshore production. OKPH was based on a six-point plan, following a classic formula of counterinsurgency strategy, combining security operations with economic and political benefits to woo the population away from supporting the separatists. The six points comprised the restoration of the rule of law, security recovery, economic recovery, new legislation for Aceh, the promotion of Acehnese culture, and social recovery.

As a clear sign of changing times, the overall responsibility lay with the police supported by the military. The police dominated urban areas and performed standard police functions with the exception of the paramilitary mobile police Brimob, which engaged in counterinsurgency alongside the military. The military had a static network of territorial units aimed at securing and consolidating the rural areas with special Rajawali antiguerrilla units fighting GAM in the jungles. Aside from "normal" difficulties in fighting an insurgency such as not always knowing who the insurgents are, and thus being able to avoid civilian casualties, OKPH suffered from disciplinary problems in the field, particularly the complete lack of professionalism of Brimob, as well as competition between the military and the police. The TNI also continued to rely on civilian defense organizations, mainly in Central Aceh, as well as collective punishment. Most important, however, the nonsecurity aspects of the comprehensive plan were not adequately implemented. While special autonomy had been legislated, the Acehnese saw no change in their everyday lives. As during Jaring Merah II, Aceh's political elite claimed that development could not be carried out because the security situation was not conducive. Thus the money Jakarta was "throwing" at the regional parliament for development and economic recovery was spent on prestige projects, such as airports and the Sabang Freeport rather than roads and schools—or went directly into the pockets of the governor and the legislators.

### Martial Law and Operasi Terpadu, May 2003–May 2004

The fourth major counterinsurgency effort came with presidential decree 28 which placed Aceh under martial law on 19 May 2003 and provided the legal framework for the Integrated Operation or Operasi Terpadu. The Integrated Operation comprised four aspects: the military operation, law enforcement, humanitarian aid, and improving local government. During the second martial law period economic recovery was added as another objective. All aspects were aimed at reducing, if not eliminating, GAM's political and military capacity, at restoring local government services, at securing the Lhokseumawe industrial complex, and at curbing Acehnese support for independence by "winning the hearts and minds" of the people.

The focus of the military operation was on reducing the strength of GAM, cutting the organization's logistics, neutralizing its territorial and psychological control, cutting its communications, and enhancing Indonesia's domestic government in Aceh. An estimated 30,000 TNI troops and 13,000–15,000 police and Brimob were assigned these tasks. Civilian defense organizations were established in every regency. The TNI strategy was broadly divided into the following phases: separation of GAM from the people, isolation of GAM, and its destruction or neutralization. The TNI claimed to have achieved a number of successes during the operation. These included securing the urban areas and the supply to the cities from Medan to Banda Aceh, breaking up GAM into smaller units, severing GAM's tactical communication lines, interruption of the movement's supply lines, cutting off GAM from its "tax base," and "significant" reduction

TABLE 3.3. ADMINISTRATOR'S ESTIMATE OF GAM STRENGTH, FEBRUARY 2004

| *Area* | *Personnel* | *Standard weapons* | Rakitan |
|---|---|---|---|
| Pidie | 791 | 365 | 118 |
| Pase | 318 | 220 | 8 |
| Peureulak | 163 | 176 | 21 |
| Batee Iliek | 86 | 172 | 21 |
| Meureuhom Daya | 30 | 25 | 20 |
| Tamiang | 26 | 58 | 0 |
| Aceh Selatan | 23 | 26 | 5 |
| Aceh Rayeuk, Sabang | 21 | 17 | 0 |
| Linge, Samarkilang, Gayo | 21 | 18 | 4 |
| Aceh Barat | 19 | 13 | 35 |
| Alas/Blangkejeren | 11 | 7 | 0 |
| Total | 1,509 | 1,097 | 213 |

in its strength. The intelligence staff of the Martial Law Administrator provided the above estimate dated 26 February 2004, showing the overall reduction in GAM's strength from 5,517 personnel and 2,137 weapons before the military emergency (see Table 3.3).

Yet the operation, like previous ones, was not without difficulties. Beyond the big picture of "crushing GAM" there was no clear definition of objectives or an exit strategy. There were problems with intelligence analysis. There were difficulties maintaining discipline in the field. While the TNI's professionalism had improved since East Timor, human rights violations were still committed. According to both domestic and international human rights organizations, the Indonesian security forces were responsible for extrajudicial killings, torture, kidnapping, forced displacement, and rape during the operation. Last but not least, the implementation of the nonmilitary elements left a great deal to be desired. During the first six months of martial law the military operation was dominant so the impact of the military operation on the civilian population was not cushioned by humanitarian aid and development, as intended. During the second six months, there was some progress on the humanitarian, law enforcement, and restoration of civil government parts of Operasi Terpadu—although not nearly enough.

## The Impact of Indonesian Counterinsurgency Operations on GAM's Support Base and the Acehnese Population

While GAM's violence has resulted in the virtual collapse of Aceh's local government structure and education system and has contributed significantly to the stagnation of Aceh's economy by deterring investment, Indonesia's counterinsurgency operations have had a detrimental impact upon the fabric of Acehnese society.

In order to weaken and ultimately isolate the GAM commanders and troops Indonesian strategy focused on cutting GAM off from its support base. During the Jaring Merah operations villagers were placed under tight control and some were relocated. During OKPH troops embarked upon a systematic effort to target suspected GAM strongholds[80]—Pidie, North Aceh, and East Aceh. Similarly, during Operasi Terpadu efforts were made to separate GAM from the people and to deny guerrilla forces access to food and information or the ability to blend with civilians.[81] In the words of TNI Aceh operations spokesman Lieutenant Colonel Yani Basuki: "We are mounting pressure on the rebel strongholds to narrow their room for movement and trying to separate the rebels from civilians."[82]

The separation of GAM from the people in this operation was pursued through a combination of different tactics. Territorially, GAM was first pushed out of the urban areas and away from the main transport routes. This was followed by the sweeping of villages and pushing GAM further back into the forest. Securing these rural areas saw some of the TNI's more controversial tactics, namely the relocation of entire villages suspected of supporting insurgents. According to senior officials interning villages would enable the soldiers to pick through emptied areas with fine-toothed combs in search of GAM members or sympathizers.[83] And it would "only be used in areas where GAM has a particularly strong influence."[84] Some 100,000 people were taken from their homes and put into 80 camps.[85]

In addition to GAM's support base, the Acehnese population as a whole was also targeted. This was partly the result of the difficulties the security forces faced in distinguishing GAM from the people. However, the people were also terrorized in order to deter them from supporting GAM. And above all, the Acehnese population was targeted because of the widespread perception that they were intrinsically disloyal. This resulted in punishment for disloyalty on the one hand and efforts to compel loyalty on the other.

Systematic terrorizing to discourage the people from supporting GAM was the preferred approach during the Jaring Merah operations. Common tactics included the burning of the homes of suspected independence supporters or sometimes their entire village.[86] This was referred to as "shock therapy," which was described as a systematic "campaign of terror designed to strike fear in the population and make them withdraw their support from GAM."[87] This also included arbitrary arrest and detention, torture, "disappearance" or summary execution.[88]

> For a period of about two years after the start of combat operations, the corpses of Acehnese victims, generally young men, were found strewn in public places—beside main roads, near village security posts, in public markets, in fields and plantations, next to a stream or river—apparently as a warning to others not to join or support the rebels.[89]

Security operations post-Suharto placed more emphasis on rules of engagement, international humanitarian law, and human rights. Their overall perception of the Acehnese, however, did not change. They continued to see them as disloyal and tried to tackle this disloyalty, above all, through "loyalization." For instance, during OKPH villages were compelled to declare their loyalty.[90] During Operasi Terpadu "loyalization" was multilayered. During the second month of martial law, in July, the military began mobilizing the people to attend loyalty ceremonies. Mass participation in the recitation of oaths of loyalty to the Indonesian state or *ikrar kesetiaan* was even broadcast on television.[91] This was followed by the mobilization of nationalist youth groups such as Pemuda Merah Putih, by demonstrations in favor of martial law,[92] and by the mobilization of civil defense organizations whose key function was displays of loyalty to Indonesia and hatred of GAM.

"Loyalization" further included the introduction of "loyalty tests." According to Governor Puteh, 67,000 civil servants were to be screened due to suspicion that many were supporting or providing funds to GAM.[93] In this context 13 district heads or *camats* were replaced by military officers. Two Acehnese councillors, one from Aceh Besar (Golkar) and one from Sabang (PPP), were also detained for collecting funds for GAM.[94] Another administrative measure was the issuing of new "red and white" identity cards in efforts to distinguish civilians from GAM.[95] These new cards needed to be produced at checkpoints, and people unable to produce them fell under suspicion of being GAM.

The other side of "loyalization" was punishment for disloyalty, which continued post-Suharto, albeit to a lesser extent. During the police operations *Wibawa* 99, *Sadar Recong* I, II, and III ,and *Cinta Meunasah* I and II, "whole villages" were "punished as retaliation for GAM attacks."[96] One of the most prominent examples is the collective punishment of the residents of the East Aceh town of Idi Rayeuk in March 2001. This followed the February 28 GAM occupation of the town, during which GAM burned down the police barracks and the jail and bombed the police station. After the Indonesian security forces had recaptured Idi Rayeuk, they burned down the center of the town.[97] They also torched six surrounding villages.[98]

During Operasi Terpadu punishment for disloyalty came in the form of beatings, summary killings, and torture of unarmed civilians despite efforts to curb human rights abuses.[99] Many of these came at the hands of frustrated soldiers who felt that they were being lied to by the people and who suspected that the people sympathized with GAM. For instance, on 27 May 2003, soldiers from Battalion 144 entered the village of Lawang, Bireuen, in search of GAM. They shot dead one man suspected of being GAM and beat up another three in search of further information.[100] In the subsequent court-martial, the soldiers testified that they felt they had been lied to, that the villagers were protecting GAM, and that they got emotional so they hit them.[101] Lawang was not an isolated incident. In fact, as interviews with Acehnese refugees in Malaysia by Human Rights Watch revealed, beating villagers seemed to be the standard response by the security forces to noncooperative, "disloyal" villagers.[102]

## Special Autonomy for Aceh

Indonesia's post-Suharto approach to resolving the conflict in Aceh has included three nonmilitary elements: special autonomy, negotiations, and legal proceedings. In April 1999, under President B. J. Habibie, the Indonesian parliament adopted Laws 22 and 25 on decentralization, aiming at forestalling the rise of separatism, especially in resource-rich regions. These laws, which did not come into effect until the beginning of 2001, devolved extensive governmental powers to the regions. They also allowed regional and local governments to retain some of the net income from the exploitation of natural resources, including 15 percent from oil, 30 percent from natural gas, and 80 percent from timber. In addition Aceh, under Law 44, was given autonomy with respect to culture, religious affairs, and education.

In August 2001, under President Megawati Sukarnoputri, special autonomy was given to Aceh under Law 18, which formally changed the province's name to Nanggroe Aceh Darussalam (NAD). While this was not officially part of the negotiation process, Indonesia considered autonomy as a concession with the hope that GAM would lay down its arms and give up its struggle for independence. Special autonomy allowed for the introduction of Islamic law, but most important, it provided Aceh with control over 70 percent of its oil and gas revenues for the next eight years. Special autonomy became effective in January 2002 but was not fully implemented. One problem was GAM's opposition to it. It actively worked to undermine implementation. The far greater obstacle was the provincial government—in the form of lack of transparency and accountability, corruption, and mismanagement. In 2001, more than Rp 1,118 billion humanitarian aid money was corruptly appropriated.[103] According to Acehnese civic leaders and political activists, in 2003 an estimated Rp 5.5 trillion was squandered by provincial officials.[104] On 1 May 2003, newspaper *Sinar Harapan* published a list of Aceh's corruption projects, which included corruption and mark-up in the purchase of a speedboat for Rp 8.6 billion, misuse of Rp 100 billion flood assistance money, misuse of Rp 43.7 billion aid money from Pertamina, and lack of transparency in the use of flood assistance from the UN exceeding Rp 176 million.[105] On 8 October 2003, Aceh's *Serambi* newspaper reported that the provincial government had even admitted to the misuse of funds for humanitarian assistance during the Integrated Operation.[106] The main result of the provincial government's corruption was that special autonomy became discredited in the eyes of the average Acehnese, who saw no improvement in his life as a result of decentralization.

## The Geneva Peace Process, 2000–2003

GAM and the Indonesian government under President Abdurahman Wahid entered into a negotiating process in January 2000 aimed at finding an end to the conflict in Aceh. This process was facilitated by a Swiss-based NGO, the Henry Dunant Center (HDC), through its head office in Geneva as well as a local office in Banda Aceh. The actual negotiations took place outside Indonesia, mostly in Geneva.

The first "result" of the talks was the 12 May 2000 Humanitarian Pause, which was a ceasefire, accompanied by the establishment of two joint committees—one on humanitarian action and one on security modalities—and a monitoring team. The implementation of the Pause lacked commitment from both sides and while violence actually escalated, the Pause was extended until 15 January 2001 as the Moratorium on Violence, and then renamed Peace Through Dialogue. The negotiations broke down in all but name in July 2001 when the Indonesian government "froze" the security modalities committee and GAM's Banda Aceh-based negotiators were arrested and jailed.

Talks resumed again in February 2002. A new element, foreign "wise men" was added. At the same time, Indonesian security operations continued and were stepped up following an ultimatum by the coordinating minister for security and political affairs, Susilo Bambang Yudhoyono, on 19 August for GAM to accept special autonomy. Throughout October, the TNI encircled GAM troops in several North Aceh locations, and in November it laid siege to the village of Cut Trieng. To this exercise in the stick was added a carrot in the form of economic rehabilitation of Aceh by the U.S., EU, Japan, and the World Bank should another agreement be reached. On 9 December 2002 the Cessation of Hostilities Agreement (COHA) was concluded.

The COHA called for the cantonment or storage of GAM weapons, the relocation and reformulation of the role of the Indonesian security forces, and the establishment of peace zones. It set up a Joint Security Commission (JSC) under the leadership of Thai major general Tanongsuk Tuvinun, including 50 Thai and Filipino soldiers to work alongside 50 GAM and 50 TNI troops. The first signs of trouble came when GAM failed to meet the February deadline for the cantonment of its arms. This was followed by the TNI's refusal to relocate and the paralyzing of the JSC through TNI-inspired systematic attacks on all its offices outside of Banda Aceh. By April the COHA was dead in all but name. Efforts to resuscitate it at a meeting in Tokyo on 18 May 2003 collapsed when GAM refused to agree to Indonesia's demands of recognizing Negara Kesatuan Republik Indonesia (Unitary State of the Republic of Indonesia, NKRI), accepting NAD, and relinquishing its struggle. The following day, 19 May, the Indonesian government placed Aceh under martial law and launched Operasi Terpadu.

Overall, the Geneva peace process saw more failures than achievements, and it has even been argued that the Acehnese would have been better off without it, as it polarized the people. Civil society did not have a voice of its own but was only involved in the dialogue as appointees by GAM or the Indonesian government to the various committees. Its organizations were forced to choose sides, eroding the middle ground and reinforcing the zero-sum nature of the conflict. The population as a whole was cut off from the talks, which were held outside Aceh. The process failed to build confidence and trust between the two negotiating parties and, above all, failed to bridge the gap between GAM's position of "*nothing* but independence" and Indonesia's position of "*anything* but independence."

## The Role of the International Community in the Conflict and the Geneva Peace Process

The international community as a whole did not play a big role in the Aceh conflict since 1976 or the peace process from 2000 to 2003. It was not, however, absent. In terms of the conflict, the only direct international support for GAM came from Libya, from 1986 to 1989. More indirect "support" was offered by the countries providing the insurgents with the safe havens that have allowed GAM to continue its struggle. Foremost among these were Sweden and more recently Norway, which have given political asylum to GAM's top political leadership, as well as Malaysia, which is home to a sizable Acehnese diaspora, among whom the GAM military leadership found sanctuary in the 1990s. The diaspora kept the struggle going by lobbying for an independent Aceh, while GAM in exile actively pursued greater involvement of the international community to level the playing field with Jakarta. Both the diaspora and GAM in exile were more hard-line than the population in Aceh and this made a compromise settlement more difficult.

With the beginning of the peace process the international role increased. Direct and formal involvement came in the form of the HDC as the facilitator. Over the course of the negotiations foreign "wise men" advisers—retired U.S. Marine general Anthony Zinni, former Thai foreign minister Surin Pitsuan, former Yugoslav ambassador to Indonesia Budimir Loncar, and former Swedish diplomat Bengt Soderberg—were added. During the COHA, Thai and Philippine military were part of the ceasefire monitoring team, while a quartet of the World Bank, Japan, U.S. and EU pledged to underwrite the reconstruction process. Finding an appropriate role for the international community was difficult, as the whole notion of international involvement became highly politicized with GAM making internationalization the focus of its political strategy. One key element of this strategy was creating an East Timor-like scenario that would compel the international community to pressure Indonesia into letting Aceh go.

To achieve this GAM lobbied human rights groups, UN, U.S., and EU. The darker side of the East Timor blueprint included striking at Indonesian security forces in populated areas in order to create as many civilian casualties as possible.

The second element of this strategy was the peace process itself. From the beginning GAM's participation in the dialogue was less motivated by what it could receive from Indonesia than by what it could receive from the international community. The United States, in particular, captured GAM's imagination. For instance, in February 2002, GAM minister of state Malik Mahmud pointed out that when the Americans ask Jakarta "to do something they have to do it because they depend on the Americans"[107] and Hasan di Tiro went even further stating that "I depend on the UN and the U.S. and EU. . . . We will get everything. I am not interested in the Indonesians."[108] When the "wise men" joined the dialogue process, GAM singled out Zinni and Pitsuwan. While each of the "wise men" was participating in a purely personal capacity, GAM saw them respectively as "the representative of the U.S. in these talks"[109] and the representative of UN secretary general Kofi Annan.[110] Moreover, according to GAM "the wise men support Acehnese independence, and the members of the UN will follow."[111]

Similarly, GAM saw the foreign monitors during the COHA as UN peacekeeping forces. According to Malik Mahmud, the monitoring "operation had UN backing because individual governments sending monitors would not support it otherwise."[112] On the ground in Aceh, GAM used the space created by the peace zones to tell the Acehnese population not only that independence was imminent but that GAM's aspirations had the backing of the UN. By March GAM's misinformation campaign had reached such heights that the head of OCHA, Michael Elmquist, issued a public statement that "we are deeply concerned to read statements by the spokesperson of GAM implying that GAM is expecting the United Nations to assist them in their quest for independence."[113]

After the peace process collapsed on 18 May, the official GAM statement released by Malik Mahmud expressed its "deepest gratitude to the international community . . . for their tireless efforts towards realizing peace in Aceh" and appealed "to the United Nations for its immediate involvement in the resolution of the Aceh conflict, and for an international fact-finding mission to be sent to Aceh to investigate the crimes against humanity that have been and are being committed in Aceh."[114]

While GAM saw the international community as its savior, Indonesia, still reeling from the trauma of the international role in the independence of East Timor, was suspicious of any international involvement from the beginning. President Wahid's decision to open dialogue with the exiled GAM leadership, to involve a foreign facilitator, and to hold negotiations on an internal problem outside the country found little understanding in the Indonesian political elite and was not supported by the military. Yet, while they disagreed with the way the process was being conducted, the moderates in both the political elite and the military were willing to give dialogue a chance, hoping that GAM would sign up to special autonomy. Its behavior in and its strategy of internationalization alienated the moderates and confirmed the views of the hard-liners. As a result, when martial law was declared in Aceh in 2003 this was supported by an overwhelming majority of the Indonesian people.

GAM's strategy of internationalization had a detrimental impact on how the role of the international community was perceived in Indonesia. Until today Indonesians believe that the HDC was pushing a GAM agenda. Similarly, calls for a return to the negotiating table, and reports of human rights violations during martial law, confirmed perceptions that the international community was biased against Indonesia. Many believe the international community, in particular the U.S. and Australia, are pushing for the territorial disintegration of Indonesia. Not surprisingly, Aceh during martial law was closed to foreigners, in particular NGOs.

## Impediments to a Negotiated Settlement

There are a number of reasons why the negotiations between GAM and Indonesia never went beyond agreeing to two ceasefires, which both collapsed. At the individual level GAM's negotiators lacked capacity and sophistication. At an ideological and political level, GAM proved inflexible and unimaginative. Convinced that Indonesia would implode anyway, and that the negotiations were going in GAM's favor, it did not make concessions. In fact, the leadership made it blatantly clear that it was not interested in the negotiations as a way to find a compromise with Indonesia but only as a means to internationalize the conflict, to draw in more and more foreign players, all of whom would eventually coerce Jakarta to give up Aceh in the same way it had been coerced to permit a referendum in East Timor. GAM was not and is not prepared to give up its aim of independence, and the negotiations did not succeed in getting it to put its aim on hold or in transforming GAM from a military into a political organization. GAM's political leaders did not believe GAM had anything to gain from "going political" within an Indonesian context, and GAM's military commanders still believed that they had a viable military option.

Disjointedness was the main problem for Indonesia. Indonesia's main interest in the political dialogue was the reduction of violence in Aceh. At the core of its negotiating strategy was compliance, "forcing" GAM to give up the armed struggle and to accept autonomy. Indonesia's negotiating position was undermined from the beginning because of discord between President Wahid who supported negotiations and the military, which did not believe in talking to rebels. Indonesia's position was hampered by disunity on Aceh within the government and weakened by the erratic behavior of Wahid who, for example, first promised a referendum and then reversed his promise. His decision that negotiations on an internal issue would be conducted outside the country was another problem. Indonesia's aim of an internal solution by getting GAM to agree to autonomy was fundamentally at odds with the structure of the negotiations. Last, but not least, Indonesia's negotiating position was damaged by the disconnection between the dialogue and special autonomy process.

Throughout the Geneva peace process, Indonesia believed that it had made all the concessions without receiving anything in return. It had agreed to negotiations on an internal problem outside the country, on foreign facilitators, foreign "wise men" advisers, and foreign monitors, as well as granting Aceh special autonomy. As far as Indonesia was concerned, it had given all it could give. What it had received in return was GAM repeatedly signing up to accepting autonomy as the starting point for negotiations, which each and every time was followed by explanatory statements that this in no way meant acceptance of autonomy or relinquishing its struggle for independence. As far as Indonesia was concerned, GAM was not negotiating in good faith.

Other impediments to settlement can be found in the failure by both sides to fully implement the two ceasefires. While the COHA significantly reduced the daily violence, GAM did not commence with the cantonment of its weapons but instead regrouped, recruited, trained, and rearmed. Similarly, the Indonesian military and police did not relocate or reformulate their roles. Once the first deadline for GAM cantonment of weapons passed without "product," Indonesia's security forces proceeded to "encourage" the systematic dismantling of the monitoring mechanism, which they saw as working against Indonesian interests.

Arguably, one of the reasons for this dynamic was the failure of the facilitator, the HDC, to build confidence between the two parties. GAM claimed it did not disarm because it did not trust the Indonesians to abide by the agreement. Handing over guns would leave them and the Acehnese people unprotected. In the eyes of some, cantonment also translated into surrender, and why should GAM surrender when it had not lost the war? GAM's argument was mirrored by that of the TNI, which claimed that it would have started relocating once GAM had handed over its first guns. That was the test of GAM's sincerity. Since GAM not only refused to give up any weapons, but continued to increase its arsenal through shipments via Malaysia and Thailand, GAM's commitment was clearly not genuine.

## Legal Proceedings Against GAM

In June 2003, Indonesia for the first time in the history of the conflict went down the legal route to deal with GAM's exiled leadership. The Indonesian police issued a "red notice" to Interpol in an effort to arrest seven GAM leaders: Hasan di Tiro, Armea, Malik Mahmud, Zaini Abdullah, Tgk Muhamad Syafi'i, Zakaria Zaman, and Muhammad Nur Djuli bin Ibrahim.[115] This was followed by the visit of a team of Indonesian police to Thailand to find Zakaria and a government team to Stockholm. The Indonesian government asserted that the exiled GAM leadership in Sweden had "been sending instructions to their forces in Aceh, including orders to burn schools, kidnap village chiefs and carry out bomb attacks."[116] It asked the Swedish government to initiate legal proceedings against Hasan di Tiro, Zaini Abdullah and Malik Mahmud on charges of "perpetrating violent acts and aiding, abetting, and leading a rebellion in a foreign country."[117]

On 15 March 2004, a team from the Swedish prosecutor's office came to Indonesia and interviewed 19 witnesses in Jakarta, Medan, and Aceh.[118] In April 2004, the Swedish government announced that it would investigate the GAM leaders residing in Stockholm. This investigation focused on "the involvement of Tiro and associates in the Senen Atrium, Jakarta Stock Exchange, and Cijantung Mall bombings as well as the killings of Teungku Nazaruddin Daud and Professor Dayan Daud, the kidnapping of 243 civilians, along with the burning of at least six schools."[119] At the end of June, the Swedish prosecutors took Zaini Abdullah and Malik Mahmud into temporary custody only to be released three days later as "the evidence presented was not strong enough."[120] However, in August 2004, following the confiscation of documents, a laptop, seven cellular phones, and $10,000 cash as well as pictures and videocassettes of GAM military training from the residence of di Tiro, Mahmud, and Abdullah, the head of the Swedish prosecutor's office, Thomas Lindstrand, announced that Mahmud and Abdullah would stand trial in December.[121] By the end of December, no court proceedings had started. In January 2005, as Aceh moved into another peace process, all charges were dropped.

## The Post-Tsunami Helsinki Peace Process

On 26 December 2004, Aceh was struck first by an earthquake and then by a tsunami that took more than 200,000 lives. This natural disaster paved the way for another round of peace talks, starting with calls for the Indonesian government and GAM to set aside their differences and return to the negotiating table. The international community sent clear signals to Jakarta that relief and reconstruction funds would flow more freely if the situation on the ground was stable. GAM, which had been pushing for a resumption of the talks since May 2003, immediately seized upon the tsunami to push for new negotiations. These were needed as the counterinsurgency operations had destroyed GAM's civilian government structure and reduced its military capacity. Moreover, the exiled GAM leadership was challenged with maintaining relevance. Not surprisingly, they quickly integrated the natural disaster into their strategy of internationalization. As Malik Mahmud told Reuters in an interview: "While we talk about natural disaster in Aceh, human tragedies and things like that, we also talk about the political aspects of Aceh and the problems we have with the Indonesian government. . . . This is an opportunity. . . . Whatever aid or attention we get from the international community will help Aceh survive."[122]

The tsunami did in minutes what GAM had failed to achieve since 1976: it put Aceh on the map and raised international interest in the conflict. Moreover, the sheer scale of the human tragedy provided a face-saving opportunity for already existing secret, back-channel talks to go public. Back-channel talks between the exiled GAM leadership and the Indonesian government had started after the election of Susilo Bambang Yudhoyono as Indonesia's new president in September 2004. These contacts focused on a political solution in which GAM explored alternatives to independence. In parallel, Indonesian vice president Jusuf Kalla initiated talks about an economic solution with GAM in Aceh.

In October Kalla's team—Aceh governor Abdullah Puteh, Aceh businessman Rusli Bintang, Information Minister and Acehnese Sofyan Djalil, and former Aceh deputy commander Major General Syarifudin Tippe—went to Malaysia to meet with GAM members Mohamed Daud Syah and Harun Yusuf, who claimed to represent GAM Aceh commander Muzakkir Manaf. This was followed by at least another two meetings in Batam in November. Informal negotiations continued until early December.

On 31 October 2004, agreement was reached on nine points, including economic compensation, according to which each GAM regional commander would receive 20 hectares of land while lower ranking GAM would get 5 hectares of land. GAM would also receive some 1,500 hectares of land for religious schools or *dayah*[123] as well as Rp 60 billion to compensate beneficiaries to be selected on the recommendation of Muzakkir Manaf.[124] The state-owned plantation areas of North and East Aceh would be handed over to GAM. The movement would also be given two Boeing 737–700 and 10 smaller planes for their own airline. All mosques and *dayah* would receive free electricity. And last but not least, GAM would hand over 1,000 weapons in turn for full amnesty.[125]

Manaf was not directly involved in these talks but he was aware of their contents and according to one GAM source, he agreed, providing that all 17 regional commanders approved and the Swedish leadership approved. Underlying Kalla's initiative was the notion that the conflict could be resolved purely economically, bypassing a political solution. However, when the tsunami hit, Indonesia felt under pressure to revive the political negotiations and thus the back-channel political contacts were merged with Kalla's economic initiative and his group became the core of the Indonesian delegation.

The Helsinki process started in January 2005 and was facilitated by former Finnish president Martti Ahtisaari and the Crisis Management Initiative (CMI), a Finnish NGO. The first meeting focused on aiding relief and reconstruction. It was not until the second round in February that it became clear that two important changes had occurred within GAM's approach to negotiations. First, GAM was willing to discuss arrangements other than independence and, second, it wanted to establish a political party. It had rejected both during the 2000–2003 Geneva talks.

According to GAM, during this second round, the Indonesian delegation agreed to set aside special autonomy while GAM set aside independence. Between the second and third round, on 23–24 March, one of GAM's foreign advisors, Australian academic Damien Kingsbury, flew to Jakarta and met with Kalla's team—justice minister Hamid Awaluddin and Dr. Farid Husein—to explore GAM's idea of self-government. GAM's position as put forward by Kingsbury was as follows: GAM wanted full TNI withdrawal from Aceh, full police withdrawal from Aceh, the security vacuum to be filled by 5,000 foreign military monitors from western countries, the establishment of an indigenous police force comprising GAM and others, change in the legislation so that GAM could form a political party, immediate elections, full revenue of all resources in Aceh, and a special passport, new identity cards, GAM's own flag, and an anthem.[126] Indonesia would retain sovereignty.

In the third round of talks, economic issues were discussed, and in the fourth round security arrangements were addressed. While there were few difficulties on economic issues, the fourth round saw some backtracking on the Indonesian side. Most notably, the Indonesian delegation reverted to its "old" position insisting on special autonomy and started emphasizing the informal nature of the dialogue. As minister of defense Juwono Sudarsono pointed out, informality meant that if the talks failed the government would not be held responsible.[127] In the fifth and final round in July, negotiations almost collapsed over the issue of local political parties for Aceh. Indonesia's parliamentarians feared that local parties would open Pandora's box and lead to the formation of ethnic and religious parties everywhere, ultimately resulting in the fragmentation and disintegration of the state. Moreover, as Fuad Bawazier, deputy head of the PAN party, explained, to hold "local elections is the same as a referendum. . . . The DPR [parliament] must oppose the negotiations."[128]

In the end, however, GAM and the Indonesian government agreed to a Memorandum of Understanding (MOU), which was officially signed a month later on 15 August 2005. This MOU stipulated for GAM to decommission an agreed number of weapons and to demobilize its guerrillas. Indonesia, in turn, would withdraw its nonorganic police and TNI, grant a general amnesty for GAM, provide compensation in the form of money and land for GAM, compensate the Acehnese population for the loss of property resulting from the conflict, rehabilitate GAM, change legislation to allow for the formation of local political parties, and set up a truth and reconciliation commission. The implementation of the MOU would be overseen by the Aceh Monitoring Mission, comprising European Union and Association of Southeast Asian Nations (ASEAN) monitors.

Compared to the Geneva talks, the Helsinki peace process achieved progress in a number of areas. For one, there were discussions on issues other than sovereignty with attempts to actually address Aceh's governance as well as some of the root causes of the conflict, particularly economic ones. The talks also had greater focus as there was a regular schedule with monthly rounds and a clear deadline: August 2005. Moreover, the CMI managed to get both parties in the same room for face-to-face talks rather than the shuttle diplomacy conducted by the HDC in the Geneva dialogue. And both GAM and the Indonesian government saw the CMI as a more professional facilitator.

Yet, at the same time, the Helsinki process did not manage to break out of the zero-sum trap. GAM made a half-hearted attempt at being inclusive by holding a series of meetings with Acehnese civil society groups from the third round of the talks onward. However, the groups invited were carefully selected and did not include those who disagreed with GAM. Overall, the Acehnese people remained as excluded from the Helsinki talks as they had been from the Geneva negotiations. And this is clearly reflected in the MOU, which focuses on GAM and the Indonesian government.

There were other "familiar" stumbling blocks as well. From the beginning, the Indonesian government was split on the resumption of talks. The driving force was clearly the vice president while Yudhoyono opted to observe. Foreign minister Hassan Wirayuda and coordinating minister for security and political affairs Widodo (Adi Sucipto) were highly critical of the talks and the TNI and parliament rejected negotiations outright. They were only brought on board in the fifth round. Similarly, GAM in East Aceh and Aceh Rayeuk saw anything less than independence as a sellout and opposed the decommissioning of its weapons. In the end the exiled GAM leadership obtained their acquiescence but not their support.

Implementing the MOU will thus face many potential challenges. Both GAM and the Indonesian security forces contain ideological hard-liners as well as individuals who benefit economically from the conflict. There are other potential spoilers as well such as the civil defense organizations, which are not even mentioned in the MOU and were not represented at the talks. An even greater challenge is managing expectations and the incompatibility of long-term aims. The Acehnese are expecting instant peace and prosperity. GAM believes it will obtain a majority of the Acehnese votes in the next elections. Indonesia believes that the MOU signifies a permanent end to the conflict and demobilization means GAM ceases to exist. Yet, GAM clearly sees these negotiations as a stage, and any form of agreement short of independence as a halfway house. As GAM information minister Bakhtiar Abdullah stated at the closing of the second round when the notion of self-government was introduced: "To be clear, GAM has not given up independence."[129]

## Evaluating Indonesia's Strategy

Looking at Indonesia's strategy, it becomes clear that its greatest strength lay in the fact that Indonesia, according to international law, has legally recognized sovereignty over Aceh and the legally recognized right to defend the unity and integrity of its territory. While the international community may not always agree with the means deployed for this defense, every single state as well as the UN has supported Indonesia's right to do so. Any future secession of Aceh will require the consent of Indonesia, and that is a highly unlikely scenario. In addition, Indonesia possesses greater military capacity than GAM. It has at its disposal some 300,000 TNI—although most of these are tied up in administrative functions or are committed to other conflict areas—who are better equipped, better trained, frequently rotated, and better supported logistically and medically. Moreover, Indonesia's security forces in a narrow sense have to do no more than hold the territory. GAM simply does not have the capacity to take Aceh by force.

Yet it can be argued that Indonesia's strengths were often outweighed by its weaknesses. One of the greatest was the lack of discipline of the security forces. While there is no doubt that the TNI and the police since 2000 have been making considerable efforts to professionalize, there is equally no doubt that breaches in discipline and human rights abuses were still occurring. These abuses were compounded by the propensity of the TNI and the police for roadside extortion, theft, and destruction of property. As a result, the security forces alienated the population whose hearts and minds it was necessary to win.

Another weakness on the military side was the reliance on civil defense organizations. These groups were problematic for three main reasons. First, they are not as well as trained as soldiers and are not formally part of the military command structure. This means that they are less disciplined, less accountable, and can easily get out of control, undermining the security operations. Second, the "franchising" of violence blurs the line between combatants and noncombatants, turning the civilian population into targets and creating horizontal on top of vertical conflict. This, in turn, makes conflict more difficult to resolve. And third, since GAM information warfare drew heavily upon the comparison with East Timor, the existence of civil defense groups, irrespective of whether or not they are like the militias in East Timor, played into GAM's hands.

These military weaknesses were compounded by political weaknesses in Indonesia's counterinsurgency strategy. Every single operation since 1977 suffered from the failure to implement the nonmilitary aspects. This partly seems to have been an "attitude" problem among the civilian leadership who still expected the military to do everything even after the end of the New Order. Inability or unwillingness to assume responsibility for providing meaningful development and effective governance was compounded by lack of capacity. Finally, more often than not, the nonmilitary aspects of the counterinsurgency operations fell victim to greed and corruption. Ironically, this has increased with the post-Suharto decentralization and special autonomy for Aceh. The unresponsiveness of the civilian leadership at all government levels to the local needs of the Acehnese undermined counterinsurgency efforts as much as the lack of discipline by the security forces.

Another political weakness was the failure to integrate counterinsurgency operations into a broader political strategy. This was most clearly seen during the peace process of 2000–2003, which overlapped with OKPH. There was no obvious connection between the two. OKPH was almost exclusively a response to the deteriorating security situation in Aceh rather than a carefully designed means to pressure GAM into being more flexible at the negotiating table. Similarly the autonomy legislation, which was passed during this period, was disconnected from both the peace process and OKPH. Unilaterally decided in Jakarta (with some input from the Aceh provincial legislature), it was without ownership by the people of Aceh who neither featured in the peace process nor in the changes to the governance of the province.

The failure to integrate counterinsurgency operations into a broader political strategy was no less evident when there were no negotiations. No exit strategies were developed. Kolakops Jaring Merah lasted for ten years. It was concluded not because it had achieved its aims but because of the fall of Suharto. Similarly, it is unclear where Operasi Terpadu fits into a greater political strategy for resolving the conflict in Aceh or whether, in fact, such a political strategy exists.

Between 1977 and 1998 there was no serious attempt, and between 1998 and 2004 no successful attempt, to address the issues at the heart of the conflict. The primary causes of the conflict—the loss of dignity as well as political, cultural and social expression with the effective removal of *daerah istimewa* status, economic and social inequalities, the feelings of exploitation—not only remained unresolved but were exacerbated by secondary causes such as the brutality by the security forces, injustice, and the decline into poverty of many parts of Aceh.

## The Impact of External Events: The End of the Cold War, the Asian Financial Crisis, the "Global War on Terror"

One of the more interesting questions in the present context of the "global war of terror" is the impact of events outside Aceh on the conflict within.

Here three events need to be considered: the 1989/90 end of the cold war, the 1997 Asian Financial Crisis, and the "global war on terror" from September 2001 onward.

The end of the Cold War affected GAM more than it did Indonesia. It could be argued that the end of the Cold War did not really register with Indonesia until after the fall of Suharto, when Indonesia realized that the "allies" who had supported its 1975 invasion of East Timor were now backing Timorese independence. In comparison, GAM took note of the changing dynamics from superpower rivalry to "Pax Americana." When GAM was established one of its ideological subcurrents was anticapitalism and anti-Westernism. Indeed, GAM saw itself very much part of the broader Third World revolutionary movement. This changed with the end of the Cold War. It moved away from its anticapitalist rhetoric and embraced the language of human rights. It sought alliances with human rights organizations and looked toward the West for salvation.

The greater impact on the conflict in Aceh came from the 1997 Asian financial crisis. It set in motion the fall of Suharto and the end of the New Order in May 1998 as well as the subsequent democratization process. Negotiations became possible for the first time. While the end of the New Order had not resulted in resolving the conflict in Aceh, it had clearly broadened Indonesia's approach from relying only on the military option to a comprehensive strategy including negotiations, autonomy, and Islamic law.

The events of 9/11 and the "global war on terror" had four effects on the conflict in Aceh. First was an international shift toward enforcing existing state boundaries, and looking less sympathetically at Muslim-based national liberation movements. Not surprisingly, GAM lost some Western support when stories of links with al-Qaeda emerged. (These reports were rejected by GAM and have remained unsubstantiated.) Second, the need for cooperation with the Indonesian police and intelligence—less so, the military—following the 2002 Bali bombings as well as their own experience of political violence shifted the sympathies of many governments toward Indonesia. When the peace process collapsed in May 2003 every single state reiterated Indonesia's right to defend its unity and integrity. Third, the sudden need for security somewhat reversed popular Indonesian attitudes toward the military, which had previously been blamed for the ills of Suharto's New Order. This strengthened the position of the police, military, and intelligence organizations. And fourth, the global war on terror partially explains GAM's redefinition of its future state from an Islamic Sultanate to an Acehnese democracy.

## Explaining the Duration of the Insurgency

Twelve factors explain the duration of the insurgency. First, during Suharto's New Order the regime relied solely upon the security approach. While each military operation initially reduced GAM's strength, the roots of the conflict and the grievances were not addressed. Second, the human rights violations perpetrated by the regime created additional grievances and reasons for the Acehnese to join GAM. Third, the impunity of the security forces even after the fall of Suharto ensured that many Acehnese continued to believe they would never receive justice from Jakarta. Fourth, the exploitation of Aceh's economic resources mainly benefited the central government to the detriment of the economy and development in Aceh. Most key positions in the oil industry were occupied by non-Acehnese. Fifth, endemic corruption alienated the average Acehnese from both the regional government—and ensured that it has been ineffective and unresponsive to local needs—and Jakarta. Sixth, regional autonomy was never truly implemented. Most Acehnese did not see or believe that there was a difference between centralization and decentralization, so many supported GAM because independence was the option that had not yet been tried. Seventh, low education standards especially among the rural population made the latter susceptible to GAM propaganda claiming that if Aceh were independent every Acehnese would be as rich as every Bruneian. Eighth, GAM was able to continue its struggle through extortion of the oil industry from multinational companies to third party contractors and through funding its struggle from *ganja* cultivation. Ninth, the Indonesian security forces have vested business interests in Aceh—including illegal logging and *ganja*. Tenth, GAM's exiled leadership kept the option of independence alive not only in Aceh but also in the international community, particularly among NGOs. Eleventh, Indonesia's security forces proved unable to cut the flow of illegal small arms to Aceh from Thailand and Malaysia. And twelfth, the exiled GAM leadership until recently was not interested in a compromise solution and, arguably, incapable of it.

## Conclusions and Policy Recommendations

Aceh is a microcosm of the problems facing Indonesia as a whole: endemic corruption, lack of implementation of policies, lack of law and order, ineffective government, and increasing unemployment and impoverishment. But unlike other regions Aceh has a history of prior independence, a history of "separateness" since 1945, and a history of human rights abuses. The Acehnese sense of identity, entitlement, and grievance is greater than that of most other peoples in Indonesia, and this has sustained the insurgent movement. The insurgency, however, has also been kept alive by increasing criminalization.

These factors present considerable obstacles to conflict resolution. Most important, the zero-sum dynamic, which has characterized both the conflict and the various peace processes, must be broken. This requires not just the full-hearted implementation of the MOU but broadening the process to include all elements of Acehnese society.

Moreover, the MOU should not be treated as an agreement ending the conflict but as the beginning of conflict transformation. It must be followed by committed peace building, which addresses the original grievances—political, social, and economic overcentralization and exploitation—as well as additional grievances such as corruption and human rights abuses. Truth and reconciliation, moreover, should not just focus on the Indonesian security forces but should also include GAM's abuses, in particular, the shooting of parliamentarians, judges, and teachers as well as the ethnic cleansing of Javanese migrants.

Furthermore, in order to stabilize the province, internally displaced persons from both the tsunami and the conflict must be fully supported in the return to their villages or chosen area of resettlement, including the estimated 125,000 Javanese IDPs in North Sumatra, who were forced out of Aceh between 1999 and 2001.

Similarly, the MOU should be underwritten by broad bottom-up development of the infrastructure, and the health care and education systems. The economy needs to be revitalized, investment encouraged, and unemployment reduced. The younger generation, in particular, needs jobs, skills, vocational training, and education.

And last but not least, should the MOU break down, the Indonesian government should focus unilaterally on addressing the root causes of the conflict and fully implement autonomy and developing Aceh's infrastructure and rural economy. Governance at all levels needs to be cleaner, more transparent, more accountable, and more effective. It must also be more responsive to grassroots political needs, more inclusive, and more reflective of the aspirations of the average Acehnese. Lastly, the province's education system must be reconstructed to provide the next generation of Acehnese with knowledge, skills, and real prospects for a better future.

## Glossary

AGAM: Angkatan Gerakan Aceh Merdeka (Forces of the Free Aceh Movement). GAM's military wing.

AM: Aceh Merdeka. Name of GAM in the 1980s.

ASNLF: Aceh Sumatra National Liberation Front. Official name of GAM.

Brimob: Brigade Mobile. Paramilitary mobile police brigade whose main function is counterinsurgency and counterterror.

CMI: Crisis Management Initiative. Conflict resolution NGO under the auspices of former Finnish president Martti Ahtisaari.

COHA: Cessation of Hostilities Agreement. Signed 9 December 2002, collapsed 18 May 2003, it called for the cantonment of GAM weapons, reformulation of the role of the Indonesian security forces, and an all-inclusive dialogue at a later stage.

*daerah istimewa*: Special area. Status given to Aceh as part of the 1959 agreement that ended the Darul Islam rebellion. It conferred upon Aceh autonomy in education, religion, and customs.

Darul Islam: Muslim political movement that sought to transform Indonesia into an Islamic state. Aceh joined the Darul Islam rebellion in 1953; Aceh's insurgency ended in 1959 through a negotiated settlement.

DOM: Daerah Operasi Militer. Military Operations Area. Popular name for the Jaring Merah operations in Aceh from 1990 until 1998.

EMOI: ExxonMobil Oil Indonesia.

GAM: Gerakan Aceh Merdeka (Free Aceh Movement). Established by Hassan di Tiro on 30 October 1976 with the aim of liberating Aceh from Indonesian "neocolonial control."

GWOT: Global War on Terror.

HDC: Henry Dunant Center, later Center for Humanitarian Dialogue, based in Geneva. Facilitator in the dialogue between GAM and the Indonesian government.

Kolakops Jaring Merah: Red Net Operations Command in Aceh from 1990 to 1998. More commonly referred to as DOM.

Kopassus: Komando Pasukan Khusus. Indonesian army special forces.

MOI: Mobil Oil Indonesia.

NAD: Nanggroe Aceh Darussalam. The name Aceh obtained under the special autonomy law in 2001, but more commonly used to refer to special autonomy itself.

New Order: Authoritarian regime under President Suharto from 1967 to 1998.

nonorganic troops. Indonesian troops that are centrally recruited, such as the Kostrad special reserve and the Kopassus special forces, as well as troops recruited in one region and sent to another. Locally recruited troops are organic.

OCHA: UN Office for the Coordination of Humanitarian Affairs.

OKPH: Operasi Pemulihan Keamanan dan Penegakan Hukum. Security recovery operation in Aceh from May 2001 to December 2002.

Operasi Terpadu: Integrated Operation. In Aceh from May 2003 to August 2005, it comprised a humanitarian, local government recovery, a law and order, and a military operation. In November 2003 an economic recovery operation was added.

*pajak nanggroë*: Aceh state tax, or GAM extortion.

*Pancasila*: Five Principles. A religiously neutral form of nationalist philosophy adopted in 1945. Its principles are belief in God, nationalism, humanitarianism, social justice, and democracy.

*rakitan*: Home-made or traditional weapons.

SGI: Satuan Gabungan Intelijen (Indonesian Military Intelligence).

*sishankamrata*: Sistem pertahanan keamanan rakyat semesta (Total People's Defense and Security System).

Stavanger Declaration: Issued by the July 2002 exiled GAM leadership meeting in Stavanger, Norway. GAM's aims were reformulated from an Islamic sultanate to a democratic Acehnese state, GAM's leadership became the State of Aceh government in exile, and AGAM became the State of Aceh military (TNA).

TNA: Tentara Negara Aceh (State of Aceh Military). AGAM was renamed TNA in the Stavanger Declaration.

TNI: Tentara Nasional Indonesia (Indonesian National Military).

## Timeline

1873: Aceh is invaded by the Dutch and incorporated into the Dutch East Indies.

1942: Aceh is invaded and occupied by the Japanese, ending the Dutch presence.

1945: Japanese occupation ends with the Japanese defeat in the Second World War. Indonesian nationalist leaders Sukarno and Hatta declare Indonesian independence. Aceh is the only part of the Dutch East Indies the Dutch do not even try to reclaim, making Aceh key to the Indonesian independence struggle.

1949: After four years of war the Netherlands formally transfers sovereignty to Indonesia. Aceh is awarded provincial autonomy in recognition of its contribution to the Indonesian war of independence.

1951: Aceh's autonomy status is revoked as Aceh is amalgamated with the neighboring province of North Sumatra. The Acehnese feel betrayed.

1953: Aceh under the leadership of Daud Beureueh joins the Darul Islam rebellion, already going on in parts of Java and Sulawesi with the aim of turning Indonesia into an Islamic state.

1959: Aceh's Darul Islam rebellion is ended by negotiated settlement that confers on Aceh special status with respect to religion, education, and customs.

1965: President Sukarno is ousted by Major General Suharto and later placed under house arrest.

1967: Suharto assumes the presidency and embarks on a policy of political, economic, and cultural centralization. This de facto reverses Aceh's special status.

1971: The Arun gas field is discovered in North Aceh. This leads to the establishment of the Lhokseumawe industrial zone, enclave development, dispossession of farmers, pollution, an influx of foreign and migrant workers, and social dislocation of the Acehnese. Moreover, the gas revenue accrues to the central government with little being spent on development in Aceh.

1976: Hassan di Tiro returns to Aceh from the United States in October and establishes the Aceh Sumatra National Liberation Front (ASNLF), more commonly known as the Free Aceh Movement (GAM). His aim is to liberate Aceh from the neocolonial Javanese exploitation.

1977: In October GAM calls on all foreign workers to leave Aceh. In response the Indonesian military launches its Nanggala intelligence operation. In December: Three foreign contractors for Bechtel, one American and two Korean, are ambushed by GAM. The American is killed and the Koreans wounded. In response, Indonesian security operations against GAM intensify.

1979: Hostilities in Aceh come to an end when di Tiro and several other GAM leaders flee into exile. Indonesian military operations succeeded in killing, arresting, or pushing out GAM. Security is restored but Acehnese grievances are not addressed.

1979–1986: The exiled GAM leadership now based in Stockholm tries to garner international support for its cause.

1986–1989: Some 700 GAM guerrillas receive training in Libya. Di Tiro joins his troops to provide them with ideological education.

1989: The Libyan-trained GAM guerrillas return to Aceh and start attacking the Indonesian security forces.

1990: GAM starts attacking civilians, in particular Javanese transmigrants. In response, the Indonesian military launches its Jaring Merah operations more commonly known as DOM.

1990–1998: During DOM the Indonesian security forces perpetrate widespread and systematic human rights abuses against the Acehnese population. GAM's military command structure relocates to Malaysia.

1997: The Indonesian banking sector and economy collapse as a result of the Asian financial crisis. Students start demonstrating against collusion, corruption, and nepotism.

1998: President Suharto resigns in May and is succeeded by his vice president, B. J.

Habibie. Habibie ends DOM and nonorganic Indonesian troops are withdrawn from Aceh.

1999: Indonesian reforms include Laws 22 and 25 on decentralization. They also include the withdrawal of the security forces from politics, the separation of the police and the military, and the professionalization of both. GAM exploits the emerging democracy and the withdrawal of troops from Aceh to regroup, recruit, and push its independence agenda. GAM's military command returns from Malaysia. Other GAM members benefit from Habibie's amnesty and are released from jail. New members flock to GAM seeking vengeance as a result of the human rights abuses. GAM pushes from its traditional base on the east coast into the rest of Aceh. Following general elections in June, B. J. Habibie is succeeded as president in October by Abdurahman Wahid. Wahid wants to resolve the Aceh conflict through negotiations.

2000: Talks between the Indonesian government and the exiled GAM leadership begin in Geneva in January, facilitated by the Henry Dunant Center (HDC). In May, GAM and the Indonesian government agree to the so-called Humanitarian Pause. A Joint Committee on Security Modalities, a Joint Committee on Humanitarian Action, and a Security Modalities Monitoring Team are established to implement the Pause. On the ground the ceasefire is soon violated by both GAM and the Indonesian security forces (usually Brimob).

2001: In January the Humanitarian Pause is extended as the Moratorium on Violence. Violence on the ground increases. In February the Moratorium on Violence is renamed Peace Through Dialogue. In March GAM cuts the gas pipelines and increases its attacks on the gas industry. ExxonMobil can no longer guarantee the safety of its employees and shuts down its onshore operations in Aceh. In April President Wahid issues presidential instruction 4 to secure Aceh. In May Indonesia launches a security recovery operation, OKPH. In July the political dialogue collapses, the Joint Committee on Security Modalities is frozen, and GAM's Banda Aceh-based negotiators are arrested and charged with rebellion. They are later released. President Wahid is impeached and succeeded by his vice president, Megawati Sukarnoputri. In August special autonomy is given to Aceh under Law 18. Special autonomy provides for the introduction of Islamic law and provides Aceh with 70 percent of its oil and gas revenues.

2002: In January special autonomy (NAD) becomes effective. GAM Aceh commander Abdullah Syafi'i is killed by the Indonesian military and succeeded by Muzzakir Manaf. In February talks between GAM and the Indonesian government start again, including the foreign "wise men' advisers. In May another round of talks takes place in Geneva. It results in a joint statement in which GAM accepts NAD as a starting point, the HDC will facilitate a democratic all-inclusive dialogue, and both GAM and the Indonesian security forces will work toward another ceasefire to permit humanitarian assistance. On returning to Sweden, the GAM leadership from Sweden issues a statement that it will never give up the independence struggle and does not accept NAD. In August Indonesian coordinating minister for security and political affairs Susilo Bambang Yudhoyono issues GAM an ultimatum to accept NAD by the month of Ramadan (4 November–6 December). In December Japan, the United States, the European Union, and the World Bank sponsor a preparatory meeting in Tokyo on peace and reconstruction in Aceh. Days later, GAM and Indonesia sign the Cessation of Hostilities Agreement (COHA) in Geneva. This agreement does not attempt to resolve the crucial issues, but only to instate another ceasefire. Crucially it includes two major demilitarization measures. GAM will place its weapons in placement sites over a five-month period starting February 2003. Indonesia will simultaneously relocate and reformulate the mandate of its security forces. It also sets up a Joint Security Committee (JSC) to monitor the ceasefire.

2003: GAM's deadline for the placement of weapons passes in February without a single gun being handed over. At the same time GAM is raising taxes and using the peace zones to tell the Acehnese that independence is imminent and will come at the hands of the UN. In March the Indonesian military starts organizing demonstrations against the ceasefire monitoring mechanism. The JSC is confined to the provincial capital Banda Aceh. Clashes between GAM and the security forces escalate. In May attempts to revive the COHA in Tokyo fail. GAM and Indonesia are unable to reconcile their differences and the COHA collapses. Indonesia places Aceh under martial law and launches the Integrated Operation. The Indonesian military lays siege to several GAM strongholds in October and November. One such area is a camp near the village of Cut Trieng, where GAM Aceh commander Muzakkir Manaf is believed to be hiding. However, when the siege is lifted it becomes clear that GAM managed to slip away. In November martial law is extended for another 6 months.

2004: Martial law is downgraded to civil emergency in May. In September Megawati Sukarnaputri loses the presidential elections and is succeeded by Susilo Bambang Yudhoyono. Back-channel contacts between GAM and the Indonesian government open up in September and intensify in November. In December the Asian tsunami devastates large parts of Aceh. Foreign military contingents and NGOs rush to Aceh. GAM declares a unilateral ceasefire and invites the Indonesian government to talks.

2005: A new peace process is convened in Helsinki in January; GAM and the Indonesian government discuss aiding the tsunami relief process. During the second round in February, GAM put forward its idea of self-government; secret talks in March between GAM adviser Damien Kingsbury and Jusuf Kalla's team in Jakarta explore GAM's idea. In April, economic issues are discussed at the third round of talks. In May 2005 GAM meets with select Acehnese civil society groups in Sweden. In the subsequent fourth round of negotiations security arrangements are discussed. On 15 August GAM and Indonesia signed a memorandum of understanding bringing an end to the conflict.

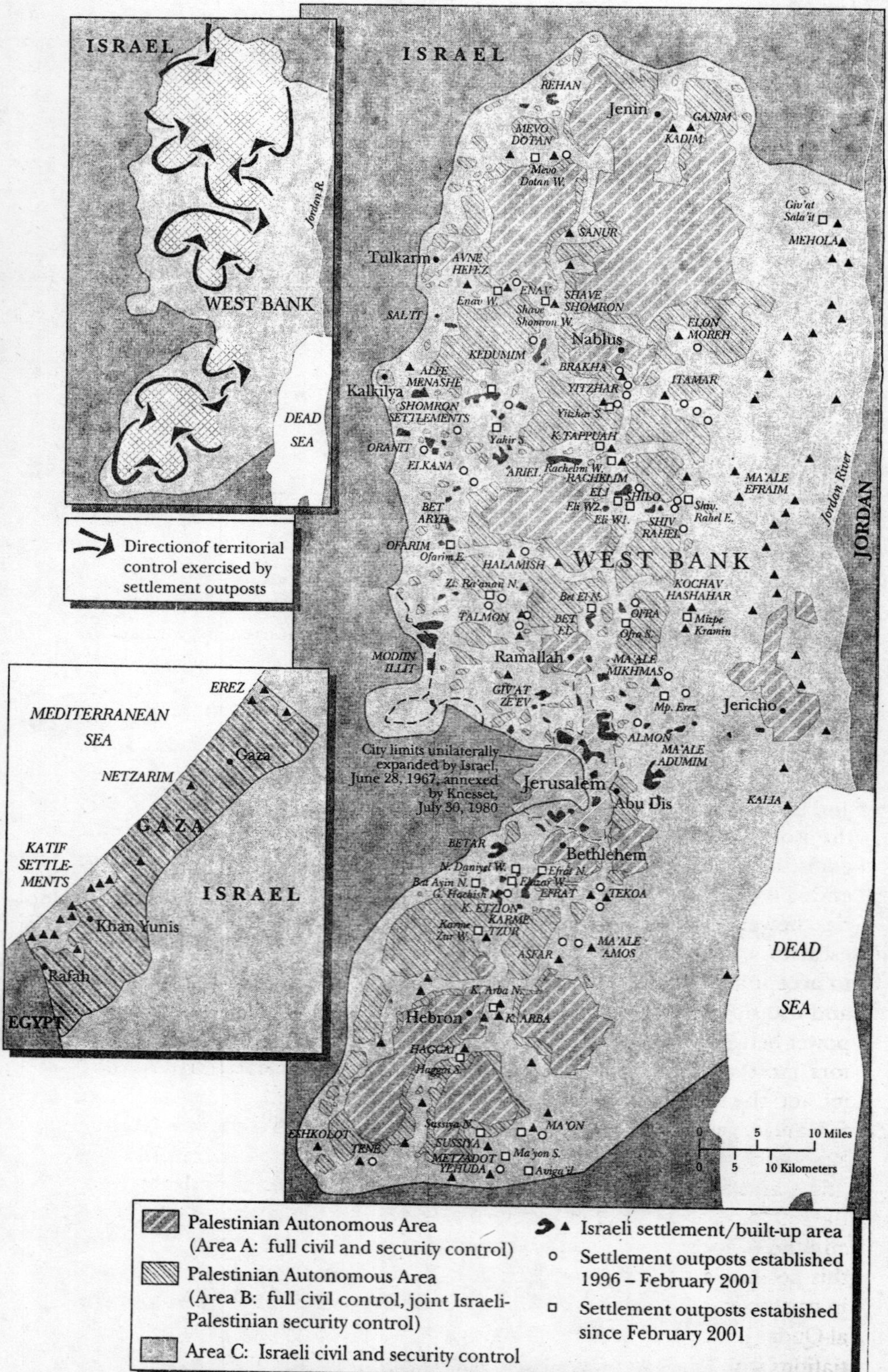


Map 4.1. Israeli settlement outposts.

*Chapter 4*

# Hamas: Socialization and the Logic of Compromise

JEROEN GUNNING

This chapter analyzes the development of the Palestinian Islamist movement Hamas, from its creation at the start of the 1987 Intifada to 2005. Hamas has begun a shift from an absolutist, reactionary resistance movement to a more pragmatic, politically oriented resistance organization, which, at least domestically, has become increasingly accommodationist. The chapter charts the origins of the movement and explores how changes in the composition of its support base, the Palestinian political system, and regional conditions have affected its goals and behavior. Particular attention is paid to the effects of Hamas's participation in the political system and to the impact of Israeli state strategies and tactics. Partial inclusion into the political system has had a moderating effect on Hamas's domestic goals, but it has not dimmed the leadership's opposition to Israel, nor ended its practice of targeting civilians. Participation in the political system has, however, introduced a logic of electoral accountability that has made escalatory resistance operations more costly and increased the incentives to accept a ceasefire. Whether Hamas will accept a compromise solution and transform itself into a political party depends on both the balance of power between pragmatists and hard-liners within Hamas, and external factors, most important the policies adopted by Israel, the Palestinian Authority, and the international sponsors of any peace process.

Hamas, the acronym for Harakat al-Muqawama al-Islamiyya (Islamic Resistance Movement), which also means "zeal," emerged out of the Palestinian Muslim Brotherhood in response to the Intifada in 1987. Its goal was the total liberation of all of historic Palestine, including what is now Israel, and the establishment of an Islamic state in the liberated lands.[1] It justified this position by arguing that Palestine is an Islamic *waqf*, a territory given in trust to all generations of Muslims, centered on Islam's third holiest city, al-Quds (Jerusalem). Since no single generation may give it away, any negotiations with Israel were framed as acts of betrayal.[2]

Initially, Hamas refused to operate under the umbrella of the secular Palestine Liberation Organization (PLO), ran its activities in direct opposition to the PLO, and refused to enter into power-sharing arrangements. In its first years, its actions revolved around organizing strikes and demonstrations, targeting Israeli soldiers, settlers and occasionally civilians, distributing leaflets, and clamping down on deviant behavior within Palestinian society. Some of its members were as concerned that women wore the *hijab* or with punishing drug pushers as they were with resisting the Israeli occupation.

Present-day Hamas has evolved into a political party, surpassing the original Muslim Brotherhood and inheriting the charitable structures established by the Brothers. Since 1991, it has delegated resistance activities to its military wing, the Izz al-Din al-Qassam Brigades, which in 1994 began carrying out suicide operations against civilians inside Israel. It has established a political presence in most of Palestine's subnational political institutions and is on the brink of participating in the second national elections since the establishment of the Palestinian Authority. Like the Brothers before it, it participates in the professional and student elections that function as the focus of political life in the absence of regular national elections. But unlike many of the Brothers (and most other political activists of the 1980s, including the dominant Fatah movement), Hamas now accepts electoral defeat without violence, refrains from intimidating the opposition, and enters coalitions with ideological co-thinkers. It has generally refrained from using violence against fellow Palestinians, even in the face of increased repression by the Palestinian Authority (PA), and has adopted a more conciliatory approach to those who dress differently or espouse different ideas.

Though Hamas still calls for the liberation of all of Palestine and the establishment of an Islamic state, it has become more open to compromise. It has made increasingly credible ceasefire offers on the basis of a return to the borders of 1967,[3] most prominently during the ill-fated 6-week ceasefire declared in June 2003, and some leaders hinted at the possibility of peace if such a ceasefire were to hold and a viable Palestinian state were to emerge. It has expressed readiness to operate within a secular political system if that system reflects the will of the people. It has engaged in numerous cross-party summits and conferences and has become an integral part of the resistance committees of the current al-Aqsa Intifada. Its rhetoric has become more secular, though it is still infused with Islamic imagery.[4]

To explain Hamas's shift from an absolutist, reactionary resistance movement toward a more pragmatic, politically oriented resistance organization with an accommodationist potential, I examine its origins, the profile of its support base, its ideology, its political culture, and the power resources at its disposal. Having reflected on what factors drive the organization's goals and methods, I then explore how these factors have changed. To better conceptualize these changes, I use Stephen Stedman's typology of "spoilers." The term "spoiler" is problematic because it suggests that blame for failure of a peace process lies with the spoilers, never with the peace process itself or with those not labeled "spoilers." Nevertheless, Stedman's distinction between a "total spoiler"—incapable of compromise because of the immutability of its demands and its unyielding desire for total power—and a "limited spoiler"—(potentially) capable of compromise because its demands are more limited and its leadership more willing to consider power-sharing—is useful to capture the evolution Hamas is undergoing.[5]

Following Stedman, if Hamas is a "total spoiler," as its absolutist rhetoric on total liberation and its initial reluctance to enter into power-sharing arrangements suggest, exclusion from the peace process and the use of force are the two most effective options available. If, however, Hamas is a spoiler of a more limited kind, as its current approach to coalition politics and its experiments with ceasefires suggest, acceptance of exclusionary and coercive strategies are likely to be counterproductive, and policies involving inducement and socialization should be adopted. In the following, I will show that Hamas has shifted from a "total" to a more "limited" type of spoiler and that policy responses should shift accordingly. I argue, with John Darby, not only that "a lasting agreement is impossible unless it actively involves those with the power to bring it down by violence" but that "zealot groups can be neutralized only with the active involvement of former militants."[6]

## Origins of Hamas

Although the original Palestinian Muslim Brotherhood was established in 1946, it had become largely marginalized by the time the Israelis had occupied Gaza and the West Bank in 1967. It reemerged in the mid-1970s with a focus on social welfare—echoing the Brotherhood's original commitment to the welfare of the approximately 700,000 refugees who had been driven out of what is now Israel during Israel's "war of independence." It refused to engage in resistance activities, arguing that Palestinian society was too weak and that it needed to return to its Islamic roots as the loss of land was regarded as a punishment for loss of faith. At first, the Brotherhood refrained from entering the political arena, which had been dominated by the PLO since the late 1960s. However, following the success of the 1979 Islamic revolution in Iran, and inspired by the actions of the Afghan mujahidin, the Palestinian Brothers began to challenge the PLO's hegemony on university campuses and in professional associations. Their program was primarily domestic, challenging the right of the PLO to be the sole legitimate representative of the Palestinian people, and focusing on issues of social morality.

The reemergence of the Muslim Brotherhood was facilitated by the existing nascent structures and personnel left over from the pre-1967 era and by the return of Islamist "exiles" to the occupied territories in the 1960s and 1970s. Its subsequent growth, especially following the 1977 election of a Likud government in Israel, was in part because of the favorable political opportunities created by the Israeli government, which sought to facilitate the Brotherhood's growth to undermine the PLO. Its reemergence was, however, also a function of changing social and economic structures in the occupied territories.

Israel's occupation of the West Bank and Gaza Strip in 1967 had had a profound effect on the traditional power of the notable families. Access to Israeli labor markets, a sharp increase in per capita income, and increased mobility weakened traditional bonds. With the increase in wealth came a demographic expansion, followed by a rapid increase in the number of universities, which both exacerbated the breakdown in traditional structures and created new opportunities for the lower and lower middle classes.[7] One outcome of this process was the demise of the traditional municipal leadership and the rise of a new class of leader, ideologically and organizationally bound to the PLO.[8] Simultaneously, though less noticeable, a second counter-elite was emerging. Both skeptical of the narrow secular nationalist claims of the PLO and inspired by the ideological promises of region-wide Islamism, this group consisted primarily of outsiders to the PLO power structures—including poorer, conservative members of the refugee communities and upwardly mobile refugees and urbanites from lower- and middle-class backgrounds. It was driven by a desire for meritocracy and social justice, in opposition to the perceived nepotism and corruption of the PLO elites. It was strengthened by financial resources available from the conservative and antisecular Gulf States whose revenues had multiplied with the sharp rise in oil prices following the oil embargo of 1973.[9]

The structural changes of the 1970s accelerated in the 1980s. Between 1977 and 1987, the population grew by 23 percent, resulting in around half the population being under fourteen. At the same time, the number of university graduates rose from 2,600 in 1977–1978 to 16,000 in 1987–1988. Because recession had hit Israel, the occupied territories, and the Gulf States (where many Palestinians worked) in the early 1980s, by the late 1980s most university graduates were underemployed—creating a surplus of well-educated, ambitious youths frustrated in the attainment of their expectations.[10] It was these youths who were among the leaders of the 1980s protests, which culminated in the Intifada. And it was these youths, dominated by the upwardly mobile lower classes, who pressed the more cautious, conservative old guard of the Muslim Brotherhood into allowing them to join the Intifada under the umbrella of a newly created resistance wing, Hamas.[11]

The initial goals of Hamas, as declared in its 1988 Charter,[12] were reflective of the environment from which Hamas had emerged and the socioeconomic background of its support base. The high percentage of refugees among its ranks was one of the driving factors behind its call for the total liberation of Palestine.[13] Its refusal to join the PLO as a junior partner was partly because its supporters were both outside the political elite structures and saw themselves as a counter-elite. Its focus on social morality was reflective of the conservative and religious background of its support base. The struggle with Israel was cast in almost eschatological terms, both in reaction to the increasingly harsh Israeli occupation policies before the Intifada, and to distance Hamas from Israeli leniency toward the Brotherhood during the 1980s. The precise formulation of these goals was shaped by the particular ideology that Hamas had inherited from the Muslim Brothers. But that ideology was itself largely a product of the particular situation from which Hamas emerged—and thus it is likely to be affected by changes in Hamas's support base or political environment.

## Sources of Power

Hamas's power is derived from four interrelated sources. Its original power base was its network of affiliated charities. Rebuilt during the 1970s, these charities have gained Hamas a reputation for financial integrity, incorruptibility, commitment to social justice, and responsiveness to the community's needs. Recipients of these charities have come to believe that Hamas, as a political organization, would champion their concerns. As the network of charities has expanded and grown in professionalism, Hamas's reputation has grown—even though the charities are independent entities over which Hamas, as a political organization, has no formal control.

The second source of Hamas's power is its political activities. Though Hamas is not registered as a political party, it has a political party organization made up of district, regional and national consultative councils. This organization defines party policy, organizes rallies, liaises with Hamas representatives on the numerous professional and student union councils, mediates on behalf of its supporters and negotiates with other political parties. In professional and student elections, Hamas representatives have come to receive anything between 20 and 80 percent of the votes, while Hamas representatives have dominated student unions across the occupied territories for much of the past decade. In the absence of regular national elections these electoral victories carry a high symbolic weight, giving Hamas real political standing—even though in opinion polls it has typically been supported by only 10–25 percent of respondents (20–25 percent since the outbreak of the al-Aqsa Intifada).[14]

Hamas's resistance activities are its third source of power, though not primarily in "military" terms. In a direct confrontation with the PA's security forces, because the Brigades comprise only an estimated few hundred operatives,[15] Hamas would stand little chance. Rather, political influence is derived indirectly, either through the ability to foil negotiations, or through increased domestic political prestige stemming from popular admiration for the Qassam Brigades and their success in paying Israel back in what many Palestinians believe to be its own currency. Because of this, Hamas is dependent on maintaining popular support to ward off PA repression—which is one of the reasons the Brigades cannot act wholly without restraint, especially when popular support for a political compromise is on the increase. Conversely, a high level of political support for Hamas means its military wing can operate with some impunity.

Last, Hamas derives power from the place it occupies in the Arab-Israeli conflict and the international support it can garner as a result. Because of its continued commitment to resistance it can count on the support of states such as Syria and Iran. It has similarly received support from those seeking to counter Fatah or the PA, as when King Hussein of Jordan negotiated the release of Hamas's then figurehead, Ahmad Yassin, in 1997. It is also supported by those who share its Islamist goals, as reflected in the steady stream of gifts from Saudi Arabia. The latter two types of support are not necessarily dependent on Hamas's refusal to compromise on Israel—King Hussein, after all, was a tireless supporter of compromise. Hamas is thus likely to continue to draw support from these sources even if it reached agreement with Israel.

Each of these power bases provides Hamas with bargaining power vis-à-vis the PA, Fatah, and other political parties. Its social network surpasses that of other political movements and in some areas outperforms the PA's institutions. Consequently, the PA is dependent on the proper functioning of Hamas's social network and cannot afford to shut it down if it wishes to avoid a humanitarian crisis—as proven when it tried to do so.[16] Similarly, because Hamas has a significant political following, the PA cannot afford to clamp down on the movement, however much the Israeli and American administrations would desire it to do so. The central role the Qassam Brigades play in the popular resistance committees of the al-Aqsa Intifada underlines Hamas's pivotal position in the Palestinian struggle—as does the fact that suicide operations, originally pioneered by the Brigades and Islamic Jihad, have become the hallmark of most resistance groups.

Each source also generates financial income. The charities are funded by local donations (e.g., *zakah*) and international humanitarian organizations, including Western charities. Hamas's political activities generate support from both local and regional political benefactors. The operations of the Qassam Brigades appear to be funded primarily from abroad, through the offices of Hamas's leadership in exile, which is currently centered in Damascus and Beirut. In each instance, local donations are typically augmented by donations from the Palestinian diaspora, although estimates regarding the share of the diaspora's input vary widely. Underlining the importance of its charitable agenda, particularly compared to its resistance activities, of Hamas's estimated annual budget of $10–20 million, 80–90 percent is believed to be spent on social service programs.[17]

## Socioeconomic Profile of Hamas's Leadership and Support Base

Hamas continues to draw its support primarily from the lower and lower middle classes. A significant proportion of these have a good education and expectations to match. Its leaders are typically professionals—engineers, teachers, and doctors. Students dominate its youth wing. Many of these come from upwardly mobile families.[18] That Hamas's constituency is centered on those who feel excluded from the current political system is illustrated by the fact that a relatively high percentage of Hamas supporters became poorer after the arrival of the PA.[19] Similarly, very few trust the PA.[20]

A second characteristic of Hamas's constituency is that many are from the refugee community. Most of its leaders in Gaza are refugees from what is now Israel, or descendants thereof. A survey I conducted in 1997 among students at the Islamic University in Gaza found that Hamas supporters were twice as likely as Fatah supporters to live in refugee camps, and a significantly higher proportion of Hamas supporters lived in Gaza City—many of whom would have been of refugee descent.[21] In sharp contrast, Fatah supporters were twice as likely to come from villages or smaller towns where the ratio of refugees is typically low.[22] This pattern is replicated in the West Bank, though to a lesser extent.

Third, Hamas supporters tend to be highly religious. Of those respondents to my 1997 survey who said they supported Hamas, 73 percent stated that "all" their family members were religious, against 0.2 percent saying that "none" were religious. Similarly, 78 percent of Hamas supporters stated they considered themselves to be religious while 68 percent said they never missed morning prayers.[23] Religiosity, however, does not necessarily mean the same thing to all supporters. Asked to name "the most important issue facing Palestine now," 38 percent selected "Islamization" against some 15 percent each naming "peace," "human rights," and "economy." In sharp contrast, Fatah supporters accorded "peace" the highest importance (37 percent), with economy a close second (31 percent). However, if we combine the choices of "peace," "human rights," and "economy," 44 percent of Hamas supporters ranked these over "Islamization." Moreover, when asked what religion meant to them, 33 percent of Hamas supporters singled out "integrity"—signifying a relatively secular understanding of "religion." Similarly, 56 percent stated that they believed modernity to be very to moderately good for Palestine and only 5 percent said that "religious people" were the institution that most influenced their political views.

## Ideology and Strategic Calculations

Given the ambiguity surrounding a Hamas supporter's interpretation of Islam, neither Hamas's advocacy of an Islamic state nor its insistence on casting the Israeli-Palestinian conflict in religious terms necessarily preclude a change of strategy, thus opening up the possibility that despite its absolutist rhetoric Hamas may be a "limited spoiler." Advocacy of an Islamic state appears to be as much a political and socio-economic as a religious choice, representing a determination to reshape the existing political landscape by those outside the established elite. The incumbent elite's emphasis on its secularist credentials makes advocacy of an Islamic state all the more attractive. Because this is a contextually situated response, changes in the political environment are likely to induce a change. If Hamas were to become part of the political establishment, and corruption and unaccountability were dealt with, a significant number of Hamas's supporters might divert their energies from promoting an Islamic state to improving social justice in the existing state. The fact that Hamas leaders liken their proposed Islamic state to an American-style presidential democracy suggests that a compromise between a secular and an Islamist solution is attainable.[24]

Hamas's insistence on total liberation is similarly contextually situated. Its readiness to observe a five-month ceasefire prior to the first national elections of 1996 to facilitate the election process, and its recent declaration of intent to participate in the legislative elections of 2005—despite both processes belonging to a political framework that recognizes the right of Israel to exist—indicate that Hamas's opposition to the peace process is not as absolute as its absolutist rhetoric suggests.

In the same vein, Hamas's resort to radical methods is not inevitable. The fact that the Brotherhood largely refrained from resistance before 1987 and that Hamas only turned to suicide operations against civilians in 1994 suggests that the organization's resort to violence is situational rather than purely ideological.

The composition of its support base does render Hamas prone to supporting radical solutions. Refugees, youths, students, professionals, and those economically affected by the peace agreement between the PA and Israel have all been shown in national surveys to be more supportive of violence than the general population.[25] However, support for violence is heavily influenced by the status of negotiations between the PA and Israel, and people's perceptions of what this means for them. In the early years following the 1993 Oslo Agreement, support for armed attacks was inversely related to support for the peace process (see Figure 4.1). This link is not inevitable as the simultaneous rise in support for armed attacks and the peace process in a December 1996 poll underlines.[26] It is nevertheless often perceptible.

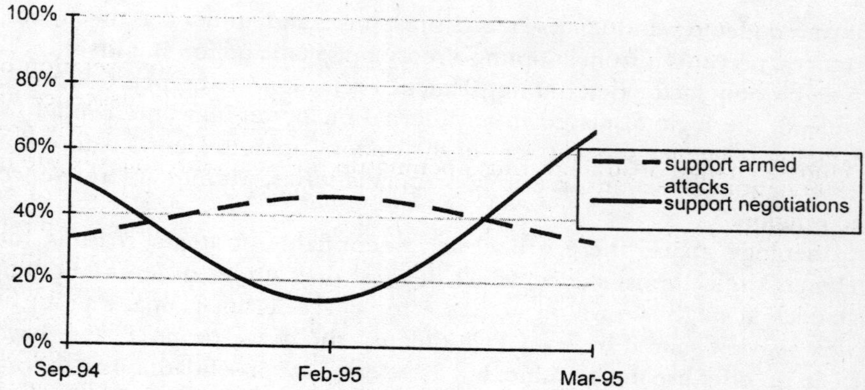


Figure 4.1. Support for negotiation and armed attacks among Palestinians, 1994–1995. Based on CPRS Polls, Nos. 12, 15, 16.

That radical methods have been used at all does not necessarily equate with an absolute opposition to compromise. Not all resistance operations that have in fact disrupted the peace process were apparently intended to do so. The 1996 suicide operations, which contributed to the election of the hawkish Binyamin Netanyahu in place of Shimon Peres, were carried out by cells within the Qassam Brigades in revenge for the assassination of their mentor and bomb-maker, Yahya Ayyash. The declared goal of these operations was to force Israel to end its practice of targeted assassinations and to "reach a truce" between the Israeli government and Hamas "through the mediation of the Palestinian Authority."[27] Their immediate goal was a realignment in the balance of power, rather than to affect the Israeli election. Indeed, it was far from clear at the time that the operations would shift Israeli opinion sufficiently for Peres to lose the elections.

Similarly, not all resistance operations were carried out with the authorization of the leadership. In an unusual display of internal division, the 1996 operations were subsequently disowned by Hamas's political leadership, suggesting that the acts were carried out by rogue cells, or at least cells that did not act on behalf of Hamas's (internal) political leadership.[28] During 1997, Hamas likewise tried to distance itself from a number of operations, while the suicide operation that ended Hamas's 2003 ceasefire was carried out without authorization from the senior leadership by a local Hamas operative in revenge for the assassination of his personal friend, a leader from Hamas's rival organization Islamic Jihad.[29]

Given that Hamas's practice stands in some tension with its absolutist rhetoric, it seems plausible to surmise that the purpose of its rhetoric is primarily to differentiate itself from the "compromised" PA as the "uncompromising" defender of the national interest. Actual policy seems to be primarily determined by strategic calculations. Absolutist, religiously inspired ideology influences Hamas's responses and, under certain circumstances, prevents it from adopting a more pragmatic policy. But ideology is not the only factor determining Hamas's rejection of the peace process. Indeed, the logic displayed in an internal memorandum, intercepted by Israeli intelligence services, set out the options open to Hamas before the 1996 national elections in purely pragmatic terms, without any reference to religion.[30]

Ideology apart, there are clearly identifiable strategic reasons for Hamas's rejectionist stance, which suggest that, under different circumstances, it might be willing to settle for peace. From Hamas's point of view—a view shared by many Palestinians—the peace proposals that have been on offer are not genuine, but an attempt at consolidating Israeli control of Palestinian territory.[31] Hamas does not believe that Israel will voluntarily dismantle the Israeli settlements on the West Bank, share control over Jerusalem, give up the water resources it now controls, or agree to lift the economic restrictions currently in place vis-à-vis Palestine's trade with third countries. Instead, Hamas believes that Israel will prevaricate indefinitely while using the PA as a substitute security force. That calls for the suppression of Palestinian militants are seldom matched with equally urgent calls for an Israeli withdrawal to its 1967 borders only serves to strengthen this belief. Thus Hamas views Israel as a "spoiler." In the absence of a powerful external "custodian" with the political will to force Israel to make sacrifices, Hamas deems violence necessary to force Israel to compromise, since security is the one "commodity" that Israel desires and the Palestinians can withhold.

Hamas's rejectionism has also been motivated by its power struggle with the PA. When Arafat endorsed the Oslo route in 1993, he was politically emasculated. His support for Saddam Hussein during the 1991 Gulf War had deprived the PLO of the financial support from the Gulf it had hitherto enjoyed—much of which now found its way into Hamas's coffers. On the ground, Hamas had made significant gains, becoming a serious threat to the PLO's hegemonic position. The Washington peace process, initiated in the wake of the Gulf War, had ground to a standstill, further undermining Arafat's authority. Oslo provided a golden opportunity to salvage his state dreams, stay in power, and keep Hamas and other contenders (including Fatah's local cadres) out. To Hamas, the peace process appears in part as a tool to exclude counter elites from power. Thus each attack on Israel is also an attack on this elite arrangement. This is underlined by the fact that Hamas's reluctance to declare a ceasefire under less than perfect conditions in June 2003 decreased as the PA's willingness to offer Hamas a post-conflict political future increased, following the ascent of Mahmud Abbas to the premiership.[32]

Hamas's increasing willingness to accept a ceasefire is also a reflection of its (pragmatic) recognition that the State of Israel cannot be destroyed, and that Palestinian society lacks the political will to continue fighting for total liberation. A ceasefire would enable Hamas to recognize Israel *de facto* without having to recognize it de jure. Hamas could maintain its position as the defender of the ultimate national interest while heeding public opinion and accepting a compromise. Hamas would gain a reprieve from Israeli counterinsurgency measures, while reserving the right to resist if Israel reneges on its commitments.

Within Hamas's discourse on ceasefire options lies a further suggestion that Hamas may not be immutably rejectionist or anchored in an unchanging religious imperative. According to senior pragmatists within the movement, a ceasefire would facilitate the establishment of a Palestinian state and the normalization of Palestinian society—eventually rendering a genuine peace accord acceptable to the population at large, beyond the political elite that now benefits from peace agreements, including the majority of refugees who form an important part of Hamas's constituency.[33]

Hamas, finally, consists of more than its Qassam Brigades, and its goals encompass more than the eradication of Israel. Its political wing and the charities affiliated to it have a greater interest in survival and long-term institution building than in the destruction of Israel. The projects of Islamizing society and furthering social justice are as important to Hamas's political leaders and welfare personnel as the liberation of Palestine. If pursuing the liberation of all Palestine means sacrificing these other goals, the resulting conflict of interest may well be resolved in favor of the latter among those involved in politics and welfare.

Despite Hamas's religiously inspired rhetoric, neither peace nor the establishment of a secular state are necessarily fundamentally threatening to its interests. A change in the content of the peace deal, the realization of a peace dividend, an increase in the PA's readiness to accommodate Hamas, or an increase in the international custodians' commitment to enforce an agreement on both sides might cause Hamas to rethink its opposition to "peace." Its tentative experiments with ceasefires and its readiness to stand in the forthcoming legislative elections suggest its leadership has already embarked on this process. To understand why Hamas has inched closer to becoming a "limited spoiler" requires a closer look at the structures and political culture that shape its decision-making process and at the influences that are transforming its political culture.

## Decision-Making Structures and Political Culture

The decision-making structures for each of Hamas's three "wings" answer to that particular section's needs. The charities are autonomous and answer to their Trustees who elect an executive board every four years (circumstances allowing). Hamas's political body consists of a series of regional councils, a national council, and a political bureau. Members of each of the decision-making organs are elected in biennial elections (circumstances permitting), and both the national council and the political bureau include members of both Hamas's internal leadership and its leadership in exile. The Qassam Brigades are highly decentralized to minimize the chance of detection. They are hierarchical, requiring obedience rather than transparency. Because of their decentralized nature, individual cells have a high level of autonomy, to the point that some have independent links with the leadership in exile that bypass both the Brigades' own hierarchy, and the political leadership within the territories.[34] This partly explains the contradictory claims regarding operations emerging from Hamas and the Brigades during the late 1990s.

Hamas's structures are to some extent a reflection of its political culture. Though far from monolithic, this culture has come to be dominated by two overriding characteristics: consultation and pragmatism. It is based on a notion of leadership that regards consultative practices and the ability to compromise as the basis for legitimate authority.[35] Hamas's commitment to internal elections is a manifestation of its consultative tendency as is its practice of consulting the wider membership on particularly significant decisions—such as whether or not to participate in the 1996 national elections.[36] The fact that pragmatists such as Ismail Abu Shannab and Ismail Haniyyah are able to occupy key positions in Hamas's leadership structure is a manifestation of Hamas's recognition of the importance of compromise—as is its readiness to consider a ceasefire.

These characteristics are shaped by Hamas's particular place in the socioeconomic and political spectrum of Palestinian society. To differentiate itself from the incumbent regime's reputation for corruption and autocratic leadership, Hamas has sought to display financial integrity and egalitarian ideals. Lacking the access to power which Fatah operatives enjoy, Hamas has had to find power elsewhere and has opted to increase its power through popular legitimacy. Consultation is one way of augmenting one's popular standing.

Another factor is Hamas's charitable network. To sustain this network, the charities rely heavily on local donations and religious alms. Proper consultation, in addition to financial integrity, is integral to maintaining popular trust in Hamas-affiliated charities.

To an upwardly mobile yet politically excluded clientele, autocratic leadership, especially in the face of an autocratically minded Palestinian Authority, has little appeal while notions of democratic accountability and egalitarianism are particularly attractive. The fact that the majority of Hamas's supporters are religiously-inclined, combined with the fact that Sunni Islam has a consultative tradition that can be tapped, strengthens this dynamic.

A similar argument can be made for Hamas's adoption of a pragmatic approach. To an upwardly mobile, politically excluded counter-elite pragmatism may seem the best way forward, in the absence of ready access to society's centers of power. To those involved in charitable activities, particularly if they do not have ready access to the elite's resources, pragmatism is similarly often necessary for the furthering of their goals.

The composition of Hamas's leadership also encouraged consultation and pragmatism. Until 1989, Ahmad Yassin was by far the most influential figure in Hamas. However, any temptation to rule autocratically was tempered by his paraplegic condition, forcing him to rely on others, and by the fact that he neither had the religious credentials nor the elite background to command an unquestioning following. Though he was charismatic, others, like Abd al-Aziz al-Rantisi, had charisma too. The modern education Hamas's younger leaders had enjoyed similarly encouraged a more skeptical attitude toward autocratic authority. From 1989 onward, the incentive to pragmatism and consultation increased with the imprisonment of Yassin and the senior leadership inside the occupied territories and the ascendancy of an external leadership, centered on the U.S.-based Musa Abu Marzouk and Hamas exiles in Jordan (now based in Syria).[37] The emergence of two centers of power, in addition to the emergence of a lower level leadership inside the territories to replace the imprisoned leaders, meant that consultation became essential for maintaining the unity of the movement. The professional background of Hamas's leaders, such as Abu Marzouk's business experience, also encouraged pragmatism. However, Hamas, and the Muslim Brotherhood before it, were not always as pragmatic or consultative as the Hamas leadership is at present. There are various factors accounting for this change and it is important to understand these to understand Hamas's future.

## Transforming Influences

One factor affecting Hamas's political culture has been a change in the ideological composition of its constituency since its creation in 1987. Hamas was established separate from the Muslim Brotherhood to enable Brothers who did not wish to engage in resistance to remain with the Brotherhood, and to protect the Brotherhood if the Intifada, or Hamas, failed. One effect of this decision was an influx of activists from beyond the Brotherhood's core constituency.[38] They sympathized with many of the Brotherhood's core beliefs but their level of commitment to these beliefs was less than that of the original Brothers. This change is well illustrated by the fact that a surprising 16 percent of pro-Hamas respondents to my 1997 student survey stated that they "did not know" whether they considered themselves religious.

Some of the more conservative, ideologically rigid Brothers opposed the creation of Hamas and withdrew into the background, making way for a younger leadership, many of whom had a Western-style education. Many of these also spent time in prison during the first Intifada where they encountered ideological opponents, particularly leftists, without fear of betrayal, triggering a process of mutual reevaluation.[39]

The net result of these internal changes, from a homogeneous to a more heterogeneous movement, was the introduction of a more pragmatic political culture. Absolutist logic made way for a more pluralist understanding of "truth," enabling Hamas to attract a wider constituency. It is upon this "culture" that the present-day Hamas has been built. And it is this wider constituency that has further affected Hamas's political practice and ideology, through both the rise of less ideological members, and the moderating influence exerted by a wider constituency. Both of these processes encourage consultation and pragmatism.

The broadening of Hamas's constituency has simultaneously resulted in a diversification of interests and of the sources of potential legitimacy. Many of those who give their religious alms to Hamas-affiliated charities do so, not because they support Hamas's stance on Israel, but because they believe that the money they give to Hamas-affiliated charities will reach its destination. Similarly, electoral support is not necessarily because of Hamas's stance on Israel. The now assassinated Ismail Abu Shannab, who had been repeatedly elected as head of the Engineers Union, enjoyed the trust of a wide ideological cross section of engineers because of his integrity and leadership skills.

The pragmatic and consultative turns have been further encouraged by the expansion of Hamas's charitable affiliates. Though independent, affiliated charities typically contain a high proportion of Hamas members among their governors and staff. As the charities have become more embedded in their local communities and as investments have risen, the incentive to pragmatism and consultation for those among Hamas's political leadership who are involved in the charities has increased.

Changes in Palestinian political culture and in the political system have also been pivotal. During the 1980s, a culture of ideological rigidity prevailed, leading to regular clashes between Fatah, the various Marxist groups, and the Muslim Brotherhood. This culture was partly a function of the practices of Israeli occupation, partly a result of internal Palestinian dynamics, best described as a process of de facto state-building in which the dominant group, Fatah, tried to establish its hegemony.[40] Fatah's temporary loss of authority following its ignominious 1982 defeat in Lebanon at the hands of the Israeli army only served to heighten the tensions generated by this process. Though the Brotherhood was equally reluctant to share power, the PLO's hegemonic attitude meant that the Brothers received little incentive to compromise or consider power-sharing and pragmatic solutions.

The 1990s, by contrast, saw the introduction of a more pragmatic political culture in the occupied territories, in which differences were more readily resolved through dialogue than violence—leaving aside the PA incarceration policy—and power-sharing became increasingly acceptable. This change was to a certain extent the combined result of the ending of the Intifada, Israel's withdrawal from the main Palestinian urban centers, and the arrival of the PA. The transformation of Fatah's senior leadership-in-exile into an internationally recognized political authority in possession of protostate structures (including security forces) laid to rest some of Fatah's 1980s ghosts and made it sufficiently confident to allow for (limited) opposition. At the same time, the arrival of the PA introduced a dynamic of accountability, which had been largely absent under Israeli occupation. Another factor was Hamas's evolution into a political force with sufficient popular following to render repression impractical for the PA. The aforementioned prison encounters, meanwhile, helped to bridge the ideological chasms between Islamists, nationalists, and Marxists and facilitated the emergence of a more cooperative political culture.

Illustrating these changes, whereas Brotherhood electoral victories in the 1980s were regularly met with Fatah mobs,[41] Hamas victories in the 1990s were largely honored. Similarly, after an initially tense relationship, resulting in the death of 15 Hamas activists in an anti-Oslo demonstration in November 1994, the PA and Hamas established channels of communication to discuss and resolve political tensions.[42] The effect of this changed political environment on Hamas was to increase the incentive to compromise and accept power-sharing. The cost of not finding a modus vivendi with the PA was amplified as initial popular support for the peace process was high, and opposition to internal violence had increased dramatically following the end of the Intifada.[43] The resulting shift from absolutism to pragmatism and (limited) pluralism is best observed in Hamas's attitude toward other Palestinian factions.

During the 1980s, leftists were condemned as unbelievers. Coalition building was frowned upon, and ideological disagreements regularly resulted in pitched battles. In sharp contrast, the Hamas leadership of the 1990s and beyond has embraced coalition-building in numerous professional and student bodies, and has entered into alliances with its erstwhile leftist enemies. Its internal rhetoric vis-à-vis the Left has undergone a dramatic change, from denouncing them as unbelievers to, by and large, according them a legitimate place in the politics of any future Islamic state. One of the most revealing reflections of this internal transformation is the tentative cooperation between Islamist women and leftist feminist groups.[44]

The regularization of political competition, Hamas's dependence on popular support, and its adoption of consultation as an electoral "selling point," have all meant that Hamas has become increasingly hostage to changes in popular opinion. In the process leading up to the 1996 elections, the leadership was as, if not more, concerned with maintaining popular support and political influence as it was with safeguarding ideological purity.[45]

Hamas's 2003 ceasefire declaration was similarly in part a response to a sustained change in public opinion toward support for a unilateral ceasefire. Before their declaration, Hamas leaders were seen canvassing the opinions of worshippers after Friday sermons. A national opinion poll conducted just before the ceasefire was declared—and certain to have influenced Hamas decisions—similarly found that 73 percent of the respondents favored a ceasefire while 67 percent were concerned that Hamas's refusal to agree to a ceasefire would lead to internal conflict.[46] Also significant was the fact that public tolerance for continued violence, and its inevitable repercussions, had become limited to violence aimed at achieving a viable two-state solution. In the same poll, 80 percent supported the mutual cessation of violence, while 52 percent expressed willingness to recognize Israel as "the state of the Jewish people" once a Palestinian state had been established. Among poll respondents who supported Hamas, 38 percent supported ending the armed struggle—only 19 percent behind the national average—while an October 2003 national survey found that 56 percent of pro-Hamas respondents supported a two-state solution—only 8 percent behind the national average.[47] Add to that the findings of a recent (controversial) survey suggesting that 38 per cent of refugee respondents—one of Hamas's key constituencies—were willing to settle in a Palestinian state alongside Israel in return for compensation,[48] and one can appreciate that the pressure on the Hamas leadership to accept a compromise had increased markedly.

## Assessing Israeli Policies

Until now, I have focused on the Palestinian context to Hamas's behavior. Yet both Hamas's actions and its popularity have been profoundly affected by Israeli policies, suggesting that any Israeli policy change will strongly affect Hamas's evolution.

The initial creation of Hamas was an indirect outcome of Israeli strategies. While the socioeconomic changes detailed above played a significant role in the creation of a frustrated, youthful counter elite ready for political mobilization, the actual form this mobilization took and the direction of its anger were largely a function of Israeli counterinsurgency practices during the 1980s. The various "Iron Fist" policies adopted by the Israeli Defense Forces (IDF) to break the will of the resistance—from collective punishment practices (such as the beating of a father in front of a "delinquent" son) and house demolitions, to detention without trial and a relaxation in the firing rules[49]—were a major factor in the radicalization of those who were to fight the Intifada and in rendering Hamas's rhetoric plausible to a significant section of the population. Israel's earlier policy of facilitating the expansion of the Muslim Brotherhood as a strategy to undermine the PLO was also a factor, both in the emergence of a movement strong enough to sustain a resistance organization like Hamas, and in increasing the resentment of the Brotherhood's younger members.

Counterinsurgency practices were not the only contributing factor. Israel's policy of land confiscation—by 1987 over half of the West Bank and one-third of the Gaza Strip had been confiscated[50]—settlement expansion, and talk of mass transfer all convinced the Palestinians that theirs was an existential struggle. The casting of Israeli policies in increasingly religious terms, as reflected in the discourse of the Likud Party, contributed to the development of a climate supportive of a religiously inspired framework. The Israeli government's decision to continue to outlaw any form of contact with the PLO and shun negotiations, despite the fact that the more pragmatic among the PLO leadership had begun to explore the diplomatic option from as early as the mid-1970s, did much to persuade those who were to lead the Intifada that nonviolent solutions lacked credibility.

Once Hamas was created, Israeli policies typically enhanced Hamas's political standing while only temporarily weakening it organizationally. From 1988 onward, Israel adopted a policy of eradication through incarceration, in addition to collective punishment. In 1989, most of Hamas's senior leadership was imprisoned, forcing the organization to restructure. In 1992, 415 alleged leaders of Hamas and Islamic Jihad were expelled to Lebanon. In both instances, Hamas's popularity increased. The 1989 mass incarceration resulted not only in increased popularity for Hamas but also inadvertently provided the leadership with the opportunity to bridge their differences with the other resistance groups and learn from their experience. The 1992 expulsion resulted in the temporary suspension of Israeli-Palestinian negotiations in Washington—even though Hamas was not part of the negotiations—and caused an upsurge in Hamas's political profile in the Palestinian territories. It also gave the expelled Hamas leadership the chance to learn first-hand from Hizballah how to conduct successful suicide campaigns. With the incarcerations and expulsions Hamas experienced the same process of radicalization and professionalization that the PLO's cadres had undergone earlier through Israeli incarceration.[51]

Israel's border closure policy, in response to Hamas's suicide operations against civilians inside Israel from 1994 onward, similarly failed to marginalize Hamas—or to stop suicide operations. In each of the two suicide "campaigns"—1994 (following the Hebron massacre) and 1996 (following Ayyash's assassination)—the first operation triggered a comprehensive border closure. Yet in each instance, Palestinians from the occupied territories succeeded in entering Israel despite the closure to execute the operations.

Besides stopping suicide operatives from entering Israel, closure of the borders between Israel and the occupied territories was intended to turn the population against Hamas by disrupting cross-border trade and pre-

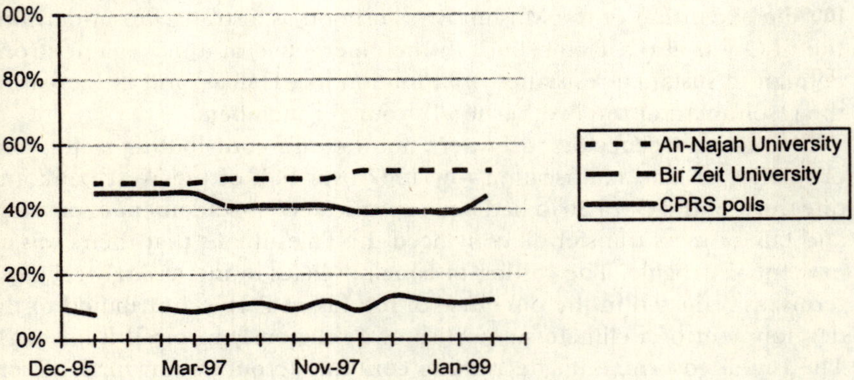


Figure 4.2. Support for Hamas among Palestinians, 1995–1999. Based on CPRS polls Nos. 19–40 (selection), Jerusalem Media & Communication Centre polls No. 20–21 (May–July 1997; http://www.jmcc.org/publicpoll/results/1997/no20.htm, accessed 21 January 2005) and student election data.

venting the 40 percent of the Palestinian workforce who had day jobs inside Israel from earning an income.[52] The comprehensive closures of 1996 caused an estimated daily loss of U.S.$1.35 million in "direct household income" alone, and an unemployment increase of 20 percent.[53] As such, it was a classic form of collective punishment.

Immediately following the 1996 closure, 31 percent of respondents to a national survey did indeed blame Hamas for the imposition of the closure.[54] However, not only did a much higher proportion (50 percent) blame Israel but this number increased to 72 percent by September 1997.[55] Hamas's political support, meanwhile, did not suffer greatly. In the spring 1996 student elections at the universities of Bir Zeit and al-Najah, pro-Hamas students defeated Fatah supporters and maintained their hold over the student councils until the end of the 1990s. Surveys meanwhile showed that throughout the period of closures Hamas support remained steady (see Figure 4.2). However, one variable that changed dramatically was popular support for suicide operations, rising from 21 percent in March 1996 to around 40 percent for much of 1997 (see Figure 4.3).

Israel's latest closure strategy—the "security fence"—has been billed as more effective. According to the Israeli Ministry of Defense, the erection of the wall north of Jerusalem (an area referred to as Samaria by the ministry) resulted in a 90 percent decrease in the "ability of these [Samaria-based] terrorist groups to perpetrate attacks within Israel".[56] However, the success of Qassam operatives in breaking out of Gaza to carry out a suicide operation in Ashdod underlines that no fence is impenetrable, as do the various incursions of Palestinian groups across the heavily fortified Israeli-Lebanese border and the tunnels across the Israeli-controlled Egyptian border with Gaza.[57] Moreover, given that the closure of borders contributed to an

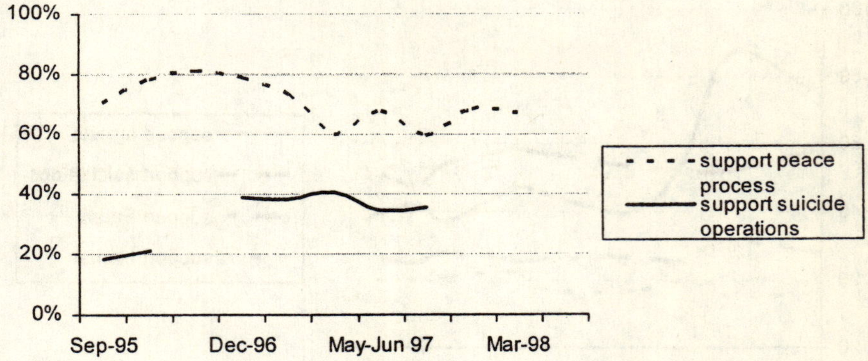


Figure 4.3. Support for suicide operations and peace process among Palestinians, 1995–1998. Based on CPRS polls Nos. 19–40 (selection), Jerusalem Media & Communication Centre polls No. 20–21 (May–July 1997; http://www.jmcc.org/publicpoll/_results/_1997/_no20.htm, accessed 21 January 2005) and student election data.

increase in support for radical solutions, the creation of a security fence deep inside the West Bank, cutting off tens of thousands of Palestinians from their land and livelihood, is likely to make radical solutions seem even more plausible—increasing, among other things, the incentive to perfect indiscriminate rocket attacks—while providing a pool of potential volunteers among those cut off on the Israeli side.[58] To offset the humanitarian disaster that would result from total closure, Israel would have to allow Palestinians to work inside Israel or access their land on the other side of the fence—thus providing further opportunities for suicide operatives to cross the fence.

Targeted assassinations have also had little success in eradicating the movement through decapitation. After each campaign of assassinations, Hamas has typically regrouped. The targeted assassination campaign of July–August 2001—during which 12 Hamas members were assassinated, including 5 senior leaders and a bomb-maker—was followed by an increase in suicide operations, from one failed suicide operation in July, to four successful operations in August and September, killing 18 and wounding 234 Israelis. The same pattern was repeated in the autumn of 2001 when the assassination of 11 Hamas members (including 4 senior members and the head of the military wing in the West Bank) was followed by two suicide attacks inside Israel, killing 26 Israelis and wounding 248.[59] Each assassination appears to swell the ranks of Hamas and the Qassam Brigades. In the words of a senior member of the Brigades, "After every massacre, every massive violation of our rights and defilement of our holy places, it is easy for us to sweep the streets for boys who want to do martyrdom operations. Fending off the crowds who demand revenge and retaliation and insist on a human bombing operation—that becomes our biggest problem!"[60]

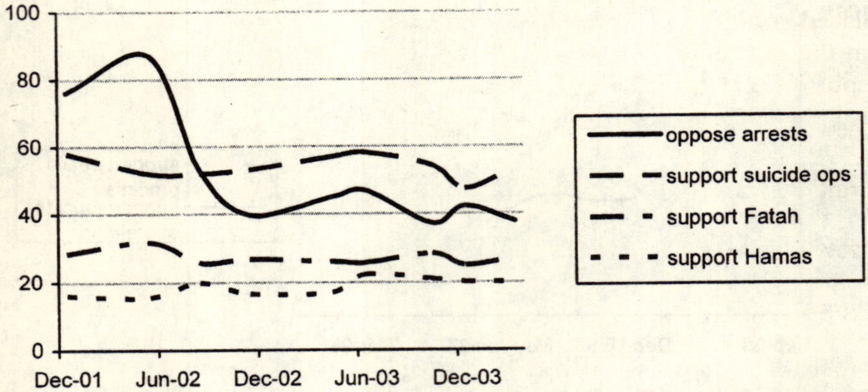


Figure 4.4. Palestine public opinion, 2001–2004. Based on PSR Polls Nos. 3–11.

Military incursions into Palestinian-controlled areas to eliminate suspected activists have similarly had ambiguous results. According to the IDF, the most notorious of these—the April 2002 invasions into the major West Bank towns—resulted in a significant immediate reduction of suicide operations.[61] However, the three months following the invasions saw roughly the same level of activity as the three months preceding the offensive: four successful operations compared to three.[62] In addition, the indiscriminate nature of military incursions—in Nablus, at least 50 civilians were killed in the incursion while the historic city center was irreparably damaged[63]—appears to have resulted in an increase in support for the militants. Though overall support for suicide operations and the different political parties appears to have remained relatively unaffected, opposition to the PA "taking measures" against militants shot up to 87 percent in the immediate aftermath of the incursions (see Figure 4.4).

Until 2004, neither military incursions nor targeted assassinations were successful in dissuading Hamas from carrying out suicide operations. The absence of successful suicide operations following the assassination of Ahmad Yassin and Abd al-Aziz al-Rantisi in early 2004 could be interpreted as an indication of success. However, as Hamas has continued to attempt to stage suicide operations following Rantisi's assassination, the absence of successful operations appears to be the result not primarily of Israel's assassination policy or even the creation of the security fence (though both have arguably contributed to it) but rather of the level of intelligence penetration that the IDF has achieved—reflected in both the betrayal of Rantisi's whereabouts and the foiling of operations in the months surrounding his assassination.[64]

Targeted assassinations have failed in part because of the horizontal nature of Hamas's leadership structure. This is particularly so with regard to the political wing where assassinated leaders have typically been replaced seamlessly by others of equal standing or members promoted from the next echelon down. A second reason is that those who control the purse strings and thus exert considerable influence over the Brigades' resistance operations, Hamas's leadership in exile, are more difficult to assassinate because they reside outside Israel's jurisdiction. Third, rather than frightening off volunteers, each assassination appears to swell the ranks of Qassam volunteers. This is partly a function of the radicalizing effects of Israeli policies, giving credence to both Hamas's struggle and its methods, and partly the result of Hamas's, and by extension the Brigades', standing in the community. Hamas's ideology, which promises great rewards, both in the afterlife and posthumously in the community, also plays a role.

The policy of targeted assassinations has not succeeded in eradicating the movement—neither militarily, as Hamas's subsequent successful operations against IDF posts in the Gaza Strip indicate, nor politically, as underlined by Hamas's success in the municipal elections of December 2004–January 2005 and the concessions of newly elected President Mahmud Abbas toward the militants in the run-up to the presidential elections.[65]

There are various reasons why these different strategies have not resulted in decapitation or created what Jeffrey Ross and Ted Gurr call "backlash"—a drop in popular support that potentially leads to the demise of an insurgent organization.[66] One set of reasons revolves around the violent and humiliating everyday practices that together constitute an occupation and Israeli noncompliance with the commitments it made within the Oslo framework. The former encourages radicalization; the latter has given credence to Hamas's argument that the Oslo process was aimed at consolidating Israeli control over the territories.

Between 1993 and 2000, despite Oslo's stipulation that no further facts on the ground be created that could jeopardize "final status" talks, the West Bank settler population expanded by 77 percent, triple the average rate of the period 1967–1993.[67] During the closure of 1996, settlement building continued unabated, as did house demolitions, land appropriations, military incursions and roadblock humiliations. Settlement activity and controversial land confiscations were stepped up following the election of Netanyahu in May 1996, causing heated demonstrations, clashes and violence.[68] For these radicalizing policies, Hamas could not be blamed. Moreover, given that one typical reason for an insurgent movement's turn to terrorism is the absence of credible alternatives,[69] Israeli noncompliance, facilitated by the leniency accorded it by the custodians of the peace process, sustains Hamas's resort to terror tactics and facilitates an increase in popular support for such practices.

Another reason for the absence of a significant "backlash" against Hamas has been the perception among many Palestinians that Israeli responses are disproportionate. The April 2002 invasions of West Bank towns caused the death of around 500 Palestinians.[70] The number of Israelis killed by the suicide operations that triggered the invasions was 56.[71] From the outbreak of the al-Aqsa Intifada in September 2000 until November 2004, a total of 3,039 Palestinians were killed. At least 1,656 of these were confirmed by the Israeli human rights organization B'Tselem as noncombatants; 606 were confirmed as minors. By contrast, 640 Israeli citizens werekilled over the same period, 112 of them minors.[72]

Palestinians felt that the intensity and duration of the 1996 closures were similarly disproportionate to the damage caused by the suicide operations. The resulting economic hardships both undermined popular trust in the Israeli government's commitment to peace and made radical solutions more defensible, as reflected in the fact that support for suicide operations remained around 40 percent in the following years, up from 20 percent before the 1996 closures.[73]

One of the chief reasons why Israeli collective punishments tend to drive people to Hamas rather than alienate them from the movement; why Hamas's justifications, explanations, and methods resonate with a sizable section of the population; and why membership of the Qassam Brigades accords social status rather than pariah status to its members concerns the fact that Hamas is a socially embedded organization reflecting the aspirations of a sizeable section of the Palestinian population.

On the other hand, it is precisely because Hamas is an embedded organization that it must attune its behavior to its support base. Collective punishment may serve to increase popular support for Hamas if it is seen as disproportionate. However, it may equally cause discontent among Hamas's supporters and increase popular pressure to change resistance tactics so as to minimize the costs of such punishment, as was the case in the late 1990s, and again in the latter half of the al-Aqsa Intifada. In this vein, collective punishment has had both a moderating and a radicalizing effect on Hamas.

A final strategy that warrants appraisal is Israel's attempt at contracting repression out to the PA. By making Israeli security the chief criterion by which PA behavior was judged, Israel in effect turned the PA into a proxy repressive force. Until the ascent of Abbas, this policy was unsuccessful. Initially, the PA lacked local legitimacy as it consisted largely of formerly exiled "outsiders" and already had a reputation for corruption. Furthermore, by forcing the PA to clamp down on militants while continuing to carry out provocative occupation policies, Israel undermined the legitimacy of the PA to the point where the PA was arguably too weak to confront the militants. Whether the reforms instituted by Abbas and changes in Israel's occupation policy, such as the imminent withdrawal from Gaza, will have the effect of rendering the PA strong enough to suppress militants remains to be seen. In recent months, the PA's popular legitimacy has soared while popular support for suicide operations has dropped from 77 percent in September 2004 to 29 percent in March 2005.[74] At the same time, support for Hamas participating in negotiations with Israel has soared to 79 percent while those supporting arrest of the perpetrators of suicide attacks does not exceed 40 percent. Repression alone is thus unlikely to succeed without serious political concessions.

## Effects of 9/11 and the War on Terror

The events of 9/11 and the subsequent War on Terror have affected Hamas in conflicting ways. The rhetoric and mindset of the global War on Terror have facilitated the Israeli government's pursuit of increasingly draconian measures with relative impunity. By claiming that it is at the forefront of the international War on Terror, and depicting Hamas as part of the international Islamist coalition against the USA—both Yassin and Rantisi were variously labeled "Palestine's Bin Laden" while Hamas was branded "Palestine's al-Qaeda" and depicted as a natural ally of al-Qaeda (despite profound strategic and ideological dissonances)[75]—the Sharon government has successfully tried to gain a level of international acquiescence in its practices.

Since 9/11, the U.S. has shown greater leniency toward Israeli policies than during the preceding decade, occasionally endorsing practices it had previously condemned. When Israel assassinated two of Hamas's senior political leaders in the West Bank six weeks before 9/11, the State Department rebuked the Sharon administration.[76] In 2004, by contrast, the assassinations of Yassin and Rantisi were defended by the Bush administration on grounds of self-defense.[77] Similarly, against decades of principled opposition by the State Department to Israeli settlements in the West Bank and Gaza, President Bush has on numerous occasions appeared to have given his blessing to existing settlements—directly contravening the principles behind his earlier "roadmap" to peace.[78] Given that past condemnations of Israel did not result in material penalties, this shift in U.S. rhetoric may be more cosmetic than substantial. But it does appear to have facilitated Israel's use of highly controversial policies. The sheer size of the Israeli assault on Hamas's political leadership would arguably have been more difficult to carry out with political impunity had the U.S. remained rhetorically opposed to the practice of political assassination.

Like most EU states, the UK has been more reluctant to change its position in the wake of 9/11, despite its central involvement in the War on Terror. It continued to condemn targeted assassinations after 9/11, including the assassinations of Yassin and Rantisi.[79] It has also maintained its stance on the issue of settlements. However, signaling that the War on Terror has begun to affect the British government too, it chose to abstain from a UN resolution condemning Israel's practices in the wake of Yassin's death.[80]

Whether Israel's policies toward Hamas and the Palestinian resistance more broadly have changed significantly as a direct result of 9/11 is difficult to ascertain. The years 2003–2005 have witnessed a radicalization of the IDF's actions compared to the 1990s. The repeated and ruthless destruction of whole segments of Rafah in the southern Gaza Strip, to destroy tunnels dug underneath the Egyptian border, is an escalation of previous policies of house demolitions. The systematic assassination of political leaders is a departure from Israel's previous sporadic targeting of leaders directly involved in resistance activities. The various invasions into Palestinian controlled areas are a departure both in breaching the boundaries set by the Oslo Accord and in the scale of destruction and the numbers of unarmed civilians killed. The fact that three times as many Palestinians were killed in the first four years of the al-Aqsa Intifada as in the entire six years of the first Intifada is similarly indicative of a process of radicalization.

However, most of these practices appear to be a direct result of either the immediate conflict or, to a lesser extent, the characteristics of the players involved. The presence of a significant number of arms on the Palestinian side and the fact that suicide operations had already become an acceptable method of resistance, both in sharp contrast to the first Intifada, have been two factors in the radicalization of the conflict. The election of Sharon, with his history of ruthless tactics, similarly played a part. Behavior on both sides seems furthermore to be dominated by a local tit-for-tat logic rather than global concerns. Moreover, the practices of both the al-Aqsa Intifada and the various Israeli policies of targeted assassinations and house demolitions predate 9/11.

The War on Terror has undermined Hamas's international position with implications for both its fundraising potential and the continued support of allies. In 2003, President Bush froze the bank accounts of individuals and charities believed to be involved in fundraising for Hamas's resistance activities.[81] In 2001, Bush had already frozen the assets of the Holy Land Foundation, America's largest Muslim charity, on similar charges.[82] In September 2003, the EU succumbed to pressure from the U.S. and Israel to place Hamas on its list of prohibited "terrorist organizations," after years of refusing to do so on the grounds that a distinction should be made between Hamas's political and military wings.[83] This move undermined the back-channel negotiations in which the EU had been engaged to persuade Hamas and Israel to enter a ceasefire.[84] It has also complicated Hamas's fundraising program in Europe—although no charities have been frozen since and only one prior to this shift.[85]

Hamas's standing with Arab governments also appears to have been affected. Syria's willingness to shut Hamas's offices in Damascus,[86] and its role in pressuring Hamas into proposing a ceasefire in June 2003,[87] are indications of Syria's increasingly precarious position in the new "Middle

East order." The fact that an (unidentified) Arab government was willing to share detailed security information on Hamas's political leadership in exile with Israel's intelligence services is similarly indicative of a shift in loyalties.[88] Changes in regional loyalties may encourage Hamas to accept compromise. The removal of the Baath regime in Iraq, a key supporter of the resistance in Palestine and generous benefactor of the families of suicide bombers, coupled to initial Iranian caution since the arrival of U.S. troops in Iraq, placed further pressure on Hamas. The shift in Hamas's external leadership's enthusiasm for a ceasefire may be indicative of this changed reality.

In the months immediately after 9/11, Hamas appeared to have been keenly aware of the potential fallout. The campaign of suicide attacks against civilians inside Israel, in which it was engaged to avenge a series of political assassinations in July and August, was suspended and not restarted until December—despite an increasingly relentless campaign of assassinations instigated by the Israeli government from October onward. However, Israel's decision to use the War on Terror to step up its campaign against Hamas, and the world's overall silence in the face of this campaign, persuaded Hamas's leadership that attempting to distance itself from al-Qaeda by ceasing its suicide campaign carried no benefits.

Paradoxically, the War on Terror has simultaneously increased support for Hamas, both locally and worldwide among certain sections of the Muslim population. The combination of the al-Aqsa Intifada and the War on Terror appears to have generated more sympathy among Muslims worldwide for Hamas's struggle. The fact that two British Muslims volunteered to carry out suicide operations on behalf of Hamas is indicative of this—although it remains to be seen whether this incident will become a trend, and whether Hamas will welcome the operational dilemmas concomitant with such international volunteers. More immediately significant is the financial support Muslims worldwide may be willing to give as a result of their increased awareness. Though no comprehensive data are available regarding the post-9/11 donation patterns of Muslims worldwide, Hamas's heightened profile has arguably resulted in an increase in financial support—possibly offsetting the negative effects of the freezing of affiliated charities in Europe and America.

Whether as a result of the radicalization caused by the War on Terror, or as a result of local developments, Hamas is politically stronger than ever before. A June 2004 poll found not only that 90 percent of those questioned supported Hamas's participation in the administration of the Gaza Strip after Israel's proposed withdrawal but also that the median suggestion for the level of power-sharing with Fatah was 50 percent.[89] Hamas's success in gaining 9 municipalities, against Fatah's 16, in December 2004's first round of municipal elections is similarly significant, particularly since the municipalities involved were considered Fatah strongholds.[90] Its success in

7 of the 9 municipalities contested in January 2005 speaks for itself, as does the aforementioned fact that 79 percent of people polled in March 2005 supported the notion of Hamas being included in negotiations with Israel.

Local factors have played a significant part, ranging from an increase in popularity following the high-profile assassination campaign to the fallout from Israel's continued commitment to occupation practices and settlement expansion. However, the War on Terror has helped increase Hamas's popularity by eroding people's belief in negotiations and nonviolent solutions—at least until recently. Indicative of this erosion are the findings of a poll taken in Palestine shortly after the invasion of Iraq, in April 2003, which found that 46 percent of respondents believed that "the war in Iraq will make it possible for Israel to carry out mass expulsion of Palestinians" while 61 percent assumed that "the war in Iraq will make it more difficult for Palestinians and Israelis to return to the peace process." An astonishing 78 percent believed that the war "will strengthen Palestinian motivation to carry out armed attacks against Israelis."[91]

The conduct of U.S. forces in Arab Iraq after the invasion has further alienated the general Palestinian population from the U.S. administration and its potential role as a "custodian" of the peace process. In June 2003, only a few months into the occupation of Iraq, half of all respondents to an opinion poll in the Palestinian territories stated they believed that President Bush "was determined to implement the Roadmap." By October 2003 none believed this was the case, while 96 percent believed that the U.S. "is not sincere when it says it works toward the establishment of a Palestinian state alongside Israel."[92] Atrocities in Iraq are merged in Palestinian public perception with atrocities committed by Israel and vice versa, creating a mutually reinforcing spiral of hatred and fear.[93] For a significant number of Palestinians the occupation of Iraq constitutes a regionalization of the conflict, potentially making their own situation less significant and its resolution less realistic. The resulting sense of helplessness is a powerful source of radicalization, and supports Hamas's argument that the (Western) international community—and the peace initiatives emanating from it—is unlikely to provide the Palestinians with a viable state.

The election of Abbas in January 2005 and the subsequent period of relative calm have served to somewhat increase popular faith in the peace process. The above-mentioned drop in support for suicide operations from 77 percent to 29 percent in March 2005 is a clear reflection of this upsurge in hope, as is the fact that 79 percent of those polled in March 2005 preferred "to see more active American involvement in the search for a peace agreement" (despite earlier cynicism concerning America's motives).[94] Whether this new climate of hope is sustained is profoundly dependent on how the peace process proceeds and in particular whether the U.S. administration will have the courage to force the Israeli government to freeze Israeli settlements in the West Bank. If it is sustained, it will put pressure on Hamas permanently to abandon suicide operations, as it has done since Abbas's election, and consider nonviolent solutions. However, even if it is sustained, it is unlikely to drastically affect Hamas's popularity, given the high percentage of people supporting the strategy of involving Ḥamas in future negotiations with Israel.

## Conclusion and Policy Recommendations

A number of observations emerge from this analysis. Israeli policies toward Hamas have typically consolidated or increased the movement's political standing. Decapitation policies such as incarceration and targeted assassination may have temporarily weakened Hamas organizationally. But the record suggests that in each case the organization recovered relatively quickly while the damage inflicted heightened its political profile. The policy of border closure came closest to eroding popular support for Hamas. But because its duration and intensity were perceived among Palestinians as disproportionate to Hamas's original attacks, and because occupation practices and settlement expansion continued unabated, blame for the ensuing economic deprivation swiftly shifted from Hamas to Israel. In short, though coercive responses may limit the options available to Hamas, a purely coercive response within the context of a democratic state is unlikely to be effective in preventing an organization such as Hamas from perpetrating violence, let alone in eradicating it.

One reason for the ineffectiveness of purely coercive policies is that Hamas is an embedded organization with a high level of grassroots support. Because both its resort to violence and its political goals are supported by a significant section of the population, any attack on Hamas is likely to strengthen the resolve of its supporters. Since Hamas has furthermore been careful to portray itself as the champion of all Palestinians and has built up a reputation for integrity and selfless leadership (rather than amassing wealth as other such organizations have done), an attack on Hamas is more likely to unite people behind it than alienate them.

A second reason is that the structural factors underlying the conflict—most prominently occupation, economic deprivation, political marginalization and degradation of human life—have been left largely unchanged. Though Hamas's rhetoric and actions undoubtedly bear partial responsibility for the radicalization of those who support it—whether through rendering violent solutions ideologically plausible, or by eliciting increasingly violent responses from Israel—the fact that large numbers of Palestinians have consistently supported violent solutions, well beyond Hamas's core support base, suggests that these attitudes are shaped by wider underlying structural causes. That support for violence has steadily increased since the 1993 signing of the Declaration of Principles, while Hamas's rhetoric and actions have been largely consistent (particularly after 1994), similarly suggests that this change in attitude was a function of underlying factors, rather than of Hamas's persuasive powers. This reading is corroborated by the fact that Hamas now operates in a semicompetitive political environment where political influence has become increasingly dependent on maintaining electoral support, and, consequently, the construction of grievances has become more explicitly a two-way process between the organization's ideologues and its supporters.

That Hamas has shown an increasing readiness to accept a compromise solution on the basis of an Israeli withdrawal to the 1967 borders, and a domestic power-sharing arrangement within the new Palestinian entity, underlines the fact that it is responsive to changing popular attitudes and has moved away from a "total spoiler" position. Extension of its involvement in the various electoral systems is likely to enhance this responsiveness, as power becomes increasingly dependent on maintaining popular support. Under these conditions, Hamas is likely to become an ever more "limited spoiler." If this is so, and if Stedman's generalizations are valid, a policy of inducement and socialization would be the most effective way for local and international policymakers to approach Hamas.

Inducement would involve addressing Hamas's chief "limited" (as opposed to its total) demands, which, unsurprisingly, concern the main structural factors that encourage radical attitudes: an end to occupation, an end to all settlements, the establishment of a Palestinian state, a power-sharing arrangement based on a free vote that allows Hamas to be politically represented, and a viable development program that is capable of meeting Palestine's economic needs. By both addressing Hamas's grievances and providing a post-conflict role for Hamas as a purely political organization, it becomes possible to bind Hamas to the compromise agreement. The fact that Hamas has multiple goals and an increasingly diversified support base will facilitate its (potential) transformation into a purely political party. Its recent gains in the municipal elections will have increased the attraction of such an option. Hamas's performance in the upcoming legislative elections, and whether the PA allows it to electioneer freely, will significantly influence this process of transformation.

Ensuring that Hamas is party to a future agreement is important for two reasons. Without Hamas, and as long as the PA's grassroots supporters are divided between it and the more radical al-Aqsa Martyrs Brigades, the PA is likely to lack the popular legitimacy needed to make an unpopular compromise agreement acceptable to the Palestinian people. With Hamas, the PA would not only gain much needed additional legitimacy but it would marginalize those who continue to reject compromise. Because of its track record, Hamas is in a better position to persuade persistent "spoilers" to suspend violent activities—particularly if the al-Aqsa Brigades have adopted a similar position. In this, it would play the role of precisely the type of "local norm entrepreneur" Steven Simon and Jeff Martini are searching for in the context of the War on Terror (although Simon and Martini restrict their focus to secular, liberal partners and advocate the marginalization of Hamas).[95] Violence by dissidents may well continue for some time following a cross-party agreement. But as long as the main "spoilers" have a stake in the agreement and the general population supports it, dissidents would have little popular support, allowing the government to crack down on them.

Socialization would involve changing the incentives and disincentives to violence in such a way that acceptance of a compromise becomes the preferred option. Because Hamas is embedded, one way to deradicalize Hamas is through the deradicalization of the population. A general process of deradicalization—which is likely to occur when occupation practices are ended, a commitment is made to the dismantlement of settlements, and a peace dividend, or even the real possibility of a peace dividend, becomes visible—is likely to result in a decrease in popular support for radical solutions, as the recent drop in support for suicide operations illustrates so eloquently. My case study of Hizballah (in Chapter 5) similarly underlines that the more extensive the peace dividend people experience, the less willing they typically are to jeopardize their new gains. Because Hamas must maintain a popular support base, and has billed itself as a consultative movement, a deradicalization of the general population will increase the pressure to adopt compromise solutions—just as it did in the case of Hizballah, and appears to have done in the lead up to Hamas's (short-lived) ceasefire of June 2003 and its current adherence, despite sporadic lapses, to a de facto suspension of operations. It is also likely to result in a decrease in the number of suicide volunteers.

Allowing Hamas to participate freely in Palestinian politics while prohibiting it from participation if it continues to engage in violence will similarly increase the incentive to adopt a nonviolent approach—just as Mahmud Abbas's tacit offer of a post-conflict role appears to have facilitated Hamas's 2003 ceasefire declaration. However, such a policy is only likely to work if the underlying structural problems are being addressed. Indeed, one of the reasons that Hamas's (partial) integration into the political system has not resulted in more circumscribed resistance practices, as it has done, up to a point, in the case of Hizballah, appears to be the fact that a large constituency for radical solutions continues to exist, at least until recently.

Of Hamas's chief (limited) demands only the issue of the right of return remains fundamentally unresolved. The rest of its (limited) demands approximate what was agreed to in principle between the Barak government and the PA during the Taba conference of January 2001.[96] The fact that Hamas is moving closer to accepting, de facto, the principle of a two-state solution suggests that a compromise on the refugee issue is within reach—especially if the remainder of Hamas's core demands are addressed satisfactorily, thus increasing the cost of intransigence on the right of return.

The success of a conditional policy of political inclusion on the basis of "good behavior" is also dependent on the level of faith among the general population and opposition groups in Israel's commitment to honoring its promises. Since Hamas's recourse to violence is in part motivated by its belief that Israel will not voluntarily withdraw to the 1967 borders or dismantle the settlements, a more active and, where necessary, forceful, commitment from the peace process's international sponsors is vital. Only when there is some guarantee that Israel will address Hamas's core concerns without the continued threat of violence is an increase in the severity of penalties for violent insurgency likely to result in a cessation, rather than an escalation, of violence.

Finally, continuing to label Hamas a "terrorist organization" is likely to undermine the process outlined above. It prevents dialogue between Hamas leaders and officials of the international community and Israel, removing an important element of the process of socialization necessary for the success of this approach. It disincentivizes Hamas from accepting a political compromise because such labeling signals a lack of interest on the part of the international community in taking Hamas's concerns seriously. And because the "terrorist" label implies immutable intransigence on the part of the labeled organization, the very essence of the socialization process—transformation—is precluded, thus both removing the incentive to transform and encouraging the false belief that Hamas is incapable of transformation.

## Glossary

al-Aqsa Intifada: Palestinian uprising of September 2000 until the present.

CPRS: Center for Palestine Research and Studies, Nablus, Palestine. Predecessor of PSR.

Declaration of Principles: principles agreed upon in Oslo between the Israeli government of Itzhak Rabin and Yassir Arafat's team of negotiators

Fatah: largest Palestinian nationalist movement. Established by Yassir Arafat in the 1950s; dominates PLO.

Gaza Strip: 363 km² strip of land around Gaza City, between Egypt's northern border and Israel's pre-1967 southwestern border

Hamas: Harakat al-Muqawama al-Islamiyya (Islamic Resistance Movement), meaning zeal.

*hijab*: headscarf.

IDF: Israeli Defense Forces.

intifada: Palestinian uprising. Usually refers to the uprising of December 1987, which ended with the Oslo Accord of 1993.

Islamism: Ideology of those seeking to establish an Islamic state and society based on Islamic law and principles

Izz al-Din al-Qassam Brigades: Hamas's military wing.

Muslim Brotherhood: Transnational Islamist movement, first established in 1928 in Egypt by Hassan al-Banna, with (autonomous) branches in numerous Arab states.

Oslo Accord: Officially the Declaration of Principles, principles agreed upon in Oslo between the Israeli government of Itzhak Rabin and Arafat's team of negotiators.

PA: Palestinian Authority. Established in 1994 as a result of the Oslo Accord, initially only in Gaza and Jericho, subsequently in all major Palestinian towns in the occupied territories.

PLO: Palestine Liberation Organization. Umbrella organization of secular Palestinian nationalist movements.

PSR: Palestinian Center for Policy and Survey Research, Ramallah, Palestine (formerly CPRS).

Qassam Brigades: Izz al-Din al-Qassam Brigades.

"roadmap": President George W. Bush's blueprint for achieving an Israeli-Palestinian peace settlement.

West Bank: area on the western bank of the river Jordan encompassing all the land between Israel's pre-1967 eastern border and the Jordan (5,900 $km^2$).

## Timeline

1917: Balfour Declaration, laying down the British government's intent to create a "national home for the Jewish people" in Palestine. British forces take control of Palestine.

1920: British government granted mandate over Palestine by the League of Nations.

1936–1939: Arab Revolt; Sheikh Izz al-Din al-Qassam becomes one of the first self-consciously "Islamic martyrs."

1946: Muslim Brotherhood established in Palestine.

1947–1948: British hand Palestine Mandate to UN, which drafts Partition Plan; outbreak of first Arab-Israeli war and establishment of State of Israel.

1948: Egypt establishes military administration in the Gaza Strip.

1950: Jordan annexes West Bank; West Bank Muslim Brotherhood becomes part of Jordanian Muslim Brotherhood.

1954: President Nasser of Egypt clamps down on Gazan Muslim Brotherhood.

1956–1957: Israel occupies Gaza Strip during and after the Suez crisis.

1957–1959: Fatah founded by Yassir Arafat and others.

1964: Palestine Liberation Organization (PLO) established by Arab League; Gazan Muslim Brotherhood further decimated by Nasser.

1967: Six Day War; Israel occupies West Bank and Gaza Strip; West Bank Brotherhood in disarray following separation from Jordanian headquarters.

1969: Fatah takes control of the PLO.

1970: PLO headquarters forced to move from Jordan to Lebanon.

1973: Ahmad Yassin establishes al-Mujamma' Islami in Gaza, first of a new generation of Muslim Brotherhood charities. Yom Kippur war between Israel and Arab states triggers OPEC oil embargo and surge in oil prices, dramatically increasing the money available for Islamist projects.

1974: Arab summit declares PLO sole legitimate representative of the Palestinians; Arafat addresses the United Nations.

1979: Galvanized by the Iranian revolution and Soviet invasion of Afghanistan, Brotherhood supporters enter student politics. Throughout 1980s, Brotherhood supporters and PLO student activists clash.

1980: (Palestinian) Islamic Jihad established by activists who disagree with the Brotherhood's quietist attitude toward occupation.
1982: Israel invades Lebanon and forces PLO out to Tunisia.
1987: Outbreak of first Intifada and creation of Hamas.
1988: PLO renounces terrorism and promises to recognize the State of Israel, paving the way for U.S.-PLO dialogue.
1989: First wave of arrests of Hamas leaders, following the kidnapping and killing of two Israeli soldiers.
1990: Al-Aqsa Mosque massacre triggers escalation in Islamist resistance, followed by a renewed Israeli crackdown into early 1991.
1990–1992: Series of clashes between Hamas and Fatah supporters.
1991: Izz al-Din al-Qassam Brigades established as Hamas's separate military apparatus (in part in response to Israeli crackdown); Madrid Conference held under U.S. auspices, hosting first direct Israeli-Palestinian negotiations.
1992: 415 Hamas and Islamic Jihad members are exiled to Lebanon, following kidnapping and killing of an Israeli border policeman.
1993: Leading Hamas official declares Hamas's readiness to accept ceasefire if Israel withdraws to the 1967 borders; Fatah and Hamas meet in Khartoum to end armed disputes; Israel implements general border closure policy; Declaration of Principles (Oslo Accord) signed by PLO, rejected by Hamas and dissident PLO groups.
1994: Ibrahimi Mosque massacre triggers first wave of suicide operations against civilians and comprehensive closure of Palestinian border; Palestinian Authority established in Gaza and Jericho; 15 Hamas sympathizers killed by new security services.
1995: Hamas observes a tacit ceasefire in the lead-up to the 1996 elections.
1996: First Palestinian national elections; Yahya Ayyash assassinated, triggering second wave of suicide operations and comprehensive closure of Palestinian border.
1997: Arafat closes 20 Islamist charities causing humanitarian hardship.
1998: Bomb kills Hamas bomb-maker Muhyideen Sharif, triggering calls for the resignation of Arafat and imprisonment of Hamas leaders and activists.
2000: Palestinian-Israeli final status negotiations at Camp David fail; outbreak of al-Aqsa Intifada; suicide operations become central to all resistance organizations, including the newly established Fatah affiliate, the al-Aqsa Martyrs Brigades.
2003: Hamas declares unilateral ceasefire; Israel refuses to accept ceasefire and continues policy of political assassination, causing the ceasefire to unravel.
2003–2004: Hamas's three most senior Gazan leaders assassinated (Ismail Abu Shannab, Ahmad Yassin, Abd al-Aziz al-Rantisi); Hamas operative assassinated in Syria.
2004–2005: Arafat dies; first Palestinian municipal elections in which Hamas performs well; Mahmud Abbas elected president; Hamas largely observes an undeclared ceasefire.

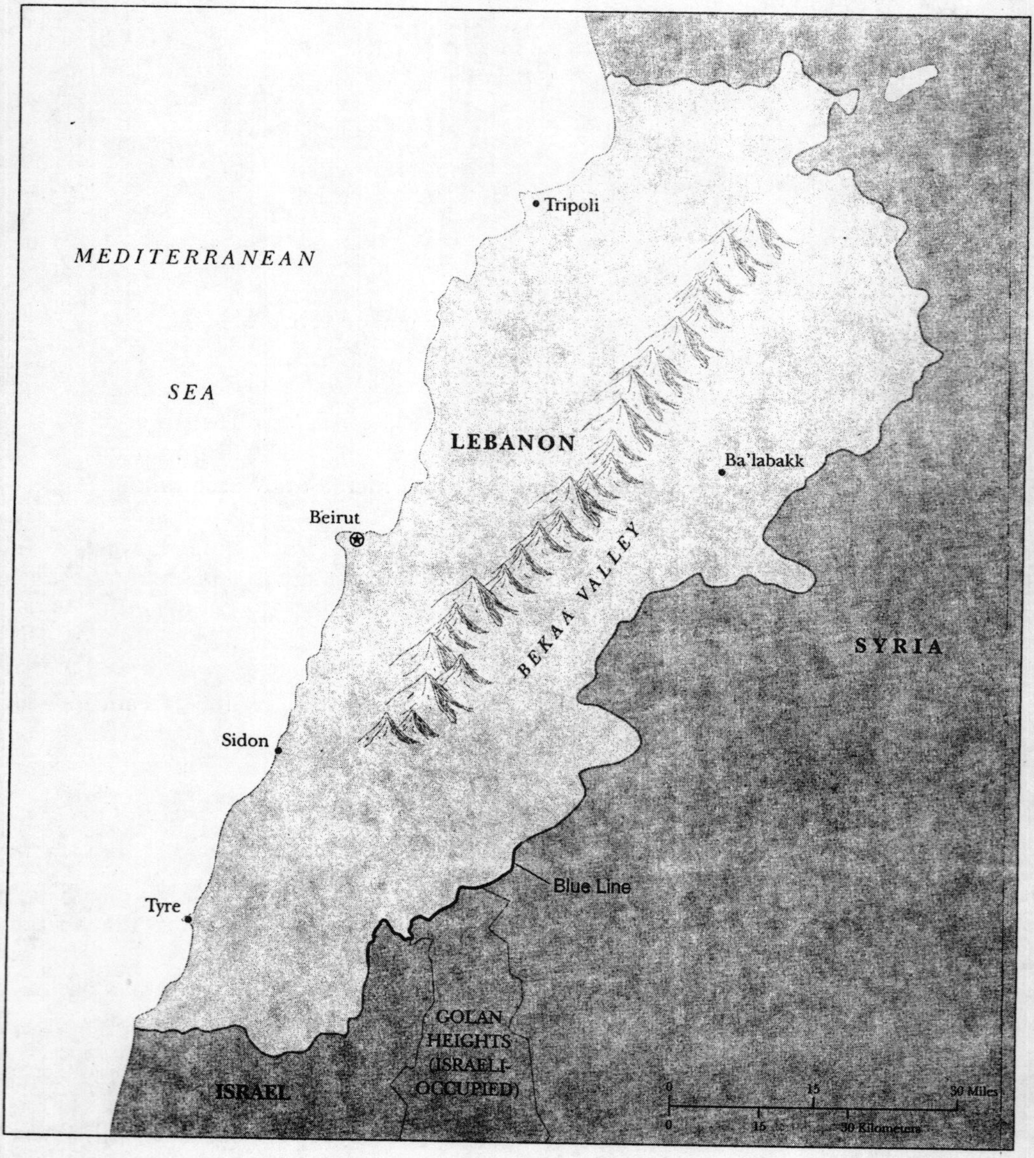


Map 5.1. "Blue line" in Lebanon.

*Chapter 5*

# Hizballah and the Logic of Political Participation

JEROEN GUNNING

This chapter focuses on the development of the Shi'i Islamist movement Hizballah from its inception in 1982 in response to the Israeli invasion of Lebanon until the present. Hizballah is undergoing a transformation from a radical, absolutist resistance movement to an increasingly accommodationist political organization. To explain this transformation, what follows charts the origins of the movement, and explores how changes in the composition of its support base, the Lebanese political system, and regional conditions have affected its goals and behavior. Particular attention is paid to the effects of Hizballah's inclusion into the political system of postwar Lebanon, and to the impact of Israeli policy on Hizballah's evolution. Among other factors, including changes in the foreign policies of Iran and Syria and the attainment of a limited balance of power between Hizballah and the Israeli army, it is maintained that inclusion into the political system has had a moderating effect on Hizballah's domestic goals and methods and to a lesser extent its resistance operations. It has not dimmed the leadership's opposition to Israel, or its support for the Palestinian resistance, including its controversial tactic of targeting civilians, but participation in the political system has introduced a logic of electoral accountability that has made escalatory resistance operations more costly.

Hizballah emerged in direct response to the Israeli invasion of Lebanon in 1982 and for much of the 1980s, its main activity consisted of resistance—including the then locally innovative tactics of suicide bombing and hostage-taking (although the precise extent of its involvement in the latter is disputed). It called for an Islamic revolution and an Islamic state in Lebanon, under the aegis of the Islamic Republic of Iran and modeled on Ayatollah Khomeini's *wilayat al-faqih* (rule of the supreme jurisprudent). To realize such a state, Lebanon had to be freed from Israeli occupation. But it also had to be "liberated" from its secular, sectarian structures and shed its imperialist roots as an "artificial" Christian-dominated client state.[1] From its inception, Hizballah refused to accept the legitimacy of the Lebanese state, or its rigid sectarian system of allocating political quotas to each of the religious communities ('corporate consociation'). Lebanon was to be abolished and subsumed under the soon-to-be liberated areas of the Middle East—starting with Iraq, which, in Hizballah's eyes, was at that time in the process of being freed by Iran from its U.S.-sponsored secular regime. Hizballah was messianic on foundation, infused with an optimism created by the Iranian revolution and its own early successes against the Israelis and the multinational force stationed in Lebanon.[2]

Although Hizballah still proclaims theoretical allegiance to the notion of an Islamic state, in practice it has abandoned calls for its establishment in Lebanon. Instead, it advocates the return of "humanitarian" values such as integrity, accountability, and noncorruptibility to public life and for the discriminatory practice of political sectarianism to be replaced with a meritocratic democracy. Calls for the abolition of the Lebanese state have been replaced with impassioned defenses of Lebanon's territorial integrity, its national interest, and the right of all its citizens, including Christians, to return. The party's campaign themes have become largely secular, focused on Lebanese concerns, and devoid of messianic content.[3]

At a practical level, Hizballah has expanded from an underground militia to a political party with a highly efficient apparatus, an extensive welfare network and a small semi-professional resistance organization. Its resistance activities have become circumscribed by rules of engagement agreed upon indirectly with the Israeli armed forces. Though Israel's withdrawal from Lebanon in May 2000 has not caused Hizballah to cease operations, it has limited its activities largely to a small disputed border area called the Shebaa Farms and carefully calibrated them so as not to escalate the conflict. It has by and large accepted the sovereignty of Lebanon's coercive apparatuses, the police and the army, and only challenges this sovereignty in its insistence on the right to resist. It has entered the political system and repeatedly won around 8 percent of Parliamentary seats, constituting the largest opposition party bloc. It has been one of the most successful parties in the municipal elections.[4] The composition of its constituency has changed to include secular supporters, while the profile of its top leadership has changed from predominantly clerical to a mixture of clerics and professionals. It has reached out to Christians and entered into alliances with both Christian and Sunni politicians.

To explain Hizballah's evolution from a radical, absolutist underground resistance to an increasingly accommodationist political party with a resistance agenda, I will take a closer look at the origins of Hizballah—the reasons behind its emergence, the profile of its support base, its ideology, its political culture, and the power resources at its disposal. Having explored the factors that can be seen to drive the organization's goals and methods, I will then examine how these factors have changed.

## Origins of Hizballah

Hizballah emerged out of three converging phenomena: the 1970s political revival among Lebanon's Shi'a; the Islamist euphoria created by the 1979 Islamic Revolution in Iran; and the resistance to Israel's 1982 invasion of Lebanon.

Marginalized socially and politically,[5] Lebanon's Shi'a were galvanized into action by a number of separate events. Modernization and the onset of civil war in 1975 had begun to undermine the authority of the Shi'i notable families and led to an expansion of the proportion of Shi'a available for political mobilization.[6] Socioeconomic changes created both a new counter-elite and an impoverished underclass within the Shi'i community. Increased proximity, as a result of urbanization, highlighted the discrepancy between the status of the Shi'a and that of the other religious communities, reinforcing their sense of communal injustice.

Politically, these changes found expression in two movements: one emanating from the Shi'i clergy as they were shedding their traditional political quietism, the other from the various left-wing political movements emerging regionwide. This second trend, represented by Lebanese parties such as the Communist Party and the numerous Palestinian militias of the PLO that had descended on Lebanon following their ousting from Jordan in 1970, played a secondary role in the emergence of Hizballah by serving as a catalyst for political mobilization among the Shi'a.[7]

The religiously inspired trend—out of which Hizballah emerged—was dominated by two social movements: the Movement of the Disinherited and the Lebanese Islamic Da'wa Party, a branch of the regionwide Da'wa Party which had its headquarters in Najaf, Iraq. The first was established in the 1970s by Imam Musa al-Sadr, son of a prominent religious leader. Its goal was to counter the corruption and ineffectiveness of the Shi'i political elite and to improve the social and political position of Lebanon's Shi'a. It did not question the legitimacy of the Lebanese state or its multiconfessional nature, but sought to change the inter-confessional balance of power. Following the outbreak of civil war in 1975, the movement established a political party and militia called Amal. Dwarfed initially by the multiconfessional militias to which the majority of Shi'a were drawn, Amal expanded exponentially after 1978.[8]

During the 1970s, Amal attracted both religiously minded and secular Shi'a. Following Sadr's disappearance in 1978, the party began to abandon its religious roots and, under the leadership of lawyer Nabih Berri, became increasingly secular, creating a dilemma for its religiously minded supporters. The process leading up to Berri's 1983 decision to join the National

Reconciliation Committee (the de facto national government of the day) without demanding significant reforms was for those already disenchanted with his secular direction the final straw. Hussain al-Musawi, one of the co-founders of Hizballah, is a good illustration of this trend. Vice president of Amal until 1982, he was ousted following a dispute with Berri over Amal's direction and formed "Islamic Amal,"[9] one of the organizations to coalesce under the umbrella of Hizballah. Each of Hizballah's three secretaries general was similarly once a member of Amal.[10]

The Lebanese Da'wa Party, and its affiliate the Lebanese Association of Muslim Students, was closely linked to Sayyed Muhammad Hussein Fadlallah, the son of an Ayatollah from South Lebanon and well known across the Shi'i community for his charisma and erudition. Inspired by Da'wa founder Sayyed Muhammad Baqr al-Sadr, Fadlallah believed that (Shi'i) Islam contained the solution to the region's problems and advocated the creation of a society based on Islamic principles. In contrast to Amal, Fadlallah and his followers questioned the very legitimacy of the Lebanese state. Theirs was a regional vision, based on affiliation to Islam.

Fadlallah was one of the main forces behind the growth of the Lebanese Da'wa Party. But similarly significant was the steady expulsion of Lebanese clerics studying in Najaf under the increasingly anti-Shi'a Iraqi Ba'th regime, culminating in the deportation of more than a hundred in 1977. Having studied under Da'wa founder Baqr al-Sadr, many gravitated toward the Lebanese Da'wa Party and established *hawzats* (Shi'i religious academies) which propagated al-Sadr's philosophy. Initially concentrating their activities in the social and spiritual realms, Da'wa supporters became progressively politicized, spurred on by the successes of Amal and the Communist Party, the socioeconomic changes that drove these trends, the Iranian revolution of 1979, and the Israeli invasion of 1982.[11]

The Iranian revolution galvanized both Amal and the Da'wa Party, serving as an inspiration for religiously inspired political activism, and making available new financial and political opportunities for specifically Shi'i parties. It sealed the shift from quietism to activism among the Shi'a regionwide. And it brought to power a regime that was both self-consciously seeking closer links with Shi'i communities elsewhere and had a particular interest in countering Israeli influence in the region, regarded as the local face of American imperialism. Lebanon thus became an important focus of Iranian foreign policy.

The Israeli invasion of 1982 both provoked resistance among the Shi'a, who suffered disproportionately, and annihilated the Palestinian militias—the invasion's objective—leaving a power vacuum. It precipitated Iran's sending a contingent of Revolutionary Guards. And it helped resolve the tension Da'wa supporters experienced between rejection of the system and the desire to affect political change, by providing a political focus away from the debate surrounding the legitimacy of the Lebanese state, and by finalizing the enclavization of Lebanon—thereby enabling dreams of establishing an Islamic order within the enclaves where activists were dominant.[12]

The 1982 invasion also encouraged the Syrian regime to cultivate a new proxy resistance force. The Syrian army had been in Lebanon since Syria's 1976 intervention yet it sought to avoid engaging the Israeli army directly. Amal, Syria's long-time ally, had initially sided with the Israelis because of its own struggle against the Palestinian militias, leaving Syria without a proxy to counter the Israeli occupation. The various religiously motivated groups that were to become Hizballah were ideal candidates because of their zeal, their roots in local society and their access to an external state sponsor, Iran, which would field the expenses.[13]

Hizballah stepped into the vacuum created by these various trends. It replaced the Palestinian militias as a dedicated resistance force. It replaced Amal as Iran's, and briefly Syria's, favored Shi'i party and as the new champion of religiously inspired Shi'a, whose number had grown since the Iranian revolution. At the same time, the seeds were laid for Hizballah to take up Amal's mantle of championing the marginalized—secular as well as religiously oriented—as Amal became increasingly absorbed into the elite pact governing the country.

Hizballah's early goals and behavior can be explained in part by the profile of its support base and the political climate it emerged from. The bulk of Hizballah's activists came from the ranks of the Da'wa Party and from among the more religiously inclined of the secularized Amal movement. Some switched from the Communist Party or the leftist Palestinian militias, disillusioned by their ineffectiveness in confronting the invasion or inspired by the Iranian revolution to rethink their secular orientation. The majority of Hizballah's leaders and supporters were not members of the traditional elite families. Most of its members came from lower- to lower-middle-class backgrounds,[14] and while an increasingly significant number of these were university graduates or people with professional aspirations,[15] few belonged to the nouveau riche class that Amal had come to represent.[16]

The less reason Hizballah's members had to be loyal to the existing system, the more attractive Iran's radically different system became. Amal's cooption into the political system confirmed their belief that only a full-scale revolution would end Shi'i marginalization within the Lebanese system. The Iranian model of self-consciously Shi'i activism was particularly attractive because it claimed to be a global movement ushering in a new age of justice. Thus, not only did membership of Hizballah transform a marginalized, local youth into a partner in a global revolution, but it also translated the local humiliations of Israeli occupation into symbols of global imperialism and offered a means of becoming part of a global jihad against American-Israeli imperialism.[17]

The fact that Hizballah consisted largely of a network of clerics and their followers, and had emerged in opposition to an increasingly secular Amal, partly explains the particular attraction of Khomeini's rule of the jurists. For the clerics, Khomeini's system offered either the prospect of political power or the comfort that power would be in the hands of fellow clerics. For their followers, the rule of the jurists offered the prospect of access to power. For both, Khomeiniism was a way to distance themselves from Amal.

Hizballah's early radicalism was in part a function of the situation in which it arose. It emerged in the aftermath of a bloody invasion, which according to one estimate caused 19,000 deaths, 32,000 casualties and damage to 80 percent of villages in the south.[18] The increasingly brutal nature of the ensuing occupation consolidated the initial sense of outrage. Because Hizballah was conceived in the midst of Lebanon's brutal civil war, its methods reflected the prevailing violent climate—although Hizballah typically limited its violence to Israelis and Shi'i rivals, while refraining from targeting other religious communities in the conflict. The presence of Iranian Revolutionary Guards and the support Hizballah received from the hard-liners in the Iranian regime ensured that the hard-liners within Hizballah prevailed. It is thus not surprising that Hizballah's initial approach was one fueled by utopian and uncompromising radicalism and that its methods were those made popular by the violent practices of the civil war.

## Transforming Influences

To understand Hizballah's transformation, it is necessary to analyze the changing nature of Hizballah's three main sources of power: local popular support, Iranian sponsorship and Syrian patronage. Hizballah's initial goals can be shown to be at least in part a reflection of the nature of these different sources and the prevailing political climate at the time, so changes in the political environment and its sources of power are likely to affect the organization's direction. A fourth factor concerns Israeli policies toward Hizballah, which have affected both the establishment and the evolution of the organization profoundly. I will discuss these separately.

Though Iran was instrumental in creating Hizballah and has been one of its main sponsors, Iran's influence has diminished. If intelligence estimates are to be believed, not only have Iran's financial contributions dropped to but a third of Hizballah's overall estimated income but also Hizballah's power has come to rest increasingly on the popular and financial support it enjoys within Lebanon and the Lebanese diaspora, and the backing of the Syrian government.[19] Consequently, Hizballah has become less dependent on Iranian support for its survival. In addition, after the death of Khomeini, Iranian support for Hizballah's initial, radical goals became more muted. Moderates came to circumscribe the power of the hard-liners, particularly in the Foreign Office (at least until the Ahmadinejad election). Iran's relations with the Lebanese state also improved, particularly since the end of the civil war.[20] Though the foreign policy goals of Iranian hard-liners and moderates differ, both have abandoned the active pursuit of spreading the Islamic revolution—which is one reason why Hizballah has ceased calling for an Islamic state in Lebanon.[21] Iran's support for the resistance has also become somewhat more muted. While Iran still encourages Hizballah's hostility toward Israel and continues to arm Hizballah's resistance wing, it has no interest in provoking a full-scale confrontation with Israel. The pressure exerted by Iran on Hizballah to cease shelling northern Israel in an attempt to prevent another Israeli invasion in 1992 illustrates the point [22]—as did the intervention of Iran's foreign minister in April 2002, urging Hizballah to end its worst confrontation with the Israeli Defense Forces (IDF) since the latter's withdrawal from Lebanon in 2000.[23] The fact that Iranian relations with the Palestinian resistance have improved since the outbreak of the al-Aqsa Intifada in 2000 also means that Iran has less need of a "second front" in Lebanon to maintain its influence in the Levant and keep pressure on Israel—although this development has increased the incentive for Hizballah to become directly, if covertly, involved in the Palestinian resistance.

Hizballah's capacity to continue functioning as a resistance movement remains largely dependent on Syrian acquiescence—even after Syria's withdrawal. Syrian support for the resistance is circumscribed by realpolitik. It can no longer count on the support of the Soviet Union, a fact that has affected the state of its army and made it more dependent on international investment. Its hegemonic position in Lebanon until 2005 had been partly dependent on Western acquiescence. At the same time, Syria continues to need a proxy resistance force—both to keep pressure on Israel to return the Golan Heights and because it has built its ideological identity on resisting Israel. In the absence of economic development and political liberalization, the Syrian regime is likely to continue to rely on resistance as a legitimizing tool.

Syria's support for Hizballah's resistance activities comes at the price of restrictions in the political realm. Until recently, Hizballah has been prevented by the Syrian government from capitalizing electorally on its military successes, in line with Syria's policy of divide and rule. In each national election, Hizballah has sought to forge an alliance in opposition to Amal. On each occasion, the party was forced into an alliance with Amal to prevent Hizballah from usurping Amal's political position. As Hizballah's support base has expanded since its entry into politics in 1992, Syrian control over Hizballah has weakened. Syria's withdrawal from Lebanon has further diluted Syria's ability to control Hizballah. But Syria can still restrict Hizballah's ambitions and influence its future direction. Hizballah's decision to ally itself to Amal in the June 2005 elections—even after Syria's withdrawal—may partly be indicative of this influence (even though the logic behind the alliance was largely informed by the need to maintain a united

Shi'i front in the face of a strong Christian anti-Syrian coalition and an upsurge in calls for Hizballah's disarmament, both locally and internationally).

Locally, Hizballah's relationship with its support base has changed with its expansion from a small underground militia to a political organization encompassing a political party, an extensive welfare network and a semi-professional resistance wing. Where once its popularity depended solely on its military prowess, it now depends on the performance of all three wings of its organization.

Hizballah's resistance force is of limited significance in "military" terms. Though strong enough to oust Amal from Beirut's southern suburbs during the civil war and to affect the IDF's withdrawal in 2000, it fails to match the separate or combined strength of the Lebanese and (until recently) Syrian armed forces present in Lebanon. By the late 1990s, Hizballah's resistance arm was estimated at 300–500 experienced fighters and a body of up to 3,000 "reservists." By contrast, the Lebanese and resident Syrian forces numbered 53,300 and 25,000–35,000 respectively in 1999.[24] Not only do these armies dwarf Hizballah's erstwhile opponent, the IDF, which only had around 1,500 soldiers in Lebanon during the 1990s, but the skills Hizballah developed in this struggle are of little use against either the Syrian or the Lebanese army. The Syrians lack the democratic constraints placed on the Israeli forces (as illustrated by the bloody 1982 massacre inflicted upon the insurgents of Hama),[25] while attacking fellow Lebanese, including Shi'i co-nationals, would greatly undermine Hizballah's political standing.

Hizballah's resistance wing has proven invaluable for gaining political legitimacy and continues to be of central importance to the party's self-image. Hizballah has gained in political standing from its early successes in driving the IDF from Beirut, through to winning the right to remain armed when all other militias were disarmed at the end of the civil war and its role in contributing to the chaotic withdrawal of the IDF in 2000. Its parliamentary candidates have consistently run on a "resistance ticket," calling themselves the Loyalty to the Resistance Bloc, asking voters to repay the sacrifice of martyrs with their vote. To the Shi'a, Hizballah's resistance success is particularly empowering. But because of Hizballah's attempts to represent the resistance as Lebanese and because of Israel's heavy-handed policies, Hizballah's continued commitment to the resistance has gained it respect beyond its Shi'i constituency.

In the context of the "war on terror," the presence of foreign forces in Iraq, and the continuation of hostilities in neighboring Israel/Palestine, resistance is likely to continue to play an important part in Hizballah's rhetoric. Hizballah's victory in the 2005 national elections has indeed been interpreted by Hizballah's leadership as an endorsement of its resistance agenda.[26] However, rhetoric notwithstanding, the actual activities of the resistance, when compared to Hizballah's welfare and political efforts, have become increasingly significant in terms of their impact on Hizballah's political clout only, rather than in and of themselves.

Hizballah's welfare services have become an important source of popularity because of their extensiveness, their efficiency and their reputation for integrity. Where the state or Amal fail to deliver basic services, Hizballah steps in—whether it is a Christian village in the Bekaa valley cut off by an avalanche, or impoverished Shi'a in Beirut lacking water, electricity and sewerage services. Welfare activities are only indirectly translated into political capital, because those benefiting from the services do not necessarily support Hizballah. However, there is no doubt Hizballah benefits politically from its charitable investments. Almost from its inception, Hizballah has employed charities to offset the negative effects of Israeli offensives, partly from a sense of civic duty, inspired by Islam and a long clerical tradition of charitable activity among Shi'a, and partly to gain sufficient credit among the population to continue its resistance efforts. One of the reasons Hizballah has recently invested heavily in the south has been to counter the influence Amal has through its control over the government's reconstruction fund for the South. The services Hizballah provides in the southern suburbs of Beirut similarly seek to outperform Amal, not only among the Shi'a who are registered to vote in Beirut, but also among the many displaced residents who are still registered, and thus vote, in the South.

Funding for these activities comes from religious and charitable donations from allied states—in particular Iran which, especially in the early stages, funded most of Hizballah's charities[27]—and from individuals, both from inside Lebanon and from the Lebanese diaspora and Iranians with Lebanese links. The process of fundraising, whether for the resistance or for Hizballah's welfare institutions, plays an important role in the political mobilization of the community. Local fundraising is carried out with the help of small colored metal boxes on poles in strategic places throughout the urban landscape, or by volunteers standing with boxes and flags by the roadside. Though funds are being raised for particular charities associated with Hizballah, Hizballah benefits politically from the "brand" recognition.

The expansion of Hizballah's welfare services has introduced a conservatism that militates against radical resistance activities. The extensive investments Hizballah has made in the South, for instance, render Israeli retaliatory strikes more costly. The growth of those involved in charitable activities within Hizballah has expanded the constituency of those more interested in institution building and networking than in resistance per se. The movement's decision to expand its investments in areas most likely to be hit by Israeli strikes suggests that Hizballah as a whole has become more interested in, and reconciled to, a post-resistance phase—suggesting its adherence to the goal of eradicating Israel may be tempered by pragmatic considerations.

The creation of a political party organization, finally, has done more than anything to change the relationship between Hizballah and its support base. That it was established at all was to a large extent a function of the ending of the civil war, the opening up of an autonomous political space and the Lebanese state's willingness (under Syrian tutelage) to invite Hizballah into the political realm—although internal changes and events in Iran similarly played a part. The reasons behind Hizballah's decision to play a full part in the new political system, and the effect of Hizballah's entry into that system are of such importance that they will be discussed in detail below.

## Factors Facilitating Hizballah's Political Incorporation

Incorporation of the erstwhile rejectionist Hizballah into the Lebanese political system was made possible by a number of developments. One factor was the transformation Hizballah was already undergoing as a result of both internal and external dynamics. The end of the Iran-Iraq war, spelling the end to the dream that the Islamic revolution would spread through Iraq to the Levant, and the death of Khomeini—and the subsequent rise of a less dogmatic elite in Iran—made it possible for internal debates and tensions to come to the surface. The routinization that any revolutionary movement undergoes and the expansion of Hizballah's welfare network had already encouraged the emergence of a more pragmatic trend. The expansion of charitable efforts had begun to change the composition of Hizballah's supporters and the very effort of setting up charities in cooperation with local communities had begun to have a moderating effect.

By the late 1980s the more fervent among Hizballah's supporters had begun to realize that Iran's brand of revolutionary Islam did not necessarily translate to Lebanon with its intensely multisectarian, pluralistic environment. Hizballah, moreover, lacked the power to enforce its vision without consent once the central state reemerged. During the civil war, when Hizballah had imposed its brand of puritanical Islam in the areas where it was dominant, it had alienated large sections of society. Within the enclaves, Hizballah had sufficient military muscle to weather local alienation, but when the civil war came to an end and the enclaves began to be reincorporated into the central state, Hizballah's control became increasingly conditional upon gaining popular support—just as all erstwhile militias were now forced to learn to resolve their differences without resorting to arms.

The pragmatic among Hizballah's leaders realized that both the resistance project and the dream of reshaping society according to Islamic principles would become untenable unless Hizballah adapted itself to the multiconfessional state that was likely to reemerge out of the civil war. In the new political climate, a dogmatically Islamist resistance would not carry the support of the national government of Lebanon, potentially pitting Hizballah against both the Israelis and the Lebanese army. In a unified Lebanon, moreover, the prospects for establishing an Islamic state would be remote, particularly now that the expansion of the Iranian Islamic revolution had stalled. It was far from clear whether the secular regime in Damascus would be willing to back a dogmatically Islamist resistance at the cost of losing influence with other pro-Syrian parties in Lebanon. Willingness to compromise made political sense. A similar conclusion was reached by the pragmatic members of the government in Tehran who threw their weight behind the pragmatists within Hizballah.[28]

The 1989 restructuring of Hizballah's command structure, which sought more local accountability and less revolutionary "aloofness," was a reflection of these internal and external changes, as was the (electoral) ousting of Hizballah's hard-line secretary general Subhi al-Tufayli in favor of the more pragmatic Abbas al-Musawi in 1991. Musawi began the process of preparing Hizballah for entry into the political system in earnest—a move opposed by the Tufayli camp on the grounds that participation would legitimate the Lebanese state and compromise the Islamic state ideal. When Musawi was killed by an Israeli air strike in 1992, a candidate with an equally pragmatic disposition, Sayyed Hassan Nasrallah, was elected, suggesting that the pragmatists had won out over the dogmatists. Supporting this conclusion is the fact that the election boycott Tufayli and his followers organized fell spectacularly flat.[29]

Hizballah's entry into the political system was eased by the movement's increasing, though far from uniform or complete, commitment to consultative politics.[30] Parallel to the structural reforms of the late 1980s, Hizballah's political culture appears to have undergone a subtle change, away from a rigid centralism centered on the will of Khomeini, to a more consultative style of decision-making, still hierarchical but more responsive to the views of both a larger section of leaders and Hizballah's support base. Consultation with members and supporters in the process of policy formation has increased—as illustrated by the survey carried out to aid the leadership in deciding on whom to field as candidates for the 2000 national elections[31]—although consultations tend to follow a top-down rather than a bottom-up pattern and decisions are still taken centrally and without much transparency.[32]

The consultative approach took an institutional form in 1991 when the party resolved to encourage "the formation of residential and professional groups in each quarter of the southern suburbs," to gather local information, and facilitate the process of advocacy.[33] The institution of a triannual party conclave gathering together all members above the rank of district representative to elect those who will govern the party for the next three years was another manifestation of this shift.[34] Ideologically, this approach is supported by the Qur'anic command to consult.[35] It is tempered, however, by the hierarchical nature of the clerical structure in Shi'i Islam.

A number of structural factors have facilitated Hizballah's shift toward consultation although none are determinant in and of themselves. One has been the expansion of Hizballah from a pure militia into the civic realm, introducing an operational logic that favors consultation for instrumental reasons. A charity is likely to be more effective—both in fundraising and in gaining grassroots cooperation—if it responds to the needs of its clientele. Another factor is Hizballah's position in the political system. As an outsider to the elite pact between the leading Maronite and Sunni players and Amal, and without a formal military to back up its claims to power, Hizballah must derive power from other sources and has turned to popular legitimacy to boost its political standing. It pays to canvass constituents' opinions regarding who to field for upcoming elections, so as to heed constituents' views if one wishes to retain their vote. That Amal portrays itself as a non-ideological party deriving its power primarily from traditional patron-client networks—often associated with corruption and nepotism—provides Hizballah with a ready-made "identity niche" for gaining popular legitimacy as Amal's supposed opposite: an ideologically motivated, incorruptible, meritocratic and more egalitarian party. The Qur'anic emphasis on consultation, equality and integrity offers a ready ideological framework. The need to distinguish itself from Amal provides an incentive to activate this framework—however incompletely.

This logic has been reinforced by the origins and composition of Hizballah's leadership. From its inception, none of Hizballah's leaders have been of particularly high standing in their religion's clerical hierarchy. The only person with such a profile, Sayyed Fadlallah, was never part of the day-to-day running of the movement and sought to stay aloof from party politics. The absence of a dominant, hierarchical figure facilitated the emergence of a more egalitarian and consultative style of decision-making—although this process was tempered by the need for "military" obedience, secrecy and the clerically inspired disposition toward hierarchy. The increasing heterogeneity of Hizballah's leadership has similarly encouraged a shift toward consultation by increasing the need to maintain party unity across differences.

The socioeconomic profile of Hizballah's constituency has reinforced this path. The majority of Hizballah's members come not from the traditional elite families, but from lower- to lower-middle-class backgrounds, and increasing numbers of these are university graduates or people with professional aspirations—particularly since the end of the civil war.[36] These qualities make Hizballah a typical counter-elite movement, outsiders with aspirations for power. For such a movement, the experience of exclusion may render the notion of organizational inclusiveness, and with it consultative practices, attractive. Particularly if those in power practice a more autocratic form of politics, consultative practices become a favorable option, not just for instrumental but also for constitutive reasons, which make the idea of "consultation" a core element of the movement's identity—if not always its practice.

A final factor encouraging consultative politics has been the effect of the end of the civil war on Hizballah's relationship with its constituency. During the 1980s, a level of popular support was necessary for securing logistical assistance and hiding places. But in the general climate of war, not only had political activity become largely insignificant but also dissent was difficult to express. Ensuring high levels of popular support was thus unnecessary. With the reintroduction of a functioning central authority and regular elections, the calculus of popular support changed. In this new political environment, dissent could be expressed through a change in voting behavior. Silencing dissent became more difficult, not only because central authority had been restored but also because criticizing the resistance had become more acceptable for those not under occupation. At the same time, winning over new supporters became easier, as the arena of political contestation widened from the civil war enclaves to the entire liberated part of the country and as people began to feel more at ease with changing political persuasion. Consulting constituents was one way to gain support.

Internal changes aside, Hizballah's entry into the political system would have been impossible but for four further enabling factors. The constitutional changes agreed upon in the Ta'if Agreement of 1989, which signaled the beginning of the end of the civil war, facilitated Hizballah's incorporation. Under this agreement, hammered out under Syrian patronage by the existing elites (and thus excluding Hizballah), the ratio of Christian to Muslim in government was partially readjusted to reflect demographical changes and the office of Speaker, allocated to the Shi'a, was given more weight—thus beginning to address Shi'i grievances. The agreement also reiterated the original constitution's commitment to ending political sectarianism.[37] Because the Shi'a generally regard political sectarianism as one of the causes of their marginalization—though the Shi'a are the largest minority in Lebanon, comprising some 40 percent of the population, the division of power is still skewed in favor of the Christians and the Sunnis—the reiteration of this commitment offered Hizballah the opportunity to make this its central goal rather than its earlier, unconstitutional goal of working toward an Islamic state.

Second, the Syrian regime, the unofficial hegemon in Lebanon until recently, needed a Shi'i opposition party in parliament to keep its, at times, truant ally Amal in check. Hizballah was the ideal candidate if it could be persuaded to tone down its Islamist goals. The fact that Syria and Iran had been close allies throughout the Iran-Iraq war and shared an aversion to Israel facilitated Syria's task of persuading Hizballah to accept the new situation—even if this meant political compromise and accepting closer Syrian control over the resistance.[38]

The third enabling factor was the fact that neither the Lebanese constitution and electoral laws nor Hizballah's own "constitution" prohibited the participation of Islamist clergy in the electoral system. Though Lebanon's constitution was modeled on the French constitution, the French state's unbendingly secular dogmatism was not adopted. Instead, building on Ottoman practices, the Lebanese state recognized the political role clergy had historically played in their communities and allowed them to run for political office. This flexibility allowed an Islamist party such as Hizballah, which, at least in principle, rejects the separation of religion and politics, to enter Lebanese politics and field clerical candidates. Hizballah's "constitution," meanwhile, established from the start that participation in elections was an Islamically legitimate way to conduct politics.[39] The fact that Hizballah's goals included more than simply conducting an "Islamic resistance" and establishing an Islamic state, and could be restated in terms of a program for social justice, Shi'i emancipation, and continued national resistance facilitated the process of compromise for Hizballah's leadership.

Finally, the Lebanese state had a vested interest in binding Hizballah to its fate. Syria, of course, demanded that the Lebanese government welcome Hizballah into its system. But, Syrian interests aside, the government had two further reasons to coopt Hizballah. Its initially fierce opposition to both the very basis of the Lebanese state, and the way Lebanon was ruled by its elites, made the party a potential threat to the status quo. Cooption, it was hoped, would curb Hizballah's more radical impulses and induce it into accepting the multisectarian basis of the state.[40] At the same time, the Lebanese state needed a proxy resistance force that could exert pressure on Israel to withdraw, independently from the Lebanese state, thus making Israeli retaliatory actions against the state more problematic.

## Effect of Hizballah's Incorporation

Hizballah's entry into the political system has had two significant consequences. Incorporation entailed a commitment to refrain from violence against domestic rivals and submitting to the official mediation organs of the state—despite Hizballah being the only remaining armed militia in postwar Lebanon. Since 1992, Hizballah has by and large refrained from using violence to settle disputes with other parties, in sharp contrast to the intra-sectarian infighting of the 1980s between Amal, the Communist Party and Hizballah. When clashes do erupt between Hizballah and Amal, as they did in March 1993, Hizballah typically cooperates with the authorities in bringing the culprits to justice.[41] Similarly, when the Lebanese army killed 16 pro-Hizballah demonstrators in September 1993, the party refrained from using arms to seek revenge.[42] Though Hizballah's submission to state authority is in part a function of the military imbalance between its forces and the Lebanese and, until recently, Syrian armies, cooperation would arguably not have been as extensive without the added disincentive of electoral losses.

Hizballah's turn to politics also profoundly affected the composition of its constituency. During the 1980s, members and supporters of the organization were predominantly religiously minded, and ideologically committed to the notion of *wilayat al-faqih*—although even then some were more interested in defending Lebanon and improving the lot of the Lebanese Shi'a. Though tensions existed from the start—as illustrated by the 1989 debate between "hard-liners" and "moderates" following the death of Khomeini—the movement was relatively homogeneous.

The 1990s saw the introduction of a new type of supporter. Once Hizballah's reputation as an efficient party of principle grew, nonpracticing or nominally religious Shi'a began to turn to Hizballah. Secular-minded businessmen became interested in Hizballah's anticorruption drive. Scions of old elite families realized that an alliance with this new party might prove advantageous.[43] Those benefiting from Hizballah's services, particularly if Amal had let them down previously, began to vote for Hizballah, as did those who were critical of the corrupt status quo or the lack of political will among the elites to confront the continuing Israeli occupation in the south. At the same time, an increasing number of Hizballah members were educated at secular institutions and pursued secular, as opposed to clerical, careers, resulting in a more heterogeneous membership profile.[44]

Once the Hizballah leadership realized that it had succeeded in attracting this ideologically heterogeneous constituency, it sought to both preserve and expand its influence among these "swing voters" in a process which social movement theorists call "frame alignment."[45] This process was encouraged by the Lebanese electoral system, which rewards cross-sectarian, cross-ideological alliances and penalizes sectarian or ideological isolation.[46] Those parties that succeed in building an electoral list that is supported by candidates from all the relevant sectarian backgrounds tend to do better in the elections. The need to woo non-Shi'i electoral allies encourages frame adaptation, reinforcing the incentives for adaptation emanating from the increase in Hizballah's internal heterogeneity and its attempts at expanding its constituency.

One of the concrete results of this "frame alignment" has been the dropping of the call for an Islamic state in favor of an emphasis on humanitarian values derived from Islam, enabling nominal Shi'a and, to a lesser extent, people of other religions to subscribe to Hizballah's vision. The shift away from a focus on Iran and the Islamic revolution to a recognition of the legitimacy of Lebanon and a focus on building coalitions with Lebanon's Christians and other Lebanese parties is similarly an outcome of this process, as is Hizballah's increased focus on social justice and its use of a purely secular language in parliament.[47] Though Islam is important to many of Hizballah's supporters, whether Hizballah strengthens Islam's hold over the public realm is of less significance to others than whether Hizballah tackles corruption and nepotism. The fact that, in a 1993 student survey, 70 percent of those who described themselves as having a low or medium level of religiosity supported Hizballah only serves to underline this observation.[48] It is therefore no surprise that Hizballah's insistence on the *hijab* or on working toward an Islamic state has lessened over the years.[49]

Hizballah's ability to carry out resistance operations against Israel has also been affected. Many of those voting for Hizballah representatives voted for them because of their reputation for good governance. Though the issue of continued resistance looms large in the mind of Hizballah's leaders, it does not necessarily loom as large in the consciousness of the general electorate—particularly since the withdrawal of the IDF in 2000. Whether or not Hizballah steps up its resistance activities is of potentially less relevance to them than whether Hizballah representatives will improve basic services—despite Hizballah's concerted efforts at creating a "society of the resistance" or resistance culture.[50] This is particularly pertinent to those with either a medium or a low socioeconomic status—for the former because they have much to lose in retaliatory strikes, for the latter because economic stability is vital for their very survival. Given the preponderance of both these categories among Hizballah supporters, Hizballah must pay close attention to the views prevalent among these categories to retain their support.

Before the IDF's withdrawal, a certain level of material damage and loss of life was acceptable to a sizable section of Shi'a, and Lebanese generally, even outside the occupation zone. The continued existence of a collective memory of suffering, the many links binding Shi'a across the line of demarcation, national pride, and the fact that Hizballah poured significant amounts of money into local welfare, all served to bolster support for the resistance. Even Christians who were often more concerned about the presence of Syrian troops than about the occupation of the south could give qualified support because the continued presence of Syrian troops was linked, in their minds, to the continued presence of Israeli troops in the south. However, qualified support for the resistance was unlikely to survive a protracted Israeli offensive in areas where a postwar "normality" had returned (unless Israel could be unambiguously blamed).

The changed dynamic between Hizballah and its electoral constituencies meant that the party increasingly had to weigh up the costs of its resistance activities to the electorate. Its willingness to agree to the tacit establishment of rules of engagement with the IDF can in part be explained by this change in dynamic. The agreement, negotiated verbally in 1993 in the wake of Israel's Operation Accountability and reaffirmed in writing (on the part of Israel) in 1996 following Operation Grapes of Wrath,[51] stipulated that the conflict be confined to combatants and spare civilians. Given that, over the course of the conflict, Hizballah has killed only a handful of Israeli civilians in rocket attacks on northern Israel, against Israel's killing hundreds of Lebanese civilians, the agreement—if adhered to—was in Hizballah's favor in limiting the costs to the general population. The seriousness with which Hizballah took its commitment to avoid unnecessary escalation can be gleaned from the fact that between 1993 and 1996 its resistance wing reportedly breached the agreement on only 13 occasions—against Israel's 231 violations.[52] Hizballah's commitment to limit the cost to the civilian population did not prevent it from breaching the agreement in retaliation to what it saw as clear provocations—even if this provoked an escalation as it did with Operation Grapes of Wrath. However, it was typically careful to breach the agreement only when unambiguously provoked so that it could lay the blame for any escalation on the IDF.

Another outcome of this changed dynamic was an increase in the political will to end the hostage crisis. Though the extent of Hizballah's involvement in the hostage crisis is disputed,[53] it was unquestionably in a position to exert pressure on the hostage-takers, as the latter operated in Hizballah-controlled areas and often had familial links with party members. A number of external factors played a role in bringing the crisis to an end, including changes in the Iranian leadership, and in the position of Syria vis-à-vis the United States. Indeed, according to one analyst, Hizballah used its leverage over the hostage-takers to boost its post-conflict position in negotiations with Syria, which needed to secure the hostages' release to cement its newfound proximity to the Western alliance of the 1991 Gulf War.[54] But the prospect of having to present itself to the electorate as a political party dedicated to social justice and reform was another factor encouraging Hizballah to end the hostage crisis.[55]

Since the IDF withdrawal in 2000, the level of popular tolerance for Israeli retaliatory action has dropped markedly. In response, Hizballah has limited its actions largely to the Shebaa Farms area. It has cooperated with the Lebanese Army in preventing Palestinian groups from attacking Israel.[56] It has stuck closely to the established rules of engagement (at least concerning the Lebanese-Israeli border) and has calibrated its attacks so as not to provoke large-scale retaliations.[57] When a Hizballah leader was assassinated in Beirut, Hizballah's response was markedly muted.[58] Only once did hostilities escalate to pre-withdrawal levels of intensity—intriguingly not in retaliation for Israeli actions in Lebanon but in response to the IDF's March 2002 invasion of Palestinian towns and refugee camps in the West Bank. Even then Hizballah was careful not to escalate the hostilities beyond a localized border conflict. Syrian and Iranian pressure played a role in this. But so arguably did electoral calculations—a reading that is tentatively supported by the fact that Hizballah began deescalating hostilities before the Iranian Foreign Minister's above-mentioned intervention.[59]

Hizballah has also begun to reinterpret the concept of resistance, subtly shifting the emphasis from military to social action. The annual "military reserve" training each Hizballah member must undergo appears to have become a vehicle for building esprit de corps and corporate identity as well as an attempt at keeping Hizballah's political and administrative personnel in military shape. The annual report of Jihad al-Binaa, Hizballah's construction company set up originally to repair the structural damage resulting from Israeli offensives, refers to farmers as "the well of resistance" and says the charity seeks to "boost the resistance of farmers . . . through guidance orientation and agricultural rehabilitation." Its focus, moreover, is overwhelmingly on building for the future, and a peaceful one at that.[60] Thus, even while maintaining a "resistance culture," Hizballah seems to be engaged in a process of redefining what "resistance" entails—although the continuing crisis in Israel/Palestine and the ongoing violence in Iraq has provided Hizballah with ample opportunity to revert to the original meaning of "resistance."

Partly because of the ongoing conflict in Israel/Palestine, partly as a result of the war in Iraq, there still appears to be sufficient popular support for maintaining a military wing—as long as it is not seen as provoking "unavoidable" Israeli retaliations. Active opposition to Hizballah's right to bear arms is typically confined to Lebanon's non-Shi'i communities and has not seriously affected Hizballah's electoral chances among the Shi'a—as Hizballah's gains in the 2004 municipal and 2005 national elections unambiguously show. Continuation of the resistance, moreover, has given Hizballah tangible benefits as it can capitalize on its status as the only Arab force to have successfully repelled the IDF. It has permitted Hizballah to maintain a high profile regionally and expand its influence inside the neighboring Palestinian territories, as the "godfather" of resistance against Israel. As long as Hizballah succeeds in limiting Israel's response, continuing its resistance efforts and rhetoric will only serve to remind its constituencies of Hizballah's victory over the IDF and so strengthen Hizballah's political appeal.

## Effect of Israeli Policies

One factor that has been pivotal in both the establishment of Hizballah and its subsequent popularity has been Israel's behavior. Hizballah's electoral gains cannot be understood without considering the impact of Israel's various offensives. To understand what impact Israel's actions have had on Hizballah, and why, more specifically, Israel's policies have not only failed to eradicate the movement but contributed to strengthening it, I will briefly explore the rationale behind Israel's policies and the response they provoked.

Israel's goal was the eradication of Hizballah's military capacities through the destruction of its military infrastructure. Because Hizballah operated as a small-scale guerrilla force, its infrastructure was typically well hidden among the general population, confronting Israel with the dilemma of either limiting itself to acting reactively to guerrilla attacks to avoid civilian casualties or taking the battle to the guerrillas and incurring civilian casualties. The IDF decision to opt for the latter was in part motivated by the calculation that the general population would turn against Hizballah. Such an approach was inspired by the notion of "collective punishment" which Israel had deployed in various guises throughout its conflict with the Palestinians and which was based on the premise that the general population could not sustain the costs of a protracted offensive.[61] Israel's two major offensives in 1993 and 1996 were premised on the notion that the material destruction and mass displacement of civilians would alienate the population and force the Lebanese government to act decisively against Hizballah. The three minor offensives carried out between 1999 and 2000 in the lead-up to Israel's withdrawal were inspired by similar notions.[62]

One of the reasons the IDF adopted this policy was the success of the 1982 invasion in turning the general population against the PLO, destroying the PLO's infrastructure in South Lebanon and ousting the PLO from Lebanon.[63] What this comparison overlooks, however, is not only the fact that, far from eradicating resistance against Israel, the invasion triggered a new resistance force, but also that this resistance thrived every time the IDF attempted to eradicate it. Operation Grapes of Wrath illustrates this process well. It was launched in 1996 to destroy Hizballah's camps, arms caches, and rocket launching facilities, but not a single rocket launcher was destroyed and only 13 Hizballah fighters were killed in the fighting. Instead, the bombing killed at least 165 civilians, including 109 refugees sheltering inside the UN compound at Qana, while thousands of civilians were forced to flee to the capital.[64] Rather than weakening Hizballah, the offensive caused Christians who had previously been ambivalent about the resistance effort to donate money and encouraged Christians, Muslims, and politicians not previously supportive of Hizballah to join demonstrations against the occupation and help raise funds for the resistance.[65]

There are various reasons for the failure of the IDF's policy of collective punishment to eradicate Hizballah. Unlike the PLO, Hizballah could not be isolated from its support base. Despite the limited appeal of Hizballah's Iranian associations and ideology, its resistance aims resonated strongly with the general population, and its leaders were well connected to their local communities. Hizballah's investments in local welfare and, post-1992, its commitment to championing the interests of its electoral constituencies ensured that Hizballah had enough popular credit to survive Israeli offensives.

Syria also played an important part in ensuring that the Lebanese government continued to back Hizballah, sometimes against its will. Israel believed, correctly, that there was a fundamental tension between Hizballah's resistance goals—liberation at any cost—and the Lebanese government's interests—economic recovery and the reassertion of sovereignty. However, it underestimated Syria's control over the Lebanese government and Hizballah's willingness to accept the state's sovereignty in all areas but resistance, thus allowing the government to save face.[66]

A third reason was the fact that Israeli offensives were typically disproportionate to Hizballah's initial resistance acts. Both the 1993 and 1996 offensives which killed around 150 each and displaced thousands were launched in response to Hizballah firing rockets into northern Israel, killing two people in 1993 and none in 1996.[67] In each case, the rockets had been Hizballah's response to Israeli attacks involving civilians outside the occupation zone—a breach of the rules of engagement agreement. Because the discrepancy between the initial act and the final response was so glaring, Hizballah had little difficulty in persuading the Lebanese public that fault for their suffering lay with the IDF.

A fourth reason was the high ratio of civilian to combatant casualties. The initial war of 1982–1985 left an estimated 19,000 dead, the majority civilians. The 1993 and 1996 offensives killed some 300 civilians between them, while each of the 231 recorded Israeli breaches of the rules of engagement between 1993 and 1996 typically resulted in civilian deaths. In most instances, few guerrilla fighters were killed. The high ratio of civilians to combatants killed was in part because of the nature of the conflict—a popular resistance movement against aerial bombardments. However, it was also a direct outcome of Israel's policy of collective punishment and its active pursuit of increasing the cost of conflict to the general population. Rather than isolating Hizballah, this policy led to an increase in general hatred of Israel and rendered Hizballah's rhetoric more resonant with the electorate.

A fifth factor was the belief that Israel lacked the political will to eradicate Hizballah. From the start, Israeli public opinion was divided regarding the right course of action in Lebanon. The IDF's phased withdrawal to the south in 1983–1985 was in part due to the unexpectedly bloody counteroffensive of the local Shi'a, in part due to contradictory views within successive Israeli governments (which in turn fueled the Shi'i offensive).[68] Having been forced to withdraw once, the IDF, and the Israeli public, were loath to reoccupy Lebanon beyond the southern buffer zone—limiting the IDF's options to aerial bombardments and covert infiltrations. This, and the fact that the occupation force only numbered 1,500 soldiers, reinforced the notion that Israel lacked the political will to eradicate Hizballah. Israel's vacillation between major offensives and containment, and its willingness to agree to a set of rules of engagement, sent out a similar message—as did the increasing level of domestic protests. Hizballah played on these domestic differences and was strengthened by them in its resolve to resist.

A further factor was Israel's willingness to negotiate with the Lebanese government. Though the negotiations were ostensibly between two sovereign states, they revolved around ending hostilities between Hizballah and the IDF, effectively giving Hizballah an indirect presence at the negotiating table. Since Hizballah was juggling local, Syrian, and Iranian interests, it had limited room to maneuver and could not fully exploit its advantage. Nonetheless the organization's political profile was boosted and the notion that Israel lacked political stamina was reinforced. The various negotiations Israel has entered into via third parties over the release of hostages and soldiers' bodies have had similar results.[69]

That Israel was willing to negotiate and agree to a set of rules of engagement was partly because of the attainment of a limited balance of power between Hizballah and the IDF—or what one Hizballah leader called a "balance of horror."[70] Within the occupation zone, and following a typical pattern of protracted conflict between unequal forces, Hizballah had succeeded in reducing the casualty ratio from 10:1 to between 1: 2.7 and 1:1 by the late 1990s.[71] Because Israel's occupation of southern Lebanon was increasingly contested domestically, the rising number of Israeli casualties hurt the Israeli government particularly hard while boosting the resistance's morale. By the late 1990s, Hizballah had also perfected the art of psychological warfare. It filmed successful assaults and broadcast them in Hebrew into Israel via its satellite station, al-Manar. It carried out a number of targeted assassinations against high-ranking Israeli officers and their Lebanese allies, and ambushed a covert IDF operation on Lebanese territory, showing that it had managed to infiltrate Israeli intelligence.[72] To soldiers who were already ambivalent about their presence in Lebanon, this type of psychological offensive was deeply demoralizing.

Outside the occupation zone, Hizballah attempted to provide a deterrent to Israel's aerial bombardments by expanding its arsenal of surface-to-surface rockets. Though the damage caused was typically material rather than involving human casualties, the terror factor was of some importance in restraining Israeli offensives.[73] Both the 1993 and 1996 offensives culminated in negotiations aimed at persuading Hizballah to stop firing rockets into northern Israel while the absence of any major Israeli offensive since 1996 can in part be ascribed to an increase in Hizballah's rocket arsenal, now rumored to stand at 7,500–10,000. Hizballah's ability to neutralize an Israeli listening post on the Golan Heights in retaliation for the IDF's targeting Syrian installations inside Lebanon was another instance of this new balance of power.[74]

Of particular significance was the belief among Israeli intelligence analysts that Hizballah had acquired rockets with a range of 120 miles, which, if true, would have increased Hizballah's firing range tenfold—bringing major Israeli cities such as Haifa within range. It is disputable whether Hizballah has acquired control over such rockets, or whether these rockets would be effective in causing serious harm given their lack of controllability. But the fact that it is possible that Hizballah might hit Israeli cities means that the IDF must take into account that an offensive might be met with an extended counteroffensive. The fact that Sharon, rumored to have considered using the Iraq war to deal Hizballah a decisive blow, did not carry out any such plans is a possible illustration of this new reality.[75]

Finally, although collective punishment has been counterproductive as a means of eradicating Hizballah, it has arguably been one of the factors deterring Hizballah from escalating the conflict. However, it would not have been as effective in doing so if Hizballah had not become partially dependent on maintaining popular support by having entered the political system. Furthermore, if the policy of collective punishment had not been adopted and Israel had withdrawn earlier, it is debatable whether Israel would have needed such a policy in the first place to deter Hizballah, as the organization's support base would arguably have been significantly less militant.

Israel's attempts at negotiating an end to its two major offensives of the 1990s would also have been less successful if Hizballah had not become part of the political system in Lebanon. Because Hizballah had a vested interest in the system, the Lebanese government had leverage over Hizballah, however limited, which it would have otherwise lacked. Moreover, because Hizballah's relationship with its supporters was now regulated by an electoral dynamic, Hizballah had an increased incentive to prevent the conflict with Israel from turning into a protracted war, thus making it more agreeable to accept a negotiated mutual containment policy.

## Effects of 9/11 and the War on Terror

The events of 9/11 and the subsequent "global war on terror" have affected Hizballah in various and conflicting ways. On the one hand, 9/11 has renewed the West's fascination with the question of whether Hizballah is a terrorist organization. Allegations concerning Hizballah's alleged cooperation with al-Qaeda abound, placing Hizballah in an internationally precarious position. It has responded to this accusation with typical self-confidence, mounting a series of operations against the IDF in the immediate aftermath of 9/11 as if to underline that its leaders believed theirs to be a just cause carried out with legitimate means, and that they would do as they saw fit, regardless of the world's views. To date, besides the U.S. and Israel, only Canada among Western states has placed Hizballah in its entirety on its list of proscribed "terrorist organizations" (as opposed to listing only Hizballah's so-called "External Organization"). The EU has so far refused to bow to U.S. pressure—allowing EU politicians and diplomats to keep channels of communication open with Hizballah. Because so few states have responded to pressure from the U.S. and Israel, and because Hizballah has been listed as a terrorist organization by the U.S. for some two decades already, the placing of Hizballah on the U.S.'s post-9/11 list has not had a significant impact. However, this situation could change if the EU—which has signed a Neighborhood Agreement with Syria and Lebanon and is seriously involved in Lebanon's postwar reconstruction—succumbed to pressure to blacklist Hizballah. The fact that the European Parliament has already called on the EU to blacklist Hizballah in its entirety may be significant in this respect.[76]

The war on terror, and particularly the U.S. invasion of Iraq, has affected both Syria and Iran, which in turn has had an effect on Hizballah. Hizballah's two main state sponsors are well aware of the fact that they are next on the list of potential targets of the U.S. administration. However, Hizballah is so integral to both their foreign policies that it would take more than the mere possibility of a threat to significantly affect their support. Developments in Lebanon following the February 2005 assassination of former prime minister Rafiq Hariri and Syria's subsequent withdrawal may affect Syria's long-term commitment to Hizballah but so far Syrian support has remained unwavering.

The war on terror has opened up new opportunities. Though Syria and Iran need to tread more carefully, both regimes appear determined to fully exploit the possibilities opened up by the U.S. difficulties in Iraq. Iran is well aware that the U.S. recognizes Iran's potential for undermining the U.S. efforts at rebuilding Iraq by stirring up the majority Shi'i population. Syria has a similarly pivotal kingmaker role through its influence over the Sunni minority and the remnants of the Ba'th party. The fact that Iran continues to refuse to bow to international pressure regarding its nuclear program suggests that the Iranian regime is, until now, not taking the threat of U.S. intervention seriously. The election of hard-liner Mahmood Ahmadinejad to the presidency is only likely to strengthen Iranian resolve. The Syrian regime is in a weaker situation because of the precariousness of President Bashar Assad's position. The fact that Syria has succumbed to international and local pressure to withdraw from Lebanon is indicative of this weakness. But Syria too has shown few signs of allowing this to affect its support for Hizballah—as evidenced by its decision to allow Hizballah to oppose Amal in the 2004 municipal elections, thereby sending the message that Hizballah is not only an organization with a grassroots mandate but also would be a much stronger force were it not for Syria's curbing hand.[77]

Hizballah itself has similarly been strengthened by the opportunities offered by the war in Iraq. The overwhelming presence of Hizballah flags at various Shi'i demonstrations at the start of the occupation indicated how many Iraqi Shi'a look to Hizballah as the role model of a successful Shi'i political-cum-militia party. Little is known for certain concerning the extent of Hizballah's actual involvement in Iraq. In Lebanese terms, whether the organization is directly involved in Iraq is of relatively little direct relevance. What counts is the fact that Hizballah can increase its support base by championing the downtrodden Shi'a of Iraq and rhetorically linking the latter's plight to the plight of the Palestinians and the plight of the Lebanese Shi'a before May 2000.[78] The fact that Hizballah succeeded in attracting 250,000 people—or 1 in every 8 Lebanese—to declare their readiness to die as martyrs during a demonstration denouncing the U.S. invasion of Iraq, only vindicates this observation.[79]

The events of 9/11 have also served to reinforce the regional position Hizballah has gained as a result of its success in ousting the IDF from Lebanon and its subsequent role as the "godfather" of the al-Aqsa Intifada in Palestine. Before the outbreak of the al-Aqsa Intifada, Hizballah was engaged in a heated debate about the future of the resistance, one wing arguing that Hizballah's future lay in politics, the other insisting that the struggle against Israel and Western hegemony should remain Hizballah's core task.[80] With the outbreak of the Intifada, the wind was taken out of the sails of the politically oriented wing. The U.S. response to 9/11 has made the position of this wing even more untenable, while offering the pro-resistance party unprecedented opportunities to capitalize on Hizballah's regional standing as the only Arab force capable of repelling Israel (and by implication, U.S. forces in the region).

## Conclusion and Policy Recommendations

A number of tentative conclusions can be drawn. Hizballah's case suggests that incorporation into the electoral process can under certain circumstances have a moderating effect on an insurgent group. The group in question must be sufficiently embedded and representative of a section of the population to envisage an electoral future for itself. Its leadership, decision-making structures and ideology must be able to support the notion of compromise. If the leadership is responsive to popular opinion, and popular opinion favors a moderate course, this facilitates both the process of incorporation and the process of moderation. Whether incorporation is likely to occur and lead to moderation is in part dependent on the composition of the movement. In Hizballah's case, the increase in highly educated and upwardly mobile supporters appears to be positively correlated to the movement's incorporation and relative shift toward moderation—despite the fact that recent research on political violence suggests that an increase in education and wealth is positively correlated to an increase in support for political violence.[81]

Some democratization theorists, most famously Seymour Martin Lipset, have long argued that an increase in per capita income facilitates the process of democratization. If democratic peace theory has any validity, this means that an increase in per capita income is likely to lead to a reduction in support for violence.[82] The relationship between socioeconomic status, democratization, and support for violence is far more complex than these theories suggest.[83] However, Hizballah's case still appears to indicate that, under conditions of electoral competition and a functioning political system in which the insurgent organization has a political stake, an increase in the overall socioeconomic condition of that organization's support base is positively correlated to moderation in the organization's conduct.

A further necessary condition appears to be a sufficiently strong central government—or external force backing up the government—to enforce compliance. Of particular importance is the relative balance of power between the insurgents and the government. If either is too weak, there is little incentive for either party to compromise. Instead a level of stalemate is necessary. This conclusion is echoed by Dankwart Rustow's classic theory of democratic transition which stipulates that for democratization to occur a stalemate must exist between at least two contending forces, typically an elite and an emerging counter-elite.[84] It is also echoed by Dietrich Rueschemeyer and colleagues' structural theory of democratization which contends that democratization is the product of the emergence of a "balance of class power" between state and landed elites on the one hand, and a coalition of working and middle classes on the other.[85] Hizballah is precisely such a coalition and thus, if Rueschemeyer is correct, a "natural" force for democratization (regardless of its views on democratization).

A second lesson lies in the observation that, in Hizballah's case, the policy of collective punishment served to consolidate rather than eradicate the movement—echoing the findings of this book's chapters on Hamas (Chapter 4), the Kashmiri insurgents (Chapter 7), and the IRA (Chapter 6). In the cases of Hamas and Hizballah, the organizations in question are socially deeply embedded, and consequently reflect the socioeconomic composition as well as the aspirations of a significant section of society. In both instances, insurgent violence was preceded by state violence in the form of invasion and occupation, creating a shared set of grievances among the larger population. Under such conditions, collective punishment, with its twin characteristics of being disproportionate to the original offense (to deter future offenses) and targeting innocent bystanders, reinforces the original grievances and grants legitimacy to the insurgents' rhetoric and methods, playing into the insurgents' hand. While it may help to deter escalatory attacks, it appears to do this only if the insurgents incur a significant political cost from escalating the conflict—in Hizballah's case, by being part of the electoral system. The benefits of deterrence, though, do not necessarily outweigh the costs of increased popular legitimacy for the insurgents, and increased popular support for militant practices.

The level of an organization's embeddedness appears to play an important determining role. The more embedded an insurgent movement, arguably the more difficult it is to eradicate it by military means alone—particularly if those means are limited to aerial bombardments and covert operations. If the state were prepared to use all coercive means at its disposal without regard for human rights, it might be able to suppress an insurgent organization through brute force alone, as President Assad of Syria did in 1982 in Hama, killing 10,000–30,000. For a democracy, total disregard for human rights is neither desirable nor electorally feasible. But even Assad's ruthless suppression was accompanied with socioeconomic and political strategies to weaken popular support for the insurgents and bind citizens to the state.[86]

When a movement is embedded, its aspirations are to a certain extent a reflection of the aspirations of a section of the population. Although an insurgent movement can manipulate its constituency's aspirations, it can only do so to a limited extent. Hizballah's particular evolution suggests that an embedded organization such as Hizballah must heed the views of its supporters if it is to retain its influence. The construction of grievances is a two-way process between the organization's ideologues and its supporters—particularly so if the organization in question operates in a competitive electoral system where support can be both gained and lost, and competition is conducted by nonviolent means. If an organization such as Hizballah reflects, even to a limited extent, the genuine views of a significant section of the population, its goals and grievances cannot be ignored if an end to violence is desired. While it is impossible for Israel to meet Hizballah's demand that it dismantle itself, Israel can meet Hizballah's calls for its withdrawal from the disputed border areas, and for an end to violations of Lebanese airspace. Such a response is likely to decrease popular support for radical solutions which will increase the pressure on Hizballah to adapt its rhetoric and practice if it is to maintain its popular backing.

That such a move is unlikely to result in Hizballah increasing its demands (as those opposing accommodation might argue) can be inferred from the fact that Hizballah, despite its continuing call for the liberation of Jerusalem, has only laid claim to border areas whose legal status is ambiguous. The Lebanese population are not interested in suffering for the liberation of Palestine, denying Hizballah the popular support needed to expand the conflict (although they may attempt to continue to covertly support Palestinian resistance groups). Once Israel has met Hizballah's demands concerning Lebanon, domestic and international pressure on Hizballah to rein in the resistance is likely to increase dramatically—especially if, in the absence of fear of Israeli reprisals, Lebanon's economy were to recover. If such a move were to be accompanied by a negotiated settlement stipulating Israel's withdrawal from the Golan Heights, Syria's support for maintaining an autonomous resistance force would similarly weaken. Syria's withdrawal and the resurgence of a vocal antiresistance movement inside Lebanon has made such a scenario more likely—even though Hizballah's success in the 2005 national elections (winning 11 seats by itself and 35 in coalition with Amal) has enabled Hizballah to claim a popular mandate for continued resistance. The fact that Hizballah leaders have begun, for the first time, to express willingness to discuss the future of the resistance is a possible indicator of things to come.[87]

A third observation concerns the importance of not viewing Hizballah as a rigid, eternally hostile, unchangeable organization. Such an approach is inspired by both the "terrorism paradigm" that Western leaders too often adopt, and by the more essentialist writings on Islamism or political Islam. The evolution charted above suggests that an embedded organization like Hizballah can be responsive to external pressures and capable of change and compromise. Adoption of a paradigm that assumes ideological rigidity is likely to affect state policies negatively. In the case of Israel, the policy of collective punishment was arguably sustained by a view—derived from Israel's contemporary understanding of the PLO—that saw Hizballah as immutable, bent on the total destruction of Israel and thus in need of eradication. Such a view ignores the fact that Hizballah needs a level of popular support to be successful and that popular support for eradicating Israel, if this incurs personal costs, is largely lacking. Conversely, adoption of a paradigm that acknowledges that Hizballah is an ideologically mutable organization facilitates a state response which seeks to understand the factors shaping Hizballah's behavior and attempts to change these to transform the situation, and with it, the organization, into one that sustains peace, or at least a permanent ceasefire. Such an approach would focus among other things on ensuring a general increase in economic and educational opportunities, and a political future for the moderates among the insurgents in question.

Labeling an organization like Hizballah "terrorist" unnecessarily complicates reaching a resolution. As long as Hizballah is publicly discredited as a "terrorist organization," Israel must resort to indirect and contorted negotiations that both limit the chances of a successful resolution and bestow the very legitimacy on Hizballah that Israel's policy of branding it as "terrorist" is seeking to avoid. Conversely, if Israel (and the U.S.) were to drop its policy of labeling Hizballah "terrorist" and propose negotiations that included Hizballah, pressure on the latter to accept the invitation would increase dramatically and allow Israel to take the moral high ground.

Finally, the case of Hizballah contains particularly compelling lessons for the case of Hamas. Hamas, like Hizballah, is a movement composed of an upwardly mobile counter-elite, an increasingly heterodox constituency, with similar goals and a comparable position within the community's political hierarchy (though Palestine lacks Lebanon's multisectarianism). That Hamas's behavior has not become more moderate in response to its political inclusion in the Palestinian system is to a large extent a function of the fact that its inclusion was only partial; that until recently a political future for Hamas was not seriously envisaged by either the Palestinian Authority or the peace process's international sponsors; and that the general population had not experienced a significant peace dividend, either in economic terms or in personal security. As a result, and in particular because Hamas's post-conflict prospects are uncertain while public opinion has until recently supported the practice of suicide bombing, the incentive to become more accommodating has not been as great as has been the case with Hizballah. The case of Hizballah suggests that if Israel were to cease its occupation of the West Bank and Gaza (and in particular its hated occupation practices); allow the Palestinian economy to grow; and encourage the Palestinian Authority to secure a post-conflict political future for Hamas, then Hamas might be socialized into becoming more moderate as a result of its constituency becoming more accommodating.

## Glossary

al-Aqsa Intifada: Palestinian uprising of September 2000 until the present.

Amal: Hizballah's chief rival among the Shi'i parties, established in the 1970s by Musa Sadr, subsequently led by Nabih Berri, and a partner to the ruling coalition since the 1980s.

Bekaa Valley: Lebanon's furthermost valley to the east, bordering Syria and populated largely by Shi'a; one of Hizballah's heartlands.

Da'wa Party: transnational Shi'i Islamist movement calling for the establishment of an Islamic state, founded in Iraq but with a local branch in Lebanon

Golan Heights: Syrian land bordering Lebanon, occupied by Israel during the Six Day War of 1967.

Hizballah: literally "Party of God," referring to a passage in the Qur'an which predicts that the party of God will be victorious.

*hijab*: headscarf.

IDF: Israeli Defense Forces.

Islamism: the ideology of those seeking to establish an Islamic state and society based on Islamic law and principles.

Jihad al-Binaa: literally "reconstruction jihad (effort)," Hizballah's network of agricultural, construction and engineering services, initially established to repair structural damage caused by Israeli offensives.

Levant: the area of the Middle East bordering on the Mediterranean, encompassing Lebanon, Syria, Palestine and Jordan.

Maronite: refers to the largest Christian denomination in Lebanon; the National Pact allocated the presidency to the Maronites.

Movement of the Disinherited: Shi'i revival movement, established by Imam Musa Sadr in the 1970s to address the socioeconomic marginalization of Lebanon's Shi'a.

Multinational Force: coalition of U.S., French and Italian forces initially dispatched to Lebanon to oversee the withdrawal of the PLO from Lebanon; following the Sabra and Chatila massacres, the MNF returned and became embroiled in the Lebanese civil war.

Operation Accountability: July 1993 Israeli air offensive aimed at curbing Hizballah; more than 130 civilians were killed, 600 wounded, 200,000–300,000 displaced.

Operation Grapes of Wrath: April 1996 Israeli air offensive aimed at curbing Hizballah; 165 were killed (mostly civilians), 300–400 wounded, an estimated 500,000 displaced.

PLO: Palestine Liberation Organization, umbrella organization of secular Palestinian nationalist movements.

Shi'a (adjective: Shi'i): minority denomination within Islam, originating in the dispute over the Prophet's succession in the seventh century C.E.; the Shi'a form the largest denomination in Lebanon; the National Pact granted them the post of House Speaker

Sunni: the majority denomination within Islam; the Sunnis were allocated the Premiership by the National Pact

*wilayat al-faqih*: rule of the supreme jurisprudent (Ayatollah Khomeini's blueprint for an Islamic state in Iran)

## Timeline

1920: France is granted mandate over Lebanon and Syria by League of Nations, following collapse of Ottoman Empire.

1943: Lebanon is declared independent; National Pact establishes division of power between Maronites, Sunnis, and Shi'a.

1959: Imam Musa Sadr arrives in Lebanon.

1966: Muhammad Hussein Fadlallah arrives in Lebanon, which becomes a center for Shi'i activism.

1970: PLO establishes headquarters in Lebanon, having been ousted from Jordan.

1970s: Lebanese branch of (Iraqi) Da'wa Party is established by activists close to Fadlallah, following the steady expulsion of Lebanese clerical students from Najaf, Iraq.

1974: Movement of the Disinherited is established by Imam Musa Sadr.

1975: Civil war breaks out in Lebanon; Amal is established by Imam Musa Sadr.

1978: Israel invades Lebanon to curb PLO; Imam Sadr disappears in Libya.

1979: Shah is toppled in Iran; Ayatollah Khomeini establishes the Islamic Republic of Iran, providing political inspiration for Lebanese Shi'a.

1982: Israel invades Lebanon, forces PLO out to Tunisia, occupies southern Lebanon and Beirut; Iranian Revolutionary Guards arrive in Lebanon; foundations of Hizballah are established; Multinational Forces arrive; first suicide operation is carried out against IDF headquarters in Tyre.

1983: Suicide operations are carried out against U.S. Embassy, U.S. Marines, and French paratroopers; first Western hostages are taken by activists close to Hizballah; Multinational Forces leave.

1984: Further suicide operations are conducted against IDF headquarters in Tyre and Sidon.

1985: IDF completes withdrawal to self-declared "buffer zone" in the south; Hizballah publishes its "Open Letter"; suicide operations gradually stop.

1986: Hizballah establishes Majlis al-Shura (consultative council).

1987: Subhi al-Tufayli emerges as Hizballah's first secretary-general.

1988: Height of Amal-Hizballah clashes; end of Iran-Iraq war marks end to dream of Iraq becoming second Islamic republic.

1989: Ta'if Agreement signed by major Lebanese factions, signaling beginning of the end of the civil war; Hizballah initially condemns the agreement as an undemocratic elite pact; Ayatollah Khomeini, supreme head of the (Iranian) Islamic revolution to which Hizballah subscribes, dies; Hizballah undergoes restructuring.

1991: Secretary-General Subhi al-Tufayli deselected in favor of more pragmatic Abbas al-Musawi; hostage crisis begins to come to an end.

1992: Secretary-General Abbas al-Musawi assassinated by the IDF; Hassan Nasrallah elected as Hizballah's third secretary-general; Israeli Embassy in Argentina bombed, killing 32, wounding 252, allegedly in retaliation for Musawi's assassination (available evidence remains speculative, pointing if anything to Iran rather than Hizballah); final hostages released; Hizballah participates in the first postwar national elections and wins 8 out of 27 Shi'i seats (plus 4 allied seats out of a total of 128).

1993: Israeli air offensive Operation Accountability kills over 130 civilians, wounds 600, displaces 200,000–300,000; Hizballah and Israel agree upon "rules of engagement."

1994: Suicide car bomb kills 96, wounds 127 at the Argentine-Israeli Mutual Association headquarters in Argentina; Hizballah blamed though available evidence remains speculative.

1996: Israeli air offensive Operation Grapes of Wrath kills 165 (mostly civilians), wounds 300–400, displaces an estimated 500,000; Hizballah wins 7 seats (plus 3 allied seats) in national elections.

1998: Hizballah participates successfully in first postwar municipal elections.

2000: Israel withdraws from Lebanon leaving only a few disputed border areas; Hizballah wins 9 seats (plus 2 allied seats) in national elections; outbreak of al-Aqsa Intifada in Palestine enables Hizballah to continue playing the resistance card.

2002: Worst flare-up of cross-border violence since 2000 erupts in response to the IDF invading Palestinian towns and refugee camps.

2004: Hizballah stages a 250,000-strong march protesting the invasion of Iraq.

2005: Rafik al-Hariri, former Lebanese prime minister, assassinated; calls for Syrian withdrawal intensify, domestically and internationally; Hizballah organizes a pro-Syria demonstration involving an estimated 400,000 demonstrators; Syrian forces withdraw; Hizballah wins 11 seats (plus 3 allied seats) in the national elections, Amal-Hizballah coalition wins 35 seats.

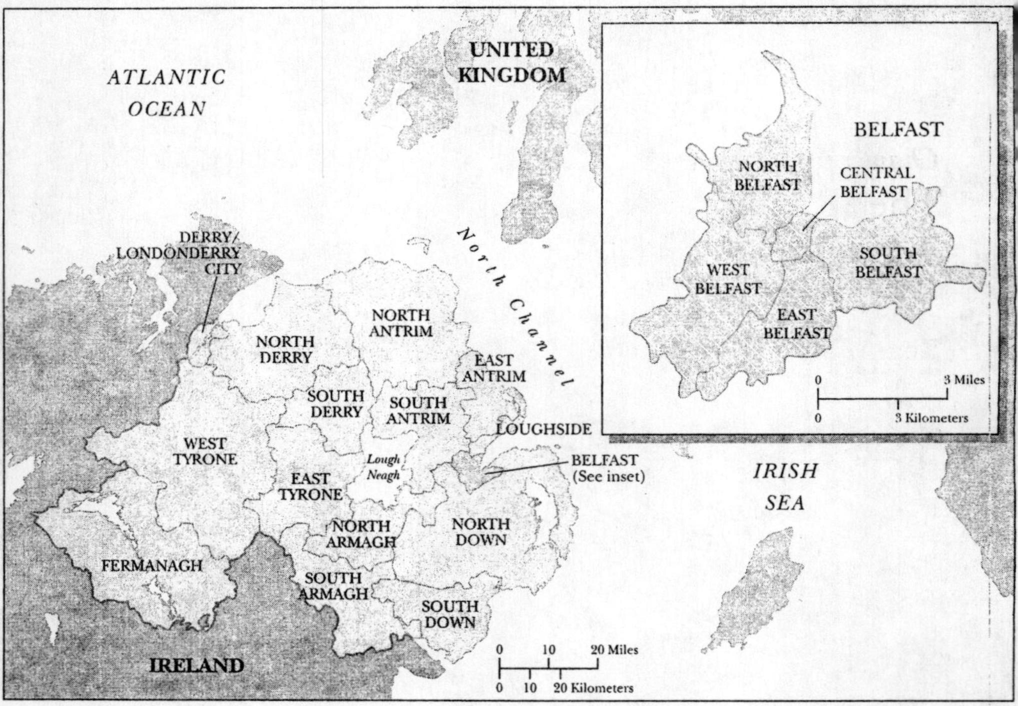


Map 6.1. Northern Ireland and Belfast.

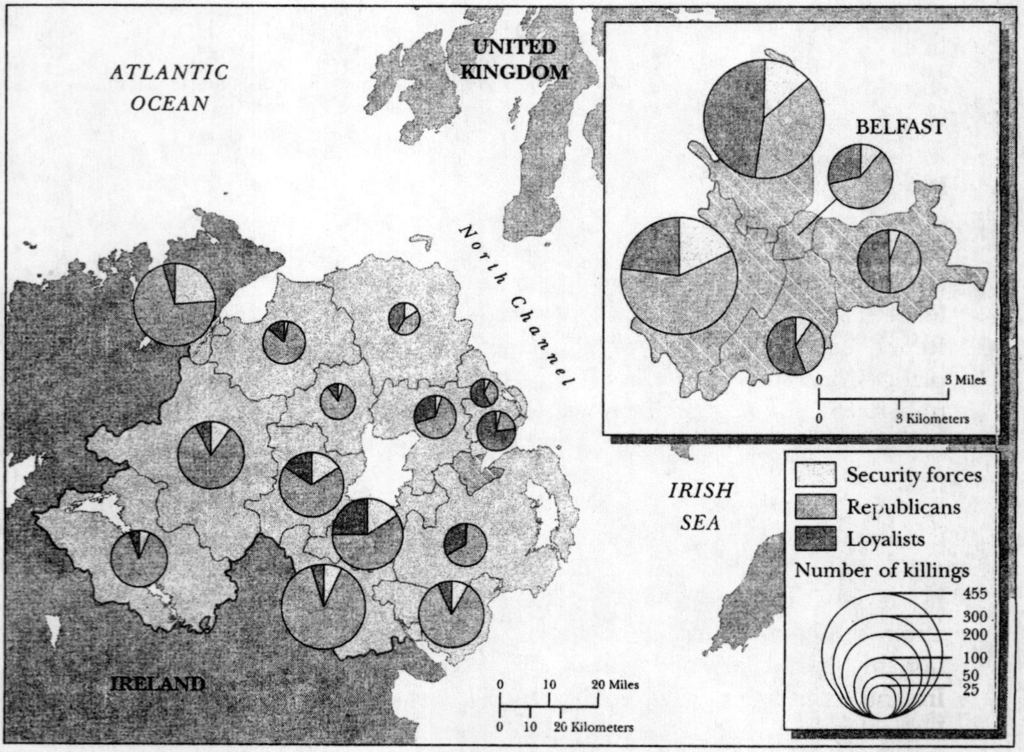


Map 6.2. Spatial distribution of killings in Northern Ireland, 1969–1989. Adapted from McKeown (1985) and IIP (1989).

*Chapter 6*

# The IRA: Looking Back; Mission Accomplished?

BRENDAN O'LEARY

> *The full implementation, on a progressive and irreversible basis by the two governments, especially the British government, of what they have agreed will provide a political context, in an enduring political process, with the potential to remove the causes of conflict and in which Irish republicans and unionists can, as equals, pursue our respective political objectives peacefully. In that new context the IRA leadership will initiate a process that will completely and verifiably put IRA arms beyond use. We will do it in such a way as to avoid risk to the public and misappropriation by others and ensure maximum public confidence.*
>
> —*IRA Statement, 6 May 2000*

People voluntarily kill, or die, for collective causes that register their group's esteem, dignity, and honor. Actions that provoke or rekindle resentment catalyze violence. Group-honor often matters more than material self-interest, or material group interest in provoking and sustaining violence. These propositions govern what follows. Flatly stated, the Irish Republican Army (IRA) of 2005 has fulfilled its original volunteers' pledges, and since its mission is accomplished, consistent with its constitution, it may, should, and likely will disband. More controversially, this dissolution will occur because the governments of Ireland between 1922 and 1949, and subsequently the governments of the United Kingdom and Ireland, have removed the constitutional resentment that created and maintained the IRA's reason for being.

The IRA's existence after 1922 expressed two constitutional resentments: (1) at the Treaty of 1921 between Great Britain and Ireland, which provocatively required the Irish Free State to imbibe the relics of British constitutionality, particularly the oath of allegiance to the Crown by members of Ireland's parliament, Dáil Éireann, and (2) at the denial of the people of Ireland as a whole of their right of self-determination, usurped by the unilateral decision of the government of Great Britain to partition Ireland in 1920. These related resentments have now been substantively redressed. The final and full implementation of the comprehensive Belfast/Good Friday Agreement of 1998 can be seen as the culmination of the IRA's mission, though it is not just that.[1]

## Óglaigh na hÉireann

Analysis of the IRA must begin with its first name, Óglaigh na hÉireann, its title in Irish, and its self-description in its official communiqués signed by "P. O'Neill" on behalf of the Irish Republican Publicity Bureau.[2] IRA activists sometimes refer to the organization as ONH, the acronym of its Gaelic name. The etymology of Óglaigh na hÉireann is significant: *laoch* means "hero, champion, warrior, soldier" and *óg* means "young," and so *óglaigh* came to mean "vassals," "youths of military age," "soldiers," and finally "volunteers."[3] Óglaigh na hÉireann therefore comprises the "Volunteers of Ireland," or the "Irish Volunteers." Óglaigh na hÉireann was founded in 1913, in response to the formation of the Ulster Volunteer Force (UVF), a militia loyal to the Ulster Unionist Party and opposed to the granting of home rule to Ireland by the Westminster parliament. Its formation was the idea of the secret Irish Republican Brotherhood (IRB), otherwise known as the Fenians, who tried to run it as a front organization. Formally it was created by the Ancient Order of Hibernians, the Gaelic Athletic Association (GAA), and Gaelic League revivalists, that is, by the major cultural bodies of the Irish nationalist revival.

The Volunteers divided shortly after the start of the Great War. The National Volunteers, following John Redmond, the leader of the Irish Parliamentary Party, took the majority into the British army—on the understanding that Great Britain would honor its commitment to implement home rule when the war was over. The minority retained the founding organization's title deeds and rejected service in another English war, not least because home rule had been postponed because of the resistance of the Ulster Unionists. Óglaigh na hÉireann organized military training. Its members were subsequently partly mobilized, through an IRB conspiracy, in launching the insurrection of Easter 1916—in which a Republic was proclaimed in arms, but put down by forces of the British Crown. At the start of the insurrection Óglaigh na hÉireann was renamed (in English), together with the Irish Citizen Army, as the Irish Republican Army, and it was as commandant general of that army that Pádraig Pearse surrendered.[4] It was "Irish" because of its national identification; "Republican" because militant Irish nationalists since the late eighteenth century have opposed British Crown authority; and an "Army" because only such an organization is the legitimate defender of a state or nation.

The Volunteers remained known by their original English title for a while, and ever since rank-and-file IRA members have been known as "volunteers." In October 1917 Sinn Féin, the political party that had originally stood for a separate Irish parliament under the British Crown, was revitalized by an influx of Volunteers, who elected Eamon de Valera, the surviving leader of the 1916 insurrection, as the party's president. Then "Under the cover of the meeting, 250 delegates met in an Army Convention in the GAA grounds, Croke Park. De Valera was elected President, and Cathal Brugha Chief of Staff, but the IRB was prominently represented in the Staff: [Michael] Collins was Director of Organization."[5] The IRA was now, in principle, subordinated to political control by a party—which claimed the right to speak for the nation, although it was in practice significantly controlled by Collins, now president of the Supreme Council of the IRB. While subordinated to civilian authority, the IRA had established its internal democracy—a general convention, and the election of the senior officers. The IRA subsequently spearheaded Ireland's War of Independence between 1919 and 1921, in conjunction with Sinn Féin, which was victorious in Ireland in the Westminster general elections held in 1918—the first held under full male suffrage and the franchise for women over thirty. Sinn Féin won on an explicit platform of "abstentionism."[6] Its members of parliament would not take their seats at Westminster but instead would constitute the deputies of the Irish parliament.

Two significant entities today call themselves Óglaigh na hÉireann because both claim to be the army of Ireland. Ireland's prime minister, Bertie Ahern, in October 2004 pointedly said, "our Constitution states there can be [only] one Óglaigh na hÉireann. At the moment there are two." One is the official name of the army of the sovereign, independent, and democratic Republic of Ireland that comprises twenty-six counties of the island and is a member-state of the European Union and the United Nations. This Óglaigh na hÉireann has never fought a foreign or defensive war; it serves a state that is not (yet) a member of NATO; and it is typical of the resource-starved military of a small European democracy, best known for participation in UN peacekeeping missions. Under the Irish Free State (1922–1937) it was known only as Óglaigh na hÉireann and had no official English name. The other Óglaigh na hÉireann is the secret army, *the* IRA. The two Óglaigh na hÉireann, official and unofficial, sprang from the winners and losers respectively of the Irish Civil War (1922–1923). That war was precipitated by the implementation of the Treaty between Great Britain and Ireland, which led to a division within the ranks of the IRA, then over 100,000 strong. After April 1922, there were two armies, one loyal to the Free State's provisional government, the other to the IRA executive. Pro-Treaty volunteers joined the army of the Irish Free State; anti-Treaty volunteers insisted they constituted the true IRA.

## Initial Constitutional Objectives

The reformed anti-Treaty IRA's initial constitution, drafted in the spring of 1922, before the onslaught of the Civil War, stated that

> The Army shall be known as the Irish Republican Army. It shall be . . . a purely volunteer Army. . . . Its objects shall be:
> 1. To safeguard the honor and maintain the independence of the Irish Republic.
> 2. To protect the rights and liberties common to the people of Ireland.
> 3. To place its services at the disposal of an established Republican Government which faithfully upholds the above objects.[7]

Having "dumped arms"—acknowledging defeat in the Civil War in May 1923—the IRA amended its constitution in November 1925 to specify four objectives: guarding the Republic's honor and upholding its sovereignty and unity; establishing and upholding a legitimate Irish government with total control over the Republic; securing and defending citizens' civil and religious liberties and their equal rights and opportunities; and, lastly (a new item), reviving the Irish language and "promoting the best characteristics of the Irish race." Aside from this fresh ethnonational agenda, the content was the same as that of spring 1922.[8]

It is vital to understand the original three quoted "objects." The IRA was reformed by those republicans, a majority of the Volunteers, who regarded the Treaty signed by Sinn Féin's delegates in 1921 as a fundamental betrayal of "the honor and independence of the Irish Republic." This was, among other things, because the Treaty acknowledged a continuing role for the British king and his successors as the (constitutional) monarch of Ireland, gave Great Britain a right of ratification over the permanent constitution of the Irish Free State by requiring that the latter comply with the Treaty, restricted Ireland's international sovereignty, and required the Free State to make its key naval ports available to the forces of the Crown. The failure of the Treaty immediately to reverse the partition of Ireland into two entities, "Northern" and "Southern," which the Westminster parliament had authorized in the Government of Ireland Act of 1920 without the consent of a single Irish MP, was regarded by some, but not all, opponents of the Treaty as an equally fundamental betrayal of Ireland's national honor, rights, liberties, and independence.

"To protect the rights and liberties common to the people of Ireland" meant that the IRA's mission was to defend the right of the people of Ireland to what today would be called their human rights, a statement of inclusive civic republican nationalism for Irish citizens, whatever their origins, and of their collective right to national self-determination.

The third object of the IRA, "to place its services at the disposal of an established Republican Government which faithfully upholds the above objects," warrants detailed parsing. The IRA endorsed republican—and democratic—government, and, in principle, the subordination of the army to an "established Republican Government," *provided* that government faithfully upheld the honor and independence and the rights and liberties of the people of Ireland. "Established Republican Government" was code for the government created by Dáil Éireann—the Assembly of Ireland—formed by the Sinn Féin members elected to the Westminster parliament of 1918, who had then proclaimed Ireland's own parliament. Its successor, the Second Dáil, elected in 1921, had "established" and sworn its members' loyalty to the Irish Republic proclaimed in the rebellion of 1916.

In 1919, Cathal Brugha, minister of defense in the government created by Dáil Éireann, had insisted that the IRA take an oath of loyalty to Dáil Éireann—thereby formally establishing civilian control of the military in the new and emergent state, and attempting to reduce the influence of the IRB (and Collins) within the IRA. The Treaty precisely required members of Dáil Éireann to swear an oath of allegiance to the British Crown, thereby repudiating the establishment of the Republic. The provocative British insistence on this new oath, requiring deputies to forswear their solemn commitments, stuck in the throat of republicans, many of whom were otherwise prepared for political compromise, for example, Eamon de Valera, president of Dáil Éireann, who had sought for Ireland to have "external association" with, but not membership in, the British Commonwealth, and was willing to recognize the British king as the head of the Commonwealth. In the perspective of the new IRA's constitution, the deputies of Dáil Éireann who obliged the Treaty by taking the oath had done what they had no right to do, namely, disestablish the Republic at British insistence: they had dishonored the independence, rights, and liberties of the people of Ireland.

The Treaty, made under the duress of British prime minister David Lloyd George's threat of "immediate and terrible war," had been accepted by a bare majority (3 to 2) of Ireland's negotiators (who had then signed *en bloc*), and by a bare majority of the cabinet of Dáil Éireann (4 to 3). The deputies who accepted the Treaty included the majority of the second Dáil Éireann, led by Michael Collins (president of the IRB), and Arthur Griffith, founder of Sinn Féin, who had endorsed the Treaty as members of the negotiating team and the cabinet. The deputies of Dáil Éireann later dissolved themselves into the new parliament (also called Dáil Éireann) of the Irish Free State, which had "dominion status" within the British Empire, with the British king as head of state. The defeated minority of deputies became, in the vision of the new anti-Treaty IRA, the upholders of Ireland's honorable independence, the "established" Republic—and they, as the rump "Second Dáil," provided the legitimate democratic authority for the IRA to oppose the Treaty. After losing the Civil War, the IRA did not disband, but endured as a significant organization of trained soldiers opposed to the Treaty and its consequences, including the partition of Ireland. The split within the IRA was mirrored at party level. Sinn Féin divided: the majority forming Cumann na nGaedheal (and the first government of the Irish Free State), while the minority maintained the title deeds to Sinn Féin.[9] Most of the members of Cumann na nGaedheal would later become, in the 1930s, members of Fine Gael, the party that was most committed to the Treaty.

The majority of the deputies of Sinn Féin left its ranks in 1926 to join the new Fianna Fáil party, which was prepared to work the dominion system while being committed to removing every obnoxious vestige of the Treaty from the constitution of independent Ireland.[10] In the meantime the IRA was pledged, by its revised 1925 constitution, provided the Republic was fully established, to acknowledge the authority of such an emergent entity: "The Army Council shall have the power to delegate its powers to a government which is actively endeavoring to function as the *de facto* government of the republic. . . . When a government is [thus] functioning . . . a General Army Convention shall be convened to give the allegiance of Óglaigh na hÉireann to such a government."[11]

## The IRA Between Two Wars in Ireland

The volatile, labyrinthine public and secret history of the IRA (or, as some would have it, of the many IRAs) between 1923 and 1969 is not traced here. It is chronicled in a range of journalists' narratives, in the memoirs of former IRA volunteers and sympathizers, and in more systematic appraisals by contemporary historians.[12] The story in the standard accounts, of course, is not one of complete coherence. Contradictory dispositions in and actions by the IRA abounded in the fifty years between the onset of Ireland's War of Independence and the extensive "return" of British troops to Northern Ireland in 1969. The IRA apparently did not believe that a majority, even an Irish majority in *the* Dáil, had the right to be wrong on the constitutional status of Ireland—evidence of "vanguardism" and "elitism." Yet its successive leaders genuinely sought to lead (or assist) a popular revolution against three regimes (in Belfast, Dublin, and London). In the 1920s and 1930s, the IRA commended parliamentary abstentionism, which for many became an article of faith as opposed to a tactic, but one of its Army Council members was elected to the Northern Ireland parliament in 1933, and the organization actively canvassed for Fianna Fáil (which described itself as the "Republican Party" in English) in two critical general elections in 1932 and 1933—both of which saw the anti-Treaty party returned to power. The IRA's membership was mostly Catholic in its origins, but the Catholic clergy and bishops of Ireland regularly condemned it. The IRA proclaimed a civic Irish republicanism, true to the heritage of the eighteenth-century revolutionaries, the United Irishmen, in which Protestants and other minorities would have full citizenship rights. Yet its leaders and members were often regarded as "sectarian" in practice. The IRA was described as comprised of highly localized sectarian militias, defenders of Northern Irish Catholics, but also as centralized internationalist left-wing revolutionaries. In one decade, the 1930s, the leadership of the IRA went from being the Comintern's closest ally in Ireland to conspiring with Nazi Germany, under Sean Russell, several years later, before returning in the 1960s to an accommodation with Marxists.[13] In the early and mid-1930s, the IRA "denounced partition, yet remained very much an organization focused on the overthrow of the southern rather than the northern state. It trained for warfare, yet often tried to prevent its members involving themselves in confrontation with their enemies."[14]

Yet despite multiple zigzags, not least in orientation toward socialist politics in this fifty-year interval, one can observe a unifying theme across the IRA's history before 1969, namely, the comprehensive constitutional rejection of British determination of Ireland's constitutional arrangements. Here is a sketch of five partially overlapping phases, which correspond to the received history learned by IRA volunteers.

First, after the glorious defeat and surrender of 1916, came sudden and surprising success in guerrilla warfare against the British. The IRA refers to this moment as the Tan War, after its engagements with the Black and Tans (uniformed in black and khaki), emergency reserve police recruited from Great Britain. Success affirmed for many the merits of armed struggle, particularly guerrilla warfare, which had done more to create a self-governing Ireland than fifty years of parliamentary pursuit of home rule.[15]

The second phase, 1923–1948, opened after the equally sudden defeat of the bulk of the IRA in the Civil War over the Treaty. The IRA was decisively defeated militarily: significant numbers of volunteers were killed, injured, or incarcerated. Of those subsequently released, many left the organization. The IRA's explicit or tacit electoral supporters became a minority in the South.[16] It became an anti-system oppositionist underground army organization in the Irish Free State—and was weaker still in Northern Ireland.[17] There was a progressive diminution in both the strength of and the support for the IRA, even though its membership in the 1930s has been estimated as high as 30,000.[18] Volunteers were intermittently repressed, subjected to extensive surveillance, interned without trial, and gradually marginalized, even though the veterans of the Tan War retained public admiration in the South. This loss of support was largely because the IRA progressively lost its rationale in the South. Successive political leaders of political parties in independent Ireland, under Cumann na nGaedheal, Fianna Fáil, and later Clann na Poblachta, were to prove Michael Collins's perception of the Treaty to be true: it could be used as a "stepping stone" to establish Ireland's formal—and republican—independence from Great Britain.[19] A Cumann na nGaedheal-led government confirmed the equality and independence of all the British dominions in the Statute of Westminster of 1931. From 1932 Fianna Fáil governments, under the leadership of de Valera, who had led most active republicans away from the abstentionist policies of Sinn Féin and the IRA, progressively dismantled most of the objectionable features of the Treaty. They removed the oath, abolished the post of governor general, recovered the Treaty ports, and established Ireland's external sovereignty—to the extent that it was able to remain neutral in World War II (formally in protest at the maintenance of partition). The removal of the requirement that deputies take an oath of allegiance to the British Crown, according to de Valera, removed the case for abstentionism in the South: deputies were now free to argue for the republican platform without British imposed impediments. Ireland freely established its popularly endorsed constitution (Bunreacht na hÉireann) in 1937 without British interference and created an elected president as head of state and external association with the British Commonwealth, that is, a republic in all but name. Later, a Fine Gael- and Clann na Poblachta-led coalition government proclaimed Ireland a Republic in 1949. The 1937 constitution vested sovereignty in the people of Ireland, made it plain that the institutions established were a product of Irish will, and (implicitly) repudiated the Government of Ireland Act (1920), which had partitioned Ireland. In Articles 2 and 3 of its constitution, it affirmed that the whole island of Ireland was "national territory," and reserved to the Irish parliament the right to govern all of Ireland, including the lost six counties. The 1949 declaration that independent Ireland was a Republic—it then left the British Commonwealth because that organization did not then accept republics—meant that the IRA was left with no meaningful grievance against Ireland's constitutional status. In short, the constitutional resentment at the Treaty in sovereign Ireland had been substantively resolved by 1937, in the view of one former IRA anti-Treaty man, who had become prime minister, de Valera, and by 1949, by another former anti-Treaty IRA man, Seán MacBride, who had become minister for external affairs.

The third phase, 1939–1956, saw a strong reorientation of the rump IRA, abandoned by many of its southern leftists, toward achieving Irish unification. Reversing partition was the last extant objectionable feature of the Treaty of 1921, arguably after 1937, and certainly after 1949. This reorientation began with a bombing campaign in England, after a formal declaration of notice and war, in 1939–1940. The campaign was a failure and the upshot was the imprisonment and the near extinction of the IRA's volunteers in both parts of Ireland as well as of its activists in England.[20] The IRA had to be rebuilt almost from scratch after World War II.[21] The logical corollary of the orientation toward ending partition was seen in an Army Convention resolution of 1948 that there would be no military action by the IRA in the twenty-six counties—which should in retrospect be read as the IRA's first step toward formal recognition of what it called the "Leinster House Parliament" (the site of Dáil Éireann). It was followed, shortly, by General Army Order No. 8, which forbade volunteers from defending their arms in the South or from any defensive actions in the South. In short, the IRA was no longer at war with independent Ireland. That armed struggle had been abandoned.

The fourth phase, the IRA campaign of 1956 to 1962, within Northern Ireland, launched from both the North and the South, was intended to liberate the six counties and to reunify Ireland using guerrilla warfare and armed propaganda. It was preceded by significant evidence of Northern Irish nationalist discontent with the Belfast regime, expressed in successive elections of Sinn Féin candidates. But it was a small-scale conflict, quickly repressed on both sides of the border, and ended in a thorough defeat, publicly acknowledged by the IRA's Army Council.[22]

The comprehensive failure of the IRA's armed struggle to liberate the North led to a fifth phase, between 1962 and 1969, when an emergent left wing-oriented leadership tried to take the IRA, South and North, strongly in the direction of communist politics, to make "reds" out of "greens." They were ready to abandon militarism and to shift toward recognition of Ireland's parliament and the abandonment of principled abstentionism.

This capsule history is, at first glance, one of comprehensive military, political, and strategic failure for the IRA. It went to war against the government of the Irish Free State (1922–1923), against the government of Great Britain in 1939, and against the Northern Ireland government in 1956. It was defeated in all three instances, had acknowledged each defeat, and by the early 1960s appeared to have a rendezvous with a coroner. Politically most of its members had been moral conservatives, Jeffersonian republicans rather than hard-line socialists—although socialists had been consistently the most ideologically driven of them, believing their position had been legitimated by the incorporation of Marxist James Connolly's Irish Citizen Army into the IRA in 1916. By the late 1960s in both parts of Ireland, and within the Irish diaspora, the IRA appeared to be a relic, a group of obsessives disconnected from contemporary politics. It had never repeated its successful symbiosis with Sinn Féin of 1919–1921, when a military and democratic political movement had combined and forced the UK government to negotiate with Irish republicans.

But failure was not the whole story. The IRA's founding agenda had been substantively realized in the South.[23] All southern governments from 1922 had former senior IRA men in their ministerial ranks. With the notable exception of Kevin O'Higgins, most were republicans with kindred beliefs to those of the IRA.[24] They progressively addressed its constitutional agenda, which was neither insane nor unprincipled, even if it was dogmatic, and even if it refused the right of a majority to be wrong on the constitutional status of the state. However, resentment did lead the IRA into increasingly bizarre ideological deductions. The deputies of the rump Second Dáil who had taken the anti-Treaty side, and who had withdrawn from participation in the "partitionist" Dáil Éireann, continued to meet until the late 1930s as if they were the valid parliament of Ireland. This, in turn, meant that the IRA's mandate stemmed from the last all-Ireland parliament—one that was increasingly, as time passed, demographically as well as chronologically removed from the current preferences of the people of Ireland, North and South. The demos from which the IRA derived its authority was frozen in time, increasingly virtual. Eventually, the aging deputies, the rump Second Dáil, authorized the IRA Army Council to be the government of Ireland until the Republic could be reestablished—although in the IRA's theory it had never been validly de jure "disestablished." It was, for example, in its capacity as the alleged government of the Irish Republic that the IRA declared war on Great Britain in January 1939.[25] Ideological, arcane, and progressively dated mandates did not stop with the view that the IRA was the Government of Ireland pending (the reestablishment of) the Republic and a validly constituted Dáil. The last surviving member of the rump Dáil, General Tom Maguire, was to live long enough to be twice asked to decide which section of the republican movement was the true inheritor of the mandate of the last valid Dáil (and thereby the valid government of the Republic of Ireland). In 1969, he decided that the mandate belonged with the Provisional IRA, and in 1986 that it belonged with those who rejected the decision of Sinn Féin to recognize the legitimacy of the Dublin parliament. On his death Maguire handed the baton on to Michael Flannery.[26]

This excursus into the repercussions of republican constitutional ideology might occasion laughter if the stakes were not so serious. In considering policy responses to political violence, it is too customary for analysts and policymakers to treat ideology and normative constitutional doctrine as masks for other interests or grievances, or as easily molded plasticine that can be rapidly reshaped as and when a movement requires. Policymakers tend to focus either on the incentives or opportunities that encourage or discourage the use of political violence, or on the material grievances held to underpin insurrectionary movements. These are not pointless dispositions. But ideologically barricaded organizations may be best induced to withdraw from violence if an internally principled path can be found for their members to abandon their use of violence. Governments that directly engage the ideological propositions and the constitutional norms of such movements may have greater success in promoting their internal transformations. That is one lesson one can extract from the progressive termination of the IRA as a serious subversive threat to the government of the Irish Free State, and its successor, the government of the Republic of Ireland. By progressively eliminating the obnoxious features of the Treaty of 1921, by transforming Ireland's constitutional status and laws, successive Irish governments rendered outmoded the IRA's constitutional objections to the "actually existing" Republic of Ireland. This assisted in the demobilization and constitutionalization of the IRA's members in the South, and their withdrawal from the politics of armed struggle. There is a forgotten logical counterfactual to this proposition. Had Irish governments not followed this path, and had British governments not reconciled themselves to it, whether by accident or design, independent Ireland's Civil War over the Treaty would have been renewed, and the IRA would have had greater support for attempting a coup d'état in the South.

Normative constitutional engagement with insurgents is not sufficient for making political settlements and peace, nor is what might be termed "constitutional appeasement" always appropriate or sufficient. The long-run success of Irish governments in marginalizing the IRA in the South owed a great deal to the regularly renewed democratic and majority mandates of such governments, their successful use of civil policing, extensive surveillance, intermittently severe repression under the rule of law, and the imposition of multiple hardships that induced many IRA veterans to leave the organization or to emigrate. One must not forget that the institutionalization of the Irish state, supported externally by Winston Churchill, was preceded by the thoroughly brutal—and frequently lawless—suppression of the majority of the IRA in the Civil War, including executive-authorized executions. Nevertheless, where military nationalist movements have constitutions that guide their conduct, and are organized around coherent constitutional resentment, constitutional engagement may be a necessary condition for conflict resolution. Having shown how the argument applies to the IRA in the South, I will later attempt to show that a similar argument can be used to interpret the IRA's willingness to sustain ceasefires in the 1990s and presently to consider its own disbandment.

## Provisional IRA: Objectives and Nature

The IRA could, and did, object to the failure of Irish governments to achieve Irish unification, but its volunteers knew that the major obstacle to Irish unification did not lie with what they persisted in calling the Free State. After all, governments of Ireland had diplomatically campaigned for Irish unification after 1937. Rather the obstacles lay with the UK government, and with the wishes of Ulster unionists, the strongest beneficiaries and supporters of the Treaty settlement.[27] The Provisional IRA was created in December 1969 in full knowledge of these facts, its twin sister, Provisional Sinn Féin, shortly afterward. The new IRA's first declaration affirmed its allegiance to "the Thirty-two County Irish Republic proclaimed at Easter 1916, established by Dáil Éireann in 1919, overthrown by force of arms in 1922 and suppressed to this day by the British-imposed Six County and Twenty-six County partitionist states," a restatement of the IRA's traditional stance.[28] The "Provisional" title served three functions. It echoed the "Provisional Government of the Irish Republic" proclaimed in 1916; it repudiated the "Official" IRA leaders, who had just sought to maneuver the IRA to end political abstentionism, and had, it was thought, used unconstitutional means to do so; and, last, "Provisional" suggested a temporary designation, pending the reorganization of the IRA. This mission was proclaimed accomplished in September 1970, but the name "Provisional IRA" and its derivatives "Provos" and "Provies" stuck.

The split between the Provisionals and the Officials is generally attributed to three cleavages. The Officials were Marxist, or on the verge of becoming so; the Provisionals were more nationalist; and the Officials preferred to build a political liberation front to military struggle.[29] There is truth in this characterization. The historian Roy Foster further maintains that the Officials were "woolly radicals dreaming of a national liberation front," whereas the Provisionals are typecast as "Defenderists" and "fundamentalists."[30] The Defenderist motif is commonplace in accounts of the Provisional IRA.[31] It suggests a lineage from the clandestine eighteenth-century agrarian Catholic nativist militia of Ulster who defended their coreligionists from Protestant settler vigilantes, the "Peep o' Day Boys," organized killers and expellers of Catholics. It insinuates that the Provisionals are more sectarian than ideological, and less committed to the civic citizenship agenda of Ireland's first eighteenth-century republicans, the United Irishmen (who fused the Defenders into their organization before the 1798 insurrection). It treats the Provisionals as atavistic.

The Defenderist motif appears to make sense because the impetus for the formation of the Provisional IRA was the unpreparedness of the IRA, North or South, for the assaults on Catholics, especially Belfast Catholics, by Protestant mobs, in collusion with the Royal Ulster Constabulary (RUC) and its auxiliaries, the B Specials, in August 1969. These assaults, which led to deaths, injuries, and expulsions, and the burning out of Bombay Street, are standardly described as "pogroms" in the memories of post-1969 Provisional IRA volunteers.[32] These assaults were responses to the then peaceful civil rights movement, which republicans had helped organize from 1966 to mobilize against deep injustices within Northern Ireland, modeling the protests on the U.S. civil rights movement.[33] The Provisionals were organized in immediate response to urban defenselessness, and to remonstrative graffiti on Belfast walls that declared "IRA = I Ran Away." But the post-1969 Provisionals were not atavistic throwbacks. Their new members were, mostly, urban working-class activists who saw themselves, initially, as defenders of their communities against contemporary loyalists, partisan police and partisan British troops. Their founding leaders soon persuaded them that active offense against the British state was the only or at least the best way to address the unreformable polity of Northern Ireland. To typecast the Provisionals as religious "fundamentalists" is as misleading as reading them as throwbacks. Their early and their later members included many self-styled socialists; and although the Provisionals have been overwhelmingly Catholic in social origin they have not, generally, been pious believers, have not followed the political advice of their Church's bishops—or the Pope—and are less overtly and traditionally Catholic than the volunteers of 1916 or the 1920s. There has never been a serving priest, let alone a bishop, in the IRA's Army Council or, to my knowledge, among its volunteers.[34] The IRA's symbolism may be suffused with a Catholic heritage, as some maintain, but it is the Irish nation rather than the Roman Catholic Church which they affirm, and to which they pledge allegiance. That said, the Provisionals were founded by "republican" fundamentalists, men who had fought in the failed 1956–1962 campaign, such as Ruairí Ó Brádaigh, Dáithí Ó Conaill, Seán Mac Stiofáin, and Joe Cahill, and who believed in the republican traditions, that is, in rejecting the Treaty's institutions and undoing partition by force.[35]

The Provisionals soon declared themselves at war with the British army, which had been deployed in Northern Ireland in 1969 in "support of the civil power," apparently in a peacekeeping role, and to head off a potential intervention by the Irish government, which had arranged at least one clandestine supply of arms to protect Northern Catholics.[36] The new IRA, which some wrongly maintain was brought into being through the active planning of the Irish government, argued that only British disengagement would resolve the conflicts on the island, but focused its initial attention on removing the Stormont parliament—through which the Ulster Unionist Party had organized systematic discrimination for nearly fifty years.[37] In 1970–1971, the Provisionals rapidly surpassed the Officials in militancy and recruitment among Catholic youths; and from 1969 until 1997, with breaks in 1972, 1974–1975, and 1994–1996, this new IRA organized a sustained insurrection. It has not succeeded in unifying Ireland, but regards itself as having removed the majoritarian and tyrannous Stormont parliament in 1972. It was not militarily defeated by what is widely acknowledged as the most capable European army, nor, after 1976, by an extremely large, armed, reorganized, and well-funded police force, the Royal Ulster Constabulary.

Operating mostly within a territory with just over a million and a half people, and for most of that time within a support base of a minority of the minority cultural Catholic population of approximately 650,000, the IRA's organizational endurance was impressive. It survived the efforts of five UK prime ministers to crush it—Harold Wilson, Edward Heath, James Callaghan, Margaret Thatcher, and John Major. The IRA's leaders negotiated, directly or indirectly, with all these prime ministers. The leader of the UK opposition, Harold Wilson, who was to be prime minister again between 1974 and 1976, met the IRA in Dublin in 1971. In 1972, an IRA negotiating team, including the young Gerry Adams and Martin McGuinness, met with Heath's deputy prime minister, William Whitelaw, in London. The IRA would later indirectly negotiate with Wilson's government in 1974–1975, and with Major's between 1990 and 1996. Thatcher must have authorized

Peter Brooke, then secretary of state for Northern Ireland, to open negotiations about negotiations by proxy with the IRA in 1989.[38] And since 1997 the IRA has been indirectly—directly on some interpretations—negotiating with another British prime minister, Tony Blair. In the same period it has negotiated, indirectly or directly, with four Irish prime ministers—Charles Haughey, Albert Reynolds, John Bruton, and Bertie Ahern. In short, "talking to terrorists" has been considered a necessary risk by six British premiers, and at least four recent Irish premiers.

What is known about the contemporary IRA? Transparency cannot be the dominant trait of an underground army. The names of the IRA Army Council and Executive leaders, although widely guessed, reported, and denied, are organizational secrets, which Ed Moloney claims to know. Presently many of its serving volunteers freely supply journalists with extensive information about intra-IRA debates, apparently in violation of IRA General Army Order No. 3, "No member . . . shall make any statement either verbally or in writing to the press or mass media without General Headquarters permission."[39] Most studies of the IRA are dependent on authorized interviews.[40] There are, of course, some documentary materials. The IRA, since its first effective organizer Michael Collins, has been textual. Its 1979 "Green Book" is a manual of lectures on constitutional commitments, rules for recruits, and guidance for volunteers facing interrogation.[41] The IRA tries to keep fastidious records in notebooks and electronic media. This trait has, of course, often compromised secrecy. Peter Taylor's remarkable account of an interview with Ruairí Ó Brádaigh shows that the IRA's leaders keep extensive minutes, and that these minutes are authoritative.[42] It is equally clear that no journalist, let alone historian, has had access to full copies of such records, and whether they will eventually become available or revelatory cannot be known. They are, however, more likely to be reliable than some of today's literature and pulp fiction. For source materials on the IRA, serious analysts are dependent on the organization's formal communiqués; transcripts of its authorized interviews with journalists and academics; public police and court records of volunteers and prisoners; stolen, lost, or leaked British or Irish army, police, MI5, MI6, and Ministry of Defense intelligence reports; accounts of conflictual incidents and victims of incidents; and what can be gleaned from the memoirs, autobiographies, and authorized and unauthorized biographies of the IRA's leaders and volunteers, or from the National Graves Association, which provides a roll call of the republican war dead.[43] There are also the suspect but potentially informative accounts of volunteers turned spies, or of those who have abandoned the cause.[44] What follows is a provisional summary of what is known about the IRA from a critical but impartial appraisal of these sources.

## Structure: Division of Labor, Recruits, and Numbers

Until 1977 the IRA was organized, as it had been since the Irish Civil War of 1922–1923, as a shadow or underground version of the British army, complete with officers, staff and line, and territorial brigades, battalions, and companies. In 1976–1977 it was reorganized in smaller cellular structures, active service units (ASUs), each intended to be specialized (e.g., in sniping, executions, bombings, robberies), and to comprise a small number of volunteers. The idea was to intensify the division of labor and create a more compact organization, less vulnerable both to volunteers' surrendering information and to intelligence losses through informants.[45] In this reformation, several hundred volunteers, especially many ex-prisoners, were excluded from the ASUs as security risks because they were easily monitored or otherwise regarded as unreliable. Nevertheless, after the change some of the old nomenclature of battalions and brigades was preserved—and in Crossmaglen and Tyrone lip service was paid to the change.[46]

Presented in a formal organizational chart, the top tier of the IRA consists of the Executive (12 members), elected by the General Army Convention, which did not meet between 1970 and 1986, because of the danger of mass arrests. As the agency responsible for the IRA's constitution, the Convention is its sovereign. The Executive elects and, nominally, holds to account the Army Council (7 members), the operational executive chaired by the chief of staff. The General Headquarters (GHQ) of the IRA staff is organized functionally into "offices": quartermaster general, operations, engineering, intelligence, finance, training, security, publicity, and political education. Operations are organized by area: England, Europe, and, since reorganization, two Irish commands, "Southern" and "Northern."[47] The role of Southern Command is to act as the supplier and stockist for Northern Command—and for many operations in England. To judge by arms, guns, ammunition, explosive devices, and bomb-making equipment found by the Garda Síochána (the Irish police) in the decade preceding the ceasefires of the 1990s, most matériel was kept in the border counties, or in the Greater Dublin region, which makes logistical sense, although extrapolating from the location of "finds" may be misleading because matériel may be more successfully hidden elsewhere in rural Ireland. Before and after reorganization the IRA sought to establish a pyramidical command and control organization, like a functioning army. But, of necessity, the IRA has been extensively decentralized, reliant on the initiatives and flair of its semiautonomous units:

> The Army Council and the GHQ were engaged in oversight, not command. Operational matters were often controlled by those close to the target. Intelligence was apt to arrive rather than be sought. GHQ spent a great deal of time balancing demands and seeking resources rather than in directing a war. All the strategic deci-

sions had been made. Most tactical decisions were shaped by opportunity and vulnerabilities. Initiative was seldom punished . . . in reality the IRA ran on a consensus achieved largely unconsciously. . . . Operational freedom often meant blunders, innocent people killed, incompetents sent in harm's way, bombs detonated when quiet was needed; but there was every indication that tight control from the centre would hardly have changed matters.[48]

The IRA has its own internal security, colloquially known as the "nutting squad," whose mission is to interrogate, court-martial, and, where deemed necessary, execute suspected spies or informants.[49] It also organizes vigilante justice through punishment squads of auxiliaries, a lower tier of generally lower caliber volunteers, who are not members of the ASUs, although they can graduate to them.[50] The administration of "punishment beatings," what I call policing without prisons, may take the form of brutal beatings of limbs with baseball bats or iron bars, or of "kneecappings" with gunshots. This is one of the most politically and morally sensitive subjects for the IRA's supporters and apologists. It is clear from interviews that republican leaders would be delighted to be divested of any association with the system—even though one standard analysis is that the IRA's leaders support punishment beatings to entrench their local power. The punishment beating system, which has its counterpart among loyalists, has been both a demand and a supply problem for the IRA. Rough justice is demanded for alleged offenders and petty criminals in nationalist working-class communities, especially where the IRA is dominant, and where calling on the services of the police, especially the unreformed RUC, has been unimaginable—not least because police officers have often been unwilling to go where they might be set up and shot. IRA leaders in Belfast felt it necessary to meet some of this demand—and at least some auxiliaries have performed punishment beatings with sadistic enthusiasm. The supply problem has been occasioned when the IRA has a surplus of potential volunteers who might otherwise either join other republican organizations or dilute the caliber of the core organization. Organizing the surplus in auxiliaries and punishment squads solves some of this problem. The system is one of the grisliest byproducts of the absence of legitimate state institutions.[51]

The IRA's finances are, of course, not "known" but are subject to extensive speculation. Journalists regularly report Irish police and RUC estimates as authoritative, but they cannot be, at least not without confirmation from the IRA's internal "accountants" and "auditors."[52] Albeit dated, the most interesting evaluation, precisely because it was not intended for publication, remains that of the stolen report of Brigadier James Glover of 1978.[53] It estimated IRA annual income at UK£950,000, and expenditure at £780,000, that is, with an annual surplus of £170,000, 17.9 percent, available for arms, ammunition, and explosives.[54] Glover estimated expenditure as devoted, in descending order of importance, to four items: volunteers' pay, travel and transport costs, propaganda, and prisoner support. He considered the IRA had four principal sources of income, in descending order of importance: theft and robbery in Ireland, racketeering in Ireland, overseas donations, and the Green Cross (a prisoners' aid organization). "Overseas donations" were estimated at £120,000, 12.6 percent of revenues, and were not expected to rise.[55] Glover assumed that the IRA's commercial undertakings were marred by "dishonesty and incompetence" and were poor sources of revenue, other than its black taxi service. He listed no domestic Irish donations at all, which seems incredible. His estimated outlay per volunteer assumed that a £20 per week supplement was paid to 250 volunteers drawing UK unemployment benefits, and that a further 60 were paid £40 per week (implying a partly or fully paid cadre of just over 300 volunteers). More recent estimates of the IRA's annual income range from U.S.$10 million to the figure of £10 million usually cited by contemporary police sources to journalists.[56] These figures imply a significant growth of revenues since the mid-1970s, even allowing for inflation. Sources of income, contra Glover's expectations, have included commercial undertakings—social clubs and service and and hospitality centers also serving as money-laundering operations—as well as extortion, armed robberies, and, no doubt, domestic donations. Kidnapping, as Glover makes clear, has been regarded as counterproductive and unauthorized, although it took place in the 1970s.

If one compares Glover's report with subsequent estimates of IRA income and expenditures, three judgments cannot be avoided. First, running the IRA is a relatively cheap operation, primarily dependent on the donated time and sacrifices of its volunteers.[57] Second, the IRA demonstrates the power of the weak. It does not need large expenditures to have dramatic and powerful impacts. Small numbers of determined militants can build and use relatively cheap "homemade" or improvised explosives (fertilizer and mortar bombs), install custom-made sleeper-devices with devastating effects, and own, maintain, and use relatively cheap guns. Third, the low estimates of the IRA's financial surplus and of resources available per volunteer strongly suggest that "rent-seeking" or "greed-based" accounts of its maintenance lack empirical foundation—Glover acknowledged that "we cannot accurately judge the extent to which they line their own pockets."[58] In short, the focus of policymakers on closing down or squeezing the IRA's finances, while a necessary and predictable response, was never likely to be pivotal in affecting its performance.

Who volunteered to join the IRA? First of all, most volunteers have been young males, although there are female members, and there is a long-standing women's republican organization, Cumann na mBan. Second, the founding membership of the Provisionals was from families with long ties to the IRA, dating back to the 1920s, and in some cases back to the Fenians of the 1860s.[59] This core provided the nucleus around which the

IRA had survived after the 1940s. (Familial socialization, of course, is not pervasive: many males with such relatives did not become volunteers.) Third, IRA recruits are nearly all young males of Catholic origin, mostly from working-class, small farmer, or lower-middle-class occupations. The list of the occupations of 95 IRA prisoners imprisoned for more than three years in Belfast Prison between 1956 and 1960 is revealing.[60] It included just one businessman. Construction workers, farmers, clerks, and industrial apprentices predominated. They were neither prosperous professionals, nor "lumpenproletarians." Twenty years later the Glover Report (1978) stated: "Our evidence of the calibre of rank and file [IRA] terrorists does not support the view that they are mindless hooligans drawn from the unemployed and the unemployable."[61] Two surveys of republican offenders coming before the courts found that the data "beyond reasonable doubt" established that the bulk of them were young men and women "without criminal records in the ordinary sense, though some have been involved in public disorders [but] in this respect and in their records of employment and unemployment they are reasonably representative of the working class community of which they form a substantial part [and] do not fit the stereotype of criminality which the authorities have from time to time attempted to attach to them."[62]

IRA recruits are therefore not criminals, gangsters, or mafiosi, despite the aforementioned auxiliaries involved in punishment squads. The gangster motif, as former IRA volunteer Patrick Magee, known as the "Brighton bomber," shows in an intelligent published doctoral thesis, is the most stale cliché in the popular or pulp fiction generated by the conflict.[63] It is also a theme highlighted in British press, broadcasting reportage, and cartoons. Journalist Scott Anderson wrote under the heading "Making a Killing" to popularize the gangster idea in the U.S.[64] It is more startling to find the contention reproduced by a thoughtful liberal intellectual, my friend Michael Ignatieff, who has lived in the UK and reported on Northern Ireland. His *The Lesser Evil* maintains "there will always be a gap between those who take the political goals of a terrorist campaign seriously and those who are drawn to the cause because it offers glamour, violence, money and power. It is anyone's guess how many actual believers in the dream of a united Ireland there are in the ranks of the IRA. But it is a fair bet to suppose that many recruits join up because they want to benefit from the IRA's profitable protection rackets." He footnotes Taylor's *Provos* and Coogan's *IRA*, without pagination, before continuing, "The IRA bears as much relation to the Mafia as it does to an insurrectionary cell or a radical political party and the motivations that draw young people into the movement are often as criminal as they are political. . . . The criminal allure of terrorist groups and the cynicism of those who join them are additional reasons why it is a mistake to conciliate or appease a group like the IRA with political concessions."[65]

There is no serious empirical warrant for these views, certainly not in the books of Coogan and Taylor. "Believing in the dream of a united Ireland" is not an impartial characterization, and while this belief may not be the primary motivation for all members to join, affirmation of the goal is a condition of membership. Ignatieff's knowledge of volunteers' private inner desires is just speculation, and he appears unaware that experience of state repression or of attacks by loyalists is the most widespread shared feature of post-1969 IRA recruits.[66] These considerations undermine the "criminal" characterization of the IRA's volunteers. Robert White's interviews, and statements by republican leaders, show convincingly that surges in applications to join the IRA are directly linked to political events, rather than to "rent-seeking" opportunities. Attacks on the civil rights movement, loyalist mobs burning out Catholics from their homes in Belfast, the Falls Road curfew by the British army, internment without trial, Bloody Sunday, and the British government's response to the hunger strikes of 1980–1981, were more potent sources of recruitment than the meager material "rewards" facing volunteers. The evidence is in fact strongly against the criminal motivation thesis.[67] IRA "surpluses" do not enrich its leaders, and if they did, this would be a major UK media theme. Gerry Adams has doubtless become prosperous, after the peace process, but from his published writings. There is no evidence that he was enriched through his IRA or Sinn Féin roles. IRA members do not personally profit from takings; if they do, they are excluded from the organization, punished, or suffer moral disapproval. This can be seen in the critical accounts of Martin McGartland (1997) and Eamon Collins (1997). Volunteers in ASUs rely on minimal support, as do those "on the run," and the auxiliaries' role is to punish petty criminals, not to lead them—though, of course, some may behave contrary to the organization's norms. Earning respect from local peers rather than profits is a better explanation of membership of vigilante and punishment squads.[68] The IRA's resources, however dubiously or criminally obtained, are overwhelmingly channeled back into mission-related activities. The IRA recruited those willing to risk their lives or long jail sentences for what they warned would likely be a dangerous and short career. In short, group-oriented, nonpecuniary, and nonegoistic motivations have been key to both recruitment and retention.

The costs of membership have been high: the risks of death or long-run imprisonment are plain, and the costs have also been borne by family and loved ones, even if support is provided to the families of imprisoned volunteers. Famously, IRA volunteers have been resistant to prison management techniques that "ordinary criminals" generally accept without organized protest or rancor.[69] This is not to say that all IRA recruits epitomize austere republican virtue, merely to affirm that personal criminal opportunism among volunteers is punished. The IRA, famously, does not "do drugs," and has attempted to "close down" a rival republican organization, the

Irish National Liberation Army (INLA), when it started this mode of "self-financing." Northern Ireland, by contrast with the rest of the UK and Ireland, as many have observed, has been politically rather than criminally violent.[70]

Ignatieff and others have the direction of causality wrong. Defeated violent nationalist organizations may become mafias, but they do not originate as such, nor will they have extensive legitimacy if they become such. One priority of the Irish peace process is to ensure the rehabilitation of former republican paramilitaries—and, to date, rates of recidivism, political or criminal, among ex-IRA prisoners have been strikingly low and further evidence against the criminal motivation thesis. The IRA, INLA, and Continuity and Real IRAs may come to resemble mafias in the course of their respective dissolutions, but this will constitute the corruption of their missions, not their starting motivations. Indeed one may argue that the policy implications of the criminality thesis have been tested to destruction in Northern Ireland.[71] The hunger strikes of 1980–1981, which led to the revitalization of support for both the IRA and Sinn Féin, were a demand for recognition as political prisoners and not as criminals. The authorities faced the obvious problem that most of those incarcerated were incarcerated under "scheduled offences," that is, special procedures for politically motivated special offenses. Precisely because the IRA was a political agency, it needed to be treated politically as well as legally (though plainly any politically violent agency in a liberal democratic state violates the criminal law). Had Ignatieff's counsel—not to conciliate or appease the IRA with political concessions—been followed, there would never have been a Good Friday Agreement in 1998, and perhaps another thousand people would have died since 1994 because of a false theory of motivation.

There is no sustained evidence that the IRA's recruits are psychologically abnormal. Studies comparing the murderers committing political as opposed to nonpolitical killings in Northern Ireland confirm this appraisal, and thereby support the general finding in research on political violence and terrorism that ethnonational terrorists are "normal," that is, representative of their social bases.[72] Yeatsian-tinged psychological portraits of Irish republicans nevertheless abound in the literature. Patrick Bishop and Eamonn Mallie title the Prologue to their *Provisional IRA*, "Fanatic Hearts," after Yeats's lines, "Out of Ireland have we come / Great hatred, little room / Maimed us at the start / I carry from my mother's womb / A fanatic heart." It is good poetry; it is not social psychology. Kevin Toolis claims to have journeyed "within the IRA's soul"—fine words, but not convincing science. Bishop and Mallie see IRA violence as an inevitable psychological product of partition: "Even if the leadership were to abandon violence, another violent organization would spring up in its place. As long as Ireland is divided, violent republicanism will be an ineradicable tradition."[73]

This is an extreme psychopolitical claim that will be tested when the IRA disbands.

The spatial origin of IRA recruits has changed. In the 1956–1962 campaign significant numbers of southerners were involved. Today, except, of course, in Southern Command, northerners predominate at all ranks—although there are still significant numbers of volunteers from or living in the southern border counties. The IRA's evolution is, in part, the story of it being taken over by northerners, those with most to complain about the long-term repercussions of the Treaty of 1921.

IRA volunteers are Irish nationalists, in identity and as a result of experience. They did not all grow up in Irish nationalist households, and, indeed, there have been a small number of Irish Protestant and English-born volunteers, but most are Irish nationalists by birth or by culture and learning. They believe that Great Britain denied the Irish people its right to self-determination when it partitioned Ireland, that Northern Ireland is an artificial entity which cannot function as a democracy, and, until recently, that it is unreformable, that is, Catholics or nationalists cannot be treated as the equals of Protestants and unionists within the UK. The IRA's nationalist character bears emphasis because it is so often portrayed in international media as religiously motivated. It is vital to preserve the distinction between nationalist agents who use political violence (whether in democratic or undemocratic settings) and the salvationist violence of religious fundamentalists (such al-Qaeda). The distinction is not just important for analytical accuracy. Nationalists prepared to use force may be repressed (but rarely fully), or negotiated with (successfully or otherwise), or both. By contrast, cosmopolitan religious fundamentalists can be thoroughly repressed in some circumstances, because they are likely to be territorially infrequent and isolated, but they cannot be negotiated with as long as they retain their beliefs. It is an error, into which Ignatieff slips, to conflate liberal opposition to nationalist violence with liberal opposition to religious fundamentalism.

A last word about the IRA's recruits since 1969 regarding numbers: we do not have the IRA's personnel records; none of the major books on the IRA list "numbers" in its index (some do not have indexes).[74] It is standard to estimate between 300 and 500 volunteers in ASUs, a measure of the "stock" of militant activists that probably derives from leaks of the IRA's own organizational planning changes of 1976–1977, which informed the Glover Report. It seems reasonable to assume approximately an equivalent number of "cadets" in training, and in the auxiliaries, at any one time, suggesting an annual stock of ASUs and reserves and auxiliaries of about 900. As for total flow, Martin McGuinness, a former chief of staff, is widely cited as having suggested that more than 10,000 people have been in and through the IRA's ranks since 1969. One journalist, Eamonn Mallie, reports that the IRA told him that between "eight and ten thousand" of its personnel had been imprisoned before 1987.[75] The gap between estimates of current stock and total flow make sense when one recognizes the high attrition rate of volunteers, through death, injury, incarceration, flight—or resignation. The IRA is not like "Hotel California"—one can leave. Most volunteers are expected to retire after having served a sentence. A formal check on the 10,000 estimate of the total flow is the stock and flow of the prison population. The average daily number of prisoners in Northern Ireland's jails in 1969 was approximately 600; by 1979 it had reached nearly 3,000—a figure that excluded IRA volunteers in jails in Great Britain and Ireland, but included loyalist prisoners. From 1985 until 1997 the Northern Ireland prison population stabilized at around 2,000 as a daily average.[76] The cited estimate of a total flow of IRA volunteers of 10,000 is therefore credible (especially given that a significant number may never have been incarcerated). It suggests that an extraordinarily high proportion of Northern Irish working-class Catholic males who matured after 1969 have been through IRA ranks.

## Tactics, Strategy, Costs of Conflict

Between 1919 and 1921 the IRA improvised to create a standard template in modern violent politics, inventing contemporary guerrilla warfare, flying columns that avoided facing the imperial power in the field of formal war, and modes of resistance and rejection that attacked the state's sovereignty and its core functionaries, especially its police and intelligence agencies, but in conjunction with a wider democratic movement, of which the most important component was a political party, Sinn Féin. This party's name, standardly translated as "Our Selves," can also be translated as "Ourselves Alone," or even as "Self-Determination," according to Bill Kissane.[77] Sinn Féin, backed by the IRA's cutting edge, established a parallel state, creating what is nowadays known, after Trotsky, as a situation of "dual power." The forte of the IRA, orchestrated by Collins, was killing policemen and intelligence officers—which broke the imperial state's surveillance and control capabilities. It ensured that the IRA was far more effective than all previous Irish insurrectionary movements; it showed how a war of the flea could confound an imperial elephant, provided that the elephant felt restrained from destroying the habitat of the flea.

The contemporary IRA also innovated. It invented new modes of urban guerrilla warfare, donating the "car bomb" to the known repertoires of political violence. Political murders, assassinations, tit-for-tat shootings, and "human bombs" made the IRA infamous, as did "tarring-and feathering" and kneecapping. It was arguably less effective than the old IRA in killing senior military, police, and intelligence officers. It failed to assist its party in creating dual power or a parallel state—unless one counts the vigilante system. It also showed greater political and moral weakness than its predecessor by its expanded conception of legitimate targets—including nonuniformed off-duty police and soldiers, retired police and soldiers, and workers in organizations supplying nonmilitary services to the army and the police. (But, as Glover noted, it generally has not attacked the families of police and soldiers.)

The IRA is not proud of its techniques of disciplining its own membership and community, but it has undoubtedly been resourceful. The IRA's campaign has been conducted in Northern Ireland, Great Britain, and in places as far apart as Gibraltar and British military bases in Germany, leading to the deaths of approximately 200 people outside the main "war theater." Fundraising and weapons running were organized in places as distinct as Carter's and Reagan's United States and Colonel Qadhafi's Libya.[78] It tied down tens of thousands of UK soldiers for three decades, imposed immense economic damage on the region and on the UK exchequer, assassinated key members of the British political elite, including Lord Louis Mountbatten, a member of the royal family, and twice came within a whisker of blowing up the UK prime minister and cabinet. The bulk of the IRA's violence, of course, was organized within Northern Ireland, where it was spatially concentrated, notably in Belfast. Allowing for the ceasefires, the IRA's thirty-year campaign is one of the longest nationalist insurgencies in the postwar world, certainly the most enduring in the established liberal democracies.

The Provisional IRA developed a fearsome capability and reputation. Between 1969 and 1994 it was responsible for more deaths, over 1,750, than any other agency in the conflict (see Figure 6.1).[79] It outkilled all other republican organizations, all "loyalist" (pro-regime) paramilitaries combined, and all loyalist *and* all other republican paramilitaries combined. It significantly outkilled the individual and combined official forces of the UK: the British army, the Royal Ulster Constabulary, the B Specials—and their successors, the Ulster Defence Regiment (UDR) and the Royal Irish Regiment (RIR). According to *Lost Lives*, by David McKittrick, Seamus Kelters, Brian Feeney, and Chris Thornton, the (Provisional) IRA was responsible for 48.5 percent of the more than 3,600 deaths arising from the conflict between 1966 and 2001. By contrast, the IRA lost nearly 300 volunteers, 8 percent of the total victims. Richard English, using an earlier version of the same data source, maintains that civilians formed the largest single category of IRA victims (642), followed by the British forces (456), the RUC (273), the Ulster Defence Regiment or Royal Irish Regiment (182), republicans (162), loyalists (28), prison officers (23), and others (12).[80] His conclusion depends upon disaggregating the security forces and aggregating civilians. A different way to frame the same data, as I have done in Figure 6.1, is to observe that 967 of the IRA's victims were military, police, prison officers, or loyalist paramilitaries—that is, the IRA killed more of its self-defined targets than civilians. But that still means that only just over 54 per-

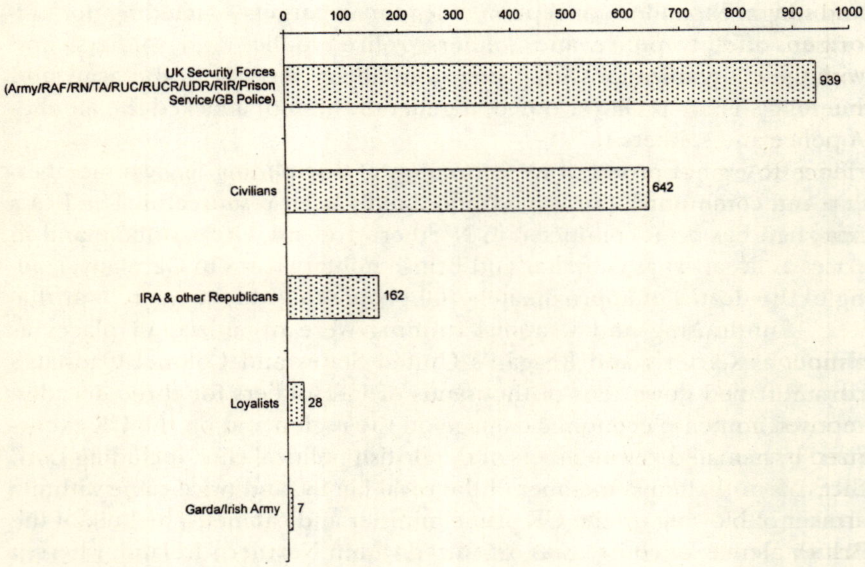


Figure 6.1. Deaths for which the IRA was responsible, 1969–2001 (total: 1778). Adapted from McKittrick et al., *Lost Lives*, 1504.

cent of its victims fell within its official legitimate targets, roughly one in two. In any military appraisal of its war, this must constitute the strongest indictment.

The IRA's violence made Northern Ireland the most politically violent region in the European Community (later the Union). The numbers killed between 1969 and 1990 exceeded those killed as a result of political violence in all other EC countries put together. In 1973–1982 violence in Northern Ireland alone placed the UK at the top of a league table of nineteen western European states in deaths from political violence and political assassinations.[81] The absolute death toll naturally pales in contrast with the major civil, colonial, and ethnic wars of the postwar authoritarian world. The British authorities have not suppressed the population that explicitly or tacitly supports the IRA in the manner experienced by Algerian Muslims, Kurds of Iraq, Kashmiri Muslims, Palestinian Muslims and Christians, South African blacks, or Sri Lankan Tamils. The British authorities treated incarcerated IRA prisoners relatively mildly by contrast with what was meted out in Latin American, African, or South Asian jails. Yet these observations can mislead. Nearly all wars and civil wars between 1945 and 1990 were exacerbated by superpower rivalries, or by regional powers and neighboring states. These factors did not operate in Northern Ireland—which proves how deep ethnonational conflict can become in geopolitically isolated regions. The U.S. government deplored violence in Northern Ireland

and sought to prevent unofficial support from Irish-Americans, in the form of guns and money, from reaching the IRA. The "special relationship" with the UK consistently proved more important for American geopolitical interests during the Cold War than the ethnic sentiments of some Irish-Americans. The Soviet Union, by contrast, used the Northern Ireland experience to embarrass the UK, for example, in reference to the jailing of innocent Irish people in Great Britain, like the Guildford Four, the Birmingham Six, and the Maguire Seven, but played no role in fomenting the conflict. The two states with most at stake, the UK and Ireland, despite multiple disagreements, generally sought to cooperate to contain the conflict. The IRA did not champion and were not championed by Ireland—although the British regarded Ireland as the IRA's "safe haven." Loyalist paramilitaries embarrassed British politicians—and such support as they received from the security forces (so far) appears to have been unauthorized by ministers. The sole third-party state that sought to inflame the conflict, Libya, was neither a regional power nor a neighbor. Its supplying of arms in 1974–1975, and again in 1988, was retaliation for American and British actions against the régime of Colonel Qadhafi. The conflict of the last thirty years has therefore been extremely intense given that it took place in a small region, in the presence of moderately amicable relations between the relevant neighboring states and regional powers, and in the absence of operational superpower rivalries. In duration, the present conflict easily outranks all others in twentieth-century Ireland, and only the Irish Civil War exceeds it in intensity.

How did people die? In assassinations (a plurality of all deaths); gun battles, crossfire, snipers' bullets, and ambushes; explosions or from antipersonnel devices; and a small proportion in riots or affrays. Over half of republican killings, mostly by the IRA, took place during gun-battles/crossfire, sniping incidents, ambushes, or through explosives and antipersonnel devices; by contrast, most loyalist killings were assassinations.[82] But a third of deaths caused by republicans were assassinations. There were, in effect, two wars. First, a war of national, ethnic, and communal assassination, executed by IRA volunteers, loyalist paramilitaries, and some UK security personnel. There was also a guerrilla and counterinsurgency war, with riots and affrays, especially in the early years, enhancing the numbers killed. In aggregate, paramilitary killings of civilians outnumbered those killed in the guerrilla war between republican paramilitaries and the security forces. The number of civilians killed through targeting, or through "collateral damage," by republicans loyalists, and UK security forces amounted to approximately half of the total number killed. The paramilitary "defenders" of the two major communities had dramatically fewer casualties than the civilians they claimed to be defending. (See Figures 6.2 and 6.3 for the annual death tolls and responsibilities for them.) The IRA failed to make and present the war as a clean fight between Irish republicans and the Brit-

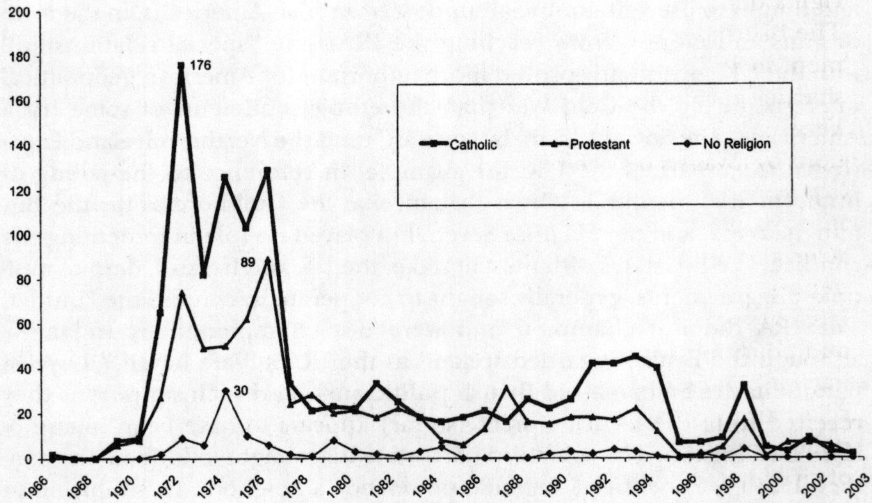


Figure 6.2. Civilian casualties from conflict, 1966–2003. Adapted from McKittrick et al., *Lost Lives*, updated.

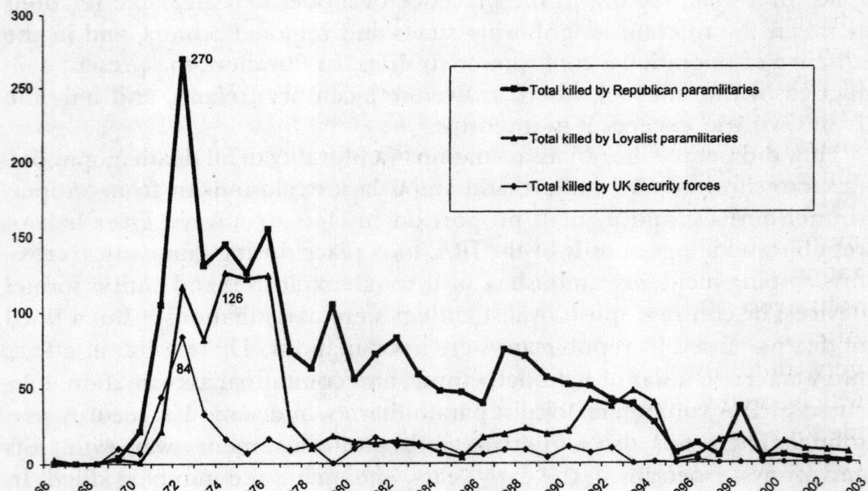


Figure 6.3. Responsibility for killing by year, 1966–2003. Adapted from McKittrick et al., *Lost Lives*, updated excluding killings by "others/civilians/not known."

ish state; the British state failed to make and present the conflict as just a dispute between two unreasonable communities, but had some success in doing so; loyalists helped veto a British disengagement.

The high death toll in the early years is explained by three factors. The first was the "loyalist backlash," both proactive and retaliatory, against civil rights demonstrations in the late 1960s, and then against the IRA's war. The British government's decision to abolish the Northern Ireland parliament in 1972 and its efforts between 1973 and 1976 to establish a power-sharing government with all-Ireland institutions increased loyalist fears. Very high numbers of Catholic civilians were victims of sectarian assassinations by loyalists between 1971 and 1975. The intention was to deter Catholics from supporting the IRA, but because loyalists did not have reliable information on IRA volunteers, "representative" killing of randomly selected Catholic civilians, identified by their first names, surnames, or residences, predominated. The second factor was the decision by the IRA to launch its war, employing classical guerrilla techniques against UK army and police personnel. But it also extensively engaged in large-scale bombings of commercial targets, such as factories and shopping centers. Guerrilla warfare produced large numbers of casualties among inexperienced police and soldiers, while commercial bombings led to significant numbers of civilian deaths, especially in Belfast; Martin McGuinness, by repute, organized the urban bombing of Derry with far less collateral damage. The third factor was the repressive—and counterproductive—policy of internment without trial of suspected terrorists, which lasted between 1971 and 1975. Initially targeted (inaccurately) exclusively at republicans, the policy produced widespread resentment throughout the Catholic population, acted as a recruiting agency for the IRA, and added fuel to the fire.

Explanations for the fall-off in deaths after 1976 complement this analysis. Loyalists reduced their killings of Catholics, both absolutely and as a share of the total death toll, because their fears of a British withdrawal had diminished—and were not revived until the Anglo-Irish Agreement of 1985. Loyalists were arrested and jailed and their organizations became more factionalized, corrupt, and directionless. The IRA changed its organization, and strategy, in ways that reduced the annual death toll. Many of its volunteers had been jailed; and in response the ASUs were developed. After 1976 the IRA primarily aimed to attack "military" and "police" targets, and until the early 1990s reduced its urban commercial bombing, which had threatened to undermine its support. The IRA became responsible for a lower annual death toll, but a higher share of the total death toll. Furthermore, more effective surveillance and intelligence among the security forces reduced the levels of violence. The authorities abandoned internment in 1975–1976. A battery of new containment techniques was employed. Up to 30,000 personnel patrolled the countryside and city streets, establishing armed "checkpoints." Forts and observation posts with the latest surveillance technologies were established in the heart of nationalist districts, including in school premises. House searching and civilian screening took place on a massive scale, backed up by computerized databases on over one quarter of the population. Armored vehicles, bomb-disposal robots, and "jelly-sniffers" were used to protect security force personnel. Entire "town centers" were cordoned off, and everybody entering such areas subjected to rigorous searching. Emergency legislation weakened civil liberties and facilitated the apprehension and sentencing of suspected paramilitaries.

Finally, all experienced "learning curves." In 1970, the IRA had to make an average of 191 attacks to kill a single member of the security forces; by 1984, 18 were sufficient.[83] The security forces became more vigilant to defend themselves. They also, formally, became more restrained: in the early 1970s they were permitted to shoot at identified petrol bombers but now are supposed to use "minimum force" weaponry, like plastic bullets. The return to "police primacy" in 1977 was associated with a reduced level of killings. Armed police are more restrained than soldiers trained to kill in combat. Personal and collective surveillance and security management by ordinary citizens also increased. They traveled warily in "shatter-zones" or "frontiers," or avoided them altogether; and migration from "mixed areas" to ethnically segregated residences in the 1970s reduced the opportunities for "soft" or "easy" killings. The time series show a dramatic falling off in the number of deaths sustained by the British army—excluding the locally recruited regiments. The local security forces (UDR, RIR, RUC, and RUC Reserve) suffered an increasing proportion of the deaths sustained by the security forces. This was the predictable product of "Ulsterization," the UK's post-1975 policy preference for local security forces—which reduced the UK's vulnerability to the loss of British-recruited troops, but increased its dependency upon local Protestants who were less likely to be impartial. It also occasioned a switch in the targets chosen by the IRA: it was easier to kill local security force members, at their homes, or off duty, than to kill soldiers in fortified barracks or in armored vehicles.

Who suffered most in the conflict? Who was most sectarian among the paramilitaries? These questions are not amenable to easy empirical treatment. Estimates of numbers of victims are available, under various labels (see Figure 6.4). Since each choice of label affects numbers, all appraisals are contested.[84] It is extremely difficult to code motivations, or even the primary motivations of the killers. Taking civilians alone, the largest single category of victims has been Catholic, and since Protestant civilians outnumber Catholic civilians by approximately 3 to 2, Catholic civilians suffered more deaths, absolutely and relatively, than Protestant civilians. Appraisal cannot rest there. Catholic civilians were the primary targets of loyalist paramilitaries, and the security forces were the primary targets of the IRA, but these facts obscure an important consideration. The local security forces were recruited primarily from Protestants. A simple comparison of Catholic and Protestant civilian death rates therefore obscures the casualties suffered by the Protestant community. That said, the nearly 300 dead mostly Catholic IRA volunteers almost directly match the over 300

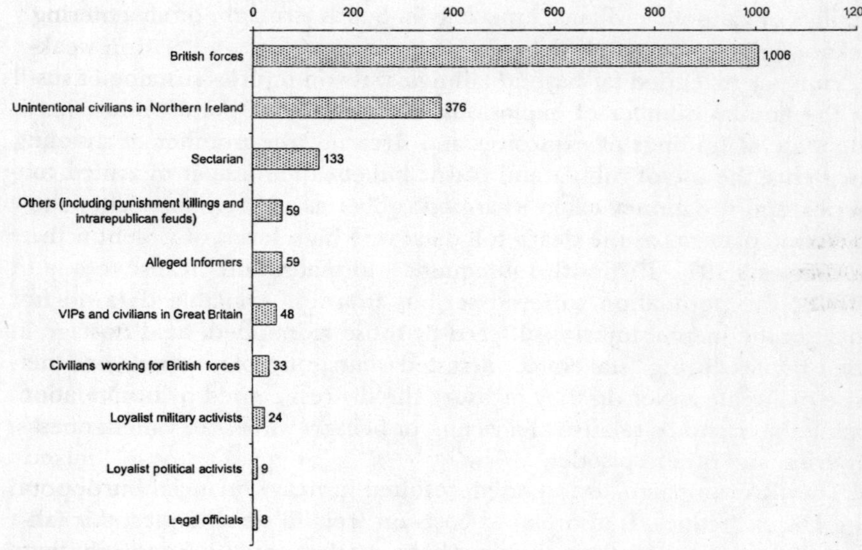


Figure 6.4. Killings by the IRA, 1969–1993 (total: 1755). Adapted from Sutton, *Bear in Mind These Dead*, 196–204.

mostly Protestant dead police in the RUC and its reserves. The dead in the B Specials, UDR, and RIR also nearly match the other republican dead. The data and interpretation of Malcolm Sutton (1994), presented in Figure 6.4, with slight adjustments, suggest that IRA violence has been primarily strategic, aimed at its official legitimate targets, rather than sectarian, that is, the deliberate killing of Protestant civilians: he classifies 12.4 percent of IRA killings as sectarian, and a very high proportion of these occurred in 1975–1976. This viewpoint is supported in the sophisticated analyses of Brendan O'Duffy (1995) and Robert White (1997). The IRA killed far more security force members than Protestant civilians, partially fulfilling its mission of fighting "a war of national liberation." But, that does not definitively settle the question of IRA "sectarianism"—even if one codes the IRA as less sectarian than loyalists, as the death evidence warrants. Protestants interpret and will interpret the targeting and killings of Protestant members of the local security forces as sectarian. White points out that the small proportions of Catholic members of the security forces killed matched their numbers in these forces (which suggests no special effort on the part of the IRA to target Protestant members of the security forces), but such killings are simply coded as sectarian by unionists, loyalists, and their sympathizers.[85] The IRA unquestionably carried out some overt and intended killings of uninvolved Protestant civilians—as opposed to killing such persons through "collateral damage." These actions were defended by IRA volunteers as necessary acts of deterrence against loyalist killings of Catholic civilians, especially in South Armagh, or shamefacedly acknowledged—or simply denied.

Violence extended far beyond killings. Data on injuries sustained as well as the annual number of explosions, the number of bombs neutralized, the scale of findings of explosives and firearms, the number of shooting incidents, the use of rubber and plastic bullets, the number of armed robberies, and the money taken in armed robberies are available. They show the same patterns as the death toll data: very high levels of violent activity in the years 1971–1976 with subsequent "normalization." Close to one in fifty of the population suffered serious injuries. Available data do not include the mental injuries suffered by those kidnapped, held hostage in their homes during "stakeouts," arrested when guilty of no crime, or otherwise maltreated. Nor do they measure the distress caused by intimidation, being the friend or relative of a victim, or being a witness to violent deaths, injuries, and other episodes.

The IRA campaign, as intended, resulted in heavy financial burdens on the UK exchequer. It also placed costs on Ireland's exchequer: the extra security costs ensuing from the crisis between the years 1969 and 1982 were estimated at over IR£1.05 million. For the same period additional expenditure on security incurred by the UK government was estimated at UK£4,150 million. One 1985 audit estimated that the annual direct costs of violence of the conflict incurred ran at £1,194 million—a figure that excluded the indirect economic costs of lost output and employment arising from the political crisis.[86] Providing security in Northern Ireland in the fiscal year 1990–1991 cost just under £1 billion—more than three times the per capita UK average, and certain costs were not apparently calculated, for example, those entailed in tightening security at military bases in Great Britain and Germany, intelligence-gathering and surveillance in Great Britain, and protecting the political and civil establishments. Other economic costs included the stress on and infrastructural damage to the public services: health and welfare and housing administration, public utilities, and the penal services. Telephone exchanges, post offices, railway networks, bus garages, gas depots, power stations, and reservoirs were bombed or robbed and their staffs intimidated. Frauds against public-sector organizations ran into millions of pounds. Compensation payments to victims of violence or owners of destroyed properties ran much higher. Claims for compensation exceeded 13,000 cases per annum. Protection rackets affected the profitability of many private-sector organizations; as did the requirements imposed by insurance companies upon shops and offices. The insurance costs of private transport rose to reflect the high numbers of vehicle thefts, hijackings, and car bombings. The incredibly high proportion of the population involved in security led economist Bob Rowthorn to describe the Northern Ireland economy as a "workhouse," in which most were employed in controlling or servicing one another.[87] The most obvious economic costs are the least measurable: the "opportunity costs" of three decades of conflict, in lost investment, output, and productive employment.

The human rights costs and the impact on liberal democratic institutions must also be counted. The legal authorities of Northern Ireland, Great Britain, and Ireland were granted formidable emergency powers. The ratios of arrests to charges, and of charges to convictions, were relatively high, suggesting large-scale screening and systematic deprivation of many innocent citizens of their liberty. Departures from traditional legal procedures become normal. No-jury courts were used because jury trials were not safe from perverse verdicts or the intimidation of jurors and witnesses. Confessions became admissible as the sole basis for conviction on charges of having committed scheduled offences—including confessions subsequently retracted. In 1988 the UK government abandoned the traditional common law "right of silence"—courts and prosecutors were entitled to draw inferences from the silence of suspects. Delays of several years became routine in holding inquests on persons killed by the security forces. Belief in the impartiality of British justice was severely damaged. The most notorious cases of wrongful imprisonment demonstrated police fabrication of evidence against innocent Irish people; incompetent or malevolent forensic practices; judicial wishful thinking and partisanship; and ethnic bias in media reporting. The conflict impaired other key institutions. Certain sections of the British intelligence services ran amok in the 1970s. Believing that the authorities were "giving in to terrorism," they plotted directly against the elected Labour government, and spread false rumors.[88] Collusion with loyalist paramilitaries also occurred on a significant scale from the late 1980s. The media were censored in both jurisdictions.

What was the IRA's strategy, and how could it justify such costs? Appraisals of its strategy are rare.[89] The simplest answer is that had no single strategy, but multiple strategies. In the first phase of conflict, 1970–1975, the IRA expected a short war, a replication of what had happened in 1919–1921, in which the British government would be forced to negotiate its withdrawal from the remainder of Ireland. It overestimated its capacity to hurt the UK state, underestimated the costs that loyalists and the security forces could impose on its volunteers, neglected the rooted determination of the majority unionist population within Northern Ireland to oppose a compulsory united Ireland, and overvalued southern support for an offensive—as opposed to a defensive—IRA. The IRA played a role in the overthrow of Stormont, but over-reached in thinking it could produce a quick British disengagement, and lacked any overt evidence of a popular mandate. It was also completely unsuccessful in negotiations—and outmaneuvered in 1975. In the second phase of conflict the IRA's leadership foresaw and organized for a long war of attrition. It was capable of maintaining itself, but underestimated the extent to which it could be contained within Northern Ireland. Taking the war to Great Britain and Europe involved spectacular activities, but these could not be as logistically sustained as those in Northern Ireland. The IRA initially lacked a convincing political strategy to match its military activities.

A new and apparently more effective strategy emerged almost by accident, in 1980–1981, when the impact of the republican hunger strikes on public opinion created opportunities for Sinn Féin to emerge as an electorally significant political party in the North.[90] To continue the novel electoral momentum and search for broader allies the republican movement was obliged to reconsider abstentionism, first within local government in the North, and then toward Leinster House in the South. It endorsed change, and modified its constitution. That led to the first significant split in the movement—though not within the IRA. Older pre-1969 southerners in protest formed Republican Sinn Féin. The strategy of combining the ballot box and the Armalite, as Danny Morrison described it, superficially resembled the Sinn Féin and IRA alliance of 1918–1921, but with a major difference: the lack of a majority mandate within the North, not even among the Northern nationalist population, or among the nationalist population in Ireland as a whole. The IRA was persuaded to accept the end of abstentionism by Sinn Féin in the belief that the army would not be run down—and hard-liners were temporarily sweetened by the prospect of major arms supplies from Libya. Sinn Féin, the IRA's party, because originally it was little more than that, then placed limits on the IRA. It gained greater autonomy, and sometimes its needs had to be placed first. Bobby Sands and his colleagues had died on hunger strike "to broaden the battlefield" and had succeeded beyond their expectations. Sands's hunger strike, his victory in a parliamentary by-election, and his death, followed by the deaths of nine other prisoners, cemented the political status of the IRA but would end up limiting its military actions and subjecting it to electoral discipline.[91] The party gathered one in three northern nationalist votes on a platform of supporting its army, the IRA, but to grow later on, it had to distance itself, or place constraints on its army. In the interests of electoral gains, reinforced by their materialization, Sinn Féin has, therefore, slowly displaced the IRA as republicans' preferred organizational means of struggle, and not without dissent within the ranks of the volunteers—and the creation of two small breakaway organizations, the Continuity and Real IRAs.[92] The party now has many members, probably an overwhelming majority, with no record of service as volunteers; and many of these are now prominent parliamentarians. Combining the ballot box and the Armalite, contrary to what Morrison thought at the time, proved unsustainable. Success with one undermined use of the other. From being the inspirer of the party, the army became a constraint. The IRA's decision to organize a ceasefire in 1994, and later to renew it, had one primary beneficiary: Sinn Féin. The party doubled its vote share in the North within a decade, recently winning four seats in the Westminster parliament, five in Dáil Éireann, and becoming, just, the largest nationalist party in the (suspended) Northern Ireland Assembly—and it has had one of its former chiefs of staff serve as a minister of the Northern Ireland Executive.

How did this transformation happen? First, the IRA was not winning its long war to compel the UK state to disengage, even if it was not losing, and even if it could plant devastating bombs in the city of London. No victory on the "battlefield" meant that there could be no victory at the negotiating table. Second, demographic transformations pointed to the possibility of a Northern nationalist majority that could create a constitutional path to end partition—and to a currently large enough nationalist bloc to leverage a power-sharing settlement given existing UK policy commitments to the Irish government. Third, republicans began properly to assess the full recalcitrance of unionists and loyalists toward the idea of a unitary Ireland, and the possible development of indifference toward reunification in the newly prosperous Ireland. Fourth, political agents inside and outside the republican movement persuaded sufficient IRA leaders, volunteers and prisoners that a peace process, building up a wider alliance of nationalists, was the best way to advance the IRA's objectives, even if that meant the IRA's disbandment before the attainment of a unitary Ireland. Key sections of the IRA leadership eventually settled on a peace process without express assurances that their declared war objectives would be met through negotiations, and called for a "complete cessation" of military operations in August 1994, after a careful and protracted process of negotiation among Irish nationalists, and then between the UK and Irish governments, had produced the Joint Declaration for Peace of December 1993. The divided IRA resumed military operations by a majority vote of its Army Council in February 1996 in protest at the Conservative government's unwillingness to engage with Sinn Féin, but formally declared a ceasefire again in 1997. The full complexity of this transformation, its necessary ambiguities and consequences, is beginning to emerge in a range of studies and publications, and we will likely not know the full details of intra-IRA maneuvers and disputes for some time.[93]

Given space constraints I will use just two texts to complement my earlier argument on the end of the old IRA, those of Richard English and Ed Moloney. English, a unionist with roots in Northern Ireland, and a professor at Queen's University, Belfast, has written a dispassionate evaluation in *Armed Struggle.* He identifies seven arguments that motivated the IRA. First, its resurgence "began primarily in response to defensive need," providing "muscular defence" in 1969–1970 for oppressed nationalists in Belfast and Derry against a partisan RUC and loyalist sectarian mobs. Second, there was deep-rooted unfairness toward the nationalist minority in Northern Ireland, where the Ulster Unionist Party ruled without interruption from the formation of the regime until 1972, and which created, thereby, the social base of the IRA. Third, and relatedly, there was the cause of Irish national self-determination—to which he arguably pays insufficient attention. Fourth, the IRA regarded Northern Ireland as "unreformable." The treatment of the civil rights demonstrations of the 1960s confirmed this belief, as had the introduction of internment without trial between 1971 and 1975, and events such as the Falls Road curfew of 1970 and Bloody Sunday in 1972. Fifth, IRA volunteers defined the conflict as a national liberation struggle, and for over two decades stressed socialist as well as republican commitments. Sixth, they saw unionists as "a residue of British colonialism in Ireland." Last, they regarded themselves as, and often succeeded in behaving as, nonsectarian republicans committed to creating a common democratic state for all of Ireland. One of the many merits of English's treatment is that he evaluates these arguments seriously, and shows that these convictions were sincerely held and were sane.

Naturally, he addresses the deficiencies and disputable elements in the IRA's arguments, dealing seriatim with the IRA's frequently offensive role, and its contribution to serious injustice in Northern Ireland and elsewhere, both through actions and provocations. He adds minor (unionist) qualifications to the picture of a discriminatory unionist regime before 1972; observes that Ulster Unionists have a case for self-determination and regarding Northern Ireland as legitimate; argues for the empirical (and normative) importance of the autonomous dispositions of unionists and loyalists, who often resisted the policies of Westminster and Whitehall; and stresses the counterproductive nature of the IRA's violence in stiffening unionist resistance to Irish reunification and in inhibiting a political settlement; and, not least, emphasizes the IRA's intermittent descent into sectarian killings. But, English scrupulously acquits the IRA of sole responsibility for the conflict of the past thirty years, distributing blame across a range of political groups and on British and unionist policies and dispositions without which the IRA's actions or persistence would have made little sense. None of his writing avoids the elemental emotions and tragedies involved in IRA actions and their repercussions for both the organization's target-victims and its members. He forgets neither the "Fanonist rage" of some volunteers nor the local status and petty power sometimes achieved through being in the "RA," but he refuses to overemphasize the tabloid components of the IRA, which he treats as neither corrupt nor as ruthlessly efficient as it would have liked to have been. From this measured study we may conclude that the IRA has failed militarily to drive the British state out of Ireland and to achieve a united Ireland in the immediate future. If Ireland is to be reunified in the future, it will be through ballot boxes and institutionalized negotiations.

But what English misses is the constitutional path through which the IRA must disband itself, if it is to dissolve itself in good order. That requires its volunteers not only to believe that military means cannot win their objectives and are therefore best replaced through democratic—and consociational—politics, but changes consistent with their own constitution, to which they are pledged, or else face the danger of further splits and the departure of their materiel into the hands of irreconcilables. Thanks to Ed Moloney's *A Secret History of the IRA*, the current IRA constitution, as amended in 1986 and again in 1996, is a matter of public record. It has five objects, recognizable successors to the founding aims, namely, "to guard the honor and uphold the sovereignty and unity of the Irish Republic as declared by the First Dáil"; "to support the establishment of an Irish Socialist Republic based on the 1916 Proclamation"; "to support the establishment of, and uphold, a lawful government in sole and absolute control of the Thirty-Two County Irish Republic as constituted by the First Dáil"; "to secure and defend civil and religious liberties and equal rights and equal opportunities for all citizens"; and "to promote the revival of the Irish language as the everyday language of the people" (Art. 3.1–5). Until these objects are achieved the organizational integrity and cohesion of the IRA, and its military capabilities must be maintained (Art. 8.5.1–2); and "until a settlement has been agreed, leading to a united Ireland" the IRA must retain its arms (Art. 8.5.5).[94] So the question presently before all is this: how may the IRA constitutionally disband itself if the sovereignty and unity of the Irish Republic, "as declared by the First Dáil," has not been achieved?

Before answering this question let me sweep aside some side issues. Let us assume that socialism on the basis of the 1916 proclamation, civil and religious liberties, equal rights and opportunities for all, and promoting the Irish language, do not require the existence or use of the IRA's arms—a proposition that the current Irish prime minister, who has declared himself a socialist, would certainly affirm. Note, second, that it is now the First—not the Second—Dáil's mandate (for an autonomous Ireland that would exercise its self-determination) that is defended by the IRA. It is this constitutional change that has enabled the IRA not to oppose Sinn Féin's participation in elections to and membership of Leinster House.

One way the IRA's constitutional self-transformation may go in future would be to argue that since the Belfast/Good Friday Agreement of 1998, endorsed by the people of Ireland, North and South, and now on the verge of full implementation, the partition of Ireland presently rests on a decision of the people of Ireland, as do the power-sharing institutions, agencies, and policies embedded in that Agreement. In short, the Agreement is the necessary act of Irish national self-determination that repairs the constitutional wound of 1920. That was certainly how constitutional nationalists, North and South, defended the Agreement, and in instructing its voters to endorse it in the two referendums, Sinn Féin became complicit with that argument. The Agreement recognizes (present) partition as an Irish, not a British decision, recognizes Ireland's right to achieve (re-)unification through consent in both jurisdictions. It also, of course, establishes consociational institutions within Northern Ireland and cross-border all-Ireland arrangements that may legitimately be construed as harbingers of a federal Ireland.[95] Once the Agreement is on the verge of being fully implemented, notably with the withdrawal of British troops to barracks, comprehensive police reform, major changes in the administration of justice, and the Northern Ireland (Suspension) Act of 2000 removed from the UK's statute book, then it becomes possible to argue two things. One is to say that "a settlement leading to a united Ireland," without any British external interference over Irish self-determination, has already been accomplished. A united Ireland has been achieved through the Agreement, but not a unitary Ireland, rather an Ireland united by the institutions of the Agreement. The people of Ireland, North and South, have the right of national self-determination, but also the right to choose how to exercise national self-determination, and if that involves having one territorial unit with revisable linkages to the United Kingdom, that need not be a denial of the underlying principle. This would probably be too much for most republicans to stomach—it may seem lawyerly, or specious, although it has its attractions. Second, and probably more persuasive to most republicans, it is possible to argue that "a settlement has been agreed [and implemented] leading to a united Ireland," even though the latter has not (yet) occurred—"leading to a united Ireland" is not the same as the "attainment of a united Ireland." Either of these arguments permit republican volunteers in good conscience to amend the IRA's constitution to say that the object of the First Dáil has been met—which would then authorize the ratification of decommissioning by an Army Convention (required by Art. 8.5.5), and the subsequent disbanding of an organization which had met its constitutional mission.

A united Ireland need not necessarily be a unitary Ireland; and a sovereign Ireland may take many forms, including a divided form, through a federation or confederation, or through two units within a European confederation. Moreover, a Northern Ireland Assembly—and legal system, and even UK parliament—which does not require oaths of allegiance to the Crown on the part of ministers is surely in some respects like a Dáil Éireann, which has no such requirement. The new Northern Assembly and North-South Ministerial Council create forums in which all the objects of the IRA may be pursued without recourse to arms, and with some prospects of success (although the chances of the Irish language must be less than those of a unitary state). Arguments of this nature may have occurred—or be anticipated—if the IRA is, as is clear, willing comprehensively to decommission its weapons. We shall find out. If such an internal constitutional transformation occurs the IRA will not have failed politically to the degree that it failed militarily. The IRA, in action or on ceasefire, made it necessary for a political settlement to address the denial of Ireland's right to self-determination in 1920—and, for that matter, to undertake the radical police reform that has been negotiated since 1998, as well as range of other antidiscrimination measures that might not otherwise have materialized. The IRA did not fight for power-sharing in a Stormont parliament, nor did it design those institutions, nor did it initially endorse the Good Friday Agreement. But its existence, and the skilled trading of its capacities for constitutional and political concessions, obliged others to create comprehensive power-sharing institutions in and across Northern Ireland, Ireland and Great Britain, all of which are consistent with the core idea of Irish national self-determination. In that idea the "Irish" include both Irish nationalists and Irish unionists who identify with Great Britain. In that idea self-determination may take a concurrent as well as a unitary form. The IRA may in good faith amend its constitution to accomplish its own dissolution in a manner that the majority of the ghosts of the First Dáil would approve, although the vote might be too close to call among the ghosts of the rump Second Dáil.

## Glossary

Ancient Order of Hibernians: Traditional Irish nationalist organization, especially strong in the U.S.

ASU: Active service unit of the IRA, small specialist cell.

B-Specials: Ulster special constabulary, reserve RUC constables, disbanded 1970.

Continuity IRA: Breakaway organization from the IRA.

Cunann na mBhan: Women's republican organization.

Cunann na nGaedhael: Pro-Treaty party formed from Sinn Féin, led governments of the Irish Free State, 1922–1932, dissolved into Fine Gael.

DUP: Democratic Unionist Party.

Emergency Provisions Act: Emergency antiterrorist legislation applied in Northern Ireland.

Fianna Fáil (lit., Soldiers of Destiny): Republican political party formed by de Valera, breakaway from Sinn Féin, now dominant party in independent Ireland.

Fine Gael (lit. Family of the Gaels): Pro-Treaty party of independent Ireland.

INLA: Irish National Liberation Army, Marxist rival to the IRA in Northern Ireland, formed from ex-Officials and others.

IPLO: Irish People's Liberation Organization, breakaway from the INLA.

IRA: Irish Republican Army.

ONH: Óglaigh na hÉireann (Volunteers of Ireland).

MI5, MI6: Military Intelligence, official UK spying and intelligence agencies.

NICRA: Northern Ireland Civil Rights Association, formed with republican support in the 1960s to protest discrimination by the Stormont Parliament.

O-IRA: (Official) IRA, now disbanded.

PIRA: (Provisional) IRA.

PTA: Prevention of Terrorism Act.

PUP: Progressive Unionist Party.

Real IRA: 1998 breakaway from the IRA.

RIR: Royal Irish Regiment (fusion of the UDR and Royal Irish Rangers).

RUC: Royal Ulster Constabulary.

SF: Sinn Féin, Irish Republican political party, formed in 1905 by Arthur Griffith as a party advocating a dual monarchy, radicalized after 1917.

Stormont: Site and name of the building of the Northern Ireland Parliament after 1932.
UUP: Ulster Unionist Party.
UDA: Ulster Defence Association.
UDR: Ulster Defence Regiment.
UVF: Ulster Volunteer Force.

## Timeline

This brief chronology does not list bombings, atrocities, or killings by the IRA.

1913: Formation of Óglaigh na hÉireann (Volunteers of Ireland) is formed in response to formation of the UVF, a paramilitary organization that opposed home rule for Ireland.

1914: Volunteers divide; Óglaigh na hÉireann opposes Ireland's participation in World War 1.

1916: The IRB organizes an Irish nationalist insurrection at Easter; Óglaigh na hÉireann is renamed the Irish Republican Army (IRA) in English; IRB and Irish Citizen Army are incorporated.

1919–1921: IRA spearheads successful insurrection against the British Empire while nominally accepting the authority of Dáil Éireann, the Irish parliament.

1920: Parliament of Great Britain partitions Ireland into Northern and Southern Ireland.

1921: Treaty between Great Britain and Ireland recognizes the Irish Free State, gives the Northern Ireland parliament the right to opt out of a unified Ireland, but does not give the Free State either full sovereignty or republican status. Northern Ireland parliament begins fifty years of domination by the UUP and presides over systematic discrimination.

1922–1923: IRA splits over terms of the Treaty negotiated between Sinn Féin and the government of Great Britain; the pro-Treaty faction becomes part of the official Óglaigh na hÉireann, the army of the Irish Free State; the IRA becomes the military organization of the anti-Treaty side and loses the Irish Civil War.

1923–1932: Irish Free State government accepts the 1921 Treaty but seeks to modify it. IRA remains intact.

1932–1949: Irish governments negotiate away or break elements of the 1921 Treaty, establishing an Irish Constitution free of British determination of its contents, and eventually proclaim a Republic. Significant sections of the IRA accept this constitutional transformation.

1939–1945: IRA declares war on Great Britain with the aim of obtaining a united Ireland; its bombing campaign in England and actions in Northern Ireland are failures.

1956–1962: IRA declares war on the government of Northern Ireland. Its campaign is a failure.

1962–1968: Republicans play a role in the formation of the Northern Ireland civil rights movement protesting discrimination by the UUP government.

1969–1970: IRA splits; the Official IRA evolves toward being a Marxist organization, and later dissolves; the Provisional IRA comes into being as a defensive response to attacks on Catholic urban districts, then goes on the offensive.

1970: IRA begins its twenty-five-year guerrilla war; insurgency tactics include assassinations against the government and security forces of Great Britain, as well as punishment beatings in its own security system; the war is punctuated by ceasefires in 1972, and 1975–1976.

1971–1975: The Northern Ireland government introduces internment without trial.

1972–1984: The Northern Ireland parliament is prorogued; Westminster undertakes direct rule, punctuated by intermittent efforts to establish a power-sharing devolved parliament (in 1973–1974, 1975–1976, 1979–1980, 1982, 1985, 1991–1992).

1975–1976: After a ceasefire, the IRA fails to achieve its objectives in negotiations; reorganizes in a cellular structure; Northerners become dominant in its leadership; IRA settles in for what it calls "a long war"; abolition of internment and of "special category status" prompts prison protests by IRA personnel.

1976–1981: IRA prisoners go "on the blanket"; "dirty protests" and hunger-strikes culminate in the death by self-induced starvation of 10 prisoners.

1982: Sinn Féin emerges as an electoral force, winning 10 percent of the vote in Northern Ireland, and openly supports the IRA.

1984: New Ireland Forum publishes its report; constitutional Irish nationalist parties propose new arrangements for Ireland and Northern Ireland, rejected by UK Prime minister Thatcher; negotiations continue.

1985: Governments of Ireland and Great Britain negotiate the "Anglo-Irish Agreement," a treaty giving the Irish government consultative rights on all matters of public policy affecting Northern Ireland—to the consternation of most Ulster Unionists.

1986: IRA receives significant arms supplies from Libya.

1988–1993: Intermittent negotiations between moderate nationalist leader John Hume and president of Sinn Féin Gerry Adams begin, culminating in proposals for a peace declaration in December 1993.

1991–1992: UK government organizes cross-party negotiations in Northern Ireland from which Sinn Féin is excluded.

1992: Sinn Féin publishes *Towards a Lasting Peace in Ireland.*

1993: The British and Irish governments issue their "Joint Declaration for Peace."

1994: IRA announces a ceasefire in August.

1995: The British and Irish governments publish "Frameworks for Peace" outlining the details of a possible constitutional settlement.

1996: IRA breaks its ceasefire, impatient at failure of negotiations to begin.

1997: Labour Party wins landslide victory in UK elections; IRA recommits to its ceasefire.

1998: Good Friday Agreement is negotiated. It is endorsed in referendums in both jurisdictions in Ireland and supported by Sinn Féin, moderate nationalists, and moderate unionists.

1999–2004: Partial implementation of the Good Friday Agreement begins. The IRA engages in partial decommissioning of its weapons, but maintains its organizational and military capacity. IRA personnel are accused of criminal murders and criminal activity. IRA criticizes UK government for breaching the Agreement on police reform and for adopting suspension power. Sinn Féin benefits dramatically from the peace process in successive elections.

2004–2005: IRA's failure to decommission and disband weakens position of moderate unionists; leads to extensive international and domestic criticism of the IRA.

2005: Before the UK general election Gerry Adams issues what is widely understood as a call for the IRA to meet and consider its own dissolution.

Map 7.1. Various outcomes of political division of Kashmir.

*Chapter 7*

# The JKLF and JKHM: The Kashmir Insurgents

SUMANTRA BOSE

Armed insurgency in Kashmir is now seventeen years old. The durability of insurgency is closely linked to the policies of India and Pakistan, the two states involved in the international conflict over Kashmir. Indian counter-insurgency forces have taken a heavy toll of insurgents, killing approximately 19,000 between January 1990 and December 2004. In the process Indian forces have eliminated the JKLF as an insurgent formation and have to some extent weakened and contained the JKHM. But the state violence and repression this has entailed has also wrought radicalization among the population and sustained insurgency by producing a constant stream of recruits for insurgent groups, since the mid-1990s mostly for JKHM and other, even more militant "jihadi" groups originating in Pakistan. The insurgency has also crucially been sustained by various forms of Pakistani sponsorship and support, whose precise nature and extent has varied over the past seventeen years. Pakistani policy, mostly executed through the military's Inter-Services Intelligence (ISI), which has a dedicated Kashmir department, has been instrumental in the marginalization and destruction of the once-dominant JKLF as a fighting force, and in the resilience of JKHM, which has survived and continued to operate as the leading insurgent group in the field.

The changed global scenario post-11 September 2001 has had significant implications for the Kashmir conflict, although three years later it remains to be seen how these implications will play out. After the attacks, Pakistan—specifically its military regime led by General Pervez Musharraf, in power since October 1999—emerged as a key ally in the American "war on terror." At the same time India seized the opportunity to tar Kashmir's Muslim insurgency with the terrorist brush, characterizing Kashmir as one of the major fronts of the global war on terror. Indian officials and propagandists pointed to the contradiction between the U.S. embrace of Musharraf's Pakistan and the Pakistani military's role in sponsoring and supporting Islamist guerrilla activity in Kashmir, which involves, in addition to JKHM, smaller but even more radical groups with pan-Islamist ideology (Lashkar-e-Taiba) and al-Qaeda links (Jaish-e-Mohammad). Under American and Indian pressure, the Pakistani junta has sought since early 2002 to deal with this contradiction by promising to curtail support for militants in Kashmir, but India has treated this pledge with skepticism. The ISI's leadership has since October 2001 been purged of officers with radical Islamist proclivities and connections—the ISI was the principal conduit for American assistance to the mujahideen effort in Afghanistan in the 1980s and later played a key role in the rise of the Taliban in the mid-1990s—and its Kashmir operations have been curbed. But insurgency and counterinsurgency continue in Kashmir.

The United States is the only external power with the clout and leverage to nudge and prod India and Pakistan into a serious peace process over Kashmir. But the potential American role is complicated by the deep suspicion and distrust of the U.S. that is widespread among both elites and masses in India, Pakistan, and Kashmir. Anti-American feeling has deepened since the invasion of Iraq in almost exclusively Muslim Pakistan, Muslim-majority Kashmir, and Hindu-majority India. After seventeen years of armed conflict in Kashmir most Indian and Pakistani elites, as well as Kashmir secessionist leaders now publicly recognize that the conflict can only be settled through a sustained peace process leading to a complex compromise between rival claims and agendas, that is, through dialogue and negotiations. But peace in Kashmir is still only a glimmer on the horizon and could yet turn out to be a mirage. Kashmir is not only one of the world's most protracted international conflicts but also a complex, even convoluted conflict *within* the contested region, which is diverse and has many social groups and political factions. As and when a serious, multidimensional peace process comes about, the inclusion and involvement of former (JKLF) and current (JKHM) insurgent groups with sizable popular support will be crucial to its prospects.

## The Kashmir Conflict

Jammu and Kashmir (often referred to simply as "Kashmir") has been the subject of a sovereignty dispute between India and Pakistan since 1947.[1] Two of the three India-Pakistan wars, in 1947–1948 and 1965, have been caused by this dispute (the 1971 war resulted from India's military intervention in support of the Bangladesh independence movement in then East Pakistan, although it also involved combat in Kashmir). The two countries also fought a two-month border conflict limited to Kashmir in 1999. The disputed territory is internally divided by a "Line of Control" (LOC) into a larger and more populous area of more than ten million people under Indian control and a smaller and less populous area of about three million under Pakistani control. The LOC originated as a ceasefire line in January 1949 and was renamed by intergovernmental agreement in 1972 (see Map 7.1).

Insurgency and protracted guerrilla warfare are, however, relatively recent phenomena in Kashmir. Since the beginning of 1990, Indian-controlled Jammu and Kashmir (IJK) has been in the grip of such conflict, which has claimed at least 40,000 lives according to Indian figures and double that number according to pro-insurgent sources.[2] Between 1990 and December 2004, about 19,000 guerrillas have been killed in Kashmir, according to Indian counterinsurgency statistics, along with over 6,000 Indian soldiers, paramilitary troopers, and police.[3] The growth and radicalization in the late 1980s of long-simmering opposition to Indian authority among a substantial section of the population were primarily the consequence of a forty-year history of abuse by Indian governments (often operating in collusion with client local elites in IJK) of citizens' civil liberties and democratic rights to participation and representation, and the effective revocation by the mid-1960s of IJK's autonomous status within the Indian Union.[4] The immediate catalyst to violence was an egregiously rigged election to IJK's legislative assembly in 1987, which a broad spectrum of pro-"self-determination" groups had contested as an opposition coalition called the Muslim United Front (MUF). This event, and a wave of police repression of MUF supporters that followed, fatally damaged the tenuous legitimacy of Indian rule, especially in the Kashmir Valley, an overwhelmingly Muslim and predominantly Kashmiri-speaking region that constitutes slightly over half of IJK's population. The client IJK government installed by New Delhi in 1987 collapsed in January 1990 as massive demonstrations calling for *azaadi* (freedom) from Indian rule broke out throughout the Kashmir Valley, centered on its capital city, Srinagar, which is located in the geographical center of the Valley.

Violence by an armed underground of embittered young men consisting mostly of former MUF activists and volunteers, mainly bomb blasts targeted at sites and symbols of government authority and selective assassinations of local pro-India political figures and Indian intelligence personnel, had been steadily escalating during 1989. In early 1990 a popular insurrection against Indian rule erupted in the Kashmir Valley. The indiscriminately repressive response of a panicked Indian government, including the killing of hundreds of demonstrators in the Valley's towns, sharply exacerbated the crisis and armed activity by previously small groups of militants rapidly acquired the form of a popularly backed revolt involving thousands of young men as combatants. From early 1990 onward, the Kashmir Valley closely resembled an occupied territory, as overwhelmingly nonlocal (and non-Muslim) Indian security forces battled a spreading and intensifying armed rebellion strongly supported by local society.[5]

The Jammu and Kashmir Liberation Front (JKLF) and the Jammu and

Kashmir Hizb-ul Mujahideen (JKHM) emerged as the major insurgent organizations in this context of ferment and uprising. Both are significant groups, albeit for somewhat different reasons, explained below. Unlike Sri Lanka or Northern Ireland, no single organization has achieved unequivocal, long-term political and military predominance in the seventeen-year history of the insurgency against the incumbent regime.

## Origins and Orientations: JKLF and JKHM

The JKLF was the agent of post-1987 insurgency in Kashmir. The movement was formed in Pakistani-controlled Jammu and Kashmir (PJK)[6] in 1964 with the avowed aim of reuniting the two parts of the disputed territory into a single independent state. Some of its first-generation members were among several thousand men who infiltrated IJK from PJK in 1965 as part of a failed plan, code-named Operation Gibraltar, developed by the Pakistani military to seize large areas of IJK, especially the Kashmir Valley. Since its inception, the JKLF's secessionist movement has had a turbulent relationship with Pakistani regimes, particularly the military, which has been in either direct or indirect control of the Pakistani state since the late 1950s and has always had the decisive say in determining policy on Kashmir. The secessionists and the Pakistani armed forces have alternated between episodes of collaboration against the common foe, India, and the more usual condition of tension, mistrust and even outright hostility and confrontation (secessionist groups routinely suffer various forms of persecution in PJK). This is not surprising since the vision of a "united, neutral, secular, federal republic" of J&K is fundamentally at odds with both Pakistani state ideology and strategic objectives with regard to Kashmir.[7]

For more than two decades after its formation, however, the JKLF had negligible presence in IJK, which it refers to, in common with official Pakistani terminology, as "occupied" or "held" Kashmir. This was because the pro-*azaadi*—a term which is open to multiple meanings and interpretations, independence but also substantial autonomy or self-rule short of sovereignty—political space in IJK was occupied by a deeply rooted Valley-based movement founded in the 1930s. This was the Jammu and Kashmir National Conference (NC) party, which operated under the name of Plebiscite Front between the mid-1950s and mid-1970s. Its name has simple origins: the sovereignty dispute over Kashmir was supposed to be settled by a plebiscite administered under United Nations supervision, and a number of UN Security Council resolutions passed between 1948 and 1957 called for such a referendum. The NC's top leader, Sheikh Mohammad Abdullah (1905–1982) was the most important political figure in modern Kashmir's political history. The NC decisively lost this mass base only after 1987, when Sheikh Abdullah's successor, his elder son Farooq Abdullah, was seen as having sold out this historic political legacy through unconditional, power-hungry collaboration with New Delhi and the then ruling Congress party.

Until that radicalization, however, the JKLF's declared stance of achieving full independence, through armed struggle if necessary, was too militant for the vast majority among the very substantial numbers of discontented IJK residents. Only an isolated handful of young men from IJK were attracted to the JKLF. The JKLF's actions were sporadic in nature. In 1971, for example, as India-Pakistan tensions severely escalated because of the East Pakistan/Bangladesh crisis, a Srinagar youth, Hashim Qureshi, hijacked an Indian Airlines plane to Lahore in Pakistan in a bid to highlight the Kashmir cause. Qureshi became an instant hero in IJK, especially the Valley, a sign of widespread discontent with Indian rule seen as based on force and fraud. But his fame was short-lived; he languished, largely forgotten, in a Pakistani prison for years afterward. The best-known IJK recruit to the first-generation JKLF is Maqbool Butt, born in 1938 in a village in the northern Valley district of Kupwara, close to the LOC with PJK. Butt was hanged in a Delhi jail in 1984 for allegedly killing a police officer during a botched bank robbery in 1976, and subsequently became an icon for independence supporters on both sides of the LOC. Butt's execution sparked unrest in the Valley but no major trouble ensued. JKLF activists (of PJK origin) living in the United Kingdom then shot themselves in the foot by kidnapping and murdering a junior diplomat attached to the Indian consulate in Birmingham in retaliation for the execution. The main JKLF leader Amanullah Khan was subsequently deported to Pakistan by the British government amid much unfavorable publicity.

The first JKLF organizational unit was established in Srinagar only in early 1988, by a new generation of radicalized young men inflamed by what they viewed as incessant Indian or Indian-inspired repression, deceit, and denial of their rightful aspiration to decide their own political status and future. This core of militants made contact with the existing JKLF organization across the LOC during 1987–1988, as well as with the Pakistani military's premier intelligence and covert operations arm, Inter-Services Intelligence (ISI), which had by then acquired vast resources and autonomy as the coordinator of the United States-backed and Pakistan-based mujahideen war against the Soviet occupation and its client regime in Afghanistan. The objective was acquisition of weapons and combat training. Within two years, the previously marginal JKLF emerged as the vanguard and spearhead of a popular uprising in the Kashmir Valley against Indian rule. It dominated the first three years of the insurgency (1990–1992), after which it was displaced from that position by the JKHM.

JKLF leaders and activists like to think of themselves as a secular-nationalist liberation movement. Indeed, the JKLF flag is patterned on that of the Palestine Liberation Organization (PLO). Nonetheless, the JKLF has never managed to acquire any cadres or support among non-Muslims in Kashmir, whose allegiance is overwhelmingly with India. Non-Muslims were 23 percent of the population of undivided Jammu and Kashmir in 1947. In IJK today, non-Muslims, principally Hindus but also Sikhs and Buddhists, comprise more than one-third of the population; by contrast, PJK is almost 100 percent Muslim. A sense of Muslim identity is embedded in secessionist politics—the JKLF constantly deployed an emotive rhetoric of jihad when it dominated the insurrection—although it is a form of Muslim identity which at its most benign is relatively nonsectarian and tolerant toward non-Muslims.[8] It upholds a brand of Kashmir regionalism that defies and resists the state-led nationalisms of both India and Pakistan. JKLF adherents in the Kashmir Valley, in particular, draw spiritual inspiration from the Valley's specific, centuries-old traditions of mystical and syncretistic Sufi Islam.[9]

The JKHM is significantly different. As its name, "Organization of Holy Warriors," suggests, it has an explicitly Islamist orientation, free of secularist leanings or pretensions. Specifically, the JKHM is closely linked with a party known as the Jama'at-i-Islami (JI; "Islamic Solidarity").[10] The JI represents a conservative religious tendency that preaches an orthodox, Wahhabism-influenced version of Sunni Islam,[11] and the movement has separate but fraternal wings in Pakistan, Bangladesh, IJK, and Pakistani-controlled "Azad" Kashmir. In Pakistan and Bangladesh as well as Kashmir, the JI shows a uniform pattern: a committed, hard-core following that amounts to only a small fraction of the population. Thus, as a political party the JI has consistently fared poorly in electoral contests in Pakistan, Bangladesh, and Kashmir, incapable of mustering more than a few percentage points of the popular vote. Nonetheless, all these JI branches have a long-standing reputation for committed cadres and organizational acumen, which partly offsets limited popular support, as well as for theological dogmatism and, in Bangladesh and Pakistan at least, a predilection to violence against political opponents. In Bangladesh and Pakistan, the JI has also expanded its influence in recent years by forming alliances with like-minded or compatible groups—in Bangladesh it is currently a junior partner in a coalition government led by a much larger right-wing party, and in Pakistan it is one of the six religious parties that comprise the Muttahida-Majlis-e-Amal (MMA), an alliance which has increased its popular support since September 2001, particularly in areas close to Afghanistan.

It is too simplistic to regard the JKHM as simply the armed wing of IJK's JI unit, as has often been presumed. Nonetheless, the relationship between the two organizations is close. The JI was founded in Kashmir in 1942 and its traditional core activity is teaching—critics say indoctrinating—children and adolescents through a network of religious schools run by the party. In the 1970s and 1980s the party repeatedly contested elections to the IJK legislative assembly and was revealed to be a marginal player in electoral politics, with a thin base of support and only a few pockets of substantial influence. The JKHM was formed as a guerrilla organization in 1989, under the rallying cry "Kashmir banega Pakistan!" (Kashmir will be part of Pakistan), in contrast to JKLF's slogan, "Kashmir banega khudmukhtar!" (Kashmir will be sovereign). Indeed, the JKHM was launched in 1989, during the countdown to the uprising, to provide a rallying point for pro-Pakistan elements in IJK, especially those of a Jama'ati or similar Islamist orientation, who were alarmed by the growing popularity of the JKLF and its goal of independecne. As explained below, the JKLF declined as an insurgent force after its peak period from 1990 to 1992 and ceased to be active in the armed struggle from the mid-1990s. The JKHM took its place, demonstrated significantly greater resilience as an insurgent outfit, and has maintained its position as the single largest guerrilla group active in Kashmir.

The JKHM owes this resilience to several factors, among them consistent Pakistani/ISI support in provision of weapons, logistics, finances, and training (which the JKLF lost from 1991 onward); the existence of well-organized JI networks in IJK as well as in "Azad" Kashmir and Pakistan, far superior to anything the JKLF could muster; and a supply of young recruits ensured by the brutality of Indian counterinsurgency to the largest guerrilla group active in the field and the only one since the mid-1990s with strong roots *within* IJK. Other even more militant Islamist groups that entered the Kashmir war from the mid-1990s onward, such as Harkat-ul-Ansar, later known as Jaish-e-Mohammad, and Lashkar-e-Taiba, have also recruited some locals, but are organizationally centered in Pakistan, have Pakistani leaderships and a majority of Pakistani fighters who are "guests" in IJK; the leadership and rank and file of JKHM is by contrast composed largely of IJK people, supplemented by a sizable contingent from PJK.

Yet the sources of JKHM strength and resilience have also been its most serious limitations. The group's ideological commitment to Pakistan renders it suspect at best and unacceptable at worst to the mainstream of pro-"self-determination" opinion in IJK, with whom the idea of independence or at least some form of self-rule, *not* incorporation into Pakistan, carries great appeal. Compounding the problem are JKHM's linkages with the JI, which is viewed by the vast majority of people in the Valley and other pro-"self-determination" areas of IJK as a sectarian, "fundamentalist" party at odds with the dominant, Ṣufism-influenced regional culture of *kashmiriyat*, "Kashmiri-ness." The JI connection has thus been both asset and albatross to the JKHM. But it is a fact, since there is a clear pattern of top positions in the JKHM hierarchy being occupied by JI members, usually of long standing, and of JI families and schools contributing their sons and pupils to the JKHM. Nonetheless, JKHM is both politically more moderate and more broadly based in Kashmir in comparison to the zealot groups of Pakistani provenance active in Kashmir insurgency since the mid-1990s, especially Lashkar-e-Taiba (LeT), which specializes in suicidal attacks, and Jaish-e-Mohammad (JeM), which has al-Qaeda links.

An organization that combined the strengths of the JKLF and the JKHM would have been a dream ticket for the politics of self-determination in Kashmir. But that is an imaginary scenario. In reality, the JKLF and the JKHM embody and express two competing, indeed inherently conflictual conceptions of the meaning of *azaadi*. There have been other (locally based) insurgent groups in Kashmir, especially during the peak period of guerrilla war in the first half of the 1990s, and the political organizations that gave rise to these groups—such as the People's League, the Awami Action Committee, and the People's Conference—are still in existence in IJK, particularly in the Valley, where politics, especially self-determination politics, is deeply factionalized. Some of these parties are pro-Pakistan, others are inclined toward independence, and many have a history of either fluctuating between the two positions or of occupying the gray zone between them. But the JKLF and JKHM are the major and the most credible representatives of their respective interpretations of the *azaadi* concept: the JKLF because of its role in pioneering the armed struggle and the resilient popularity of its professed goal (although not necessarily of the JKLF itself, which has suffered splits and organizational decimation); the JKHM because of its resilience as a fighting force on the ground and the sacrifices made by its militants. Both groups and their supporters will be critical in any serious peace process in Kashmir.

Despite their fundamental differences, the JKLF and the JKHM both emerged from a shared disillusionment with the Indian state's democratic credentials and disgust at its treatment of Kashmir. In the infamous IJK elections of March 1987, a middle-aged JI veteran called Mohammad Yusuf Shah, a village schoolteacher by profession, contested from a high-profile electoral district in the heart of Srinagar under the MUF banner. His election manager was a young man called Mohammad Yasin Malik, twenty-one, a resident of that Srinagar neighborhood. This was Yusuf Shah's third attempt to be elected to the IJK legislature—he had lost badly on two previous occasions standing as a JI candidate. According to locals and eyewitness media reports, he won by a landslide in 1987, but his opponent, a National Conference candidate backed by Congress, was declared the winner. Blatant rigging and fraud also happened in numerous other constituencies in the Valley and some parts of IJK's other populous region, Jammu. Both Yusuf Shah and Yasin Malik were then arrested and jailed for a number of months; their sole crime appeared to be their beliefs (pro-Pakistan and pro-independence, respectively) and their attempt to organize a political opposition within the officially sanctioned institutional framework and process.

In 1989–1990, Yasin Malik reemerged as one of the top commanders of the insurgent JKLF, and he continues to be the JKLF's political leader in

IJK today. In the early 1990s, Yusuf Shah also reappeared, as the chief commander of the JKHM under a nom de guerre, Syed Salahuddin. In late 1992 Salahuddin told an Indian interviewer that experience had convinced him that "slaves have no vote in the so-called democratic set-up of India." In mid-1989 Malik recalled his months of post-election captivity to an Indian journalist: "They called me a Pakistani bastard. I told them I want my rights, even my vote was stolen. I am not pro-Pakistan but have lost faith in India."[12]

## Insurgents and States: JKLF, JKHM, India, and Pakistan

The trajectory of armed conflict in Kashmir from early 1990 onward, involving pro-independence and pro-Pakistan insurgents, has been decisively influenced by the policies of both states embroiled in the Kashmir dispute. During 1990, the JKLF emerged as the dominant militant organization. It is not possible to estimate numbers of insurgents with any degree of reliability in the conditions of turmoil that prevailed at that time, but in 1990–1991 thousands of local youths in the Valley carried guns under the JKLF flag. From 1991 onward, however, the JKLF's domination of the armed struggle began to erode. This was the cumulative result of Indian and Pakistani policies toward the independentist insurgents.

First, the JKLF bore the brunt of a ferocious Indian counterinsurgency campaign. Although severely beleaguered by the explosion of insurgency and the hostility of almost the entire local population in the Kashmir Valley, Indian security planners as well as field officers and soldiers proved tenacious in their response. The primary theaters of armed conflict during the first half of the 1990s were the city of Srinagar and the Valley's other towns. Most neighborhoods in the Valley's urban centers were infested with guerrilla fighters in the early 1990s. The grim task of taking on the insurgents in unfriendly urban terrain[13] fell to paramilitary forces under the control of India's federal government[14]—the Border Security Force (BSF) played the frontline role—with backup support when necessary from the regular Indian army[15] units deployed in strength in rural and border areas. The local Jammu and Kashmir police virtually disintegrated, as some of its personnel became insurgents while others disappeared from work or became inactive, and the force was only revived with the relative waning of insurgency in the Valley in the second half of the 1990s.

Despite the adverse odds, the Indians succeeded in "neutralizing" three of the four top JKLF commanders between 1990 and 1992. Ashfaq Majid Wani, aged twenty-three, was killed in an "encounter" (gun battle) in Srinagar in late March 1990, and Yasin Malik, who led a charmed existence for several months, was wounded and captured in August 1990. A third key leader, Hamid Sheikh, was also captured. Released in the autumn of 1992 by BSF intelligence, which was increasingly concerned about the growing clout of pro-Pakistan elements (particularly the JKHM), he was killed in November 1992, along with five fellow fighters while riding a boat on Srinagar's scenic Dal Lake, by the Indian army, which apparently did not agree with the BSF's decision. Javed Mir, the fourth commander, was the sole survivor. In all, 2,213 guerrillas were killed between 1990 and 1992.[16] The majority of the 1990–1992 casualties belonged to the JKLF. The group thus lost almost all its top commanders and the cream of its fighting cadres, while hundreds more were captured.

Indian counterinsurgency strategy relied on cordon-and-search operations known as "crackdowns," on information extracted through routine and often horrific torture of civilians and guerrilla suspects picked up during such raids and, during 1992–1993, on an apparent policy, called "catch and kill," of simply executing captured insurgents and suspects. By 1993, the JKLF had been severely weakened by this onslaught. In October 1993, a contingent of JKLF insurgents were surrounded by Indian security forces in one of their last strongholds, Srinagar's Hazratbal shrine, a major Kashmiri spiritual center in which a hair of the Prophet is preserved as a relic and which was once Sheikh Mohammad Abdullah's political headquarters. The insurgents eventually accepted an offer of safe passage and the standoff was resolved without a bloodbath, but this episode was effectively the JKLF's last major stand as a fighting force.

Second, the Pakistani military and its ISI deliberately and systematically undermined the JKLF. From 1988 to 1990, the ISI and the JKLF were complicit in launching the insurgency. Raja Mohammad Muzaffar, a senior JKLF leader in "Azad" Kashmir, was the key figure in this joint venture, which began with sporadic bombings and targeted shootings in Srinagar and other Valley towns in the second half of 1988 and escalated sharply in the second half of 1989. But both the militants and their irredentist ISI patrons were pleasantly surprised by the extent and intensity of anti-India feeling that overwhelmed the Valley in the first half of 1990. As the insurgency rapidly acquired a popular character during 1990, largely because of the brutal and indiscriminate nature of the Indian response, the Pakistanis decided that the time was opportune to take control of the spreading and intensifying insurrection and shape it in accordance with Pakistani interests. The JKLF became an obstacle to this design. Most of its leaders and prominent activists could not be persuaded, in spite of repeated efforts, to renounce the idea of independence and become Pakistan's proxies in Kashmir. From 1991, the ISI more or less cut off assistance—weapons, finances, training, logistical support for infiltration across the LOC into IJK—to the JKLF. It also began to engineer defections from the JKLF by its more pliable elements and the reconstitution of such elements as pro-Pakistan *tanzeems* (guerrilla groups). By 1991, several such splinter groups had emerged, invariably with Islamist-sounding names such as Ikhwan-ul-Muslimeen ("Muslim Brotherhood"), Al-Umar Mujahideen, and so on.

The trump card in the Pakistani strategy of taking over the Kashmir insurgency was, however, the JKHM. From 1991, the Pakistanis concentrated on building up the JKHM as a force that could first rival and then displace the JKLF in the insurgency. A policy of all-out support to the JKHM was put into effect, at the same time as the JKLF, under siege from the Indian security forces, was starved of resources and assistance. Even as the JKLF splintered with Pakistani encouragement, the ISI facilitated the merger of some smaller pro-Pakistan *tanzeems* into the JKHM. One such group, the Tehreek-e-Jehad-i-Islami (Movement for Holy War), which merged with JKHM in 1991, provided the JKHM with Abdul Majid Dar, who became the JKHM's top field commander in the Valley for most of the 1990s. Also in 1991, the commander-in-chief of JKHM since the group's formation in 1989, Ahsan Dar, was removed and replaced with the reliably pro-Pakistan Jama'ati, Yusuf Shah, alias Salahuddin.

The JKLF decline and JKHM ascendancy was consolidated during 1993. In early 1992, the JKLF organization in "Azad" Kashmir made an attempt to arrest the decline by organizing a pro-independence march to the LOC to emphasize the unity in struggle of the two Kashmirs. The Pakistani authorities and pro-Pakistan groups on both sides of the LOC condemned the march as an irresponsible act that could provoke a massacre by Indian forces stationed on the LOC. Some 30,000 people joined the controversial march, which was broken up by Pakistani border guards who opened fire near the LOC and killed at least twenty marchers. The incident sparked large-scale pro-JKLF and pro-independence demonstrations in Srinagar. But the reprieve proved to be temporary. During the second half of 1992, unsuccessful attempts were made by both groups to stem the rapid growth of armed clashes between JKLF and JKHM fighters in the Valley. The JKHM tended to initiate most of these clashes, although JKLF members also hit their rival *tanzeem* hard when and where they could. Between 1992 and 1994, a number of prominent figures in the Srinagar intelligentsia with JKLF sympathies were murdered; in some cases at least JKHM gunmen were responsible. Other eminent citizens with JKLF connections fled Kashmir fearing assassination by JKHM. While it is not possible to conclusively establish what part the JKHM's ISI nexus played in this violence, some involvement and even direction is more than plausible.

When Yasin Malik was released by the Indian government in mid-1994, he returned to a Srinagar very different from the city he had last seen in August 1990. As a guerrilla force, the JKLF, which effectively controlled Srinagar in 1990, was on its last legs by 1994. Within days of his return, Malik narrowly escaped an apparent assassination attempt by the now dominant JKHM's gunmen. Other significant changes were unfolding in the war-torn Valley. A new term with a pejorative connotation had entered the local vocabulary: "gun culture." The first four years of insurgency had led to an alarming proliferation of armed groups in the Valley. In the early 1990s, with revolution in the air, it was highly fashionable to become a "freedom fighter." With the Valley awash in weapons coming across the LOC, it was also easy for newly minted "commanders" to gather a band of AK47-toting gunmen from their native village, urban neighborhood, or extended family and float a *tanzeem*. The Valley's history of political factionalism played a part in this—different pro-"self-determination" political groups from the pre-1990 period, and factions thereof, tended to spawn their own *tanzeems*, many of them nonserious outfits, at an alarming rate—as did the ISI-sponsored fragmentation of the armed struggle, intended to facilitate Pakistani control and manipulation. Intimidation, extortion, rape and other anti-social and criminal activities by armed militants were becoming a problem, tarnishing the mujahideen's original halo of heroism. Meanwhile, Indian repression was as real as ever; the guerrilla war had posed a major challenge to the Indians but, it was becoming increasingly clear, was very far from bringing the Indian state to its knees. Public opinion in the Valley was noticeably beginning to shift in 1994 from the mass pro-*azaadi* fervor of the preceding years. Realising this creeping change in the public mood and the JKLF's enfeebled state, Malik declared an indefinite, unilateral JKLF ceasefire soon after his release. This was effectively the end of the JKLF's armed struggle, although a minority faction of JKLF militants refused to accept Malik's re-oriented approach. This faction was eliminated when thirty-seven of its members were killed in an Indian counterinsurgency action against their base in the Hazratbal shrine in 1996.

Malik's new pacifism was partly motivated by a desire to save what remained of the JKLF's decimated cadre. He was not particularly successful. After the JKLF effectively ceased insurgent activity, approximately three hundred of its members were hunted down across the Valley and killed by Indian security forces, in the estimate of one respected journalist from IJK. According to the same source, many of these JKLF members were tracked down on the basis of information supplied to the Indians by JKHM members. The JKLF also suffered from its own limitations, in particular its overly Srinagar-centric and Valley-centric focus and organization. All four of the JKLF's top commanders in the early phase of the uprising were from Srinagar (the JKLF's other stronghold in the early 1990s was Anantnag, the main town in the southern part of the Valley) and the group failed to develop and sustain an effective organizational structure outside Srinagar, in the smaller urban centers and the rural areas. This was in stark contrast to the JKHM, which put great emphasis on recruitment and organization in the Valley's smaller towns and villages, and put the JI's grassroots network to good use in this effort. Once the Indian counterinsurgency forces gradually reasserted control over Srinagar, the erstwhile JKLF bastion, the group had no "Plan B" to fall back on. In contrast, the JKHM, which in 1992 "liberated" Sopore, a large town in the northern part of the Valley, was able to carry on a protracted guerrilla war of ambushes and improvised explosive device (IED) attacks elsewhere in the Valley and beyond after its fighters were evicted from Sopore by a massive Indian army/paramilitary operation in 1993. In the late 1980s and early 1990s, the JKLF benefited from the radicalization of the established National Conference/Plebiscite Front mass constituency, but it lacked the strategic foresight and planning to use this to put down lasting roots in society. The JKLF also failed to develop its own financial networks. The movement enjoys widespread sympathy among the Kashmiri diaspora settled in the United States and United Kingdom, and received generous contributions during the first half of the 1990s from wealthy members of this diaspora, particularly Kashmiri doctors living in the U.S. But unlike the Liberation Tigers of Tamil Eelam in Sri Lanka (see Chapter 8), it failed to build on this goodwill and turn the diaspora into a vital source of financing. Once the ISI ceased helping the JKLF, the movement was almost literally left high and dry. On the other hand, the JKHM could draw on massive funding from Pakistan, not just from the ISI but also the JI party.

The JKLF's insurgency also remained confined to the Kashmir Valley. As the 1990s progressed, however, extensive areas of IJK's other populous region of Jammu,[17] south of the Valley—which at 26,293 square kilometers is significantly larger than the Valley's 15,948 kilometers and has hilly, mountainous and forested areas well-suited to guerrilla operations and large areas with Muslim-majority populations (although the Jammu region has an overall non-Muslim, principally Hindu majority)—became a hotbed of insurgency. The JKHM was successful in establishing and sustaining units in the Jammu region, and these units, as well as the *tanzeems* of Pakistani religious radicals who infiltrated in large numbers into IJK from the mid-1990s onward, have posed a major and continuing challenge to Indian security forces in the Jammu region.

Malik was also not successful in getting the Indian government to deal with the JKLF on respectable terms as a political movement. It appears that Indian officials and leaders were interested in getting Malik, a pioneer militant and high-profile independentist leader, to essentially capitulate in the manner of many pro-self-determination Kashmir figures before him, after which he would be suitably rewarded with political office and other perquisites (formal proscription of the JKLF expired several years ago and the ban was not renewed by the Indian government). Malik, who is known for his fiery nature and courage of conviction, refused to do this and was rewarded instead with repeated arrests and imprisonment between the mid-1990s and late 2002. The JKLF also suffered an embarrassing split in the mid-1990s between Malik's IJK-based group and Amanullah Khan, the senior leader on the Pakistani side of the LOC, although Malik eventually gained the loyalty of most JKLF activists in PJK as well as those based overseas in the United States and Britain.

Also in the mid-1990s, the JKLF permanently joined the All-Parties Hurriyat (Freedom) Conference (APHC), an umbrella body of over two dozen pro-"self-determination" groups in IJK formed with Pakistani encouragement in 1993, and Malik became an important figure in this fractious conglomerate. The APHC has been vertically split since late 2003 between factions inclined to rapprochement with the Indian government and more hard-line groups who distrust Indian motives intensely. The dispute is compounded by intense, almost byzantine factional intrigues and personal rivalries. By 2004 the coalition had practically ceased to function because of the split, and in August 2004 the more hard-line elements formed their own grouping under the leadership of Syed Ali Shah Geelani, a hawkish JI leader in the Valley who is the spiritual mentor to JKHM. Malik and the JKLF have been fence-sitters in this ugly divide. Malik is a frequent visitor to Indian cities, especially Delhi, and has become well known among liberal intelligentsia in urban India as a spokesman of the Kashmiri self-determination cause. In 2001, he was granted a passport by the Indian government, after years of waiting, to travel abroad for treatment for various medical problems; he has injuries from his guerrilla past as well as other health problems created or aggravated during detention. He spent most of his time in the United States, where he spoke at major universities and think-tanks as well as to U.S. government officials and leading human rights groups, invariably reiterating the independentist stance. The Indian government was annoyed and he was incarcerated again shortly after his return.

In late 2002, a reformist and liberalizing party of pro-India orientation (the People's Democratic Party, PDP, formed in 1999) assumed charge of the government in IJK, after elections more or less limited to the pro-India spectrum of political groups. Malik was then released from his most recent spell in prison, followed by releases of a number of senior JKLF activists prominent in the early phase of the *azaadi* insurrection, some of whom had been continuously incarcerated under antiterrorist laws for a decade or more. During 2003, the JKLF launched a new political initiative—a mass signature campaign in the Valley asking citizens to sign a statement calling for the representation of Kashmiris in any peace process, on the grounds that an intergovernmental India-Pakistan process is necessary but not sufficient, and the opinions and aspirations of people who live in Kashmir should be taken into account. Malik and his colleagues took this campaign to the smaller towns and remote rural areas of the Valley, in addition to canvassing support in Srinagar. The popular response was good. Malik and other JKLF leaders were for the most part warmly received by citizens, especially in villages, and addressed numerous public meetings, including some sizable gatherings. By the end of 2004 the JKLF claimed to have gathered 1.5 million signatures from all sections of society, and its renewed attempt at mass contact and grassroots organization seems to have been a limited success.

While the group rejects participation in Indian-sponsored electoral processes and institutions as a sellout, it has come a long way from its insurgent phase, and is groping for a strategy which will make it a viable political player. Malik made this clear to me when I met with him in Srinagar in September 2004. Coinciding with a thaw in abysmal India-Pakistan relations in early 2004, Malik addressed a New Year letter jointly to India's then prime minister Atal Bihari Vajpayee and Pakistan's president General Pervez Musharraf, once again calling for the meaningful inclusion and participation of Kashmiris in any peace process. The legacy of the JKLF's armed struggle and the role of independentist representatives in a Kashmir peace process are assessed in the final section of this chapter.

The JKHM's dominance of the armed struggle came at a price, both for the group and for the *azaadi* movement. Because most supporters and sympathizers of the self-determination demand in Kashmir are of a pro-independence or at least a pro-autonomy mindset, the JKHM could not aspire to the same degree of spontaneous popular support enjoyed by JKLF insurgents in their prime. Conscious of this limitation, JKHM leaders, fortified by Pakistani/ISI backing, decided to try to impose their own understanding of the *azaadi* concept through the gun. The ascendancy of JKHM during 1993–1994 was marked by a rash of killings not just of JKLF cadres and intelligentsia figures (mentioned above), but also of numerous ordinary civilians deemed unfriendly or unreliable, of commanders and members of other, smaller insurgent factions (mostly pro-Pakistan ones, ironically), and of prominent religious leaders who dared to criticize JKHM or were simply considered potential rivals. As early as May 1990, JKHM gunmen killed the *mirwaiz* (religious head) of Srinagar and the northern Kashmir Valley, Maulvi Farooq, in his home in Srinagar. In addition to discharging his religious duties, Maulvi Farooq led a pro-Pakistan political group, the Awami Action Committee (he was succeeded as *mirwaiz* by his son, Umar Farooq, who is a leading APHC figure). JKHM also murdered Maulana Masoodi, an aged cleric who had been a top leader of the historic National Conference and a major figure in pro-independence politics for three decades from the 1940s into the 1960s. In June 1994, JKHM gunmen assassinated Qazi Nissar, *mirwaiz* of the southern part of the Kashmir Valley, in his home near the town of Anantnag. Qazi Nissar had been a prominent MUF leader in 1987 and had been openly critical of the JKHM shortly before his assassination. His murder shocked the public and enraged his spiritual following. Furious denunciations of JKHM and its sponsor, Pakistan, erupted among the 100,000 mourners at his funeral, and a strike called throughout the Valley to protest the murder was successful.

In 1995–1996, a new phenomenon emerged in the armed conflict. Increasing numbers of former guerrillas switched sides and joined the Indian war on insurgency as auxiliaries. Some of these were criminal types, while others were opportunists and men of shallow political commitment who had joined the insurgency at the peak of *azaadi* fervor and discovered in due course that they had no appetite for a protracted struggle against the huge Indian state-security apparatus, which numbers approximately half a million personnel if all military, paramilitary and police forces inside IJK and along the LOC are taken into account. But others had been serious militants who were disillusioned by what they viewed as Pakistan's ruthless interventions in and corrupting influence on their struggle and the willingness of the pro-Pakistan hardcore, represented above all by JKHM, to perpetrate violence against those among their own people who did not agree with the "Kashmir banega Pakistan" slogan. To this day, many JKLF activists, other former insurgents, and ordinary citizens are convinced that the JKHM aimed not just to dominate but monopolize the insurgency as part of a wider ISI game plan.

Thus in May 1996 four senior insurgents, including three former commanders of Muslim Jaanbaaz Force, Al-Barq, and Muslim Mujahideen (all pro-Pakistan *tanzeems* smaller than JKLF and JKHM) and one commander of JKHM publicly gave up the gun, resumed civilian lives, condemned Pakistan and called for dialogue between local "separatists" and the Indian government to resolve the Kashmir problem. Others followed, and as a result a number of smaller guerrilla outfits active in the first part of the decade became defunct. This, together with the JKLF's withdrawal from armed struggle, meant that the insurgency lost much of its steam and bite. But many former foot soldiers in the JKLF and the other groups did not renounce the gun. Motivated by fear and hatred of the JKHM, these fighters—often joined by their relatives and friends—sought protection, or vengeance, or money (or some combination thereof) through active collaboration on the ground with the Indian counterinsurgency campaign.

It was this collaboration that enabled the Indian security forces to reassert control over Srinagar and other Valley towns, as well as over some rural areas in the Valley. Insurgency continued at a significantly lower intensity in the Valley, remained unabated in the Jammu region's vast and mountainous Doda district (which has a Muslim majority, mostly Kashmiri-speaking as in the Valley, and where insurgency in general and JKHM units in particular have proved very resilient since 1992) and spread to Rajouri and Poonch, two other Muslim-majority districts on the LOC in the Jammu region where infiltrating fighters of Pakistani religious-radical *tanzeems* established a menacing presence in the second half of the 1990s. The upper hand over insurgency made it possible for the Indian government to conduct dubious elections in IJK in autumn 1996 that restored Farooq Abdullah—the discredited politician who headed IJK governments in 1982–1984 and the disastrous 1987–1989 period—from oblivion to office.

The new breed of pro-India gunmen, known variously as "renegades," "counterinsurgents," "pro-India militants," "surrendered militants," "reformed militants" and "Ikhwanis" soon became a law unto themselves.

Their activities, including intimidation, smuggling, robbery, extortion, rape and murder—all under the protective umbrella of the Indian security forces—generated revulsion among the public. But these groups also played a key role for several years after their emergence in the Indian war on the JKHM. The largest contra concentrations, located just north of Srinagar and around the southern Valley town of Anantnag, respectively, were led by a former JKLF insurgent and a former Muslim Mujahideen (a breakaway JKHM group) fighter. These and other "renegade" groups unleashed a savage vendetta against the JKHM, which retaliated by killing the pro-India gunmen and sometimes their entire families when and where they could. The "renegades" in turn targeted known activists of the JI, and hundreds of JI members were killed in the major renegade-active zones. This slaughter caused a faction of the JI leadership in IJK to rethink the closeness of its nexus with the JKHM. By the late 1990s this faction, urging a return to traditional JI activities centered on Islamic teaching and a delinking from JKHM insurgency, emerged as the majority group within the JI, although the party remains divided on the issue; the JI's single most influential leader, the septuagenarian Syed Ali Shah Geelani, is a pro-JKHM hawk.

Between the middle and late 1990s, according to Indian counterinsurgency sources, the core JKHM combat strength fell from over 3,000 to under 1,500 because of casualties and desertions. This is a plausible estimate but must still be regarded with caution, and it is unclear whether the latter figure includes the sizable JKHM contingents active in the Jammu region (if it does, the estimate seems too low to me). The group's commander-in-chief, Syed Salahuddin, decamped to "Azad" Kashmir and Pakistan from the Kashmir Valley in end-1994 and is not known to have returned at all since. He was probably wise; in 1998 Ali Mohammed Dar, a former senior IJK police officer who became a top JKHM "military adviser" after the outbreak of insurgency, was eliminated by special counterterrorism police—raised since 1996 from turncoat insurgents and IJK Hindus and Sikhs as well as some pro-India Muslims—when he returned to the Valley from across the LOC.

In 1998, the Hindu nationalist Bharatiya Janata Party (BJP) came to power in India at the head of a polyglot coalition government. This government tested five nuclear devices in May 1998, and Pakistan responded by testing six (thereby equaling India, which tested its first atomic bomb in 1974) within weeks. A short-lived thaw in India-Pakistan relations in early 1999, initiated by India's Prime Minister Vajpayee who made a trip to Pakistan, was rudely interrupted in the summer, when units of the Pakistani army infiltrated IJK's Ladakh region in the vicinity of the border town of Kargil. The operation was, according to the Indian government, masterminded by the then army chief, Pervez Musharraf, and touched off heavy fighting—terminated after two months only when U.S. president Bill Clinton and his colleagues talked tough to Pakistani prime minister Nawaz Sharif in Washington[18] and secured a Pakistani withdrawal—and a precipitous deterioration in intergovernmental relations ensued. In October 1999, Musharraf deposed Sharif and seized power in Pakistan; in the same month, the BJP-led coalition returned to power after a midterm parliamentary election in India. Vajpayee reinitiated intergovernmental contacts by inviting Musharraf to a summit meeting in India in mid-2001. The meeting was inconclusive and was regarded as a disappointment by both sides. After September 11, 2001, Pakistan returned to favor as a front-line ally of the United States, a traditional status it had largely lost—even as India expanded its relations with the U.S. through the 1990s—since the end of the Afghan war and especially after Musharraf's military coup. Clinton visited India for five days in March 2000 and stopped over at Islamabad airport for a few hours on the way back, where he lectured Musharraf and his fellow-generals on the virtues of democracy.

In December 2001, a squad of five men, allegedly jihadi extremists from Pakistan, mounted a suicide attack on the Indian parliament building in New Delhi in connivance with two men from the Kashmir Valley resident in Delhi. The attack was fortunately thwarted by Indian security personnel and unarmed parliament stewards, eight of whom (and a gardener tending the lawns) lost their lives during a 45-minute battle with automatic rifles and grenades in the building's courtyard and portico. India's relations with Pakistan plunged to the lowest level since the 1971 Bangladesh war, India mounted a major military show of force on its borders with Pakistan during 2002, and war clouds seemed to loom over the subcontinent. The crisis eventually passed. In April 2003 Vajpayee once again turned the page when he delivered a speech in Srinagar calling for better relations with Pakistan and a peaceful approach to the Kashmir conflict. The renewed thaw was consolidated when Vajpayee and Musharraf met at a summit of South Asian leaders in Islamabad in January 2004, and a slew of measures to normalize intergovernmental relations were rapidly put into effect. In late January, a delegation of the "moderate" APHC faction met both Vajpayee and his deputy prime minister and home (interior) minister, the right-wing Hindu hard-liner L. K. Advani, in the first such face-to-face encounter between leading Kashmir "separatists" and the highest officials of the Indian state. Advani made commitments on accelerated release of political prisoners and improved enforcement of human rights standards during and after the meeting.

In February the first round of intergovernmental talks were held in Islamabad between the Indian and Pakistani foreign secretaries (the top career foreign service officers of the two countries) and an eight-item agenda, including Kashmir, was agreed on for substantive talks. Further meetings were held in the second half of 2004, after the conclusion of India's general elections in May, which in a shock outcome ousted the BJP-led coalition, headed by Vajpayee, from power and restored a Congress-led coalition in New Delhi. The agenda included nuclear risk-reduction measures and the commencement of a trans-LOC bus service between Srinagar and Muzaffarabad, the capital of "Azad" Kashmir. The Srinagar-Muzaffarabad bus service proposal aroused great excitement on both sides of the LOC in Kashmir, especially among families divided by the de facto border since 1947 but also the general populace. An exciting and competitive series of cricket matches—cricket is *the* mass sport in the subcontinent—played in Pakistan during March-April 2004 between the Indian and Pakistani national teams had contributed to normalization and an atmosphere of optimism. But a meeting in Delhi in early September 2004 between the Indian and Pakistani foreign ministers failed to produce any concrete forward movement. A meeting in late September on the sidelines of the United Nations annual meetings in New York between Musharraf and the new Congress prime minister, Manmohan Singh, occasioned a spirit of bonhomie, but like the stalled bus service proposal the Kashmir peace process remained incipient in at the end of 2004.

As this tumultuous, seesaw series of events unfolded in the subcontinent, the insurgency in IJK entered a deadly phase from mid-1999 onward (as the Kargil fighting wound down), as radical Islamist groups based in Pakistan assumed center stage, their fighters—mostly infiltrated Pakistanis, supplemented by local recruits—using *fidayeen* (suicidal) tactics against Indian military camps, police stations, government and official buildings, and civilian targets in a psychological war of attrition with the Indian state.[19] The JKHM, however, continued to be the most important insurgent organization, for two reasons, although it does not generally practice *fidayeen* tactics. First, the size and field presence of the JKHM, and its support network in IJK, are significantly larger and more extensive than any of the more radical *tanzeems* like LeT and JeM, which rely on a smaller cadre (likely to be in the low to middle hundreds for JeM and upper hundreds for LeT) of fanatical fighters. Second and even more important, the JKHM is the only active guerrilla group composed largely of, and led by, IJK people, augmented by some from "Azad" Kashmir. The radical Islamist groups have recruited some locals but still have predominantly Pakistani cadres, as well as Pakistani leaders and Pakistan-based organizations (LeT leader Hafiz Muhammad Sayeed and JeM leader Maulana Masood Azhar are from Lahore and Bahawalpur, respectively, both cities in Pakistan's dominant Punjab province, and LeT is headquartered near Lahore and JeM in Karachi).

Moreover, despite difficult times and setbacks, the JKHM has, unlike the JKLF, survived as an insurgent force and continued guerrilla warfare, albeit increasingly reliant on IED attacks against the security forces. Indeed, the JKHM has over time wreaked a terrible vengeance on its tormentors during the second half of the 1990s, the "renegades"—several top renegade commanders have been assassinated by JKHM hit squads since 2002. In recognition of this role, the JKHM occupies the chair of the Muttahida Jehad Council (MJC; United Jehad Council), an umbrella body of *mujahideen* groups headquartered in Muzaffarabad, which includes all active *tanzeems* (about a dozen) other than the LeT, which is a maverick and exceptionally violent group.

At the same time, the JKHM has experienced considerable internal upheaval over the past few years. This began in July 2000, when the JKHM declared a general ceasefire in IJK. The man behind the move was Abdul Majid Dar, the group's top operational commander in the Valley, known until then to be a hard-liner and long-standing favorite of the ISI. But in 2000 Dar announced that "even if this violence continues for another ten years, ultimately the concerned parties will have to sit around a table and find a solution through talks. So it is better that a serious and meaningful dialogue begin now, so that further bloodshed is stopped."[20] The other groups in the MJC, who had apparently not been informed about the decision, were enraged and Salahuddin was temporarily suspended from his post as MJC chairman. The Indian government welcomed the move and said its forces would reciprocate. Dar and several other JKHM commanders then met in Srinagar—where the ceasefire was announced—with an Indian delegation led by a senior official of the federal government's interior ministry. On the ground in IJK, jihadi insurgents responded by going on a killing spree, and more than one hundred Hindu civilians died in a series of massacres, mainly in the Valley but also in the Jammu region. Under pressure in Muzaffarabad from the radical Islamists and probably also the ISI, Salahuddin declared that the ceasefire would be rescinded after two weeks unless the Indian government categorically admitted that Kashmir is a "disputed territory" and not an "integral part" of India (as Indian officialdom likes to claim) and conceded that talks would immediately begin with Pakistan on the dispute. The Indian government refused to respond to such an ultimatum, and Salahuddin rescinded the ceasefire in a press conference held in a hotel in Islamabad. Within days of the collapse of the truce, a major car-bomb attack took place in central Srinagar, the JKHM claimed responsibility, and the war resumed.

Despite this failure, the episode was rife with implications. It exposed the existence of a sizable "peace faction" and an internal rift in the JKHM. One year later, in August 2001, Dar and his supporters, including several senior commanders, were purged. Almost all of those expelled abandoned active militancy, and one purged commander was later killed in his Valley hometown by counterterrorist police for unknown reasons. Dar was among a number of pro-self-determination figures who were courted by the Indian government to take part in Indian-sponsored IJK elections in autumn 2002 but did not do so.[21] In March 2003 he was shot dead in his house in Sopore, a northern Valley town, by two gunmen. Their identity is unclear, but JKHM militants are the prime suspects. After Dar's murder, some of his followers formed an armed group called the Hizb-i-Islami, but it remains marginal. A week after Dar's assassination, the man who had replaced him in 2001 as JKHM's operational commander in the Valley—Ghulam Hassan Khan, alias Saif-ul-Islam—was tracked down and killed by Indian security forces, leading to speculation that Dar supporters had facilitated his elimination to avenge their leader's murder. The JKHM's vulnerability to Indian decapitation attacks based on "real-time intelligence" was further underscored in January 2004 when Khan's successor as JKHM operational chief, Ghulam Rasool Dar alias Ghazi Nasiruddin, was also tracked down and killed in Srinagar by Indian forces, along with the group's head of finance.

But while the former JKHM chief Abdul Majid Dar was quietly laid to rest by his family in Sopore, with no sign of public mourning despite his contribution to the "freedom struggle," the burial of the incumbent chief Ghulam Hassan Khan barely a week later in his southern Valley hometown was a mass event attended by many thousands from the area and beyond, underscoring the base of the JKHM and the respect commanded by its "martyrs"—despite all the flaws and misdeeds of the group and its many enemies. The JKHM's reaction to the recent thaw in India-Pakistan relations, which may represent the beginning of a Kashmir peace process, is lukewarm and somewhat skeptical, but not dismissive. Ambivalent statements from the group's Muzaffarabad headquarters typically exhort the Indian government to abandon intransigence, withdraw or at least reduce its troops in IJK, and so on. But the APHC's implosion during 2003–2004 has meant that "self-determination" politics, always fractured and fractious, is presently in a shambolic state. Mysterious assassinations of middle-level leaders of both APHC camps have occurred during 2004, further poisoning the situation.

## Conclusion

Since the Kashmir conflict has multiple layers and dimensions, any peace process needs to involve multiple, interlocking, and mutually reinforcing tracks: New Delhi-Islamabad, New Delhi-Srinagar, Srinagar-Jammu, Islamabad-Muzaffarabad, and Srinagar-Muzaffarabad.[22] Of these, normalization and progress at the international, intergovernmental level is crucial to prospects of building a substantive, sustained peace process. But institutionalized intergovernmental cooperation, however essential, is in itself insufficient. Peace building is incomplete and unsustainable without strong legitimacy *within* the contested territory and its society. A Kashmir peace process needs the participation of the broadest possible spectrum of sociopolitical forces and actors from the highly differentiated and fractured social and political space of Jammu and Kashmir. It is particularly crucial to include representatives of former or current insurgent groups. In this regard, the incorporation of both the JKLF and the JKHM are important.

The JKLF is the group that put the largely dormant Kashmir question back on the global map of major regional conflicts in 1990, and it has been the most consistent voice of independence, an aspiration that has mass appeal on both sides of the LOC, particularly in IJK and within IJK in the Kashmir Valley. The JKHM has been the main organization that has kept insurgency going since the mid-1990s, thereby ensuring that the Kashmir question does not fall off that map again or recede into the background. The as yet nascent peace process in Kashmir will be significantly strengthened if Yasin Malik and Syed Ali Shah Geelani (the Valley-based JI figure who is JKHM's spiritual mentor) become actively engaged. As the single largest group in the MJC and the only one with strong roots within IJK, the JKHM's decisions will be critical to reducing the still ongoing daily violence and death toll in IJK to negligible levels. There have been reports since late 2003 that Pakistani officials, especially from the ISI, have been discussing the possibility of a ceasefire declaration with MJC leaders. The JKLF's demand for Kashmiri representation in any process to tackle the Kashmir conflict is well known and of long standing. But even the JKHM, which has largely acted as the Pakistani state's surrogate and agent in the armed conflict, may have a mind of its own. Its commander in chief Salahuddin could have been mistaken for a JKLF spokesman when he told an Indian interviewer in late 1992: "No settlement can be reached without the active physical participation of the representatives of Kashmir. Kashmir is the real party in the case. India and Pakistan will not decide by themselves. It is not possible."[23]

At the same time, after seventeen years of armed conflict, JKLF supporters and independence-minded people in general are fully aware, although they may be reluctant to openly admit it, that their maximalist conception of *azaadi* is unrealizable. India and Pakistan are tacitly united in their opposition to a sovereign authority in Kashmir or in any part of Kashmir. The independence idea is also unacceptable to the substantial pro-India and pro-Pakistan segments of the population in IJK, and to the substantial pro-Pakistan segment in PJK. The JKHM's war cry, which parrots Pakistani propaganda that Kashmir is the "jugular vein" of Pakistan is, in turn, unacceptable to India, to the pro-independence and pro-India segments of the population in IJK, and to the pro-independence segment in PJK. While both JKLF and JKHM have tended in their rhetoric to swear by the plebiscite called for by the United Nations more than fifty years ago to decide the question of rightful sovereignty, the JKLF has stood for the "third option" of independence, while JKHM (and JI) have been insistent that the choice be restricted to India or Pakistan—a very fundamental difference. India dismisses the idea of a plebiscite altogether: its governments have done so since 1956. Pakistan has been formally in favor of such an exercise, but Musharraf has become the first Pakistani leader to publicly acknowledge that the plebiscite is not a viable option and an alternative path to an honorable peace needs to be found. I have argued elsewhere that the plebiscitary approach is both infeasible and deeply flawed as an idea, while a range of suggested partitionist formulas are equally flawed and rife with risks of exacerbating conflict.[24] Both near-term agendas such as reduction of Indian troop presence (a demand JKHM raises) and longer-term goals such as self-rule and an end to the hard division of Kashmir along a heavily militarized LOC (central JKLF concerns) can only be advanced through multitrack negotiations as part of a structured peace process.

The support of major states, regional blocs, and multilateral organizations in the international system would be a considerable asset to such a peace process, although the initiative and momentum have to come from within India, Pakistan, and Kashmir. The constitution of a contact group-like consortium that includes representation from major states like the U.S., Russia, and China (all of which have a declared interest in stability in South Asia), regional blocs such as the European Union and the Association of Southeast Asian Nations, and international organizations like the UN is an idea worth consideration. But any extraregional role in a Kashmir peace process would have to be *supportive* rather than *interventionist*, if it is to be acceptable to all protagonists and of benefit to a peace process, given the largely negative stance of governments (particularly India) and of public opinion (in India, Pakistan, and possibly Kashmir) to external, especially Western intervention. The United States, as the global superpower with direct influence on Pakistan and leverage with India, may play a vital role, but most effectively behind the scenes.

The nascent peace process on Kashmir could either move forward or stagnate (and eventually dissipate). The list of obstacles and complications is long and daunting. Pakistani and Indian perceptions and expectations of the yet incipient intergovernmental dialogue process differ significantly. Formally, Kashmir is only one among eight issues on the agenda of "composite" talks. This is consistent with the long-standing Indian view that intergovernmental talks ought not to be "unifocal"—about the Kashmir dispute alone. While Pakistan has conceded to the Indian preference on the structuring of intergovernmental talks, its officials and spokesmen, from Musharraf downward, continue to emphasize that without discernible forward movement on Kashmir the whole exercise will be rendered meaningless. Moreover, the Pakistani and Indian leaderships have different timeframes in mind in assessing whether or not progress has been made. Musharraf, who survived two assassination attempts in December 2003 by apparent al-Qaeda/Jaish-e-Mohammad elements who were helped by low-ranking members of the military, presides precariously over an unstable polity and is noticeably keen if not impatient that the Kashmir conflict be thrashed out within two to three years at the most. The Indians, one the other hand, prefer a tortoise-like pace, not surprising since India has for the last five decades been the status quo power in the territorial dispute over Kashmir, while Pakistan has been the revisionist party.

The change of government in India in May 2004 has introduced a further element of uncertainty into prospects of tangible progress. Atal Bihari Vajpayee, the moderate Hindu nationalist who was prime minister until May 2004, had invested a great deal of personal effort and prestige into the normalization and improvement of relations with Pakistan, and appeared to have some sort of vision for peace and security in the subcontinent. Before the fall from power, Vajpayee and his national security adviser Brajesh Mishra had laid the groundwork for a substantive peace process and built good rapport with their Pakistani counterparts. Vajpayee also enjoys high standing among the population of Indian-controlled Kashmir, not a mean feat for an Indian politician. The Congress, the emasculated dinosaur of Indian politics, is on the other hand a deeply conservative, status quo-ist party not known for either tactical initiative or strategic vision. Some of the leaders of India's new government may be complacent and shortsighted enough to let the peace process stall, although Prime Minister Singh is personally interested in taking it forward. After Singh met with Musharraf in New York in late September 2004 rumors circulated about a deal to end the two-decade confrontation between the two armed forces on the Siachen glacier, north of the LOC at altitudes of 18,000–20,000 feet above sea level. But the rumors of an Indian pullback and subsequent demilitarization of the area were angrily dismissed by India's Congress foreign minister. In November 2004 the Indian government announced a minor, practically token reduction of its troop levels in Kashmir. The much-awaited Srinagar-Muzaffarabad bus service, which would probably have materialized before the end of 2004 had the Vajpayee government been returned to office, began only in April 2005.

The international context remains equally uncertain. The United States is the only country with the influence and leverage to nudge and prod India and Pakistan into a peace process over Kashmir. Yet U.S. credibility is at an all-time low in India, Pakistan, and Kashmir in the wake of the invasion and occupation of Iraq. The JKLF leader Yasin Malik, in private conversation, speaks with deep empathy of the "Iraqi resistance" to America and its satellites; Malik, it should be reiterated, is a moderate Muslim who traveled across the United States in 2001 canvassing support for his cause and was in that country when the September 11 attacks occurred. Antipathy to the U.S. is scarcely limited to Muslims, however; in India, where only 13 percent of the population are Muslim, 87 percent of the population opposed the Iraq invasion. Restoring American credibility among Muslims and in most of the world, especially Europe and the developing world, appears to be a task of near-Herculean proportions. U.S. policy on the Palestinian-Israeli conflict would be a litmus test in this regard. As of mid-2005 peace in Kashmir is just a glimmer on the horizon, which could yet turn out to be a mirage.

## Glossary

AJK: Azad (Free) Jammu and Kashmir, the more populous of two regions of the disputed territory of Jammu and Kashmir that are under Pakistani control.

APHC: All-Parties Hurriyat (Freedom) Conference, a coalition of about two dozen pro-independence and pro-Pakistan parties in Indian-controlled Jammu and Kashmir. Formed in 1993, the APHC disintegrated because of factional feuding in 2004.

BJP: Bharatiya Janata Party, a Hindu nationalist political party that led India's coalition government from 1998 to May 2004.

Congress: India's oldest political party, which heads the coalition government formed in May 2004.

IJK: Indian-controlled Jammu and Kashmir. This includes the bulk of the territory and population of the disputed territory of Jammu & Kashmir and consists of three regions: Kashmir Valley, Jammu and Ladakh.

ISI: Inter-Services Intelligence, the Pakistani military establishment's elite covert operations agency. It has a dedicated Kashmir department and has been deeply involved in insurgency in IJK since the late 1980s.

JI: Jama'at-i-Islami, a conservative Islamic movement active in India, Pakistan, Bangladesh, and Kashmir.

JeM: Jaish-e-Mohammad, a militant Islamic group led by Pakistanis that has been active in insurgency in IJK since 2000.

JKHM: Jammu and Kashmir Hizb-ul Mujahideen, IJK's largest and most resilient insurgent group. Formed in 1989, it has a pro-Pakistan orientation and political links with the JI.

JKLF: Jammu and Kashmir Liberation Front, formed in AJK in 1964. It stands for the independence of the entire disputed territory of Jammu and Kashmir. The JKLF pioneered insurgency in IJK in 1989–1990 but has been militarily inactive since the mid-1990s.

LeT: Lashkar-e-Taiba, a radical Islamic group active in insurgency in IJK since the mid-1990s and responsible for the majority of *fidayeen* (suicide) attacks by insurgents since 1999.

LOC: Line of Control, the 742-kilometer dividing line between the Indian-controlled and Pakistani-controlled parts of Jammu and Kashmir. It originated as a ceasefire line in 1949 and was renamed the LOC by intergovernmental agreement in 1972.

MJC: Muttahida (United) Jehad Council, the coordinating body of about a dozen insurgent groups active in IJK. It does not include LeT and is chaired by the JKHM.

MUF: Muslim United Front, a coalition of pro-"self-determination" parties that contested elections, rigged by Indian authorities, to the IJK legislature in 1987. Forerunner of the APHC.

NC: National Conference, a political party historically dominant in the Kashmir Valley and until the outbreak of insurgency the linchpin of politics in IJK. It has a pro-India orientation.

PJK: Pakistani-controlled Jammu and Kashmir. It consists of two regions: AJK and the high-altitude, thinly inhabited "Northern Areas."

## Timeline

1947: The Kashmir dispute is born as the newly independent states of India and Pakistan both claim the territory and its population. Fighting breaks out in Kashmir in October.

January 1949: A ceasefire ends the first India-Pakistan war over Kashmir. Most of the territory and its population are on the Indian side of the ceasefire line.

1964: The Jammu and Kashmir Liberation Front is formed by independentist Kashmiris living in Pakistani-controlled Kashmir.

August–September 1965: India and Pakistan go to war for the second time after a Pakistan-sponsored force infiltrates Indian-controlled Kashmir in a failed attempt to spark a mass uprising.

December 1971: India and Pakistan go to war for the third time. Pakistani forces are routed by the Indians in eastern Pakistan, which emerges as a sovereign state, Bangladesh. The ceasefire line in Kashmir is slightly altered during the hostilities.

July 1972: The ceasefire line in Kashmir is renamed the Line of Control (LOC) by intergovernmental agreement, pending a negotiated settlement of the Kashmir dispute. The LOC is nominally more stable than a ceasefire line but lacks the permanent, juridical status of an international border.

September 1982: Sheikh Mohammad Abdullah, Kashmir's most prominent political leader since the 1940s, dies in Srinagar.

March 1987: Indian authorities blatantly rig an election to form the legislature and government of Indian-controlled Kashmir. This crystallizes intense popular grievance, especially in the Kashmir Valley, where young men begin to drift toward insurgency.

1988: A JKLF organization comprising local youth is established in Srinagar. Its members receive weapons and training from the JKLF organization in Pakistani-controlled Kashmir as well as from the Pakistani military's Inter-Services Intelligence (ISI) agency.

1989: Pro-Pakistan elements in Indian-controlled Kashmir form the JKHM as a pro-Pakistan insurgent group to fight Indian forces and compete with the independentist JKLF.

1990: A popular uprising for *azaadi* (freedom) erupts in the Kashmir Valley in January. Insurgency, spearheaded by JKLF militants, intensifies sharply in response to Indian repression of the civilian population.

1993: The JKHM displaces the JKLF as the dominant insurgent group. The JKLF's decline is the cumulative result of Indian counterinsurgency, Pakistani interventions in the Kashmiri armed struggle, and the organization's own weaknesses.

1994: In May and June, the JKLF's top surviving commander, Yasin Malik, is released after almost four years in Indian captivity and declares a unilateral, indefinite ceasefire. This is effectively the end of the JKLF's armed campaign against Indian rule.

1998: In May, India and Pakistan conduct nuclear tests in rapid succession.

1999: In February, Indian prime minister Atal Bihari Vajpayee travels to Pakistan on a peace initiative. A framework declaration is issued by Indian and Pakistani leaders affirming the need for mutual restraint in a post-nuclear context and reiterating the need for a political solution to the Kashmir dispute. In May–July, the nascent peace process collapses as Pakistani military units are found to have infiltrated the Indian side of the LOC along a 140-km stretch in the high-altitude, sparsely inhabited Ladakh region. A fierce border war ensues with hundreds of military fatalities on both sides. The fighting winds down after President

Clinton talks tough to Pakistani prime minister Nawaz Sharif in Washington and secures a Pakistani withdrawal.

2000: Field commanders of the JKHM in Indian-controlled Kashmir declare a ceasefire. The group's central leadership based in Pakistani-controlled Kashmir rescinds the ceasefire after two weeks and violence resumes.

2001: In July, Pakistan's military ruler General Pervez Musharraf visits India on Vajpayee's invitation. The summit proves inconclusive and is regarded as a disappointment by both sides. In the wake of the 9/11 attacks in the United States, Musharraf emerges as a key ally in the American "war on terror." In December, the Indian parliament complex in New Delhi is attacked by a five-man terrorist squad alleged by the Indian government to be Pakistani nationals. All five are killed by security guards after a fierce battle in the parliament building's compound. Nine security personnel and parliamentary staff are also killed. An infuriated Indian government commences a massive military buildup on Pakistan's borders in response.

2002: A tense year for the subcontinent as the Indian and Pakistani militaries face off on the international border and the LOC. The war clouds blow over by late 2002, as India begins to demobilize and Pakistan follows suit. The United States once again has a role in defusing the crisis, as its officials urge Musharraf's regime to curb the activities of radical Pakistani Islamic groups directed against India.

2003: In April, Vajpayee delivers a speech in Srinagar during a visit to Indian-controlled Kashmir. He calls for better relations with Pakistan and a political settlement to the Kashmir conflict. In November a ceasefire between Indian and Pakistani forces comes into effect along the LOC. Insurgency and counterinsurgency, however, continue inside Indian-controlled Kashmir, as Indian security forces remain locked in combat with both the JKHM and jihadi groups of Pakistani origin such as the LeT. In December, Musharraf survives two assassination attempts in quick succession. Radical jihadi elements involved in the Kashmir insurgency are implicated in at least one of the attempts.

2004: In January, the emerging thaw is sealed when Vajpayee and Musharraf meet in Islamabad on the occasion of a regional summit of South Asian leaders. In February, an eight-point agenda for intergovernmental dialogue, including Kashmir, is agreed to by the two countries. In May, Vajpayee's BJP-led coalition government unexpectedly loses parliamentary elections in India. A Congress-led coalition government takes over. In September, Musharraf and India's new prime minister, Manmohan Singh, meet on the sidelines of the United Nations annual meetings in New York. In December, the incipient India-Pakistan peace process appears to be running out of momentum. While talks continue at several levels, there is a noticeable failure to make progress on Kashmir-related issues, such as a proposed bus service connecting the capitals of Indian- and Pakistani-controlled Kashmir across the LOC. Prospects of peace in Kashmir hang in the balance.

2005: In April, the Srinagar–Muzaffarabad bus link begins. Progress in the intergovernmental dialogue remains slow and halting, however, despite professions of good intent and flexibility by the leaders of both countries. In June, a delegation of pro-"self-determination" leaders from IJK visits "Azad" Kashmir and Pakistan. The delegation includes JKLF leader Yasin Malik, who uses the opportunity to reiterate the importance of Kashmiri participation in crafting a Kashmir settlement. Malik and Mirwaiz Umer Farooq, another member of the delegation, meet with Syed Salahuddin, the JKHM chief commander, during the visit. In the second half of June JKHM militants carry out two major car-bombings in the Kashmir Valley, killing at least a dozen Indian military and paramilitary personnel. Twelve civilian bystanders are also killed in one of the attacks.

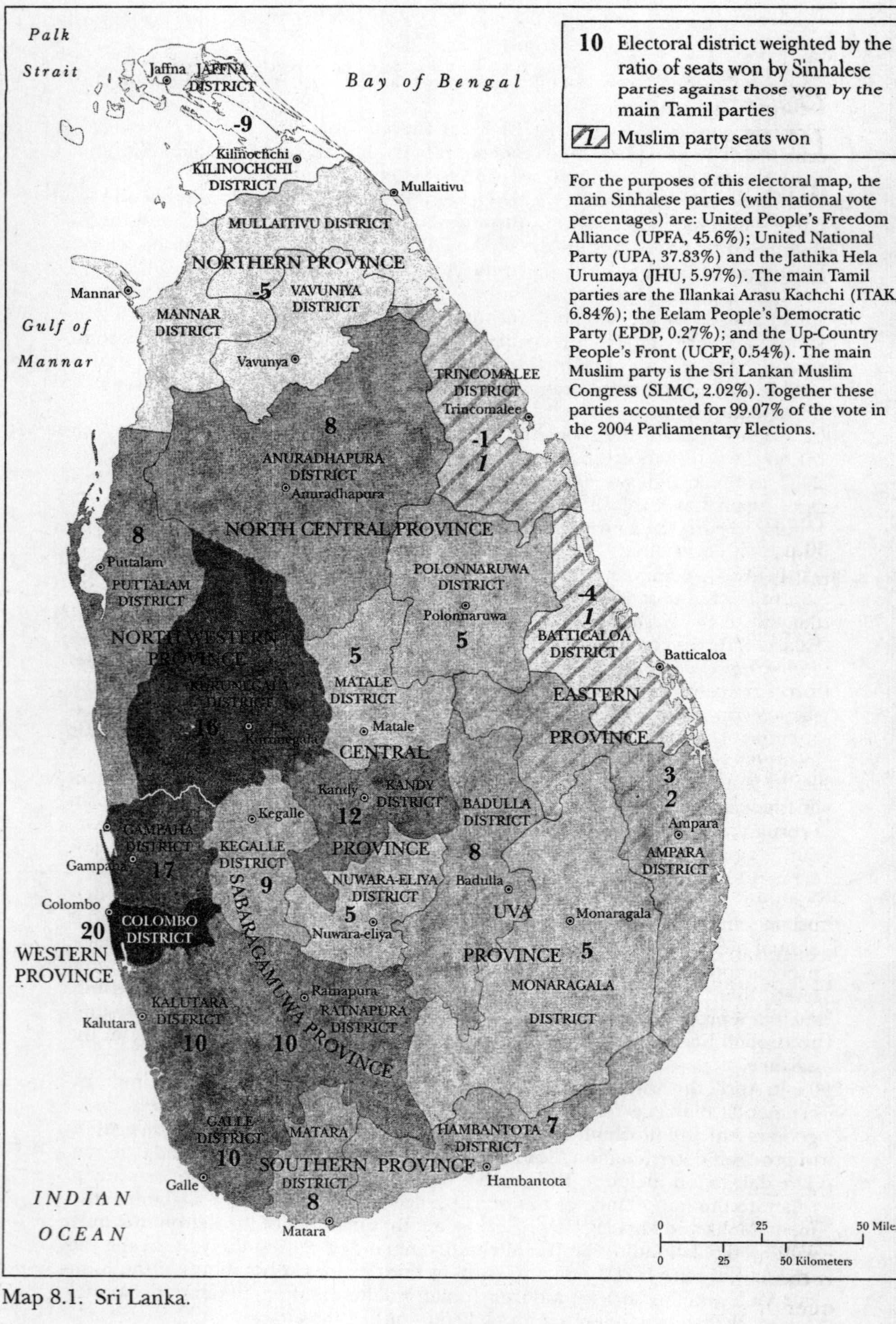


Map 8.1. Sri Lanka.

*Chapter 8*

# LTTE: Majoritarianism, Self-Determination, and Military-to-Political Transition in Sri Lanka

BRENDAN O'DUFFY

The rise of the Liberation Tigers of Tamil Eelam (LTTE) from a group of 30 poorly armed dissidents in 1983 into one of the world's foremost paramilitary groups by 1991 demonstrates what may happen to states that attempt to ignore ethnonationalism and impose majoritarian democracy. Despite a rare peaceful transition from colonial rule in 1947, high levels of literacy, and significant basic development in health, housing, and education, Sri Lanka's independence has been marred by the deaths of nearly 100,000 people from political violence, including the successful assassinations of a prime minister, a president, and numerous other politicians, the displacement of nearly one million of its 18 million inhabitants, and the widespread destruction of homes and property.

Conflict has not been limited to Sri Lanka, but in 1987 involved India in a "peacekeeping" operation that led to the deaths of more than 1,000 of its soldiers and ended in the ignominious retreat of the world's fourth largest army at the hands of the emboldened LTTE, which proceeded to assassinate Rajiv Gandhi the following year and to continue its fight for an independent homeland state (Eelam). The impact of the conflict has spread farther to influence other secessionists and insurgents—including the use of suicide jackets, naval suicide attacks against large craft, improvised mortars and landmines, and integration with sophisticated worldwide arms suppliers.[1]

This chapter examines the failure of the majoritarian institutions of independent Ceylon, as it was known, to accommodate the grievances of the Tamil-speaking minorities or the rising expectations of those members of the Sinhalese majority who felt marginalized by the economic modernization experienced in the 1960s and 1970s. The LTTE as an organization is then examined. Policy responses to the LTTE's emergence are subsequently evaluated, as are the costs of the conflict that had led by the late

1990s to a discernible "hurting stalemate." The conclusion suggests how this stalemate might be converted into a viable, mutually accommodating negotiating process. The key argument is that the LTTE's status as the vanguard of Tamil nationalism can and should be recognized in a negotiating partnership with the Sri Lankan government, but that it need not concede the long-term recognition of the LTTE as the "sole representatives" of the Tamil people. Since the costs of military containment are so high and avenues for a federal compromise have not been exhausted, the inclusive process of a negotiated settlement should continue on the basis of the Memorandum of Understanding reached between the LTTE and the Sri Lankan government in November 2002.

## From Ceylon to Sri Lanka: Legacies of Majoritarianism and Presidentialism

Conflict in Sri Lanka shares with other conflicts included in this book a popular majority in one sovereign territory threatened by a minority with ethnic (including cultural and religious) links to a dominant neighbor, and ethnonational aspirations that challenge existing state sovereignty. Just as Israelis fear the support given to their Arab minority by neighboring Arab states and as Northern Ireland unionists fear the support for Irish nationalists by the Irish Republic, so Sri Lankan Sinhalese Buddhists fear cultural, political, and economic domination by India and support for Tamil separatists from 60 million (Hindu) Tamils in the southern Indian state of Tamil Nadu.

Sinhala Buddhist nationalism has a mission to protect both the Sinhala language (derived from Sanskrit) and Theravada Buddhism. These cultural components of Sinhala identity have been threatened historically by Christian missionary projects and their colonial sponsors since the seventeenth century: the Portuguese, Dutch, and British. It is understandable, therefore, that Sinhalese leaders embraced majoritarian political institutions upon achieving independence on 4 February 1948, and most analysts of the origins of conflict, both Sinhalese and Tamil, retrospectively emphasize the conflict-generating properties of the majoritarian ethos of the Westminster system inherited at independence.[2] A principal contributor to the drafting of the 1947 Constitution was British constitutional authority Sir Ivor Jennings, who was convinced of the superiority of ordinary law in protecting the rights of minorities as individual citizens. "In Britain, we have no Bill of Rights; we merely have liberty according to law and we think—truly I believe—that we do the job better than any country which has a Bill of Rights or a Declaration of the Rights of Man."[3] He ended up exporting the defects in the Government of Ireland Act of 1920 to Sri Lanka.[4]

Predictably, given the similarity of ethnonational cleavages and territorial disputes in another former colony, these minimal minority rights provisions failed in Ceylon. Jennings himself subsequently admitted that the antidiscrimination provisions of Section 29 (2) were insufficient, and advocated in the early 1960s for a "comprehensive chapter of fundamental rights."[5] He reconsidered his original proposals because the minimalist protections had been nullified by the emergence of a Sinhalese-Buddhist nationalist movement that insisted on instituting majoritarian supremacy. To no avail. Indeed, Sri Lanka's British majoritarian legacy was given a French magnification in 1978 with the introduction of a Gaullist semipresidential system.

The Sinhalese felt discriminated against under colonial rule: Tamils were given a disproportionate share of administrative posts. They reacted accordingly with independence. Minority safeguards were interpreted in ways that emphasized formal, procedural interpretations over substantive rights protections. For example, the provision for a two-thirds majority to amend the constitution was adhered to but was substantively undermined in 1949 when the "estate Tamils" (invited from India by the British colonial administration as cheap labor, primarily for tea cultivation) were disenfranchised, thereby removing effective minority veto provisions for Tamil-speaking minorities because the Tamil-speaking "bloc" in parliament was reduced to less than 20 percent.[6] According to an Indian observer, S. Manivasakan, the judiciary was politically partisan and gave constitutional legitimacy to acts of the legislature at the expense of individual minority rights.[7]

The logic of "winner takes all" competition under the Westminster system encouraged extremist outbidding that deepened competition along linguistic and religious lines. Plurality rule combined primarily with single-member districts gave seat bonuses to the winning party (as intended), producing large swings in seats from small swings in votes, and therefore tempted the two dominant Sinhalese parties—the liberal United National Party (UNP) and socialist Sri Lanka Freedom Party (SLFP)—to make populist appeals for Sinhalese voters. In K. M. de Silva's interpretation, "once the state was in their [Sinhalese-Buddhist nationalists] hands it was treated as the source of redistributive justice with its own inner logic guided more by political will than concerns for economic growth."[8]

The "Sinhala Only" Act[9] of 1956, making Sinhalese the sole official language, was the key tipping point. This policy was a considerable reverse for the Tamil Federal Party (FP), which was committed to parity status for Tamil. The language issue directly affected two core institutions: the state bureaucracy and education. In both domains, Sinhalese governmental policies were designed to redress the imbalances that favored Tamils during the colonial period. While government apologists such as K. M. de Silva essentially blame Tamils for over-dependence on government-sector jobs, Tamil sympathizers such as A. J. Wilson document the subjective sense of collective insult, objective blocked upward mobility, and the perceived inefficacy of constitutional means to protect Tamils.[10] Whichever interpretation is favored, it was a significant reversal for Tamils. The percentage of Tamil-speakers employed by the state declined from 30 percent at the time of independence to 5.9 percent by 1990.[11] In education, Tamil representation in science-based disciplines fell from 35 percent in 1970 to 19 percent in 1975.[12] Riotous violence accompanied each phase of policy reform or failed constitutional compromise—with severe riots in 1958, 1965, 1971, 1978, and especially 1983.

Both Radhika Coomaraswamy and K. M. de Silva, representatives of Tamil and Sinhalese scholarship respectively, recognize the passage of the Republican Constitution of 1972 as both the culmination of Sinhala-Buddhist nationalism that began in the 1950s and the decisive moment in the march of Tamil separatism.[13] This first autochthonous constitution changed the name of the country from Ceylon to the Republic of Sri Lanka. Among the most contentious provisions, from a Tamil perspective, Buddhism was given the "foremost place" among the religions and the state was entrusted to protect and foster Buddhism (Art. 6). Sinhala was made the official language, thus, in one interpretation, enshrining the 1956 Sinhala Only Act as an inviolable and nonnegotiable constitutional principle (Art 7);[14] and Section 29 of the Soulbury constitution (1946) was deleted and not replaced by explicit judicial protections for minorities. Last, the 1972 constitution subjugated the judiciary to the control of the legislature by eliminating appeals to the (British) Privy Council on constitutional issues. This measure was a response to a supreme court finding against the 1956 Sinhala Only Act; it exemplified for moderate Tamils the futility of constitutional politics.[15]

Following the subsequent 1978 constitution, the politicization of separate branches of government, the judiciary and the bureaucracy, created significant obstacles to the state's ability to respond to violent ethnic conflict. The creation of a Gaullist executive presidency (semipresidential, with a prime minister and cabinet elected separately by the legislature) further undermined the separation of powers by vesting supreme authority in the president, elected by absolute majority using a unique form of the supplementary vote (SV).[16] Allegedly intended to force presidential candidates to seek votes outside their core ethnic constituencies, according to Ben Reilly, "there is little evidence that appeals for preference votes have ever played a major part in determining the results of Sri Lankan elections" because each successful candidate has won by first preferences alone.[17]

The majoritarian ethos of the 1972 and 1978 constitutions was exaggerated further by the SixthAmendment of the constitution. In response to the Tamil United Liberation Front's (TULF) Vaddukoddai Resolution of 1976 (discussed below), the Sixth Amendment "prohibited political parties and individuals from demanding or advocating a separate state for the Tamil-speaking people as a solution to the intractable ethnic conflict in Sri

Lanka."[18] This measure led the TULF to boycott parliament as it attempted to limit loss of support to nascent and more militant Tamil groups, including the LTTE.

Finally, forms of internal colonization have been used in association with development projects to supplement constitutional control by territorial control over areas of traditional Tamil settlement. These territorial restructurings have been central to Tamil grievances and have shaped their conceptions of self-determination. State-sponsored irrigation schemes led to significant movements of Sinhalese settlers to the southern "border" of the Northern Province, the Weli Oya (or Welioya) region in the east of the Northern Province, and the Ampara District of the Eastern Province under the Gal Oya irrigation and colonization projects. Under the guidance of Israeli military advisers in the mid-1980s, the UNP government attempted to subsume the Muslim districts into an enlarged Uva Province—leading to a breakdown of alliances between local Muslim leaders and the governing UNP. Tamils and Muslims generally interpret the schemes as purposeful strategies of internal colonialism, to claim or reclaim national territory for the Sinhalese and challenge Tamil claims for a national homeland in the North and East.[19] Professor Pon. Balasundarampillai, vice-chancellor of Jaffna University, argues that the Welioya region was created with the intention of "bifurcating the traditional Tamil homeland of North and East by [a] series of Sinhala villages coupled with defense establishments . . . a Sinhala land corridor [has been] created between the North and the East."[20] Sinhalese scholars, like G. H. Peiris and K. M. de Silva, by contrast, assert that Tamils migrated voluntarily away from old or underdeveloped irrigation schemes and sought employment in coastal towns like Trincomalee and Batticaloa.[21]

Whatever the ultimate motivations guiding the policies, the results have been contested, both politically and militarily, especially when the LTTE's campaign escalated in the 1980s. Sinhalese settlers were frequently attacked by the LTTE in their attempt to control territory. Fighting was particularly fierce in the Welioya district, a particularly important settlement because of its strategic position relative to both Trincomalee port and the mineral-rich section of the eastern coast of the Northern Province.[22] The Sinhalese population of this area has declined from 10,000 to approximately 3,000 heavily defended people. Under the current ceasefire, the Sri Lankan Army and the LTTE remain positioned to contest parts of the Eastern Province containing substantial Sinhalese populations, particularly the strategically important port of Trincomalee and Ampara District.

## Tamil Political and Militant Responses to Majoritarian Subordination

The demands made at Thimpu, Bhutan, on 13 July 1985 by groups representing constitutional and militant Tamil organizations (including the

LTTE, though not represented by its leader) were fourfold: recognition of the Tamil people as a distinct nationality; guarantee of the territorial integrity of an independent Tamil homeland; recognition of the inalienable right of the Tamil nation to self-determination; and safeguards of the fundamental rights of the Tamil people outside the independent Tamil homeland.[23] These proposals, first enunciated in the Vaddukoddai Resolution of 1976, reflected the cumulative, cyclical experience of Tamils as a subordinate and subjugated minority in post-independence Ceylon/Sri Lanka. As enunciated, for example, in October 2003 in the LTTE Proposal by the Liberation Tigers of Tamil Eelam on Behalf of the Tamil People for an Agreement to Establish an Interim Self-Governing Authority for the Northeast of the Island of Sri Lanka, the armed struggle for independence (Eelam) was considered "a measure of self-defense and as a means for the realization of the Tamil right to self-determination [that] arose only after more than four decades of nonviolent and peaceful constitutional struggle proved to be futile and due to the absence of a means to resolve the conflict peacefully."[24]

Nevertheless, the dominant view has been that the LTTE, led by Velupillai Prabhakaran, will now settle for nothing less than an independent state. Prabhakaran's own comments had been unambiguous until the November 2002 statement on internal self-determination. In 1987 Prabhakaran addressed a crowd of 50,000 on the LTTE's position toward the Indo-Lankan accord, which proposed a settlement based on devolution: "I have unrelenting faith in the proposition that only a separate state can offer a permanent solution for the problem of the people of Tamil Eelam. Let me make it clear to you here, beyond the shadow of a doubt, that I will continue to fight for the objective of obtaining Tamil Eelam."[25] In the first "Heroes' Day" speech of 1990, in honor of those cadres lost in the struggle, Prabhakaran vowed never to give up the struggle and declared, "our homeland needs to be liberated. The chains that bind us have to be broken. Our people shall live in dignity, with honor, safety and independence."[26]

Given this unswerving commitment, Prabhakaran's previous commitments to a negotiated settlement have been interpreted as purely tactical: to relieve pressure and allow the LTTE to rearm for the next phase of struggle. Examples include the acceptance in the early 1980s of training by the Research Analysis Wing (RAW) of the Indian army, while preventing the RAW from confirming the identity of LTTE cadres; verbally acquiescing to the Indo-Lankan accord in 1987 to allow Prabhakaran physically to escape from Delhi and return to Sri Lanka, from where he subsequently denounced the accord as a coerced treaty; entering into an arms pact and negotiations with the Sri Lankan government in 1989, only to pull out of negotiations and continue the war, eventually assassinating the national leaders responsible for the talks initiatives (former Indian Prime Minister Rajiv Gandhi in 1991 and Sri Lankan president Ranasinghe Premadasa in

1993). Similarly, the LTTE called a ceasefire in 1995 and entered into negotiations on the basis of a federal system, only to stonewall in the negotiations and eventually launch what became known as Eelam War III. This experience left Sri Lankan prime minister and subsequent president Chandrika Kumaratunga convinced that Prabhakaran was a "merciless megalomaniac who is insincere about a negotiated settlement, and determined to eliminate any LTTE rivals interested in peace."[27]

Can the preeminent Tiger change stripes? Are the ceasefire and peace process merely a tactical ploy, a prelude to Eelam War IV? The current Sri Lankan political establishment, represented by a new coalition, clearly does not trust the LTTE's commitment to an internal solution. Chandrika Kumaratunga believed in 1995 that Prabhakaran had killed too many people to believe he could have a future in less than an independent state. Less extremely, a senior defense official interviewed for this study felt in 2004 that Prabhakaran would need jurisdictional separation to provide sufficient immunity from prosecution.[28]

Against the view of Prabhakaran's unceasing commitment to an independent state, we need to consider the basis of the proposed compromises he and his leadership have rejected. The Indo-Lankan accord of 1987 was, as the name suggests, between the two sovereign states of India and Sri Lanka. As such, it was exclusive of any formal involvement of the LTTE or other Tamil groups (though others were consulted). The lack of LTTE consent or participation in the development of the accord was then the major source of criticism by Prabhakaran. He accused both governments of attempting to divide and conquer by recognizing and involving rival Tamil paramilitary groups and political parties. In addition, the devolution proposals that were the centerpiece of the accord fell short of a federal constitution, as they did not entrench the devolved powers. Moreover, in practice, the implementation of devolution was dictated by a Sri Lankan government that was, given the dissent from Sinhalese Buddhist extremists, reluctant to allow the North and East to achieve substantial autonomy. A promised referendum on the merger of the Northern and Eastern Provinces was suspended by a presidential order after both the LTTE and the Janatha Vimukthi Peramuna (JVP, People's Liberation Front) denounced the accord.[29] Similarly, the talks initiative of 1989–1990 was based on a tactical alliance between the LTTE and the UNP government against the Indian Peace-Keeping Force (IPKF). Once the IPKF withdrew on 24 March 1990, the LTTE turned against the government. The LTTE perceived that the Sri Lankan government's commitment to a just peace was belied by its overtures to both Sinhalese Buddhist groups[30] and to rival Tamil groups, especially the Eelam People's Revolutionary Liberation Front (EPRLF). Finally, the ceasefire and negotiations of 1994–1995 could not be interpreted as a consensual and mutual recognition negotiating process. Kumaratunga's government took a rigid stance on military positions in Jaffna and insisted on the precedence of ceasefire monitoring over engagement of the LTTE in talks. The LTTE complained that the government was sending lower-level intermediaries rather than ministerial-level negotiators. The government also made immediate humanitarian relief a condition of prior agreement to a political settlement designed and proposed unilaterally by the Sri Lankan government.

None of the initiatives described above could be interpreted as a mutual process of consensual negotiation satisfying the minimal recognition of internal self-determination. On the contrary, all initiatives were based on unilateral or external, bilateral (Indo-Sri Lankan) imposition of settlements.[31] For example, at a press conference in March 1995 Kumaratunga claimed that her government offered "a solution to the *ethnic* problem of Sri Lanka. *We* [the Sri Lankan Government] have worked out a solution. Perhaps the LTTE does not seem willing to discuss it."[32] The LTTE rejects the assumption that the conflict is merely an "ethnic problem"—along with the implication that such a problem can be solved merely by restoring full civil and political rights to minority communities.[33] Instead, the LTTE, along with most Tamil parties, insists that the Sri Lankan conflict is an ethnonational conflict, in which aspirations for national self-determination have to at least be recognized.[34] By extension, the LTTE has consistently asserted that a settlement has to be negotiated between the representatives of the respective nations, a principle that also will force them over time to recognize more explicitly the distinctive interests of Muslims and Sinhalese in any jurisdictions granted autonomy. The ceasefire and negotiations begun in 2002 were based on the premise that the government of Sri Lanka and the LTTE are of equal status *as negotiators*. The LTTE political leader in Jaffna, Illamparithi, emphasized in an interview for this research that the negotiations would not have been possible without recognition of LTTE as "equal partners." He also emphasized that subsequent problems were caused by the government's failure to maintain that equality of status.[35] The principle of equal status also guided the establishment of joint committees and joint task forces and subcommittees established to deal with military/paramilitary, humanitarian relief, refugee resettlement and constitutional issues.

Failure to recognize the nationalist basis of the conflict is likely to perpetuate further conflict. The foundation of the ceasefire established in November 2002 included a LTTE agreement to *consider* a federal settlement based on a unified Sri Lanka. The LTTE leader qualified this commitment in his annual Heroes' Day speech (27 November 2002): "But if our people's right to internal self-determination is denied and our demand for regional self-rule is rejected we have no alternative other than to secede and form an independent state."[36] The conditional adherence to a negotiated, internal settlement was reiterated in the 2004 Heroes' Day Speech when Prabhakaran reviewed the failure of previous attempts at a negotiated compromise, arguing that "The Sinhala nation neither assimilates and integrates our people to live in co-existence nor does it allow our people to secede and lead a separate existence." He then warned: "If the Government of Sri Lanka rejects our urgent appeal and adopts delaying tactics, perpetuating the suffering of our people, we have no alternative other than to advance the freedom struggle of our nation." Prabhakaran remained ambiguous about the form the freedom struggle would take, but given the LTTE's continued recruitment, past record, and organizational structure (discussed next), there is little doubt that militancy remains the most likely option in the event of a breakdown of talks.

## LTTE Organizational Structure

The organizational structure of the LTTE is extremely hierarchical, with a Central Governing Committee, headed by "the leader" Vellupillai Prabhakaran (b. 1954), overseeing both military and political branches. The organization is command-driven, with "the leader" dictating, in consultation with a select group of military and political leaders, all aspects of policy. The LTTE's military wing, which is clearly in the ascendant over the political wing, is divided into an elite fighting wing (Charles Anthony Regiment), an amphibious group (Sea Tigers), an airborne group (Air Tigers), a suicide commando unit (Black Tigers), and an intelligence group. S. P. Tamilchelvan and Prabhakaran's political adviser Anton Balasingham head the political office. While the political wing has risen in prominence in light of the ceasefire and negotiations since November 2002, it remains clear to most observers that the political leaders remain subordinate to Prabhakaran.[37]

The specific ideological orientation that has created solidaristic bonds within the LTTE combines ethnonationalism and Maoism. Prabhakaran's own asceticism pervades the organization, reflected in the Spartan administrative, police and judicial institutions operating in Kilinochchi and Jaffna town. According to M. R. Narayan Swamy, Prabhakaran was particularly influenced by the militant thoughts and deeds of Subhas Chandra Bose, whose Indian National Army challenged Gandhi's nonviolent anticolonialism in the 1940s.[38] The training and indoctrination process is based on a high degree of mental and physical discipline.

The cult of personality at the apex of the organization is reflected in the pledge of allegiance made by cadres to the Eelam struggle *and* also specifically to Prabhakaran. Interviews with senior LTTE leaders reinforce the mythic, reverential perceptions of the leader. The senior LTTE administrator in Kilinochchi (Sanappah Master) told me that he and others considered Prabhakaran as "God become man."[39] Other cadres have also emphasized their devotion not only to the cause of Eelam but also to their sense of personal duty and obligation to the leader.

The extent of ideological commitment to the cause is represented by the cyanide capsule worn by all cadres, including the leader, which are bitten to avoid live capture by the Sri Lankan security forces. Suicide is the expected fate of those carefully chosen cadres who become Black Tigers, dedicating their lives to the cause as suicide bombers or deep-penetration assassins. Land- and sea-based suicide attacks killed 521 people between 1987 and 2003, making the LTTE one of the world's most lethal proponents of suicide attacks.[40]

The handling of dissent within the organization reveals the dominant position of Prabhakaran. Apart from the comprehensive and ruthless elimination of rival Tamil paramilitary organizations, two cases of internal dissent reveal the totalitarian grip of the leader. Prabhakaran's elimination of Mahattaya, one of his closest allies and confidants, surprised many because of the latter's popularity and established credentials in furthering the struggle. Prabhakaran justified Mahattaya's elimination by accusing him of collaborating with the Indian army's Research and Intelligence Wing (RAW) and planning to assassinate Prabhakaran and 10 other LTTE leaders in the early 1990s. More recently, the ejection of Vinayagamoorthy Muralitharan (alias "Karuna"), an important military leader in the Eastern Batticaloa region, is a contemporary indication of the intolerance of dissent. The outcome to what many have considered the most serious split in the LTTE is an indication of the continued dominance of the Northern leadership under Prabhakaran. Karuna, the leader of the split, went to ground after a brief though indecisive defeat in April 2004. Since then, the Northern and Eastern rival Tamil groups have continued to attack each other with lethal grenade and gun attacks. The Northern-based LTTE accuses the Sri Lankan government's Special Task Force of providing sanctuary and arms to Karuna's breakaway faction.

Any encouragement of a transition from a paramilitary movement into a political movement must take into account the extent and ideological orientation of the LTTE's popular base. While the organization is extremely hierarchical, it has a very thick middle stratum of leaders equally committed to Eelam, making a decapitation strategy against Prabhakaran, as attempted by the IPKF in 1989, unlikely to succeed as the domestic and international support networks for the LTTE are so formidable. On the other hand, the encouragement of divisions between Northern LTTE supporters (mainly in the Jaffna peninsula and in the jungles of the Vanni) and Eastern LTTE (mainly in the Batticaloa area) could weaken the LTTE negotiating position in the short term by undermining the LTTE claim to autonomy over a combined North and East Province. But, in the longer term, a split would increase the complexity of negotiations of a final settlement (by the inclusion of more parties) and increases the likelihood, should hostilities resume, of a Northern LTTE land grab of Trincomalee town and its strategically coveted deep-water harbor.

## The Popular Base: Greed over Grievance

The most convincing explanations for the emergence of the LTTE and Tamil separatism emphasize the interactions among economic, political, and cultural forces. Additionally, we need to distinguish between popular support in the first phase of mobilization in the early 1970s, and the second phase of mobilization under conditions of internal war from the early 1980s.

The radicalization of Tamil youth resulted from the interaction of political, economic and cultural reverses experienced by Tamils. Politically, the marginalization of Tamil elites, both elected officials and civil servants, led to outflanking by radical Tamil youth movements by the early 1970s. The reversals of elite pacts between Tamil and Sinhalese leaders in 1957 and 1965, and especially the consolidation of Sinhalese-Buddhist ascendancy in the 1972 constitution, convinced many Tamil youths that the constitutional approach based on federalism and language rights protections was futile.[41] Given the previous dependence on civil service sector jobs, the reverses in Tamil opportunities created higher unemployment in Jaffna and other dry-zone areas of the North, North Central and East—where alternative sources of employment were scarce. Tamil grievances were by-products of an island-wide tension between increases in higher education participation and lack of employment opportunities. Overall unemployment among the younger sections of society (ages fifteen to twenty-four) decreased only marginally, from 35.6 percent of active job-seekers in 1969/70 to 30.9 percent by 1985/86. Among those in the twenty-five to thirty-four age bracket, unemployment nearly doubled, from 7.4 percent in 1969/70 to 13.7 percent in 1985/86.[42] Employment prospects were inversely related to educational attainment, that is, those with higher degrees suffered worse employment prospects. The result was a radicalization of both Tamil and Sinhalese youth. While the former radicalized the TULF into demands for separatism, the latter flocked to the JVP, leading to severe levels of violence between 1987 and 1990 that further limited the governing UNP's ability to compromise with Tamils.

In the North and East, economic competition was intensified by the relatively high rates of population growth of the dry zone brought about by a combination of natural increase and state-assisted colonization of Sinhalese (mainly from the Kandyan highlands and the southwest). The differential impact of irrigation schemes, which were the engine of internal colonization, reinforced Tamil antagonism against the state. As Amita Shastri has documented, the main areas of Tamil population (Jaffna and Batticaloa) had the lowest proportion of state-generated irrigation (approximately 30 percent).[43] In addition, the Sinhalese colonists were more fully integrated into the district-level administration and benefited disproportionately from input and consumer subsidies to the disadvantage of the surplus-producing Tamil and Muslim farmers.[44] In Jaffna, economic development in the post-independence period was achieved with little input or investment from the central state, apart from government loans. The agricultural productivity gains (mainly in chili and onion cultivation) in Jaffna occurred because of fortuitous market conditions and despite the relative neglect in investment and infrastructure development by the center, which concentrated services and industrial development strategies in the more populous Western Province including the capital Colombo.[45] Thus, the social base of the earliest separatist movement stemmed from a combination of rising expectations from the expansion of higher education, "standardization" policies limiting access for Tamils, and high unemployment affecting both Tamil and Sinhalese youth. In this context, it is not surprising that lower-middle classes with most to lose from restricted access to education were the strongest supporters of separatism in the first, nonviolent phase, with middle and upper-middle classes more reluctant secessionists, using the threat of secession to increase bargaining power with the center.[46]

Under conditions of economic competition and absence of constitutional redress, caste conflict was exacerbated as mainly English-educated, higher caste Tamils (Vellala), who were dominant in the Federal Party, faced outflanking pressures by lower or competing castes. Of particular relevance is the competition between the dominant Vellala caste (up to 50 percent of Tamils) and the Karaiyars (10 percent).[47] The nucleus of the LTTE leadership, including Prabhakaran, emerged from a subset of the Karaiyars, the higher status Kadalodiekal, who are traditionally prominent seafaring traders (and smugglers). Their strategically important role in seafaring trade links, as well as domestic links to Karaiyar landlords in the Batticaloa region of the East, have been vital assets to the LTTE.

The second phase of mobilization and the LTTE's growth from the early 1980s was caused primarily by the sense of victimization and threat to physical security following the outbreak of violent confrontations with Sinhalese extremists and eventually Sinhalese-dominated governments. In part, the LTTE leadership embarked on a purposeful strategy of provoking state violence to generate popular support for the LTTE among Tamils. Thus, Sinhalese commentators have interpreted the killing by the LTTE of 14 Sri Lankan soldiers in July 1983 as an intentional provocation that resulted in the anti-Tamil pogroms in Colombo and other parts of the south in July/August 1983. These events, in which between 1,000 and 2,000 Tamils were killed, were a pivotal moment in the modern conflict as tens of thousands of educated Tamils with the means to emigrate fled to Europe and North America, establishing an aggrieved Tamil diaspora with particular concentrations in Madras, London, Paris, New York/New Jersey, and Toronto. The cycle of violence continued through 1984 with LTTE attacks against Sinhalese "colonists" in the East and North leading to retaliation by the Sri

Lankan army against Tamil civilians. Furthermore, the outcry among Tamil sympathizers in the south Indian state of Tamil Nadu created intense pressure on the Indian (Congress) government to intervene, leading to the training of Tamil paramilitary groups (including the LTTE) by the RAW, and the eventual intervention of the Indian army. Similarly provocative tactics were used to galvanize Tamil opposition to the IPKF, once Prabhakaran decided to go to war against it. According to Swamy, Prabhakaran admitted that the IPKF was attacked in populous urban areas to draw fire against civilians. "He [Prabhakaran] argued that innocent men and women who suffered at the hands of Indian soldiers for no fault of theirs would be forced to sympathize with the LTTE and even join them eventually."[48] The flight of the middle classes and the devastation of local agriculture and fisheries caused by war meant that the peasantry and fishing communities became the main targets for LTTE recruitment.[49] More generally, studies have demonstrated how, under conditions of war, environmental conditions, market restrictions, and security fears have entrenched ethnic solidarity at the expense of "bridging social capital" that could otherwise cut across ethnic divisions.[50]

Yet if the mobilization of support was partly based on Prabhakaran's brutal tactical ingenuity, followed by war-driven solidaristic bonds, it was also dependent on a clear sense of national identity and perceived national injustice at the hands of Sinhalese majoritarians since independence,[51] and reinforced by the opposition to the Brahmin-led machinations of India following the IPKF period. It is doubtful that the majority of supporters in the diaspora have merely succumbed to the cult of Prabhakaran.[52] The deep, cultivated sense of Tamil identity has all the hallmarks of nationalism: collective identity based on shared culture (including language and religion), myths of descent, and entitlement to political authority on a self-defined national homeland. While Sinhalese scholars and politicians have challenged the claim to national self-determination,[53] there is little doubt over the collective, *subjective* sense of the legitimacy of Tamil national self-determination, if interpreted broadly to include internal self-determination.

Interviews with current and former cadres, conducted for this research, suggest that initial reasons for joining the movement stem from a mixture of anti-Sinhalese grievances, produced by Sri Lankan army bombings of villages, witnessing of atrocities committed against family and friends, and displacement interrupting both family life and educational opportunities. For many volunteers, the disruptions of civilian life in a war zone are replaced by the stability (if ultimately a precarious one) of paramilitary organization. One former female cadre reported that once she joined she felt that the discipline and training gave her a sense of confidence that she lacked previously. She also claimed that the movement liberated her from the subservient position typical of women in rural Tamil societies. She was motivated principally by the desire to liberate her people from Sinhalese and army oppression and above all, she wanted to fight for the leader (Prabhakaran). "The leader does everything honestly, straightforwardly. He is a man of correct judgment and a man of justice. Compared to the Sri Lankan army which goes on rampages, LTTE only kills soldiers for a reason."[54]

This cadre (Jenitharathy Sivasithambaram), who had lost a leg in combat, declared that she supported the peace process, but would also be willing to fight again if the leader so commanded. Other cadres interviewed were less hopeful about the prospects of a negotiated solution, as they were skeptical that a Sri Lankan government would or could deliver the degree of autonomy and immediate humanitarian assistance that the LTTE demanded. Their zeal, determination, and ideological purity contrasted sharply with the attitudes of former Sri Lankan officers and soldiers interviewed for this research.

The social functions of the LTTE are also attractive to some women for their effects on liberating them from the strictures of traditional Tamil society. In an interview, K. Sudarshini, director of the LTTE-supported Centre for Women's Development and Rehabilitation in Kilinochchi, emphasized the LTTE's progressive role in breaking down caste barriers, mobilizing against the dowry system, and promoting equality of sexes and awareness of other social and family problems.

On the other hand, many Tamils who were not indoctrinated by the LTTE complained—mostly anonymously for fear of retribution—about the totalitarian nature of LTTE control over political, economic, and social life. Businessmen and civil servants paid by the government complain bitterly of the onerous "revolutionary tax" burden imposed by the LTTE and also against the monopolization of commercial contracts, stifling of non-LTTE political parties, absence of open debate, and use of violence and intimidation against those who oppose the LTTE. The leader of the TULF, V. Anandasangaree, has refused to comply with the LTTE's demand to subjugate his candidacy to the LTTE-dominated Tamil National Alliance (TNA, an umbrella organization for Tamil parties in the North and East, effectively controlled by the LTTE). Anandasangaree openly declared, "we have helped the LTTE establish a dictatorship. The LTTE misled 18,000 youths to their deaths.[55] They think they can use their guns to control politics and economics in the North and East. They are fixing prices, grabbing all agencies [commercial contracts]. Everyone has a grievance against them [LTTE]. Everyone here [Jaffna] has been reduced to a pauper. The government should not have allowed LTTE to control territory. It should have forced both sides to lay down arms."[56]

Equally strident criticisms have been made by groups like the University Teachers for Human Rights (Jaffna), whose main spokesman, Rajan Hoole, has been forced into exile to the south for his regular reporting, particularly of the LTTE's recruitment of child soldiers in the Eastern Province, while balancing his reports with criticism of government rights abuses (see below).[57]

This brings us to the major societal level challenge confronting the LTTE in its transition to constitutional politics. The 2004 split of the Eastern leader Karuna represents a deeper set of ethnopolitical cleavages in the Eastern Province, claimed by the LTTE as integral to the homeland of Tamil speakers. The LTTE's command-led domination of the Northern Province is not as easily maintained in the East, mainly because of the trinational ethnic structure of the East, divided roughly three ways into Sri Lankan Tamil (40.9 percent), Muslim (32.5 percent), and Sinhalese (25 percent) communities. While the Sinhalese are primarily concentrated in the Gal Oya development of the Ampara District, the populations of the Batticaloa and Trincomalee areas are extensively mixed. Despite the considerable internal divisions among Hindu Tamils, and between them and Muslims, a degree of unity has been forged by the perception of common external threats or enemies. Tamil speakers (both Tamil and Muslims) have felt commonly threatened by Sinhala-only language legislation, and Tamils in the North and East have become united in opposition to Sinhalese colonization of their traditional homelands.[58]

Nevertheless, significant divisions exist between Eastern and Northern (primarily Jaffna) Tamils. Anthropologists have studied the cultural and sociological distinctions between Tamils in these two regions that have evolved during the pre-colonial and colonial periods: "The high caste Jaffna Tamils, especially the aristocratic Jaffna Velalars (sic), look down upon the Batticaloa Tamils for their alleged lower caste origins and for their less Sanskritic forms of Hindu ritual. The Batticaloa Tamils reciprocate with an ambivalent view of the northerners: while the 'Jaffanese' are admired for being ambitious and highly educated, they are also viewed as arrogant, exploitative, and exclusivist."[59]

Tamil versus Muslim tensions arose in the early 1990s as the Eastern command allowed local conflicts to escalate, just as Northern LTTE leaders ordered the expulsion of 55,000 Muslims from the Jaffna Peninsula. Resentment has been consciously generated by successive governments' tactic of keeping a light touch on the Muslim community relative to that of Hindu Tamils. Dennis McGilvray summarizes the effects of the war on relations between the two groups, generalizing from his anthropological research on the Batticaloa area: "Many of the Muslims I have spoken with since 1993 seem to wish the Tamils well in their quest for some form of self-determination and political autonomy, but they vehemently oppose being hijacked or punished in the name of the Eelam cause. Many people share my astonishment at the LTTE's brutality and short-sightedness in their relations with the Batticaloa Muslims—as well with the Muslims of Mutur, Mannar, and Jaffna—who otherwise might have provided solidarity and support for a geographically and linguistically united, but ethnically and religiously pluralistic, Eelam or Northeastern Province."[60]

Interviews with Muslim representatives in Trincomalee expressed a similar sense of determination to avoid succumbing to the one-party dominance of the LTTE, especially the imposition of the LTTE legal system that would hinder attempts to promote the sharia law, and the potential ethnic cleansing by LTTE of Muslims in the strategically important Mutur area, near Trincomalee.[61]

## International Support Networks

The LTTE is one of the most sophisticated insurgent groups in the world, with international financial and shipping networks, extensive procurement routes, and links with other terror networks. Current estimates of LTTE strength range from 10,000 to 14,000 cadres. Each cadre requires approximately 180 Sri Lankan rupees, just under two U.S. dollars, to clothe and feed daily, amounting to costs of $6,570,000 annually. The remainder of the estimated U.S.$24 to $36 million LTTE budget[62] is used to buy weaponry, ammunition and to promote the cause abroad. The amount and sophistication of LTTE weaponry and transport equipment approach that of a small conventional army. These costs are met through a sophisticated international network, based on legal merchant shipping acting as a front for smuggling of fuel, weaponry and ammunition, and, allegedly, drugs. Donations are raised from the approximately 650,000-strong Sri Lankan Tamil diaspora in 60 countries, operating through LTTE branches (where legal), and a series of front organizations that separately funnel humanitarian aid, sophisticated electronic equipment, and weapons.[63]

From the July/August riots of 1983 until the assassination of Rajiv Gandhi in 1991, the LTTE's main external refuge and support base had been in the Indian state of Tamil Nadu, just 30–50 kilometers (depending on the route) from the northern tip of the Jaffna Peninsula. Its population of 60 million was naturally concerned with its co-ethnics across the Palk Strait. After the 1983 anti-Tamil pogroms the Sri Lankan Tamil separatist cause became an important political issue in Tamil Nadu politics, with notable leaders like former Indian film star turned politician M. G. Ramachandran competing with rivals like M. Karunanidhi for LTTE favor and the mantle of the sponsor of Tamil rights of self-determination. Significant funds, safe houses, training facilities, and medical care for injured cadres were provided during the formative period of LTTE growth. Ramachandran admitted allocating 3.2 million rupees of Tamil Nadu state funds to Sri Lankan "freedom fighters," ostensibly for humanitarian relief.[64]

After the Indo-Lankan accord of 1987 and especially after the assassination of former Indian Prime Minister Rajiv Gandhi in 1991, it became more difficult for the LTTE to access sanctuary and supplies from Tamil Nadu.

The LTTE shifted toward other sources of support. A key development was the maritime shipping fleet that developed both as a legitimate enterprise and as a front for smuggling weapons, fuel, and narcotics. The fleet ranges from small, outboard-powered craft operating in the Palk Strait and the maritime boundary, acting as transshipment vehicles moving supplies, up to ten deep-water freighters.[65] The sophisticated networks in Southeast Asia also produced SAM-7 surface-to-air missiles from Cambodia (via Thailand). Extensive arms networks have been developed to procure arms through Hong Kong, Singapore, Afghanistan, Middle East (Lebanon, Cyprus, Greece, and Turkey), Ukraine, and Southern Africa.[66] The narcotics trade has allegedly been an important source of funding for these expensive weapons, though little firm evidence has emerged to link the LTTE with large-scale trafficking. Robert Oberst and others have investigated the emergence of the "Tamil connection" that grew from the traditional smuggling routes based on the Palk Strait to become "one of the largest sources of heroin and cocaine in Western Europe and North America in the 1980s."[67]

A second organizational asset has been the development of propaganda and dissemination networks connecting the main diaspora centers in London, Switzerland, Toronto, Paris, and Australia. This network has evolved sophisticated communication technology and produces high-quality video, literature and print and electronic journalism, sponsors front organizations to lobby western governments to condemn "Sinhalese chauvinism," and cultivates Tamil solidarity through social and political activities.[68]

## Military/Security Responses

Three themes dominate the discussion on Sri Lankan military strategy toward the LTTE since the withdrawal of the Indian Peace Keeping Force in 1990. First, the politicization of the Sri Lankan bureaucracy affected negatively the capacity of the security forces to respond to the capacities of the LTTE. On the one hand, defense contracting, accounting for 5 percent of the GDP in 1997, is a major source of the endemic corruption that characterizes the Sri Lankan state.[69] With margins on procurement of heavy equipment being greater than for equipment needed for "counter-revolutionary warfare," there has been a supply-led tendency to reinforce conventional military approaches and a sectoral interest in sustaining war. On the other hand, the politicization of the bureaucracy has affected the ability to train and motivate agents required for intelligence gathering at home and abroad.[70]

Second, conventional military tactics based on the establishment of fortified garrisons leading to expansion and control of territory failed in the end to consolidate positional advantages. The battles for Jaffna were examples of the counterproductivity of these tactics because the LTTE twice relinquished control of the town and peninsula and melted into the jungles of the Vanni, south of the Elephant Pass. From bases there, and in the interior along the east coast, LTTE was able to threaten and at times overrun even the most heavily fortified garrisons.

Naval capacity or operational capability did not achieve dominance over the LTTE, whose fleet of small and medium-sized craft, armed with high-caliber machine guns, outclassed the more conventional Sri Lankan navy. While recent developments in naval cooperation between Sri Lanka and India are likely to redress the LTTE's naval advantages, it will remain very difficult to curb smuggling because of the sophistication of LTTE naval units and the extensiveness of the coastline being contested: the LTTE's self-declared homeland in the North and East includes 28 percent of Sri Lankan territory and 40 percent of the coastline.

Third, a knock-on effect has been the demoralization of high-ranking officers who felt that the recruitment and promotion strategies needed to shift toward results-based counter-insurgency strategies had been sacrificed to political patronage. Thus, while recognizing that the military had considerable success with its use of forward bases, sending out mobile units for "long range patrolling" into LTTE-held territory, an official in the defense ministry recognized that the military was unable to activate and train sufficient forces necessary to sustain this high-risk approach.[71] The same handicaps of politicization and insufficient professionalism have hindered Sri Lankan intelligence capabilities. The National Intelligence Bureau (NIB), which monitors and collates military and diplomatic intelligence and runs its own agents, has been criticized for its lack of ability to retain specialists on the LTTE and for failing to reciprocate with agencies of other states because of the poor quality of its own agents.[72]

Wider intergovernmental intelligence sharing occurs in a network involving the Research Analysis Wing (RAW, India), CIA (U.S.), MI6 (UK), DST (France), and CSIS (Canada). Since the assassination of Rajiv Gandhi, RAW has been the most committed in infiltrating and defeating the LTTE. While some notable successes against the LTTE have been achieved, such as the seizure of several large weapons consignments in the mid-1990s, the Sri Lankan intelligence agencies were wary of overreliance on Indian intelligence cooperation because of the ambivalent posture of RAW toward Tamil separatists in the recent past. More recently, however, this ambivalence appears to be shifting toward a more solid anti-LTTE alliance between Sri Lanka and India, in part because of the post-9/11 fear of the spread of terrorist networks that may lead to collusion between the LTTE and potential separatists in Tamil Nadu. At the time of this writing, a new defense pact was being negotiated with India that represents a culmination of naval cooperation and procurement, and adds army training and intelligence sharing. There are also reports that the Congress government in Delhi may be encouraging the split in the LTTE by providing sanctuary and support to Karuna's new rival political party, the Tamil Eelam People's Liberation Tigers (TEPLT).[73] More recently, India has insisted that the terms being negotiated to create a joint mechanism for the distribution of Tsunami relief aid do not recognize the LTTE as the sole representative of Tamils. India has also called for the joint mechanism to include "equal representation" for Muslims in the Eastern Province.

It is too early to tell if such Indo-Lankan cooperation will have significant effect, but it is likely that the LTTE will continue to respond with its own deceptive shipping and procurement tactics. Equally, the past record has shown how difficult it has been for India or Sri Lanka to sustain anti-LTTE Tamil parties.

So, despite the perceived ability to decapitate the LTTE leadership, the squeeze on finance and procurement developing from the proscriptions in the U.S., Canada and UK, and the improvements in intelligence gathering and processing, militarily, the conflict definitely has reached a hurting stalemate. The LTTE felt it could make most of the North and East ungovernable and could penetrate the financial heart of Colombo, causing massive explosions with car bombs at the Central Bank in 1996, the World Trade Centre in 1997, destroying large oil complexes outside Colombo in 1995 and 1996, and attacking the main airport outside Colombo in 2001, while continuing to target political and military elites with embedded Black Tiger units in Colombo and elsewhere in the south.[74] The "War for Peace" promised by the president may have recaptured Jaffna (at the cost of the destruction of much of the old city), but the government struggled to defend Colombo. At the same time, for the LTTE, the strategy of sickening Sinhalese society into accepting a separate Eelam has led to war weariness and resentment among non-indoctrinated Tamils and Muslims. Sustaining the revolution requires a heavy hand.

## Economic and Human Costs

Saman Kelegama's conservative estimate of the economic costs of the war between 1984 and 1994 identified three main components: primary costs (loss in economic output due to loss in investment) between 1984 and 1994 of $12 billion; secondary costs (damage to infrastructure, loss of capital from production and services, including tourism) of $3.6 billion; and tertiary costs (mainly rehabilitation of displaced persons) of $315 million.[75] The primary costs do not include the "missed bandwagon" effects of competitive disadvantage with countries like Malaysia, Thailand, Indonesia, and Vietnam that are emerging as financial and manufacturing centers. Sri Lanka's average economic growth rate of 4.5 percent between 1970 and 1995 compares reasonably well with the South Asian countries (Bangladesh, India, Pakistan) average of 4.9 but less well with the East Asian average of 7.5. Nor do these costs include the incalculable psychic and

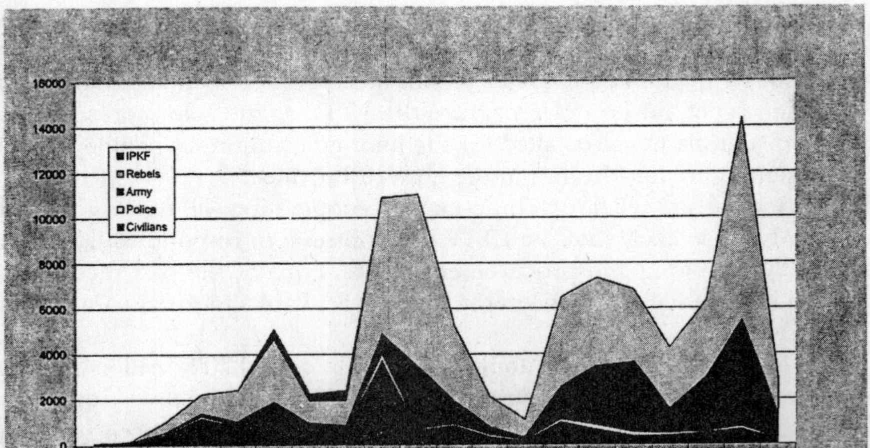


| | 1972-82 | 1983 | 1984 | 1985 | 1986 | 1987 | 1988 | 1989 | 1990 | 1991 | 1992 | 1993 | 1994 | 1995 | 1996 | 1997 | 1998 | 1999 | 2000 | 2001 |
|---|---|---|---|---|---|---|---|---|---|---|---|---|---|---|---|---|---|---|---|---|
| IPKF | 0 | 0 | 0 | 0 | 0 | 433 | 301 | 456 | 29 | 0 | 0 | 0 | 0 | 0 | 0 | 0 | 0 | 0 | 0 | 0 |
| Rebels | 4 | 6 | 438 | 823 | 1363 | 2755 | 959 | 1067 | 5962 | 7583 | 3326 | 1307 | 737 | 3914 | 3850 | 3157 | 2684 | 3388 | 8912 | 1645 |
| Army | 6 | 15 | 36 | 136 | 194 | 280 | 38 | 84 | 899 | 2730 | 1004 | 358 | 151 | 1422 | 2824 | 3106 | 1064 | 2386 | 4661 | 1037 |
| Police | 35 | 5 | 78 | 87 | 43 | 53 | 29 | 25 | 315 | 53 | 68 | 84 | 60 | 122 | 185 | 162 | 103 | 46 | 118 | 34 |
| Civilians | 44 | 140 | 473 | 1188 | 827 | 1568 | 921 | 776 | 3891 | 669 | 859 | 375 | 189 | 1013 | 683 | 391 | 404 | 535 | 681 | 220 |

Figure 8.1. Deaths from political violence (victims), 1972–2001.

emotional toll of death, injury, and detention (or the export of suicide bombing technology and tactics).

Figure 8.1 reveals the Lincoln Project estimates of deaths from political violence between 1972 and 2001.[76] These figures, the most reliable in existence, suggest that the actual level of violence was nearly one-third more severe than the most frequently cited government figure of 64,000. The trend over time shows that violence (as measured by deaths) has increased in each of the three successive phases of war since 1972, peaking in 1987 (5,142 deaths), 1990 (11,092) and 2000 (14,562). In ethnic terms (Figure 8.2), Tamil speakers have suffered disproportionately. As 18 percent of the population, they have suffered 69 percent of the deaths (including members of rebel groups), compared to Sinhalese speakers, who are 72 percent of the population and suffered 29 percent (including security forces) of casualties. In organizational affiliation (see Figure 8.3), "rebels" (mainly the LTTE plus other Tamil groups) have accounted for 57 percent of deaths, more than double the 25 percent suffered by security forces (army, 23 percent, and police, 2 percent). Civilians suffered 17 percent of all deaths. In addition to deaths, 120,000 people have been disabled as a result of conflict, 650,000 refugees (mainly Tamil) have left the country, approximately 1,000,000 people have been internally displaced, 327,000 homes (90 percent of homes of internally displaced persons in the Northeast) have been partially or completely damaged during war (58 percent uninhabitable as of May 2003)[77], 125,000 non-Tamils have had their land occu-

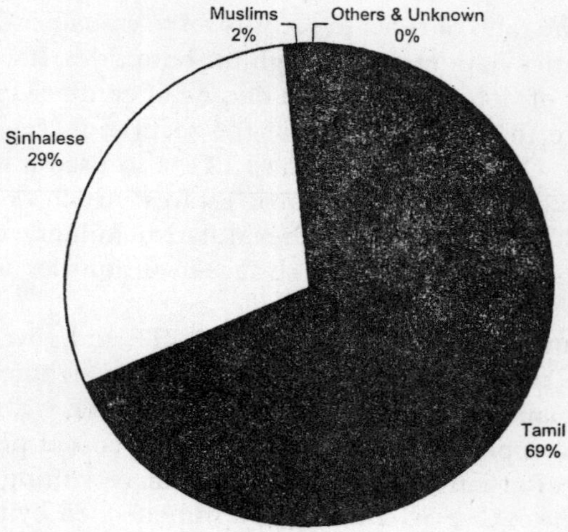


Figure 8.2. Victims of conflict, 1972–2001 (by ethnonational affiliation). From Robert Oberst, Lincoln Project, 2004.

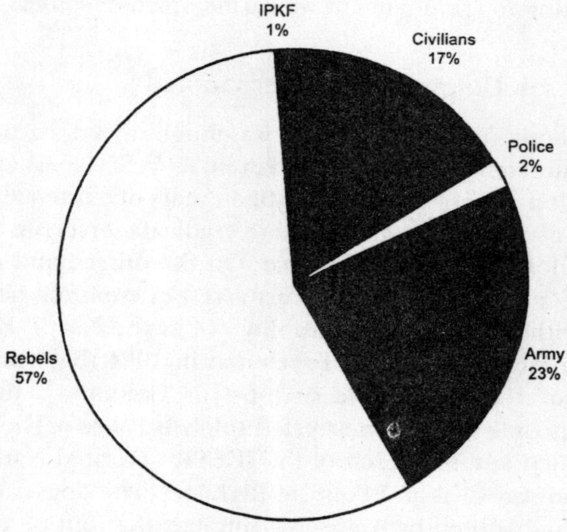


Figure 8.3. Victims of conflict, 1972–2001 (by organizational affiliation). From Robert Oberst, Lincoln Project, 2004.

pied,[78] 700,000 land mines have been placed, most in Jaffna and Vanni, of which only 54,846 had been cleared by August 2003, according to the International Congress to Ban Landmines; 30 percent of the area of internally displaced people's homes are occupied by the Sri Lankan army in "high security zones" in the North and East.

From a strategic point of view, the efficacy of militancy and defense could be analyzed by the ratio of rebel to security force casualties. In this respect the costs of violence have remained high for both sides. If we focus on the three peak years of violence in the last decade of conflict, 1991, 1996, and 2001, we can see that one member of the security forces was killed for every two rebels. Over this period, the LTTE also used a wider range of weaponry, combining "ceaseless [human] waves" (such as in the LTTE's successful amphibious assault on the Mulativu military complex) and improvised land mines, mortars with surface-to-air missiles, and heavy artillery.

Given the human cost of the war for the LTTE and government in the Eelam III phase, it is no wonder that both have had significant difficulties recruiting and maintaining force strengths. The LTTE is able to maintain force strength of approximately 14,000 but at the cost of political damage internally and externally—because of forceful recruiting, especially of child soldiers. Successive Sri Lankan governments, led by the SLFP, have also paid a high political price for casualties, offsetting the limited military gains in the "war for peace" from 1995 and contributing to its electoral defeat in 2001. The Sri Lankan army has also had a very high rate of defection, contributing to criminality by well-armed former solders.[79]

## Legal Responses: Domestic and International

While the expensive military campaign was fought to a draw, the erosion of civil liberties threatened a wider degradation. As V. S. Ganeshalingan noted of the Prevention of Terrorism Act, "Fifteen years of existence of this [Act] has not in any considerable way helped to eradicate terrorism or to weaken the ranks of those engaged in violence. On the other hand it had led to accusations of 'state terrorism', arbitrary arrests, detention, deaths, dissent and tension within the Sri Lankan polity . . . in the North, East and elsewhere."[80] Amnesty International concluded in 1994 that "the indiscriminate nature of the large scale arrests [in Colombo], during which thousands of people have been arrested solely because of their ethnic origin, is unjustified and in breach of the ICCPR" (United Nations International Covenant on Civil and Political Rights).[81] The abuse of emergency legislation is highlighted by Amnesty's findings that out of 15,711 arrests made in Colombo between June and December 1993, sufficient evidence was found to continue holding a person in only 8 percent of cases under Emergency Regulations, and 0.1 percent under the Prevention of Terrorism Act. Furthermore, in only 17 cases out of 15,711 (0.1 percent) were charges brought against detainees.[82] In Sri Lanka, as in other conflicts studied by this author, there is considerable evidence that unjustified detention has had a direct negative effect on conflict resolution by alienating moderate citizens from government and contributing to support for groups advocating political violence.[83]

In 2000, attorneys J. C. Weliamuna and Dhananjay Tilakaratna wrote a review of the new Emergency Regulations.[84] While noting that these measures were a response to the escalation of conflict between the government of Sri Lanka and the LTTE, they concluded that "the situation does not warrant the imposition of certain of these provisions that deprive persons who are accused of offences under the Emergency Regulations of their basic rights in connection with their arrest and detention, as well as with the investigation of their culpability and the judicial proceedings relating to their offence."[85] Not only is it alleged that Sri Lanka's human rights regime violates international treaty obligations (ICCPR) but also that these violations have contributed to a continuation of a cycle of human rights abuses by both the state and nonstate actors. The UN Human Rights Commission reported in 1998 that more than 12,000 people had been reported as disappeared at the hands of the Sri Lankan security forces.[86]

## Sowing Intra-Tamil Rivalry

Kethesh Loganathan, head of the Conflict and Peace Analysis Unit of the Centre for Policy Alternatives (Colombo), describes the symbiotic relationship between state repression and anti-state militancy: "In a nut shell, the Tamil militant youth movement with a strong egalitarian and ideological content in its formative period, soon became subordinated to the compulsions of Tamil Resistance in the face of increasing state repression."[87] For Loganathan, the lurch toward extremism that resulted in the "fratricidal" conflict between the LTTE and opposing Tamil organizations was a byproduct of the state's policies of cultivating anti-LTTE paramilitaries. "Successive governments and their military-intelligence apparatus also contributed to the rot through the creation of "paramilitaries" accountable to no one but their "handlers." The tendency by the Sri Lankan state to use the ex-Tamil militant organizations as instruments in the military campaign against the LTTE, instead of empowering them as political parties by evolving a package based on substantial autonomy for the northeast, further discredited the non-LTTE Tamil organizations and impeded their process of transformation."[88]

The cultivation of intra-Tamil conflict, whether intentional or not, has contributed directly to a major source of dispute in the current peace process. Since the ceasefire agreement of 2002, the LTTE is alleged to have assassinated over 100 members of opposing Tamil political parties,[89] has engaged in violence, intimidation, and extortion of Tamil-speaking Muslims in the Eastern Province, and is accused of widespread recruitment of child soldiers despite commitments made to curtail such practices. As a result, the UNP government faced considerable political pressure from the SLFP and JVP opposition over the continuation of LTTE violence, despite the fact that both major parties have cultivated intra-ethnic rivalry by supporting anti-LTTE Tamil groups.

Following the change of government in 2004, the new United People's Freedom Alliance (UPFA) governing alliance, formed between President Kumaratunga's SLFP and the Janatha Vimukthi Peramuna (JVP), appeared to be content to allow intra-Tamil conflict to escalate to justify delays in restarting negotiations with the LTTE. This position reflected the new government's internal difficulties as the main coalition partners disagree over the principle of federalism as the basis of renewed talks. Equally worrying was the new government's apparent shift away from treating the negotiations as based on parity of status between the Sri Lankan government and the LTTE. Instead, the UPFA decision to delay a restart of negotiations and their alternative creation of National Advisory Council for Peace and Reconciliation (immediately boycotted by the main opposition UNP and the LTTE-affiliated Tamil National Alliance) reflected a return to asymmetrical negotiations, with the Sri Lankan government placing itself at the apex of a process in which the LTTE is one of several minority interests, rather than a direct partner in the negotiation of a comprehensive settlement. This development threatened to repeat the mistaken attempts to marginalize the LTTE rather than cultivate it as a partner in conflict resolution.

The Asian Tsunami of 26 December 2004 had a substantial effect on relations between the Sri Lankan government and the LTTE. This natural disaster killed over 30,000 people on the island and devastated homes, infrastructure and the fishing industry along the wartorn Eastern Province and the populous south coast. A silver lining to this humanitarian disaster had been a resumption of bilateral relations between the UPFA coalition and the LTTE, producing in June 2005 a formal agreement between these parties (approved in advance by India) to share the $3 billion in relief funds that poured into the country. The silver lining was eclipsed by a Sri Lanka supreme court ruling that the temporary autonomy agreement breached sections of the Constitution that defined Sri Lanka's unitary status. The LTTE returned to its jungle bunkers to prepare for war.

## The Impact of the Global War on Terror

A similar process of marginalizing the LTTE has been encouraged by the Sri Lankan defense establishment (including the president, who has overall responsibility for defense), regional powers (namely India), and the United States. Legal actions and proscriptions against the LTTE followed the escalation of Eelam War III from 1995. In that year India formally indicted Prabhakaran for the murder of Rajiv Gandhi, although they have yet to submit a formal request for extradition. In 1997 the U.S. placed the LTTE on its proscribed list of terrorist groups. In 2001 the UK also proscribed the LTTE. The effectiveness of these measures is unclear. On the one hand, a senior LTTE officer admitted that the proscriptions hurt the reputation of the LTTE, particularly in the post-9/11 context. The London-based *Economist* reported in July 2002, without citing a source, that freezing LTTE-controlled bank accounts worldwide had prevented $ 4 billion from reaching the Tigers.[90] This figure must be treated with caution given the reported estimates of LTTE finances. On the other hand, London-based LTTE activists have suggested that the ban on the LTTE was a temporary inconvenience that has been circumvented by channeling activity through existing and new front organizations.[91]

As for any specific "9/11 effect," it is important to emphasize that important matters predated the U.S.-led "Global War on Terror": the long-standing grievances and cyclical experience of conflict, and the LTTE's realization of its hurting stalemate and the necessity of a negotiated settlement. The LTTE declared a temporary 3-month suspension in late 1999 and the same year the leader's Heroes' Day speech made a clear reference to the LTTE's willingness to enter negotiations. While international cooperation against terrorist financial and procurement networks is bound to cause problems for the LTTE, it is unlikely to affect substantially the resolve to achieve a form of self-determination that meets historical aspirations and contemporary interests of Tamils.

## Conclusion: Policy Implications

Five policy implications result from the analysis of interaction between LTTE and the Sri Lankan state. First, the social base of the secessionist movement could be limited by policies from the center that give lower classes a sense of viable upward mobility and middle- and upper-class Tamils a greater stake in the distributive and regulative policies of the central state. Policies based on the ethos of the original elite pacts of the 1950s and 1960s, based on Tamil language rights and regional autonomy, combined with equitable access to higher education and more equitable regional development policies, could have reduced Tamil grievances and increased their stake in the central state.

Second, recognition of the principle of internal national self-determination as the basis for the ceasefires and currently stalled peace process must be combined with a shift away from strategies aimed at fostering inter-Tamil rivalries. In the short term, accepting the LTTE's sole representative status is the price for consolidating negotiating blocs. Previous talk processes have shown that attempts to "divide and rule" through territorial settlement of Sinhalese in the North and East or through cultivating anti-LTTE groups among Tamils has been counterproductive. At the same time, this approach does not preclude inclusion of non-LTTE groups, particularly the primary Muslim party, the Sri Lankan Muslim Congress (SLMC), as recently demonstrated by their coalition with the last UNP government.

The broader point is that the recognition of LTTE as national representatives is the only way to force the LTTE to recognize the national rights of Sinhalese and Muslims in areas they hope to govern in a federal settlement. This will in turn force them to recognize the need for power-sharing institutions at the central and provincial levels and the need for an agreed collective and individual human rights regime.

Third, a combination of federalism and power-sharing at the provincial and central government level remain viable remedies for core Tamil grievances. These forms of conflict regulation have the potential to solve or at least regulate the conflict over opposing national aspirations.[92] While there remains considerable difference between the LTTE's essentially confederalist ideals, as proposed in their Interim Self-Governing Authority proposals, and the Sri Lankan government's federal reforms, as proposed in the draft Constitution of 2000 on the North-Eastern Region, the opposing positions are compatible as the basis of negotiation. The threat of secession has been substantially modified to a conditional rather than absolute position for the LTTE, and the principle of federalism has gained wider acceptance among the Sinhalese majority.[93] Despite the continuation of violence and ceasefire violations[94]—the LTTE has killed more than 100 alleged informers and suspected security-force agents, continued to procure arms and reinforced and developed new bases—it appears to this observer that the LTTE is using its power as leverage in negotiations and internal party management rather than as leverage to renew secessionism. Moreover, federalism and power-sharing have the potential to meet the separate rights of self-determination of Muslims and Indian Tamils, through guaranteed proportionality in representation at the Provincial level as well as at the center, through either an upper house or coalition participation in the federal/confederal executive. The experience of the Sri Lankan Muslim Congress as coalition partner with the UNP, the continued potential of a UNP-TNA alliance, and the recent SLFP-JVP coalition (the UPFA, which subsequently dissolved over the tsunami relief agreement) represent precedents for managing conflict by the inclusion of erstwhile extremists into negotiations based on the principles of federalism and power-sharing.

Fourth, while there is clear potential for the above-mentioned policy approaches to regulate the conflict, there remains uncertainty over both the commitment of the LTTE to a federal solution, and over the ability of the main Sinhalese parties to evolve sufficient bipartisan agreement to move toward a form of federalism that meets Tamil and Muslim expectations. There remains a clear need for the maintenance of an international safety net to prevent either side from perceiving positional advantage through a return to war. Given the failure of substantive cooperation to emerge in the South Asian Association for Regional Co-operation, the most effective international relations are likely to be made in strengthened and perhaps institutionalized bilateral ties with Norway (as the talks mediator and through the continued role of the Sri Lanka Monitoring Mission), India (defense and trade), and Japan (trade, humanitarian aid and development assistance). The price of this safety net will be to open up Sri Lanka to Indian and Japanese economic competition, as already witnessed in the oil services industries.[95]

Finally, the international safety net should be modulated to encourage and sustain the transition of the LTTE from a military to a political movement *and* the transition of the Sri Lankan state from a quasidemocratic state to a more transparent, accountable, and efficient state. This requires a continuation of the need to tie humanitarian and development assistance for both the government and any interim authorities to both accountable financial management and adherence to the rule of law. At the same time, in humanitarian relief there needs to be a shift from an "incentives approach," which rewards the majoritarian status quo, to a peace-dividend approach, which addresses immediate needs. Since the Tamil-concentrated North and East were most heavily affected by the war and the 2004 tsunami the LTTE carries a larger burden of immediate expectation from its grass roots. The incentives approach favored by the donors at the Tokyo conference (boycotted by the LTTE *after* it was barred from a preliminary aid conference in Washington) ties the disbursement of aid to the achievement of "road-map" targets such as disarmament and commitment to human rights. On balance this approach advantages Sri Lankan governments because the LTTE is expected to make a very quick transition from a military organization to a political organization capable of implementing complex agreements. A "peace-dividend" approach offers better incentives for such a transition by providing more immediate relief to resolve grievances and remove excuses for not facing difficult constitutional and security issues. An important aspect of a peace-dividend approach is the role of the Tamil diaspora in developing civil society and development assistance in the North and East. Reducing transaction costs of remittances and migration policies developed by diaspora host countries to facilitate knowledge and human capital circulation between the diaspora and Sri Lanka are important.[96]

Recent evidence has also shown that the legal proscription of the LTTE has been detrimental in consolidating the shift into constitutional politics. The system of "purdah" that prevented the LTTE from attending an important donors' meeting in Washington in 2003, or LTTE delegates from traveling to the United Kingdom to learn about devolution and the Northern Ireland agreement, should be replaced by a form of probation in which proscribed "terrorist" groups that have shown a sincere engagement in a negotiated compromise should be temporarily exempt from proscription, or at least allowed special visas for specific quasi-diplomatic missions.[97] Rigid adherence to a blanket maxim of total opposition to "terrorism" is a self-defeating policy.

## Glossary

BC Pact: Bandaranaike-Chelvanayakam Pact (1957). The pact provided regional autonomy for the Tamil-dominated Northern and Eastern Provinces, but was never implemented because of strong opposition from within Bandaranaike's own governing coalition.

CWC: Ceylon Workers' Congress, representing Indian (estate) Tamils.

DC Pact: Dudley Senanayake-Chelvanayakam Pact. An unpublished 1965 pact that attempted to restore Tamil language rights and the principle of devolution at district council level.

EPRLF: Eelam People's Revolutionary Liberation Front. An Indian-backed, Marxist Tamil party formed between 1981 and 1984 that became the focus of Indian-led attempt to achieve devolved government between 1987 and 1990.

FP: Tamil Federal Party (Federal Freedom Party of the Tamil-Speaking Peoples), formed in 1949 and led by S. J. V. Chelvanayakam.

ICCPR: International Covenant on Civil and Political Rights.

IPKF: Indian Peace-Keeping Force, introduced as part of Indo-Lankan accord (June 1987). Initially welcomed by war-weary Tamils in the North and East, the IPKF was eventually drawn into war with the LTTE, suffering nearly 2,000 casualties before exiting in March 1990.

JVP: Janatha Vimukthi Peramuna (People's Liberation Front), a Marxist Sinhalese party led by students and unemployed youths in the southwest. JVP launched revolutionary uprisings in 1971 and 1989–1990 that were suppressed brutally by Sri Lankan governments.

LTTE: Liberation Tigers of Tamil Eelam, established by Velupillai Prabhakaran in 1976 as successor to the Tamil New Tigers, which in turn derived from the Tamil Students' Federation (1970). LTTE became the dominant Tamil political and military movement after the anti-Tamil pogroms of 1983 and the marginalization of the constitutional Tamil United Liberation Front (TULF) with the passage of the Sixth Amendment to the constitution in 1983.

PA: People's Alliance. Coalition formed 1994, led by the center-left Sri Lanka Freedom Party.

PTA: Prevention of Terrorism Act, passed as temporary legislation in 1979, made permanent in 1982. The Act was modeled on the draconian anti-terrorism legislation then in place in Northern Ireland and South Africa, giving the security forces wide powers of arrest, long-term detention without trial, single-judge, juryless trials, and press censorship.

RAW: Research and Analysis Wing of the Indian Army. RAW trained and armed a variety of Tamil separatist groups in the late 1970s and early 1980s. RAW's strategy was to cultivate rival Tamil groups, both to pressure the Sri Lankan government into granting concessions to Tamils and to limit the ability of any one Tamil militant group to gain the upper hand. The LTTE carefully avoided becoming too dependent on RAW and was able to marginalize the rival Tamil groups.

"Sinhala Only" Act: Exclusive Sinhalese language provision that outraged Tamils.

SLFP: Sri Lanka Freedom Party. Post-independence socialist party dominated by the Bandaranaike family, including prime ministers S. W. R. D. Bandaranaike (assassinated by a Buddhist monk in 1959), the world's first female prime minister Sirimavo Bandaranaike (elected in 1960), and president Chandrika (née Bandaranaike) Kumaratunga.

SLMM: Sri Lankan Monitoring Mission, led by the Royal Norwegian Government. Established by the "Agreement on a Ceasefire Between the Government of the Democratic Socialist Republic of Sri Lanka and the Liberation Tigers of Tamil Eelam," 22 February 2002.

TELO: Tamil Eelam Liberation Organisation, a "high-caste" Vellala-dominated organization strongly supported by India's RAW. The LTTE ruthlessly eliminated the organization and its military wing (Thamil Eelam Liberation Army) in 1984–1986.

TEPLT: Tamil Eelam People's Liberation Tigers. The organization founded in mid-2004 by Vinayagamoorthy Muralitharan (alias "Karuna") the Eastern LTTE commander who defected from the organization over the Northern command's alleged disregard for the disproportionate sacrifices of Eastern cadres.

TNT: Tamil New Tigers (see LTTE above).

TULF: Tamil United Liberation Front, formed in 1976 to unite Tamil parties including the Federal Party (see FP above).

TNA: Tamil National Alliance, formed in 2001 to unite the main Tamil political parties, including the TULF, All Ceylon Tamil Congress (ACTC), Tamil Eelam Liberation Organisation (TELO), and a faction of the Eelam People's Revolutionary Liberation Front (EPRLF).

TUF: Tamil United Front, comprising the FP, the All Ceylon Tamil Congress, and other smaller parties formed in 1972 in opposition to the SLFP government's drafting of the Republican constitution.

TULF: Tamil United Liberation Front, evolved from the TUF. The TULF made an explicit demand for a sovereign state of Eelam, which was supported overwhelmingly in Tamil areas in the 1977 parliamentary elections. The TULF won all 14 seats in the Northern Province and three of four in the Eastern Province. After the escalation of conflict from the early 1980s the TULF was largely eclipsed by the LTTE. Under the latter's influence, the TULF joined the Tamil National Alliance in 2001, apart from a faction led by TULF leader V. Anandasangaree, who continues to defy the LTTE control of the TNA.

UNP: United National Party, the center-right party that has alternated in power with SLFP-led coalitions since independence.

## Timeline

1948: Ceylon granted independence 4 February after 150 years as British Crown Colony.

1956: Official Language Act No. 33 ("Sinhala Only Act") makes Sinhalese the only official language, provoking Tamil political protests and severe ethnic rioting.

1957: Bandaranaike-Chelvanayakam Pact (B-C Pact) provides regional autonomy for the Tamil-dominated Northern and Eastern Provinces. The pact is never implemented because of strong opposition from within Bandaranaike's own governing coalition.

1958: Severe ethnic rioting erupts in wake of the failure of the B-C Pact.

1959: S. W. R. D. Bandaranaike is assassinated on 25 September by a Buddhist monk

1960: Sirimava R. D. Bandaranaike elected world's first female prime minister.

1961: Federal Party launches satyagraha campaign in the Northern Province. Government declares state of emergency amid severe ethnic rioting.

1965: Dudley Senanayake-Chelvanayakam Pact (DC Pact) is signed in March, increasing language rights for Tamil speakers. The pact is aborted due to Sinhalese opposition.

1971: Marxist uprising by People's Liberation Front (JVP) leads to approximately 6,000 deaths.

1972: On 22 May, SLFP-led government passes new constitution transforming Ceylon into Democratic Socialist Republic of Sri Lanka. Changes to university admissions policy provoke student uprising in Jaffna by Tamil Students' Movement (Tamil Manavi Peravi).

1974: Formation of Tamil New Tigers (TNT), led by Chetti Thanabalasingham as political leader and Velupillai Prabhakaran as military leader.

1975: On 27 July, Velupillai Prabhakaran, military leader of TNT, assassinates Tamil mayor of Jaffna Alfred Duraiappa.

1976: Vaddukoddai Resolutions passed calling for a sovereign Tamil state. Tamil United Front (TUF) changes name to Tamil United Liberation Front (TULF). TNT becomes Liberation Tigers of Tamil Eelam (LTTE), which then begins campaign of violence against policemen and other public officials in Jaffna.

1978: UNP Prime Minister J. R. Jayewardene legislates new constitution to convert government into a Gaullist semipresidential system.

1981: Escalation of violence against police in Jaffna leads to police retaliation in which the Jaffna library, an important repository of Tamil literature, is destroyed by arson.

1983: On 23 July, in retaliation for the killing of 13 Sri Lankan Army soldiers by the LTTE, an outbreak of severe ethnic rioting targeted at Tamils in Colombo spreads to other areas, leading to the deaths of between 1,000 and 2,000 Tamils.

1983: On 5 August, Parliament passes law banning political parties that advocate separatism, leading to the exile of the TULF to the southern Indian state of Tamil Nadu as well as the beginning of training of Tamil militant groups by the Indian government Research and Analysis Wing (RAW), which lasts until June 1987.

1984: LTTE 30 November massacre of 62 Sinhalese civilians leads to retaliation by army, who kill 63 Tamils.

1985: On 14 May, LTTE kills 120 pilgrims in the sacred city of Anuradhapura.

1985: India mediates talks in Bhutan between LTTE and Sri Lankan officials, 8–13 July. The talks fail to reach agreement.

1986: Sri Lankan air force begins aerial bombardment of Tamil areas, leading to increases in LTTE recruitment of relatives of victims of bombings.

1986: On 3 May, LTTE bomb kills 16 people (mostly foreigners) and destroys Airlanka aircraft at Colombo airport, representing the first major attack in the capital and a tactical shift toward economic targets.

1987: On 21 April, LTTE car bomb kills 113 and injures over 200 people in a market in Colombo.

1987: In May, Sri Lankan army launches major offensive to gain control of LTTE-controlled territory in Jaffna. Indian government responds by entering Sri Lankan airspace to drop supplies to Tamil civilians in Jaffna.

1987: On 2 June, LTTE kills 29 Buddhist monks and 4 others in a gun attack on a bus near Arantalawa, Eastern Province.

1987: Indo-Sri Lankan Peace Accord is signed 29 July, providing for an Indian Peace-Keeping Force (IPKF), a devolution package for a combined North-East Province, and the disarmament of Tamil militant groups. LTTE leader Prabhakaran resents the lack of involvement of the LTTE in negotiations and eventually reneges on verbal pledges to honor the accord.

1987: LTTE declares war on IPKF on 10 October.

1988: In November, North-East Provincial Council is (NEPC) established as part of Indo-Lankan accord.

1988: R. Premadasa elected president of Sri Lanka in December. Premadasa requests the withdrawal of IPKF.

1989: On 19 September India and Sri Lanka reach agreement on withdrawal of IPKF.

1990: Peace talks between UNP government and LTTE collapse in June, leading to start of Eelam War II
1991: Former Indian prime minister Rajiv Gandhi killed on 21 May by LTTE suicide bomber in southern Indian state of Tamil Nadu.
1993: LTTE suicide bomber kills Sri Lankan President Ronasighe Premadasa and 23 others at 1 May Colombo political rally.
1994: Chandrika Kumaratunga becomes president, pledging to open peace talks with LTTE.
1995: Peace talks between government and LTTE collapse, leading to start of Eelam War III and government campaign to regain control of Jaffna peninsula.
1996: On 31 January LTTE suicide bomber devastates Central Bank (Colombo), killing 91 people and precipitating nationwide state of emergency.
1997: On 15 October LTTE suicide bomber severely damages World Trade Centre (Colombo) killing 18.
1998: LTTE bombs Temple of the Tooth (Kandy), the holiest Buddhist site.
1999: President Kumaratunga partially blinded in LTTE suicide assassination attempt during election rally. Despite injuries, Kumaratunga wins second presidential term.
2000: In April LTTE recaptures strategic Elephant Pass linking Jaffna Peninsula to mainland.
2001: 5–9 December, United National Party (UNP) forms government under Prime Minister Ranil Wickremesinghe, pledged to open negotiations with LTTE.
2002: Ceasefire agreement signed 22 February by Prime Minister Ranil Wickremesinghe and LTTE leader Velupillai Prabhakaran.
2002: Peace talks in Norway in December lead to an agreement to seek a solution based on principle of federalism.
2003: In April LTTE suspends participation in peace talks, citing failure of government to fulfill pledges to relieve immediate humanitarian needs of people living in the North and East. Government blames LTTE for demanding too much autonomy prior to a final constitutional settlement.
2003: In November President Chandrika Kumaratunga precipitates political crisis by suspending three ministers, accusing Wickremesinghe's government of conceding too much sovereignty to LTTE.
2004: In April United People's Freedom Alliance (UPFA, coalition dominated by President Kumaratunga's People's Alliance and the JVP) forms government under Prime Minister Mahinda Rajapakse. New government is pledged to resume peace talks, but coalition differences over talks agenda leads to continued stalemate.

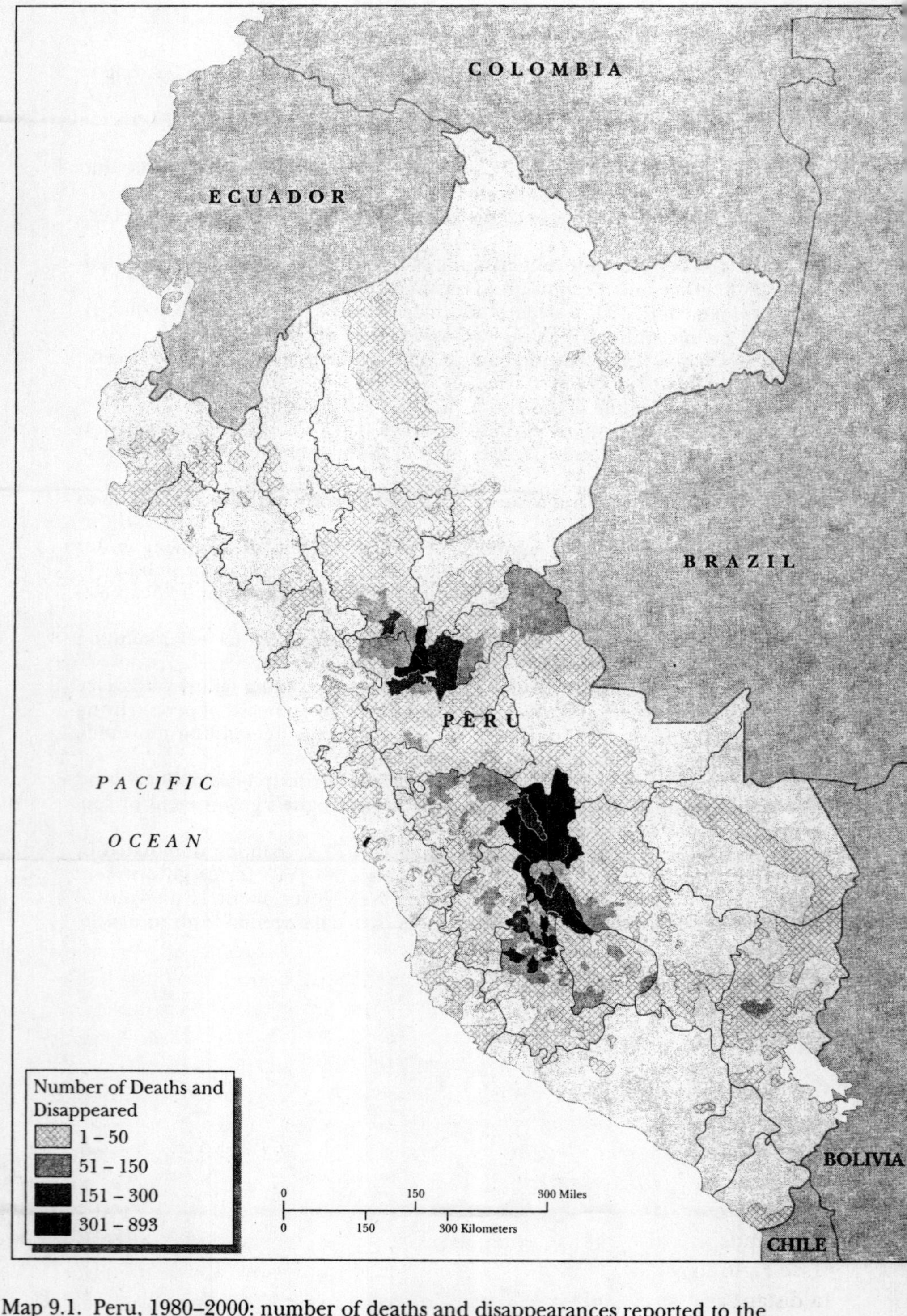


Map 9.1. Peru, 1980–2000: number of deaths and disappearances reported to the TRC according to districts.

*Chapter 9*

# PCP-SL: The Defeat of Sendero Luminoso in Peru

MARC CHERNICK

On 17 May 1980—the eve of the first democratic elections in 16 years—an obscure Maoist group, the Communist Party of Peru-Sendero Luminoso (PCP-SL), announced that it was initiating its armed struggle. Its first action was to burn the ballot boxes in the remote Andean town of Chuschi, in the southern Andean highlands in the Department of Ayacucho. The group's leader, Abimael Guzmán, viewed himself as the "fourth sword of Marxism" and believed that Peru had become the epicenter and vanguard of world revolution, particularly after the death of Mao and the rise of the reformist Deng Xiaoping in China.

Sendero's rebellion quickly became the central axis of Peruvian politics during the 1980s and early 1990s. The insurgency spread from its base in the southern Andean Department of Ayacucho, where Guzmán had been a professor for many years, into the lowlands east of the Andes, into the coca-growing regions in the northeastern jungles,[1] and then into practically every region of the country, including the capital city of Lima on the Pacific coast. During the first two years of the war, the government was slow to respond. When it did react, it overreacted. President Fernando Belaúnde, elected in 1980 following a twelve-year period of military rule, declared a state of emergency in the largely indigenous and Quechua-speaking conflict zones and sent in the armed forces to put down the rebellion. The army and marines carried out operations like an occupying army in enemy territory. Some generals spoke of inverting the Maoist dictum that a guerrilla moves among the people like a fish in water. If this is so, they asserted, their duty is to drain the sea. The military actions further terrorized the population and, in so doing, aided Sendero.

Yet Sendero's violence against the civilian population in the southern highlands was ultimately greater than that of the Peruvian Armed Forces (see Figure 9.1). Many in the civilian population, historically distrustful of a distant and neglectful state, at first inclined toward Sendero. By the late

1980s, however, most of this support had vanished and Sendero was faced with a social rebellion against its brutal methods, militarism, and ideological demands. Furthermore, the armed forces reexamined their counterinsurgency strategy and demonstrated a capacity to learn from mistakes and adjust their methods and tactics. Over time, they learned to operate effectively among the local population, and, with the support of lightly armed self-directed civilian patrols, the army succeeded in dislodging the PCP-SL from most of its original bases of operations.

This chapter provides a brief history of the origins, escalation, and precipitous collapse of Peru's violent armed conflict, as well as the organization, ideology, financial structures, and social base of Sendero Luminoso. Unlike many of the other chapters in this book, this chapter recounts a story of a war that has effectively been concluded. It ended not through negotiations but through military defeat and social rejection of the insurgency. There was no history of talks, and there was practically no international involvement except for the U.S antinarcotics program, which often proved to function at cross purposes with Peru's counter insurgency objectives.

Since the end of the Cold War, few internal conflicts have ended so decisively with one side victorious and the other defeated. Even in Guatemala, where the guerrillas were severely weakened militarily, hostilities did not fully end until an internationally brokered peace settlement was concluded in 1996.

However, in analyzing the defeat of Sendero Luminoso, this chapter cautions against drawing the wrong lessons. The Peruvian experience is not easily replicable; attempts to implement similar counterinsurgency strategies in other sociopolitical contexts could prove disastrous. The example I have in mind is Colombia, where the government of Alvaro Uribe, elected in 2002 on a hard-line platform of defeating the insurgents, has attempted to pursue some of the military and political strategies that were successful in Peru. But Uribe is unlikely to achieve similar results (see Chapter 2). Peru's insurgency was unlike any other guerrilla war experienced in Latin America.

The chapter also examines the consequences of ending an internal armed conflict through military victory and not through negotiations. For a decade following the defeat of the insurgency, Peruvians chose not to address the consequences of the internal war. These included not only deep psychological scars among the victim population but also a political system that had jettisoned the normal checks and balances of democratic government while empowering the president and armed forces to defeat the terrorists.[2] Worse, following the capture of Abimael Guzmán and the defeat of Sendero, the triumphant president, Alberto Fujimori, proceeded systematically to consolidate state power into his own hands by suborning and marginalizing other powerholders and political branches of government.

Yet the Fujimori administration came to an abrupt end in November 2000, when videos emerged showing the president's intelligence chief bribing congressmen, judges, and others. Fujimori faxed in his resignation from Japan. As Peruvians attempted to take stock after more than a decade of Fujimori's enigmatic rule, the subject of the violations and crimes during the war years quickly rose to the surface. Interim president Valentín Paniagua (November 2000–July 2001) approved the establishment of a Truth and Reconciliation Commission (TRC) charged with investigating the political violence between 1980 and 2000. The commission began work in 2001 under Fujimori's elected successor, Alejandro Toledo (2001–2006) and presented its findings in August 2003.

By 2005, only two small bands of Senderistas still operated in the remote areas in the foothills and jungles east of the Andes and did not represent an immediate terrorist or insurgent threat to the nation. Nevertheless, the conditions that gave rise to Sendero have not been adequately addressed. The TRC's final report urged the nation to confront the long history of social, economic, political, regional, and ethnic exclusion that created the conditions under which such a violent, nihilistic, and ideological insurgency took root. The country is still struggling with these questions as well as with the commission's recommendation to provide reparations to individuals and families victimized by the war. Yet the experience of the TRC, established almost a decade after the defeat of the insurgency, represents a powerful first step in recovering the historical memory of the period. It also provides a blueprint in its section on recommendations for the construction of a more integrated, pluri-ethnic nation that, even if only partially enacted, would help ensure that a violent insurgent group does not again launch a "popular war" fueled by the resentments of those who have been excluded from national development.

## Origins and Early Phases of Sendero's "Popular War"

The Peruvian novelist Mario Vargas Llosa wrote a novel called *The Real Life of Alejandro Mayta* in which he parodied the Peruvian left for its incessant factionalism, pitting Maoists, Stalinists, Marxist-Leninists, Trotskyites, and other Marxist iconic figures against each other before dividing again over "correct" interpretations of particular schools of thought. Vargas Llosa's story of internal divisions and deadly confrontations could be the story of the founding of Sendero Luminoso.

The genealogy of the PCP-SL can be traced to the original socialist party in Peru founded by one of Latin America's foremost Marxist thinkers, José Carlos Mariátegui, in 1928. Mariátegui sought to adapt Marxism to the realities of Peru. In his most famous writings, *Seven Interpretive Essays on Peruvian*

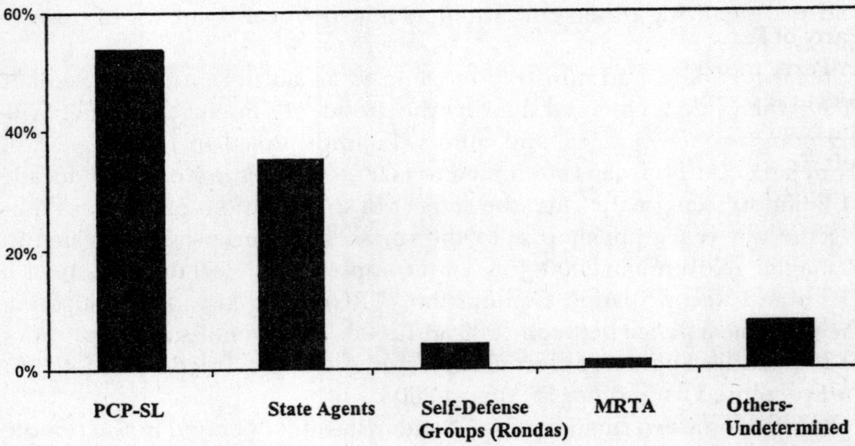


Figure 9.1. Percentage of deaths and disappeared reported to the TRC according to presumed responsible agent. TRC *Final Report*, vol. 1, 133.

*Reality* and in particular an essay entitled "The Problem of the Indian" published in 1928, he argued that because Peru was underdeveloped and lacked an industrial proletariat, the equivalent of the proletariat was the nation's indigenous peoples. For Mariátegui, the Indian problem, as he referred to it, was not cultural or ethnic. It was economic and caused by the problem of land.[3] The indigenous question was reduced to a class issue and the indigenous population, representing about 35 percent of the population, was portrayed as the primary revolutionary class that needed to be organized and led by a Leninist vanguard party. Four decades later, Abimael Guzmán would assert that Mariátegui anticipated Mao in emphasizing rural rebellion as the motor of revolutionary change in less developed economies.

Following Mariátegui's death as a young man in 1930, the Socialist Party was renamed the Peruvian Communist Party (PCP) and joined the Soviet-led Communist International or Third International, known as the Comintern. In 1964–1965, the PCP split into pro-Chinese and pro-Soviet PCP factions following the geopolitical tensions of the times. The division also reflected a fundamental difference over the role of Communist parties within the broader context of Latin American politics. The pro-Soviet parties emphasized the "peaceful road to socialism," participation in national elections and alliances with bourgeois and middle-class parties. This path culminated in the election of Salvador Allende in Chile at the head of a coalition of leftist parties in 1970.

Many Maoist parties, however, believed in the centrality of violence as a necessary tool of class struggle. Abimael Guzmán, then a university professor in Ayacucho, was a founding member of the pro-Maoist Communist

Party of Peru—Bandera Roja (Red Flag). Maoism was particularly resonant in Peru, more so than in any other Latin American nation. The emphasis on rural politics and the glorification of the traditional culture of the peasants and agricultural laborers seemed appropriate to many on the Peruvian left. In 1967, a dissident Maoist group separated from Bandera Roja and founded the PCP-Patria Roja (Red Fatherland). Patria Roja went on to take over the national teachers union. In 1970, following the struggles in China over the Cultural Revolution—personally experienced by Abimael Guzmán in a trip to China where he viewed Mao from a distance and received guerrilla training—Guzmán led a breakaway faction and formed the PCP-Sendero Luminoso (Shining Path). The name evoked the "Shining Path of Mariátegui." But for Guzmán, returning to the tradition of Mariátegui was a way to reinterpret Mariátegui in light of Mao. He soon supplanted the idea of Mao and Mariátegui with his own teachings, which he branded "Gonzalo Thought" after his revolutionary name, Comrade (later Presidente) Gonzalo.

As a political force, the left in Peru was not a central protagonist of politics during most of the early and middle periods of the twentieth century. It was the populist APRA (American Popular Revolutionary Alliance) party, under the leadership of Victor Raúl Haya de la Torre, that came to present the greatest challenge to oligarchic rule. However by the 1960s, many younger Apristas (followers of APRA) had gravitated to the left as the country witnessed an upsurge in strikes and campesino mobilization. In this period, at least four groups took up arms, drawn from militant campesino movements, from dissident and radicalized Apristas, and from youth attracted to the new left inspired by the example of the Cuban Revolution.[4] This bourgeoning guerrilla activity and social confrontation in the early and mid-1960s was to have a profound impact on the country and in particular the Peruvian armed forces.

Like their counterparts throughout the region following the Cuban Revolution, the Peruvian generals too began to link national security with economic development and reoriented their focus from external threats to internal security.[5] However, unlike the militaries in Brazil and the Southern Cone, where internal unrest led to the rise of repressive authoritarian regimes in the 1960s and 1970s, the Peruvian military turned leftward. After defeating the guerrilla insurgencies and peasant rebellions, the Peruvian Armed Forces themselves seized power in 1968 and initiated a "revolutionary military government." In power, they enacted a sweeping land reform that rivaled Cuba's revolutionary agrarian program. The generals effectively beheaded the power of the rural oligarchy and *gamonales* (political bosses) and attempted to create state-sponsored organizations that would channel labor and campesino unrest.

However, the left-wing military experiment failed. It destroyed the old order but was unable to institutionalize a new one dominated by the armed forces. The result was a vacuum of authority in the countryside that unintentionally opened up a space for independent leftist parties, campesino groups, and NGOs that refused to recognize the military as a legitimate force despite its rhetoric and far-reaching reforms. It was in this context that Abimael Guzmán began to plan to launch a "popular war" based on the Maoist idea of a prolonged war beginning in the countryside and encircling the cities.

By the late 1970s, as the economy contracted, investment declined, and social protests soared, culminating in a national strike in 1977, the military began to prepare for a withdrawal from power. A Constituent Assembly was held in 1979 and the military returned to their barracks in 1980. Peru's democratic transition revealed a surprising realignment in the national electorate. In the 1978 elections for the Constituent Assembly, the nation's many leftist parties collectively gained 29.4 percent of the vote and went on to become a powerful electoral force throughout the 1980s.

Yet while the majority of the left—Maoists, pro-Soviet Communists, fidelistas (pro-Cuban), mariateguistas (pro-Mariátegui), and others—participated in the Constituent Assembly, the Communist Party of Peru-Sendero Luminoso swam against the current. Isolated in Ayacucho, with little contact with national politics or even the broader currents of Peruvian Maoism, Sendero continued to prepare for the initiation of a "popular war." In comparative Latin American terms, the timing of the guerrilla war to coincide with a democratic transition was unprecedented.[6]

The PCP-SL's initial base was the San Cristóbal National University of Huamanga, UNSCH, a university founded in Ayacucho in colonial times that was closed in the nineteenth century and then reopened in 1959. Abimael Guzmán, a philosophy professor in the faculty of education, was one of many professors who moved to this poor highland city to staff the new regional university. Guzmán was convinced that Peru in the 1970s resembled China in the 1930s—rural, feudal, backward, and ripe for revolution. The experiences of the left military government, the extensive agrarian reform, the electoral rise of the left in the Constituent Assembly, and the return to civilian elected government in 1980 were all dismissed as irrelevant by Guzmán.

For more than fifteen years, Guzmán prepared the terrain for war, first as the regional leader of the PCP-Bandera Roja and then as the maximum ideologue and leader of Sendero Luminoso. The PCP-SL came to dominate student, administrative, and faculty politics at UNSCH. Graduates of UNSCH were sent back to their villages or to towns throughout Ayacucho to serve as schoolteachers and to recruit, organize, and prepare the population for the coming prolonged "popular war."

Sendero initiated its first armed action on 17 May 1980. Guzmán stated in the only public interview he gave before his capture that he chose the date of the 1980 elections to initiate the armed struggle for a specific strate-

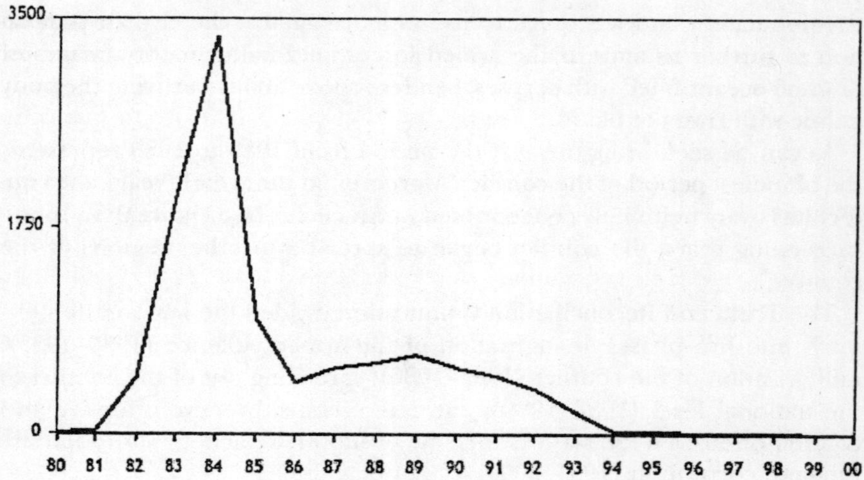


Figure 9.2. Number of deaths and disappearances reported to the TRC for 1980–2000. TRC *Final Report*, vol. 1, 133.

gic reason: after twelve years of military rule, the newly elected civilian president would be reluctant to call on the armed forces and reengage them in national politics and would thus delay for months or years their deployment to fight an insurgency.[7]

The calculation proved prescient. President Fernando Belaúnde of the Conservative Acción Popular viewed the uprising as an inconsequential disruption of public order and relied primarily on the police to confront it during his first two years in office. As a result, between 1980 and 1982, Sendero was able to greatly expand its activities throughout Ayacucho. For most of the population in Lima and the more modernized urban centers, the rebellion in the southern highlands seemed exotic and marginal to the prevailing current of democratic transition. Sendero was left relatively uncontested for two years and was able to consolidate and extend its influence. The PCP-SL proclaimed that the aim of the "popular war" was to destroy the state and the vestiges of the corrupt, semifeudal, oligarchic society.

As can be seen in Figure 9.2, between 1980 and 1981 the state barely responded to the spreading insurgency. Finally in 1982, the president felt compelled to act and turned the problem over to the armed forces. From 1982 to 1985, the army effectively initiated a scorched earth strategy, sending up specialized units that viewed most indigenous people as terrorists, supporters or sympathizers. Most troops did not speak the dominant language, Quechua, and remained culturally and socially isolated in an Andean world that was difficult for them to comprehend.

Sendero for its part, demanded support, recruits, and obedience from the population and was quick to use violence against the civilian population to further its aims. If the armed forces held hallucinatory images of drained oceans filled with corpses, Sendero spoke about purifying the body politic with rivers of blood.

As can be seen in Figure 9.2, the period from 1983 to 1985 represents the bloodiest period of the conflict. Moreover, in these early years, the conflict was overwhelmingly concentrated in Ayacucho (see Figure 9.3). In the succeeding years, the conflict began to spread into other regions of the country.

The Truth and Reconciliation Commission divided the war and its aftermath into five phases: inauguration of the armed violence (1980–1983); militarization of the conflict (1983–1986); spreading out of the conflict to the national level (1986–1989); extreme crisis: subversive offensive and counter-offensive (1989–1991); decline of subversive action, authoritarianism, and corruption (1991–2000).

In the first phase, Sendero initiated armed actions and consolidated its influence throughout the villages and towns of Ayacucho, from the high altitude villages of Huanta down to the Apurimac Valley in the tropical jungle lowlands to the east that bordered the Department of Cusco. In the second phase, the army and marines unleashed a brutal counterinsurgency campaign and military intelligence units began a program of selective assassinations. From speeches and newspaper accounts of the era, it is evident that the government was uncertain who the enemy was. Belaúnde and senior military officials blamed foreign states such as Cuba or the Soviet Union. In fact, Sendero had no ties to foreign states and was only loosely tied to the extreme Maoist international organization Revolutionary International Movement.

A second guerrilla movement, the Túpac Amaru Revolutionary Movement (MRTA), also took up arms during these early phases of the war. The MRTA was more in the mold of the traditional Latin American guerrilla groups of the 1960s and grew out of the union of two small groups with roots in that period, the Revolutionary Socialist Party-Marxist-Leninist (PSR-ML) and the Movement of the Revolutionary Left-Militant (MIR-EM). It began urban actions in 1984 and then launched a general war in June 1985, choosing a date to commemorate the 1965 MIR guerrilla uprising.[8] The MRTA soon after allied with another surviving faction of the MIR, MIR-Voz Rebelde (Rebellious Voice). The groups that came together to form the MRTA viewed the moment as propitious following the triumph of the Sandinista Revolution in Nicaragua and the advances of the Salvadorian and Colombian guerrillas. They also were influenced by the spectacular growth of Sendero. Throughout this period, the MRTA was forced to fight in the shadow of Sendero. In a few key regions of the country, particularly in the coca-producing regions of the Alto Huallaga valley, Huancayo, and

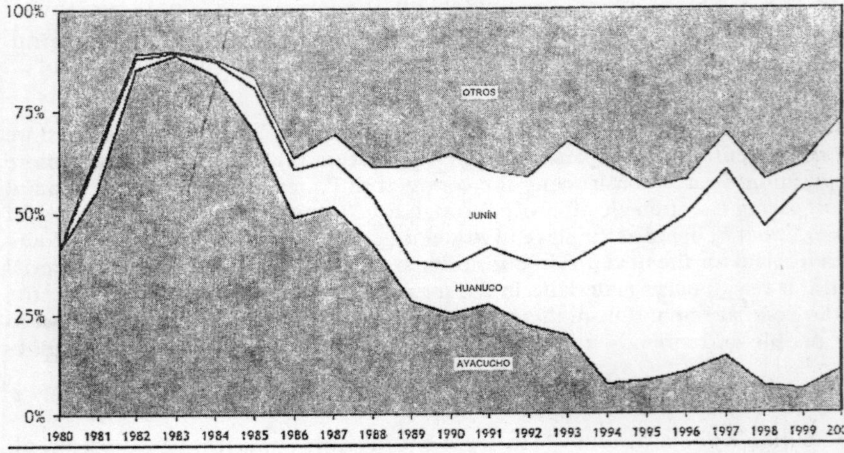


Figure 9.3. Percentage of deaths and disappeared reported to the TRC according to department of occurrence of the incident, by year, 1980–2000. TRC *Final Report*, vol. 1, 134.

in universities across the country, the MRTA had to engage Sendero militarily and politically for popular support and influence.[9]

By 1985, after a presidential election won by APRA under its new young leader Alan García,[10] the army retreated from its scorched earth policy in the southern highlands. The troops withdrew to their barracks and suspended many of their efforts to form civilian antisubversive patrols. In the next phase, the war spread into the lowlands along the Apurimac and Ene River Valleys and into the Alto Huallaga River Valley, which in the 1980s was transformed into the world's largest coca producing area. Sendero also successfully moved into the Montaro Valley in the central highlands that controlled the food and energy supply of metropolitan Lima, causing disruptions in the food supply and regular blackouts following the bombing of electrical pylons. The PCP-SL also began to infiltrate the shantytowns and poorer, unorganized areas of Lima as well as public universities throughout the country (see Figure 9.3 and Map 9.1).

In the First Plenary Congress of the PCP-SL, held in 1988 and 1989 in Lima, Presidente Gonzalo declared that the first phase of the popular war had been fulfilled and that the military conditions of the country now warranted the development of the next phase: a war of positions fought on equal ground with the enemy forces of the state, what he declared Mao had called a state of "strategic equilibrium." Guzmán emphasized this view in his 1988 interview in *El Diario* and also spoke of preparing for the next and final stage, the "strategic offensive" that would result in their taking power. These are Maoist categories of the popular war. Yet for Mao, strategic equilibrium was just a turning point in the transition from defense to offense. Guzmán transformed this into a stage of the struggle.[11]

In the 1988 interview, speaking with the prophetic syntax worthy of someone who believes that he represents the "fourth sword of communism," he described the strategy as follows:

> Since the Congress, we have proposed to construct the conquest of Power and we are constructing this conquest. Strategic equilibrium is a political fact, not a mere lucubration; we are constructing the conquest of Power. . . . We also are mindful of preparing the strategic offensive through the "Construction of the Conquest of Power," that is, being at the stage of strategic equilibrium it is here where the foundation is laid for the next phase: our strategic offensive. . . . We insist, it is a material fact. It is real, it exists materially, in the society, in the class struggle of the country, in the popular war and from there we reflect these facts in ideas. Make it known to the people and embody it: we have entered into the phase of strategic equilibrium.[12]

Guzmán's declaration of "strategic equilibrium" was not based on a realistic assessment of the facts on the ground. In certain regions of the country, particularly in Ayacucho, the campesinos were in open revolt against Sendero's domination. Moreover, the Army had reentered the rural zones in force, but this time with a more enlightened strategy to work with the peasant communities. By the time Sendero had entered Lima, it had already lost most of the countryside with the exception of the coca-growing areas of the Alto Huallaga and parts of the Rio Ene in the eastern jungles. It entered Lima not from a position of strength, as many in Lima believed at the time, but from a position of weakness. As Comandante Feliciano, a member of the Sendero's governing council, emphasized in an interview with the TRC from his prison cell in the naval base of Callao, Sendero did not have the military capacity to engage the military in a war of positions. "Abimael Guzmán made a Nintendo war," he declared. He was deploying fictitious columns and battalions.[13]

The view from Lima was that Sendero's long-planned assault on the capital city had begun. The guerrillas' weakness was not evident to those who lived in the capital. In the mid-1980s, Limeños had been subjected to blackouts that would reveal an enormous bonfire in the shape of a hammer and sickle etched into the desert mountains and silhouetted against the sky. Following the First Congress, Sendero made a major push into Lima. The PCP-SL increased its assassination of leftist, NGO, and state officials throughout the greater metropolitan area and tried to take control of popular organizations and impoverished neighborhoods. The group stepped up terrorist attacks on the nation's infrastructure and against defenseless civilian targets, killing and maiming randomly. The year of Guzmán's capture, 1992, was the most violent year in Lima. A car bomb exploded in an upscale section of the city, Miraflores, killing bystanders and incinerating houses. After almost a decade of a popular war in the countryside, residents feared that the Maoist war had arrived in the city.

## Organization and Recruitment

The PCP-SL at the time of the "popular war" was a Leninist vanguard party, not a mass party. Its members were chosen to lead the revolution and were organized in secret cells.[14] The party was deliberately kept small. Its followers were generally not party members. According to the TRC, the party had 520 militants and close collaborators at the moment that it initiated the armed conflict in 1980. By 1990, when the violence had extended to most regions of the country, it had about 2,700 militants, not including those in the coca-growing region of the Alto Huallaga.[15]

Authority emanated from the person of Abimael Guzmán, who was head of the central committee of the party and head of the revolution and who was later declared "President of the Republic of New Democracy." Although the PCP-SL literature does not refer often to Stalin, his influence can be seen in the cult of personality around the figure of Presidente Gonzalo and the understanding that only the official party carries truth. Rivals should be liquidated.

The party was organized with a permanent committee that consisted of Abimael Guzmán, his wife, Augusta LaTorre, Compañera Nora, and his future companion after the death of his wife, Elena Iparraguirre, Compañera Miriam. Below this was a politburo, with the three members of the permanent committee plus two others. At the time of Guzmán's capture in 1992, the structure remained the same with the exception that Oscar Ramírez Durand, Feliciano, had replaced Guzmán's deceased wife on the permanent committee and in the politburo. When Feliciano was later interviewed in prison by the TRC about his participation in the central committee, he stated that his membership was strictly formal since he was in the countryside and could not attend the meetings of the central committee to take decisions. Below the national committees there were eleven regional committees that also had little independent protagonism.

Guzmán was also head of the military commission that oversaw the guerrilla army that was subordinate to the party, the Ejército Guerrillero Popular (EGP) or Popular Guerrilla Army. The guerrilla army was comprised of a principal force, a local force, and a base force. The principal force in 1990, excluding the Alto Huallaga, consisted of 816 guerrilla fighters. It operated like a guerrilla army, assaulting police stations, taking over towns, and defending strategic zones, and was armed with more modern weapons than the other two forces. The PCP-SL was slow to develop its armed wing. According to captured documents, in 1987 the principal force had only 83 combatants.[16] The local force was only lightly armed and operated in areas where Sendero had taken over the positions of authority in a town, replacing traditional and state authorities. Combatants drawn from the town would continue with their normal work activities between operations. The base force consisted of all residents in guerrilla zones capable of military

TABLE 9.1. RESOURCES OF THE POPULAR GUERRILLA ARMY, 1989–FEBRUARY 1990 (DOES NOT INCLUDE HUALLAGA)

| | |
|---|---|
| Manpower | |
| Principal force | 816 (283 party militants) |
| Local force | 4,650 (385 party militants) |
| Base force | 17,940 (1,958 militants) |
| **Weaponry** | |
| Long weapons | |
| FAL | 68 |
| HK | 50 |
| AKM | 43 |
| Mausers | 43 |
| Carbines | 77 |
| Shotguns | 413 |
| Machine guns | 97 |
| Short weapons | |
| Pistols | 40 |
| Revolvers | 195 |
| Rudimentary arms | 8,496 |
| Dynamite | 66,000 sticks |

Source: "Balance de desarrollar las bases en función de Conquistar el poder Campana impulsar," document written by Abimael Guzmán, captured by Dincote, reprinted in TRC, *Final Report*, vol. 2, 99.

activities, including children beginning at age twelve and older people able to endure the strains of long marches. The base force was used as a reserve force and was armed with makeshift weapons, sticks, or machetes. Their numbers in 1990 totaled 17,940 (see Table 9.1). Those who showed promise were elevated to the local or principal force.[17]

After the "initiation of the armed struggle" in 1980, the party essentially closed its membership to avoid infiltration. New militants were recruited through what it called the "engendered organizations" first founded in the 1970s to create a "mass" base for the party. These included such Senderista organizations as the Movimiento Femenino Popular (Popular Women's Movement), Socorro Popular (Popular First Aid), Movimiento Clasista de Obreros y Trabajadores (Class Movement of Workers and Laborers), and Movimiento de Campesinos Pobres (Movement of Poor Campesinos). Even the EGP fighters, as can be seen in Table 9.1, were mostly not party members.

The party recruited initially from its base in the University of Huamanga. Ayacucho in this period was experiencing profound social upheaval as a large percentage of the region's youth for the first time had increased access to secondary and university education. All of Peru was undergoing a similar phenomenon. The opening of the UNSCH in 1959, after having

TABLE 9.2. ENROLLMENT AND DEMAND FOR UNIVERSITY EDUCATION, PERU, 1960–1990

| *Students* | *1960* | *1970* | *1980* |
|---|---|---|---|
| High school graduates | 19,305 | 66,199 | 153,100 |
| University applicants | 14,665 | 64,312 | 239,485 |
| Registered university students | 5,429 | 23,914 | 58,744 |
| Registered students as % of all applicants | 37 | 37 | 25 |

Source: TRC, *Final Report.*

been closed since 1886, reflected this national expansion and opened up new educational opportunities in one of the poorest and isolated areas of the country. However, as Table 9.2 shows, the availability of places at the university did not meet the growing demand. By 1980, there were 239,485 applicants for the 58,744 available spaces nationwide.

The period witnessed a radicalization of the teachers' unions and university professors. Sendero Luminoso grew and thrived in this environment as Guzmán systematically took over student, faculty, and administrative politics and used the university to prepare the terrain for armed struggle. The TRC described the phenomenon in the following terms:

> Guzman propagated a fundamentalist Marxist historical materialism that consisted of a closed diagnosis and circular analysis with little disposition for debate, with a vision that was inconsistent with reality but that was expressed as being based on scientific and universal truths. As such, the PCP-SL presented itself as a caudillo-teacher, as the motor for change, and as the armed educator who can use language and violence as instruments on which to base his power. How did they move beyond rhetoric to practice? The answer was through didactic education.[18]

Sendero Luminoso represented a pedagogical project as well as a party. Its control of the regional university and its assertion of authority based on greater knowledge represented a Leninist-style (vanguardist, "democratically centralized," distrustful of the masses) pedagogy of revolution.

In addition to teachers, PCP-SL also sent out revolutionary anthropologists, historians, archaeologists, and others from the UNSCH who conducted field research and worked with the local populations to prepare for the armed struggle.[19] As the TRC observed, Sendero recreated the vertical hierarchy of authority that had traditionally ordered social relations in the countryside and had subordinated the region's campesinos. Guzmán, in portraits and murals painted on walls and buildings across the country, was always portrayed as a revolutionary figure, bespectacled, with a book—not a gun—in his hands, looking toward the future, larger than life, and leading the masses who were depicted as sprouting from his coattails.

However, the revolution was not made just with the vanguard party. It was made by the party *with* the masses. In order to understand, then, how such an ideological and regionally specific revolutionary project could spark a national insurgency that quickly moved beyond the conditions of Ayacucho, one has to examine the relationship between the party and the "masses."

Most analysts agree that initially Sendero was able to garner a significant degree of support in Ayacucho, principally from the region's youth. Ponciano del Pino, a historian at the UNSCH, noted that many in the Andean communities of Ayacucho, particularly the young people, initially welcomed the arrival of Sendero. The party offered education, a more just order, and a degree of dignity and hope. "Shining Path, moreover, offered a system of order, in contrast to the arbitrary rule of the authorities, police, merchants, and teachers. Sendero seemed to buttress ethical and moral values in crisis by punishing adultery, alcoholism, vagrancy, robbery, and cattle rustling. It seemed to offer not only a just and ordered society, but solutions to concrete problems that the state and capitalism had not addressed. . . . Within this general context, generational and ethnic factors held significance. Youth more readily identified with the party and seemed disposed to join and to fight while adults from more traditional and ethnically identified communities were most skeptical of such sacrifices."[20]

In a detailed case study of one town, Sello del Oro, del Pino described the initial reception of the guerillas:

> In the beginning, the population provided food to the guerrillas, took them in, and participated in "people's assemblies." The peasants had lacked such services as health and transportation. They suffered economically from the low prices of produce (such as coffee, *cube*—a plant used to make poison and insecticide—cacao, and *achiote*, which were monopolized by large merchants) and from constant devaluations and rises in the cost of living. All of this meant that the inhabitants looked favorably on those who offered new hope for their lives.[21]

For all of its ideological rigidity documented so thoroughly by the TRC and others, [22] the PCP-SL consistently demonstrated a degree of flexibility and adaptability when it moved into new regions, revealing an ability to identify community needs and regional enemies and aligning its war with the villager's war. The result was, at a minimum in the early stages, a passive tolerance of the guerrillas' actions.

One author summed it up this way, citing a strategy document of Sendero:

> Although Sendero has earned a reputation for being ideologically dogmatic and fanatical, it is highly versatile in fitting its strategy and tactics to the demands of Andean ecopolitics. Sendero itself expressed this concept subconsciously when it called the current revolutionary phase, "The War of Little Wars" in its pamphlets—a thousand little wars across the Andes. Each skirmish is fought on its own terms, without the adversaries necessarily being aware that war has broken out.[23]

But Sendero was not content to engage in a thousand little wars. Its strategy in each village and town was to penetrate and then destroy the local authorities and substitute its own authorities. The TRC described the strategy in the following terms:

> When the PCP-SL took control of a community, it was declared a liberated zone (LZ) and the traditional authorities were replaced by authorities named by the party. Many communities of the region were declared LZ between 1980 and 1982; however, the approach of the PCP-SL in each was different; there were variations and nuances in the local organizations that the PCP-SL established. In some cases, the PCP-SL made use of the community's leaders, who became those who were locally responsible for the new Senderista organization.[24]

Del Pino describes a harsher reality:

> Shining Path's hardening political line and authoritarian attitudes led to problems with the peasantry even before the military occupation. Early in 1982, Shining Path intensified actions oriented to "hammer" (*batir*) the countryside. The idea was to expel the state from the guerrilla zones and to mount its first People's Committees as a new governing structure. The guerrillas tied to "sweep out" (*barrer*) the authorities, the traditional bosses (*gamonales*) and the police. . . . This meant imposing revolutionary authorities and organizational structures to replace expelled and assassinated officials."[25]

The TRC outlined the organization of the "new State" as follows:

> Besides using local conflicts to exercise justice in the communities, the PCP-SL instructed the youth in strategies of war in popular schools, thus forming militants who could join the Popular Guerrilla Army (EGP). . . . The young people assumed the main responsibilities in the popular committees. Each popular committee, with some variations, had a primary person who was responsible, a security commissar, a production commissar, a communal affairs commissar, and an organization commissar.

As detailed in the TRC, many resented the usurping of authority of the traditional elders and authorities by young people without experience and lacking respect.[26] Yet in this way, Sendero succeeded in eliminating the state from vast areas of the countryside. These new authorities organized the local and base forces. They regulated social relations among townspeople and prohibited religious and many traditional cultural practices, often punishable by death. They attempted to regulate market relations, particularly through their prohibitions of the *ferias campesinas* (farmers' markets), and administered "popular justice," meting out capital punishment for minor crimes.

## Finances

Although the Peruvian war occurred at a time when the cold war was flourishing in the western hemisphere, Sendero received no external funds. It opposed the politics of other socialist nations—Cuba, the recently victorious Nicaraguan revolution, the Soviet Union, and China—and was one of the first insurgencies to fund itself entirely from internal sources. Yet in practice, PCP-SL did not resemble the type of post-cold war insurgencies that came to blur the boundaries between war and crime. It did not participate in kidnapping for economic reasons or extort national and multinational companies and rob banks as the Colombian guerrillas have done for the last two decades.

Yet all insurgencies need to mobilize resources, and Sendero was no exception. For twelve years, it was able to wage war throughout the Peruvian national territory. It reportedly paid party members comparatively good salaries, $250 to 500 a month,[27] and helped sustain a wide array of the Senderista "engendered organizations" discussed above.

Sendero raised its funds through the drug trade that boomed in Peru in the 1980s as the country was transformed into the world's largest producer of illicit coca. Coca paste was sold to Colombian traffickers, then transported to Colombia for processing into cocaine before being transshipped to consuming regions, particularly the United States. In some ways, Sendero's relationship to the coca trade in the 1980s in Peru resembled the FARC's relationship to the coca growers and drug-traffickers in the 1990s and 2000s in Colombia.

Even before launching the armed struggle, the PCP-SL had entered into the coca producing zones of the Alto Huallaga River Valley in the northeastern jungles. As the coca trade boomed and the coca growers were increasingly placed outside the law and in an adversarial relationship to the state and its antinarcotics policies, Sendero quickly won support among the growers. The U.S. war on drugs only aided Sendero. Sendero was able to provide armed protection from Peruvian and U.S. antinarcotics programs. During the course of the 1980s, somewhat like the FARC in the 1990s, Sendero served as an armed union for the coca growers, negotiating better prices for their crops with drug traffickers and imposing order in the zone. As in other regions, the communities initially welcomed Sendero.

One *cocalero* activist declared in an interview with a Peruvian journalist:

> What the growers want is protection and money. The traffickers kept telling them that the coca price was down because of overproduction. They know it is not true, but they had no one to protect them. That's what Sendero gives them: protection. . . . Besides, in the area, as long as there is a lot of money, there is alcohol, laziness and violence. . . . Sendero put an end to all of that and made everybody work. It also closed all the discos, the whorehouses, killed the homosexuals, and expelled the prostitutes.[28]

The difference when compared to other regions is that Sendero maintained this symbiotic and relatively cooperative relationship with the *cocaleros* of the zone throughout most of the 1980s. The area's principal function was to generate resources, not provide the political and military support for the "popular war."

Some have placed Sendero's income from the drug trade at between $20 million and 250 million between 1987 and 1993. This was raised through landing fees ($3,000–10,000 per flight) plus "revolutionary tithes" in exchange for armed protection and controls on the market price of coca.[29] One should caution that these numbers are difficult to determine and generally widely inaccurate (see similar discussion of the FARC in Chapter 2).

On the surface, then, the case of Sendero appears to support the general arguments on resource mobilization and falls within the parameters of the debates on the economics of internal wars generally framed as "greed versus grievance." These arguments assert that economic factors—greed—largely explain the presence and duration of internal armed conflicts.[30] Indeed, one scholar argues that the rise and fall of Sendero correlates almost exactly with the rise and fall of the price of coca in Peru.[31] Sendero first took up arms precisely at the point when the illicit coca/cocaine trade took off. It collapsed when the Peruvian coca trade went bust and most coca production moved to Colombia—and benefited the FARC.[32]

Such correlations are intriguing but a closer examination reveals that the price of coca and the scope of guerrilla activity are unrelated. Sendero's demise had little to do with the collapse of the price of coca or the U.S. war on drugs, as will be discussed in the next two sections. If anything, the Peruvian case seems to refute the greed versus grievance thesis. Sendero clearly had access to substantial resources as a result of its control of the coca-producing regions. Yet Sendero did not invest its resources in the war effort or visibly accumulate or horde capital. Table 9.1 reveals that the EGP, the guerrilla force of Sendero, had 816 full-time combatants at the height of the war and a total of 97 machine guns, 281 vintage assault rifles and semiautomatic weapons, and 413 shotguns. Most of its arms were acquired through overrunning police stations and ambushing army patrols. Dynamite was the principal weapon.

Compare Sendero's war-fighting capabilities with those of the FARC in Colombia. As the FARC's income increased, it was able to expand its army from about 4,000 combatants in the early 1990s to approximately 18,000 combatants equipped with modern weaponry. Their monies were invested in building a large and expensive war machine. Sendero made no such investment. Its spectacular growth in the 1980s and later its precipitous fall in the early 1990s seem to be unrelated to its ability to mobilize resources. The demonstrated ability to mobilize resources seems to have been a negligible factor in the success or failure of its "popular war."

## The Defeat of Sendero (1): Campesinos Revolt Against the Insurgents

Sendero lost the war principally because it lost the support of its social base.

Even at a time of severe economic crisis with negative growth, increasing indebtedness, and hyperinflation that reached 2500 percent per year in 1990, Sendero's support had eroded throughout its original zones of operation, with the possible exception of the Alto Huallaga. Another revolutionary movement, more attuned to the social crisis around it, would have taken advantage of the extreme weakness of the state. Sendero managed to turn the population against it and, ironically, ended up strengthening the presence of the state in regions that had long been abandoned by the central government in Lima.

In one study in the region of Andahuaylas, Ronald Berg captures the key moment that practically all communities who suffered through the war seemed to have experienced: the moment when support for Sendero began to waver, before doubts turned to passive and eventually active resistance:

> When Sendero first emerged in Andahuaylas in 1981, peasants were unclear about the guerrillas' aims. Discussing this, people often remarked simply, "We do not know what the terrorists want." After political assassinations began in 1982, opinions began to be more strongly felt and more polarized. On the one hand, there was some question about whether the choice of targets was always just. As a number of people stated, "I have nothing against their killing the rich, but I don't like it when they kill peasants."[33]

Through its strategy of liquidating local authorities, Sendero was able to gain influence in towns and villages across the country. However, the townspeople were resistant to the idea of a broader war or a wholesale reorganization of their daily lives. The villagers accommodated Sendero's authority up to a point but slowly began to resist when they viewed that their moral values, sense of proper order, and dignity were violated.[34] Like the peasants and rural laborers described by James Scott in his classic text *Weapons of the Weak,* the Peruvian campesinos at first had limited means or instruments of resistance to confront Sendero, so they engaged in "everyday forms of resistance."[35]

Yet in region after region, the population began to turn against Sendero. They had initially welcomed Sendero's "little wars" against village enemies, thieves, and corrupt townspeople and officials. However, they were not prepared to accompany Sendero in its "popular war" of a new social order and "new State." After about 1984, passive resistance turned into active resistance in some communities. A few formed *montoneras,* a term that harks back to guerrilla bands in the time of the wars of independence.[36] In the coca-growing region of the Apurimac Valley in the lowlands of Ayacucho and Cusco, peasants also took the initiative to form self-defense committee years before the Army formally founded the *rondas.*[37]

In Huanta, peasants acknowledged their early cooperation with Sendero. According to the TRC, Huanta was the province that suffered the most deaths and disappearances during the war. In 1993 when I first visited the region, practically all the villages were organized into peasant self-defense committees or *rondas campesinas.* A State of Emergency remained in effect throughout the district, and the civilian leaders were all subordinated to local military officials. In a collective interview in San José with leaders of the *rondas campesinas* and of the Mothers' Club (Club de Madres), the principal organization for women in the village, I asked about the village's relationship with Sendero. The assembled group told of how Sendero had long had a presence in the area and mentioned the fieldwork of Osmán Moróte in the nearby village of Chaca.[38] In the early years of the armed struggle, the village had basically supported Sendero for many of the reasons cited earlier. But then they went on to describe the alienation and rejection that had caused them to eventually take up arms against the terrorists. They enumerated three primary reasons.

First, they mentioned the strong village opposition to the closing of the *ferias campesinas* (farmers' markets). Sendero had forcefully divided up the few estates in this area and distributed the land, but then had prohibited the selling of produce at market. Sendero had insisted that the campesinos were to grow only what they could consume. They were forbidden to engage in capitalism. The edict was incomprehensible to the community. The *ferias* in the different villages were the lifeblood of the region. Over several years, Sendero would shut down the markets and when their forces left the traditional village authorities would reopen them, ignoring the new authorities designated by Sendero. When the Senderistas returned, they would punish those responsible for disobeying their orders. Sendero never succeeded in completely eliminating the markets.

Second, the villagers opposed and resisted Sendero demands that the community send more of its youth to fight in the wider war after Guzmán declared the start of the next phase of the war, "strategic equilibrium." The leaders from the Mothers' Club found this strategy of forced recruitment to be the most reprehensible, and indicated that it represented a significant turning point in the resistance.

Finally, after an hour of complaints about the *feria* and forced recruitment, I mentioned Sendero's violence. While the principal *rondero* leader and the president of the Club de Madres were animated in discussing the other two issues, they barely wanted to discuss the violence. They acknowledged my concerns when prompted, confirmed that Sendero was violent, and left it at that. It was by then nighttime. The room was cold and someone had lit candles. We sipped coffee. Two in the room were former Senderistas, *arrepentidos,* those who had accepted the government's offers to desert in exchange for leniency or amnesty. They were leaving for night patrols shortly. The war was not over.[39]

## The Defeat of Sendero (2): The Tension between Counterinsurgency and Local Resistance and the Uniqueness of the Peruvian Case

The state, particularly the army, was not passive as the campesinos took the lead in expelling Sendero. Several policies implemented across two administrations—Alan García and Alberto Fujimori—were critical in ending the war, including improved police and military intelligence and the capture of Abimael Guzmán, which will be discussed in the next section. However, the most significant factor in the defeat of Sendero was the ability of the army to reexamine its strategies and learn from the growing peasant rebellion.

In the late 1980s, the armed forces returned to communities that had rejected their actions just a few years earlier. In Huanta, the marines, a division of Peru's naval forces, had unsuccessfully tried to organize the upper mountain regions in 1984 and 1985. By the late 1980s, it was the army that took the initiative and returned to the zone. Some of the officers were Quechua-speaking and most of the recruits came from the region. The new policies put into place were designed to assist the peasant resistance while keeping most of the arms in the hands of the army. Alan García had authorized the first civilian self-defense committees or *rondas campesinas*. The policy was vastly expanded under Fujimori. Between 1992 and 1994, according to the TRC, the army formed 4,628 self-defense committees, integrating 232,668 *ronderos*.[40]

The idea of military forces arming civilian "self-defense groups"—literally *paramilitary* groups—is on its face quite disturbing. Anyone familiar with the excesses of other counterinsurgency programs should have raised more than an eyebrow by now. In Colombia, as detailed in Chapter 2, the policy of the armed forces to arm civilians led to a human rights and humanitarian crisis. It gave birth to a third actor in the conflict—semiautonomous paramilitary groups—that contributed to a significant escalation of the violence. The paramilitaries provoked a dramatic increase in extrajudicial killings, forced displacements, and massacres of unarmed civilians. They turned their guns not only on poor campesinos and alleged guerrilla sympathizers, but also on politicians, judges, academics and others when it served their interest. In Guatemala, the Historical Clarification Commission declared that the program of forcing peasants into special villages and into civilian self-defense patrols in certain areas of the country between 1981 and 1983 constituted genocide against the Guatemalan indigenous population as defined by the 1948 Genocide Convention.[41]

Why, then, did the Peruvian experience differ from these other two countries as well as from the experiences in other countries around the world? The answer lies in the structure of rural social relations in the 1980s in Peru and the direct relationship that the armed forces were able to establish with the campesino communities. This point needs to be underscored because it explains much of the difference between Peru and some other Latin American countries, most notably Colombia. In Peru, the 1968 military government enacted the most sweeping land reform on the continent after Cuba. The result was that large estates and landowners were eliminated from the countryside. In the few remote highland areas that the generals did not reach, Sendero did. The Peruvian countryside in 1980 was populated by small peasant villages with small and medium-size landholdings, particularly in the Andean highlands. When the army set up civilian self-defense groups in the late 1980s and early 1990s, it engaged directly with the small peasant communities who were already in direct revolt against Sendero.

In Colombia, in contrast, the countryside is characterized by a diversity of land tenure, including a sizable and growing number of large estates in north, central, and eastern cattle regions and the southern colonization zones. Worse, since the mid-1980s, the country has experienced what one Colombian sociologist called a counteragrarian reform: land and power have become more concentrated, not less, as drug traffickers have purchased an estimated 5–6 million hectares of land and expelled small and medium peasants from neighboring lands through the use of violence.[42]

When the army moved in to arm civilians beginning in the 1980s, the paramilitary groups acted not in defense of small peasant groups, but on behalf of the interest of the large estates, *gamonales,* and large business interests. They inserted themselves into a complex social conflict that has fueled Colombia's internal war for over half a century. [43] In Colombia, the paramilitaries do not represent a peasant revolt against the guerrillas, as in Peru. They represent a revolt by the traditional rural powerholders, landowners, *gamonales,* large—agribusinesses—many of which have been strengthened by large infusions of narco-investments—against the guerrillas, a phenomenon that has long and deep roots in Colombia. Creating private paramilitary armies linked to both the armed forces and rural landowners only served to further fuel the conflict.

The size of land holdings and the organization of rural society do not by themselves ensure fewer violations. The early experiences of the armed forces, particularly by the marines in Huanta between 1983 and 1985, echoed elements of the extreme abuse of the Guatemalan experience. Yet in Guatemala, the policy severely weakened the insurgency. Even in Colombia, the paramilitaries had some success in expelling the guerrillas from zones that they had long dominated. However in Peru, the "scorched earth," "drain the ocean" strategy of the early years did not achieve results. It alienated the population and strengthened the insurgency. The armed forces evaluated and learned from this experience. When they returned, the counterinsurgency strategy was more discriminate and expressly designed to channel the deep and growing resistance of the peasantry, a factor that did not exist or was only nascent in the earlier period.

The return of the army to the Peruvian highlands was fraught with tensions. The army sought to ally its interests with those of the campesino communities. Both groups shared a common objective of defeating the insurgents. But the army also wanted to maintain and assert control of the counterinsurgency effort. Under Fujimori, the army was granted the authority to name and remove local officials, powers it had sought since the days of Alan García. To show some deference to community leader, in each zone, the military-political chief, the senior army officer in the zone would designate a committee of notables to recommend personnel decisions. But ultimate authority lay with the armed forces.

Unlike the Colombian paramilitaries, the Peruvian civilian self-defense committees did not turn into an independent source of violence or a third actor in the conflict. As Figure 9.1 shows, they were involved in less than 5 percent of the human rights violations. They were only lightly armed. In San José de Secce in the Santillana District of Huanta, there were about 100 *ronderos,* all men. Women were prohibited from joining. For 100 men, the committee had access to about twenty World War I-era Winchester and Mauser rifles, which were stored on the military base located just outside the large stone-gated entrance to the town. The rifles had been personally given to the town by President Fujimori. Those without rifles carried sticks, machetes, or homemade weapons on patrols. Their poor equipment mirrored that of Sendero. As a military force, they were negligible, again in great contrast to the Colombian paramilitary armies bristling with modern weaponry. They were basically used to patrol the area and serve as a trip wire and intelligence network. The central military activity was monopolized by the army.

Peru's internal war was primarily a "dirty war," as are most guerrilla wars. There were very few instances of military clashes or armed engagements between Sendero forces and the army. Both sides conducted the war through ambushes of small military targets or assassinations, extrajudicial killings, disappearances, and massacres of defenseless civilians. As Figure 9.4 demonstrates, although the army's involvement in human rights violations declined significantly as compared to the 1983–85 period, the "dirty war" tactics of the armed forces did not end when they returned to the highlands. In 1988 and 1989, Peru led the world in forced disappearances. Most of these were attributable to the Peruvian armed forces.[44]

The second experiment in Peru with civilian self-defense groups was decisive in defeating the insurgency. It was most distinguishable for the way it took advantage of the peasants' own resistance. Contrary to my expectations formed as a result of long experience in Colombia, the creation of the *rondas* did not lead to an escalation of the violence. The experience created a new relationship to the state that was somewhat more respectful

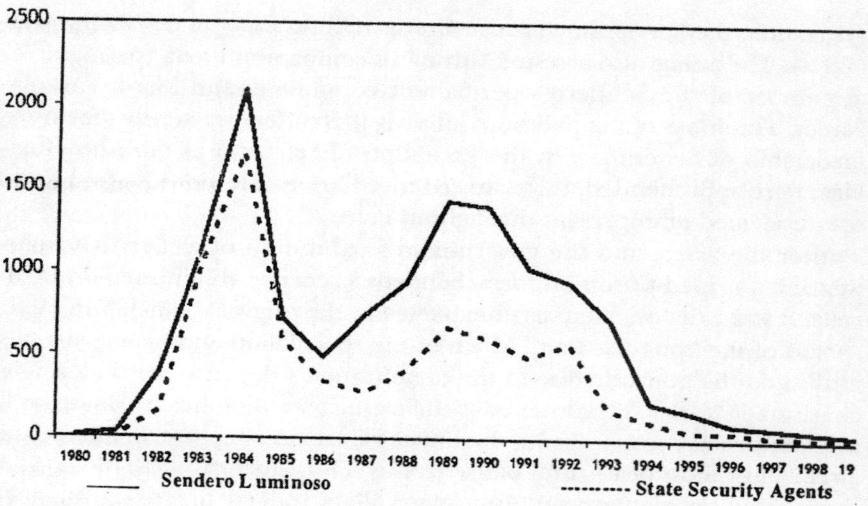


Figure 9.4. Deaths and disappearances reported to the TRC, according to the actor that is responsible, by year, 1980–1996. TRC, *Final Report*, vol. 1, 137.

of the communities' needs. Furthermore, as several Peruvian intellectuals have argued, the *rondas* began to plant the seeds of a new civil society with a more direct access to the state and its resources.[45] But the experience was less beneficial for the armed forces or the state. The army continued to participate in extrajudicial killings and disappearances even after the conflict had diminished and it acted with practically no civilian oversight in the emergency zones.

In 2004, I returned to Huanta and again visited San José. The army had long since abandoned the zone, and the military base outside the village gates was reduced to rubble and ruins. A few stone walls remained exposed to the sun and rain. There were overgrown weeds everywhere and children were playing soccer in the open areas. In the town, I interviewed the mayor. I asked about the *rondas.* He answered, yes, they were no longer needed against Sendero, but that there was still need to organize against the growing crime in the area. Some of the *ronderos,* he explained, had moved on to positions of authority in the town and the region. Others had returned to their previous lives and yet others had migrated to the cities of Huanta, Ayacucho, or Lima.

## The Capture of Guzmán

Abimael Guzmán was captured, practically alone and unguarded, hiding in a room above a dance studio in Lima on 12 September 1992. Although Fujimori had emphasized the army in the fight against Sendero, the final blow was delivered not by the army but by a new and efficient police intelligence unit, the Special Intelligence Group (Grupo Especial de Inteligencia, GEIN). The police also arrested Guzmán's companion Elena Iparraguirre, a member of the Sendero's permanent committee, and María Pantoja, Nancy, a member of the politburo. Shortly thereafter, practically the entire leadership of Sendero, with the exception of Feliciano in the Alto Huallaga, were apprehended. It was an effective blow to a leader who had heretofore seemed omnipresent throughout Peru.

After the arrest and the government's exhibition of a caged Guzmán wearing a striped prison uniform, Sendero's activities diminished dramatically. It was a denouement as unexpected as the original launch and rapid spread of the "popular war." Much of the speculation and expert analysis attributed the quick demise to the organization's dependence on a single charismatic leader.[46] Undoubtedly, the capture was significant. However, it also obfuscates the fact that at the time of Guzmán's capture, Sendero had already lost most of its rural bases in Ayacucho, Huancavelica, Junín, and throughout the Mantaro and Apurimac Valleys. Indeed, practically the only area where it maintained some strength was in the coca-producing zones of the Huallaga River Valley. Guzmán's arrest did not cause Sendero's defeat. It was the coup de grace. It represented a final blow to the Senderista militants who had deified Guzmán and had pledged to give their lives in his name.

## Impact of Political Violence

Sendero's "popular war" shook the foundations of Peruvian society and left a river of blood in the highlands. According to the official Truth and Reconciliation Commission (TRC), out of a total of 69,280 people killed or disappeared in the conflict between 1980 and 2000, 54 percent of all deaths were caused by Sendero and 34 percent by the armed forces (see Figure 9.1).[47] In comparative Latin America terms, these percentages are startling. The Guatemalan Historical Clarification Commission, the equivalent of the Peruvian TRC, found that 95 percent of all human rights violations were committed by state forces and less than 3 percent by the Guatemalan guerrillas.[48] In Salvador, the figures were 93 percent by the state and 2 percent by the guerrillas. Even in Colombia, a conflict that is more protracted and still enduring, paramilitary groups with ties to state security forces have been responsible for roughly 75 percent of atrocities—massacres and extrajudicial killings—from the late 1980s to 2004 (see Chapter 2). In the case of the repressive military dictatorships in Argentina (1976–1982) and Chile (1973–1989), the respective Truth Commissions found that state agents were responsible for practically all the violations.[49] The PCP-SL, however, not only took up arms against the state; it massively killed individuals from sectors it claimed to represent, targeting other leftist parties, civil society organizations, peasants who disobeyed orders,

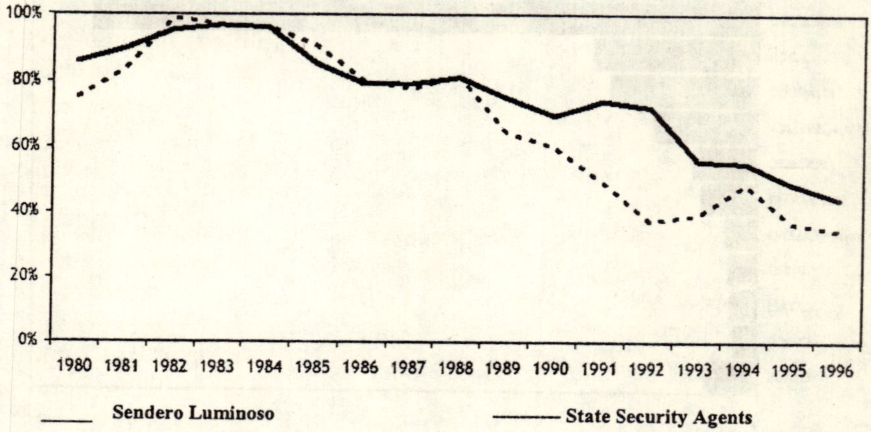


Figure 9.5. Percentage of deaths and disappeared reported to the TRC, whose maternal language in Quechua, according to year and responsible agent. TRC, *Final Report*, vol. 1, 138.

accused collaborators, and those deemed social misfits or political or class enemies.

Sendero first took up arms in the indigenous highlands and many assumed that the rebellion represented an indigenous uprising. But although many of the followers were Quechua-speaking, Sendero spoke the language of Marx and Mao, not of indigenous rights or ethnic exclusion. Ethnicity stands out in the conflict only when focusing on the victim population: 75 percent of all the victims spoke Quechua or another native language compared with 20 percent of the overall population. In the early years of the war, almost the entire victim population was indigenous (see Figure 9.5).

The Truth and Reconciliation Commission underscored the deeply rooted racism in Peruvian society that made such wanton killing possible by both sides:

> The TRC has not found the basis to affirm, as some have, that this was an ethnic conflict. But there is enough evidence to assert that these two decades of destruction and death would not have been possible without a profound contempt toward the most dispossessed population of the country, as demonstrated equally by members of the Communist Party of Peru –Sendero Luminoso (PCP-SL) and agents of the State, a disdain that is interwoven in each moment in the daily lives of the Peruvian people.[50]

From Sendero's initial actions in 1980 through its decline beginning in 1992, the war spread throughout the country. However, when the national death toll was calculated by the TRC, the victims were not only overwhelmingly indigenous. They were also predominantly rural, poor, and concen-

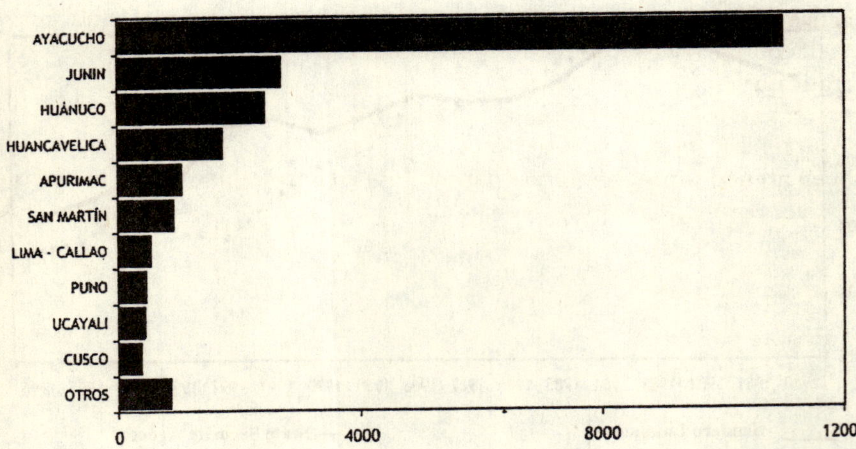


Figure 9.6. Deaths and disappearances reported to the TRC, according to department (state) where events occurred, 1980–2000. TRC, *Final Report*, vol. 1, 120.

trated in one underdeveloped, sparsely populated region of the country: Ayacucho, the area where the PCP-SL initiated its "popular war" (see Figure 9.6). Of the 69,280 total deaths caused by the armed conflict, 26,259 were concentrated in Ayacucho.

To help the majority of Peruvians comprehend the magnitude of the tragedy, the TRC labeled one section of its report, "If We Were All Ayacuchans" and wrote:

> If the proportion of victims estimated for Ayacucho according to its population in 1993 had occurred in the same proportion in the entire country, the armed conflict would have caused nearly 1.2 million victims in all of Peru, of which approximately 240,000 would have taken place in metropolitan Lima, the equivalent in 2000 of the total population of the Limeño districts of San Isidro, Miraflores, San Borja, and La Molina. Such magnitudes might seem unfathomable for a considerable sector of Peruvian society. But they would not be if we were all Ayacuchans, or if, at least, one made the effort to understand the meaning of the sociodemographic profile of the vast majority of the victims. Analyzing this profile, it is clear that most of the bloodletting of these years was experienced by the Peru that is rural, Andean and jungle, Quechua and Asháninka, peasant, poor, and with little formal education, without the rest of the country even feeling or realizing the true dimensions of this tragedy for these "other people within Peru."[51]

The twelve years of war not only traumatized the society and destroyed families, communities, indigenous tribes, and entire regions, it weakened the country's political institutions. By the time Alberto Fujimori was elected president in 1990, the war had not managed to destroy the principal vestiges of democratic governance. Nevertheless, in April 1992, the president shut down the Peruvian Congress and seized dictatorial power with the active support of the armed forces. The novel action was quickly dubbed a "self-coup." Fujimori effectively led a coup d'état against his own democratically elected government. The coup helped Fujimori consolidate power and for almost a decade, Peruvians mostly assented. But the counterinsurgency campaign did not require the destruction of democracy, as has been argued throughout this chapter. Indeed it would have benefited from greater democratic oversight.

## Overcoming the Legacy of War

Fujimori was to stay in power from 1990 to 2000. During his decade in power, he blocked investigations into accounts of human rights abuses perpetrated by the state's security forces during their counterinsurgency efforts as well as inquiries into his own complicity in authorizing antiterror operations that involved extrajudicial killings and massacres. In June 1995 he approved a broad amnesty that covered all violations of human rights committed by state forces in the fight against terrorism.[52]

Fujimori was forced to resign in 2000 after his intelligence chief Vladimir Montesinas was implicated in scandals involving large-scale corruption and abuse of power—including the illegal sale of arms to the Colombian guerrilla group FARC and the videotaped bribing of key members of the legislative and judicial branches, as well as prominent representatives of business and the media. Only in the aftermath of the Fujimori years did the country begin to come to terms with the legacy of the war.

In 2001, interim president Valentín Paniagua established a Truth Commission; his successor, Alejandro Toledo, modified and implemented the original decree. The commission was charged with investigating the causes of violence in Peru between May 1980 and November 2000 and clarifying crimes and human rights violations during this period. Its mandate was to identify those responsible, elaborate proposals for reparations to the victims and their families, and recommend preventive and follow-up measures to implement its recommendations.

The Commission began its work in January 2002 and submitted its findings in August 2003. Like all truth commissions in post-conflict and post-authoritarian situations, questions remain as to the relationship of the Commission's findings and the process of bringing to justice perpetrators of war crimes and crimes against humanity from all sides of the conflict. Nevertheless, the Commission's report can now be used in the Peruvian criminal justice system.

The Commission hopes that its *Final Report* will be used as a guide to help Peruvians overcome the legacy of such horrific violence. At a time when some elements of the international community speak of a "global war on terror," the world community also needs to continue to assist Peru in overcoming its violent ordeal with "terrorism." In Peru, the "terrorism" was perpetrated by nihilistic ideologues in the remote Andean highlands; it was sustained by the historic exclusions of Peruvian society.

## Epilogue

After the capture of Guzmán, a small dissident faction under the command of Feliciano continued to operate in the Alto Huallaga. Feliciano rejected Guzmán's public calls to suspend operations. He led a faction known as Sendero Rojo. He was eventually captured in 1999.

In 2005, there remained only two small factions. One operates in the Alto Huallaga and Rio Ene Valley and is led by "Artemio." In 2003, the group unilaterally proposed a peace settlement with the government but was rebuffed. The other operates in the Rio Ene and Rio Apurimac Valleys and is led by "Alippio." During my visit to Huanta in August 2004, I traveled the road from Huanta to Chaca, the village where Osmán Morote conducted his field research, and then on to San José. Since my previous visit, a road had been constructed from Chaca, in the high mountains, down to the tropical forest and coca-producing areas of the Rio Apurimac. The road is unpaved and runs precariously along the sides of mountains with vast drops below. The campesinos report that there are bandits along the road and that it is best not to drive at night.

We stopped to spend the night in the small village of Carhuahuran. My traveling companions knew the townspeople and the mayor agreed to let us stay in the village meeting room. There we talked throughout the night. The mayor told us that Sendero had entered the town only six weeks earlier. They seized all the village's weapons and then ordered the villagers to meet. They asked for medicines from the village clinic and stated that they were not there to harm them. The medicines were provided and the Senderistas returned the weapons and left the town.

The mayor shook his head. He had been a *rondero.* He did not trust the terrorists. "But," he said, "if they don't bother us, we won't bother them."

Throughout 2004 and 2005, the Huanta press reported accounts of similar incursions by Sendero throughout the lowlands of Huanta. Today Abimael Guzmán and Vladimir Montesinos are housed in the same prison. The Sendero that terrorized Peru no longer exists and has few prospects of returning. The same cannot be said of the social and political violence that engulfed the country from 1980 to 1992.

## Glossary

Accion Popular: Popular Action Party. Conservative party whose candidate Fernando Belaúnde won the 1980 presidential elections.

Alto Huallaga: Region in northeastern Peru along the Huallaga River in the Amazon Basin that in the 1980s became the world's largest producer of coca, the traditional Andean plant used to make cocaine.

APRA: Alianza Popular Revolucionaria Americana (American Popular Revolutionary Alliance). Populist party founded by Victor Raúl Haya de la Torre in 1924 that became Peru's largest and most institutionalized party during most of the twentieth century but did not reach power until 1985.

*arrepentido*: Former insurgent who abandoned subversive activity and accepted the individual amnesty or lenient treatment authorized by the government's Law of Repentance.

*autogolpe*: Self-coup. Term used to describe the actions by Fujimori when, as the elected president, he closed congress with the support of the armed forces and further concentrated power in the presidency.

Ayacucho: Region in the southern highlands of Peru where Sendero was founded and which was the center of the political violence in Peru.

CAC: Comité de Autodefensa Civil or Comité de Autodefensa Anti-Subversiva (Civilian Self-Defense Committee or Antisubversive Self-Defense Committee). Formal names of the peasant self-defense groups commonly called *rondas campesinas,* organized to confront Sendero.

*cocalero*: Farmer who grows coca.

EGP: Ejéricto Guerrillero Popular (Popular Guerilla Army). The military arm of Sendero Luminoso.

ELN: Ejéricto de Liberación Nacional (Popular Liberation Army). Guerrilla movement that took up arms in Peru in the 1960s inspired by the Cuban Revolution.

*gamonales*: Traditional term for "political bosses."

GEIN: Grupo Especial de Inteligencia (Special Intelligence Group of the National Police), responsible for the capture of Sendero leader Abimael Guzmán.

Gonzalo Thought: Pensamiento Gonzalo, body of thought propagated by Sendero leader Abimael Guzmán as the fourth stage in the development of Marxism after Marx, Lenin, and Mao. Named for Guzmán's revolutionary name, Presidente Gonzalo.

IU: Izquierda Unidad (United Left). Coalition of leftist parties that formed an electoral alliance in the 1980s, winning the mayoralty of Lima and exerting a strong impact on electoral politics throughout the 1980s.

Law of Repentance: Ley de Arreptentimiento, part of antiterrorism legislation passed under President Fujimori that provided amnesty or lenient treatment to subversives who surrendered to the authorities.

Mariátegui, José Carlos: Marxist thinker and founder of the Peruvian Communist Party.

MIR: Movimiento de la Izquierda Revolucionaria (Movement of the Revolutionary Left). Short-lived guerrilla movement founded in the 1960s by former APRA militants inspired by the Cuban Revolution.

MIR-EM: Movimiento de la Izquierda Revolucionaria-El Militante (Movement of the Revolutionary Left-The Militant). Faction of the original MIR that in the 1980s united with other small revolutionary parties to form the MRTA.

MIR-VR: Movimiento de la Izquierda Revolucionaria-Voz Rebelde (Movement of the Revolutionary Left-Rebellious Voice). Faction of the original MIR that joined the MRTA after its founding.

MRTA: Movimiento Revolucionario Túpac Amaru (Túpac Amaru Revolutionary Movement). Guerrilla movement that took up arms in the 1980s, formed by factions of earlier guerrilla movements and revolutionary parties of the 1960s.

PCP-Bandera Roja: Partido Comunista de Perú-Bandera Roja (Communist Party of Peru-Red Flag). First Maoist party that broke away from the pro-Soviet Peruvian Communist Party following the Sino-Soviet split in the1960s.

PCP-Patria Roja: Partido Comunista de Perú-Patria Roja (Communist Party of Peru-

Red Fatherland). Maoist party that broke off from the PCP-Bandera Roja over ideological clashes.

PCP-SL: Partido Comunista de Perú-Sendero Luminoso (Communist Party of Peru-Shining Path). Maoist party that broke off from the PCP-Bandera Roja following differences over the Chinese cultural revolution. Name signifies "for the Shining Path of Mariátegui."

PCP-Unidad: Partido Comunista de Perú-Unidad (Communist Party of Peru-Unity). Pro-Soviet Communnist Party.

popular war: Maoist concept of guerrilla war that calls for a prolonged war of national liberation beginning in the countryside and advancing on the cities.

Presidente Gonzalo: Revolutionary name of Sendero leader Abimael Guzmán.

PSR-ML: Partido Socialista Revolucionaro-Marxista-Leninista (Revolutionary Socialist Party-Marxist-Leninist). Small revolutionary party that joined with other parties to form the MRTA.

Revolutionary International Movement: International movement of small Maoist parties that includes Sendero Luminoso, the Communist Party of Turkey/Marxist Leninist (TKP/ ML), and the Maoist Communist Party of Nepal.

*rondas campesinas*: Peasant self-defense committees, popular name used to refer to the CACs.

*ronderos*: Members of the *rondas campesinas.*

Sendero Liminoso: Shining Path, name used to refer to the Communist Party of Peru-Shining Path.

Socorro Popular: Popular First Aid. Senderista front organization that became principal coordinating body in Lima for Sendero Luminoso.

strategic equilibrium: Period in the Maoist conception of popular war when defensive guerrilla warfare has achieved a strategic balance with government forces and conflict is transformed into a war of positions.

TRC: Truth and Reconciliation Commission (Comisión de la Verdad y Reconciliación, CVR). Commission established to investigate the facts of the conflict between 1980 and 2000 and to make proposals for national reconciliation and reparations to victims.

UNSCH: Universidad Nacional San Cristóbal de Huamanga (National University of San Cristóbal de Huamanga). University in Ayacucho where Abimael Guzmán was a philosophy professor and where Sendero was founded.

## Timeline

1928: José Carlos Mariátegui founds the Socialist Party of Peru.

1930: Socialist Party becomes the Communist Party and joins the Third International.

1959: The Universidad Nacional San Cristóbal de Huamanga in Ayacucho opens after being closed since 1886.

1964–1965: Short-lived guerrilla insurgencies by the ELN and MIR.

1965: The Communist Party of Peru divides into the pro-Chinese Communist Party of Peru-Bandera Roja) and the pro-Soviet Communist Party of Peru-Unidad.

1967: Maoist division results in the founding of the Communist Party of Peru-Patria Roja).

1968: The democratically elected government is overthrown and and the left-leaning Revolutionary Armed Forces Government under General Juan Velasco Alvarado is inaugurated.

1970: The Communist Party of Peru-Sendero Luminoso is founded by Abimael

Guzmán in Ayacucho to advance the "Great Proletarian Cultural Revolution" following the death of Mao.

1979: An elected Constituent Assembly is organized by the armed forces to rewrite the constitution and prepare for the military's withdrawal from power and the transition to democracy.

1980: Ballot boxes in Chuschi (Ayacucho) are destroyed on 17 May, on the eve of presidential election, initiating the "popular war" by Sendero Luminoso. On 18 May former president Fernando Belaunde of the Conservative Acción Popular party wins the first presidential election in 16 years. This first phase of Sendero's war plan (initiation of armed struggle) would last until 18 December.

1981: The second phase of Sendero's war plan—to expand expand guerrilla war, "hammer the enemy," "recover" arms from the police and military, create liberated zones (LZs), construct a "new state" through creation of popular committees in zones where there was a power vacuum—begins in January and will last for the next two years. On 12 October President Belaúnde declares a state of emergency in 5 provinces of Ayacucho (Huamanga, Huanta, Cangallo, La Mar, and Victor Fajardo). On 31 December Belaúnde names an army general the senior political and military authority of the emergency zones of Ayacucho.

1983: The marines, a division of the Navy, enter Huanta (Province of Ayacucho) on 21 January and begin to attempt to establish the first civil defense committees. In March Sendero launches the third phase of the war plan: formation of organization committee of the Popular Republic of New Democracy, declaration of Abimael Guzmán as Presidente Gonzalo, formation of Ejército Guerrilero Popular (EGP), implementation of more aggressive tactics, and expansion of the war into new regions of the country.

1984: In January the MRTA takes its first armed action, an attack on a police station in Villa Salvador, one of the poorer sectors of Lima founded, originally by squatters.

1985: Alan García of the APRA Party is elected president of Peru. The marines withdraw from Huanta and military strategies change in the emergency zones.

1986: Senderista presence increases in universities and marginal barrios in Lima, as do attacks on electrical system to create blackouts, yet over the next two years Sendero remains weak in Lima.

1987: The army begins the policy of creating a civilian self-defense force authorized by President Alan García.

1988–1989: First Plenary Congress of the PCP-SL and declaration that war had reached the phase of "strategic equilibrium" between state and guerrilla forces.

1990: Alberto Fujimori, running as the candidate of a new party founded by him, Cambio 90 (Change 1990), is elected president. The Special Intelligence Group of the National Police (GEIN) is created.

1992: On 5 April Fujimori stages an *autogolpe* or self-coup and suspends democratic governance with the support of the armed forces. Subsequently, military authority expands in the emergenzy zones and organization of civilian self-defense committees or *rondas campesinas,* under the authority of the armed forces, increase in 1992–1993. In May the government decrees the Law of Repentance and other measures designed to weaken the insurgents. In June Victor Polay, leader of the MRTA, is recaptured. On 12 September Abimael Guzmán is captured by the GEIN with the simultaneous arrest of senior members of PCP-SL's central committee.

1993: Abimael Guzmán signs a "Peace Accord" from his prison cell and calls for the suspension of the armed struggle. Óscar Ramírez Durand "Feliciano," the only member of Sendero's permanent committee still at large, forms Sendero

Rojo (Red Sendero) and continues limited operations in the Alto Huallaga and Ene River Valleys.

1995: In June the government approves a general amnesty for state officials convicted of human rights violations in the antiterror war. The amnesty subsequently declared invalid by the Inter-American Court of Human Rights.

1996: In December MRTA takes over the residence of the Japanese ambassador to Peru during a diplomatic reception, taking more than 600 guests hostage. Fujimori retakes the residence by force, rescuing all but one of the hostages and killing all insurgents.

1999: Feliciano is captured.

2000: Fujimori is reelected to third consecutive term, despite allegations of fraud. In November Fujimori faxes his resignation from Japan after scandal erupts involving charges of corruption and abuse of power by the president and his intelligence chief.

2001: Interim president Valentín Paniagua decrees formation of the Truth and Reconciliation Commission.

2003: The Truth and Reconciliation Commission presents its *Final Report* in August.

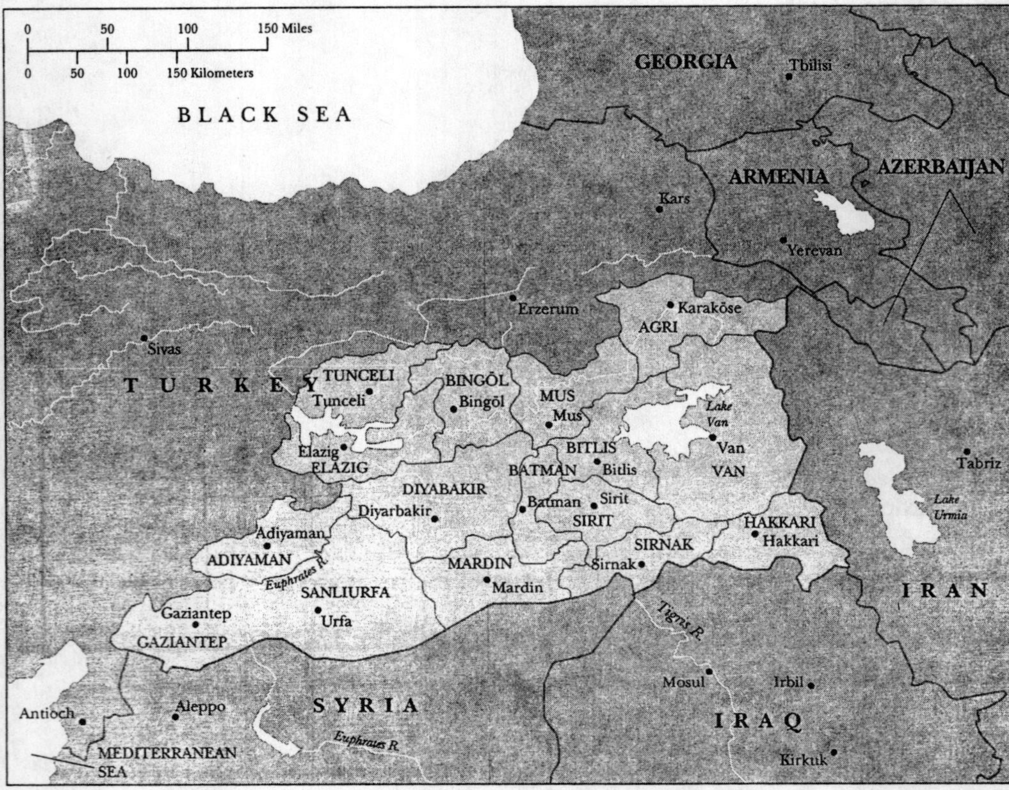


Map 10.1. Zones of heaviest PKK activity.

*Chapter 10*

# PKK: The Kurdistan Workers' Party

DOĞU ERGIL

One of the most important factors retarding the consolidation of democracy in Turkey has been the country's treatment of its Kurdish citizens. Although Kurdish is the mother tongue of as many as one in five inhabitants of Turkey, until 2004 the government prohibited the teaching of Kurdish in schools and the broadcasting of Kurdish radio and television programs. These restrictions attest to a continuing refusal on the part of the Turkish state to recognize the cultural identity of its Kurdish citizens, a policy that has generated widespread discontent among the country's Kurds. Although about half the Kurdish population of Turkey now lives in other parts of the country and in Europe (one million strong), the rest are still concentrated in their ancestral region in the southeast, where they predominate. This region has had a long history of Kurdish insurrections, but none so deadly and lengthy as the struggle waged during the past two decades by the Workers' Party of Kurdistan (PKK), led by Abdullah Öcalan. Though precise figures are difficult to come by, there is little doubt that nearly 35,000 people have lost their lives in clashes between government security forces and PKK militants.[1] Turkey's inability to come to grips with its Kurdish citizens' demand for cultural recognition not only prevented a peaceful resolution of the Kurdish problem but also impeded improvement in the country's legal and political standards. The European Union (EU), which Turkey is seeking to join, has consistently maintained that Turkey's human and minority rights record should be improved.

The Kurdish problem is but one symptom of a more general weakness of Turkish democracy: the failure or deliberate refusal of the state to acknowledge ethnocultural minority groups. Although the plight of the Kurds has attracted international attention, other ethnic and linguistic groups that differ from the official culture of Turkish society—Armenians, Greeks, Alevite Arabs, Romani, Domari, and Lazi speakers, for example—have also suffered from discrimination and repression. The root of this intolerance is to be found not in the character of the Turkish people or their political leaders but in the nature of the modern Turkish state. This state is based on a conception of nation-building that calls for standardizing the citizenry to make them Turkish in language and nationality, secular in orientation, and obedient to the state. Turkey's constitution does not accept the fact that there are minorities in the country, other than non-Muslim religious groups. This denial of diversity has led to policies that repress the expression of any group identity other than the officially defined citizenship. The Turkish official mentality invariably confuses unity with uniformity. Tension and conflict have been the inadvertent results of the uneasy relationship between the tutelary central authority and the populace.

Another important factor behind the Kurdish problem is economic. Whether or not the persistent pattern of uneven development within Turkey has resulted from deliberately disriminatory policies, economic backwardness has hampered eastern Turkey's integration into the rest of the country. Average per capita annual income in the Kurdish southeast is only U.S.$3,360, which is much less than in the rest of Turkey, especially eastern and central Anatolia. This impoverished region must be brought up to par with the rest of society. Turkey's overall economic performance must also be improved. There can be no popular satisfaction—or, for that matter, democracy—without a decent standard of living for all social groups.

The bloody struggle that went on for years has sharpened both Turkish and Kurdish nationalism. Many Kurds feel that they are not recognized under their own name as the legitimate son of an authoritarian father. Some Kurds go farther than protesting this negligence and want to leave home, but take their dowry with them. This radical group, which in 1978 organized as the PKK, employed violent means to achieve its end: an independent or autonomous political entity carved out of Turkey. The PKK has become a significant actor in the Middle East, and Kurdish nationalism has become an international phenomenon. This polarization is a destabilizing force and creates opportunities for outside intervention.[2]

Because the Turkish state has seen the Kurdish problem as a security issue and not as a social conflict, the people of Turkey have suffered from an unnamed war fought on their own lands among themselves. When a complex social problem is treated at as a matter of security, one party to the dispute must be treated as an enemy. An internal enemy cannot benefit from political or institutional solutions; instead, it is declared illegal and repressed militarily. In the name of security, the state has carried out extrajudicial killings and forced evacuations and destruction of villages. It created an emergency law for the Kurdish region that differed from the rest of the country, while at the same time claiming that Turkey is faced with the threat of division. None of these facts has been open to popular or legislative discussion.

What Turkey has not realized is that it has violated many fundamental human rights and democratic freedoms while fighting the PKK. Not only did it reinforce the very separatism it sought to suppress, but it restricted democratic rights, using the excuse that these measures were necessary to combat internal and external threats. It did not understand that, rather than reconciling with Europe, it was alienating itself from the international community. Now, when reminded of the distance between itself and Europe, Turkey displays anger toward the West and the Kurds, whom it blames for the rift.

The Kurdistan Workers' Party has recently turned from nationalist politics and practice advocating separatism achieved through armed struggle to a pluralistic, multicultural, and democratic vision of the future.[3] This development, while resulting from the imprisonment of the PKK's leader, Abdullah Öcalan, and the military situation on the ground in the region, has created new opportunities for a political solution to the Kurdish problem.

The history of the conflict between the PKK and the Turkish state, as it played out within Turkey and in the broader regional and international setting, demonstrates that the Kurdish problem cannot be resolved by a military solution imposed by either side. Before the 1980 military coup in Turkey, Öcalan and his close associates sought refuge in Syria. Damascus sheltered, trained, and equipped the PKK, using it as a bargaining chip against Turkey in its disputes over territory and the sharing of the waters of the Tigris and Euphrates rivers. The PKK grew rapidly in size and popularity, thanks in part to the Turkish government's dismantling of rival democratic Kurdish organizations and its prohibition on all expressions of Kurdish identity. Trapped in a traditional society marked by tribalism, economic backwardness, and social inequality, young Kurdish men and women found in the PKK an appealing and unifying cause. The organization was a means to personal emancipation as well as political recognition. The PKK was ready to pay the price in persecution and sacrifice that armed struggle requires, and it gained considerable support for its strategy of seeking control over territory inhabited primarily by Kurds.[4]

At first, the PKK seriously hurt regular Turkish troops, who were inexperienced and ill equipped for guerrilla combat. By employing hit-and-run tactics from their mountain hideouts, PKK guerrillas were able to maintain military superiority over Turkish security forces throughout the 1980s. Only in 1995, after the Turkish army had trained and equipped commando troops and special police forces, was the army able to gain the upper hand, first in the cities and later in the rural areas of the southeast. At the same time, Turkish military incursions into the area in Northern Iraq referred to as Kurdistan, facilitated by U.S. consent and the cooperation of Massoud Barzani's Kurdistan Democratic Party (KDP), thwarted the PKK's efforts to gain a footing or a broker's position there. Öcalan's entrenchment in Syria, however, made it impossible to eradicate the PKK completely.[5]

In 1998, the Turkish army, having lost patience with Syrian president Hafez al-Assad, threatened to attack Syria if it continued to harbor Öcalan. Assad had little alternative but to comply, and Öcalan was evicted from Syria in the autumn of 1998. After a brief period of exile in Europe, he was captured in Kenya and brought to Turkey in February 1999. Öcalan's imprisonment initiated a new phase in Turkey's struggle with the PKK. During his trial, Öcalan did not offer a legal defense. "There are enough reasons to accuse me of wrongdoing," he stated; "We must learn from our mistakes and learn to achieve peace."[6] He declared that violence and fighting for an independent state were wrong and that Turks and Kurds, who had shared the same homeland for a thousand years, ought to work together toward reconciliation and democratization. He offered his services to the state in order to achieve these ends, provided that he were allowed to live. To add credibility to his statements, he ordered PKK fighters to stop engaging with army troops, and a short time later called on them to leave Turkey. A "Peace Group" headed by Ali Sapan, former PKK spokesman in Europe, assembled in Europe and Northern Iraq (referred to as Kurdistan) and surrendered to Turkish authorities at the Iraqi border and in Istanbul in October 1999. The state chose to ignore these symbolic gestures, remaining adamant in its resolve not to bargain with a terrorist organization.

The PKK could not legitimately demand democracy, human rights, or recognition of Kurdish ethnic identity by way of armed struggle. The method betrayed the cause. Terrorism is not a sufficient means to accomplish a broad political transformation, although it is an effective way to attract the public's attention to a significant political problem, a fundamental social demand, or a widely held grievance. Although the PKK's leader has been in a Turkish prison since 1999, the organization has not laid down its arms, disbanded, and shed its character as a terrorist organization. If the Kurdish problem is to be solved, the Kurds must believe in and practice democracy and peaceful methods of conflict resolution. So far, the PKK has waited and expected the government to change and abandon its harsh methods. This impasse has hindered the normalization of politics and the extension of democracy in Turkey.

The Kurds of Turkey must not be satisfied with merely ethnic politics; concessions that start and end with ethnic recognition are not enough. They must contribute to the development and globalization of those countries of which they are citizens. They must struggle to democratize Iran, Iraq, and Syria and work together to bring Turkey closer to membership in the EU, whose standards will be beneficial to all the citizens, Turks and Kurds and others alike.

Today, as before, not less than one-fifth of the Grand National Assembly (parliament) of Turkey comprises members of Kurdish origin. A quarter of the top business people of Turkey are Kurdish.[7] These figures point out the fact that there is no discrimination at the individual or civil societal level. The problem is in the public domain, which does not allow the expression of ethnic, cultural, religious, and/or ideological identities other than the designated and approved official identities. This restriction is not a handicap for Kurds only. Over time, Leftist, Liberal, Kurdish, and Muslim identities have all been barred from public visibility and subjected to legal prosecution.

The majority of the Kurdish population of Turkey desires to live in peace and harmony. But, just like their Turkish brethren, who are proud to be Turkish, they want to be respected for what they are—Kurdish—and be included in the mainstream society as such. Otherwise, their support for the violent PKK could have turned every city with Kurdish enclaves into a war zone. Considering that Kurds constitute a quarter of Istanbul's population of eleven million and that the leading Kurdish political party, the People's Democratic Labor Party (HADEP), received only a small fraction of the Kurdish votes in this metropolis in the 1995 national elections, Kurds seem inclined to integration rather than separation. This fact must be fairly considered by the authorities, and unnecessary suspicions must cease in order to devise more constructive policies that will normalize politics. Now it is time to respect cultural differences and protect them legally, while affording no special privilege to any ethnic or religious group.[8]

## Political Goals, Leadership, and Organization

The PKK was founded largely by a group of university students of Kurdish origin, all of whom were citizens of the Republic of Turkey, on 7 November 1978, in the Diyarbakir Province of Turkey. Influenced by the rising tide of student movements taking place elsewhere, especially in Europe, they began with a Marxist-Leninist interpretation of their society and the world. Their political career, like that of many other Kurdish groups and organizations, started within the framework of the surging left-wing politics that fundamentally affected Turkey in the 1960s and 1970s. However, the failure of the Turkish left to create a genuinely domestic agenda by which it could mobilize different sections of the society (except for some intellectuals, students, and urban labor unions), in combination with punitive official pressure on the left (which officials saw as a fifth column of international communism), led the Kurdish elements to seek a different venue. Left-wing politics had emphasized solidarity among diverse ethnic and cultural groups and was internationalist in orientation. Repression and internal weakness of the leftist movement in Turkey released a more nationalistic, or at least ethnocentric, offshoot. Several radical Kurdish organizations were founded, mostly by young people. Soon they were all declared illegal and closed down; their members were tried and imprisoned. The most tenacious of them, which could bear the heat of official repression and competition from other Kurdish organizations, survived—namely, the PKK.

The founders of the PKK were deeply influenced by Lenin's principle of "self-determination of nations" and Stalin's book *The National Question.* The government's prohibition of any form of Kurdish collective expression, no matter how peaceful, and its systematic denial of Kurdish cultural identity led to a very reactive response. Ther pride wounded, the Kurds perceived official repression as a form of imperialism and the Kurds as the victims of internal colonialism. The hierarchical ordering of Turkish and Kurdish ethnic identities called for a struggle for liberation. These concepts led the founders of the PKK to hope for a "united and democratic Kurdistan" in southeastern Turkey and those parts of Iran, Iraq, and Syria with Kurdish enclaves.

In 1997, the organization abandoned the idea of a separate Kurdish nation-state because of failure to create the conditions for founding one and called for a federal state in Turkey where Kurds would have political equality through autonomy and shared sovereignty. After Öcalan's capture, he floated the idea of a "Democratic Republic and Peace Project." During his trial, Öcalan admitted: "I wish I had the level of consciousness that I have today in 1973. Then, this method [violence] would not have been followed. . . . Indeed this people have suffered the most. War does not have a basis; a foundation. . . . A peaceful life [together] may be pursued in a democratic republic."[9] The PKK started out with the maximalist aim of carving out a Kurdish "motherland" from Turkey to establish an independent nation-state and used systematic violence to attain its political objectives. It employed "low-intensity warfare," with a well-trained and highly organized guerrilla force supported by a civilian front encompassing organizations serving various purposes, such as propaganda, logistics, recruitment, and fund-raising. It also created or affiliated with civic organizations in Europe through the Kurdish diaspora, which grew to nearly a million migrants. However, in 1999 the PKK gave up its irredentist aim and began to advocate for cultural rights and wider democratic and legal standards by which ethnic, linguistic, and political differences may be respected and protected. Advancing Turkey's candidacy for membership in the European Union became a major part of the PKK program.

Öcalan ordered armed PKK militia to leave Turkey for Northern Iraq referred to as Kurdistan to support his rhetoric advocating a democratic republic in which Turk and Kurd could live in peace and harmony. However, after the abolition of capital punishment during the summer of 2002, Öcalan claimed that he was unable to prevent his organization from resuming armed struggle. He wanted the government to act swiftly to improve the Kurds' conditions and pardon imprisoned PKK members. In the winter of 2005, inspired by developments in post-Saddam Iraq, Öcalan's thinking took yet another radical, even fantastical turn; he suggested a "stateless confederation of the Kurdish enclaves and their host states in the Middle East," encompassing Turkey, Iran, Iraq, and Syria.[10] Once again, the PKK began to act as a stumbling block to further democratization, the rule of law, and Turkey's rapid admission to the EU. In pursuit of such unrealistic goals, the PKK may not only consume itself but also delay many of the processes set in motion to make Turkey into a European-style democracy and an affluent country that can resolve problems such as the Kurdish issue.

## Leadership and Structure

The PKK was founded by Kurdish university students from rural areas who studied in major cities of Turkey. At the outset there were also Turks in the organization, because they believed that Turkey's problems could not be overcome by relying on only one ethnic group. Öcalan, the key leader and ideologue, was born in the Omerli village of the Halfeti Township of Turkey's Diyarbakir Province. After primary education in the region where he was born, he graduated from a technical high school. Then he went to the prestigious Faculty of Political Science of Ankara University, from which Turkey's prominent bureaucrats, administrators, and diplomats have graduated. He dropped out during the third year because of his political activities. Most of the founders of the PKK resemble Öcalan, coming from a traditional rural society divided by tribalism and feudal landlordism that left little room for individualism.[11] Studying in modern towns brought them face to face with a much more liberal value system and gave them freedoms of thought, action, and association that they had never experienced before. They adopted Marxism as a vehicle of emancipation, both for themselves and for the social group with which they identified—the Kurds as a whole. They wanted to liberate first the Kurds of Turkey and, later, what they called North Kurdistan, carved out of Iran, Iraq, and Syria, to create an independent, united Kurdistan.

Leadership was initially a shared responsibility. However, given their background in tribal communities, the founders needed a leader to personify the group and the movement. In 1974–1977, the group was called Revolutionaries of Kurdistan, and Öcalan was the first among equals. Following the founding of the PKK as a party and the naming of Öcalan as the general secretary on 27 November 1978, he became the undisputed leader of the organization and the Kurdish rebellion in general.[12]

The PKK is organized both hierarchically and horizontally. Öcalan has delegated operational leadership to paramilitary commanders at various levels in different geographical locations, but he has retained political and ideological leadership, leaving no room for challenge. Authority is absolutely vertical. There is a strict chain of command, which can under no circumstance be broken or questioned. Any aberration is severely punished. Local guerrilla leaders have occasionally acted independently of the leader, for example by ambushing unarmed soldiers going out of the region on leave. Öcalan reprimanded the commanders who committed the crime and never permitted such a thing to happen again. Those who are accused of betraying the cause or the organization are executed. Many of Öcalan's early comrades and hundreds of PKK members have been liquidated for not meeting the absolute demands of the leader obediently and efficiently. The same fate has been shared by other Kurdish organizations, armed or democratic, which have not bowed to the leadership of the PKK and its Stalinist leader.[13] This pattern of domination over and submission by his followers is so powerful that, even after six years of incarceration in a Turkish prison, Öcalan is still the undisputed leader of the PKK and the wider network that has emanated from its affiliated civic organizations.

Subleaders with delegated powers all derive their authority and legitimacy from the supreme commander—even though Öcalan has never personally engaged in armed combat. The social profile of these subleaders exhibits several common patterns. Most of them come from the rural parts of southeastern Turkey; others have some urban experience. A small minority comes from the Kurdish diaspora in Europe. Members of the third group, who are generally better educated, organize and manage civic organizations both at home and abroad. Guerrilla leaders are generally appointed from the first and second groups. The rank and file of the PKK were comprised of peasant boys and girls who had little to lose but much to gain in pride and a meaningful role in their immediate communities during their short lives as fighters.

Öcalan's power is absolute, but the organzation's positions are theoretically debatable. Discussion of important matters occurs to the extent that the leader allows it. Any thought or deed that is not ordered by the leader is subject to censure and self-criticism. Everyone is accountable to Öcalan. Verbal reports from founders who have fled the organization and those who have turned themselves in or been arrested attest to the severity of retribution in case of dissent. There have been real differences of opinion within the group, especially regarding the form and extent of violence. Before 1999, however, the leader constantly denied that enough violence had been committed and that it was time to engage in politics. No room was left within the organization to discuss the wisdom of continuing armed struggle or substituting nonviolent means of political action.

Two methods were used to get rid of internal dissent. First, forceful persuasion, constantly reinforcing the cult of the unique and matchless leader and exalting the organization, its goals, and the sacrifices of those who fell earlier. The cause of national liberation and its materialized form, the organization, were presented as the ultimate value, a reason to be and to sacrifice one's being. Both the leader as the bearer of the cause and the organization that was the instrument to realize that cause were absolute values, larger and more precious than life. Long sessions of criticism by the leader were followed by self-criticism before the group. When persuasion failed, dissenters were brutally punished. Many accounts attest that Öcalan himself has ordered the execution of hundreds of his followers for failing to do what he ordered them to do or for using their own judgment and doing it in another way.[14]

## Ideology of Insurgency and Politics

The PKK has legitimized its armed activities by using three arguments: First, Turkish Kurdistan is a colony of Turkey and the Kurdish people are colonized by the Turkish state. Second, Kurds are the largest stateless minority in the world and they are entitled to a nation-state. Western imperialism has divided wider Kurdistan among a number of nation-states that deny Kurdish identity and rights. These pieces must be brought together in order to create an independent, united Kurdistan. Third, war against Turkey is just.

Kurdish activists have frequently been arrested and imprisoned. Not only have they have been treated roughly in prison, but they have lost the opportunity to complete their university studies and the legal right to work as government employees, the most prestigious careers for rural youth. The repression they suffered, the sacrifices they made, and the time they spent in prison convinced them that there was no way to go back. The organization's commitment to violence was reinforced by the relentless counterviolence of the Turkish state, which left no room for legitimate political activity. Other states in the Middle East have used the PKK as a proxy to settle their scores with Turkey. Indeed, the PKK could not fully act of its own will from the moment it settled in Syria and set up training camps in Lebanon's Bekaa Valley, which was under Syrian control. Later, the PKK had camps and strongholds in Iraq and in Iran. Cooperating with these rogue states was a matter of survival and symbiotic interdependence. Greece supported the PKK overtly and covertly. The PKK had to render services to these patrons and sponsors, which allowed it to continue in order to settle their own lingering scores with Turkey.[15]

The situation on the ground began to change in March 1995. Guerrilla warfare on familiar terrain among a friendly local population is quite different from facing a well-trained and well-equipped regular army on the field of battle. The PKK tried this twice, in 1992 and 1995, and lost bitterly both times. During the early 1990s, the Turkish army trained and armed its personnel to deal with guerrillas. After the first Gulf War, international circumstances allowed hot pursuit and preemptive strikes on PKK forces located in and operating out of camps in Northern Iraq referred to as Kurdistan. The effectiveness of the PKK was drastically reduced. Frustration led to suicide attacks on selected official targets, but also to a search for ways of gaining political influence in Turkey, the Middle East, and the international community.

The desire to recruit suicide bombers led the PKK to flirt with religious groups, which it had refrained from doing previously. It set up three organizations, each to encompass a group with specific religious convictions, namely Sunni Muslims, Alevite (Syrian) Muslims, and Yezidi (Zoroastrians). The PKK leadership thought a nationalist and fundamentalist approach would be more attractive to a broader spectrum of the Kurdish population because the predominant majority of the Kurds were rural, traditional, and religious.

While fierce fighting was going on in eastern and southeastern Turkey's plateaus and mountains, Öcalan encouraged the members of the People's Labor Party (HEP), the only legal Kurdish political party, to run in the October 2001 national elections on the ticket of the Kemalist Social Democratic People's Party (SHP). HEP won 18 seats in the parliament. Leyla Zana became a center of controversy because she insisted on taking the oath of office in Kurdish with a tricolor band on her head, signifying the PKK's traditional Kurdish colors. Sentenced to fifteen years in prison for being a member of a terrorist organization and put into prison in December 1994, Zana served ten years, together with three of her comrades to be released in June 2004. HEP was closed down and replaced by the Democratic Labor Party (DEP), which was also banned, and then by the People's Democratic Labor Party (HADEP). Behind these transitions was the will and guidance of the PKK leadership, which was seeking a legitimate political organ to voice its views and demands.[16]

At the same time, the PKK never wanted to give up violence or the threat of violence to promote Kurdish interests. The group believed that an independent Kurdistan could only be attained by armed struggle. The organization weighed two options: an immediate and widespread uprising, or a gradual and more grassroots popular movement supported and pushed forward by low-intensity warfare. The organization began forging alliances with ultra-left-wing illegal armed organizations in 1992 and in 1998 attempted to conduct spectacular operations in the cities and create a safe haven for the PKK in the northeast Black Sea region. As the party leadership acknowledged, this failed strategy was based on the model of Vietnam. Building a network of alliances for both political and military aims went hand in hand with the use of force.

The PKK's stance toward insurgency and politics shifted decisively in 1999. The rationale for these changes was articulated by its founder and leader during his trial:

> I told [my comrades] . . . especially after . . . 1996 that the problem could be solved through the development of democracy within the framework of a unitary state. It

> wasn't easy. I, myself, have reached this conclusion in 20 years. . . . If the government makes a call for peace it will definitely receive a positive answer. . . . We have taken a decision on peace. [We hope] our State calls for peace as well.
>
> We can all live in peace under a democratic republic. If it is necessary for Turkey, I can sacrifice my life. I will bring [the PKK militia] off the mountain, give me three months. . . . I believe and struggle for a democratic republic. I believe the future of the country lies not in war but peace. . . . Irredentism is not correct. . . . The best way is to unite on the basis of a democratic republic. There is no problem other than [lack of] cultural rights. . . .
>
> If the main aim is freedom, why this conflict? You may ask, "did you realize this just now?" Yes, I realized it now, recently. We are together with the Turkish nation; we cannot part with them. These people [Kurds] to whom I belong cannot part and live on a piece of mountain by themselves. Neither rebellion nor quarrel, this problem must be solved on the basis of democratic culture.[17]

Öcalan's statements soon transformed the party's rhetoric, principles, and practices. In January 2000, the PKK's Seventh Congress adopted a resolution to change its program and bylaws to fit to its leader's new directives. The strategic goal became constitutional citizenship in the context of a democratic, pluralist, and multicultural republic. The name of the party's military wing, which had been called the Kurdistan People's Liberation Army (ARGK), was changed to the less military People's Defense Units (HPG). The Vietnam model was abandoned in favor of *serhildan*, Kurdish for *intifada*, adopted from Palestine. All forms of democratic protest would be tried, including civil disobedience.[18]

In undertaking political activity, the PKK increasingly began to feel the handicap of bearing the name of an internationally recognized terrorist organization. Its followers could not go far with this notorious name, as the group was banned everywhere. Nor could it compete with new and untarnished democratic Kurdish organizations, which it had stifled for so long. When the PKK convened its Eighth Congress in April 2002, the group adopted the name Kurdistan Democracy and Freedom Congress (KADEK). The congress once again unanimously elected Abdullah Öcalan as its leader.

In spite of these changes, the organization neither gave up arms nor declared that it would do so; rather, it asserted that it would hold its forces on alert for "self-defense." In time, some guerrilla groups returned to the mountains of Turkey; their numbers are said to add up to 4,000.[19] In March 2005, during a party congress in Northern Iraq referred to as Kurdistan, the organization reverted to its original name, PKK. Was this a tactic to stimulate the Turkish government to step up reforms because of the fear of resuming armed confrontation, or a message to its supporters that they have not abandoned its initial principles and aspirations? Only time will reveal the answer. The PKK wants to hold on to its armed force for two reasons: to maintain pressure on Turkey for the realization of its demands and the release of its leader from prison; and to be a political actor in the

Middle East by seizing and holding a foothold in both Turkey and Northern Iraq referred to as Kurdistan.

Turkey declared KADEK a terrorist organization and never treated it as an interlocutor for its Kurdish citizens. Instead, the Turkish government campaigned to convince its Western allies to treat KADEK as a terrorist organization as well. The antiterrorist offensive that developed globally after 9/11 led the U.S. to agree to Turkey's request; the member states of the EU soon followed suit. In May 2002, the EU put the PKK on the list of international terrorist organizations; two years later, it added KADEK. Considered the scion of the PKK in terms of leadership, membership, and material possessions, KADEK could not clear itself from being seen as an adjunct of the PKK, which rendered KADEK inefficient and ineffective. So its members changed its name once again. In October 2003, at the second party congress held on the border with Northern Iraq referred to as Kurdistan, the name of the organization was changed to Kurdistan People's Congress, Kongra-Gel. Abdullah Öcalan was once again elected as the leader of the organization.[20]

The PKK's leader seems more flexible and resilient than the organization. Öcalan has never been on the battlefield or used arms. He has been a politician and ideologue. He can take twists and turns. But, with a large peasant base, the PKK and its sequels cannot easily adapt to political maneuvers of the day. They are mostly fighters, not politicians. They need to stay together for the cause of armed struggle, which requires strict obedience to the commander in chief. The question is whether and when Öcalan will declare that armed struggle has ended and how the guerrilla commanders who have lived for years under dire conditions in mountain camps will receive this. If uncertainty continues, a rift could develop between the political cadres, who under Öcalan's influence want a solution in Turkey, and the paramilitary forces, whose members have been conditioned to fight for the liberation of Kurdistan. Recent developments in Northern Iraq referred to as Kurdistan have whetted their appetites. Fortunately, unlike the Armenian diaspora in the U.S. and Europe, the Kurdish diaspora in Europe plays a nonviolent role and supports a democratic solution in Turkey by further liberalization of the system and expanding democratic and cultural rights.

## The Political and Social Base

The PKK quickly gained support within Kurdish society because it met several vital needs of the Kurds and successfully addressed the social and political cleavages within the community. The Kurds are traditionally divided up into tribes and denominational groups. In southeastern Turkey, a lingering feudal system of land ownership and backward methods of farming have perpetuated dependence on traditional leaders, such as the tribal chieftain, the feudal landlord (*aga*), and the sheikh, or sectarian religious leader. Clientism was the most widespread form of social and economic relations in these least developed parts of Turkey.

The PKK has built its rhetoric on the poverty, backwardness, and neglect of the region. It interpreted this situation as a form of colonial exploitation of the Kurds that kept the old traditions and institutions intact. Feudalism, tribalism, and religious obscurantism were all tools of Turkish imperialism to keep the Kurds divided and out of touch with the developed world. Kurdish nationalism was promoted to cut across all local and traditional alliances. Landless peasants, especially poorly educated and unemployed or irregularly employed young people, were attracted to the organization. If the revolution succeeded, they would all share the wealth and the privileges of the rich and powerful. Socialism gave them not only a cause to struggle for but also hope for a better future, which the Turkish leftist movement could not offer them.

Another factor that attracted popular support is the irrational insistence of the Turkish state on the denial of Kurdish ethnic identity and cultural rights. The prohibition on expressing their cultural traditions freely had frustrated the Kurds to the point of rebellion. Their previous uprisings, led by traditional local leaders, were repressed, and each time more prohibitions were imposed. Speaking their language publicly and listening to music with Kurdish words were forbidden. Personal and place names in Kurdish were not allowed, while existing Kurdish names were changed to Turkish. This policy created widespread resentment and deep feelings of victimization. The PKK-led resistance immediately found support from all social cohorts of Kurdish origin.

Those factions that condoned violence and those that supported armed struggle did not differ significantly in socioeconomic standing and geographical location. While the rank and file of the PKK were composed of peasants, rural poor, and marginal urban dwellers of Kurdish origin, there were also high school and university students and graduates in its ranks. These better-educated Kurds joined or supported the organization because they believed the PKK represented Kurdish pride and they sought the deliverance of the Kurds from the authoritarian Turkish state. People in this category came from the Kurdish diaspora in Europe as well as schools and cities in Turkey.[21]

Young Kurdish women voluntarily joined the PKK and served the organization selflessly. In traditional and religious communities, few Kurdish women enjoyed the opportunity for self-development and individual achievement. They were married young, generally in return for a sizable dowry paid to the father, thus passing from the authority of one man to another. Kurdish women in rural areas live in such a confining cultural atmosphere that they cannot speak unless they are spoken to. They are inferior to all the men of the family, including their sons. They risk punishment, even death, if they disobey the elders and go out of the homestead so much as to go window-shopping in the nearest town. Under these stifling circumstances, hundreds of young Kurdish women joined the PKK seeking both personal emancipation and collective liberation. Öcalan admits that women comprised as much as one-third of the organization's active membership. They took the same military training and engaged in battle alongside their male comrades. Their efforts to prove themselves in the organization took some to extremes; women committed 11 of the 15 suicide terrorist attacks committed by PKK militants.[22]

The number of PKK guerrilla forces rose to at least 15,000 in the mid-1990s. Many more supporters harbored and supplied the PKK guerrillas. Logistical support for the armed groups who roamed the mountainous terrain came predominantly from the peasants and small shepherd communities of eastern and southeastern Turkey. They extended this support in part willingly and in part out of fear. In the early 1990s, when PKK roamed the plateaus and mountains of southeastern Turkey, it tried to build an alternative state structure to sever local people from the state. The PKK established its own judicial system with three types of courts: independence tribunals to deal with political matters such as treason, subversion, and collaboration with the enemy; Military Tribunals to deal with the affairs and problems of the guerrilla forces; and People's Tribunals to deal with common crimes. Planned as early as 1980, these courts became operational in 1989. However, as the Turkish security apparatus gained the upper hand and prevented the PKK from controlling territory, these courts became nonfunctional within the borders of Turkey. They continued within the organization and the social groupings over which it retained control.[23]

When Turkish security forces learned that PKK militia were being supplied or hiding out in a remote mountain village or hamlet, the peasants suffered bitterly. Several thousand villages and small hamlets of herdsmen (*kom*) were evacuated by executive order and destroyed. The Maoist maxim "dry the pond to get to the fish" was applied effectively. Inhumane as the method was, it proved to be successful militarily. Tens of thousands of people were forced to migrate to other parts of the country. However, the tactic backfired politically by alienating the populace. Young people from the uprooted communities joined the PKK ranks. The remainder became sympathizers in the towns and cities where they settled; now they staff the urban underworld.

The Kurdish diaspora has played a significant role as well. Kurds began to settle in Europe as early as the 1960s, when the booming European economy needed labor. Many citizens of Turkey, Turk and Kurd alike, went to work in European countries, especially Germany. In the 1970s, an ethnically mixed group of leftists fled from the Turkish military government and took refuge in Europe. In the 1980s, economic difficulties in Turkey, exacerbated by internal strife, led many more people to leave the country for a better and safer life in Europe. During the late 1980s and 1990s, people who had been evicted from their villages or caught in the crossfire between the PKK and the Turkish armed forces applied as political refugees and victims of civic strife. Out of the 3.6 million Turkish citizens who made their way to Europe, close to a million are estimated to be Kurds. Later the PKK saw a lucrative business opportunity as well as a way to build a support network on its behalf and began to smuggle Kurds into European countries.

As the number of Kurds living in Europe rose, civic organizations were created that acted as effective lobbying and public relations bodies for the PKK.[24] A system that collected money willingly or forcibly from all citizens of the "old country" was put into effect. Another network took on the task of generating and disseminating publicity through newspapers, journals, radio stations, and a TV station that transmits via satellite (MED-TV, now ROJ-TV). These organizations and networks were so successful that they overshadowed Turkish official organizations in Europe. Furthermore, they could reach the Kurdish population in Turkey with new and innovative ideas to forge a Kurdish ethnic or national identity across continents. The Kurdish diaspora played a very active and effective role in carrying the Kurdish problem of Turkey to Europe and raising awareness of the exigencies and demands of the Kurds in European public opinion.

The popular base of the movement and organization expanded when Turkish and Kurdish ethnic identities were both sharpened by their friction. This friction was at its height when extensive armed struggle exacted blood and when massive demonstrations or celebrations of the Kurds were suppressed. Until 1995, when Newroz, the traditional festivity of the Kurds to meet the approaching spring, was officially acknowledged as a legitimate holiday, its celebration was treated as an illegal act and roughly suppressed. This policy had created widespread resentment against the security forces and the state. The PKK capitalized on the occasion as the defender of Kurdish rights. Support for the organization surged with clashes every Newroz. Fortunately, the government of Tansu Ciller heeded this author's advice and declared Newroz a holiday for all citizens of Turkey. When Turkish politicians acknowledged Kurdish identity, support for the government rose.

## Social and Political Impacts of Rebellion

The fratricidal conflict that went on in their country for so long led the Turks to develop a sense that some of their Kurdish compatriots had betrayed them and that a sinister plot had been hatched by the neighboring states, such as Syria and Iran, to weaken their country by exacerbating its internal divisions. On the whole, the average Turk never understood what the "Kurdish problem" was. Under the heavy official ideological bombardment of nationalism through the schools and political system, the Turks were strongly conditioned to accept and uphold the ideal of "one nation, one culture, one language, one common history and total obedience to the state." Any criticism, or even questioning of this monolithic understanding of state and society was perceived and treated as subversion. Even six years after the cessation of armed struggle, the Turkish people do not have a rational explanation for why, over a period of fifteen years, 2.5 million young men were drafted and sent to fight a war against a part of the national population in their own country.

This feeling of betrayal led the Turks to look the other way when the security forces used excessive force and transgressed the boundaries of legality. Turks did not develop a generalized hatred of Kurds, but on the whole believed that PKK violence was unwarranted and foreign-inspired. Under the influence of state-oriented political culture, the Turks failed to grasp the full extent of the Kurdish problem. Consequently, they have confused PKK terrorism with a problem that is basically economic, political, and cultural in nature and could have been addressed by democratic reforms and economic development. While these alternatives were regarded as concessions to terrorism, warfare was presented as "defense of the homeland." PKK violence prompted counterterrorist measures in a destructive spiral of mistrust and coercion.

Fifteen years of terrorist and counterterrorist struggle in Turkey cost dearly in economic terms as well. A rough estimate of the cost of the damage—infrastructure, plants, and facilities destroyed, dislocation in services and ongoing economic activities, the burning of forest sites—during the twenty years since the beginning of PKK attacks and counterattacks is estimated to be around U.S.$400 billion. The costs of security were also considerable. Excluding current and routine expenses to maintain a standing army of a half million troops, an informed estimate of the Turkish state's expenditures on security related to the conflict is U.S.$200 billion.[25] Exorbitant expenditures increased inflation and debt and made the economy unmanageable. This problem stalled Turkish economic development and depressed the quality of life. Lack of investment caused widespread unemployment, which is the main problem of the country today.[26]

The Kurdish community felt caught up in the crossfire between the Turkish security apparatus and the PKK. Both sides had positioned themselves as warriors and left no room for neutrality. "You are either on my side or on the side of the enemy" was the reigning mentality. The military conflict had devastating effects on the already impoverished residents of the southeast. The main economic activity of tribal communities is herding and small-scale agriculture, which requires full or seasonal nomadism. This movement became increasingly difficult each passing year. Security concerns halted migration between plateaus and mountains as well. Thousands of Kurdish families left the war zone for safer places, damaging local economies, especially animal husbandry and agriculture. Large households moved to cities, where they swelled the lumpen classes. Crime rates increased drastically, and gangs flourished.

In the countryside, the government organized those Kurdish tribes and villagers who resisted the PKK into "village guards," who played an important role in thwarting PKK attacks and regaining control of rural areas. Authorized to shoot to kill and paid by the government, they felt they could be the sole authority in the areas where they lived. Many village guardsmen settled their own personal scores and engaged in extortion, kidnapping, and smuggling. The village guard system reinforced feudalism at a time when it had been declining. By forging alliances with tribal chieftains and paying salaries to tribesmen, these traditional producers were turned into paid mountain scouts and loyal guerrillas. They became a dependent population, clients of the state. All of these problems have to be dealt with today, especially as the inhabitants of evacuated villages are gradually returning. As they do, disputes are emerging between the "loyalists" (guardsmen) and those who are accused of "failing to prove their worth under dire circumstances." News of bloody confrontations between returning villagers and village guards who occupied their homes and now till their fields often appears in the daily papers.

A final example of polarization and disintegration in the Kurdish community is the appearance of anti-PKK organizations that are equally violent. Hizballah is a characteristic example. When the "revolutionary tax" that PKK militia squeezed out of the merchants and artisans in the southeast became extortionate, these small businessmen organized to defend their interests. They were religious and anti-leftist, quite the opposite of the PKK. They found an ideological backbone to oppose the secular ethnic nationalism of the PKK in fundamentalist religion. They took on the name Hizballah (Party of God), inspired by the struggle of its counterpart in Lebanon. The belief in the region is that the PKK attributed this name to them. At the outset they had no international character or any contact with Iran or Lebanese factions bearing the same name.

Their struggle against the PKK became so effective that they threw the PKK out of such southeastern towns as Batman, Nusaybin, and Silopi. The fundamentalists were brutal and unforgiving but effective. The authorities committed the age-old mistake of looking at Hizballah as the "enemy of my enemy" and turned a blind eye to its crimes. There is widespread suspicion, which is never officially denied, that Hizballah operatives were supplied and supported by covert agencies or agents of the state. But later, this organization became the center of fundamentalist terrorism, just like the Taliban in Afghanistan, and the security forces went to great pains to liquidate most of this organization after it committed serial murders in the southeast and in Istanbul.[27]

Society broadly become more radicalized and polarized between 1990 and 1999. As warfare escalated, with scenes of funerals dominating TV screens every day, both the PKK and officialdom fomented nationalistic feelings in order to keep up the collective fervor that legitimized drafting young people and sending them to the defense of the "motherland." Ironically, both sides were fighting for and over the same "motherland." The capture of Öcalan eased tensions drastically, and nationalism declined on both sides.

Strong evidence of broad popular support for a nonviolent, pluralist political solution is provided by the decline in political support for the Turkish ultranationalist Nationalist Action Party (MHP) between 1995 and 1999. In the national elections held in 1995, at the height of warfare, the MHP won approximately 19 percent of the vote and became a coalition partner. In the subsequent national election, it won only 8.9 percent, less than the national election threshold of 10 percent, and remained outside Parliament. The election results for the only legitimate Kurdish political party are similar. HADEP won 6.2 percent of the vote in the 1992 national elections, and People's Democratic Party (DEHAP) won 5.3 percent in the March 2004 municipal elections. The Turkish and Kurdish people proved not to harbor grudges and lasting animosities. Radicalization and polarization, which were never universal, gave way to moderation and reconciliation as hostilities subsided.

## The Political Economy of Rebellion

PKK leadership has never complained about lack of funds or inadequate expenditures because of meager resources. The organization had two sources of income: monetary and in kind. In-kind support was provided by patron states that gave safe haven to the PKK and used it to promote their political and military strategy against Turkey. They provided arms and supplies, including strategic weapons such as antiaircraft missiles. When the1991 Gulf War ended, the defeated Iraqi Army left arms and supplies that were later used by the PKK.[28]

The monetary income of the PKK came mainly from donations and membership fees collected both in Turkey and abroad. Citizens of Turkey living and working in Europe paid the larger part. Turks paid dues unwillingly; Kurds, on the whole, paid fees more willingly. Many civic institutions organized by the PKK in Europe took an active role in collecting funds for humanitarian reasons. Extortion and donations were indistinguishable. People were smuggled from Turkey to European countries under the name of "political asylum seekers" in return for sizable sums, and after they were gainfully employed a portion of their income was required as a running donation to the organization. Taxing smugglers was major source of income for the PKK. Despite constant claims by Turkish officialdom that the PKK is involved in drug smuggling, there has been no substantial evidence of the organization's direct involvement. However, it is a known fact that the PKK "taxes" those who smuggle drugs, arms, and other valuable goods.

Although PKK membership is a way of life, especially in the armed faction of the organization, it is a dangerous, ascetic, and poor life. Most of the rank and file are peasants who are used to living without the benefits of modern technology. A guerrilla's life is not a desirable form of employment and source of income. The Kurdish people who have supported the PKK by contributing significant sums from their personal income cannot do it forever. The bulk of the Kurdish people who have supported the PKK for one reason or other are inclined to dissolve the organization, provided that Turkey carries out the full course of legal and political reforms along European Union standards.

The dissolution of the PKK might displease some of the "the mountain cadres," who would be rendered functionless and left adrift. The grievance that had motivated their self-sacrifice for so long would end. Greed might keep a splinter group intact. But, devoid of an exalted cause, they might soon become subcontractors for warlords and intelligence agencies. Alternatively, they might turn into mafia-type organizations to take their share in the wider network of smuggling operating in the Middle East.

## The Role and Function of Violence

Armed struggle was chosen as a result of the PKK leadership's theoretical evaluation of the state, their ethnic group, and the situation of east and southeastern provinces of Turkey where Kurds constituted the majority, which they called "Kurdistan." Marxism-Leninism at the theoretical level and the national liberation struggles of Vietnam and China at the practical level shaped their evaluation. The PKK analysis labeled "Kurdistan" a colony of Turkey. For them, while Turkey was a colony of Western imperialism, it turned Kurdistan into an internal colony. Internal colonialism sustained itself through the most backward elements in Kurdish society, namely the feudal landholders (*agas*), religious sect leaders (sheikhs), and tribal chieftains. Their collective hold on the Kurdish society was maintained by force, so their control could be ended only by counterforce.[29]

Since this backward power block did not allow the development of Kurdistan, no national bourgeoisie and modern working class could emerge. The only group that provided the basis for a national liberation struggle was the peasantry and rural landless workers. The most suitable form of struggle was guerrilla warfare, which gives the advantage to the weaker side. It was through guerrilla warfare and violence that the Kurdish nation was supposed to reinvent itself and deliver itself from colonialism.

In the final analysis, the PKK wanted to achieve the creation of an "Independent, United Greater Kurdistan" with the inclusion of Kurdish populations and the territories on which they were concentrated in Iran, Iraq, Syria, and Turkey. The particular historical mission of the PKK was to establish the "North Kurdistan State" by mobilizing the Kurds in Turkey into a national liberation movement. The Kurdish movement would aim at both liberation from the Turkish state and a social revolution that would deliver the Kurds from traditional Kurdish exploiters and institutions.

The strategy chosen to realize this end was planned with three stages. First came strategic defense: indoctrinating the Kurdish people, organizing them, and preparing the conditions for armed struggle. Guerrilla formations would engage in selective battles with the security forces, taking advantage of surprise. Next came a period of strategic equilibrium, with the creation of a broad popular front by winning the people over to the PKK's side and building a guerrilla army to fight against the regular army on its own conditions. The rugged terrain, distance from urban centers, and weak or absent government control in these remote areas would all be to the advantage of the guerrilla army of the Kurdish revolution. Third came a strategic offensive: extensive popular uprisings to unleash the power of the people and overthrow the institutions and the cadres of the "colonial government," while the guerrilla army gained the upper hand over regular army troops on familiar terrain. In the end, Kurdistan would be carved out of Turkey while other Kurdish enclaves did the same in neighboring countries.

This strategy did not work for several reasons. First, the majority of the Kurdish people did not follow the call of the PKK. They opposed assimilation but at the same time opted for equal integration with rather than separation from Turkey. Second, Turkey was a much more democratic country than its neighbors, and its European orientation could eventually make it an EU member country. European standards could be achieved much earlier here than in any other Middle Eastern country. Third, more than half of the Kurds were scattered all over Turkey, rather than living in a geographically compact enclave. This dispersion increased as violence made the eastern and southeastern provinces unsafe. These Kurds were received with no discrimination, in accordance with the Ottoman tradition, and immediately integrated into the general population. Kurds are among the most prominent politicians, businessmen, and artists.

Partitioning countries by force is prohibited by international law. Except for the rogue states of the Middle East and their strange bedfellow Greece, with its historical fear of Turkey, the rest of the international community did not support the PKK's terrorist practices. They supported the Kurds' efforts to secure cultural recognition and the expansion of Turkey's democracy, with the enhancement of human rights, further liberalization, and demilitarization, but they condemned terrorism. Kurds in Europe, including supporters of the PKK, eventually understood this contradiction, and in the end they did not want to leave these affluent, democratic, and peaceful countries to go and live in an impoverished land under a Stalinist regime. This conviction reverberated in the Kurdish community.

Finally, starting in the early 1990s, the Turkish army and the police created special forces, trained them in guerrilla warfare, and equipped them properly. With the support of air power, the army turned the tide of the armed conflict. The PKK's retreat into Iraq was pursued with multiple operations involving as many as 20,000–25,000 troops. Their ruthless tactics, which alienated local people, soon alarmed the authorities, and they were pulled back from the war zone. But they had already contributed to the military defeat of the PKK by reducing its zone of influence. Other anti-PKK Kurdish armed groups, especially village guards and community defense organizations such as Hizballah, limited the military success of the PKK.

Violence was a shared value in the PKK, central to the group's theory and practice. However, starting in 1996, some Kurds in PKK circles began to feel that violence had reached a saturation point and should gradually give way to peaceful forms of politics and reconciliation with the Turkish government. This inclination found no echo from Ankara, and the regional circumstances in which the PKK was immersed in the Middle East was unsuitable to launching a peace process.

## The State Response

In the mid-1990s, as the Turkish army reestablished control over the territory it had lost to the PKK by defeating PKK irregulars in every open confrontation, the tide began to turn. Recognizing that the PKK did not control their lives any more, people began to lean toward the government once again. This move was a matter of expediency, for the tactics of both sides were brutal and control-minded rather than compassionate and persuasion-oriented. The situation changed slowly but decisively after 1999. The government lifted the curfew in a number of provinces and then ended the state of siege in all southeastern provinces. Today no province is subject to the "Law of Extraordinary Conditions." Some provinces (Diyarbakir, Batman, Sirnak, Madin, Siirt, Hakari, Bingol, and Tunceli) are called "Critical Provinces," however, and are still administered under the provisions of the old "Provincial Administration Law." This law is reinforced with new principles that are residues of the Law of Extraordinary Conditions. These provisions are likely to end when the government feels completely safe, which will come about only when the PKK dissolves itself as an armed organization. As Turkey prepares for EU membership and accelerates reforms, the favorable environment is leading people to condemn the option of violent politics.

The Law for Fighting Against Terrorism enacted in 1991 worked more to repress the local population and the press and intellectuals who dared to speak of the "Kurdish problem" than it did to combat the PKK. The act of "terrorism" was so broadly defined that the law itself became an instrument of terror for anyone who spoke or wrote on these subjects. Even verbal infringement of the law was punishable by a prison term of up to 12 years and 6 months. Fortunately Article 8 of the antiterror law, whose broad, sweeping definition of terrorism threatened to criminalize the most innocent discussion of the Kurdish problem, was annulled on 20 July 2003.

The Law of Conditional Release, or Probation, as it was called, enacted in December 2000, allowed the release of prisoners charged with crimes prior to 23 April 2000, contingent on their not repeating the offense, and the postponement of current cases and sentences. The other clause of the law stipulated that capital punishment would not be carried out, with the exception of treason in war and terrorism with the intention of dividing the country. All death sentences were commuted to life imprisonment, and other sentences were reduced by ten years. This was a revolutionary change considering that the ultranationalist Nationalist Action Party was in the coalition government at the time, since it had been swept to power on the wave of Turkish nationalism that surged in response to PKK terrorism.

The Law for Gain for Society (Homecoming Law), put into effect in August 2003, offered amnesty to fighters who chose to lay down their weapons and return to civil society. Ramazan Er, spokesperson of the Turkish Police Department, described the outcome of the law after six months: "3,412 persons applied to benefit from the law. 1873 persons were freed. The number of persons who have applied to benefit from seven consecutive earlier Repentance Laws total 4429 persons and 832 of them have been freed. Hence while the percentage of beneficiaries of seven earlier laws was 18, it is 60 percent for the Law for Gain for Society."[30] However, all these laws have not gone far enough to persuade the armed faction of the PKK to disband.

The PKK was perceived as a separatist, terrorist organization from the very beginning. Its sequels, KADEK and Kongra-Gel, were labeled and treated similarly. In fact, Turkey's insistence led the EU countries to declare them terrorist organizations as well. What the Turkish government missed was why this organization under any name meant something to a large section of the Kurdish citizens of Turkey. Because of this failure, Turkish governments failed to distinguish between the "Kurdish Problem" and PKK-led terrorism. The Turkish establishment did not want to recognize any ethnocultural group, or "people," as a national minority because the official understanding of minorities included only religious minorities, that is, Christian groups and Jews. No assurance was provided for Muslim groups of different sects, other than the majority Sunni, and for other Muslim ethnicities. Turkish officialdom insisted that the minorities policy of the Republic emanated from the Treaty of Lausanne (1923). This constitutive treaty, which secured international recognition for the Republic of

Turkey, acknowledges the existence of religious minorities but not ethnic or national minorities. Basing their arguments on the words of the Lausanne treaty, Turkish governments refrained from extending the cultural rights to the Kurds that were afforded to non-Muslim minorities. Article 39 of the treaty reads as follows:

> No restrictions shall be imposed on the free use by any Turkish national of any language in private intercourse, in commerce, religion, in the press, or in publication of any kind, or at public meetings. Notwithstanding the existence of the official language, adequate facilities shall be given to Turkish nationals of non-Turkish speech for the oral use of language before their own courts.[31]

This pledge to respect the language rights of "any Turkish national," including citizens who are not of Turkish ethnic origin, was systematically neglected. The excuse was that Article 14 of the Turkish Constitution stipulated that "the Turkish state, its territory and nation is an indivisible entity whose language is Turkish." Article 14 prohibits activities that violate the "indivisibility of the state with its territory and nation." Article 68 provides a mold for political parties: Their programs should "not be in conflict with the indivisible integrity of the state with its territory and nation." This clause does not allow the establishment of political parties based on ethnicity (or religion, for that matter). Other laws and legal principles prohibit actions that may be deemed to endanger the unity of the nation and its territory. Article 125 of the Turkish penal code stipulates that "Any person . . . who carries out any action intended to destroy the unity of the Turkish state or to separate any part of the territory from the control of the Turkish shall be punished by death." Similarly, Article 8 of the Antiterror Law (1991) forbids propaganda in either verbal or written form and all meetings, demonstrations, or other acts that can adversely affect the indivisible integrity of the nation and national territory of the Republic of Turkey. This article was partly altered in 1995 by removing the phrase, "whatever the methods, goals and ideas thereof," which prohibited even the most peaceful forms of political discourse. This minor change allowed the freeing of many detainees and reduction of sentences on the condition that the accused should not violate the article once again in the future.

The PKK-led rebellion that flared up in 1974 is not the only Kurdish uprising. There have been many others in the Republic's history, starting with two uprisings in 1925 and 1936–1937. That is why Kurdish provinces have been administered throughout the twentieth century on the basis of a legal setup different from the rest of Turkey. A number of southeastern provinces were put under martial law in 1978. A more totalitarian form of administration was declared in 1987 called the "state of emergency." A whole generation of Kurds in the southeast has never lived under a normal legal regime because of the security concerns of the state. Both the martial law and the state of emergency have been lifted in recent years. But the population in the Turkish southeast still lives under the careful eyes of the military and the intelligence services.[32]

Between 1989 and 1996, more than 1,500 civilians affiliated with the Kurdish opposition were assassinated on the streets, victims of "unidentified" murderers. Close to 500 people were classified as missing between 1991 and 1997. Between 1983 and 1994, 230 people died under police torture, the reports of the Human Rights Foundation revealed.[33] What topped the security measures was the scorched-earth policy the government adopted. More than two thousand villages and an equal number of hamlets were evacuated, and many were destroyed in order to prevent them from offering logistical support to the PKK and providing safe haven for its guerrillas.

The threat of terrorism and Turkish governments' exaggerated perception of its risks led Turkey not to sign or ratify some international conventions and covenants. For example, concerning European conventions, Turkey placed a reservation on the concept of "national minorities" and insisted that only those minorities that are recognized in international treaties should be considered (which, under the Lausanne treaty, includes only religious minorities). Together with Spain, Turkey has emphasized that the European High Commissioner on National Minorities may not intervene in situations involving terrorism. The Turkish authorities also opposed any possible implementation of the Moscow and Vienna Mechanisms of the Human Dimension with reference to the Kurdish problem in Turkey. Turkey had signed but not ratified the International Convention on the Elimination of All Forms of Racial Discrimination. Similarly, together with a small number of countries, Turkey had not yet sıgned and accepted to be a party to the International Covenant on Civil and Political Rights. Only in 2003, after the cessation of hostilities and reduction in the authorities' perception of threat levels, were all of these conventions were signed and ratified. The only relevant conventions to which Turkey is not a party are two conventions of the European Council: the Framework Convention for the Protection of National Minorities, and the European Charter for Regional and Minority Languages. I predict that Turkey will refrain from becoming a party to these conventions until the PKK and its armed sequels disband themselves and cease to be threats to national security.

Turkish prison authorities have recently changed their policies toward members of the PKK and its sequel organizations. Initially those inmates labeled "terrorists" were put into relatively large dormitory-type halls. Dozens of inmates stayed together. Prisons became centers of ideological reinforcement and military planning. Newcomers were indoctrinated, and new strategies were developed that were later implemented on the battlefield. Authorities designed a new prison system along the lines suggested by United Nations standards. After building new (F-type) prisons with single, double, and triple cells, authorities separated inmates from their organizational comrades. This policy broke down inmates' collective solidarity and reduced the influence and pressure of their organizations on them. It also prevented friction between large and closely knit groups and the prison management, which had led to the maltreatment of inmates and the destruction of prison facilities. PKK members and members of radical leftist and religious organizations were dispersed and placed in the new type of prisons. This change met with great resistance because inmates from terrorist organizations felt like fish in a dry pond. Successive hunger strikes, death fasts, and suicide attempts occupied the public press for nearly three years. But, because the new prisons and the treatment of inmates were found to be consonant with international standards, death fasts and hunger strikes dwindled, and we hear little of such protests from the prisons today.

The Kurdish people of Turkey followed all these positive legal and policy implementations with approval and hope. They welcome reforms and normalization efforts but they also want the government to do its best to meet the reasonable demands of the organization, a resolution that could lead to its self-termination as an armed group.

There has been no official communication or negotiation between the Kurdish nationalists and the successive Turkish governments except indirect messages carried by journalists and Jalal Talabani, leader of the Patriotic Union of Kurdistan (PUK) and president of Iraq today. The late president Turgut Özal thought that American forces would enter Baghdad and terminate the rule of Saddam Hussein in the first Gulf War in 1991. If so, there could be a meltdown in the Iraqi political system and the oppressed Kurds could vie for independence. However, in a hostile environment, they could fall prey to superior neighboring forces. Then Turkey could step in and even form a federation with the Kurds of Iraq. With this embryonic idea in mind, he talked to Jalal Talabani and asked him to cool down the PKK leadership, hinting at better prospects for the Kurds of Turkey in the situation that would emerge after the Gulf War. However, the first President Bush stopped U.S. troops short of entering Baghdad, the Iraqi regime remained intact, and Özal could not develop his strategy further.

There are indications that Necmettin Erbakan, prime minister in the late 1990s, tried to send a message to Damascus where Öcalan was living to ask him to wind down hostilities with Turkey in order to ease mounting pressures on his tenure in office. Other than these unofficial and personal trials, a few journalists carried messages from Öcalan to the incumbent politicians with whom they were familiar. No formal negotiations ever took place.[34]

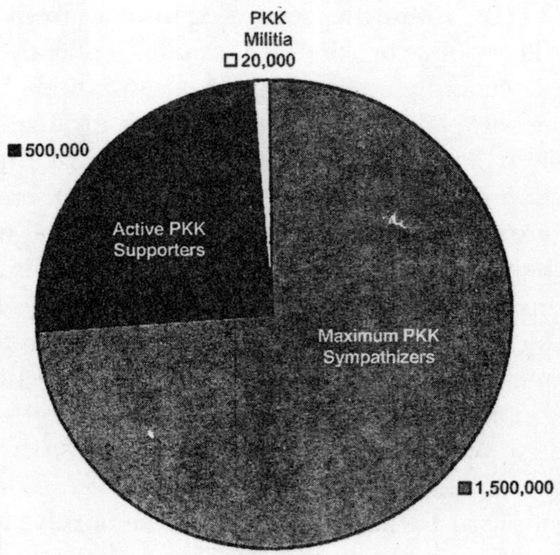


Figure 10.1. PKK membership.

## Size and Stock of Group Membership

The PKK was structured as a party, an army, and a mass or popular front, with sympathizers and political and ideological organizations supportive of its policies. Personal interviews with group members and official documentation suggest that the maximum number of people affiliated with the front was one and a half million. Party membership amounted to half a million activists. The guerrillas numbered 20,000 at the height of armed struggle, while the PKK maintained 10,000 armed militia on the ground at all times. Thus, the popular supporters vastly outnumbered party loyalists and armed fighters (see Figure 10.1).

Today, informed police authorities put the number of PKK militia bearing (but not using) arms who are hiding in the mountains of Turkey at 4,000, and another 5,000 roam the mountains of Northern Iraq referred to as Kurdistan near the Turkish border. These numbers must be compared with the total number of Kurdish citizens of Turkey, safely estimated to run between 12 and 14 million. This figure is an educated approximation because no census data on ethnicity are collected.[35] The PKK has not annulled itself and disbanded its armed forces. From time to time, it demonstrates that it is still capable of engaging in armed struggle if the Turkish government does not respond to its now more democratic and considerably more modest political demands.

After Öcalan's capture and the PKK's withdrawal from Turkey, the government, especially the security bureaucracy, became much more responsive and compassionate to local Kurdish communities. The military even took on the functions of primary education and health care in villages with-

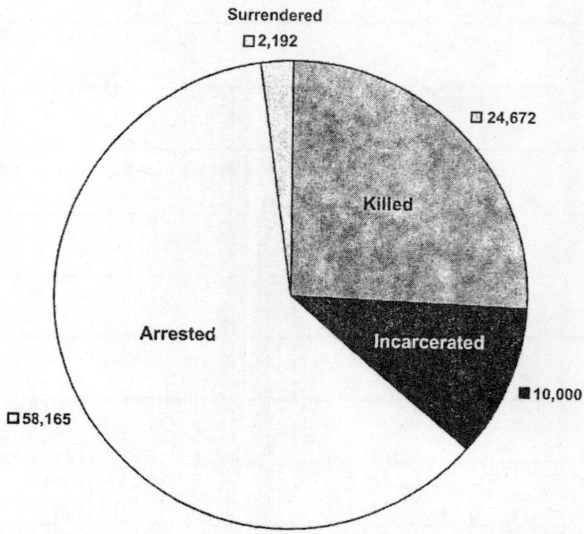


Figure 10.2. Number of PKK members killed or incarcerated, 1984–December 2003.

out sufficient numbers of schoolteachers and doctors. The government initiated a "back to the village" program. Those peasants who had been banished from their villages because of security concerns were allowed to go home and given a sum of money to rebuild their houses, herds, and farms. This drive was coupled with a legal and political push to uproot the "village guards" from the homes and villages of the peasants who had been forcefully removed during the 1980s and 1990s. Kurds and Christians began to return from Europe. All these are signs of the ongoing normalization process in the southeast.

The most decisive development in the process of normalization is the succession of legal and political reforms that have been telescoped in the last four years. With the prospect of EU membership, Turkey in general, and the incumbent Justice and Development Party (AKP) government in particular, have hastened reforms expanding individual freedoms and affording cultural rights to minorities. These reforms have made Kurds feel more secure and part of the country than at any time in the past.

The sporadic outbreaks of PKK violence that still occur are tactical moves that serve the purposes of the organization's leader. They prove that the organization is still alive and kicking. They show the Turkish government that Öcalan is the only person who can bargain or negotiate in the name of the Kurds. And they are intended to gain pardons, first for guerrillas who are still capable of fighting, and second, within a reasonable time span, for Öcalan himself.

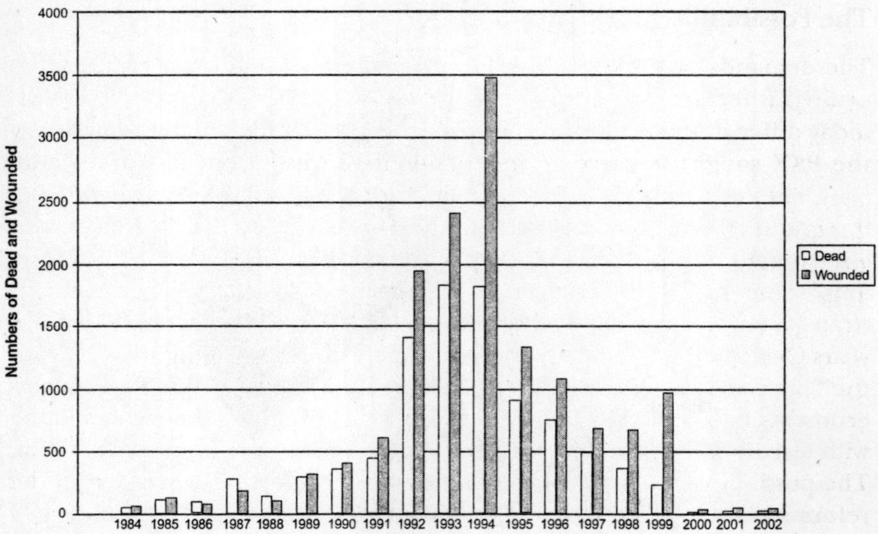


Figure 10.3. Police and soldier casualties caused by the PKK, 1984–2003.

**Casualties, 1984–2003**

| | | |
|---|---|---|
| (1) | Army regulars (professional and drafted soldiers) | 4,177 |
| (2) | Policemen | 254 |
| (3) | Village guards (loyalist village militia of Kurdish origin) | 1,265 |
| (4) | Neutral villagers and ordinary citizens of Kurdish origin who failed to obey or tried to resist the demands on the PKK, and innocent bystanders of mixed identities present at the crime scene during PKK attacks and acts of sabotage. | 5,140 |

Source: Special data provided to the author by the Prime Ministry on February 2004; official figures pertaining to the period between 1984 and 2000 only slightly differ from the above and can be found at the following publicly available official source: <http://www.byegm.gov.tr/YAYINLARIMIZ/DISBASIN/2004/06/03x06x04.HTM>

At the same time, Abdullah Öcalan is regrouping his supporters under a new political organization that will not take a party name in the early stages, but will engage in politics as a broader front called the Democratic Popular Movement. He has disavowed his brother Osman Öcalan and his supporters, who gave up arms and left PKK ranks to settle in what was the PUK-administered part of the Kurdistan region in Iraq.[36] One founding group of this new "movement" (as they call it) is Leyla Zana and her three other prison mates who were incarcerated for ten years on the grounds of aiding and being members of a terrorist organization.

In short, apart from tactical operations inspired by its leader to improve his negotiating position, the PKK is fairly inactive, and the predominant majority of the Kurdish people of Turkey no longer support politics carried on by means of violence.

## The Possibilities for Political Compromise

The demands of the PKK and the Kurdish citizens of Turkey have to be distinguished from each other. Furthermore, the demands of the PKK today differ dramatically from those of the past. Until the late 1990s, when the PKK sought to carve an independent Kurdistan out of Turkey and, later, out of Syria, Iraq, and Iran, political demands that were embedded in this grand scheme were never found to be negotiable, either by the Turkish government or by the governments of the neighboring countries. After the imprisonment of the organization's leader in 1999, the PKK changed its strategy, but not the tactic of resorting to violence when necessary. For five years Öcalan advocated taking an active part in transforming what he calls the "bureaucratic republic" to a "democratic republic." But Turkish governments have not deviated from the rule of refraining from negotiating with terrorists; instead, they adopted indirect ways to accommodate them. The possibility of a peaceful solution has arisen only in the context of the reforms enacted in preparation for EU membership.

The militant PKK leadership had two reasons to choose compromise. First, Öcalan was captured, imprisoned, and prosecuted for treason. Conviction for this high crime meant capital punishment. He chose to live and asked for a second chance to make up for his mistake. He did not want to go down in history as a defeated rebel and mass murderer. But, more than anything else, he wanted to save his own neck. And that he did, when Turkey abolished capital punishment as part of legal reforms necessary to start accession talks with the EU. Second, the Kurdish uprising under Öcalan's leadership had depleted almost all of its capital. Kurds in Europe, where most of the PKK's funds came from, did not support the continuation of futile and costly warfare. The main benefactor of the PKK, Syria, had let go of the organization under serious Turkish military threat. Other possible havens were rendered inaccessible. The Turkish army regularly conducted surgical operations into Northern Iraq referred to as Kurdistan to deny comfort to the PKK. But, more than anything else, the Kurdish people wanted hostilities to cease and to return to a normal life. Today hardly anyone in southeastern Turkey wants hostilities to resume, or to send their sons and daughters to take part in a meaningless struggle. Now they believe that they can win the political struggle by other means. The prospects of EU membership united diverse groups on a common platform and raised hopes that things will improve in the near future. Together all of these factors induced the militant leadership to compromise.

Other favorable conditions are now in effect. Torturers in the security apparatus have been arrested and punished, although not sentenced to the long prison terms they deserve. More human rights-oriented principles have been adopted in the codes that govern criminal prosecution and court procedures. Restrictions on cultural freedoms like publishing, broadcasting, and teaching in the mother tongue of the ethnocultural group have been relaxed. The "back to the village" policy allowing displaced villagers to return promotes normalization. The conflict that polarized Turkey for a decade and a half seems to be coming to an end.

These singular policies, although interconnected and serving the same end, have not yet yielded a decisive solution. Yet there is a new dynamic, which is systematic, encompassing, and affects all aspects of life in Turkey: the major transformation now being undertaken to prepare Turkey for membership in the European Union. All laws, institutions, and practices are being overhauled to fit EU standards. This process has especially benefited the Kurds. So, while 70 percent of Turks as a whole favor EU membership, fully 90 percent of the Kurds do.[37] They see EU membership as a means of salvation not only from their traditional and impoverished way of life but also from the oppressive and discriminatory practices of the present political system. For the majority of Turkey's citizens, EU membership is an accelerated journey toward "contemporary civilization." The EU prospect is the only common platform that unites almost all social groups as well as most of the main political actors in Turkey.

Like Gerry Adams and Sinn Féin's relation to the Irish Republican Army, and like Herri Batasuna's relation to the Basque separatist organization Euskadi 'ta Askatasuna (ETA), the PKK had legal political parties in order to attract wider popular support. The most recent of these, DEHAP, won three dozen municipalities in the local elections held in the spring of 2004. Like its predecessors, this party suffered from lack of support outside the southeast, where Kurdish nationalism and ethnic consciousness are sharpened by the state's suppression of Kurdish cultural identity and by Turkish nationalism, represented mainly by the security forces who constantly emphasize their Turkishness. Although more than half of the Kurdish population of Turkey lives elsewhere than their ancestral lands, Kurdish political parties receive few votes from "out-of-area" provinces. Evidence shows that those Kurds living in metropolitan areas who do not feel the brunt of ethnic tensions realize that their conditions are not dictated by their ethnic identity but rather the general circumstances prevalent in the country. Hence they do not harbor the idea that Kurdish nationalism is the panacea to their problems; they believe that such a stance is counterproductive. Kurdish political parties have never passed the national election threshold of 10 percent of the nationally cast votes and put members in the parliament, although at least one-fourth of the parliament consists of members of Kurdish origin elected from different parts of the country on the tickets of various parties.

Efforts at third-party intervention have been limited on the grounds that all PKK activities were deeds of a terrorist organization. However, there have been internal and international interventions attempting to differentiate PKK activities from the Kurdish problem in Turkey. The Turkish government vehemently refused to separate these two things until the end of hostilities. Yet, constant international pressure to rename the problem and to approach it from a political, economic, and legal perspective rather than merely with security measures has left an imprint.

Internally, the only serious effort came from a civic initiative that later crystallized as TOSAV (now TOSAM), or the Foundation for the Research of Societal Problems. Supported by the Winston Foundation for World Peace, Search for Common Ground in the United States, and the Peace Research Institute of Oslo, besides the governments of Switzerland, France, and Belgium, a group of representative Kurdish and Turkish public opinion leaders was selected and brought together throughout 1996 in different countries for lengthy discussions. Through heated discussions, the two sides developed a shared definition of the problem and possible solutions to it. Everything was negotiable except the territorial integrity of Turkey and the denial of violence as a means of exerting political leverage. At the end of the year a "Document of Mutual Understanding" was produced. TOSAV, a civic organization founded in early 1997, organized regional meetings throughout Turkey, bringing together local public opinion leaders of Turkish and Kurdish origin, along with others, in order to discuss and expand the Document of Mutual Understanding. In April 1999, the document took its final form reflecting a national civic consensus. What had to be done in order to solve the Kurdish imbroglio that had tied up Turkey for so long was laid out in the document. It was printed in Kurdish, Turkish, and English. As the latter versions were taken out of the printing shop, the police sequestered the booklets. Consequently, TOSAV was prosecuted at the State Security Court. Fortunately a lawsuit was not brought up, but the Kurdish version of the document was never recovered.[38] The other versions were widely distributed, even to the military establishment and the intelligence service. The European Parliament and all the governments of democratic countries represented in Turkey received copies. The effectiveness of this domestic intervention is difficult to assess. However, everything that Turkey has to do in order to adapt to European standards was pointed out in the document. Several of the reforms enacted since 1999 seem to be inspired by this historic document and the national consensus behind it. This was the first and only negotiated settlement exercise of a protracted conflict in republican Turkish history.

Now the EU is the driving force behind efforts of resolution, with direct and indirect effects in enhancing democratic rights and development of a more rational, inclusive economic system. Economic policies, though politically and militarily fraught, were considered important instruments of a settlement. In fact, the government made it a special policy to invest in the infrastructure of the southeast after the PKK began to argue that "Turkish Kurdistan" was an internal colony. The roads and electric system of the southeast are no worse than in many other parts of Turkey. Several economic incentive packages were put into effect for investors. However, nearly 90 percent of these so-called investors got the capital from the banks and invested elsewhere, in western Turkey, after building a few concrete blocks. Economic support was not free from discrimination. Those businessmen who were thought to be sympathetic to the PKK or supported the organization financially were excluded from government contracts and found it impossible to get credit to expand their business. The insecure atmosphere of the region did not allow a Kurdish local bourgeoisie of some significance to develop and mitigate between the radicals and moderates and between the state and the Kurdish community. Those who prospered did so elsewhere.

The government is now providing small sums of capital for the displaced villagers who are returning, but this initiative is neither sufficiently widespread nor satisfactorily funded. At the same time, the government was stretching its resources to finance the colossal Southeastern Anatolia Development Project comprised of 20 dams, multiple hydroelectric plants, and massive irrigation systems that would bring prosperity to a large section of the southeast. Politicized Kurds under the influence of PKK rhetoric interpreted this initiative as appropriating Kurdish resources, just like the Batman oilfields whose reserves and productivity have been grossly exaggerated.

The government encourages border trade with Syria, Iraq, and Iran. The most promising of these would have been trade with Iraq, had it not been for the ongoing turmoil in that country. The government encourages local merchants and transporters to take part in the border trade despite the current insecurity. Turkish businessmen are busy developing commercial concerns within Iraq. Southeastern businessmen of Kurdish extraction feel at home in Northern Iraq referred to as Kurdistan because the region is a cultural extension of southeastern Turkey and needs everything that Turkey can offer. Although a factor in alleviating the pressure of unemployment in southeastern Turkey, trade and other commercial relations with Iraq are yielding only limited opportunities to the citizens of Turkey.

The economic measures that may undermine the appeal of militancy are the reforms currently being enacted as part of Turkey's preparation for EU membership, which is expected to attract substantial foreign investment. All sectors of the economy are adjusting their positions and making future plans to take advantage of this development. Although this is a long-range plan, or at best a mid-range policy, it lays out a road map where all economic actors have to chart their positions and make plans. New investments are planned. New partnerships are formed as the system is improving and cleansing itself of corrupt and inefficient practices.

Can such policies be put in place in a preemptive manner? The answer to this question may be "yes" if the government looks at the Kurdish problem as more than a security matter. So far the problem has been viewed and dealt with only through the perspective of national security. Such a shortsighted approach prevented successive governments from considering a comprehensive solution based on winning the hearts and minds of the people as well as making life economically sustainable and offering better prospects ahead. Repressive policies may succeed, as they did, only in the short run. But this method deals only with the terrorist. Dealing with terrorism requires taking into consideration the human condition as a whole, no matter how complex it is. Until today, the Turkish government has demonstrated neither the necessary wisdom nor the resilience to approach the matter from a wider angle. Fortunately, with the ongoing paradigm shift that denotes the change from "state's nation" to "nation's state," the problem may be dealt with more humanely and by including the "one with the problem" in the "solution of the problem." In the case of the Kurdish problem of Turkey, it is imperative to start with social and economic policies that will dismantle the tribal and feudal character of the region. The second major step has to be reducing the high rate of population increase in the Kurdish countryside that rapidly renders any economic development policy ineffective.[39]

The long struggle with the PKK revealed the nature of Turkish public administration. Its capacity to solve problems without violence and the rigid stance toward cultural uniformity were put to test. The need for a pluralist and deliberative democracy and a more liberal legal system to support it became obvious. So all the suffering caused by PKK violence and official counterviolence drew home lessons of lasting impact, which, in the eyes of some, may justify the losses.

## Glossary

AKP: Justice and Development Party.
ARGK: Kurdistan People's Liberation Army.
DEHAP: Democratic People's Party.
DEP: Democratic Labor Party.
HADEP: People's Democratic Labor Party.
HEP: People's Labor Party.
Hizballah: Party of God.
HPG: People's Defense Units.
IRA: Irish Republican Army.
KDP: Kurdistan Democratic Party (Iraq).
KADEK: Kurdistan Democracy and Freedom Congress.
Kongra-Gel: Kurdistan People's Congress.
MED-TV: Media Television (now ROJTV).
MHP: Nationalist Action Party.
PKK: Workers' Party of Kurdistan (Turkey).
PUK: Patriotic Union of Kurdistan (Iraq).
SHP: Social Democratic People's Party.
TOSAV: Foundation for the Research of Societal Problems (now TOSAM).

## Timeline

1806: The first Kurdish uprising occurs in the Ottoman Empire.
1847: Bedirhan Bey, a local Kurdish notable who had come into conflict with the central Turkish authority, leads the "Bey Uprisings."
1880: The first "Sheikh Uprising" is led by the Kurdish Sheikh Ubeydullah.
1925: The last "Sheikh Uprising" is led by the Kurdish Sheikh Sait.
1930: Kurdish nationalists who had fled to Iran after 1925 stage the "Agri Uprising. Turkish troops enter Iran, ending the uprising in 1932.
1937: The "Dersim Uprising" is staged.
1959: In the "Operation of 49s," the Turkish government banishes 55 (originally 49) Kurdish feudal landlords (*agas*) to the western part of the country.
1960: The Democratic Party of Turkish Kurdistan is founded by Kurdish intellectuals. The Turkish government responds by rounding up, prosecuting, sentencing, and banishing many Kurdish leaders.
1969: The Eastern Revolutionary Cultural Hearths (DDKOs), a left-wing Kurdish group, begin to distinguish Kurdish nationalism from the leftist movement.
1970: The Marxist-oriented Turkish Labor Party (TIP) is shut down after trial because the word "Kurd" is mentioned in the proceedings of its Fourth Congress.
1973: Kurdish and Turkish university students meet to discuss the Kurdish issue, considered the beginning of the PKK.
1978: On 27 November, meeting in the village of Fis in Diyarbakir, the group takes the name PKK, Workers' Party of Kurdistan.
1979: PKK leader Abdullah Öcalan seeks refuge in Syria, where he remains until 1998.
1982: PKK holds its Second Congress in Syria and adopts the resolution that militia be sent to Turkey in order to create independent Kurdistan by armed struggle.
1984: PKK stages its first armed assault, in the Eruh-Semdin region of Siirt.
1990: Leaving behind its Marxist-Leninist past, PKK decides to replace the hammer and sickle on its party flag with a Kurdish nationalist icon.
1993: Abdullah Öcalan, together with Jalal Talabani, leader of the PUK (Patriotic Union of Kurdiştan, in Iraq), and Kemal Burkay, leader of the Socialist Party of Turkish Kurdistan, calls on Turkey to find a peaceful solution to the Kurdish problem. Germany declares the PKK a terrorist organization—the first time the organization is put on a European list of terrorists.
1998: General Atilla Ates, commander of the Turkish ground forces, makes a public statement close to the Syrian border to protest its harboring Öcalan and the PKK. Evicted from Syria, Öcalan goes to Russia, Italy, Greece, and Kenya.
1999: Öcalan is arrested in Nairobi by Turkish special forces and returned to Turkey, where he is imprisoned, tried, and condemned to death for treason. During his trial, he renounces armed struggle for Kurdish independence.
2002: In line with legal reforms to meet European Union standards, the Turkish Parliament annuls capital punishment. Öcalan's penalty is commuted to life imprisonment.
2005: From prison, Öcalan called for "a stateless confederation of Kurdish enclaves in the Middle East together with a concentric confederation of their host states."

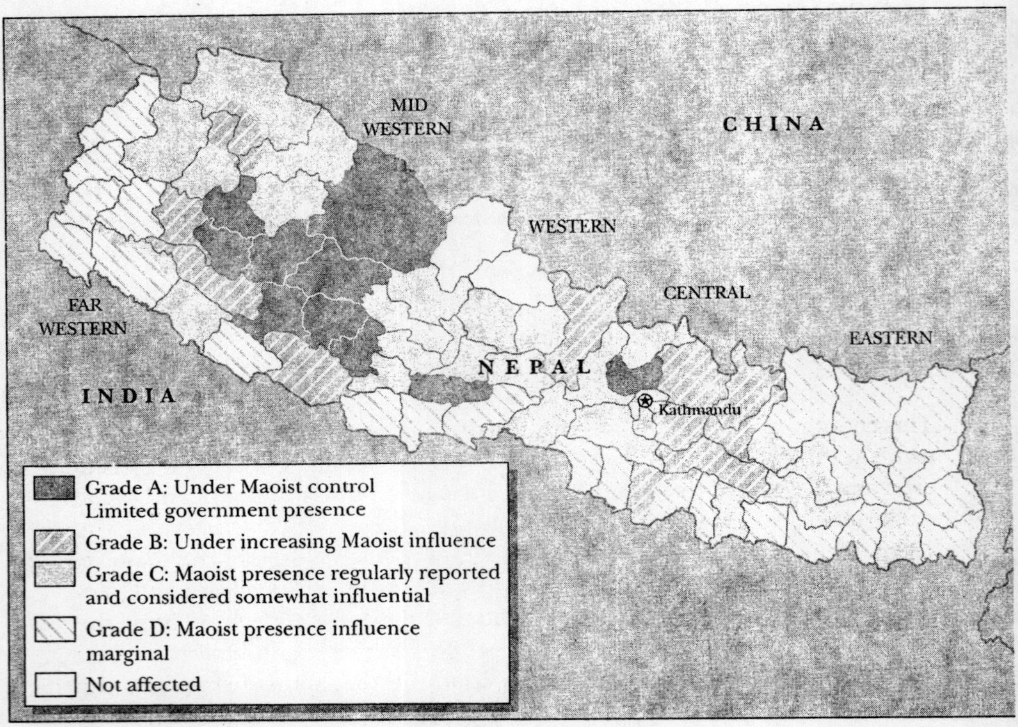


Map 11.1. Degree of Maoist control in Nepal.

*Chapter 11*

# PLA CPN (M): The Insurgency of the People's Liberation Army of the Communist Party of Nepal

HARALD OLAV SKAR

This chapter reviews the Maoist insurrection in Nepal, which began in 1996 with the "Declaration of People's War." The insurrection may be considered as a peasant uprisingand an uprising against discrimination and social exclusion.[1] Income from agricultural production fell drastically in the 1990s, while jobs in government agencies have been closed to the majority of people for centuries. Access to education and health facilities and general development have also been limited: the poor are 42 percent of the Nepalese population of 23 million people.[2] Nepal is one of the poorest countries in Asia, and is expected to continue that status because of the repercussions of the insurgency and the conduct of extremely corrupt governments over the last decade. Legal rights in Nepal have been generally limited to the upper classes, as approximately 85 percent of all judges and lawyers are high caste, while the percentage of prisoners who are low caste is the same. Where there are no fair trials, and no future sustainable work, low caste and ethnically excluded groups are open to alternatives sought through the gun.

The insurrection in Nepal has gained unexpected momentum and support as the government has drifted farther and farther away from what may be considered acceptable democratic standards. The present regime can most aptly be described as a royalist military dictatorship. The king sacked Nepal's elected government on 22 May 2002. Parliament was dissolved and the military prevent parliamentarians from meeting. Local elected bodies were not reinstated when their terms expired in 2003, and the king subsequently nominated personnel to run these positions. The king has also been using the *raj parishad* (royal advisers) to hold regional royalist support meetings ("civic receptions"), and using the powerful Thapa faction in the Rastriya Prajatantra Party (RPP), the royalist party, to appoint local leaders in rural areas.[3] The Maoists reacted vigorously against such appointees, as have the constitutional political parties. A royalist "joint command structure" was established in 2003, putting civilian authority under military control. The country is at present led by the king in person as chairman of the governing council and Nepal has been under a state of emergency since November 2001.[4] The military works with apparent impunity as they fight against "terrorists," and human rights violations have steadily and dramatically increased. Although the Maoists are also continuously violating basic human rights, Amnesty International reported in 2003 that most transgressions had been by the Royal Nepalese Army, and that Nepal now held the world record in human disappearances.[5] The army is losing popular support, but so is the Maoist People's Liberation Army (PLA), as it abducts students for training and indoctrination while financing the war through extorting money from local businesses and the industry. The conflict is slowly acquiring an ethnic dimension as the Hindu king fights the low-caste "bhote," or Buddhists, who more frequently support the Maoists. Currently young people are afraid to stay in the countryside, as one or the other of the two armies either enrols or executes them. The king has claimed that the war made it imperative that he take "benign command to protect his people," while the Maoists claim that they fight a dictator and represent the poor. Both seem to think that they can win the war which, so far, has claimed 12,000 lives. The Maoists control approximately 70 percent of the country, mostly the rural areas, while the king controls the towns and the capital of Kathmandu. The king's government has the support of the United States as an integral part of "the global war on terror."

## Communist Consolidation and Split

After Nepal's "velvet revolution" of 1990, which promised a new democratic era, the communist movement began consolidating in Nepal. Together with the Congress Party (traditionally the largest political party in the country, with strong ties to the Indian Congress Party), most of the communist factions had participated in the revolution of 1990 that led to a redefinition of the Constitution. Without unity between the communists and Congress, it is doubtful that change would have occurred. However, the changes that were made have later been manipulated or misused, in the eyes of their critics. Some say that, with the king constitutionally still in charge of the army, more trouble was only to be expected.[6]

Within the communist bloc there was considerable optimism. In 1991, the majority of the twenty two communist factions took part in the national elections under the umbrella of the United People's Front. However, the Front failed to gain the required 3 percent of the vote, and was thus excluded from the 1994 elections. Several years were to pass before war was declared because another communist group actually came to power constitutionally in 1992. Under Prime Minister Man Mohan Adhikari, the

CPN-UML (Communist Party of Nepal-Marxist Leninist) formed a minority government, which lasted for 9 months. Some UML leaders, however, incurred strange accidents, such as a roadside accident involving Chairman Bandari, and the UML split into further factions—the best known being the Marxist-Leninist (ML), which actually was voted in to head the capital, Kathmandu's municipal government, until the ML rejoined the UML in 2003. However, by 1996 the "other" CPN, the Maoist faction, had become tired of what they considered Kathmandu power games, where reportedly everyone seemed to want power so as to get a share of the action in what became known as the "kleptocratic decade" (1990–2000). (Court-cases are pending on the conduct of government officials and ministers from this time.) On 13 February 1996, the CPN (M) declared a People's War and decided to form its own army: the People's Liberation Army (PLA).[7]

The reasons for the People's War were, according to my informants in the party, threefold. First, government officials had proven themselves corrupt. Second, the CPN (M) claimed that the elections had been rigged.[8] Third, the CPN (M) argued that the focus on the poor, slaves, ethnic minorities, and casteless, initially promoted by the short-lived government of Adhikari with the support of other factions on the left, had been lost. A growing disillusionment with the gains of the 1990 "velvet revolution" had been accompanied by a general lack of trust in politicians in Nepal,—from all parties but especially from the Congress Party, which had been in government most of the time.[9] At the start of the People's War, declarations claimed that the revolution would follow the road or "path" of the Sendero Luminoso—the Peruvian Shining Path movement—and its leader Abimael Guzmán. However, with time this connection became less pronounced, and the new Path of Prachanda, the Nepalese revolutionary leader took over.[10]

The first violent clashes took place in the hilly regions of the far west of Nepal, and some say that the government at this time underestimated the movement. Subsequently, major battles have been fought between the armies of the two sides, and twice the roads were blocked to disrupd delivery to the capital (autumn 2004, February 2005). Now "the war is to become an urban guerrilla uprising," according to Maoist sources, which reportedly use the blockades to move troops and equipment closer to Kathmandu. Thus far, some 12,000 people, mostly rural peasants, have died in the insurgency. There have been no non-Nepali casualties, and the guerrillas mainly attack strategic sites guarded by the "enemy"—the Royal Nepalese Army (RNA)—or other representatives of the state. Other targets have changed over time—including undesirable individuals/informers (*suraki*), and infrastructure like the hydropower industry or U.S. interests in Nepal. The RNA became involved in the war only after the June 2001 massacre of the royal family.

The Maoist movement in Nepal is not a secessionist territorial movement, as is the case, for example, with the LTTE's war in Sri Lanka. The goal is not to free a specific area, but regime change, to take over control of the entire kingdom of Nepal and establish a communist republic. It is estimated that the Maoists currently control over 70 percent of the rural countryside, while the RNA controls the major cities and population centers. There is a potentially deepening ethnic boundary formation, between the royalists, with the king as an incarnation of the Hindu god Vishnu, and the Maoists, with their largest support among the Bhote groups of Tibeto-Burman origin. The main fighting and support forces of the PLA consist of Janajatis (middle- and low-caste ethnic groups), Magars, Tamangs, Gurungs, Tharus, and Dalits (outcastes), as well as poor high-caste Brahmins and Chhetris. The main leaders come from the latter two groups. The Maoist-controlled areas have now been separated into ethnic regions with ethnic leaders, while the government areas are controlled more and more by the army, under a "Unified Command" that overshadows civilian life. At the same time there is a power vacuum in the capital, as the country lacks an elected parliament. Furthermore, the king's refusal to reappoint elected local bodies has led to a lack of a state representation in rural areas throughout the kingdom. The appointees from the Royalist Party Rastriya Prajatantra Party (RPP) have not been able to fill this vacuum—indeed, they have often been unable to stay in the rural areas and have fled to the cities.

At present, the two largest employers in Nepal are the two armies; both pay wages. These same armies (led by high-caste individuals but formed of poor and illiterate soldiers at lower levels) have, as noted, managed to place Nepal at the top of the world in disappearances.[11] Additionally, the war has drained the country's economy, with a severe impact on industry, tourism in particular. Nepalese have also started to "vote with their feet," migrating to neighboring and other countries at an alarming rate. Almost 8 million are reported to be abroad, mostly in India as there is an open border.

There have been two rounds of peace talks. Both have failed, basically because they were not well organized and because the "participants had not been given sufficient mandate" to negotiate.[12] The talks did not include representatives of the armies and the role of the government representatives in relation to the king was also unclear[13]. In August 2004, a new "all-party" government (without ex-PM Koirala's Congress Party) was formed by a (third time) reappointed prime minister Sher Bahadur Deuba—previously sacked by the king in October 2002 for incompetence, then reinstated in June 2003. Deuba appointed an interparty High Level Peace Committee (HLPC), but this achieved little. It is widely accepted that the RNA is not under the control of the prime minister, but is loyal directly to the king and to its central command. This fact became unambiguous on 1 February 2005, when the king again sacked the Deuba government, placed all political party leaders under house arrest, and took over as chairman of a governing council. In his televised declaration that day, the army was given wider but unspecified mandates. Simultaneously the king declared a state of emergency and cut all access to telephones and the Internet. The press was censored, and a climate of fear descended over the country. The speech did not mention any further peace talks.

## Grievances and Demands

The fundamental demands of the Maoists have changed little throughout the rounds of peace talks. Their stated goal is a more egalitarian society that favors low castes and the poor. To reach this goal, they first of all have set as a minimal condition that a constituent assembly be held, as they see the present king as their main opponent, and they are seeking to replace monarchy with a communist republic. However, the new state is not envisioned to be run as a classical proletarian, that is, communist-party dictatorship: Speaking at an "interaction" organized by the party's Dalit (outcaste) wing in the capital on 1 July 2002, Mahar (Krishna Bahadur Mahara, politburo member of the CPN (M), said that "the party was going to adopt a new policy that would ensure the 'right to rebel' and delete the 'dictatorship of proletariat' clause from the party policy."[14] This proposal was presented as a new form of democracy. The leadership, respecting the "continuous revolution" (the Prachanda Path), is supposed to rule with the participation of "other democratically acceptable parties." The question that everyone is asking—especially the CPN-UML, which is sympathetic to some of the views of Maoist comrades—is whether the Maoists will respect a multiparty state, and how the decision will be made as to who is an "acceptable" ally. During rural elections in Maoist autonomous regions (January 2004), no parties with an affiliation to the king or the royalists (RPP) were allowed to take part, but individual candidates, free of party affiliations, were accepted (January 2004).[15]

According to the PN (M) *Maoist Information Bulletin*,

> A round table conference, an interim government and election to a Constituent Assembly are the minimum political tactics proposed by the Party in this context. Only a new constitution made by a Constituent Assembly can in reality institutionalize the sovereign rights of the Nepalese people. There can be no reason for anybody to disagree with this supreme modality of democracy to let the Nepalese people determine their own destiny and future."
>
> On the basis of this flexible tactical line the Party entered into negotiations with the old regime twice. However, both the times it was proved that the old regime was not in favor of a political solution but was in the path of conspiracy and regression. Rejection of the supreme democratic method of Constituent Assembly to make a new constitution by the old regime merely proves that it does not rely on the people but on armaments, army and terror.[16]

In further amplification of their demands, a unification of the two opposed armies is proposed, and a socialist welfare state is envisioned. The Maoists seem to consider the state as the steering mechanism for economic policy, and not the free market. Internationally they want to be non-aligned, while renegotiating all treaties with India, a country they seem to consider as a "big brother who has got a too large share of the natural resources"—a view with considerable support in Nepal today.[17]

Behind all these formulas we can also discern a clear ethnic policy and policy for the abolition of caste criteria, in favor of newly created ethnic "Autonomous Regions," basically represented by non-Hindu ethnic groups—despite the present multiethnic pattern in nearly all regions of Nepal. Using ethnic criteria for mobilization, the Maoists may theoretically appeal to a large section of Nepal's population. The 2001 census was held unpublished for almost a year because 51 percent, the majority of people in the only Hindu state in the world, had claimed non-Hindu religious affiliations. The census listed the diversity of Nepal—103 castes and ethnic groups were evident rather than the previously identified 59.[18] Furthermore, only 49 percent of the population had claimed Nepali as their mother tongue.

While catering to lower-level ethnic groups and promising them liberation from the Brahmins and other high castes, who own the majority of resources in Nepal, the focus of the CPN (M) is on recruiting the poor. Promising a better and more egalitarian society in one of the poorest countries in Asia has certain strategic advantages, as the potential recruitment base is large. In 2000 the United Nations Development Programme (UNDP) concluded that "Nepal ranked 144th out of 174 countries in the United Nations Human Development Program index. The people in the poorest regions of the country also have the lowest access to education and basic health services, highest rates of infant mortality, and highest rates of child malnutrition. Poverty undermines efforts at promoting human development, since it prevents many parents from sending their children to school. . . . In Nepal, about 42 percent of the population lives below the national poverty line of NRs 4,400 ($77) per capita per annum."[19]

Even though Nepal is a poor country, we cannot say that poverty is the single predominant reason why people support a violent insurgent movement. At least as important is the discrimination against minorities in decision-making positions in the state. Recruitment to public positions in the army, police, and military, except as low-grade officers, has always been closed to the poor. However, grievances related to lack of income and sustenance have made it easier for the movement to recruit soldiers. A study undertaken for the British Department for International Development (DFID) and Peace Research Institute, Oslo (PRIO)[20] indicates a close statistical correlation between poverty and support of violence per district in Nepal. The study concludes that the degree of inequality and poverty in

Nepal is directly correlated with the present civil war, and they base their conclusion on very solid statistical data.[21] However, the fact that large groups of the population are excluded from general political life in the same districts makes it difficult to make a causal link. Poverty, is however, one factor in the equation. Today as the war is increasingly prevalent it is becoming more and more difficult to survive as an agriculturalist. Production is frequently disturbed and as the government cut the subsidy for paddy at the same time as they cut subsidies for fertilizer a farmer can now rarely make a profit. This has led to a rapidly increasing poverty rate in a country where more than 70 percent are still farmers.

In analyzing the demands and grievances of CPN (M) it is important to bear in mind that what is demanded is a fundamental change in the

> total present State. This is a movement with an alternative agenda, that in other parts of the world may have become somewhat old-fashioned, but in Nepal, with its large population of poor and downtrodden castes, is still alive. As such, the Nepalese struggle has become a focal point for the International Revolutionary Movement (RIM), as they would like to see a red banner on top of the world's highest mountain. The symbolic value seems obvious. Imagine the international consequences. The radical left throughout the world would be heartened by a victory, somewhere, impressed to see the red flag planted, as the secretary-general of the CPN (M) Prachanda, likes to put it, atop Mt. Everest, the roof of the world. . . . The governments of the world—virtually all of them—would be highly displeased and mainstream intellectuals puzzled. The victory would after all constitute a challenge to the Fukuyama thesis (about the 'end of history' as a clash of ideologies) and the Huntington thesis (about 'the clash of civilizations'). We'd be back to the old capitalism vs. communism discussion, which was supposed to be behind us, all settled, and consigned to the rubbish heap of history![22]

## Organizational Capacity: Leadership, Recruitment, Social Base, and Finances; the PLA Organization and Recruitment of the Young

The most obvious measure of the organizational capacity of the CPN (M) can be seen in the fact that the PLA has managed to conquer large parts of the territory of Nepal, and in August 2004 and February 2005 held Kathmandu blocked off from the rest of the world by closing down all the roads to the capital. Some believe this to be the beginning of the final, decisive battle, while others see it as a strategic change from a rural-area approach to an urban guerrilla fight, not least since the *bandh* (general strike/ blockade) was presumably used to move troops. Increased pressure on national and international industries to shut down—eleven such, including Coca-Cola, have bowed to the demand—is another indication of CPN (M) capacity.[23] From my own observations on the organizational capacity of the Maoist movement it seems that they are well coordinated and have a clear strategy with a first-phase focus on rural areas and a second-phase focus on moving the battle to the towns. This seems to be acknowledged by the RNA, who are said to have placed 10,000 land mines round Kathmandu,[24] a practice more commonly used by the Maoists.

The rural victory is the most encompassing threat to the incumbent regimes so far. The Maoists battlefield gains pushed both the UK and the U.S. to step up military assistance to Kathmandu out of the fear that the state could actually fall.[25] According to some reports, the 70 percent figure for rebel-controlled areas is based on statistics on areas that are "not considered safe" rather than "areas under Maoist rule." In some areas the state and the military may have a presence during daytime, but withdraw at night. This means that the Maoists must remain in daytime hiding in such areas and cannot work overtly, as they would otherwise be arrested during military operations. In the Terai (southern lowlands) area, where I have a small farm, we experienced a campaign in December 2002–January 2003 that virtually pushed the government presence out from the region. Many peasants could bear witness to the brutality of the soldiers who were seen as taking vengeance on a neutral third party—the village poor. The nearby police station in Parsa was evacuated (as in most other rural areas); in March it was blown up by the Maoists in a preventive action, as the police and military had threatened to return. The only government now present is in the regional town of Bharatpur and the tourist village of Sauraha near Chitwan National Park and some command camps along the east-west highway, but they have little impact on the local communities.[26]

In December 2003, the Maoists began with intensive recruitment of soldiers. In my area they went from house to house demanding one soldier from each family and then began a multitude of coordinated attacks on selected targets while they blocked off the east-west highway. When I visited the area in March 2004, no vehicle could pass without military escorts. There were rumors of imminent attacks on the joint command headquarters in Bandara, and threats had also been made to make the joint command pull out or be attacked. A roundup of youth was taking place on both sides. The Maoists wanted fighters to take part in attacks, while the military actually detained, "disappeared," or shot youth who could be considered sympathetic to the Maoist cause.[27] For a while the area, which is close to the Indian border, became a no-man's-land, and dacoit bandits began operating in this lawless zone from India. However, abuses of any sorts were by mid-2004 reported to the Maoists who held strict control and dealt with crime and other matters by night. The main Maoist regional commander is reportedly from one of the most suppressed ethnic groups, the Tharu, and is generally regarded with respect as a fair person. Even during this difficult situation, as a foreigner I could travel freely, and tourists were still not considered a target—kidnapping of foreigners or visitors has never been on the Maoist agenda. However, kidnapping (and forceful recruitment) of local youth has become a major problem. Targeting the youth may be linked to a vision of a new "young state." As "old and older men" dominate the old regime and traditional power structures, the new state clearly focuses on youth—the largest age segment in Nepal.

Traditionally, age gives respect in Nepal, and most political leaders are accordingly older men. (The term *dai* is used of elder "brothers" and *bhai* of younger, with rights and obligations from *dai* to *bhai*). However, with new agitating movements, the young are more active and thus are becoming included as new leaders. It may be that some youth accept incorporation in the Maoist movement in opposition to the old-style family and hierarchy in daily life. Such inclusion, however, is not always voluntary. The story that follows is only one of hundreds of incidents reported during 2004:

> Maoist rebels Wednesday abducted more than 1,300 civilians from eastern districts of Ilam, Panchthar and Taplejung, reports said. In Panchthar, rebels abducted civilians from Ranitar, Sidin, Nawamidanda, Phakteb, Shiba, Lumbabung, Panchami and other VDCs. According to Nepal Samacharpatra, the rebels took one person from each family for the celebration of Lenin Day on Thursday which is going to be organized somewhere in Panchthar district. Maoist leader Dr Baburam Bhattarai is expected to attend the celebration, reports said.[28]

When youth have been kidnapped they are generally released later, but only after having been indoctrinated and told that they are expected to participate in the Maoist movement for social change. Some such "participation" has also involved acting as human shields in battle: thousands have been reportedly "rounded up" and been told to run with the soldiers during battle.[29] Many human rights organizations have protested against this type of warfare, where a small group of maybe one hundred actual solders may appear as thousands during an attack, while many civilians may be shot while carrying no weapons. In a Maoist-controlled district like Achham, the "people's mobilization" program has furthermore barred 45,000 students in the district from attending schools, according to the *Himalayan Times*, 25 November 2003.

Using humans as shields is also a strategy that may backfire on the Maoists, as the exodus of young able-bodied men toward the open border of India has exploded. Many pull and push factors are present, and reports are full of comments like these: "Most able-bodied men and women in the rural areas are now desperate, and looking for any option that come their way: migrating to towns, going to India as their fathers and forefathers had done; going to the Middle East or other overseas countries if they have the means for travel, or joining the 'Maoist' campaign if they meet its recruiting agents. It is this 'push' factor that has also sent the village girls, knowingly or unknowingly to be sold to the Indian brothels, or more recently, also to join the Maoist ranks."[30]

With the Maoists now taking some sort of control over rural areas, the question of who controls urban centers becomes paramount. Looking at the election results from all elections since 1990, it is remarkable that the city of Kathmandu (approximately 2 million people including the adjacent municipalities of Bhaktapur and Lalitpur [Patan]) has always had a communist majority. Before 4 October 2002, when the king formally took over, Marxist Leninists (ML) ran the town with a majority vote in the municipality, and a 6 percent national vote with members in Parliament. In 2003, however, they united with the larger CPN-UML,[31] which had 21 percent. This gave the new coalition 27 percent of the popular Nepal-wide vote, making them the largest party in Nepal, even greater than the Congress Party, with its 23 percent.

With a legal communist majority in the capital and major city and with 70 percent of the remaining 23 million in the hands of the underground Maoist movement CPN (M), little support is left for center-right political forces. In the areas of Ramecchap and Dolakha, districts where I had the opportunity to work as general manager for a hydroelectric company, there was an even stronger UML presence, as 49 out of 52 seats in elected offices were from this party and one candidate was running as independent. However, in the industrial lowlands of the east, the Congress Party still has a stronghold.

## Organization and Leadership

The CPN (M) is organized primarily through people's committees at various levels, as in other communist states (see Table 11.1), but also through formal and informal groups within Nepal and outside. "Mao Zedong's principle that the party, the people's army and a united front are the three weapons for a people's revolution hasbeen embraced by the CPN (M)."[32] Although "people's committees" may function at a lower level in areas where the Maoists do not have full control, we see the total structure as depicted by Sudheer Sharma only in the areas under autonomous people's governments (*jana sarkars*). Such have been formed in Seti-Mahakali Region, Tharuwan, Tamuwan, Tamang Region, Kirat, and the Madhesh terai region, as well as in 23 district level governments.[33]

Many of the new ethnic autonomous regions were formed in early 2004. On 9 January that year, the Magarat Autonomous Region People's Government was declared amid a mass meeting of reportedly attended by over 75 thousand people.[34] On 19 January, the Bheri-Karnali Autonomous Region People's Government was formed, and made public amid a big mass rally in Jajarkot district. It may be noted that western Nepal's Karnali region is the most remote and backward area of the country. This is also one of the major storm centers of the revolution. Coordination of such liberated Autonomous Regions seems to be through a special directorate for the administration of "people's power."[35]

The leaders of the "People's War" unite different factions and different regions of Nepal—an elongated country stretching from east to west including many river basins with many ethnic groups. On the area commit-

TABLE 11.1. CPN (M) ORGANIZATION

| *Party* | *People's Army* | *United Front* |
|---|---|---|
| Standing committee | Central military commission | United people's district committees |
| Politburo | Regional military commissions | United people's area committee |
| Central committee | Subregional military commissions | United people's village committees |
| Regional bureaus (five) | District military commissions | United people's ward committees |
| Subregional bureaus (in some places special subregional bureau) | Includes temporary battalions | |
| District committees | Companies | |
| Area committees | Platoons | |
| Cell committees | Squads (separate people's militias also exist under united village people's committees) | |

Source: Sudheer Sharma, "The Maoist Movement: An Evolutionary Perspective," in Deepak Thapa, ed., *Understanding the Maoist Movement in Nepal.*

tee level, the command seems to have been divided in high and low sections according to watershed, but recent reports from Ramecchap and Dolakha tell of an eastern and a western command group for each river basin, making it easier to communicate in the rainy season. In 2001, the local platoon commanders were also put under the central command of ambulatory cells to avoid local identification between cadres and local residents, and accordingly make the attack groups more able to "deal with potential targets." This made it more difficult to operate traditional development projects, as no amount of "welfare work" could satisfy these central ambulatory cells that had no ties to the region.[36]

Factional leaders within the People's War have been many and still are, especially after ethnic leaders have been put in charge of autonomous regions.[37] However, directly after 1996 the major ones united under the leadership of Prachanda to form the Communist Party of Nepal-Maoist (CPN (M)), and are today rumored to be in two main factions—a moderate one, and a more violent one—each associated with known individual leaders:

## Main Leaders: Prachanda, Baburam, Parvati, and Others

Pushpa Kamal Dahal, known as Comrade "Prachanda" (the name means awesome or powerful), leads the insurgency. Born in 1954 into a humble family of tenant farmers in the Kaski district in the Himalaya foothills, he saw the way "the money-lenders humiliated his father"[38] and later joined the Communist Party. After finishing education as a scholarship student, he graduated from Rampur Agricultural College (south Nepal) and briefly worked for USAID. Few have met Prachanda after he went underground. One exception is considered to have been during the Lucknow (India) meeting with Madav Kumar Nepal, head of CPN-UML, the largest legal political party in Nepal. Some have suggested that letters allegedly signed by Prachanda and distributed—through flyers handed out from motorbikes and on posters in Kathmandu, or texts as in statements to the foreign press, or even as letters to Kofi Annan of the UN—reflect the authorship of many.

The main leaders have a body of intellectuals as formal advisers. Little is known about this intellectual advisory board, but it is said to contain sympathizers at universities in and outside Nepal. According to Nepalese Maoist doctrine, "everyone connected to the revolution does not have to just carry a gun. According to one's proclivities, and the necessities of a revolution, some carry a physical weapon and others a mental weapon."[39] Meetings between these intellectuals are arranged through the Revolutionary International Movement (RIM), which organizes seminars on other topics and holds "sideline meetings" simultaneously. Prachanda is known as a hardliner, while his second in charge, Dr. Baburam Bhattarai, has acted as the moderate negotiator at peace talks. Bhattarai has become a well-known figure: at the last round of peace talks he appeared in a costume imitating Karl Marx with cap and so on, copying old photos. He gave interviews and held lectures in Kathmandu during the negotiations period. Just as with the "idol" Abimael Guzmán from Peru's Shining Path movement, Baburam has a background as a university professor, and has even published a book about Maoism in Nepal.[40] It is also said (as for Guzmán) that he has obtained the highest marks in his field during his academic life.

Other known leaders also include women such as Comrade Parvati (the name of a major Hindu goddess: nom de guerr*e* for Baburam Bhattarai's wife Hsila Yemi)—she wrote in the *Monthly Review* about female leadership and the revolution. Some estimate that almost 40 percent of the Maoist cadres are women.[41] Until 2003, no women could inherit from their father (and still after the new law of 2003 they can not retain "inherited property" after marriage) and their position is generally a reflection of patriarchal values—in fact, suttee or widow burning still takes place in some rural areas. Comrade Parvati appealed to women to liberate themselves and to join the underground movement to free themselves as well as the country. Some who have done so have, however, regretted this as they reportedly have been used as prostitutes for soldiers and may now not be acceptable in regular marriage, according to Nepalese traditions.

The leadership structure is relevant to any peace process that may be forthcoming: but we simply do not know how well integrated the movement is today, and if the known leaders will respect decision made by the others. Accordingly, we cannot know whether a splinter movement would occur if a main leader were to sign a peace accord.

## The Social Base in a Caste Society

If you are part of a poorer caste with a divinely allotted spot in life and earn 20 Rps (30 cents) a day, or do not even see this amount, as it is all taken from you to repay your inherited debt, then a salary, companionship, and power (arms), may seem a good offer where "little is left to lose." In Nepal we find that the CPN (M) successfully has been able to mobilize the "poorest of the poor," that is, recently liberated slaves, especially in the Far West region.[42] The Kamaiya (slavery-bonded labor) issue is still not resolved. The short-lived UML government freed the slaves in 1994, but later governments failed to give them adequate income opportunities, forcing them either to go back to their previous owner, stay in camps with inadequate housing without medical attention (8–10 are reported to have starved to death in 2003), or join the Maoists. In the 1980s and 1990s, as a member of Anti-Slavery International, I was studying Nepal and could observe the slave market every first day of the Nepalese Year (1 Baisakh/mid-April).[43] Whole families (including women and sexual rights) were for sale, as their family "debt" was transferred from one "owner" to the other. With the younger generation rapidly acquiring knowledge of the outside world (through television development projects, schooling, and so on), more and more are refusing inherited debts and are looking for any way available to start a new life.

Rebel organizations generally face severe difficulties in maintaining cohesion over a long time. "As they operate outside the law, they do not have recourse to normal contract enforcement techniques. Governments can divide a rebel movement by buying off local commanders, a technique used against the Khmer Rouge."[44] In far west Nepal (Kailali), a rural Maoist commander was granted amnesty and provided opportunity to work outside of Nepal in 2003. Later this strategy was made into a general amnesty for Maoists who surrendered. However, according to Paul Collier, "one technique for maintaining cohesion is to have a hierarchical, dictatorial decision structure, with most power vested in a charismatic leader" (cf. Guzmán in Peru and Prachanda in Nepal); when this fails, recruitment can be confined to a single ethnic group with leaders from the same clan (e.g., the Hussain Tikriti clan). However, in a country like Nepal the obvious problem is deciding which clan or tribal affiliations to proceed with. With at least 59 ethnic options, a few larger ones will have to be selected, and problems will still remain in relationship to diversity and cohesion, as subgroups exist in the hundreds. Thus Maoist support will probably depend on the way the conquered autonomous regional structures take into account the diversity within their boundaries. The possibility for split in Nepal is endless and not as straightforward as the situation envisioned by Collier.

## Financing Rebellion

The CPN (M) movement in Nepal has been involved in many episodes of bank robbery, leading to frequent news reports like this one: "In Nawalparasi, armed Maoists looted Rs 21,000 in cash from Western Region Rural Development Bank in the Shiva Mandir VDC this afternoon. Bank manager Soviet Jung Joshi said the rebels looted the cash from bank staffers returning to the bank after recovering loans from farmers in Pithauli VD."[45] However, sometimes even full-scale attacks with large numbers of people have failed: "Maoists Sunday admitted that they attempted to rob Agriculture Development Bank in Narayangadh losing some of their colleagues in the cross firing on Friday. 'P.L. commander Sagar Humagain of Chitwan, two P.L. Vice Commanders Akash from Kapilvastu and Keshav along with two Section Commanders Sushil and Rupesh were killed in the encounter,' said the statement. 'We are investigating the reason of the failure of their attempt,' it added."[46]

"Taxation of industry" has brought a certain amount of revenue to the movement—failure to pay has resulted in the destruction of power plants, offices, machinery, and vehicles. Generally, most national industry has been paying for the last few years, while foreign-owned industry and NGOs have refused. The embassies have been active in bringing foreign interests together under one ethical code, thus making a united stand against extortion. While I was working as director of the largest privately owned hydropower plant in Nepal (Khimti, 1999–2002) we constantly received letters asking for "support." We always replied that support to the local poor was already taken into consideration in our development program as we were spending approximately $2.6 million on schools, hospitals, rural electrification, and so on (NORAD grant included). In the end, however, we had to face the choice of paying for support through the military or through the Maoists; the first was logically chosen, as more than 100 soldiers became deployed, and shooting towers, tunnels, and bunkers became part of daily site life. In the Maoist-held territories there is a more directly regulated finance procedure. All households are now asked to "pay taxes" in rice or food to the Maoist army; for those who are salaried wage earners, a 10 percent tax has been introduced.

There seems to be a clear difference between CPN (M) and Latin American revolutionary groups that try to profit from the illegal narcotics trade (Peru, Colombia, etc.), with ideological factors apparently taking precedence over economic needs: "Asking the farmers of Makwanpur district to finish their marijuana stock within this month, Maoists have asked them not to cultivate marijuana anymore in the area, a daily said Monday. Marijuana cultivation is popular in ten different VDCs in the western part of the Makwanpur district for the last decade, Nepal Samacharpatra said. Maoists used to levy Rs.100 per kilogram from the farmers for the cultivated marijuana, the report said."[47]

Another financial source may be through the Nepalese diaspora, but little of this can be documented. Lastly, there is payment in kind, through the training of Maoist soldiers abroad, mainly in India (see RIM below)

## External Support and Diaspora Attitudes

External support for the CPN (M) can be seen in three areas: in the international Maoist movement (CCOMPOSA, RIM), through Nepalese student groups and refugee Nepalese, and among non-Nepalese groups sympathetic to any cause that can be considered anti-American or anti-imperialist.

The Maoist movement has broad contacts with other similar groups on the Indian Sub-continent through CCOMPOSA (the Coordination Committee of Maoist Parties and Organizations of South Asia) and also with other similar movements through RIM (the Revolutionary International Movement).[48] CCOMPOSA has issued the following declaration of support for the Nepalese Maoists:

> The U.S. has entered into a strategic alliance with India in order to extend and consolidate hegemonic dominance in the South Asian region. In this context, this strategic alliance has set out to assist the feudal comprador autocratic monarchist state in Nepal in its desperate attempt to militarily crush the blazing protracted people's war led by the Communist Party of Nepal (Maoist) [CPN (M)]. . . . The Nepalese state has suspended all fundamental human and democratic rights, whilst killing and arresting progressive journalists and activists. In its effort to centralize, concentrate and monopolize state power, the monarchy has marginalized the parliament and all other institutions and agencies of the state, whilst strengthening the role of lackey forces such as the "United Marxist-Leninists" (UML).[49]

The RIM first followed the path of Chairman Gonzalo and the Shining Path of Peru, but in 2001 (during a North India meeting), the chairmanship was rumored to have been offered to Prachanda from Nepal, with the launching of the "Prachanda Path."[50] Although remaining central in the RIM movement, Prachanda is said to have declined the chairmanship to give priority to the revolution in Nepal. RIM's direct support of Prachanda is evident in the following statement from the RIM Central Committee:

> The CPN (Maoist) led by Chairman Prachanda has integrated the universal principles of Marxism-Leninism-Maoism to the concrete reality of Nepal. . . . In this period of complex class struggle in Nepal amidst an increasingly turbulent international situation, we are confident that under the leadership of Comrade Prachanda the party will be able to navigate the turbulent waters, safeguard the fundamental

interests of the people in Nepal, complete the new democratic revolution and transform Nepal into a bright red base area of world proletarian revolution. The Committee of the Revolutionary Internationalist Movement reaffirms its full support for this process.[51]

One may ask what real importance the RIM and the CCOMPOSA have in the People's War in Nepal. First, the Maoists in Nepal use the RIM for coordinating their "Advisory Group" and to arrange meetings to discuss strategy. Second, they invite the groups involved to think regionally and internationally. In doing so they have had a clear impact on the Maoists in Nepal, and the war is spilling over to India, where the RIM facilitates contacts between groups such as the Naxalites and the CPN (M). Third, the RIM Internet and global contact network is made available to its "members," and many CPN (M) speeches by Prachanda have appeared first on their Web site. This is important, as there is a heavy penalty for being caught with Maoist propaganda material in Nepal. Last, the RIM may actually push ideas based on international agendas and not the local Nepalese ones. One example is as follows, although the source is not impartial: "The former Prime Minister Surya Bahadur Thapa on Wednesday revealed that Maoists had walked out of previous second round of peace talks following pressures from International Maoists' group RIM. "RIM had advised the Maoists to fight to finish," he said.[52]

In any case it would be a mistake to view the uprising in Nepal as an event limited to that country. The regional implications and the links with Communists in the north and the south speak not of isolation, but of larger agendas. The ties to India deserve a special focus, as the border between the two countries is open. As the king took absolute power in 2005, as many as 45 Maoist leaders met in India. At this time the Indian prime minister expressed his concern that the Nepalese king's fight in the north might lead to more problems in the south, as at this time there was a surge in Naxalite/Maoist attacks in northern India. Maoist training has been taking place in India as reported in almost all the national papers in Nepal and in Uttar Pradesh and Bihar, two northern Indian States: "According to him [captured commander Ghatri], PWG and MCC, which are banned in India, trained a batch of 17–18 Maoists for the first time in 2055 BS [five years ago]. The numbers of the second lot of the Maoists to receive military training from the two outfits were 70 to 80 in 2056/57 BS (two/three years ago), Gharti said. "The last time we received such training was in 2058 BS (two years ago). . . . Around 150 of us received the training at that time."[53]

Recent reports indicate that such training is still going on. Indian news sources tell of training-centers in the jungle area on the borders between the two countries: "Police in the Indian state of Uttaranchal have discovered a training centre being run by Nepali Maoists on Indian soil during a search operation, reports said Friday." The rebels were using the dense forest at Chorgaliya and Hanspur area in the terai region of Nainital district for quite some time, security officials said. The security sources said they have sent the report to the state police and RAW—external intelligence agency of India. The newspaper report, however, did not say if the security officials could round up Nepali rebels. Indian security personnel belonging to police, PAC and SSB, Kantipur daily reported, jointly carried out the search.[54]

## Diaspora Groups and Support for the CPN (M)

The Maoists have representatives within diaspora groups and especially at some universities abroad. Some seem to have central roles in the movement (as members of the intellectual advisory committee), and in Norway I recognize some individuals from my times in Nepal, where they acted as regional contacts in relationship to industrial firms. In Norway they seem relatively passive—perhaps spreading information and helping those who have outstayed their Schengen visa in Europe. Visa runaways seem to be constantly on the move, unable to apply for refugee status in most countries since the Maoist movement has been classified as a terrorist movement. The countries reported to have the largest number of such Nepalese without visas are the UK and Belgium. According to one informant, Britain is considered easy to hide in, due to the large diaspora there. In some countries problems incurred by people fleeing the RNA have been reported:

> A Nepali national has been found dead on 8 December in Gent of Belgium. The dead Nepali Mr. Prem Prasad Subedi, birth of 15-10-1971 in Myagdi district of Nepal was reported to have committed suicide. It is note worthy that the authority had rejected his asylum request by which he was bound to leave Europe . . . his case was dismissed and [he] was either forced to go to the country being killed by the Nepalese Royal Army, or being forced by the Authority to leave country [of Belgium]. Prem Prasad Subedi was an activist of our organisation. After his death, he is survived by Sagar Subedi a son aged 12, and two daughters—Ganga and Sarala aged 8 and 5 respectively and his wife. These children and his wife now remained hapless and without support. We urge the United Nations Organization, governments of Europe and the prosperous nations to grant Nepalese asylum.[55]

Besides asylum in Europe for "comrades on the run," jailed Maoists in India have been at the forefront oj attention among supporters of the Maoist movement abroad, especially "Comrade Gaura," one of the first to be arrested in India after UML leader Madav K. Nepal held his meeting with the CPN (M) near Lucknow in the north of India. Almost simultaneously with the meeting, the Indian communist movement issued a declaration of support for the Nepalese Maoists, and this may have changed the position of the then Indian BJP government against the Maoists, despite its earlier "no intervention" stand. From then on many Maoists have been detained in India and handed over to Nepalese authorities. Other international "anti-imperialist" movements have also picked up the case of Nepal's insurgency:

> The World People's Resistance Movement, Benelux (Belgium, Netherlands and Luxembourg) and the STOP USA (a platform of more than 50 organizations) staged a protest rally in front of the Indian Embassy, in Brussels demanding immediate release of Comrade Gaura, a political bureau member of the CPN (Maoist), and handed over a memorandum to the Indian Prime minister, Mr. Atal Bihari Bajpayee through ambassador. Nepalese students in Norway have also demanded immediate release of Comrade Gaurav. A protest letter was handed over on 10th of November to the Indian Embassy in Oslo, the capital of Norway.[56]

Besides Europe there is a major Nepali diaspora population in Korea, Thailand, and Arab states where people go for work. Brunei has a large Gurkha regiment colony. But India tops the list: it is estimated that annually more than seven million Nepalese migrate to neighboring India for job opportunities.[57] The number is increasing daily, due to the war. With the open border between India and Nepal, and the higher salaries in India, this sizable diaspora might play a vital role in financing the Maoist movement.

## Other International Support for CPN (M)

With regard to other international support for the CPN (M), Sri Lankan president Chandrika Kumaratunga reportedly said to the Nepali ambassador to Colombo (on 14 June 2003) that the Liberation Tigers of Tamil Eelam (LTTE) are training Nepali Maoists in the northern part of the country.[58] Furthermore, the *Independent* (12 May 2003) cited "Western intelligent agencies" as suspecting that al-Qaeda has been supplying "sophisticated weaponry" to the Maoists in Nepal. Both rumors seem questionable in view of the difference in ideologies, and the fact that large amounts of weapons have been captured (more easily) through attacks on RNA positions within Nepal. However, foreign involvement in this respect cannot be ruled out, and arms may even come from China: "China has arrested four persons for trying to smuggle in a sack of Chinese pistols and explosives into the country from Tibet, Radio Nepal said quoting security sources. Maoists have been using Chinese pistols in murderous attacks, particularly in Kathmandu Valley. Rebels have robbed the pistols from police, but this is the first time official confirmation of arms and explosives being smuggled from Tibet."[59]

## Actions and Policies of the State

Nepal has maintained a divided official attitude to the Maoist insurgency. First, the state overlooked them, with the exception of a highly unsuccessful police campaign in 1998, Kilo Shera 2, during the Nepali Congress/ Koirala period, which alienated the locals and increased support for the Maoists.[60] Later the state generally preferred to win the battle on the battleground, while engaging in extended peace talks. There have also been other attempts to stop the recruitment of the poor into the Maoist army, but such efforts in regard to the Dalit (outcastes), Kamayia (slaves),[61] and ethnic minorities (Janajatis) have been either too slow or too few to make sufficient impact.[62]

## Modernizing the Nepalese Army

Until 1990, the military had been a traditional army, with old-fashioned weapons and scant fighting power. As the king and the Rana family retained control over the army after the new constitution was drafted (1990), the army slowly woke up. The late king Birendra had refused to use the army within the country, whereas king Gyanendra has had no such qualms. Some (conspiracy theorists) even say that this is the main reason behind the palace massacre of 1 June 2001, when King Birendra, Queen Aiswarya, and ten other members of the royal family were killed in the Royal Palace. Others say that even Birendra was on his way toward the use of the military, and that it was the change of time and situation rather than the change of king that mattered.[63]

At any rate, the army expanded rapidly after 2001: today it incorporates approximately 70,000 soldiers. With the help and training of U.S. professional soldiers, a regular fighting force has been built. By contrast, the Maoists have approximately 30,000 soldiers according to their sources.[64] The basic RNA soldiers' salaries, at 3,500 Rps per month, are good compared with agricultural work, where the daily wage is about 80 Rps, or approximately a dollar. In addition, RNA soldiers also get free food and lodging.

Does the new RNA really want peace? Its organizational interests may point otherwise. Some critics argue that the army has become part of a carousel of escalation and corruption. The main supplier of its arms has been the U.S., and in some cases "rebels have captured such new arms," leading some to say that the upgrading of the RNA has increased the firepower on the Maoist side. With the military now in charge of a unified command, media attention has also focused on possible further military escalation. In some areas of Nepal it is now said that even the previously mighty CDO (chief district officer) will have to bow to the decisions of a low-ranking army sergeant, and that with this move the total state apparatus has become militarized, drawing comparisons to Pakistan. One may, however, also see the unified command as a natural development, as the country is in civil war and also in view of the strong tendency toward centralization present in traditional Nepalese culture.[65] Traditional police were insufficiently coordinated, and there were incidents in which they were attacked while the army nearby did not come to help. The most worrying aspect, however, is that human rights violations have increased at a rapid pace and, with abductions and abuses, the RNA's popularity is rapidly diminishing.

## Human Rights and Security Acts (TADA)

In my March 2004 interview with human rights leaders, I was told that about 80 percent of violations are perpetrated by the state forces, while the most gruesome incidents of head-cutting and torture are carried out by the Maoists. Reports of human rights abuses by both the security forces and the CPN (M) escalated after the RNA was mobilized and a state of emergency imposed between November 2001 and August 2002. Many people were arrested under the 2002 Terrorist and Disruptive Activities (Control and Punishment) Act (TADA), which empowered the security forces to arrest without warrant and detain suspects in police custody for up to 90 days. Scores of people are reported to have been held for months in illegal detention in secret army custody without access to their families, lawyers or medical assistance. Concern renewed after new repressive laws were introduced in April 2004. Amnesty International (2003) has publicly charged that the "preventive detention provisions" under Public Security Act (PSA) were being used to stop the organizers of the rallies (against the king) in continuing their campaign. "We urge the authorities to stop these mass arrests and to ensure that any future arrests and detentions are based on adequate grounds and are in line with international Covenant on Political and Civil Rights (ICCPR), to which Nepal is a party."[66]

Today human rights organizations of Nepal do not trust the government and the government reciprocates. According to one minister interviewed in March 2004, human righst groups were "all Maoist supporters." That the Maoists are also denounced by the human rights activists, especially those affiliated with the press, suggests that the warring sides are against human rights groups that make it their business to scrutinize local reality and complain to the outside about conditions in Nepal. Many human rights activists believe that both warring sides actually want a military solution—and that the rest is mere window-dressing.[67]

## Peace Talks

The peace talks held in Kathmandu were from the start destined for only limited success, mainly because those in charge of the two armies were not sufficiently involved in the talks, nor were the "real clan or ethnic leaders."[68] The RNA has repeatedly shown that it does not take orders from any democratically elected or appointed prime ministers, and not even from the country's minister for defense. The RNA, however, does take orders from the king and his advisers. Some observers maintain that the RNA actually boycotted the talks, first by insisting on PLA disarmament (first round of peace talks), and second by instigating the "Dorumba incident"[69] (second round), denounced as mass murder by many human rights groups as well as Kathmandu foreign embassies (including that of Norway). When the two sides agreed in the second round that no armies were to move more than 5 km from their barracks, the RNA refused to comply. In talks with RNA leadership (Brg. General Gurung) it was explained that compliance would be tantamount to losing hard-won ground—and show lack of respect for the soldiers who had died for it. Furthermore, the RNA would also be left with old-fashioned defensive strategies like "rabbits in the hole," and this was not acceptable. As the RNA forces had little representation in the talks and only civilian royal appointees were put in charge, the warring armies—according to informants on both sides—had no prior faith in the peace talks.

### First Round of Peace Talks, August and November 2001

Following the June 2001 royal massacre in Kathmandu, king Gyanendra took the reins. By mid-summer the army and the Maoists had come into direct combat for the first time. Next, Prime Minister G. P. Koirala (Congress Party) resigned in the face of a corruption scandal. Newly appointed prime minister Sher Bahadur Deuba and Maoist leader Prachanda called for peace talks, and the first round started. A ceasefire began in July, leading to two sequences of talks in August and September. They broke down after Maoists released 26 police officers and the government did not reciprocate. After more violence, talks were renewed briefly in November, only to lead to a declaration of a state of emergency when the government issued the Terrorist and Destructive Activities Control and Punishment Ordinance, limiting many rights, including freedom of expression, freedom of the press, and freedom from preventive detention, and named the Maoists "terrorists." The Maoists later requested further talks, but the government insisted they lay down arms and give up violence first.

The crucial issue was said to be the management of the arms possessed by the Maoists. Nepal's proposal has it that the Maoists surrender their weapons under surveillance by the UN.[70] All those that have reviewed these talks agree that they were poorly organized, that the roles of mediators sometimes were confused with those of negotiators, and that the role of the king was too diffuse to be meaningful. In talks with the facilitators for the peace talks, they maintained very clearly that they had had no clear mandate from the king, even after they had requested a written mandate, and thus did not know the limits and bounds for the talks.[71] The Maoists claim that their (PLA) military acted as advisers during the talks, but that the RNA military had not accepted the PLA as officers—only as renegade bandits. The Maoists asked for royal inclusion in the talks: "'There is no uniform voice on the state side Bahdur Mahara,' politburo member of the CPN (M) said (during the talks). "'Various interests are playing within the government.'"[72] There was also no precise agreement on monitoring of the ceasefire, which led to obvious troop movements on both sides, as they took advantage of the ceasefire conditions.

## Second Round of Peace Talks, 2003

The second round of official peace talks began in a rather unexpected way. After dismissing Prime Minster Deuba, stating that he was incompetent (in his peace efforts), King Gyanendra sent an emissary, the minister for physical planning and RNA colonel Naryan Singh Pun, for highly secret talks—even India seems to have been kept out of the loop. This resulted in the ceasefire announced on 29 January 2003. A 22-point "code of conduct" was later agreed to (on 13 March), essentially as military ground rules while peace negotiations proceeded.[73] However, even at the beginning, each side accused the other of persistent violations, and maintained that sufficient independent verification was not in place. Originally the Maoist demand was that the RNA should remain within barracks and not be deployed inside the country. The royal side insisted that the PLA should first lay down their weapons before further talks could continue. Both demands were later dropped.

The Maoists were by now openly holding meetings in Kathmandu and elsewhere for the first time, and at first the atmosphere seemed optimistic: the Maoists publicly stated that they wanted the monarch to play a role both in the talks and as a constitutional head in the new state.[74] As later reiterated, "Dr. Baburam Bhattarai, one of the two top rebel leaders who also heads the rebels' talks team, said at the time that the rebels wanted Nepal to be a republican state but are open to compromise with the monarchy on its role."[75] Initially, Gyanendra continued his role as an "active monarch," and proposed the following 7-point agenda for peace: (1) national consensus; (2) peace and security; (3) corruption control; (4) people-oriented administration; (5) national solidarity; (6) free and fair elections; (7) an all-party government.[76] This was later set aside in the royal takeover in 2005. Even at the time this agenda was seen as too loose and not specific with regards to control of the army and the role of the king. In an interview granted to *Time Magazine Asia*,[77] the king appeared not to accept a role as constitutional monarch, but only as an "active one."

Yet between January and May 2003 government officials seem to have been very forthcoming. On 9 May they agreed to restrict the RNA to a five-kilometer restraining order in relation to barracks. On the other hand, they appeared to lose the connection with the RNA, which Colonel Pun had represented, and the RNA may even have boycotted and subverted the talks. Later the government had to retract from the 5-km agreement. From then on, Maoist demands centered only on a one-point agenda, insisting on a constituent assembly to put the vote to the people on the issue of monarchy and control over the army. Not surprisingly, the king had no wish for a vote as to his own role, not least because his popularity was uncertain after the palace massacre and after he had changed one prime minister after another.

Many observers agree that the peace process was then stalled by the royal side.[78] But the actual breakdown was precipitated by unilateral action taken by the Maoists on 27 August 2003, after seven months of ceasefire and three rounds of talks. While the Maoists had been able to keep their cadres in the "peace fold," they could not continue without any realistic prospects of power-sharing. The day after the ceasefire broke down, the Maoists targeted two RNA colonels and killed the highest-ranking soldiers so far targeted. As the political parties felt that they had not been included in the peace process, they had set out on peace talks on their own. The most famous set of such talks was that between the two CPN parties. On 12 September 2003, the Maoist leader Prachanda announced his refusal to talk to "a puppet regime," after having put so much pressure on this regime to initiate peace talks. The sincerity of both sides in seeking a political solution was once again in doubt.

## The Lucknow Peace Talks Between Communist Blocs

Feeling left out of the political process, the nonviolent parties, the Congress Party, the RPP and the CPN-UML have all tried to broker agreements with the Maoists and through such efforts gain political momentum. It was the talks between the two largest communist parties that achieved most: formal meetings were held with Party heads themselves, and not only through intermediaries, as had been the case with other efforts. On 19 November 2003, Madav Kumar Nepal, party chairman of CPN-UML, together with two other central committee members of his party—Yuba Raj Gyawali and Govinda Koirala—dismissed their bodyguards and set off for the Indian city of Lucknow. At an undisclosed site in Lucknow they met with Maoist leaders including Prachanda, Battarai, Mahara, and others, according to personal information from M. K. Nepal. Nepal/UML subsequently proposed a peace plan (10 January 2004), which according to him incorporated the wishes of the two Communist parties. Later M. K. Nepal also briefed the king on his mission. Maoist leader Krishna Bahadur Mahara, however, went public and disassociated the Maoist movement from the proposal, not wanting to bind them to a closed agenda with the UML. Then, against all odds, M. K. Nepal's Communist Party joined the king's "coalition government" in June 2004.[79] With that, talks with the Maoists broke down totally.[80] The agenda document that resulted from the Lucknow meeting remains, however, probably the closest one can come to an acceptable peace plan or road map. Maoists for the foreseeable future were likely to see any appointed government as "puppet regimes for the king"—thus a future peace plan would have to originate with the king.

As the king took overt personal power in February 2005, his appointees proclaimed that now "peace talks would be easier" as the criterion of royal direct involvement had been met. The Maoists answered by saying that they would not talk to a dictator and supported the jailed political party leaders, presumably attempting to establish a united front between themselves and the democratic political parties. With the royal takeover, the jailing of all party leaders, the censorship of the press, and the limitations posed on e-mail and phones, it is hard to say what will take place. However, local Maoists in the Terai today walk more openly with their arms in daylight as they feel they have more support among other party affiliates everywhere. As the earlier governments only had to contend with the Nepalese Maoist problem, the king will now confronts all the political parties and the international opinion.

## A Long-Term Conflict

With more than 12,000 dead and a continuous struggle since 1996, the insurgency in Nepal ranks as one of the most enduring conflicts in Asia. Battles between the two armies have resulted in perhaps as many as 1,000 casualties per incident, and traditional guerrilla warfare and hit-and-run methods have become mixed with attacks between clearly defined territorial armies. The fact that the rebels can claim so much of the national territory and that security is no longer guaranteed makes the state vulnerable. Some observers have already started to call it "a failing state," both economically[81] and in security.

The impact of political violence on the people in general has been twofold. There is a sense of dread and despair as the armed forces of both sides retaliate against the civilian population, and as they feel dragged into violence, which they would rather not take part in. The particular gruesome tactic of using the local population as human shields in Maoist attacks and the fear of retaliation from the RNA make people feel squeezed between the two sides. People have been leaving the rural countryside to become internal refugees in Kathmandu or are leaving the country altogether. Prices are soaring on land and housing in the capital, with real estate prices increasing as much as 100 percent in the two past years.[82] People are "voting with their feet," in search of a peaceful life and new livelihoods elsewhere. As the war hits industry and the tourism business, traditional sources of income are dwindling and poverty is felt by larger and larger segments of the population. This again plays into the hands of the Maoists.

## Effects of Political Change and External Events

The Maoists during the peace talks utterly rejected the label of "international terrorists" that has been applied to their organization both internationally[83] and in Nepal. This label was disregarded during the talks—the government could not be seen as negotiating with terrorists—but later reapplied. Cash bounties on the heads of Maoist leaders have since been retracted.[84] Since such labeling makes the moderate Maoists lose ground—"you are all terrorists, so we cannot talk to you"—it would be prudent to avoid such labeling.

## Impediments to Settlement

Policies targeting the insurgency in Nepal have largely failed. King Gyanendra and his appointed cabinet have not come up with an agenda that can lead to peace. Enjoying the backing of the United States, Britain, and India, they seem to be in no hurry to proceed with further talks. For now it seems that a military solution is the principal choice of the king, the military, and the Maoists. That the government is not democratically elected and has changed four times in three years undermines the prospects of a peace process: the Maoists are not willing to "talk to puppets." A message conveyed to me in the summer of 2004 from the Maoists explained that "total war" had been launched and that no talks would be possible. Maoist hard-liners now want to press toward the capital. The military strategist Ram Bahadur Thapa, alias Badal, with training from Russia, Chechenya, or Libya,[85] is rumored to lead the total war.

Since the king has so far refused to allow the involvement of outside parties this has put the diplomatic professionalism of previous as well as potential new peace talks into question. U.S. ambassador James F. Moriarty held the same view: "Addressing a talk programme in the capital recently, Moriarty ruled out the need for any third party mediation in the Nepal conflict. He, however, said India had a big role to play in (resolving the conflict in) Nepal, according to reports."[86] Both the UN and the Commission of the European Union have volunteered to assist in the process toward peace,[87] Norway has had requests for its good offices,[88] and its ambassador Tore Toreng has said that Norway can "think for mediation."[89] But as the two warring sides have not reached a mutual agreement to talk, the prerequisites for mediation or internationally led peace mediation are not there. While the Maoists have accepted UN intervention—without, however, apparently taking any steps forward to make peace possible—the government has presented its case to the UN, appealing for understanding and for continued economic support, while at the same time referring to India with regard to "third-party" intervention. The role of India in any way forward would be crucial, but historical differences have long legacies.

The British conquered India, but they never conquered Nepal. If the United States discontinues its support for the king, the Nepalese fear that Hindu-dominated India may invade (or help the king to remain in power by putting Indian soldiers on Nepalese soil). Compared with that prospect, a compromise with the Maoists seems a better solution to most Nepalese. The Maoists have indicated that involving India in the fight will force them to use terrorist methods: "Maoists have warned to use suicide bombers to attack Indian leaders if India went ahead with its plan to provide military assistance to Nepal, BBC Nepali service news broadcast citing hand written pamphlets pasted on walls in Jhulaghat of Pithoragarh district said Wednesday."[90]

Constructive Indian involvement may be crucial, but the path toward peace may also become more difficult if the intervention is only through the military and not through a peace mission aimed at ending the war through dialogue. India has its own Maoist groups to consider, and the conflict may become regional rather than local: "The [military] training might bring a halt to the ongoing negotiations between the Andhra Pradesh state government and People's War Group (PWG) as intelligence agencies believe that PWG along with the Maoist Communist Centre and other revolutionary outfits have tied up with Nepal's Maoists to carve out a Compact Revolutionary Zone, including Bihar, Orissa, Chhatisgarh and Andhra Pradesh insurgents, the daily added.[91]

Unlocking the existing stalemate, and preventing either an outright Maoist victory or an Indian intervention to prop up an unpopular king, requires seven injunctions to be followed by international and domestic players. First, in the future the two armies' leaders must be incorporated in talks after properly monitored ceasefire operations are put in place. Second, a comprehensive negotiating process is required to build truly inclusive political institutions. Ethnic leaders and outcaste group leaders must be incorporated in talks—and an upper houses should be considered in Parliament for such groups). Third, human rights issues must be put high on the agenda; abuses by both armies must be monitored internationally. Fourth, professional international mediation and advice on the running of negotiations is needed. Fifth, a tailored economic aid package is essential to build confidence and consolidate any future ceasefires. Sixth, the role of king and Parliament must be made clear, the king must take part in talks, and the democracies of the U.S., UK, and India should consider why they are locked into supporting one of the last absolutist monarchies—and thereby enabling a Maoist insurgency to entrench itself in Nepal. Last, the U.S. and India encourage peaceful dialogue and reconsider the logic of their "counterterrorism" diplomacy, which currently assists the hard-line Maoists.

## Glossary

*bandh*: General strike mostly affecting traffic and commercial life, a strategy used by the Maoists to close down access to towns and town life.

*bhote*: Term predominantly used to describe the Buddhists in Nepal

Congress Party: Nepalese party affiliated with the social-democratic movement in Europe with close ties to the party of the same name in India. It has formed the government for most of the time since the 1990 revolution. The largest party until it split, it is also supposedly the most corrupt.

constituent assembly: An elected body of people with a mandate to redraft the constitution, a prerequisite for further talks by the Maoists.

CPN (M): Communist Party of Nepal, Maoist, the group attempting a revolution in Nepal.

CPN-UML: Communist Party of Nepal, United Marxist-Leninist, at the last elections the largest party in Nepal with representation in Parliament.

Dalit: A group of people in the hills and the Terai who were and are considered by many to be "untouchables."

HLPC: High Level Peace Committee for Peace. Interparty group formed during Prime Minister Deuba's second term, which never produced any results.

*jana sarkar*: Term used by Maoists for "people's government."

Janajati: Tribal groups consisting mainly of Gurungs, Magars, Rais, and Limbus, many of whom were working as soldiers in British and Indian armies.

*kamaiya*: Bonded laborers who inherit the debt of their fathers, accordingly considered as slaves, following the UN declaration of 1964. Debt and "sale" of slaves is at the beginning of the Nepalese new year.

Kilo Shera 2: Police operations against the Maoists in 1998 in the mountain districts of Rolpa and Rukum.

Maobadi: Nepali name for Maoist.

People's War: The Maoist insurrection.

PLA: People's Liberation Army; also known as the People's Revolutionary Army (PRA). The Maoist armed forces.

Prachandra: Nom de guerre for Maoist supreme leader in Nepal, Chhabilal Dahal, renamed in high school Pushpa Kamal Dahal (after the lotus) because of his supposedly high intelligence.

Prachandra Path: A proletarian revolution deemed suitable for Nepal, supposed to be a fusion of the Chinese model (encirclement of towns) and the Russian model (general armed insurrection).

RIM: Revolutionary International Movement, an international organization of communist revolutionaries.

RNA: Royal Nepalese Army.

RPP: Rastriya Prajatantra Party, the royalist party in Nepal, conservatives.

Shining Path: Maoist organization in Peru that was active in the 1980s.

TADA: Terrorist and Destructive Activities Control and Punishment Act from 2001. The act limited many rights, including freedom of expression, freedom of the press, and freedom from preventive detention, and named the Maoists terrorists.

Tharu: An ethnic indigenous group living in Terai, many of whose members, especially in the mid- and far west, have joined the Maoists.

VDC: Village development committee, lowest unit of local government in Nepal

## Timeline

1996: February, the Declaration of People's War and first Maoist attacks at Rukum, Holeri, and Sindhuli police posts.

1998: In May, Prime Minister G. P. Koirala launches "Kilo Sera 2 Operation" against the Maoists. The brutality of the operation is said to have furthered the support for the Maoists.
1998: In October, Maoists announce the establishment of "base areas."
2001: In April, the government announces the Integrated Internal Security and Development Program in Maoist areas. In the 1 June Royal Palace Massacre, the king, queen, princes, and princesses in the Royal line are killed (total 10 persons). The king's brother takes over. In July, Prime Minister Koirala resigns amid talk of large-scale corruption. Sher Bahadur Deuba becomes new prime minister on 21 July and invites Maoists for talk. Government and Maoists declare ceasefire on 25 July. First round of government-Maoist talks begin on 30 August at Godavri resort outside Kathmandu. The second round is held 13–14 September at Thakurdwara, Bardiya (lowland Tarrai)
2002: Third round of talks held 12 January at Godavri. On 19 January Maoist chairman Prachanda declares the end of ceasefire. On 21 January Maoists declares Kendriya Jan Sarkar (central level people's government) ,with Baburam Bhattari as its coordinator. Simultaneously they launch attacks in 24 districts. On 24 January the Deuba government declares a state of emergency, and declares the Maoists "terrorists." On 7 May Deuba meets U.S. president G. W. Bush and gains continued support. On 22 May Deuba dissolves Parliament and announces elections for 13 November. On 26 May he is expelled from his party (Nepali Congress), and subsequently forms his own party (Nepali Congress Democratic). On 4 October King Gyanendra sacks Deuba and assumes executive authority. Elections are postponed indefinitely.
2003: On 28–29 January the Terrorist Red Corner Notice (Interpol) is withdrawn and a ceasefire is declared. On 10 February the Chand government and Maoists agree on a code of conduct for the ceasefire. On 12 March all major political parties (NC, UNL People's Front Nepal, NWPP) agree to launch a joint movement against the royal takeover of 4 October 2002. Chand government-Maoist first round of peace talks begin on 27 April at Hotel Shankar, Kathmandu; the Maoist political agenda is not discussed. At the second round, held 9–10 May, the 5 km rule for troops is discussed but denied. Chand subsequently resigns, blaming absence of support from parties. On 4 June Surya Bahadur Thapa becomes new prime minister. At the third round of talks, 17 August at Nepalgunj (Indian bordertown), the government rejects the Maoist demand for constituent assembly elections. RNA instigates the Doramba case. Talks continue in Hapure, Dang (central Nepal), on 18–19 August; parties agree to meet again, but this never materializes. On 27 August Maoist chairman Prachandra declares end of ceasefire.
2004: In April Deuba is reinstated as prime minister and promises elections and peace talks. In May UML and RPP joins the Deuba government, which becomes a royal appointed government with participation of all major parties except the Koirala/Congress Party. In August Kathmandu is isolated by the Maoists. All roads are blocked.
2005: On 1 February the king sacks Deuba government and assumes executive power as chairman of new ministerial committee. Emergency is declared, and all media, Internet, international phone services are interrupted. All major political party leaders are put under house arrest or in jail.

*Conclusion*

# Understanding and Ending Persistent Conflicts: Bridging Research and Policy

BRENDAN O'LEARY AND ANDREW SILKE

Terrorist actions in insurgencies kill people; on that all agree. They may also inhibit, bias, or simply stop sensible thought among the targets who escape destruction. Sometimes these effects are intended. With minds numbed or outraged, the closure of adversarial debate, argument, and critical policy evaluation often follows, and a war to the death is then proclaimed. Politicians, policymakers, and mass media may respond emotionally to the detriment of reason and prudence. These human responses are not always either humane or the best. Thoughtless, rushed, or outraged responses can be perverse; counterterrorism can be counterproductive and may, according to some, produce worse consequences than that which it targets. Ill-considered reprisals certainly jeopardize the moral and political standing, and security, of the relevant states and their citizens.

The late Dr. Marianne Heiberg, who conceived this volume, but died untimely as it neared completion, recognized these features of contemporary politics. But she was not content to interpret the world correctly; she wanted to change it as best she could. She sought to bridge cross-Atlantic perspectives on appropriate appraisal and democratic policy responses toward violent insurgencies—now generally but loosely collectively labeled as terrorism. She was worried that the United States was increasingly in danger of a long-term intellectual as well as a policy rupture with its Canadian and major European democratic allies.

Dr. Heiberg's credentials for this enterprise were not in doubt. She had a worldwide reputation as an anthropologist of Basque nationalism and had long played the role of an engaged intellectual in the foreign policy of her own country, Norway. Her doctoral supervisor at the London School of Economics, Ernest Gellner, the twentieth century's major theorist of nationalism, proudly used to say that the Oslo Agreement was negotiated in the kitchen she shared with her husband, the Norwegian foreign minister.[1] Dr. Heiberg, Marianne to her friends, lived ten years after the Oslo process was initiated, long enough to see it unravel, to the point where she was prepared to regard it as terminated. She was a realist as well as a constructive thinker, and these traits are found in the contributions she encouraged and that are now published in the preceding chapters. We shall, in her spirit, advance a set of realistic but researched propositions, based on collective deliberations with our case study authors, in the hope that we may bridge the gulf between research and policy and assist both ends of the bridge.

Propositions 1, 2, and 3. *1. The "war of the flea" is almost as old as the hills from which it may be waged. 2. The horrifying consequences of terrorism should not be exaggerated. 3. Powerful conventional armies often fail to defeat insurgencies that use terrorism.*

All our contributors recognize that the use of terror, by insurgents and by governments, is neither novel nor surprising. Many conflicts in the world, on inspection, turn out to be encounters between "state terrorists" and "NGO terrorists." The attacks of 11 September 2001 and the Bush administration's "global war on terror" (GWOT) galvanized American and global attention to the repercussions of terrorist actions, and have prompted extensive debates over appropriate domestic and international policy responses. It is important, however, not to exaggerate the novelty of terrorism, or its scale, either in contemporary international relations or in domestic confrontations between states and insurgents. *Peace and Conflict 2005*, an annual report from the Center for International Development and Conflict Management at the University of Maryland, makes some careful assessments about insurgent terrorism, defined, as it has been understood by all of our contributors, as the intentional targeting of civilian, noncombatant populations:

> Terrorism is a global threat through its possible association with war. *Terrorism as a specialized form of political violence, by itself, is a technique of relatively minor effect.* Very few examples of [the] tactical form of terrorism have caused more than 100 deaths [we have documented 10 such incidents between 1997 and 2004]. The highest fatality count after the 3000 [killed in the 9/11 attacks] is the 330 officially acknowledged deaths attributed to the attack on the school in Beslan, Russia, on September 1 2004. [In] the 1990s [worldwide] there were . . . about 300 reported deaths per annum [from] international terrorism and 3,000 reported deaths per annum by acts of local terrorism. In contrast, according to calculations based on data from the *Armed Conflict and Intervention* project, there were over 300,000 deaths in the world per annum in warfare in the 1990s, the majority of which were deaths among non-combatant populations affected by wars.[2]

These are sobering metrics. Too much can be made of the "dark side of globalization," of "terrorism with global reach," or of "apocalyptic millenarian sacred terror," clichés that fill our airwaves. Insurgent terrorist actions are phenomena presently about 100 times less quantitatively important in killing human beings than recognized warfare. By contrast with the death tolls associated with HIV/AIDS or older illnesses such as malaria, insurgents' terrorist actions may arguably be regarded as lower-order problems for human welfare and global governance, but no one in elected public life is likely to stand by such comparative claims without being exposed to ridicule. It will be said that keeping things in perspective is no comfort to the victims, and, more fairly, that keeping things in perspective should be no cause for complacency. And, of course, the costs of terrorism go beyond those killed and injured, affecting all dimensions of public life.

It bears repeating nonetheless that governments have been grappling with small insurgencies, or "low intensity conflicts."[3] throughout recorded history. It is difficult to find any century in the past two thousand years of European, North African and Asian political systems—which have longer and more sustained historical documentary records than the rest of the planet—which cannot supply at least one example of what today would be described as a guerilla and/or terrorist conflict.[4] "The war of the flea," we might say, is almost as old as the hills from which it is often waged.[5] Nor have insurgents and their allies previously always confined their actions to what might seem the appropriate theater of combat. Acting "out of theater," or with "global reach," is not novel to al-Qaeda's attacks on North America. In 1866 Ireland's Fenians launched two raids on Canada, using veterans from the American Civil War. They were intent on using Canadian territory to bargain for the liberation of Ireland. In 1876 Fenians successfully chartered a ship to sail to western Australia to rescue a group of Fenian prisoners; and in 1881 they commissioned what is now recognized as the first American submarine, the *Fenian Ram*.[6] Were such episodes, remembered by these two Irish authors, fore-runners of terrorism with a global reach? Were they pioneering efforts by nongovernmental organizations to possess deadly weapons that are regarded as properly only possessed by states?

It is just as evident from the historical record that the same state that is formidable in conventional war may prove inept against insurgents that deploy terrorist tactics. Great Britain won World War I with its allies but shortly afterward Lloyd George felt obliged to negotiate a treaty with the IRA's leaders in the ranks of Sinn Féin. Great Britain won World War II with its allies but could not defeat the Irgun in Palestine. The French military won the battle of Algiers, but lost the war over Algeria's status to the FMLN.[7] The British military, usually regarded as the best in Europe, could not defeat the Provisional IRA after 1969, as O'Leary reports here (Chapter 6). The Israeli army, undoubtedly the best in the Middle East, has not been able to eradicate Fatah, Hamas, or numerous other Palestinian insurgent organizations, nor to defeat Hezballah in Lebanon, as Gunning reports (Chapter 5). The U.S. military, the world's premier fighting forces, obliterated Iraq's Ba'thist regime's formal war machine with ease, but have responded much less effectively to insurgencies led by Ba'thists, Wahhabists, and jihadists primarily recruited from the formerly dominant minority of Sunni Arabs. The U.S. and its allies were able to destroy the armies of Nazi Germany and Imperial Japan in less time than they have spent grappling with al-Qaeda and its off-shoots. These examples almost immediately suggest that insurgencies that use terrorism and that have gathered momentum cannot be easily defeated by strong militaries from democratic states, no matter how much the "gloves are taken off." Political strategy, policy and policing are often more important in ending such insurgencies and the use of terrorism within them.

Proposition 4. *There have been—and there remain—good reasons why the quality of research on terrorism has been—and will be—uneven.*

While guerilla insurgencies and the use of terrorism by insurgents may be of established vintage, systematic research on insurgents, states, and terrorism is more recent and is generally agreed to be uneven, including by its practitioners.[8] Modesty about current and past research and its promise for policy are therefore in order. None of our case authors claim that they have adequately resolved the major difficulties in systematic research in their field, no matter how well they appear to understand their particular cases. The contrast in the intellectual and financial resources devoted to the subject of terrorism is striking by comparison with the scientific, material and economic treasure poured into the preparation, defense against, and fighting of conventional warfare, that is, war between states: "real war" rather than "internal wars." To judge by the data from Maryland's auditors of death and conflict there may well be sound public policy reasons why there should be at least a hundred times less research expenditure on preparation for and defense against insurgents' terrorism than on official or "civil" warfare, but not less than that whatever that figure is.

Effective thinking and planning in response to insurgencies that use terrorism have lagged far behind the application of science to conventional interstate wars. Why might that be the case apart from the fact that the impact of insurgencies that use terrorism rarely comes close to conventional wars in numbers killed or infrastructure destroyed? Occasional rhetoric to the contrary the great powers have not taken terrorism outside their own regimes too seriously before the events of 9/11, Beslan, 3/11 (Madrid), or 7/7 (London). One obvious reason for the neglect of extensive systematic and well-funded research is that insurgencies that use terrorism are usually defeated by incumbent governments. When they are defeated they are usually defeated early; indeed, it bears emphasis that they are often crushed very quickly indeed. Many may try, but few insurgencies succeed in securing organizational maintenance and in sustaining long campaigns. One report in the early 1990s, suggested that 90 percent of terrorist organizations were entirely defeated within the first year of their conflicts.[9] Of the remaining 10 percent of groups, many had endured for long periods, in a few cases stretching over centuries. But in most cases the state, eventually, endured, persevered, and "won." Such data may explain the relative lack of well-funded social scientific research on the subject of insurgencies that use terrorism. It also suggests that comparing insurgencies that "take off" and endure, as opposed to those that are crushed early, may have fruitful implications for understanding and for policy, but that is an agenda for another project because our cases consist solely of insurgencies that "took off."

The 9/11 attacks, organized by al-Qaeda, showed that terrorist attacks can have profound and negative impacts, even on the most powerful state, and the "global war on terror" launched in its aftermath has forcibly raised the question of "what is the best way to respond to terrorism?" The non-American democracies whose elites and publics were inclined to think, despite or because of 9/11, that terrorism was an American issue, largely linked to the repercussions of U.S. foreign policy in the Middle East, have had rude awakenings. The killings of Australian tourists in Bali in October 2002, of commuters and tourists in the Madrid bombings and the London transport bombings of March 2004 and July 2005 respectively, were shocking jolts to the affected citizens and their policymakers—but they had had recent precedents in Algerian actions in Paris in the 1990s. These episodes have ensured that we can expect better-funded research on terrorism and political violence in future—as well as the possibilities of better policy and policy-evaluation. We hope this book is a step in these directions. But there will remain reasons why research in this field will be constricted.

Many democratic governments claim to be interested in "evidence-led" policy, that is, informed and guided by good science, natural or social. But we do not live in technocratic states despite such proclamations. Far from it. Many features of democratic policymaking, good and bad, stand in the way of technocracy. Incumbent party ideology, party competition, media sensationalism and its attendant repercussions (such as media management and manipulation by incumbent politicians), and the felt imperatives of reelection collectively inhibit democratic governments' willingness to be assessed in many policy sectors by fixed indicators of success or failure. That said, policymakers are nominally keen in most domains to get value for money for their inputs. They want to demonstrate positive outcomes from their outputs. They need measures to defend their actions to a varied audience, which can include an electorate, political opposition parties, the press, and foreign governments. That is why governments tend to provide lists of terrorists killed, or arrested, and plots foiled—but less frequently ratios of arrested to convicted, aborted or foiled plots to insurgent operations, or measures recording decisive shifts in public opinion among the insurgents' supporters.

In confronting the use of terrorism by nongovernmental organizations, the first question for democratic policymakers should be "what works?" Given that terrorist networks or organizations are often relatively weak, the truth is that many policies and actions can work in defeating them, but they do not all work equally well, especially when, as here, we study the larger, more enduring, and more successful insurgent organizations that have used terrorist methods. If not all policy to terminate terrorism is equally good, policymakers face difficult choices in developing or proposing policy and will rarely have carte blanche. Among other things, they face real limitations in their budgets, their constitutional and legal traditions, their international relations, and in managing profoundly difficult multi-organizational coordination and implementation. The evidence base is a problem. How does one measure treatments, or success or failure? The evidence needed for good decisions is often lacking and incomplete. It would be sensible if democratic governments could agree to research and publish a set of metrics and task independent agencies with providing data on such matters—and restrain themselves from interfering with such regular reports or indices as such agencies will produce. If it is appropriate to have independent central banks to free monetary policy from the day-to-day temptations of politicians the same protection needs to be provided for security and intelligence assessments. The measures must be public—even if some evaluations may sensibly be temporarily restricted. Shifts in such metrics should be preceded by extensive public debate, and based on efforts to establish a cross-party consensus.[10]

Propositions 5, 6, and 7. *5. Not all contemporary terrorism is new or mandates new paradigms. 6. Don't throw out babies with the bathwater. 7. There is a strong case for field research.*

There has been research on insurgents and their use of terrorist methods that can be used in intelligent democratic antiterrorism policy. It would be extremely premature, as Professor Martha Crenshaw has warned, confidently to assume that worldwide a new terrorism has superseded an old form and to deduce that consequently all research conducted before 9/11 may be safely neglected.[11] The argument that current (Islamist) terrorism is wholly novel in its goals, scope, and degree of nonnegotiability, may seduce some foundations, or publishers, or governments, but it is better treated as a hypothesis. Existing research results should be first appraised and reevaluated in the light of current debates and needs.

That said, our group would be the first to acknowledge that research on terrorism has had a troubled history and has tended to suffer from certain flaws. Too often "research" on terrorism has amounted to pro-administration propaganda, lobbying or advocacy against certain insurgents and their causes, or cheerleading the actions of the authors' favored governments, such as the U.S., UK, or Israel.[12] Bias in many cases can be found in the tacit assumption that Western democratic states have never used terrorist methods in the past, or were formed without the assistance of terrorist methods, or have never sponsored either foreign governments or foreign insurgents who have used terrorist methods. Our authors have sought to avoid these overt biases. More important for credible scholarship there has been a shortage of experienced statistically trained researchers in the field, especially ones with rigorous econometric training. It is almost satirical, but almost true to say, that much of what is written about terrorism in the liberal democracies is written by people who have never met a terrorist, or have never actually spent significant time on the ground in the areas most affected by conflict. Terrorism research has been top-heavy with desk-based accounts, where second-hand conclusions are reached based on media reports, magazine articles, and other published sources. This fact left an opening for a book by a BBC journalist, Phil Rees, pointedly entitled *Dining with Terrorists: Meetings with the World's Most Wanted Militants.*[13]

These critical observations are not intended as an indictment of all desk-based research. Careful framing and analysis of good data can produce important results in all sciences, including the study of insurgents and their methods. Marc Sageman's superb *Understanding Terror Networks* is a tribute to the high caliber of analysis that can be done with public sources, but it is difficult to believe that his work would have been so astute had Sageman not had a career as an experienced U.S. intelligence operative in Afghanistan.[14] Unlike Sageman, the authors of many works on terrorism are often unfamiliar with the protocols of careful statistical reasoning, the existing literature, or the field experience to tell good intelligence or information from the bad. A high proportion of research on terrorism has been produced by transient researchers, individuals who rarely carry out research on terrorism and who then move on to other subjects. A recent survey found that over 80 percent of research articles published on terrorism in the past decade were from "one-timers," writers who wrote only one article in the mainstream terrorism journals during the entire ten-year period.[15] One experienced Israeli researcher, Ariel Merari, has observed that

> The result has been, sometimes, an unexpected fresh look at the issue, which carried a promise of generating a new line of research, but more often it has been a superficial treatment of a singular aspect of the problem, ignorant of the complex and heterogeneous nature of terrorism, at times suffering from factual errors. Usually, a contribution of this kind is well-grounded in the empirical and theoretical findings of the writer's particular area of expertise, but lacking in knowledge on terrorism . . . it seems that the majority of the academic contributions in this area have been done by people whose main research interests lie elsewhere, who felt that they had something to say on this juicy and timely subject.[16]

A review of the literature by Andrew Silke suggests that terrorism research remains very heavily dependent on easily accessible sources of data, and that only a small minority of articles provide substantially new knowledge.[17] Taken as a whole, therefore, terrorism research in most places exists on a diet of "fast food": quick, cheap, ready at hand, and nutritionally dubious, especially in the long run. The reluctance to move away from limited methodologies and levels of analysis has a price tag. While the field may appear to be relatively active and energetic, growth in understanding of several key questions remains stunted, with consequent limitations on the caliber of policy advice that may be rendered.

Properly to understand conflicts in which insurgents use terrorism—and properly to assess what policies will and will not work—requires both good theories and reliable evidence. Worthwhile modeling requires some credible facts, rather than "stylized facts." Reliable evidence can only be supplied by good researchers using good methods. Such work is rarer than we might expect or hope for. A limited range of methodologies in data-gathering, combined with a reluctance to use more rigorous analysis and a shortage of experienced researchers, has left the field with deficiencies. The methods used by most terrorism researchers have essentially been exploratory, and as a result the field struggles to explain terrorism or to provide findings of predictive value. If "the ability to make correct predictions [is] . . . the outstanding characteristic of science," as Milton Friedman and econometricians might agree, then terrorism research has generally failed.[18]

There are no compelling reasons to be confident that this situation may improve.[19] Perhaps there are good epistemological reasons for the difficulties: predicting the formation of small groups and which ones will mushroom and then endure as long-term insurgencies is no easy modeling task. The aspiration to make "point predictions" in a field like this may be an example of hubris. Network analysis, epidemiological modeling,[20] or agent-based simulations may help us produce better forecasts, but the calls for large expenditures in support of the social, behavioral and economic sciences may fall on deaf or skeptical ears.[21]

The case study chapters here do not suffer from some of the limitations and failings of some research on terrorism and low intensity conflict. The researchers are neither novices nor only fleetingly interested in the conflict they report. In each case, the writer has spent at least a decade studying the conflict in which there has been at least one insurgent organization using violence. They have lived for extended periods in the regions involved, are able to speak the local language(s), have had access to militants, volunteers, and their immediate communities of belonging, including individuals at the most senior leadership levels. They have had access to those in government and in the security sectors combating the insurgents. None of our writers are armchair philosophers or just desktop analysts. They have trekked through deserts, mountains. and jungles, driven along modern roads, walked in slums, or lived in refugee camps, wartorn streets, or bad hotels and guesthouses in ruined towns. They have been threatened and harassed and in some cases targeted. They have been to where the action is, seen the reality of low intensity conflict, and interviewed those directly involved in (or indeed directing) the campaigns of violence. They harbor no illusions about the conflicts they write about. The first hand experience and insight they bring to the analysis is at least as good as the best journalism—their work flows from longer engagements than most journalists are able to develop, they are mostly social scientists, and they are under no immediate obligations to deliver "stories."

Our writers, though, are not simply excellent field researchers. They are familiar with the works of other academics and writers on their specific conflict and are among the best placed to judge the relative strengths and weaknesses of this literature. They should be the type of people one might want to be briefed by or take advice from if one is a non-area expert. They should be helpful to those who wish to build or evaluate a model or general theory. The strengths of their chapters do not end there. Most research on terrorism is rushed and suffers as a result. Opinion dominates; difficult research, like interviewing militants, is often avoided. The chapters in this collection try to avoid these weaknesses. The chapters themselves were not rushed, and we have not sought to bring them right up to date, which would involve endless tinkering. The process of commissioning and pulling the work together took three years. The contributors met on three separate occasions for closed three-day conferences to discuss each case study in detail, to examine progress on the research, and to discuss what generalizations seemed to hold—or not. We exchanged ideas and arguments by e-mail. Even our book's title is the result of an extended debate. Each chapter is therefore the result of the writer's own extensive experience, knowledge, and insight, but also of extensive review by highly qualified peers. The support of the SSRC and the NUPI, and the evaluation process organized by Dr. Heiberg, make possible significant confidence in these case materials.

## The Evidence from Case Studies and the Prospect of Policy Lessons

Having highlighted the value of these case chapters, we can ask what generalizations and policy lessons they sanction. An initial caveat is required before we hazard a response. All of the case studies emphasize that understanding their conflict requires awareness of its particular political context and time to immerse oneself in that context. It is dangerous to assume that a new conflict is similar to a familiar one, or that the patterns one has seen before will automatically be repeated again; but it is just as facile to assume that every case is *sui generis.* Governments and their advisors are notoriously quick to forget the lessons of history, but we must be careful to emphasize that not all lessons work equally well everywhere, and that the wrong lessons are often learned from cases. We do not counsel despair, however; we disagree with the claim that the only lesson that history has to teach is that there are none to be taught. But no conflict reported here is straightforward; all are the products of root causes, organizational resilience, and strategic responses that have produced distinct pathways to conflict between insurgents and states.

Governments respond to terrorism by insurgents and low intensity conflicts with a range of approaches. They usually attempt to deal with the onset of conflict by using existing measures to exert order and control, to emphasize that they are the monopolists of the legitimate use of publicly organized force. Frequently these approaches prove adequate to the situation and the problem is managed. The threat is eliminated, or reduced to a broadly acceptable level, its sources are "nipped in the bud." In none of the cases considered here did this scenario develop. In each case, the available responses for control failed, and governments felt forced to take extraordinary measures. In such circumstances, informed, expert advice takes on great importance, and policymakers should be interested in lessons that can be usefully applied from the experiences of other countries (and indeed even from the lessons of their own country's past).

What then are the lessons of our case studies? We shall first address causation debates. Two propositions, 8 and 9, confirm the well-established results of others. Two further propositions, 10 and 11, by contrast reject or qualify some presently fashionable arguments.

Proposition 8. *Those who employ terrorist methods are normally normal, and have learned to see themselves as soldiers.*

Those willing to plan or use terrorist methods in the service of a political idea are generally representative of the constituencies they claim to represent and, normally, normal. Our authors concur with this insufficiently known but well-established research result.[22] Insurgents who use terrorist methods are not, in general, deranged, demonic, or deeply disturbed. They act out of group honor, group commitment and out of a sense of group-service, in addition to their normal individual or self-centered motivations. They use the normal justifications associated with just war doctrines, whether these are organized in religious, secular nationalist, or class frames. They justify violence, insurgency—and terrorism—morally and strategically. Equally, however, the initiation and recruitment of people into insurgent organizations that use terrorism are not an immediate or overnight process: terrorists are made by history, they don't just attempt to make history. Usually there is a gradual process of radicalization before the use of violence can be normalized and seen as "correct." Poor public policy may play a role in that radicalization. Insurgents kill for the same reasons that other groups have killed other groups since time immemorial, that is, they kill for what Professor Clark McCauley, a leading psychologist in research on terrorism and political violence, calls "cause and comrades," for a combination of beliefs and intense small group commitments.[23] It follows that policy (or research) focused on the psychologically "abnormal" is likely pointless, and that public rhetoric on terrorists which stereotypes them as madmen, psychopaths, and lunatics is not likely to aid understanding or sensible policy. Instead, there should be a recognition that "terrorists are normal" and that insurgent organizations mimic and try to become like official armies, that is, to connect a larger group cause (of the nation or the religion or political goals) with the small group loyalties and dynamics that can deliver individuals to sacrifice themselves for the cause (but by doing so for their small group). Every insurgency imitates a formal army (or develops one) by persuading recruits that the combat unit is their family, their brothers, and persuading them that to betray their comrades is worse than death. Policy in the case of long-run insurgencies therefore has to address how to demobilize people who regard themselves as soldiers, whose constituencies see them as such, and who may be trained, like soldiers, to avoid leaking information and to resist interrogation. It would seem to follow that pure criminalization strategies are not likely to work.

Proposition 9. *Insurgents have constituencies, within which they seek both legitimacy and control.*

Consistent with other findings, the sustained insurgencies reported here have all, at least initially, been rooted in "communities of belonging" or "constituencies," within which they have sought to establish and maintain their legitimacy, and of which they have sought to become the army. The target constituency has included those who rate the value of the cause highly, and those who do not, and those who reject violence as well as those who support it. Policymakers usually eventually realize that winning the battle of ideas may be as important as the use of weapons in keeping the insurgents from monopolizing the representation of their constituency. Repressive policies may backfire to the advantage of the insurgents.

Some of the worst, most intense, and least highlighted terrorist violence of insurgents takes place against rivals within their own constituencies. Sometimes it is aimed at establishing hegemony within the constituency, either through targeting rivals—as when the LTTE sought to establish itself as the sole spokesperson of the Tamils of Sri Lanka, or through the competitive demonstration of military superiority to potential rivals—as with the Provisional IRA's takeover from the Official IRA, or with the JKHM's displacement of the JKLF. Sometimes violence by insurgents is intended to deter defection from the constituency to their rivals or to the authorities. Shining Path killed more than 80 persons, men, women and children, in a massacre in Lucanamara to deter villagers from supporting progovernment militias, "to make them understand that we were a hard bone to chew, and that we were ready to do anything, anything."[24] The PKK killed teachers of Turkish, even if they were Kurds. ETA, GAM, Hamas, Hezballah, the IRA, the LTTE, the PKK, FARC, and Shining Path have all killed informers or suspected informers. In doing so, they have not merely been protecting themselves, but attempting to establish themselves as the monopolist of security within their constituency.

The use of terrorist violence therefore is usually part of a battle for ascendancy within a constituency as well as a strategic choice against a regime. The implications for policy of this finding are not, however, straightforward. Policymakers may face a choice between making their own force more fearsome and credible (to deter the target constituency from supporting the insurgents), recruiting or encouraging "a third force" (on which more will be said), or allowing insurgents to fight among themselves, in the hope that that will weaken them, or alienate them from their constituency. In the case of Shining Path the initial fearsome repression of the Peruvian army completely backfired. Only later, after Shining Path had repulsed its own potential constituency—by seeking to terminate farmers' markets, conscripting recruits and imposing youthful cadres as authorities in villages—was the Peruvian army able to conduct an effective, targeted and successful counterinsurgency. Constituencies may independently temper the actions of rebel organizations, a phenomenon that sensible governments exploit

Proposition 10. *There is no obvious distinctive association between religion and the use of terrorist violence.*

In our cases, the proportionally bloodiest insurgents have had secular goals and leaders. Our four Marxist (three Maoist) insurgencies, those led by the FARC, the PKK, Nepal's PLA-CPN(M), and PCP-SL (Sendero Luminoso), have been especially bloody, but not religious.. The secular nationalists of the LTTE pioneered and used suicide bombings and suicide units before Hezballah and Hamas. The regimes these groups have fought have been religious (Nepal's Hindu kingdom), religiously biased (Buddhism is privileged in Sri Lanka), or secular (Colombia, Peru, and Turkey). Secularized, not religious Muslims have led GAM and the PKK. Secularized Catholics and Marxist-influenced figures have been prominent in the nationalist insurrections of ETA and the IRA.

This quick review does not, of course, support the converse proposition, namely that the religiously motivated are quietist and peaceful while secular, agnostic and atheistic insurgents are more disposed toward violence.

Catholics, Protestants, Jews, Buddhists, Hindus and Muslims have very bellicose as well as pacific histories, and we suspect no reader requires citations to be convinced on this point. Islamists have, it is true, currently been dominant or strongly influential among Hezballah, Hamas, and the JKHM in Kashmir. But, of interest, two of these organizations are parts of national liberation causes (those of Kashmir and Palestine), and they regard themselves and are regarded by others as more hard-line exponents of those causes, which explains at least part of their appeal. Hezballah has increasingly become a champion of Shi'a interests (secular and religious) within Lebanon, as Gunning reports (Chapter 5), rather than the messianic vanguard of international Shi'a Islam. In short, these three organizations owe a considerable degree of their strength in their constituencies to their national and ethnic ties, and their national and ethnic policies, as Jeroen Gunning and Sumantra Bose affirm (Chapters 4, 5, 7).

These findings of our authors replicate those of other researchers. Many groups that have used terrorism since World War II have been radical socialist groups with no religious agendas: the Red Brigades in Italy, the Baader-Meinhof Gang and the Red Army Faction in Germany, or the Weathermen in the U.S.. The anarchists and the Animal Liberation Front in the UK are not religious. Atheistic communism and the nation can galvanize groups to become insurgents and to employ terrorism, which is simply not the preserve of exponents of sacred violence, let alone of Muslims.

Conflicts between states and insurgents may indeed reinforce previously existing cultures, or the barriers between them, whatever these may be. This fixing or hardening of identities may not just be the product of those who are leading the conflict, but an existential reaction, with psychological roots. The same Professor McCauley we quoted earlier emphasizes that "Dozens of experiments have shown that thinking about our own death leads us to embrace more strongly the values of our culture" ("terror management theory").[25] Our cases, in short, suggest it is premature, at best, to assume that there is—or should be—a global war with a unified phenomenon of Islamic terrorism. There is an international extensively Sunni Islamist jihadist network, or a cluster of such networks. But many of the causes in which the clusters participate have nationalist or ethnic underpinnings (in Palestine, Kashmir, Chechnya, and the Philippines). Or, they try to root themselves in particular Sunni Muslim communities (among Arabs in Iraq and Saudi Arabia, and the Pashtun in Afghanistan). Or, in the grievances of unintegrated immigrant populations (e.g., among some Muslim immigrants in the states of the European Union). For policy purposes, it is vital to distinguish these contexts in which the jihadist networks try to grow themselves. What is left of al-Qaeda may have ambitions to establish a global caliphate, but it should not follow that U.S. or EU policy should treat all Islamist violence as cut from the same cloth, or as appropriate for identical treatment everywhere. There have been Muslim-minority nationalist rebellions against Muslim-majority regimes (in Kurdistan in Iraq and Iran, in Aceh in Indonesia, and in Afghanistan), as well as Muslim-minority rebellions against non-Muslim majority regimes (in China, Philippines, and India). These observations do not underestimate the gravity of recent Islamist urban terrorism in the U.S., UK, Spain, or the Netherlands, but they counsel against seeing them through the prism of a "clash of civilizations." The shared spectacles of a Harvard professor and Osama bin Laden do not offer the most accurate vision of reality.

Proposition 11. *Causes matter more than "greed" in initiating insurgencies; "supply-side explanations" may help explain the duration of insurgent organizations, but not their origins, their ceasefires, or their termination.*

None of our cases significantly support the "supply-side explanations" of insurgent or rebel violence popularized by Professor Paul Collier of the World Bank and his colleagues, whose publications are referenced in the introduction by Brendan O'Leary and John Tirman. ETA, GAM, Hamas, the IRA, the JKLF, the LTTE, and the PKK were formed by people influenced by nationalist and leftist doctrines, and they understood themselves to be acting in response to the repression, conquest, partition or maltreatment of their nations. The relevant case studies show, briefly, why they believed what they believed. The leaders of the Tamil Tigers were part of the cohort of Tamils who suffered exclusion from educational and job opportunities as a result of coercive Sinhala-only laws in Sri Lanka; the IRA's fresh stock of volunteers in 1969–1971, and its future leaders, included people mobilized in protest at the denial of equal citizenship to cultural Catholics in Northern Ireland and subsequently repressed by the local police; ETA was formed to respond to Franco's repression of the Basque nation; and so on. One does not need to accept that the causes articulated by these insurgents were all fair complaints or correctly understood (let alone argue that resorting to violent insurgent conduct was their optimal rational choice in the circumstances) in order to accept that the relevant reasons for violence were believed, and that these beliefs mattered in explaining the onset and maintenance of the respective mobilizations.

Likewise, class-based injustices, often understood through the frame of Marxist theories, were invoked by the rural insurgencies in our case studies (in Colombia, Turkish Kurdistan, Nepal, and Peru). Class-based injustices also account for some of the support initially enjoyed by these organizations. Marc Chernick (Chapter 9) suggests that Shining Path's initial base of support was built in the parts of the Andes least reached by the radical land reforms of the 1968 government; Doğu Ergil (Chapter 10) maintains that the PKK mobilized in a still feudal environment, and Harald Skar (Chapter 11) has much the same to say about the mobilization of the Nepalese Maoists. In Colombia, Chernick (Chapter 2) explains that the FARC emerged from an earlier period of political violence in the 1940s and 1950s where several peasant communities rejected an elite power-sharing accord excluding third parties and refused to hand in their arms. Similarly, religious convictions, combined with communal grievances about the treatment of their communities, were vital in assisting the formation of Hezballah in Lebanon and the JKHM in Kashmir. Both also enjoyed significant international sponsorship, from Iran and Pakistan respectively.

These observations do not imply that our authors naively believe that "grievances" are necessary and sufficient to explain the existence and maintenance of insurgent organizations that use terrorism. They are certainly not all exponents of "relative deprivation" explanations of violence. To the contrary. In general our case authors support economic reforms or economic development for their own sake, not because they think that antipoverty programs are magic bullets to terminate terrorist temptations. The collectively agreed observation of our authors was that there have to be niches of injustice to exploit if what the Collier school calls "violence entrepreneurs" are to make any headway. We also rejected, on the basis of our cases, the view that explanation should be limited to the choices of greed or grievance. Political sociologists and psychologists have long advanced beyond this contrast in debates over the salience of relative deprivation, resource mobilization, and opportunity structures to account for the formation of illegal or radical social movements and the use of violence.[26] Policy errors by governments, including those who supported some of our groups against their rivals (e.g., as Israel supported Hamas's development to weaken the PLO), or the overuse and misuse of repression were in some of our cases regarded as equally important in explaining who got mobilized and which organizations got entrenched.

None of our authors reported that material incentives for leaders—"greed," in the form of pecuniary advantages or lootable resources—were critical in initiating these insurgencies, or in subsequently maintaining them through the pay-off of cadres with lucre. The leaders of ETA, Hamas, Hezballah, the IRA, JKLF, JKHM, LTTE, PKK, FARC, or Nepal and Peru's Maoists have not led luxurious lifestyles, nor have their volunteers or cadres, including their forcibly conscripted cadres. The leaders of GAM, on Schulze's account (Chapter 3), were hard-liners in constitutional negotiations because of their secure status in Sweden, not because of their control over lootable resources or pecuniary stakes in conflict. The FARC is the most notorious of the organizations reported here for extracting rents from coca and cocaine production, but it is difficult to read this development, on Chernick's account (Chapter 2), as other than opportunistic conduct to support its long insurrection, as opposed to its raison d'être. He accepts, of course, that FARC may morph into a merely criminal enterprise; he does not suggest that it is one now. Closing down coca production will lead the FARC to diversify its sources of revenue rather than to end its struggle. (Incidentally, our group observed that too few economists draw the conclusion that it is the demand habits of U.S. drug-users that are the real cause of Colombian drug production that in turn has fueled the Colombian conflict.) The FARC, of course, has engaged in kidnapping and other criminal forms of resource mobilization, but the sums it extracts are almost exclusively committed to maintaining a large army and pursuing the insurgents' mission, as Chernick reports. He also notes that Shining Path extracted revenues by offering its protection services to coca producers, and indeed likens its growth to an "armed trade union" for them. But he insists that the price of coca and the scope of guerrilla activity are not causally related and that Shining Path's demise had little to do with the collapse of the price of coca or the U.S. war on drugs.

Our cases, naturally, show considerable variation in the extraction of resources to finance insurgencies, in the degrees of ruthlessness and ingenuity displayed by rebels, and in the degree to which the constituency of belonging was subjected to predatory behavior or complied with some degree of consent. But it should not be news or regarded as profound to argue that criminal actions sustain insurgents just as taxes sustain governments. Many could have told the World Bank that for free. Nor is it news to policymakers that cutting insurgents' capacities to raise resources is a sensible goal if they wish to weaken them. But that is much easier said than done, and such policies may backfire. Cracking down on voluntary contributions, especially from diasporas, or regulating informal banking systems used by migrants, may create new and less easily monitored channels of funding, increase the scale of resort to other criminal methods of finance, and damage the welfare of the innocent.[27] Neither Hamas nor Hezballah raises "taxes"; like others in our case studies, they enjoy foreign state sponsorship and diaspora support.

It was the shared view of our case study authors that the Collier school at best overgeneralizes from some West African and Great Lakes cases (that were not examined by us) and, at worst, overgeneralizes from the obvious point that insurgent groups, by definition, are illegal, and therefore likely to finance themselves by illegal means. Correlation, however, is not causation. Only the most romantic of analysts, curiously not named, could be accused of believing that insurgencies live entirely off voluntary donations from their cadres and constituencies. Just as governments tax because citizens would not supply enough voluntary donations to provide public goods, so insurgents claim to be entitled to tax—as proof of their status as a government in embryo, or as the way of eliminating free-riding within their constituents. In general our results suggest that insurgents can maintain themselves at low costs—they can live cheaply as O'Leary reports of the IRA (Chapter 6), but when well financed by the diaspora they can also organize something approximating a navy, as O'Duffy reports of the Tamil Tigers (Chapter 8).

By contrast, our case authors had fewer quibbles with the claims of James Fearon and David D. Laitin, also summarized in the introduction. Nearly all our conflicts were initiated before the end of the Cold War. Our insurgencies took place in both culturally homogeneous and heterogeneous milieus. "Rough terrain" obviously helped Shining Path, Kashmir's insurgents, the FARC, the PKK, and Nepal's Maoists. But it can't explain the endurance of the IRA, ETA, or Hamas. Fearon and Laitin's treatment of "poverty"—which they see as favoring insurgency because it suggests the state will be weakly resourced—was not universally accepted. The UK, Spain, and Israel do not display poverty in the relevant regard. All our authors thought that Fearon and Laitin failed to model the state the way they modeled insurgents—which suggested theoretical inconsistency—and that their approach, like Collier's, was too quick to reject (or neglect) insurgents' narratives of their own causes and grievances. There is no good a priori or well-founded empirical reason to suggest that "supply" matters more than "demand" in explaining the formation or the maintenance of insurgent organizations.

Propositions 8–11 largely dealt with the causation of insurgent organizations, and their maintenance. We now turn to what our case authors thought about policies that targeted insurgents, to assess what worked to reduce terrorism, or to bring it to an end, and why. Overall, eight broad policy instruments were observed, from which some circumspect conclusions are drawn. Outlining these we shall draw attention to where the lesson appeared to have no relevance, was not used, or else failed when it was attempted. In doing so we try to avoid the fallacy of saying "our theory is correct, except in country x."[28] The eight policy approaches we observed that seemed to matter were constitutional, legal emergencies, repression, incarceration, media management, negotiation, democratization, and internationalization.

Proposition 12. *Constitutional reconstruction of the regime, or engagement with the insurgents' own constitutions, may help terminate conflicts; conversely, constitutional rigidity may block the prospects for political settlements and peace processes.*

In our cases constitutional amendments have not played a significant role in most governments' reactions to serious insurgencies that have used terrorism. In most cases the constitutions of the affected states have remained unaltered. The most significant exception to this rule among our cases is Northern Ireland, as reported by O'Leary. As part of a multifaceted peace process to resolve the conflict in the 1990s, both the UK and Ireland introduced constitutional amendments in 1998. The UK abolished the Government of Ireland Act of 1920 and recognized the right of the Irish people—albeit in two jurisdictions—to self-determination. Ireland reciprocated proposing and passing a referendum that led to the amendment of

Articles 2 and 3 of its constitution (the original wording had made an irredentist claim to sovereignty over Northern Ireland). These were constitutional changes, but part of a wider political settlement and peace process. They had been preceded by a pathbreaking 1985 agreement between the UK and Irish governments intended to manage their relations over Northern Ireland and to encourage an internal power-sharing settlement among moderates. In fact the two governments eventually successfully managed both constitutional change—involving consociational, federal and confederal features—and a peace process including significant hard-liners. Political engagement and electoral incentives worked to transform the conflict, as O'Leary has shown elsewhere with others.[29] In the course of this story the IRA's own internal constitution had to be amended and reinterpreted to permit it to support these transformations, and eventually, as predicted by O'Leary, to organize its own disarmament and dissolution. Here constitutional transformation and engagement worked, though, of course, it does not tell the whole story.

This case, of course, seems like a radical outlier. So does it have any significance for the other cases? Our group answered, in general, "yes," especially for nationalist conflicts. The IRA, like ETA, GAM, Hamas, JKLF, JKHM, LTTE, and PKK, has been motivated by national self-determination. Self-determination conflicts can be read as intrinsically zero-sum, and frequently they become so. But power-sharing (be they consociational, federal, or co-sovereignty) arrangements may facilitate effective and honorable compromises in which more than one nation can believe that new institutions reflect a free choice of political status and achieve sufficient recognition for their peoples.

The Kashmir conflict, as Bose reports, is the unfinished legacy of an unresolved self-determination dispute that arose during the partition of India. It is difficult to see how it can be resolved except through constitutional negotiations that provide some role for popular consent by the people(s) of Kashmir, as well as modifications in India's and Pakistan's constitutions. India's constitutional rigidity on Kashmir's status is at least part of what blocks a negotiated settlement—as does Pakistan's irredentist claim in its constitution. The constitution of the Republic of Turkey (as amended in 2001) has irrevocable provisions, Articles 1, 2 and 3, which by virtue of Article 4 "shall not be amended," "nor shall their amendments be proposed." This has the effect of explicitly prohibiting constitutional alteration of the state's "indivisibility." It blocks any moves to propose a federation (let alone secession). Article 42 constitutionally bans teaching or training in a mother-tongue language other than Turkish—the international treaty exceptions do not cover Kurdish. Article 68 is read as banning federalist or ethnic or minority language parties. It is not the view of our group that merely altering these provisions would have stopped the PKK in its tracks, or would presently lead all its remnants to dissolve. But it is difficult to portray these articles as anything other than obstacles to a peaceful and democratic resolution of the Kurdish question in Turkey. Moderate Basque nationalists have proposed a constitutional settlement of the Basque question (the Ibarretxe Plan) in which the Basque lands of Spain would freely associate with Spain after a referendum that explicitly recognized a Basque right to self-determination. To date Spain's major party leaders, conservatives and socialists, stand by Articles 1 and 2 of the 1978 constitution, which are incompatible with this plan. Again, while none of our group would assume that ETA will necessarily abandon its armed struggle if the Ibarretxe Plan is implemented, we believe that it is clear that Spain's current constitution blocks any test of its merits. The Tamil Tigers have indicated their willingness to consider asymmetrical federal arrangements for Sri Lanka, thereby rescinding their prior hard-line secessionist stance. But, as their proposals, unformed as they may be, would require a two-thirds majority in the Sri Lankan parliament to amend the constitution there is a problem. They would require the full support of both the major Sinhalese parties, which have traditionally "outbid" one another on the Tamil question. Sri Lanka's constitutional amendment rule (adopted in a general constitutional change that Tamils did not in general ratify) currently acts as a veto on constructive and necessary institutional change.

Indonesia's leaders, by contrast, have proven constitutionally flexible—and have demonstrated willingness to adopt a highly asymmetrical autonomy arrangement, which is why there is presently some prospect that the Aceh conflict can be durably resolved. Israel's constitutional amendment process is extremely flexible: a simple majority of the Knesset would suffice for any comprehensive settlement or treaty. That means that the dispute between Israel and Hamas and other Palestinian militants is at least amenable in principle to constitutional management if some formulae can be devised for addressing their presently zero-sum disputes, though, of course, Hamas will have to modify its charter.

Our cases in which insurgents expressed class-based grievances or religious agendas have all declared, formally or implicitly, desires to transform their state's constitution. The Nepalese Maoists grew partly because of the failure to consolidate the constitutionalization of the monarchy. Hezballah has sought to revise the religious quotas in Lebanon's corporate consociation and prefers normal majority rule—although it is presently relatively satisfied with its place in Lebanon, according to Gunning. The FARC has engaged in negotiations (see below), but Shining Path, by contrast, did not make demands for reform of the constitution during its emergence.

Our group concluded that unless insurgents defeat themselves (as Shining Path and to an extent the PKK did), or are comprehensively defeated by a combination of other policies, then constitutional transformations will usually be required for sustained peace processes. Rigid constitutions, especially ones that express the past exclusion or defeat of certain communities (e.g., of Basques, Kashmiris, Kurds, Tamils) may require initial transformations, or promises of transformation, as confidence-building measures. Our view does not embrace commending a general policy of constitutional appeasement, and extends confidently solely to national self-determination disputes. We consider governments very capable of opening the possibility of constitutional change without rigid precommitments, and it is up to them whether to precondition such opening discussions on prior ceasefires or decommissioning of weapons. Governments that use the cover of the "global war on terror" to rule out any need for constitutional change may, in our view, only be sustaining conflict into the future.

Proposition 13. *Emergency legal regimes may work to stop incipient insurgent organizations, but in the long-run they degrade the human rights protections that democratic governments are supposed to support. There is a case for making such arrangements subject to regular and extraordinary levels of approval for renewal, and open to domestic and international evaluation.*

A government's best response to small-group violence from within its territory may often be a "no-response response," by which we do not mean to counsel tolerance of illegal acts or of violence that harms or kills people or damages and destroys public or private property. As Clark McCauley argued in *Terrorism and Public Policy* (1991), "doing nothing does not mean giving up on regular police and intelligence work under existing laws; it means doing nothing new, nothing different from what the same threat or violence would provoke if perpetrated by criminals without political purpose." He went on to explain, "If terrorists are normal people in abnormal groups, if terrorists are unlikely to be decisively defeated by government forces, if attempts to defeat terrorism can be more dangerous to the government than to the terrorists, if in any case antiterrorist initiatives are communications with diverse and difficult to predict effects on diverse audiences," then any other response by the government to those who contest its monopoly on legitimate violence gives up some ground to the challengers. In short, emergency regimes recognize insurgents, they give them that de facto political status that they are seeking to establish.

Our group discussed the possible truth of a paradox. Governments that carry on under normal rules—and address any negotiable and remediable grievances capable of further exploitation—may defuse insurgencies. Governments that use formidable and sustained repression—legal or otherwise—may eventually pulverize insurgents that use terrorism. But governments which inconsistently move between these positions may fail to be successful because they have lost credibility. But we decided we had insufficient evidence to pronounce on its merits.

The use of emergency legal regimes has been common across our cases. The legal amendments permissible under these regimes usually focus on three broad objectives: (1) weakening the rights and protections of individuals suspected of involvement in terrorism; (2) increasing the state's powers of investigation, surveillance, arrest, detention, and punishment; and (3) replacing the normal criminal court system with specialized tribunals. Such amendments are designed to improve the state's ability to detain and imprison suspected militants and their supporters. The burden of proof required for the conviction or detention/internment of suspects is generally drastically reduced compared to that required for other types of criminal offense.

In the UK, the Westminster government sanctioned the introduction of internment without trial by the Ulster Unionist-dominated local parliament in 1971. The quality of evidence required to intern individuals was so low, however, that large numbers of innocent civilians were incarcerated. The majority of individuals initially interned were innocent of any current involvement with terrorism. The policy was also initially strikingly partial: it targeted suspected republicans not suspected loyalists. The policy did much to enhance the IRA's recruitment.

The UK gradually provided police and the other security services with other increased powers to combat terrorism. Having initially removed the hated Special Powers Act a new emergency regime was established in Northern Ireland with the Emergency Powers Act (1973) and in Great Britain the Prevention of Terrorism Act (1974) followed after IRA urban bombings. The human rights of suspects and defendants were weakened. Jury trials were abolished for terrorism-related cases ("scheduled offences") and a special Diplock Court system (single judge, no jury) was introduced, on the grounds that the IRA and loyalist paramilitaries intimidated jurors. Ireland also abolished jury trials for terrorism-related cases and a Special Criminal Court was created, where again the judgment was made by special judges.

Post-Franco democratic Spain followed a similar pattern, as did Sri Lanka. In both countries, emergency laws broadened the state's powers of detention. In Kashmir, an emergency legal regime was introduced in 1990. This, as in Northern Ireland, was followed by a dramatic increase in the level of violence. What had already been a fairly draconian legal system before 1990 became even more oppressive. The new legislation was more indiscriminate and less focused. The authorities' use of extralegal (unlawful) methods (e.g., "disappearances") escalated at the same time as the tougher laws were introduced. Human rights protections almost disappeared and civilian government and administration collapsed. In responding to the threats posed by Hezballah and Hamas, Israel has turned to legal regimes based on military law, and applied these in Lebanon and in the occupied territories. Many of its provisions have their origins in British legal rules from colonial times (and legislation used in Ireland). Israel has legalized what other courts generally regard as torture in interrogation methods. In Turkey, extraordinary powers were granted to the military under an emergency regime. They allowed the military to evacuate and to destroy entire villages without prior notice. Torture became a routine element of interrogation, and detention without trial commonplace. The definition of who was a terrorist was greatly widened and thousands were killed by "death squads." Such was the scale of the abuses that some 2,000 cases were brought against Turkey in the European Court of Human Rights (with the government losing the vast majority). After 2000, however, the legal regime has changed and has been greatly relaxed.

Overall, the emergency legal regimes have had a mixed impact on the various conflicts. Large-scale internment has normally failed. This certainly happened in Northern Ireland, Israel, and Kashmir, where the policy led to increased radicalization and an escalation in the level of violence. The use of death squads and torture has also generally been associated with an increase in violence and increased support for the insurgents within their constituencies. In general, our group concluded that special laws, introduced to combat terrorism and insurgency by reducing human rights protections and increasing the state's ability to detain and interrogate suspects, have not by themselves significantly improved the conflict. While we considered some regimes may have had prima facie justifications, we concluded that it is best that emergency legal regimes be genuinely temporary—and that the special status of those held (or convicted) under these regimes should be recognized, with appropriate implications for amnesties and early releases. To make such laws temporary, rather than have them routinely renewed, would require governments to make their renewal subject to supermajorities and to have them publicly reviewed by judges trained in human rights protections or by international bodies to which the governments are parties.

Proposition 14. *Repression may backfire; repression is immoral and may damage democracy; targeted and selective repression damages insurgent organization, but governments rarely organize targeted and selective repression. Repression works best after insurgents have discredited themselves with their constituents.*

What is the difference between repression and introducing tougher legislation to fight terrorism? In our group repression was treated as the sanctioning of methods which are illegal under international law or the state's own constitution or legal code. Many of its forms are generally covered by the umbrella term "dirty war."

Does "dirty war" work for incumbents fighting insurgents? Its exponents would argue that it is fighting dirty with those who fight dirty, and not in accordance with the laws of war. Before we answer whether it works we should observe that in all our cases some "dirty war" tactics have been adopted by incumbents—the Nepalese police and military may be the last to get going on this front. Overall, the case studies suggest that targeted, discreet, intelligence-led repression may be effective in fighting insurgency. Provided the correct people are targeted, with reliable information, without collateral damage, then insurgents suffer and may lose morale. The almost consistent problem across our cases, however, is that governments, whether deliberately or otherwise, tend to sanction repression that is indiscriminate, ill-judged, and poorly informed, especially in the initial stages of the conflict. The Peruvian army's initial response to Shining Path is a clear example. The result in almost every situation of generalized repression has been an increase in the intensity of the violence and an increase in wider support for the insurgents.

The dirty war tactics used by governments typically involve the assassination of militants, volunteers, or insurgents ( and their suspected sympathizers) by various branches of the state, or by state-sponsored militias, or autonomous paramilitaries. In Spain, as ETA violence increased the state responded with death squads that abducted, tortured, and assassinated suspected militants. Many of those being killed had no involvement in terrorism: French businessmen with no ETA connections were among the victims. In consequence, the assassinations undermined the wider legitimacy of the Spanish government's cause, increased ETA's legitimacy and its claims that its militants were indeed fighting an oppressive and unjust regime.

In Northern Ireland, the UK government resorted to what unofficially became known as the "shoot-to-kill" policy. This was a somewhat more nuanced form of dirty war than in many other conflicts, because the security forces, at least "officially," tried to only kill IRA volunteers who had either just carried out an attack or were in the process of doing so. Scores of IRA members were killed in ambushes prepared by security special forces. Several of these ambushes were high profile: in 1987 eight IRA members were killed in an ambush at Loughgall's police station, and an innocent passerby was killed. In 1988, the SAS shot dead three unarmed IRA members in Gibraltar. Premeditated ambushes were accompanied by the passing of intelligence files on suspected IRA members to members of loyalist paramilitary groups. These activities, when they became public, enabled the IRA to argue, correctly, that there was collusion between the army, the police, and what they called "loyalist death squads."

In Sri Lanka the government waged a dirty war against many insurgents, not just the LTTE. It was especially vicious in the early 1980s when there was widespread killing of Tamils, but the policy failed to undermine the LTTE. As innocent people were targeted, support for the LTTE increased. In Colombia, a long-term legacy from dirty war campaigns by pro-regime paramilitaries in the 1980s is that FARC has been reluctant to enter into mainstream politics for fear that its representatives would be systematically assassinated once they became public figures. As Chernick observes, the

Patriotic Union (UP), founded by the FARC, was wiped out as a movement in the 1980s when thousands of its members and representatives were killed in this way. The apparent short-term success of dirty war tactics can therefore have unexpected long-term drawbacks: they are not immune to what the CIA calls "blowback."

In Kashmir, dirty war tactics initially had some success. Irregular militias seriously weakened insurgents through assassination. The JKLF was essentially forced out of the conflict in this way, but perhaps only because Pakistan colluded in the strengthening of its irredentist rival. However, repression has not, Bose reports, worked so well against the JKHM. Increasing use of dirty war tactics by state forces in Kashmir has in the past decade been followed by a growth in fedayeen warfare, with foreign fighters entering the region to play an increasing role. When the state becomes extremist so may its targets.

Graham Greene's *The Quiet American* popularized the notion of "third forces" as the favored instruments of counterinsurgency practitioners. There is some truth in this. In several of our cases governments and militaries encouraged the formation of voluntary militias among the insurgents' constituents, sometimes with considerable success (in Peru and Turkey). In other cases governments and militaries cooperated with pro-regime but otherwise illegal paramilitaries (e.g., the Colombian government). In yet other cases they raised military and police units from locals opposed to the insurgents (e.g., the British in Northern Ireland, the Israelis in Lebanon). Third forces, however, have mixed records. They can damage the government's supposed monopoly on security; the autonomy of such forces may take them out of governmental strategic control; they may engage in far more repression than expected; they may become "spoilers" of peace processes; and, in the case of ethnically differentiated forces, they are not capable of penetrating the insurgents' organizations.

The use of dirty war tactics should not be appraised in isolation. Instead it needs to be viewed within the framework of the overall counterinsurgency strategy. Both Turkey and Peru were, eventually, able to use controlled repression permanently to undermine the insurgents. In both cases the incumbent governments' armies benefited from the PKK's and Shining Path's abuse of their constituencies, and, in consequence, they were able to obtain better intelligence and recruit locals to help them. So, in some cases dirty war tactics did not eliminate violence, but they played a role in significantly reducing it and deterring support and recruits for insurgents.

Such tactics often enjoy remarkably high levels of support among those who identify with the government. Within Spain, the death squads were viewed as justified and necessary by a clear majority of the public. Ulster unionists were, in general, enthusiasts for more repression—of the IRA. Indian and Turkish governments thought they lost few votes by being hardline. Similarly, in Israel, public opinion polls consistently show high levels of support for the extralegal assassinations of alleged terrorists.[30] For a government, then, there may be immediate political or electoral benefits to taking extreme measures, beyond the objective of defeating terrorists.

Selective repression can be effective in weakening or defeating an insurgency (or in creating a stalemate that limits the ambitions of the insurgents or brings them to the negotiating table). *But* it rarely is, not least because governments are rarely selective in the ways that would be required. Moreover, such limited evidence as there is of empirically successful selective repression should not be seen to provide a normative warrant for selective repression. The converse case is prudential, lawful, moral, and better. Selective repression is never guaranteed to be successful, to put matters mildly, and unsuccessful selective repression is highly likely to be perverse for a regime: it will help the insurgents, and damage the government. For those who need reminding: Illegal acts are illegal; and, it is a good maxim that some immoral acts can never be justified on utilitarian grounds—torture is among their number. In our case studies, no one reported examples of torture as successful in achieving any particular goal. Even if someone had reported to the contrary, in our view that would not provide any policy warrant for the reversal of hard-won human rights standards. Destroying our village to save it makes no sense. Abolishing the right to life, to bodily and mental integrity, and to due process of law would destroy our village. We concluded that states rarely exercise the restraint needed to achieve a positive impact in extralegal repression. The necessary restraint is especially likely to be lacking in the early phases of a conflict, when repression nearly always leads to an escalation in violence. Generally, it takes several years of failure for governments to become convinced that repressive tactics need to be highly selective and extremely controlled. Some regimes never fully comprehend this.

Proposition 15. *Concentrated incarceration creates "insurgent universities"; dispersed imprisonment disorganizes insurgents but, in consequence, makes them less negotiable.*

The management of insurgents in custody and in prison has often been overlooked in research on terrorism. Our case studies highlight that the incarceration policies used to manage insurgents (whether they were interned, awaiting trial, or serving sentences post conviction) were often very ill-considered, inconsistent, or counterproductive.

The incarceration policies typically focused on concentrating insurgents in a small number of high security prisons. In Northern Ireland, for example, paramilitary prisoners were concentrated in Long Kesh (later called HM Prison Maze). At its height, this prison held more than 1,000 political prisoners, and it remained the primary holding facility for such prisoners throughout the conflict.[31] In almost every case, however, such a concentration policy resulted in what are dubbed "universities of terror." The incarcerated prisoners organized themselves, generally adopting the command structure of the movement on the outside. Once organized, the prisoners created classrooms and lectures that focused on practical issues such as construction of weapons, how to organize cells, and how to deal with surveillance. Prisoners were educated/indoctrinated in the history and politics of the movement. Indeed, many prisoners' understanding of the broader philosophy of their organization was often extremely basic before prison. Close proximity also allowed the prisoners to coordinate escape attempts, protests, and riots. The isolated environment of prison settings, where the inmates were living in very close proximity, engendered powerful social pressures to conform to the group. The commitment of prisoners to their cause tended to increase considerably in such circumstances, and indeed many innocent inmates—those who were innocent of involvement in the insurgency before their arrest or imprisonment—became politicized and radicalized while incarcerated and were committed supporters by the time of their eventual release.

Some governments gradually recognized the disadvantage of concentrating so many political prisoners—who were sometimes treated as criminals, sometimes as political prisoners, sometimes as hybrids. Spain is the most notable example of a dispersal strategy. Up until 1986, ETA prisoners were concentrated in only a few prisons. After this point the authorities started to distribute prisoners more widely throughout the Spanish prison system. The dispersal strategy seemed to bring quick benefits. The number of prisoners who resigned from ETA increased considerably. The level of terrorism-related training and skills development the prisoners experienced declined considerably. Over a period of time, this is believed eventually to have translated into a drop in the number and effectiveness of ETA operations on the outside. In Indonesia, the authorities also initially concentrated GAM prisoners, but this changed to a more dispersed policy especially for prisoners who had received sentences in excess of three years. But in this case the policy shift appears to have been a response to accommodation issues, rather than a conscious government policy on dispersal.

In the other cases, however, governments tended to proceed with the concentration approach. In Turkey, the state used dormitory type prisons, which essentially became schools for the PKK. The PKK, like some other insurgents, was also to use prisons to recruit and coopt nonpolitical prisoners. The high levels of abuse and torture in Turkish prisons did not undermine the commitment of PKK prisoners. Instead prisoners' commitment to the group and the cause increased, as did their hatred for the government and the authorities. The importance of the social support prisoners gave to each other can be seen in the dramatic increase in suicide rates when Turkey moved prisoners from dormitory arrangements to individual cells. Israel too followed a concentration approach. Mass incarcerations in the early 1980s radicalized a generation of prisoners—when these individuals were released en masse they became the leadership of Hamas. Mass incarceration could also have other unexpected side effects. In 1989, mass sweeps allowed Israel to imprison most of the senior leadership of the Intifada. But the organization remained relatively intact, and the detentions allowed a younger and more aggressive leadership cadre to take control of the movement. The result was a significant increase in violence.

Many militaries and police use detention to recruit informers within the movements. As well as offering incentives to potential informers, states can use blackmail and threats. Israel, for example, has taken compromising pictures of prisoners (e.g., showing the inmate in an apparently homosexual activity) and threatened to release these images if the inmate does not cooperate. In response to such tactics, insurgents learn to debrief—and be suspicious of—those released from detention especially if released early, and increase their training of their cadres on how to handle interrogation.

Overall, the management of prisoners has been rather poorly understood by most governments. Only in a few cases, and especially Spain, did governments consciously tackle the de facto "universities of terror" that result from concentration. The Spanish dispersal policy did not destroy ETA but it did weaken the organization. The policy led to a substantial increase in the number of prisoners who left ETA, and significantly hampered ETA's ability to train, supervise, and motivate prisoners who chose to remain. Thus it experienced considerable obstacles not faced by the IRA.

But this observation points to a paradox. Concentrated groups, almost by definition, become more disciplined, more soldier-like, and more likely to come under the control of their leaders and organizations. Not only does this create the possibility of an easier life for the authorities if they recognize prisoners de facto or de jure as political. It also means the authorities have bargaining leverage in two senses. First, prisoners can be used to bargain with the organization and the constituency from which they come—over issues such as amnesties, visitation rights, and so on, and second, well-structured insurgent organizations are more likely to make worthwhile partners to negotiations. The IRA perhaps became more "bargainable" because of the consequences of prison concentration; ETA is perhaps less "bargainable" because of the consequences of dispersal, which has led released prisoners to create rival ETAs and to become "hydraheaded" in the eyes of critics of the prison policy.

Proposition 16. *Successful media management requires intelligence, liberalism and sensitivity; these qualities are rare.*

Media coverage of terrorist violence is generally a sensitive issue for governments. Governments often prefer that insurgents' actions receive no coverage at all or else just coverage sympathetic and supportive of the government position. They tend to treat the media as "the terrorists' best friends" or their "oxygen supply." By contrast, insurgents are generally very keen to attract as much media interest as possible (an exception in our case studies is Shining Path, which showed very little interest in the media). Consequently, governments frequently decide on censorship to attempt to control the media coverage of a conflict. This censorship can take the form of legislation banning certain types of media reporting or of completely banning journalists from even traveling to the districts where the conflict is taking place.

In the UK, the government introduced a broadcasting ban for the representatives of the paramilitary groups. This was particularly targeted at Sinn Féin, the political party that supported the IRA (the two groups had overlapping memberships). Initially the ban was comprehensive. It prevented the UK media from broadcasting interviews or public statements from Sinn Féin members, including ones given outside the UK. However, the ban was gradually relaxed as the various media organizations began systematically to expose loopholes in the legislation. For example, the media were not allowed to broadcast the speech of Sinn Féin politicians, but they could show their images. Broadcasters started to dub the images using actors' voices. A journalist would interview Sinn Féin's Gerry Adams, then the interview would be broadcast with an actor's voice used in place of Adams's. A cottage industry developed with actors ready to carry out dubbing duties.

A tougher broadcasting ban was brought into effect in independent Ireland. Interviews, direct or indirect, with Sinn Féin members (again the main target of the legislation) were banned from the radio and television. However, censorship did not extend to print media. Paramilitary groups were able to publish their own magazines, pamphlets and newspapers. The most significant of these was (and is) *An Phoblacht/Republican News*, a weekly newspaper published by Sinn Féin and sold openly in Catholic areas in Northern Ireland throughout the conflict.

In contrast to the very uneven attempts at media control in the UK, Indonesia took a more aggressive approach. From 1989 to 1998, no media access whatsoever was allowed to Aceh. This obviously severely restricted coverage of the conflict. From 1999 on, the government relaxed media restrictions and coverage of the conflict increased enormously. In 2003, the government introduced fresh restrictions on the media making it almost impossible for foreign journalists to visit the region. Indonesian journalists could travel to the area but only if they were embedded with military units. Despite these new restrictions, media coverage of the conflict has become more balanced as members of the media have telephone numbers for many GAM representatives.

In Nepal censorship of the official national press is intense. The insurgents, who at the time of this writing control some 70 percent of the country, run their own newspapers and operate their own Web sites. Most of the general public, by contrast, are dependent on Indian media for news. In India itself, Bose reports that the media are largely self-censoring with regard to the Kashmir conflict. The main media outlets have made no serious attempt to present a balanced account of the issue. The general coverage is very pro-government. The government is primarily concerned with regulating and limiting the flow of information to the Indian public on the conflict, and media stories critical of government policies can provoke a serious reaction. One journalist from the *Times of India* filed a story highlighting abuse of the electoral system in Kashmir—reporting that large numbers of people were forced to vote at gunpoint. As the editors were absent, the story was included in the following day's issue. The journalist was recalled immediately from Kashmir by the paper and then forced to write a follow-up story denying the claims made in the previous piece. Thus, while there is no official censorship, self-censorship combined with occasional government pressure, results in very biased and controlled coverage of the conflict.

The situation in Israel, in the eyes of some, is quite similar to that in India. Israel has not imposed state censorship on the media, but there is a high degree of self-censorship. Israeli governments attempt to manage rather than gag the media. After a major incident or event, the government will hold a well-organized press conference for journalists, supply them with information packs, and give them a list of contacts within government and the security forces who are available to be interviewed. On the Palestinian side, by contrast, there are rarely any coordinated press conferences and journalists can struggle to find contacts for interviews. They are also more likely to receive conflicting accounts about what has happened. The end result is that the official Israeli government version of events tends, over time, to dominate.

Our group had no special or profound observations to make on the management of media. We agreed that in general the media do not positively report terrorist actions—indeed they generally emphasize the toll on civilians' lives and public assets. We agreed that there is little evidence that media reporting strongly affects support for or against government policy—what matters are the policies themselves. We also agreed that in general the international media report positively on ceasefires, negotiations, and peace processes. We thought there was evidence that governments that censored the media suffered some risks of loss of belief in their versions of events, especially internationally. Governments supported by their publics could rely on favorable reportage from their national media, and therefore could get by with "news management," as opposed to censorship. In general our group thought that a liberal media environment had some prospect of holding both insurgents and governments to account for their actions and of keeping open the prospects of negotiations. It was thought important that governments be held to account for their counterterrorism policies, for there to be agreed metrics to evaluate their successes and failures, and that efforts be made to prevent over sensationalized fearmongering among the general public (but no one had a formula to achieve the latter). Our group thought the Internet had played no outstandingly remarkable role in transforming terrorist networking: no more than the postage stamp did in the nineteenth century, or the telephone in the twentieth century, so went one view.

Proposition 17. *Governments and insurgents generally negotiate even though they say they never will.*

It is often assumed that governments will unilaterally reject negotiation with terrorists. It is also often assumed that negotiations will only encourage insurgents to ask for more. Most of the cases examined in this volume have seen the use of negotiations at some stage in the conflict, either directly or by proxy. These negotiations have had mixed outcomes. In many cases they have failed, but in almost all negotiation has been seen as a worthwhile option at some time.

Northern Ireland is an example of where negotiation has brought about the permanent cessation of violence on the part of the leading insurgent organization, the IRA. Aceh may prove to be another. Initial efforts at negotiations between the UK government and the IRA failed badly. In 1972 and 1974/1975 the British government entered into negotiations. Both efforts failed; the first because the IRA greatly overestimated the strength of its position and insisted on unrealistic demands; the second because it was never taken seriously by the UK government and was exploited to disorganize and undermine the IRA. The result of this second experience was to create a new IRA leadership that for twenty years was reluctant to commit to future negotiations before the UK government had met its preconditions. Despite this history, negotiations eventually played an important role in bringing about the current peace process. In 1990 secret negotiations opened between the IRA and the UK government, and via proxy with the Irish government there had been explorations of possibilities in 1987. The IRA's leaders by then were clearly aware of the limits of what they could achieve through violence and thus were far less arrogant than in 1972. The Anglo-Irish Agreement of 1985 mattered. Republican leaders feared they faced progressive political marginalization. The UK government for its part was now more interested in a genuine negotiation process and even admitted to IRA representatives that this had not been the case in the 1974/1975 negotiations. With increased interest and more realistic expectations, the renewed negotiation process nevertheless proved slow and laborious and suffered several setbacks (including most significantly the IRA's rescinding of its cease-fire in 1996–1997). Nevertheless, the negotiations laid the foundations for the 1998 Agreement. Had the government refused to negotiate (first secretly and then publicly) it is difficult to imagine that the IRA would ever have declared any ceasefires. Indeed, without the negotiations, the conflict almost certainly have continued, and another 1,000 or more people might have died in consequence.

The Irish example shows the positive role negotiations can play in resolving conflicts. But negotiations only work when both sides are genuinely interested in the success of the process, and have realistic appraisals of what the other negotiators can concede. In Colombia, for example, negotiations have been attempted on several occasions. Some partial successes were achieved with the smaller guerrilla groups, particularly the M-19, EPL and Quintín Lame, but talks have repeatedly broken down with the FARC. There are multiple reasons for these failures. The FARC has insisted on a broad agenda of far-reaching political, economic, and social reforms and has rejected a process that would only lead to its demobilization and disarmament. Nevertheless, on three occasions, the government and the FARC were able to agree on a common agenda. Yet each time the two sides reached the negotiating table, both the FARC and the government stepped up military activities, terrorism, repression, and extrajudicial killings to increase their leverage. Each time, the rise in political violence provoked the breakdown of the talks.

These repeated failures have made the Colombian government, the FARC, and the public wary of opening yet another round of negotiations, though the internal dynamics of the conflict and the inability to achieve military victory or defeat will inevitably lead the government and FARC in that direction in the future. A similar outcome occurred in the first set of negotiations between GAM and the Indonesian authorities. The election of a new Indonesian president in 2000 provided an opportunity to launch negotiations. It was not clear that GAM viewed these negotiations as a serious opportunity to reach a settlement. Instead, the group used the talks as a period to rearm and reorganize. Involvement in the negotiations also helped increased GAM's profile throughout Aceh and gave the group an increased international profile. By 2005, however, GAM had reappraised its position and settled.

There are no easily digestible lessons to take away from the various negotiation processes we have considered across the different conflicts—other than it takes at least two to make a deal. Most negotiations work on the principle of bringing moderates in the opposing camps together. This project, at the heart of the Oslo peace process, promised to resolve the Israeli-Palestinian conflict in the 1990s. This approach is vulnerable because it is relatively easy for hard-liners on both sides to sabotage the process, and gain support for their spoiling efforts, unless the moderates mutually support one another in the successful implementation of their respective commitments. In contrast, the Good Friday Agreement in Northern Ireland was, eventually, built on incorporating hard-liners, albeit hard-liners who were willing to moderate their positions. We have no general conclusion to reach on which strategy is best: circumstances may permit one or the other. Governments must appraise the possibilities and not simply assume that only a settlement with moderates is viable. Governments should not close off the prospects of incorporating hard-liners into settlements—and ensure if they do so that they neither create the suspicion that the hard-liners are being taken for a ride, or that they are about to get all that they fought for. Sri Lanka's and Spain's governments have, it seems to us, some prospects of reaching settlements acceptable to the supporters of the Tamil Tigers and ETA should they have the desire and the capacity to do so.

International actors can have a positive influence on negotiations. "Third parties" can increase the room for maneuver for negotiations between warring sides. The presence of third parties who can act as go-betweens, and also reward the success of the process, can help. One of our editors, Marianne Heiberg, famously played such a role in the early 1990s, helping mediate secret negotiations between Israelis and Palestinians in Oslo. Mediation like this can work because talking before a third party is not the same as talking to the enemy, and progress made in this way can help lay the foundation for more substantial initiatives. It helps, however, if the third party is capable of inflicting sanctions on the different sides if negotiations fail and issuing rewards if they succeed; the same applies to the implementation of what is agreed to at the negotiations—a role Norway could not play in the Middle East. A mediator with muscle is more likely to be successful than one without, but a mediator with muscle is more likely to be biased. Negotiations in Sri Lanka generally failed entirely before international involvement. The promise of some $4.5 billion in aid if substantive negotiations took place added genuine momentum to the current peace process.

Negotiations can have a positive influence on conflicts, but our cases show that both sides have to be seriously interested and realistic. The process may be abused by one party (or both) to reorganize or to attract positive publicity and legitimacy. But negotiations are frequently attempted even by states (such as Israel, Sri Lanka, and the UK) that declare publicly that they will never talk with terrorists or insurgents. Our group obviously favored constructive negotiations when these seem feasible, but did not think our cases could generally explain when they would work, or that whatever the negotiators agreed would be acceptable to their constituents. We thought, however, that governments intent on principled negotiations should seek to bring as many insurgents as possible into settlements. Splits among insurgents may look beneficial to the government in the short term, but they may reignite, prolong, and unnecessarily complicate the conflict.

Proposition 18. *Democracy is no panacea for terrorism; democratization may encourage insurgencies; and democracy is rarely sufficient to resolve national, ethnic or religious controversies.*

Does democracy help reduce terrorism? This assumption currently is present in U.S. foreign policy. What do our cases suggest? Many of them suggest a link between increased democratization and increasing levels of violence—after Franco's death in Spain; after the fall of Suharto in Indonesia; after 1968 in Northern Ireland; after elections in the West Bank and Gaza; after the 1980 alternation in Peru; after democratization in Nepal; and some might add after democratization in Iraq.

Our cases suggest a number of reasons for this outcome. One is that more democratic regimes are more restrained in using repression and force; and insurgents are freer to organize. In Indonesia, increased democratization constrained the military; it provided opportunities for a peace process, but also lifted pressures on the insurgents. In Turkey Dogu Ergil argues that increased democratization without satisfying increased expectations proved destabilizing. People may assume that democracy will lead to greater material progress, freedoms, and opportunities than under previous regimes, and if such changes are slow in coming, dissatisfaction increases and provides opportunities for extremists. Democratization may shatter previous hierarchical control systems in which one national, ethnic, or religious community has controlled and disorganized others. Attempts to smash such systems may be especially explosive. These descriptions partially fit the take off into conflict in Sri Lanka, Kurdistan in Turkey, Kashmir, Northern Ireland, Franco's Spain, and some would argue the civil war in Lebanon.

So, in short, democratization per se offers no immediate prospects of pacification and may facilitate more evenly matched contests for power. That, of course, does not mean that our group thought that antidemocratization would be a better strategic response. Some argued that careful and controlled transitions to democracy (Spain was defended as such) can be very constructive. Spain's new and large middle class already had strong vested interests in the success of the new government, and as a relatively wealthy country had experienced sustained economic growth at the same time as the transition to democratic government. Others pointed out that Sri Lanka had appeared to be the very model of a post-colonial democracy until Sinhalese politicians started to compete over which party best represented Sinhalese interests. This case suggested that in nationally, ethnically, or religiously heterogeneous environments it is vital that democratization be accompanied by federal or consociational power-sharing practices. Democracy is not enough if one wants to avoid the self-determination insurgencies found in Turkey, Sri Lanka, and Indonesia.

However, once the initial process of democratization is sustained, and provided the government does not retreat from its implications (as in Nepal), electoral processes can have restraining influences on insurgent organizations. Gunning reports that Hezballah has become increasingly moderate as it has become more embedded in the democratic process in Lebanon. Electoral alliances are essential in Lebanese politics and neither all the parties Hezballah have aligned with nor all of Hezballah's own voters are as committed to violence against Israel as it is. Hezballah has realized that it can attract support and votes from well beyond its traditional constituency because it does not suffer from the corruption and scandals found with so many other parties and it enjoys a reputation for providing good social services. Moderating its militant dimensions may help make the movement even more accommodationist, especially as Israel's withdrawal from Lebanon has reduced the incentive for popular resistance. Hezballah itself has invested very heavily in building new houses, infrastructure and services in Lebanon and continued conflict with Israel puts that work at risk. Sinn Féin is also now far less revolutionary as it bids to be the leading nationalist party in both jurisdictions in Ireland.

The central government's form of democracy is not always directly relevant to conflict-resolution. Both Kashmir and Northern Ireland are good examples. India is the world's most populous democracy but that has not prevented a series of governments from instituting highly repressive policies in Kashmir or engaging in electoral fraud. The UK is one of the world's oldest democracies but Great Britain's processes of electoral and party competition are irrelevant in Northern Ireland. In both cases inclusive regional-level democracy offers better prospects for conflict resolution. Regional-level democracy can be grossly abused: from 1920 to 1972 the Ulster Unionist Party ran a discriminatory majoritarian one party government and cabinet. India organized fraudulent elections in Kashmir. One hopes that both Delhi and London have learned their lessons.

Proposition 19. *International agents matter, but perhaps not as much as people think.*

The international dimension of terrorism is an old chestnut. Throughout the cold war it was often, on flimsy evidence, suggested that Soviet sponsorship was a major factor in driving terrorist groups. The FARC, however, did have ties with the USSR and Cuba. The Shining Path was not sponsored by the Soviets or any foreign power. It is also clear that the PKK lacked significant Soviet support. Iran, Syria, and Libya have been sponsors of organizations that have used terrorism. U.S. sponsorship of antisocialist militias in Latin America, and of Islamist insurgents in Afghanistan, during the cold war showed that there could be state sponsorship of insurgencies by democratic states, not just by communist or authoritarian regimes.

But, overall our cases suggested that international agents do not play a straightforward role, and after the cold war Soviet facilitation ceased to have a role. In most cases, in fact, international agents play relatively minor roles, whether as protagonists, victims or as inhibitors of violence. There are clear exceptions. In some cases international organizations can have relatively subtle, but still significant, leverage in conflicts. In Turkey many organizations are very keen for the state to join the European Union: the incumbent Turkish government because of the extensive economic benefits of membership (among other reasons), and Kurdish groups because of the restraints EU membership will impose on Turkish policies and laws on minorities. Such restraint is already in evidence, for example. in the manner in which the Turkish authorities handled PKK leader Ocalan's trial and sentencing. That there was a trial—and that Ocalan was not executed when it was over—were signs that the Turkish government felt the heavy gaze of the EU on its proceedings.

Thus, interested international organizations can be a significant factor in encouraging moderation, provided the conditions are "ripe"—which they plainly were not in the Turkey of the 1980s and 1990s. In Northern Ireland, the UK government eventually realized it would benefit from increased cooperation with Ireland to manage the conflict, and responded to an initiative from Ireland in 1984. This led to a number of agreements between the two countries, eventually coalescing in the intergovernmental arrangements of the Good Friday Agreement. Further afield, the U.S.A played a significant role as an intermediary for the peace process: it had clout with both governments and was able to exert considerable influence on militant Irish republicans; it could not impose a peace process but it could underwrite one. Granting Gerry Adams a visa to enter the U.S. for fundraising purposes, while controversial, rewarded Sinn Féin for the positive steps it was making toward a lasting peace settlement. In other cases, foreign governments have acted as neutral peace-brokers, bringing conflicting groups into productive negotiations: Norway in Israel/Palestine and in Sri Lanka are the best examples from our cases. Norway did not offer the huge economic incentives the U.S. or the EU (albeit less overtly) can advance for Northern Ireland and Turkey, but as a neutral party without vested interests in the success or failure of either protagonist it was able to exert a positive influence on events. Positive international involvement also aided settlements in Guatemala and El Salvador.

Foreign governments can, of course, exert negative influences. Libya, for example, provided support for the IRA in the 1980s, sending some 120 tons of weapons and explosives to the organization. The Libyan government was not especially interested in an IRA victory, but was happy simply to know that the aid would be used to inflict harm on the UK government, which had supported the U.S. attack on Tripoli. Much more committed partisanship can be seen in Lebanon, where Hezballah has been heavily dependent on Syrian support and aid and has provided Syria with a de facto means to wage war on Israel. Syria's retreat from Lebanon may cool the conflict between Hezballah and Israel. Our Middle East cases are particularly good examples of multiple external governments playing adverse (and positive) roles in conflict: viewing these situations as Israel versus Hamas, or as Israel versus Hezballah, is no route to lasting settlements.

Passive roles by international agents may have significant impacts. Schulze maintains this is especially clear in the conflict over Aceh. The Swedish government's tolerance of GAM's exiled leadership in Stockholm allowed its leaders to control of the campaign in Aceh, but protected them from the consequences of the conflict. No matter how extreme and bloody events became on the ground in Aceh, GAM's leadership was safe in Europe. She maintains that this meant that GAM's leadership became distanced from the costs of the struggle, and became much more willing to sponsor, encourage, endorse, and command continued fighting.

Diasporas have long been recognized as important components in sustaining national or ethnic based insurgencies. Basques in Latin America and the U.S.; Lebanese in Latin America or Africa; Acehnese in Sweden; Irish Americans; Palestinians in the Gulf States; Kashmiris in Pakistan; Nepalese in India; Tamils in Canada and the UK; and Kurds in Germany; all these communities have acted as resources for the respective insurgents analyzed here. But it would be simpleminded to conclude that surveillance, control, and repression of these diasporas is what is required for conflict resolution. In the first place such actions might backfire for the host governments if they are seen to mistreat their new or long-established citizens. Diasporas are rarely homogeneous; bad public policy might make them so. Second, diasporas can also be mobilized for constructive purposes: peace processes, public criticism of human rights abuses by their own insurgents in their homeland (as well as the regimes they generally oppose), and post-conflict reconstruction and investment. They also act as voices for groups whose plight might otherwise be completely ignored. Our group, in general, considered that current emphases on "globalization," diasporas, and terrorism were over-general and overdone. Large scale migrations, and the consequences of the expulsion of losers of internal or interstate wars, preceded our times. Whether these arguments hold for the Muslim diaspora in Europe we left as an open matter.

Proposition 20. *9/11 and GWOT have mattered far more in the U.S. than in the world; they have scarcely affected any non-Muslim conflicts—except in changed international discourses; their joint-effects have been far greater in the Middle East than elsewhere, but are difficult to judge.*

In the American public imagination the world changed on 11 September 2001. Terrorism had been around for a long time, but the attention focused on it in the wake of the attacks in New York and Washington was profoundly different. The "Global War on Terror" (GWOT) was presented as a sea change in American foreign policy. It ushered in two invasions, and regime changes, in Afghanistan and Iraq. It led to a range of international initiatives at the United Nations in law, police cooperation, and efforts to control the financing of insurgent groups. We asked our case researchers to consider the impact of 9/11 and GWOT on their conflicts.

The easiest assumption would have been that 9/11 had had little impact on the various conflicts. After all, al-Qaeda—and the militant organizations affiliated with its movement—has not been directly or significantly involved in the disputes considered here, although Palestine and Kashmir have figured prominently in its statements. In Indonesia, GAM is not linked with Jemaah Islamiyah. Hamas and Hezballah ( older organizations than bin Laden's al-Qaeda) do not have obvious ties with the Salafist jihadists (although many are keen to portray these disparate groups as closely linked). In our remaining cases there are no arguments whatsoever to suggest links with al-Qaeda.

Our researchers generally supported the view that 9/11 and global war on terror have not had a significant impact on their cases—and when they have it has been in quite unexpected ways. For example, violence increased in Nepal in the wake of GWOT, not because the insurgents are Islamists (or connected to al-Qaeda). They are Maoists. The Nepalese government joined the U.S. war on terror. In return the king received aid and support from the Americans, which allowed the government to increase the size of the military by nearly 40 percent; and violence increased considerably. This external support reduced the king's interest in a negotiated settlement. Here is a bizarre case where the war on teror led the U.S. to support an absolutist monarch, one much worse than George III, against communists, rather than, as one might have expected, to align with the democratic third forces intent on rejecting both absolutism and an archaic agrarian Marxism (from which the Chinese government distances itself).

In some other conflicts, the effects of 9/11 and the war on terror have been claimed to have had positive repercussions. In Northern Ireland, some observed that the IRA announced partial decommissioning in the immediate wake of the 9/11 attacks; and that its recent verified wholesale disarmament (announced as this chapter was finalized), has come after the 7/7 London bombings. But these interpretations are just false. The IRA had been preparing the announcement of its first decommissioning for several months before 9/11, while its recent disarmament owes most to the logic of the peace process—in which there is no remaining advantage to the IRA's existence, only electoral disadvantages to Sinn Féin. The stagnation in the peace process between October 2001 and September 2005 cannot be explained by the impact of 9/11 and GWOT. It had wholly local causes.

In Colombia, the war on terror led to a redefinition of the U.S. role. Before 9/11, the U.S. had invested heavily in antinarcotics programs, converting Colombia into the third largest recipient of U.S. military assistance after Israel and Egypt. However, that aid came with restrictions. The U.S. Congress expressly prohibited U.S.-supplied military equipment or specially trained forces to be used for any purposes beyond the antinarcotics mission. Congress viewed Colombia's armed conflict as an internal Colombian matter. In August 2002, Congress lifted these restrictions and allowed Colombia to use the military assistance in counterterrorism. The new policy led to a more direct role for the United States n Colombia's internal conflict in the name of fighting the "war on terror" although there are no known ties between FARC and Al Quaeda.

In Sri Lanka and Turkey little impact from 9/11 and GWOT is evident to our researchers—the remnants of the PKK in Iraq have been left alone by the U.S. military; the Tamil Tigers faced some difficulties from greater regulation of international financial transactions. The governments of Turkey and Sri Lanka have, of course, like all incumbent governments, sought to represent their local insurgents as terrorists. There has been little obvious impact on the conflict involving GAM (the Americans are only interested in Jemaah Islamiyah in Indonesia). In Spain the conservative government allied itself strongly with the U.S., in both Afghanistan and Iraq. Antiterrorism legislation was widened, and the political party associated with ETA was proscribed (but after a judge's initiative). But the 11 March 2004 bombings in Madrid resulted in a surprise defeat for the government—because it sought to blame ETA for Islamist violence. It was replaced by a socialist government that was keen to distance itself from involvement with the U.S. government, and with some of the consequences of GWOT, and it withdrew Spain from the conflict in post-invasion Iraq.

Perhaps surprisingly, in Kashmir, 9/11 and GWOT have arguably served as moderating influences, which were not expected. Tension between Pakistan and India has eventually reduced in the wake of 9/11, partly because the U.S. played a key role in bringing the two countries somewhat closer together after they had appeared to be on the verge of a showdown. Pakistan's military president curtailed his country's support for the Islamist insurgents in Kashmir and, especially important, purged the ISI of its radical Islamist sympathizers. Violence has, however, continued, but there is at least a more serious likelihood now of the two states engaging in a meaningful dialogue on the conflict than there was before 9/11. But that is because 9/11 exposed the bizarre repercussions of Pakistan's Islamist alliances in Afghanistan and Kashmir for its U.S. ally—rather than because of the impact of GWOT on insurgents per se.

The post 9/11 situation in the Middle East is very difficult to read clearly. The U.S.-led invasion, occupation, and supervised regime change in Iraq has added a significant complication to analysis of the impact of 9/11.

Before the Iraq war, the U.S. declaration of the GWOT had been accompanied by increasingly aggressive tactics on the part of Israel in dealing with Palestinian militants and by increasing militancy by Palestinians. These were not new tactics as far as the Israelis or Palestinians were concerned, but Israelis felt freer to be aggressive after 9/11, expecting less U.S. restraint. In contrast, with regard to Hezballah, Israel arguably was more restrained than would have been the case in a pre-9/11 world. Hamas's international position was weakened after 9/11. The organization has been added to many proscription lists, including in the EU. Its support from Syria and Iran has come under pressure. Yet support for Hamas among Palestinians remains strong. Israel's shift of policy, its decision to disengage from Gaza, while supported by the U.S., appears to have no direct causal relationship to 9/11 or GWOT. The removal of a strongly anti-Israel regime in Iraq, and the weakening of its Ba'thist cousins in Syria, has improved Israel's regional security with respect to states, but it has aggravated Sunni Ạrab pride, and increased support for jihadist operations among Syrians, Jordanians, Saudis, and Yeminis. The failure of the U.S. led coalition to justify its claim that Saddam's Iraq possessed imminently deployable weapons of mass destruction—and that the regime was a sponsor of al-Qaeda—has plainly adversely affected support for the U.S. reconstruction of Iraq, and it has also led to what had not existed before—a curious coalition of Ba'thists and jihadists against the new government of Iraq.

It is, in short, too soon to tell what the lasting impact of 9/11 and GWOT will be in the Middle East. Sunni Arab Iraq and Baghdad are sites of bloody insurgency occasioned by the removal from power of the formerly dominant minority. There is no indication that the largely Sunni Arab insurgencies that have mushroomed since spring of 2003 will diminish soon, or that they are significantly interested in negotiations. The fall of Saddam has, however, had some deterrence effects on Syria, Iran, and Libya. Syria has been obliged to consider policy changes that would have been considered highly unlikely four years ago; Iran is a tougher case to assess—and on one reading Iran's strength in Iraq is now at an all-time high.

Ultimately, our group concluded that treating 9/11 and GWOT as independent variables in explaining the rhythms of our cases is presently an indeterminate exercise. Their impact is likely to be greatest in the long-run on Hamas and Hezballah, and indirectly important in Kashmir, but in directions that no one can confidently predict. Their joint impact in some of our cases has been negligible (Aceh, Turkey), or grossly exaggerated (Northern Ireland); in others, so far, very odd and unexpected (Nepal, Kashmir, and Spain). They obviously have no relevance in Peru. In Colombia, despite greater U.S. involvement, GWOT is unlikely to alter the basic dynamic of conflict. What GWOT has facilitated is greater ease for incumbent regimes in labeling their respective insurgents terrorists.

Building public policy, especially foreign policy, without drawing on available evidence is to build on sand. Most policymakers recognize this and would prefer to have good evidence at hand when deciding how best to tackle any problem. Good evidence makes the policymakers life easier at every turn, provides the keys for appropriate action, and highlights appropriate measures to judge the success or failure of initiatives. It provides robust defenses of policy and challenges critics to produce more compelling reasons for alternatives. For the policymaker managing insurgents that use terrorism, the evidence base for guidance has often been poor. This book attempts to help fill an important gap in this critical area. The modest lessons we have extracted from our different conflicts merit close attention. For example, our group concluded that designating a group as terrorist is useful only if there are clear guidelines for placement on and removal from the relevant domestic and international lists—that way insurgents can be steered toward better behavior as well as condemned. Intelligent policy formulation and analysis can benefit from these studies; at least that is our hope.

# Notes

### Introduction

Epigraph: Harry Eckstein, "Introduction: Toward the Theoretical Study of Internal War," in Eckstein, ed., *Internal War: Problems and Approaches* (New York: Free Press, 2004), 1.

1. See Marie Lecomte-Tilouine, "Ethnic Demands Within Maoism: Questions of Magar Territorial Autonomy, Nationality and Class," in Michael Hutt, ed. *Himalayan People's War: Nepal's Maoist Rebellion* (Bloomington: Indiana University Press, 2004), 112–35; Pankaj Mishra, "The 'People's War'," *London Review of Books* 27 (12) (2005): 6.

2. The FARC today is the principal insurgent group but historically has competed with multiple groups that have been major players in the conflict, M-19, EPL, and still, the ELN.

3. It is better known as GIA, from its French acronym (Groupe islamique armé). For one controversial but illuminating assessment of the conflict in Algeria see Stathis N. Kalyvas, "Wanton and Senseless? The Logic of Massacres in Algeria," *Rationality and Society* 11 (3) (1999): 243–85.

4. Bob Woodward, *Bush at War* (New York: Simon and Schuster, 2002), 33.

5. We see this as a nationalist insurgency, even though both Russia's President Putin and Osama bin Laden see the Chechens' struggle as part of the Islamists' global jihad; according to bin Laden, Chechens are "A Muslim people who have been attacked by the Russian bear which embraces the Christian Orthodox faith," cited in Robert O. Marlin, IV, *What Does Al-Qaeda Want? Unedited Communiqués, with Commentary by Robert O. Marlin IV* (Berkeley, Calif.: North Atlantic Books, 2004), 36.

6. For the best explanatory research on al-Qaeda (and its affiliates) using public-source information on a large sample of its members, Marc Sageman, *Understanding Terror Networks* (Philadelphia: University of Pennsylvania Press, 2004). For key al-Qaeda communiqués see note 3 above.

7. Since al-Qaeda's agenda includes the entire historic Islamic world (as well as those it defines as part of the Crusader and Jewish alliance) a lot may seem to ride on the word "directly." It has had affiliates or ambitions in Turkey, Lebanon, Israel/Palestine, Kashmir, and Indonesia. Our research design selected cases in these last-named states where there were active insurgent organizations before al-Qaeda developed interests or affiliates there. It is more recently that al-Qaeda has had affiliates or small groups wanting to be affiliates within the European Union.

8. Cited by Charles Townshend, *Terrorism: A Very Short Introduction* (Oxford: Oxford University Press, 2002), 3. Almost all treatises note that the definitions of terrorism in most legal codes are difficult to distinguish from definitions of war (except where war is defined to be exclusively combat between recognized states) and that most laws to prevent, preempt or punish terrorism outlaw what is already illegal (e.g., killing people) under the relevant country's criminal statutes.

9. This distinction is Thomas Perry Thornton's, "Terror as a Weapon of Political Agitation," in Eckstein, ed., *Internal War.*

10. Even al-Qaeda has felt obliged to defend itself against the charge that it has committed crimes against innocent civilians. Its retort is to deny the innocence of the said civilians, or to allow Allah to decide their innocence. In bin Laden's "Letter to America" of November 2002, he uses Western democratic claims to argue that the "American people are the ones who choose their own government by way of their own free will." They are "thus" responsible for their government's support for Israel's treatment of Palestinians, U.S. bombings in Afghanistan, and for "the armies which occupy our lands in the Arabian Gulf." That, he claims, "is why the American people cannot be innocent of all the crimes committed by the Americans and Jews against us." In any case, "Allah, the Almighty, legislated the permission and the option to take revenge," Marlin, *What Does Al-Qaeda Want*, 62–63. The full text is on pp. 57–73, where the claim is maintained that the U.S. attacked "the Islamic Nation" in Palestine and in Somalia, runs the governments of "our countries" as its agents, supports "Russian atrocities against us in Chechnya, the Indian repression against us in Kashmir, and the Jewish aggression against us in Lebanon" (60).

11. Eckstein, ed., *Internal War.*

12. Mary Kaldor, *New and Old Wars: Organized Violence in a Global Era* (Cambridge: Polity Press, 1999).

13. Fortunately, much greater attention is now being given to post-conflict casualties in the assessment of the costs of wars (internal and intergovernmental); not surprisingly women and children suffer more after conflicts than adult men of combat age, see Hazeem Ghobarah, Paul Huth, and Bruce M Russett, "Civil Wars Kill and Maim People—Long After the Shooting Stops," *American Political Science Review* 97 (2) (2003): 189–202.

14. See the research of Rudolph J. Rummel, *China's Bloody Century: Genocide and Mass Murders Since 1900* (New Brunswick, N.J.: Transaction Books, 1991); Rummel, *Democide: Nazi Genocide and Mass Murder* (New Brunswick, N.J.: Transaction Books, 1991); Rummel, *Lethal Politics: Soviet Genocides and Mass Murder 1900–1987* (New Brunswick, N.J.: Transaction Books, 1990); culminating in Rummel, *Death by Government*, Foreword by Irving Louis Horowitz (London: Transaction Publishers, 1997).

15. See Barbara Harff, "No Lessons Learned from the Holocaust? Assessing Risks of Genocide and Political Mass Murder Since 1955," *American Political Science Review* 97 (1) (2003): 57–74.

16. See Victor David Hanson, *The Western Way of War: Infantry Battle in Ancient Greece.* (Berkeley: University of California Press, 1989), and Hanson, *Carnage and Culture from Salamis to Vietnam: Landmark Battles in the Rise of Western Power* (New York: Doubleday, 2001). John A. Lynn, in our view, convincingly demonstrates that the so-called Western way of war has neither been exclusive to the west, nor a continuous and universal feature of western conceptions of correct warfare: Lynn, *Battle: A History of Combat and Culture* (Boulder, Colo.: Westview, 2001).

17. David Edgerton, "Liberal Militarism and the British State," *New Left Review* 185 (1991): 138–69.

18. Carnegie Commission on Preventing Deadly Conflict, *Final Report* (New York: Carnegie Corporation, 1998).

19. Elizabeth Jean Woods, "Civil Wars: What We Don't Know," *Global Governance* 9 (2) (2002): 247–60.

20. See inter alia Paul Collier, "On the Economic Consequences of Civil Wars," *Oxford Economic Papers* 51 (1999): 168–83; Paul Collier and Anke Hoeffler, "Greed and Grievance in Civil War," Policy Research Paper 2355 (Washington, D.C.: World Bank, 2000); Collier and Hoeffler, "On the Incidence of Civil War in Africa," *Journal of Conflict Resolution* 46 (1) (2002): 13–28, and Paul Collier, V. L. Elliott, Håvard

Hegre, Anke Hoeffler, Marta Reynal-Querol, and Nicholas Sambanis, *Breaking the Conflict Trap: Civil War and Development Policy* (Washington, D.C., and Oxford: World Bank and Oxford University Press, 2004).

21. Collier et al., *Breaking the Conflict Trap,* 82.

22. Ibid.

23. James Fearon, "Why Do Some Civil Wars Last So Much Longer Than Others?" *Journal of Peace Research* 41 (3) (2004): 276.

24. James Fearon and David D. Laitin, "Ethnicity, Insurgency and Civil War," *American Political Science Review* 97 (1) (2003): 75–90.

25. Fearon and Laitin, "Ethnicity, Insurgency, and Civil War," 75.

26. Fearon and Laitin comment on Collier and Hoeffler's work in the following arresting footnote: "There are 79 wars in their sample, but they lose about 34 due to missing values or explanatory variables, which are mainly economic. Standard economic data tend to be missing for countries that are poor and civil-war torn. This highly nonrandom listwise deletion may account for some of the differences between our results." "Ethnicity, Insurgency, and Civil War," 76, n. 2. Their own data set finds little evidence for the importance Collier and Hoeffler attach to primary commodity exports (proxies for "lootable resources"). Laitin and Fearon themselves use the "commonly employed" ethnolinguistic fractionalization (ELF) index, which, as they state, is based on data from *Atlas Nardoov Vira,* a Soviet atlas from 1964 (78, n. 9), though they also develop and use other attempts to measure the possible importance of ethnic, linguistic, and religious demographic structures, most of which appear to depend on a highly individualist interpretation of ethnic conflict. Their efforts to derive measures of "state discrimination" (against regional languages or minority religions) seem in the right direction, but they have no direct measures (understandably) of public or private economic discrimination (which is not the same as economic inequality).

27. Barbara F. Walter, *Committing to Peace: The Successful Settlement of Civil Wars* (Princeton, N.J.: Princeton University Press, 2002); Walter, "The Critical Barrier to Civil War Settlement," *International Organization* 51 (3) (1997): 335–64.

28. Stephen John Stedman, "Spoiler Problems in Peace Processes," *International Security* 22 (2) (1997): 5–53.

29. Richard A. Clarke, *Against All Enemies* (New York: Free Press, 2004), 23–24.

## Chapter 1

*Editors' Note.* On 19 June 2005, ETA announced a partial and conditional ceasefire. It would "cease armed activities" against elected politicians in Spain in apparent response to Spanish prime minister Zapatero's recent offer to open talks provided ETA agreed to abandon violence. The Spanish government said the statement was not sufficient, while a spokeswoman for the Basque regional government welcomed the statement but also insisted it did not go far enough, 'businesspeople, university professors, security forces, police and journalists continue to live under threat" (*New York Times,* 20 June 2005). As of this writing, ETA has not carried out a fatal attack in over two years.

1. During its history, Herri Batasuna has changed its name on several occasions usually because it feared becoming illegal, or indeed became so. In chronological order, the party became Euskal Herritarrok, then Batasuna, and currently Sosialista Abertzaleak. In order not to confuse the reader I use the term Herri Batasuna. or HB, throughout, although the organization may have operated under a different name at the time of some of the events described.

2. Basque nationalists regard the *fueros* and the *foral* regime of which they

formed part as original Basque privileges derived from original Basque sovereignty. The *fueros* were collections of local laws and customs together with special economic and political immunities underwritten by the kings of Castile (and later Spain) in return for allegiance to the monarchy. This system was not unique to the Basque country or, indeed to Spain, but was common throughout medieval Europe before state centralization. Unlike the *fueros* in Catalonia, the Basque *fueros* never institutionalized a wider Basque unity.

3. During the period 1890–1900, Bilbao had the highest mortality levels recorded in Europe.

4. Sabino Arana, "Què caridad," in *Obras completos* (Buenas Aires: Editorial Sabindiar Batza, 1965), 296, translation mine.

5. The Church often attracted into its ranks the brightest of the rural youth. It was in the rural areas in particular that political and cultural oppression was most noticeable. Clerical discontent was generated by the resentment many of these individuals felt concerning the key role the Church played in the maintenance of the Franco regime.

6. Txillardegi, 1973, emphasis original)

7. "Nafarroa Euskadi da" (Navarra is Euskadi) has always been a central nationalist and in particular ETA slogan. It refers to the medieval kingdom of Navarre, which nationalists argue was the original Basque state although Euskera was the language of neither the administration nor the court. The original draft of the Basque autonomy statute left open the possible incorporation of Navarre into Euskadi. However, the Navarrese provincial parliament opted for a separate uniprovincial autonomy, the only Spanish province to do so.

8. Exact fatality rates are slightly uncertain since the Spanish Ministry of Interior and ETA operate with somewhat different figures.

9. José María Olarra, a leader of Herri Batasuna. ETA in a communiqué, February 2, 1999, branded all journalists who "wrote or expressed themselves in the media in the Basque country or in Spain against the construction of Euskalherria" as enemies.

10. Euskobarametro, Universidad de Pais Vasco, May 2004.

11. The figure is from Florencia Domínguez Iribarren, editor in chief, Vasco Press, interview, September 2004.

12. ETA document, July 2004.

13. Euskobarametro, Universidad de Pais Vasco, May 2004.

14. Interview, September 2004.

15. Figures do not total 100 because of rounding. All figures are based on interviews with Basque prisoners and are taken from Fernando Reinares, *Patriotas de la Muerte* (Madrid: Grupo Santillana de Ediciones, 2001).

16. These are educated guesses at best. There are two definitions of an ETA member. First, individuals who are registered ETA members; second, according to the report of Judge Baltasar Garzón, all those who operate knowingly within the command and control lines dependent on the ETA leadership, a considerably larger group.

17. HB participated in all the elections in the Basque country, local, provincial, regional, and general. Because it refused to accept either the Spanish constitution or the Basque autonomy statute as valid, its elected representatives to the Madrid parliament refused to take their seats. Its attendance at the Basque parliament in Vitoria has been irregular.

18. The organization of ETA is complex and has shifted frequently over the years. A full analysis is impossible within the limits of this chapter.

19. Figures from Florencio Domínguez Iribarren.

20. The organizations illegalized are KAS, Xaki, EKIN, Jarrai, Haika, Segi, Gestoras Proamnistia, Batasuna, all accused of "depending on and implementing directions given by ETA."

21. For instance, Xaki, which according to its statutes did advocacy work internationally on behalf of the Basque cause, was charged as operating as the communication link between the ETA leadership and ETA exiles.

22. The PNV is not the only moderate nationalist political party. There exist several more parties in what is often termed "nacionalistas democraticas." However, a more thorough description of the shifting political alignments inside moderate nationalism falls outside the limits of this chapter.

23. Euskobarametro, May 2004.

24. The Madrid Agreement on Terrorism of 1987 denied any legitimacy to ETA and reaffirmed the autonomy statute as the arena to resolve the political problems confronting the Basque country. The Ajuria Enea Pact, formally called, Agreement on the Normalization and Pacification of Euskadi, stated, among other clauses, that no dialogue with ETA was possible until violence had been abandoned.

25. Nicolas Aasheim, "The Illusion of Lizarra," master'ss dissertation, University of Oslo, 2003.

26. The PNV denies this and argues that some 37 competencies have not been devolved.

27. Izquierda Unida, formerly part of the Communist Party, also signed as the only nonnationalist representative.

28. ETA added a footnote to this agreement stating that the ceasefire in the first instance would last only four months, pending the performance of the moderate nationalists in implementing its provisions. The PNV added a codicil meant to soften some of these provisions.

29. Robert P. Clark, *The Basque Insurgents: ETA 1952–1980* (Madison: University of Wisconsin Press, 1984).

30. At times GAL would kill with exceptional brutality. In one case the bodies of two ETA members who had disappeared in 1983 were discovered in 1985. They had been tortured, possibly for months, killed, and their bodies covered in quicklime.

31. In 1998 most of the GAL command, which included high ranking police officers, were convicted for the crimes of kidnapping and murder. The former minister of interior, Barrionuevo, was sentenced to ten years imprisonment for embezzlement of funds used to finance GAL.

32. Domínguez Iribarren.

33. Interview, October 2004.

34. Article 506bis. of the Spanish Penal Code.

**Chapter 2**

1. "'En Colombia sí hay un conflicto armado interno': Comité Internacional de la Cruz Roja," *El Tiempo*, 4 May 2005, http://eltiempo.terra.com.co/coar/DER_HUMANOS/derechoshumanos/ARTICULO-WEB-_NOTA_INTERIOR-2058965.html, accessed 13 May 2005.

2. Coca is the plant used to make cocaine hydrochloride.

3. Opium poppies are the base ingredient for the production of heroin.

4. FARC-EP, *Esbozo histórico* (México: Comisión Internacional, 1998).

5. Eric J. Hobsbawm, 1963. "The Revolutionary Situation in Colombia," *World Today* 19 (1963): 246–58; Camilo Torres, *La proletarización de Bogotá* (Bogotá: Fondo Editorial CEREC, 1987).

6. According to the Uppsala definition, a civil war is defined as more than 1,000

casualties. Applying this definition strictly, Colombia would qualify as a civil war in Phases 1 and 3. Phase 2 should more accurately be viewed as a "low intensity conflict." See Roy Licklider, "How Civil Wars End," in *Stopping the Killings: How Civil War Ends*, ed. Roy Licklider (New York: New York University Press, 1993).

7. Comisión Colombiana de Juristas, *Colombia: En contravía de las recomendaciones internacionales sobre derechos humanos, August 2002 to August 2004* (Bogotá: Comisión Colombiana de Juristas, 2004).

8. Manuel Marulanda Velez is the nom de guerre of Pedro Antonio Marín, born into a peasant family in the coffee-producing region of Quindio.

9. Colombia is traversed by three cordilleras, or mountain ranges, that collectively form the Colombian section of the Andes. They are referred to locally as the Eastern, Central, and Western cordilleras and serve as basic markers of Colombian geography.

10. Unlike most areas of Latin America where communism gained strength in urban or labor-export enclaves, in Colombia the Communist Party developed its greatest influence in rural areas, particularly the coffee regions, and among landless peasants and small farmers.

11. For details of the fighting and the original assessment of the strength of government forces, see Manuel Marulanda Vélez, *Cuadernos de campaña* (Bogotá: Ediciones CEIS, 1972); Arturo Alape, *Tirofijo: Las vidas de Pedro Antonio Marin, Manuel Marulanda Vélez* (Bogotá: Planeta, 1989). Sources close to the army refute the FARC numbers. In an interview with the Colombian magazine *Cromos* in 1985, General Joaquín Matallana, the Colombian general who led the assault, claims that there were only 250 Colombian troops. Another general, Alvaro Valencia Tovar writing in the newspaper *El Tiempo* in 1999, claimed there were 1,500. The testimonial evidence from guerrillas, soldiers, and lower-ranking officers indicates a large military buildup before the assault with significant input from U.S. military advisers, followed by fierce fighting in difficult terrain during the assault that held off the final occupation of the zone for several weeks. See Eduardo Pizarro Leongómez, *Las FARC: De las autodefensas a la combinación de todas las formas de lucha* (Bogotá: Tercer Mundo Editores y IEPRI, Universidad Nacional de Colombia, 1991).

12. "Programa Agrario, proclamado el 20 de julio de 1964, corregido y ampliado por la Octava Conferencia Nacional de 2 de abril de 1993," in FARC-EP, *Esbozo histórico.* Translations taken from Center for International Policy Colombia Project, *Peace on the Table,* sponsored by International Committee for the Red Cross Colombia Delegation, Commission of National Conciliation, and Cambio 16 Colombia Magazine, 11 May 1998; www.ciponline.ort/colombia/peaceontable.htm

13. Charles Tilly, *From Mobilization to Revolution* (Reading, Mass.: Addison-Wesley, 1978), 437.

14. Interview with Manuel Marulanda Vélez, by author in La Uribe (Meta), Colombia, May 1987.

15. W. Ramírez Tobón, "La guerrilla rural: Una via hacia la colonización armada," *Estudios Rurales Latinoamericanos* 4 (2) (1981), author's translation.

16. Ibid.

*17. Ibid., 176*

*18. Alfredo Rangel, Colombia: Guerra en el fin del siglo* (Bogotá: Tercer Mundo Editores-Universidad de los Andes, 1999).

19. Most human rights reports attribute similar percentages of human rights violations, as measured by massacres and extrajudicial killings, to the paramilitaries. See http://www.wola.org/colombia_adv_certification-jointstatement_0101.ht m

20. For a decade-by-decade breakdown on the territorial growth of the ELN, FARC and AUC, see Camilo Echandía, *El conflicto armado y las manifestaciones de vio-*

*lencia en las regiones de Colombia* (Bogotá: Presidencia de la República de Colombia, Oficina del Alto Comisionado para la Paz, 1999).

21. "Over 3 Million Colombians Displaced by Violence since 1985 (CODHES 2003). http://www.db.idpproject.org/Sites/IdpProjectDb/idpSurvey.nsf/wViewCountries/BA1571472BCBCBFDC125684100331C40, accessed 5 May 2005; United Nations High Commissioner for Human Rights, "Informe del Alto Comisionado para los Derechos Humanos de Las Naciones Unidos sobre la situación de derechos humanos en Colombia," February 2004.

22. In December 2002, the AUC declared a "unilateral ceasefire" that contained no verification mechanisms and did not reduce paramilitary attacks and human rights violations during the next three years. In July 2003 and August 2004, the AUC and an affiliate group, the Central Bolívar Bloc, agreed to concentrate their forces—with arms—into a special *zona de ubicación* (location zone) in Santafé de Ralito (Córdoba) to further negotiations and begin a progressive process of demobilization. The Ralito II Agreement of 2004 set a demobilization schedule that would disarm 8,750 combatants of a projected total of 20,000–23,000 by December 2005. In June 2005, the Colombian Congress passed a Peace and Justice Law to facilitate and establish the legal framework of the demobilization process. The law sparked much controversy nationally and internationally as it provided only remote possibilities that leaders would be held responsible for war crimes and massive human rights violations. Some called it a law granting impunity. Furthermore, the law provided no mechanisms to dismantle paramilitary *organizations* even though over 30,000 individuals demobilized. See International Crisis Group, "De-mobilizing the Paramilitaries in Colombia: An Achievable Goal," *Latin American Report* 8, Bogotá/Brussels, 5 August 2005; and, Human Rights Watch, "Colombia: Bill Leaves Paramilitary Structures Intact," 15 June 2005, http://www.hrw.org/americas/colombia.php, accessed 15 June, 2005.

23. Interview with Arturo Alape by author, April 1986 (Bogotá).

24. Latinobarometer 2002.

25. Eduardo Pizarro Leongomez, *Las Farc.*

26. Stephen Stedman, "Spoiler Problems in Peace Processes," *International Security* 22 (2) (1997): 5–53.

27. Interview with Antonio Navarro Wolff, leader of the M-19, by author, *NACLA Report on the Americas* 27 (4) (January-February 1994).

28. FARC-EP, *Esbozo histórico.*

29. The CGSB also included a small dissident faction of the EPL that refused to hand in its arms in 1991 when most of the group demobilized and several EPL leaders participated in the Constituent Assembly.

30. The ELN responded to the official indifference by hijacking a civilian airliner and kidnapping its passengers and then kidnapping a large group of worshippers in a church in Cali. Throughout the four years of the Pastrana government, and despite several attempts by foreign governments and by the special representative of the UN secretary-general, talks with the ELN never got off the ground and the ELN never received the benefits or presidential attention that the FARC received in this period.

31. "Plataforma para un gobierno de reconstrucción y reconciliación nacional 3 de abril de 1993, Octava Conferencia Guerrillera, 'Comandante Javobo Arenas: estamos cumplieno,' Fuerzas Armadas Revolucionarias de Colombia, Ejército de Pueblo, FARC-EP," in FARC-EP, *Esbozo histórico.*

32. Presidencia de la República, Oficina del Alto Comisionado para la Paz, *Hechos de paz V-VI: A la mesa de negociación* (Bogotá: 7 August 1998–24 October 1999), 545–48.

33. Presidencia de la República, Oficina del Alto Comisionado para a Paz, *Hechos de paz XIII: Un recorrido por Europa construyendo la paz* (15 March 2000).

34. It is difficult to assess the impact of these public fora, known in Spanish as *audiencias públicas,* since no agreement was ever reached by the principal actors at the negotiating table on the main agenda issues. As such, these meetings were unable to serve their stated function, which was to assist the principal actors at the negotiating table. Many of the conclusions of the meetings that were held can be found on the FARC's website, http://www.farcep.org.

35. The description of the FARC's organization structures is drawn from author's interviews with Jacobo Arenas in La Uribe (Meta), Colombia, May 1987, and updated by the excellent and most complete study of the FARC, Juan Guillermo Ferro and Graciela Uribe, *El orden de la Guerra: Las FARC-EP, entre la organización y la política* (Bogotá: Pontifícia Universidad Javeriana and Colciencias, 2002).

36. The smaller central and western groups are officially designated not as divisions but as Collective Commands (Comando Conjunto Central, Comando Conjunto Occidental).

37. Arturo Alape, *Las muertes de Tirofijo* (Bogotá: Plaza y Janés, 1978).

38. Throughout 2004 and 2005, there were periodic reports that Manuel Marulanda was dying from cancer and that Alfonso Cano would become the maximum leader. On 12 June 2005, the BBC reported that Alfonso Cano had become the new leader of the FARC and speculated that this would indicate a shift to a more political orientation of the FARC. http://news.bbc.co.uk/2/hi/americas/3800601.stm, accessed 25 June 2005.

39. Ferro and Uribe, *El orden del la Guerra,* 66–67.

40. The unit had access to relevant intelligence available across Colombia's civilian, intelligence, and security bureaucracies as well as local records and commercial and banking documents. See "Las cuentas de las FARC," *Semana* 1187, 28 January 2005, http://semana.terra.com.co/archivo/articulosView.jsp?id=84475 and 84464, accessed 15 June 2005.

41. Nazih Richani, in one of the best studies of the economics of war, also places the numbers higher. According to Richani, by the 1990s coca and related activities was providing the FARC anywhere from $100 to 200 million annually, about 50–60 percent of the guerrilla revenues. The other 40–50 percent, according to him, came from kidnapping, legal investments, and extortion of other productive and commercial industries. See Nazi Richani, "The Political Economy of Violence: The War System in Colombia," *Journal of Interamerican Studies and World Affairs* 39 (2) (1997): 37–81.

42. Paul Collier, "Economic Causes of Civil Conflict and Their Implications for Policy," World Bank Policy Research Paper, 15 June 2000.

43. I have done this in more detail elsewhere. See Marc Chernick, 2005. "Resource Mobilization and Internal Armed Conflicts: Lessons from the Colombian Case," in *Rethinking the Economics of War: The Intersection of Need, Creed, and Greed,* ed. Cynthia J. Arnson and I. William Zartman (Baltimore: Woodrow Wilson Center Press and Johns Hopkins University Press, 2005).

44. Ferro and Uribe, *El orden de la Guerra,* 102–8.

45. "Los negocios de las FARC," *Semana* 879, 8–15 March 1999.

46. Chernick, "Economic Resources," 200–201.

47. Ingrid Vaicius and Adam Isacson, "The 'War on Drugs' Meets the 'War on Terrorism,'" International Policy Report, Center for International Policy, Washington, D.C., February 2003, http://www.ciponline.org/colombia/0302ipr.htm, accessed 10 May 2005.

48. Human Rights Watch, *World Report 2002: Colombia,* http://hrw.org/wr2k2/

americas4.html, accessed 5 May 2005; Human Rights Watch, "Colombia: More FARC Killings with Gas Cylinders Bombs," 15 April 2005, http://hrw.org/english/docs/2005/04/15/colomb10496.htm, accessed 5 May 2005; and Human Rights Watch, "Colombia: Letter to Rebel Leader Demands Release of Kidnapped Political Figures," 15 April 2002, at http://hrw.org/press/2002/04/farc-0415-hr.htm, accessed 19 March 2006.

49. Ministerio de Defensa Nacional, *Guia de Planeamiento Estratégico 2005–2006* (Bogotá, January 2005), http://www.mindefensa.gov.co.

**Chapter 3**

1. Dayan Dawood and Sjafrizal, "Aceh: The LNG Boom and Enclave Development," in Hal Hill, ed. *Unity and Diversity: Regional Economic Development in Indonesia Since 1970* (Singapore: Oxford University Press, 1989), 115.

2. Amnesty International, "*Shock Therapy*": *Restoring Order in Aceh, 1989–1993* (London: Amnesty International, 1993), 4

3. Human Rights Watch, "Indonesia: The War in Aceh," *Human Rights Watch Report* 13 (4) (2001): 8.

4. Amnesty International, *Shock Therapy*, 8.

5. Richard Barber, ed., *Aceh: The Untold Story* (Bangkok: Asian Forum for Human Rights and Development, 2000), 47.

6. Banda Aceh Legal Aid Foundation as cited by *Straits Times*, 29 July 1998.

7. *Far Eastern Economic Review* (Hong Kong), 19 November 1998.

8. *Suara Pembaruan* (Jakarta), 26 November 1999.

9. Data gathered by Forum Peduli HAM as cited in Barber, *Aceh: The Untold Story*, 47.

10. Hasan di Tiro, *The Price of Freedom: The Unfinished Diary of Tengku Hasan di Tiro* (Ministry of Education and Information, State of Aceh Sumatra, 1982), 84.

11. Interview with Hasan di Tiro, GAM leader, and Wali Negara, Norsborg, Sweden, 22 February 2002.

12. Michael Ross, "Resources and Rebellion in Aceh, Indonesia," Yale-World Bank Project on the Economics of Political Violence, manuscript, 2003, 12.

13. "Aims of the ASNLF," http://www.asnlf.net/asnlf_int/politics/aimsoftheasnlf.htm, accessed 20 March 2006.

14. Edward Aspinall, "Modernity, History, Ethnicity: Indonesian and Achenese Nationalism in Conflict," *Review of Indonesian Malaysian Affairs* 36 (1) (2002): ,22.

15. Di Tiro, *The Price of Freedom*, 136.

16. Stavanger Declaration, issued by the Executive Committee of the Worldwide Achehnese Representatives Meeting in Stavanger, Norway, at the closing of the 3 day meeting from July 19 to 21, 2002.

17. Ishak Daud, interview in *Jakarta Post*, 9 October 2003.

18. Interview with Malik Mahmud, GAM minister of State, Norsborg, 22 February 2002.

19. Interview with Amri bin Abdul Wahab, GAM Tiro field commander, Banda Aceh, 22 April 2003.

20. Confidential interview with first humanitarian aid worker, 25 June 2001.

21. Confidential interview with second humanitarian aid worker, 29 June 2001.

22. Interview with Malik Mahmud.

23. Interview with Hasan di Tiro and Wali Negara.

24. Interview with Malik Mahmud, 23 February 2002.

25. International Crisis Group, *Aceh: Why Military Force Won't Bring Lasting Peace.* Asia Report 17 (Jakarta: ICG, 2001), 3.

26. Data from Indonesian military intelligence (SGI), Lhokseumawe, April 2003.
27. ICG, *Why Military Force Won't Bring Lasting Peace,* 7.
28. *Tempo* (Jakarta), 17 November 2003.
29. Interview with Sofyan Ibrahim Tiba, senior GAM negotiator, Banda Aceh, 21 April 2003.
30. *Far Eastern Economic Review,* 16 March 2000.
31. Interview with second humanitarian aid worker.
32. Interview with Sofyan Dawod, GAM Pasè commander, Nisam, North Aceh, 19 April 2003.
33. Ibid.
34. Interview with Bill Cummings, public affairs manager, ExxonMobil Oil Indonesia (EMOI), Jakarta, 19 March 2003.
35. Confidential interview with contractor, Greater Lhokseumawe, 22 August 2002.
36. *Far East Economic Review,* 30 January 2003.
37. *Jakarta Post,* 4 February 2003.
38. Data from Indonesian military intelligence, April 2003.
39. Interview with Rizal Sukma, Aceh expert, Center for Strategic and International Studies, Jakarta, 24 April 2001.
40. *Joyo Indonesian News,* 9 June 2002; see also *Jakarta Post,* Jakarta, 10, 15 June 2002.
41. Agence France Presse, 15 May 2002.
42. *Joyo Indonesian News,* 28 May 2002.
43. Associated Press, 29 August 2001.
44. Dow Jones Newswires, 6 May 2002.
45. Agence France Presse, 2 July 2002.
46. Paul Collier and Anke Hoeffler, "Greed and Grievance in Civil War," Policy Research Paper 2355 (Washington, D.C.: World Bank, 2000), 2.
47. Paul Collier, "Economic Causes of Civil Conflict and Their Implications for Policy," World Bank, 2001.
48. *Jakarta Post,* 3 June 2003.
49. Testimony of Sidney Jones, Indonesia project director, International Crisis Group, before Subcommittee on East Asia and the Pacific, House International Relations Committee, Hearing on Recent Developments in Southeast Asia, U.S.House of Representatives, 10 June 2003.
50. Agence France Presse, 5 June 2001.
51. General Endriatono Sutarto, press conference, TNI headquarters, Cilangkap, 5 May 2004.
52. Press Statement, ASNLF military spokesman, 26 January 2002.
53. *Jakarta Post,* 13 September 2002.
54. *Jakarta Post,* 16 September 2002.
55. *Jakarta Post,* 4 May 2004.
56. *Kompas* (Jakarta), 19 June 2002.
57. Interview with Malik Mahmud, 23 February 2002.
58. Di Tiro, *The Price of Freedom,* 29.
59. *Jakarta Post,* 29 October 2002.
60. ICG, "Aceh: How to Lose Hearts and Minds," *Asia Briefing* 27, 23 July 2003, 1.
61. Ibid.
62. Agence France Presse, 21 May 2003
63. UN OFfice for the Coordination of Humanitarian Affairs, Integrated Regional Information Network, "Indonesia," Daily Sitrep Aceh 31, 17 June 2003

64. *Jakarta Post,* 8 June 2003.
65. *Jakarta Post,* 28 May 2003.
66. Di Tiro, *The Price of Freedom,* 78.
67. Ibid, 125–26.
68. Geoffrey Robinson, "Rawan Is as Rawan Does: The Origins of Disorder in New Order Aceh," in *Violence and the State in Suharto's Indonesia,* ed. Benedict R. O'G. Anderson (Ithaca, N.Y.: Southeast Asia Program Publications, Cornell University, 2001), 224.
69. *Sydney Morning Herald,* 3 April 2001.
70. Interview with Isnander al-Pasè, GAM spokesman, Nisam, North Aceh, 19 April 2003.
71. Interview with Lieutenant General Sofian Effendi, former Nanggala unit commander, Jakarta, 25 September 2003.
72. Interview with Major General Sjafrie Sjamsoedin, TNI spokesman, former Nanggala unit commander, Cilangkap, 4 September 2003
73. Indonesia has a territorial army system comprising regional military commands that shadow the regional government structure.
74. Amnesty International, *Shock Therapy,* 3.
75. Ibid.
76. *Editor,* 20 July 1991, 28.
77. Amnesty International, "*Shock Therapy,* 12.
78. Ross, "Resources and Rebellion in Aceh, Indonesia," 18.
79. Interview with Effendi, 25 September 2003.
80. HRW, "Indonesia: The war in Aceh," p.11.
81. *Los Angeles Times,* 31 May 2003.
82. Agence France Presse, 30 May 2003.
83. *Straits Times,* 23 May 2003.
84. *Far Eastern Economic Review,* 5 June 2003.
85. *Times,* 22 May 2003.
86. Anthony L. Smith, "Aceh: Democratic Times, Authoritarian Solutions," *New Zealand Journal of Asian Studies* 4 (2) (December 2002): 77.
87. Tim Kell, *The Roots of Acehnese Rebellion, 1989–1992* (Ithaca, N.Y: Cornell Modern Indonesia Project, 1995), 74.
88. Amnesty International, *Shock Therapy,* 6.
89. Robinson, "Rawan Is as Rawan Does," 227.
90. Interview with Col. Endang Suwarya, Danrem Teuku Umar 012, Banda Aceh, 26 December 2001.
91. ICG, "Aceh: How to Lose Hearts and Minds," 4.
92. Kontras data cited in Samsul Bahri, "Aceh: A Land of Silenced and Marginalized Voices," paper presented at World Social Forum, Mumbai, India, January 2004 6.
93. Indonesia Consolidated Situation Report No 132, OCHA, 7–13 June 2003.
94. *Jakarta Post,* 13 June 2003.
95. *Jakarta Post,* 28 May 2003.
96. Human Rights Watch, "Aceh Under Martial Law: Inside the Secret War," *Human Rights Watch Report* 15 (10) (December 2003): 9.
97. *Time,* 23 April 2001.
98. HRW, "Indonesia: The War in Aceh," 18.
99. *Jakarta Post,* 3, 11 June 2003.
100. *Tempo,* 29 May 2003.
101. *Tempo,* 10–16 June 2003.
102. HRW, "Aceh Under Martial Law," 15.

103. *Sinar Harapan* (Jakarta), 1 May 2003.
104. *Far Eastern Economic Review*, 9 October 2003.
105. *Sinar Harapan* (Jakarta), 1 May 2003.
106. *Serambi* (Banda Aceh), 8 October 2003.
107. Interview with Mahmud, 22 February 2002.
108. Interview with di Tiro and Negara, 22 February 2002.
109. Press Statement, ASNLF/GAM from Stockholm, 30 January 2002.
110. Ibid.
111. Interview with di Tiro and Negara, 22 February 2002.
112. Quoted in "Aceh Rebels Want UN Help, More Monitors," Reuters, 5 December 2002.
113. Statement by OCHA at Workshop on Aceh—Peace and Development, Hotel Indonesia, 12 March 2003.
114. ASNLF, "Official Statement on the Failure of the Joint Council Meeting of COHA in Tokyo on May 18, 2003 and the Declaration of War by Indonesia on Aceh," Stockholm, 20 May 2003.
115. *Tempo*, 10–16 June 2003.
116. *Far Eastern Economic Review*, 1 July 2004.
117. Ibid.
118. Ibid.
119. Ibid.
120. Ibid.
121. http://www.tempointeractive.co.id, accessed 27 August 2004.
122. Reuters, 31 December 2004.
123. Interview with an Acehnese source, 20 March 2005.
124. ICG, "Aceh: A New Chance for Peace," *Asia Briefing* 40, 15 August 2005, 2.
125. Ibid., 3.
126. Discussion with Damien Kingsbury, Jakarta, 23 and 24 March 2005.
127. *Kompas*, 7 June 2005.
128. Ibid.
129. Statement on the Helsinki Peace Talks by ASNLF/GAM Spokesman Bakhtiar Abdullah, at the close of the talks, 23 February 2005.

**Chapter 4**

1. Khaled Hroub, *Hamas: Political Thought and Practice* (Washington, D.C.: Institute for Palestine Studies, 2000), 59–86. For current debates, see http://www.palestine-info.co.uk.
2. For a translation of Hamas's charter, see Shaul Mishal and Avraham Sela, *The Palestinian Hamas* (New York: Columbia University Press, 2000), 175–99. Since Hamas's old guard wrote the charter, it does not necessarily reflect current positions. The original arguments outlined in this chapter are still advocated, though: see, e.g., "Youths on Gaza Frontline Keep Hatred Alive," *Guardian* (London), 23 April 2004.
3. See Hroub, *Hamas*, 69–86; Alistair Crooke and Beverley Milton-Edwards, "Costly Choice: Hamas, Ceasefires and the Palestinian-Israeli Peace Process," *World Today* 59 (12) (2003): 16.
4. Cf. Mishal and Sela, *Palestinian Hamas*, 130–71; Jeroen Gunning, "Peace with Hamas? The Transforming Potential of Political Participation," *International Affairs* 80 (2) (2004): 233–55; Gunning, "Re-Thinking Western Constructs of Islamism: Pluralism, Democracy and the Theory and Praxis of the Islamic Movement in the

Gaza Strip," doctoral thesis, Centre for Middle Eastern and Islamic Studies, Durham, 2000, 173–333.

5. Stephen Stedman, "Spoiler Problems in Peace Processes," *International Security* 22, (2) (1997): 7–16; see also Gunning, "Peace."

6. John Darby, *The Effects of Violence on Peace Processes* (Washington, D.C.: U.S. Institute of Peace Press, 2001), 118–19; see also John McGarry and Brendan O'Leary, *The Northern Ireland Conflict: Consociational Engagements* (Oxford: Oxford University Press, 2004), chap.1, for a discussion of the strategy of including the moderates among hard-liners, rather than just moderates

7. See Glenn Robinson, *Building a Palestinian State* (Bloomington: Indiana University Press, 1997), 11–37.

8. See Moshe Ma'oz, *Palestinian Leadership on the West Bank* (London: Frank Cass, 1983).

9. Glenn Robinson, "Hamas as Social Movement," in Quinto Wiktorowicz, ed., *Islamic Activism: A Social Movement Theory Approach,* (Bloomington: Indiana University Press, 2004), 117–23.

10. See Arjun Adlakha, Kevin G. Kinsella, and Marwan Khawaja,. "Demography of the Palestinian Population with Special Emphasis on the Occupied Territories, *Population Bulletin of ESCWA* 43 (1995): 5–28; Robinson, *Building a Palestinian State,* 21; Robert Hunter, *The Palestinian Uprising: A War by Other Means* (London: I.B. Tauris, 1991), 52.

11. Robinson, "Hamas," 121–23.

12. For a translation, see Mishal and Sela, *Palestinian Hamas,* 175–99.

13. Robinson, *Building,* 141.

14. See CPRS/PSR surveys of the Palestinian Center for Policy and Survey Research (PSR Polls), http://www.pcpsr.org. Surveys usually find Palestinian students more radical than the general population; student election results are thus typically inflated. National surveys are typically deflated because of the respondents' fear of declaring their support for Hamas.

15. The U.S. State Department describes the strength of the Brigades as "unknown, http://www.state.gov/s/ct/rls/pgtrpt/2001/html/10252.htm#hamas, accessed 24 January 2005. A special report in the *St. Petersburg Times* estimated in 2003 that it had 200–500 "hard-core members." "Special Report: Terror Groups," http://www.sptimes.com/2003/webspecials03/alarian/terror.shtml, accessed 24 January 2005.

16. See Frozen Accounts Jeopardize Learning, Healing in Gaza, *St. Petersburg Times,* 15 September 2003; PCHR calls upon the Palestinian Authority to Cancel Its Decision to Freeze Funds of Charitable Societies," Press Release, Palestinian Centre for Human Rights, Gaza, 28 August 2003.

17. Triffin Roule, "Post-911 Financial Freeze dries up Hamas Funding," *Jane's Intelligence Review* 14, 17–19 May 2002, 17; "Flow of Saudi Cash to Hamas Is Under Scrutiny by U.S.," *New York Times,* 17 September 2003; "Backgrounder: Israel's Adversaries: Hamas: Back-Seat Driver to Arafat Group," *Atlanta Journal-Constitution,* 24 January 2002.

18. Of the students responding to a 1997 survey I conducted at the Islamic University in Gaza, 63 percent of Hamas supporters had family members with a university education, 76 percent described their family's financial situation as "good" or "fair." Krueger and Maleckova found that support for armed attacks against Israeli targets (which would include Hamas supporters) is particularly high among students, merchants, farmers, and professionals. Alan Krueger and Jitka Maleckova. 2002. "Education, Poverty, Political Violence and Terrorism: Is There a Causal Connection?" Princeton University Research Program in Development Studies Working Paper 206, 2002, 16.

19. 63 percent of Hamas supporters responding to my 1997 survey who considered their families "poor" stated that their family's poverty had come about since the arrival of the PA (against 12 percent for Fatah supporters).

20. 4 percent of Hamas supporters (against 16 percent for Fatah supporters) singled out the PA as the institution that "most influenced [their] views on the political situation in Palestine."

21. The figures for Hamas and Fatah supporters were 27.5 and 16.4 percent for those living in refugee camps, 43.4 and 34.3 percent for those living in Gaza City.

22. For villages, the figures were 13.4 versus 7.8 percent, for smaller towns 32.8 versus 16.6 percent.

23. The figures for Fatah were 57 percent and 12 percent; 65 percent and 54 percent.

24. Gunning, *Re-Thinking,* 178.

25. See CPRS/PSR surveys, http://www.pcpsr.org.

26. PSR Poll No. 25, 26–28 December 1996.

27. "'Martyr' Leaves Perilous Legacy," *Guardian* (London), 4 March 1996.

28. Ibid.

29. See Mishal and Sela, *Palestinian Hamas,* 77–79, "Road Map Sowed Seeds of Ceasefire's Destruction," *Guardian,* 23 August 2003. See also "Middle East: Cease-Fire Producing Splinter Groups," 30 June 2003, http://www.stratfor.biz.

30. Mishal and Sela, *Palestinian Hamas,* 122–30 (details of pragmatic calculus, 49–146).

31. See critiques in Roane Carey, ed., *The New Intifada: Resisting Israel's apartheid* (London: Verso, 2001).

32. See "Sharon's Target Is Not Arafat: Hamas Must Be Drawn into a Political Role," *Observer* (London), 16 October 2003.

33. Interviews with Ismail Abu Shannab (Gaza, 1998, 2002), Usama Abu Hamdan (Beirut, 2002), Khaled Mish'al (Damascus, 2002); see also "Hamas Official Has a Vision of Living Next to Israel," *Jerusalem Post,* 25 June 2003; "Sharon Shies Away from Killing Hamas Ideologue," *Guardian,* 13 June 2003.

34. Cf. Mishal and Sela, *Palestinian Hamas,* 76–79.

35. Gunning, *Re-Thinking,* 226–66. See also my forthcoming monograph on Hamas (Cambridge: Cambridge University Press).

36. Gunning, *Re-Thinking,* 257–59; Mishal and Sela, *Palestinian Hamas,* 120–22.

37. Mishal and Sela, *Palestinian Hamas,* 58.

38. Gunning, *Re-Thinking,* 41, 327.

39. Ibid., 326–27.

40. Cf. Yezid Sayigh, *Armed Struggle and the Search for State: The Palestinian National Movement, 1949–1993* (Oxford: Oxford University Press, 1997).

41. Gunning, *Re-Thinking,* 113–41; Beverley Milton-Edwards, *Islamic Politics in Palestine* (London: I.B. Tauris, 1996), 108–16, 132–39.

42. See Mishal and Sela, *Palestinian Hamas,* 106–7.

43. Ibid., 64–72, 105–12.

44. Gunning, *Re-Thinking,* 267–69, 326.

45. Mishal and Sela, *Palestinian Hamas,* 122–30.

46. PSR Poll No. 8, 19–22 June 2003.

47. PSR Poll No. 9, 7–14 October 2003.

48. PSR Polls on Palestinian Refugees, January–June 2003. The findings are not uncontested; Gunning, "Peace," 252.

49. See Geoffrey Aronson, *Israel, Palestinians and the Intifada: Creating Facts on the West Bank.* (London: Kegan Paul International, 1990), 215–21, 315–19.

50. Robinson, *Building,* 15.

51. See Hillel Frisch, "The Palestinian Movement in the Territories: The Middle Command," *Middle East Studies* 29 (2) (1993): 254–74.

52. The estimate of 40 percent is based on the number of Palestinians working in Israel before the Intifada; see Robinson, *Building*, 14.

53. "Closure on the West Bank and Gaza," United Nations/World Bank Fact Sheet, August–September 1997, http://www.arts.mcgill.ca/mepp/unsco/closure 001097.html, accessed 26 April 2004.

54. PSR, Poll No. 22, 29–31 March 1996.

55. PSR, Poll No. 29, 18–20 September 1997.

56. "Security Fence's Effectiveness," Israel's Security Fence, News Briefs, 1 July 2004, http://www.securityfence.mod.gov.il/Pages/ENG/news.htm#news19, accessed 21 January 2005.

57. "Suicide Bombers kill 10 at Israeli Port," *Guardian*, 15 March 2004; "Two-Mile Gaza Moat to Foil Tunnels to Egypt," *Guardian*, 18 June 2004.

58. For details, see http://www.stopthewall.org, accessed 21 January 2005.

59. Details taken from Institute for Counter-Terrorism (ICT) database, http://www.ict.org.il, accessed 13 April 2004. I have only counted suicide operations inside Israel. Other episodes reveal the same pattern.

60. "An Arsenal of Believers," *New Yorker*, 19 November 2001.

61. "Successful vs. Unsuccessful (thwarted) Terrorist Attacks," Israeli Defense Forces Website, Statistics, http://www1.idf.il/SIP_STORAGE/DOVER/files/6/31646.doc, accessed 21 January 2005.

62. Data from http://www.ict.org.il, accessed 13 April 2004. Numbers killed before and after were comparable: 56 versus 45 killed, 230 versus 193 wounded.

63. "Report: Nablus Suffered Most from Israeli Invasion," BreakingNews.ie, 21 May 2002, http://archives.tcm.ie/breakingnews/2002/05/21/story50978.asp. In Jenin, at least 22 civilians were killed; see "Jenin: IDF Military Operations," *Human Rights Watch* 14 (3E) (May 2002).

64. "Successful vs. Unsuccessful (Thwarted) Terrorist Attacks."

65. "Palestinian Guerrillas Kill Four Soldiers," *Guardian*, 13 December 2004; "Six Die in Palestinian Raid on Gaza Army Post," *Independent*, 24 September 2004; for election results, see footnote 99; "Abbas turns to militants in attempt to secure power," *The Times*, London, 3 January 2005.

66. Jeffrey Ross and Ted Gurr, "Why Terrorism Subsides," *Comparative Politics* 21 (4) (1989): 408–9.

67. Mouin Rabbani, "A Smorgasboard of Failure: Oslo and the Al-Aqsa Intifada," in Carey, *The New Intifada*, 76.

68. See clashes surrounding the opening of a tunnel under the al-Aqsa Mosque complex and the building of the Har Homa settlement.

69. See Martha Crenshaw, "The Causes of Terrorism," *Comparative Politics* 13 (4) (1981): 389.

70. Between 28 February and 27 April 2002, 502 Palestinians were killed, according to the Union of Palestinian Medical Relief Committees, http://www.upmrc.org, accessed 16 January 2005. The bulk of these deaths were caused by the invasions.

71. Data from ICT, http://www.ict.org.il, accessed 13 April 2004.

72. Data from "Statistics—Fatalities," http://www.btselem.org, accessed 19 April 2005 (the figure for noncombatants is taken from "24 Nov. 04: Rules of Engagement and Lack of Accountability Result in Culture of Impunity for Palestinian Civilian Deaths"; this figure is based on earlier statistics and should thus be slightly inflated).

73. Cf. CPRS Polls post-1997.

74. PSR Poll No. 15, 10–12 March 2005.

75. Cf. "Road Map Is Forgotten at Dead End for Negotiation," *Observer,* 28 March 2004; "100 Acts of Revenge," *Mirror* (London), 19 April 2004; Yaakov Amidror and David Keyes, "Will a Gaza "Hamas-stan" Become a Future Al-Qaeda Sanctuary?" *Jerusalem Issue Brief* (Jerusalem Center for Public Affairs) 4 (7), 8 November 2004.

76. Cf. "West Condemns Israel as Gunship Attack Kills Eight," *Daily Mail* (London), 1 August 2001.

77. See "Middle East: The Legacy of Lebanon," *Guardian,* 19 April 2004; "White House Denies Giving Green Light to Israeli Operation," *Independent,* 19 April 2004.

78. See Jonathan Freedland, "Sharon's Triumph Is Blair's defeat," *Guardian,* 16 April 2004, 24.

79. See "West Condemns Israel."

80. See "An Assassination That the World Must Condemn," *Independent,* 19 April 2004; "There Is Something We Can Do About Israel," *Independent,* 27 March 2004.

81. See "Israel Urges EU to Freeze Assets of Hamas Funders," *Independent on Sunday,* 24 August 2003.

82. See "Frozen Assets Clue to Bush's Next Move," *Daily Telegraph,* 8 December 2001; "Hamas Leader Rejects Texan Charges," *Morning Star,* London, 20 December 2002.

83. See "Israel Urges EU; "EU Adds Hamas to Terror Blacklist," *Morning Star,* 12 September 2003.

84. See "Israel Must Talk to Hamas to Achieve Peace, Aays Former MI6 Man," *Daily Telegraph,* 2 February 2004.

85. Jeroen Gunning, "Terrorism, Charities and Diasporas: Contrasting the Fundraising Practices of Hamas and al-Qaeda Among Muslims in Europe," in *Financing Global Terrorism,* ed. Thomas J. Biersteker, Nikos Passas, and Sue Eckert (London: Routledge, 2006).

86. See "Mossad Blamed for Hamas Killing," *Times,* 27 September 2004.

87. "Hamas: Diplomatic Pressure vs. Popularity," 18 June 2003, http://www.stratfor.biz, accessed 1 October 2003.

88. See "Hamas Plots Revenge After Leader Assassinated," *Independent,* 27 September 2004.

89. PSR Poll No. 12, 24–27 June 2004.

90. Cf. "Fatah Versus Hamas—At the Polls," CBSNews.com, 23 December 2004; "Hamas Makes Gains in Palestinian Poll," Aljazeera.net, 26 December 2004.

91. PSR Poll No. 7, 3–07 April 2003.

92. PSR Poll No. 9, 7–14 October 2003.

93. For Hamas's view, see "Zionist Dependence on American Occupation," Political Analysis, www.palestine-info.co.uk, accessed 24 January 2005.

94. PSR Poll No. 15, 10–12 March 2005.

95. Steven Simon and Jeff Martini, "Terrorism: Denying Al Qaeda Its Popular Support," *Washington Quarterly* 28 (1) (2004): 131–45.

96. For agreed upon synopsis of talks, see "The Taba Talks, 2001," http://www.al-bab.com/arab/docs/pal/taba2001.htm, accessed 19 January 2005.

**Chapter 5**

Research for this chapter was carried out with the generous help of a British Academy Postdoctoral Fellowship, a British Academy Small Research Grant, and the Norwegian Government. The author would also wish to thank Mona Harb and Judith Harik for their insightful comments.

1. Jeroen Gunning, "Hezbollah Reappraised: A study into Hezbollah's Changing Public and Hidden Transcripts in post-Ta'if Lebanon," master's dissertation, School of Oriental and African Studies, London, 1995, 24–26.

2. Suicide car bomb operations contributed significantly to the withdrawal of the Multinational Force and the Israeli army. See Ze'ev Schiff and Ehud Ya'ari, *Israel's Lebanon War,* trans. Ina Friedman (London: Unwin, 1986), 310–15.

3. Interviews with Mohammad Ra'ad MP, head of Hizballah parliamentary bloc, Beirut, 26 September 2001; Ali Fayyad, Hizballah Shura Council member, director, Consulting Center for Studies & Documentation, Beirut, September 2001.

4. See Judith Harik, *Hezbollah: The Changing Face of Terrorism* (London: I.B. Tauris, 2004), 52, 99–110, 148–51; "Poll Results Usher in New Lebanese reality," *Daily Star* (Beirut), 25 May 2004.

5. The 1943 "National Pact" effectively divided power between the Maronites and the Sunnis, leaving the Shi'a the (then) largely symbolic position of House Speaker. In 1955, only 3.6 percent of leading bureaucrats were Shi'i; as late as 1972, only 19 of the 99 parliamentary seats were allocated to Shi'a despite their constituting an estimated 40 percent of the population. Illustrating the socioeconomic marginalization of the Shi'a, the Shi'a-dominated south received less than 0.7 percent of the 1974 state budget despite constituting 20 percent of the population. Anoushiravan Ehteshami and Raymond Hinnebusch, *Syria and Iran* (London: Routledge, 1997), 117; Richard Norton, *Amal and the Shi'a* (Austin: University of Texas Press, 1987), 17–18.

6. For detailed description see Norton, *Amal,* 13–58.

7. The majority of Shi'i activists were mobilized by left-wing organizations (ibid., 38, 48–49).

8. Ibid., 38–58.

9. Robert Fisk, *Pity the Nation* (Oxford: Oxford University Press, 1990), 520. Norton describes Musawi as merely "a member of the thirty-member Command Council" of Amal (*Amal,* 88).

10. Amal Saad-Ghorayeb, *Hizbu'llah: Politics and Religion* (London: Pluto Press, 2002), 15.

11. See Shimon Shapira, "The Origins of Hizballah," *Jerusalem Quarterly* 46 (1988): 116; Martin Kramer, "The Oracle of Hizballah," in *Spokesmen for the Despised: Fundamentalist Leaders of the Middle East,* ed. R. Scott Appleby (Chicago: University of Chicago Press, 1997), 100.

12. See the "miniature Iranian republic" created in Ba'albek. Hala Jaber, *Hezbollah: Born with a Vengeance* (London: Fourth Estate, 1997), 108.

13. See Etheshami and Hinnebusch, *Syria and Iran,* 120–25, 130–31; Harik, *Hezbollah,* 38–41.

14. The areas where Hizballah is particularly strong are typically those with a high percentage of impoverished residents, e.g., Ba'albek-Hermel, Beirut's southern suburbs.

15. No conclusive data are available. According to one study, a Hizballah martyr is somewhat less likely to be poor and ill-educated than the general population. Alan Krueger and Jitka Maleckova. 2002. "Education, Poverty, Political Violence, and Terrorism: Is There a Causal Connection?" Princeton University Research Program in Development Studies, Working Paper 206, 2002, 24–25. A 1993 student survey found that 18 percent of those supporting Hizballah had a high, 37 percent a medium and 45 percent a low socioeconomic status. Judith Harik,. "Between Islam and the System: Sources and Implications of Popular Support for Lebanon's Hizballah," *Journal of Conflict Resolution* 40 (1) (1996): 55. A 2004 survey found that 46 percent and 38 percent respectively of those naming Hassan Nasrallah, Hizbal-

lah's current secretary-general, as the most important politician in Lebanon had a higher or primary school education, against 15 percent with a secondary school education—suggesting that Nasrallah supporters come predominantly from the two extremes of education. Similarly, against 62 percent coming from the "free professions" (illustrating the aspirational nature of Hizballah's support base) 77 percent earned less than $800 a month. Statistics Lebanon, 5 May 2004, for the Lebanese political magazine *al-Kifah al-Arabi.*

16. Ehteshami and Hinnebusch, *Syria and Iran,* 120, 145.

17. Cf. Martin Kramer, "Redeeming Jerusalem: The Pan-Islamic Promise of Hizballah," in David Menashri, ed., *The Iranian Revolution and the Muslim World,* (Boulder, Colo.: Westview Press, 1990), 105–30.

18. Saad-Ghorayeb, *Hizbu'llah,* 11.

19. According to one source, $100–120 million of Hizballah's estimated annual budget of $200–500 million is believed to come from Iran. Rachel Ehrenfeld, *Funding Evil: How Terrorism Is Funded—And How to Stop It* (Chicago: Bonus Books, 2003). According to another, Iranian funding has long been surpassed by "contributions from expatriate Lebanese Shi'ates and by revenue from the movements array of commercial businesses in Lebanon." Gary Gambill and Ziad Abdelnour, "Hezbollah: Between Tehran and Damascus," *Middle East Intelligence Bulletin* 4 (2) (2002), http://www.meib.org, accessed 11 March 2002.

20. Interview with Talal Atrissi, political analyst, Beirut, 10 April 2001.

21. Other reasons concern the nature of Lebanon's election system and the need to woo votes from beyond one's own constituency, including from other sectarian communities.

22. Ehteshami and Hinnebusch, *Syria and Iran,* 149. Iran's success in persuading Hizballah to de-escalate may have come at the price of orchestrating the bombing of the Israeli Embassy in Argentina, which, many argue, has been carried out in retaliation for Israel's assassination of Hizballah secretary-general Abbas al-Musawi.

23. See "Iranian Terror Ties Disputed," *Iran Report* 5 (37), 14 October 2002.

24. See Anthony H. Cordesman, *Military Balance in the Middle East VI: Arab-Israeli Balance—Overview* (Washington, D.C.: Center for Strategic and International Studies, 1999), 30, 78, 81.

25. See Moshe Ma'oz, *Asad: Sphinx of Damascus* (New York: Weidenfeld, 1988), 149–63, 193–98.

26. See "Hezbollah Wins Easy Victory in Elections in Southern Lebanon," *Washington Post,* 6 June 2005.

27. See Harik, *Hezbollah,* 82–89.

28. Ibid., 56–60.

29. Magnus Ranstorp, "Hizbollah's Command Leadership," *Terrorism and Political Violence* 6 (3) (1994): 312–15; Harik, *Hezbollah,*. 54–57; Saad-Ghorayeb, 25–33.

30. Practices differ across the organization; see Mona Harb el-Kak, "Pratiques comparées de participation dan deux municipalités de la banlieue de Beyrouth: Ghbairé et Borj el-Brajneh," in *Municipalités et pouvoirs locaux au Liban,* ed. Agnès Favier (Beirut: Centre d'études et de recherches sur le Moyen-Orient contemporain, 2001), 157–77.

31. Interview with Atrissi, 2001.

32. Harb el-Kak, "Pratiques," 157–77.

33. Harik, *Hezbollah,* 89.

34. Interview with Ra'ad, 2001.

35. See Qur'an, vv. 3:159 and 42:38.

36. See notes 14, 15.

37. See Marie-Joëlle Zahar, . 2002. "Peace by Unconventional Means: Lebanon's

Ta'if Agreement," in Stephen Stedman *et al.* (eds.), *Ending Civil Wars: The Implementation of Peace Agreements,* ed. Stephen John Stedman, Donald Rothchild, and Elizabeth M. Cousens (Boulder, Colo.: Lynne Rienner, 2002), 567–97.

38. Harik, *Hezbollah,* 46–48.

39. Lebanon Constitution, ICL edition, 21 September 1990, http://www.oefre.unibe.ch/law/icl/le00000_.html, accessed 4 January 2005; "Text of Open Letter Addressed by Hizb Allah to the Downtrodden in Lebanon and in the World," in Norton, *Amal,* 167–87.

40. Interview with Nassib Lahoud, MP for Metn, Beirut, 2 April 2001.

41. "Defence Minister Says Calm Restored to Beirut's Southern Suburbs Following Clash," Radio Lebanon, Beirut, *Summary of World Broadcasts,* ME/1633 A/7 [9]b, 10 March 1993.

42. See "Reactions to Killing by Lebanese Troops of Anti-Peace Accord Demonstrators," Editorial Report, *Summary of World Broadcasts,* ME/1794 MED/27 [43], 15 September 1993; interview with Atrissi, 2001.

43. Harb el-Kak, "Pratiques," 161–63; interview with Philippe Adaimy, Haret Hrayk municipal councillor, Beirut, 17 May 2004.

44. Interview with Atrissi, Beirut, 11 April 2002.

45. David A. Snow, E. Burke Rochford, Steven K. Worden, and Robert D. Benford, "Frame Alignment Processes, Micromobilization, and Movement Participation," *American Sociological Review* 51 (4) (1986): 464–80; interviews with Atrissi and Mona Harb, political geographer, Beirut, April 2002.

46. See Donald Horowitz, "Conflict and the Incentives to Political Accommodation," in *Northern Ireland and the Politics of Reconciliation,* ed. Dermot Keogh and Michael Haltzel (Washington, D.C.: Woodrow Wilson Center Press, 1993), 173–88.

47. See Dalal Bizri, *Islamistes, parlementaires et libanais: Les interventions à l'Assemblée des élus de la Jamâ'a islamiyya et du Hizb Allah (1992–1996),* Document du CERMOC 3 (Beirut: CERMOC, 1999).

48. Harik, "Between Islam and the System," 56–57.

49. Interview with Harb, 2002.

50. Mona Harb and Reinoud Leenders. 2005. "Know Thy Enemy: Hizbullah, 'Terrorism,' and the Politics of Perception," *Third World Quarterly* 26 (1): 173–97.

51. For details, see Harik, "Between Islam and the System," 122–23.

52. Both UN and Western diplomatic sources in Lebanon have confirmed these claims put forward by Hizballah (Jaber, *Hezballah,* 173).

53. Ibid., 113–44.

54. Magnus Ranstorp, *Hizb'Allah in Lebanon: The Politics of the Western Hostage Crisis* (London: Palgrave Macmillan, 1997), 104–5.

55. The 1991 election of Abbas al-Musawi as secretary-general marked an increase in the party's efforts to end the hostage crisis (Ranstorp, *Hizb'Allah,* 105–6).

56. Nicholas Blanford, "Israel Scrambles Aircraft as Lebanon Hears News," *Times* (London), 5 November 2004.

57. Such support as Hizballah has given to Palestinian resistance groups—opinion is divided over the extent to which Hizballah is involved with the Palestinian resistance—has been provided in such a way that Hizballah can claim "plausible deniability" and so escape Israeli retaliation inside Lebanon.

58. Nicholas Blanford, "Sticking to the Rules in South Lebanon," *Daily Star* (Beirut), 23 July 2004.

59. 10 April, the day before Iranian Foreign Minister Kamal Kharrazi intervened, marked the height of hostilities. Nicholas Blanford, "Syria Reaffirms Role as Volatile Barrier to Mideast Peace," *Christian Science Monitor,* 17 April 2002.

60. *Jihad al Binaa in Its Twelfth Spring,* Beirut, 2000.

61. See Chapter 4 on Hamas in this volume.

62. See Ehteshami and Hinnebusch, *Syria and Iran,* 150; Harik, *Hezbollah,* 123.

63. Ehteshami and Hinnebusch, *Syria and Iran,* 120–21.

64. Jaber, *Hezbollah,* 169–204; Harik, *Hezbollah,* 122.

65. Jaber, *Hezbollah,* 196–99. Operation Accountability (1993) similarly killed over 130 civilians, wounded 600, displaced 200,000–300,000, yet left Hizballah largely unscathed and more popular than before. Jaber, 172; "Hizbollah Says Raid is 'Lesson for Israel,'" *Independent,* 20 August 1993.

66. See Harik, *Hezbollah,* chap. 8.

67. See "Guerrillas Pound Israel with Rockets," *Guardian,* 26 July 1993; "Rockets Fired into Galilee," *Times,* 1 April 1996; Harik, *Hezbollah,* 117.

68. See Itamar Rabinovich, *The War for Lebanon 1970–1985,* rev. ed. (Ithaca, N.Y.: Cornell University Press, 1985); Schiff and Ya'ari, *Israel's Lebanon War.*

69. See "Israelis Exchange Prisoners for Bodies," *Times,* 22 July 1996.

70. Mahmud al-Qamati in "Lebanon: Hezbollah Official on Relations with Iran, Syria, Israel," BBC Monitoring Service, 28 April 2002.

71. Thomas Friedman, "Pull Up a Chair," *New York Times,* 20 March 2002; "Israel Besieged on Two Fronts," *Guardian,* 4 March 1997.

72. Harik, *Hezbollah,* 130–33.

73. See 1999 survey in the border settlement Kiryat Shimona (Harik, *Hezbollah,* 145n217).

74. Harik, *Hezbollah,* 156–57.

75. See Nicholas Blanford, "Lebanon Border Tensions Raise Second Front Fear," *Times,* 4 April 2002; Larry Collins, "New Hezbollah Rockets Threaten Israeli Cities," *International Herald Tribune,* 12 March 2003; "Hezbollah's Strategic Rocket Arsenal," *Middle East Intelligence Bulletin,* November–December 2002, http://www.meib.org/articles/0211_12.htm, accessed 28 October 2004.

76. "Motion for a Resolution," European Parliament PE356.337v01–00, Strasbourg, 2 March 2005.

77. See "Hizbullah's Missives to America," *Daily Star,* 2 June 2004.

78. See "On the Rise: Why Militant Shias Are on the Rise in Lebanon too," *Economist,* 27 May 2004.

79. Ibid.

80. Interview with Nicholas Blanford, Beirut, 11 April 2002; Nicholas Blanford, "Cracks Emerge in Hizballah's Relations with Damascus," *Daily Star,* 30 October 2001.

81. See Krueger and Maleckova, "Education, Poverty, Political Violence, and Terror."

82. Seymour Martin Lipset, S.M. 1960. *Political Man: The Social Bases of Politics,* 2nd ed. (London: Heinemann, 1960); Michael W. Doyle, "Kant, Liberal Legacies, and Foreign Affairs," *Philosophy and Public Affairs* 12 (3) (2003): 205–35 (part 1); (4): 323–53 (part 2).

83. For a more recent, and critical, discussion of modernization theory, see, e.g., Gary Marks and Larry Diamond, eds., 1992. *Reexamining Democracy: Essays in Honor of Seymour Martin Lipset* (Newbury Park, Calif.: Sage, 1992); Adam Przeworski, "A Flawed Blueprint: The Covert Politicization of Development Economics," *Development and Modernization* 25 (1) (2003).

84. Dankwart Rustow, "Transitions to Democracy: Toward a Dynamic Model," *Comparative Politics* 2 (3) (1970): 337–63. For a more recent discussion, see, e.g., Guillermo O'Donnell, Philippe C. Schmitter, and Laurence Whitehead, eds., *Transitions from Authoritarian Rule,* 4 vols. (Baltimore: Johns Hopkins University Press, 1986).

85. Dietrich Rueschemeyer, Evelyne Huber Stephens, and John D. Stephens, *Capitalist Development and Democracy* (Cambridge: Polity Press, 1992).

86. See Ma'oz, *Asad*, 149–63, 193–98.

87. See "Beirut Trembles at Hizbollah's Might," *Observer*, 13 March 2005.

**Chapter 6**

This chapter is based on the author's research and fieldwork in Northern Ireland in the years since 1985. A slightly longer version was published in *Field Day Review* 1 (2005).

1. For a detailed analysis of the Agreement see Brendan O'Leary, "The Nature of the British-Irish Agreement," *New Left Review* 233 (1999): 66–96.

2. Selections of recent IRA statements may be found on Sinn Féin's Web site: http://sinnfein.ie/peace/ira_statements. The BBC has a collection of the IRA statements 1998–2003: http://news.bbc.co.uk/1/hi/northern_ireland/1144568.stm. The University of Ulster's CAIN web-site has a collection of 1994 statements: http://cain.ulst.ac.uk/othelem/organ/ira/statements.htm

3. Patrick Dinneen, ed., *An Irish-English Dictionary: Being a Thesaurus of the Words, Phrases and Idioms of the Modern Irish Language* (Dublin: Irish Text Society, 1927), 631, 807, 808.

4. The name had an antecedent: J. Bowyer Bell, *The Secret Army: The IRA*, 3rd rev. ed. (New Brunswick, N.J., Transaction Publishers, 1997), 15n.3, notes that "As early as the abortive Fenian invasion of Canada in 1866, a green flag was used with the letters IRA."

5. Bell, *Secret Army*, 17.

6. For fuller analyses of this election see John McGarry and Brendan O'Leary, *Explaining Northern Ireland: Broken Images* (Oxford: Blackwell, 1995), chap. 1, and Brendan O'Leary and John McGarry, *The Politics of Antagonism: Understanding Northern Ireland*, 2nd ed. (London: Athlone, 1996), chap. 2.

7. Tim Pat Coogan, *The IRA*, 4th ed. (New York: Palgrave, 2002), 30–31.

8. Constitution of Óglaigh na hÉireann as Amended by General Army Convention, 14–15 Nov. 1925, Blythe Papers ADUCD P24/165 (10), cited in Richard English, *Armed Struggle: The History of the IRA* (Oxford: Oxford University Press, 2003), 42–43, 394n.3. The word "race" was used the way people today use "ethnic," so it is anachronistic—and false—to interpret the IRA's mission as racist; nationalism and racism are not equivalents.

9. The most comprehensive and elegant treatment of the early Sinn Féin is provided by Michael Laffan, *The Resurrection of Ireland: The Sinn Féin Party, 1916–1923* (Cambridge: Cambridge University Press, 1999). Brian Feeney, *Sinn Féin: A Hundred Turbulent Years* (Dublin: O'Brien Press, 2002), 161–210, provides a witty dissection of its development between 1923 and 1969 (and after).

10. The Irish title of the new party, "Soldiers of Destiny," had been the slogan of the Irish Volunteers and had been embroidered in their cap bands; see Feeney, *Sinn Féin*, 159.

11. English, *Armed Struggle*, 43.

12. See Coogan, *IRA*, Part 1; Patrick Bishop and Eamonn Mallie, *The Provisional IRA* (London: Heinemann, 1987), 1–88; Peter Taylor, *Provos: The IRA and Sinn Féin*, rev. ed. (London: Bloomsbury, 1998), 1–20; Bell, *Secret Army*; English, *Armed Struggle*, Part 1; Brian Hanley, *The IRA, 1926–1936* (Dublin: Four Courts Press, 2002); Peter Hart, *The I.R.A. and Its Enemies: Violence and Community in Cork, 1916–1923* (Oxford: Oxford University Press, 1998) and *The I.R.A. at War, 1916–1923* (Oxford: Oxford University Press, 2003); Uinseann Mac Eoin, *The IRA in the Twilight Years:*

*1923–1948, History and Politics* (Dublin: Argenta,, 1997). Argenta, the name of Mac Eoin's publisher, signals the author's sympathies: it recalls the ship on which IRA members were interned without trial in Northern Ireland in 1922, on which see Denise Kleinrichert, *Republican Internment and the Prison Ship* Argenta, *1922* (Dublin: Irish Academic Press, 2001).

13. From 1933, volunteers were prohibited from belonging to the Communist Party by General Army Order No. 4: see Bell, *Secret Army,* 246.

14. Hanley, *IRA,* 26–27.

15. Hart's *The I.R.A. and Its Enemies* and *The I.R.A. at War* provide the most social scientific treatment of the IRA in these years. I cannot discuss my reservations about this excellent work here.

16. Drawing extensively on the papers of Maurice (Moss) Twomey, Hanley's *The IRA, 1926–1936* provides an analysis of the organization in this period; the idea that Ireland experienced a counter-revolution after 1921 is spiritedly advanced by John Regan, *The Irish Counter-Revolution, 1921–36: Treatyite Politics and Settlement in Independent Ireland* (Dublin: Gill and Macmillan, 1999).

17. Comprehensive historical treatments of the IRA in Northern Ireland between 1916 and 1969 are yet to be written; Jim McDermott, *Northern Divisions: The Old IRA and the Belfast Pogroms 1920–22* (Belfast: Beyond the Pale, 2001) provides a pioneering account of divisions between the pro- and anti-Treaty IRA in Belfast.

18. This figure is "safely assumed" by Coogan, *IRA,* 79, but Hanley, *IRA,* chap. 1, provides good reasons for thinking that the IRA numbered between 10,000 and 12,000 volunteers in 1932 before declining after a significant breakaway by the politically minded founders of the Republican Congress, and being reduced to fewer than 4,000 members by 1936.

19. Seán MacBride, the leader of Clann na Poblachta, was a former chief of staff of the IRA, who achieved a unique historical status as a winner of both the Lenin and Nobel peace prizes.

20. The defeat of the IRA in Northern Ireland in the 1940s was exemplified in the execution of Tom Williams, whom the Northern Ireland court identified as the key figure in a unit that killed an RUC officer. One of his reprieved comrades, Joe Cahill, later became the first chief of staff of the Provisional IRA: see Jim McVeigh, *Executed: Tom Williams and the IRA* (Belfast: Beyond the Pale, 1999) and Brendan Anderson, *Joe Cahill: A Life in the IRA* (Dublin, 2002).

21. Bell, *Secret Army,* 252n.1, observes that "The situation was so bad that the IRA Intelligence had got access to a copy of a secret [Irish] government publication, *Notes on the IRA,* and used the names to make their early contacts [for reconstruction] under the assumption that if Special Branch thought a man was a troublemaker he would be a good man."

22. Bell, *Secret Army,* chaps. 14–16; Seán Cronin, *Irish Nationalism: A History of its Roots and Ideology* (Dublin: Academy Press, 1980), chap. 5.

23. The most incisive analysis of de Valera's long-term legitimizing of independent Ireland through constitutional republicanism is Bill Kissane's *Explaining Irish Democracy* (Dublin: University College Dublin Press, 2002), 165ff.

24. O'Higgins, the strongman of the Cumann na nGaedheal government, seriously sought to have George V separately crowned as king of Ireland, following thereby the original "dual monarchy" proposal made by Arthur Griffith earlier in the century, and claimed that "republicanism" was a foreign ideal. Griffith died in 1922 so we do not know whether he would have supported this reasoning.

25. Its ultimatum addressed to Lord Halifax is reproduced in Cronin, *Irish Nationalism,* app. 14.

26. For a 90-page statement of calcified orthodoxy, see Ruairí Ó Brádaigh,

*Dílseacht: The Story of Comdt. General Tom Maguire and the Second (All-Ireland) Dáil* (Dublin: n.p., 1997).

27. In the 1950s and 1960s, to judge by their publications and statements, Irish nationalists did not consider that Ireland's progressive unwinding of the Treaty had entrenched Ulster unionists' wish to remain part of the United Kingdom. Denis Kennedy, in an analysis of unionist newspapers in 1919–1949, argues that it in fact widened the gulf between the two parts of Ireland (by which he means the gulf between Ulster unionists and Irish nationalists); see *The Widening Gulf: Northern Attitudes to the Independent Irish State, 1919–1949* (Belfast: Blackstone Press, 1988).

28. Bishop and Mallie, *Provisional IRA*, 104; Paul Arthur, "Republican Violence in Northern Ireland: The Rationale," in John Darby, Nicholas Dodge and A. C. Hepburn, eds., *Political Violence: Ireland in a Comparative Perspective* (Belfast: Appletree, 1990), 48–63 (49).

29. Bishop and Mallie, *Provisional IRA*, 89–105; Bell, *Secret Army*, 355–72; Coogan, *IRA*, 365–84; English, *Armed Struggle*, 81–147; Henry Patterson, *The Politics of Illusion: Republicanism and Socialism in Modern Ireland* (London: Hutchinson Radius, 1989), chaps. 4–6 and James M. Glover, "Northern Ireland: Future Terrorist Trends," Ministry of Defence [United Kingdom], D/DINI/2003 MOD Form 102: s25/II/82, 2 November 1978, reprinted in Cronin, *Irish Nationalism*, 339–57.

30. R. F. Foster, *Modern Ireland: 1600–1972* (London: Allen Lane, 1988), 589.

31. Kevin Toolis, *Rebel Hearts: Journeys Within the IRA's Soul* (London: Praeger, 1995), 28ff. Toolis writes of the IRA through investigative and personalized studies of "defenders," "brothers" [the Finucanes], "informers," "volunteers," "chieftains" [McGuinness], and "martyrs." In its storytelling and prose *Rebel Hearts* is the best journalistic foray into the IRA. It is, however, a social science-free zone, and its policy proposals are shallow. But it has the quality of enduring literature.

32. See the interviews in Robert White, *Provisional Irish Republicans* (Westport, Conn.: Greenwood Press, 1993), chap. 4.

33. Bob Purdie, "Was the Civil Rights Movement a Republican/Communist Conspiracy?" *Irish Political Studies* 3 (1988): 33–41; Purdie, *Politics in the Streets: The Origins of the Civil Rights Movement in Northern Ireland* (Belfast: Blackstaff Press, 1990).

34. Father Michael O'Flanagan was vice-president of Sinn Féin (1917–1921) and president in 1934. He was disciplined by the Roman Catholic Church and was the sole priest in Ireland to support the Spanish Republic against General Franco (Cronin, *Irish Nationalism*, 279n.140). Father Patrick Ryan, whose extradition to the UK was refused by the Irish courts in 1988, was accused of being a member of the IRA.

35. Hereafter, unless otherwise stated, the Provisional IRA will be treated as *the* IRA, and Provisional Sinn Féin as Sinn Féin because that is how the volunteers and members describe their organizations, and because, officially, the Official IRA no longer exists, having been disbanded by its party, the Workers Party, the heir of the defunct Official Sinn Féin.

36. James Kelly, *Orders for the Captain?* (Dublin, 1971); *The Thimbleriggers: The Dublin Arms Trials of 1970* (Dublin: J. Kelly, 1999).

37. O'Leary and McGarry, *Politics of Antagonism*, chaps. 3–4.

38. She almost certainly authorized indirect negotiations during the first batch of hunger strikes in 1980; see David Beresford, *Ten Men Dead: The Story of the 1981 Irish Hunger Strike* (London: Grafton, 1987), 40, 292–93. After the Anglo-Irish Agreement of 1985 Thatcher and secretaries of state Tom King and Peter Brooke were aware, and approved of, a "pipeline" to and from Gerry Adams via priest Alex Reid; see Ed Moloney, *A Secret History of the IRA* (New York: W.W. Norton, 2002), 246–60, passim.

39. For example, see the information in Moloney, *Secret History*, passim.

40. See Coogan, *IRA*; Brendan O'Brien, *The Long War: The IRA and Sinn Féin from Armed Struggle to Peace Talks*, updated ed. (Dublin: O'Brien Press, 1995); Taylor, *Provos*; White, *Provisional Irish Republicans.*

41. O'Brien, *Long War*, app. 1; Martin Dillon, *Twenty Five Years of Terror* (London: Bantam, 1996), 353–84; and see the commentary in Coogan, *IRA*, 544–71.

42. Taylor, *Provos*, 181.

43. For police and court records, see Kieran McEvoy, *Paramilitary Imprisonment in Northern Ireland: Resistance, Management and Release* (Oxford: Oxford University Press, 2001); for a key intelligence report, see Glover, "Northern Ireland: Future Terrorist Trends." For accounts of victims, see David McKittrick, Seamus Kelters, Brian Feeney, and Chris Thornton, *Lost Lives: The Stories of the Men, Women and Children Who Died as a Result of the Northern Ireland Troubles* (Edinburgh: Mainstream, 2001); Malcolm Sutton, *Bear in Mind These Dead: An Index of Deaths from the Conflict in Ireland, 1969–1993* (Belfast: Beyond the Pale, 1994). For autobiographical and biographical accounts of republican figures, see Gerry Adams, *Falls Memories* (Dingle, Ireland: Brandon, 1983); *Cage Eleven* (Dingle, 1990); *Before the Dawn* (London: Heinemann, 1996); *An Irish Voice* (Dingle, 1997); *An Irish Journal* (Dingle, 2001); *A Farther Shore: Ireland's Long Road to Peace* (New York: Random House, 2003); Anderson, *Joe Cahill*; Liam Clarke and Kathryn Johnston, *Martin McGuinness: From Guns to Government* (Edinburgh: Mainstream, 2003); Seán Mac Stiofáin, *Memoirs of a Revolutionary* (London: Gordon Cremonise, 1975); Laurence McKeown, *Out of Time: Irish Republican Prisoners, Long Kesh 1972–2000* (Belfast: Beyond the Pale, 2001); Shane Paul O'Doherty, *The Volunteer: A Former IRA Man's True Story* (London: Fount, 1993); Bobby Sands, *The Diary of Bobby Sands* (Dublin: Sinn Féin Publicity Department, 1981); *Prison Poems* (Dublin: Sinn Féin Publicity Department, 1981); *One Day in My Life* (Cork: Mercier, 1982); David Sharrock and Mark Devenport, *Man of War, Man of Peace? The Unauthorised Biography of Gerry Adams* (London: Macmillan, 1997). There is also Danny Morrison's prison journal, *Then the Walls Came Down: A Prison Journal* (Cork: Mercier, 1999), which I have not read.

44. Martin McGartland, *Fifty Dead Men Walking* (London: Blake, 1997) and *Dead Man Running: The True Story of a Secret Agent's Escape from the IRA and MI5* (Edinburgh: Mainstream, 1998); Eamon Collins (with Mike McGovern), *Killing Rage* (London: Granta, 1997); Sean O'Callaghan, *The Informer* (London: Bantam, 1998). Collins's book seems to me the most interesting, honest, revealing and least self-serving of the apostate accounts.

45. John Horgan and Max Taylor, "The Provisional Irish Republican Army: Command and Functional Structure," *Terrorism and Political Violence* 9 (1997): 1–32. Details of the reorganization, spelled out in a "Staff Report," allegedly thought through by Gerry Adams and others when interned in Long Kesh, became known when IRA chief of staff Seamus Twomey was arrested in December 1977. The changes may have been implemented when Martin McGuinness was chief of staff (1978–82): see O'Brien, *Long War*, 107ff; see also Coogan, *IRA*, 464–74.

46. Collins, *Killing Rage*, 83.

47. According to Moloney, *Secret History*, 573, the operational units in Northern Command are formally organized around Belfast and six other areas (Derry, Donegal/ Fermanagh, Tyrone and Monaghan, Armagh (North and South), and Down), and each has ASUs operating under Brigades; in slight contrast, O'Brien, *Long War*, 105, 110, maintains the Northern Command is organized over all of the six counties of Northern Ireland and the five adjacent border counties of the Republic (Louth, Monaghan, Cavan, Leitrim and Donegal), and has Belfast, Derry, Donegal, Tyrone/Monaghan and Armagh as the Brigade areas.

48. Bell, *Secret Army*, 468–69.

49. The IRA's internal rules of court martial procedure are documented in Coogan, *IRA*, app. 2. Collins's *Killing Rage* describes his participation in these internal courts.

50. Collins, *Killing Rage*, 84.

51. A clear-headed appraisal of vigilantism and punishment beatings is found in Andrew Silke, "Rebel's Dilemma: The Changing Relationship between the IRA, Sinn Féin and Paramilitary Vigilantism in Northern Ireland," *Terrorism and Political Violence* 11 (1) (Spring 1999): 55–93. Unlike standard critics he shows how much it is a response to local demands. Silke correctly argued that only with major police reform will the IRA and Sinn Féin be able to terminate their involvement in the system, but in my view was too pessimistic in assuming that both organizations are "irretrievably" committed to vigilantism.

52. Many of these are summarized in Horgan and Taylor, "The Provisional Irish Republican Army," Table 1.

53. Glover, "Northern Ireland: Future Terrorist Trends," published in *Republican News* and reprinted in Cronin, *Irish Nationalism*, 339–57.

54. Cronin, *Irish Nationalism*, 344. Hereafter, unless otherwise indicated, all references to pounds are to pounds sterling.

55. Foster, *Modern Ireland*, 590, writes of the Provisionals that "American money, local support and the army's record in house-to-house searches established them firmly in the urban ghettos." This implicit order of ranking is not consistent with the evidence. It would have been more accurate to write that local support for defense against loyalist and police attacks, the British army's record of repression, and donations from Ireland and America, firmly established the Provisional IRA in many nationalist dominated areas.

56. Scott Anderson, "Making a Killing: The High Cost of Peace in Northern Ireland," *Harpers Magazine* 288 (1725) (February 1994): 45–54.

57. See also Robert White, "Commitment, Efficacy and Personal Sacrifice Among Irish Republicans," *Journal of Political and Military Sociology* 16 (1988): 77–90.

58. Cronin, *Irish Nationalism*, 343.

59. White, Provisional Irish Republicans, *passim.*

60. Cronin, *Irish Nationalism*, app. 16; the list was compiled by Eamon Timoney, one of the prisoners.

61. Cronin, *Irish Nationalism*, 342; Coogan, *IRA*, 468.

62. Kevin Boyle, Tom Hadden, and Paddy Hillyard, *Ten Years on in Northern Ireland* (London: Cobden Trust, 1980), 19; see also Kevin Boyle, Robert Chesney, and Tom Hadden, "Who Are the Terrorists?" *Fortnight*, 7 May 1976 and *New Society*, 6 May 1976. Ex-IRA Volunteers Gerry Adams, *The Politics of Irish Freedom* (Dingle: Brandon, 1986), 67–68, and Patrick Magee, *Gangsters or Guerrillas? Representations of Irish Republicans in "Troubles Fiction"* (Belfast: Beyond the Pale, 2001), 16, both approvingly cite the Glover Report, and the Boyle, Hadden and Hillyard (1980) appraisal, as independent assessments of the noncriminal nature of IRA recruits.

63. Magee, *Gangsters or Guerrillas?* passim. The 1984 bombing of the Grand Hotel Brighton, the site of a Conservative Party conference, killed five people, injured senior Conservative Norman Tebbit, seriously disabled his wife, and came close to killing Margaret Thatcher. Magee received five life sentences for the bombing. He served fourteen years before being released under the terms of the Good Friday Agreement.

64. Anderson, "Making a Killing."

65. Michael Ignatieff, "The Temptations of Nihilism," in *The Lesser Evil: Political Ethics in an Age of Terror* (Princeton, N.J.: Princeton University Press, 2003), 122.

66. Robert White, "From Peaceful Protest to Guerrilla War—Micromobilization of the Provisional Irish Republican Army," *American Journal of Sociology* 94 (1989): 1277–302; White, *Provisional Irish Republicans*, passim. Collins's *Killing Rage* provides the fullest narrative of his movement into the IRA—it includes the mistreatment of his mother and the beating up and false arrest of his father, his brother, and himself by British paratroopers, knowledge of left-wing ideology and exposure to a left-wing (English) academic, disillusionment with the prospects of reform and power-sharing, and the impact of the campaign for political status by republican prisoners. "I was full of a heady mixture of anti-imperialism, anger, sympathy and self-importance" (23); greed played no role, and he despised volunteers and auxiliaries who engaged in petty theft.

67. Reviewed further in McGarry and O'Leary, *Explaining Northern Ireland*, chaps. 6–7.

68. Frank Burton, *The Politics of Legitimacy: Struggles in a Belfast Community* (London: Routledge, 1979); Silke, "Rebel's Dilemma."

69. See McEvoy, *Paramilitary Imprisonment.*

70. Ken Heskin, "Societal Disintegration in Northern Ireland—A Five Year Update," *Economic and Social Review*16 (3) (1985): 187–99.

71. See also Brendan O'Leary, "The Labour Government and Northern Ireland, 1974–79," in John McGarry and Brendan O'Leary, *The Northern Ireland Conflict: Consociational Engagements* (Oxford: Oxford University Press, 2004), 194–216.

72. H. A. Lyons and H. J. Harbinson, "A Comparison of Political and Non-Political Murderers in Northern Ireland, 1974–84," *Medicine, Science and the Law* 26 (1986): 193–98; Clark R. McCauley, "Terrorism Research and Public Policy: An Overview," *Terrorism and Political Violence* 3 (1) (1991): 126–44; Andrew P. Silke, "Cheshire-Cat Logic: The Recurring Theme of Terrorist Abnormality in Psychological Research," *Psychology, Crime and Law* 4 (1998): 51–69; Andrew P. Silke, ed., *Terrorists, Victims and Society: Psychological Perspectives on Terrorism and Its Consequences* (London: Wiley, 2003), chaps. 1–2.

73. Bishop and Mallie, *Provisional IRA*, 5.

74. For example, see Moloney, *Secret History.*

75. Bishop and Mallie, *Provisional IRA*, 1; Mallie is identified as the interviewer and Bishop as the author.

76. McEvoy, *Paramilitary Imprisonment*, 16.

77. Personal communication.

78. Jack Holland, *The American Connection: U.S. Guns, Money and Influence in Northern Ireland* (Dublin: Poolbeg Press 1989), 27–113; Moloney, Secret History, 1–33.

79. O'Leary and McGarry, *Politics of Antagonism*, chap. 1, and Brendan O'Leary and John McGarry, *The Politics of Antagonism: Understanding Northern Ireland*, 3rd ed. (London: Athlone, forthcoming).

80. English, *Armed Struggle*, 380.

81. E. Zimmermann, "Political Unrest in Western Europe," *Western European Politics* 12 (1989): 179–96, cited in O'Leary and McGarry, *Politics of Antagonism*, ch. 1.

82. See O'Leary and McGarry, *Politics of Antagonism.*

83. W. D. Flackes and Sidney Elliott, *Northern Ireland: A Political Directory, 1968–88* (Belfast: Blackstaff Press, 1989), 394.

84. Compare the evaluations of Brendan O'Duffy, "Violence in Northern Ireland: Sectarian or Ethno-National?" *Ethnic and Racial Studies* 18 (4) (1995): 740–72, and Robert White, "The Irish Republican Army: An Assessment of Sectarianism," *Terrorism and Political Violence* 9 (1) (1997): 20–55, with those of Steve Bruce, "Victim Selection in Ethnic Conflict: Motives and Attitudes in Irish Republicanism," *Terrorism and Political Violence* 9 (1) (1997): 56–71.

85. For example, see Bruce, "Victim Selection."

86. Irish Information Partnership data, cited in O'Leary and McGarry, *Politics of Antagonism*, chap. 1.

87. Bob Rowthorn and Naomi Wayne, *Northern Ireland: The Political Economy of Conflict* (Oxford: Polity, 1988), passim.

88. See Peter Wright, *Spycatcher: The Candid Autobiography of a Senior Intelligence Officer* (New York: Viking, 1987) and Paul Foot, *Who Framed Colin Wallace?* (London: Macmillan, 1989).

89. Michael L. R. Smith, *Fighting for Ireland? The Military Strategy of the Irish Republican Movement* (London: Routledge, 1995) is an unusual Clausewitzian treatment, which I examined as a Ph.D. dissertation.

90. On the blanket protest and hunger strikes, see Tim Pat Coogan, *On the Blanket: The H Block Story* (Dublin: Ward River Press, 1980), Beresford, *Ten Men Dead*, and Liam Clarke, *Broadening the Battlefield: The H-Blocks and the Rise of Sinn Féin* (Dublin: Gill and Macmillan, 1987).

91. See the discussion of the hunger strikes in Padraig O'Malley, *Biting at the Grave: The Irish Hunger Strikes and the Politics of Despair* (Belfast: Blackstaff Press, 1990), critically reviewed in Brendan O'Leary, "Review [of O'Malley 1990]" *Irish Political Studies* 6 (1991): 118–22.

92. See Feeney, *Sinn Féin*.

93. Important here are Feeney, *Sinn Féin*; English, *Armed Struggle*; Eamonn Mallie and David McKittrick, *The Fight for Peace: The Secret Story Behind the Irish Peace Process* (London: Heinemann, 1996); McGarry and O'Leary, *Explaining Northern Ireland*, chap. 10; McGarry and O'Leary, *Northern Ireland Conflict*; Anthony McIntyre, "Modern Irish Republicanism: The Product of British State Strategies," *Irish Political Studies*,10 (1995): 97–122; Moloney, *Secret History*; Brian Rowan, *Behind the Lines: The Story of the IRA and Loyalist Ceasefires* (Belfast: Blackstaff Press, 1995).

94. Moloney, *Secret History*, Appendix 3.

95. See O'Leary, "The Nature of the British-Irish Agreement."

**Chapter 7**

1. See Sumantra Bose, *Kashmir: Roots of Conflict, Paths to Peace* (Cambridge, Mass.: Harvard University Press, 2003), chap. 1; Jyoti Bhushan Dasgupta, *Jammu and Kashmir* (The Hague: Nijhoff, 1968); Josef Korbel, *Danger in Kashmir* (Princeton, N.J.: Princeton University Press, 1954); A. G. Noorani, *The Kashmir Question* (Bombay: Manaktalas, 1964).

2. These estimates were cited during the author's personal interviews in Srinagar in September 2004 with members of the Indian counterinsurgency command and with leaders of the All-Parties Hurriyat Conference.

3. Personal communications with members of the Indian counterinsurgency command (Srinagar), December 2004.

4. See Bose, *Kashmir*, chap. 2.

5. Ibid., chap. 3.

6. PJK consists of two distinct regions. The more populated region is known as "Azad" (Free) Jammu and Kashmir and comprises a long sliver of land running on a north-south axis, across the LOC from IJK's Kashmir Valley and Jammu regions. "Azad" Kashmir has its own institutions, but is subject to heavy-handed control and regulation by the Pakistani civilian and military authorities. The second, sparsely populated but vast region is known as the Northern Areas and lies in the remote high Himalayas. The Northern Areas are governed directly by the Pakistani central government.

7. See Amanullah Khan, *Free Kashmir* (Karachi: Central Printing Press, 1970), esp. 139–49. Khan, a JKLF cofounder and ideologue, was born in 1933 in Gilgit, a town in PJK's Northern Areas, and lives in Rawalpindi, Pakistan, although his political activism is centered on "Azad' Kashmir.

8. The bulk of the Kashmir Valley's small Hindu minority (4 percent of the population) fled the Valley for the Hindu-majority city of Jammu in IJK's south, or farther to Delhi, during the first months of the insurrection in 1990. These refugees frequently blame the JKLF for their plight.

9. See Muhammad Ishaq Khan, *Kashmir's Transition to Islam: The Role of Muslim Rishis* (Delhi: Manohar, 1994).

10. See Seyyed Reza Vali Nasr, *The Vanguard of the Islamic Revolution: The Jama'at-I-Islami of Pakistan* (New York: I.B. Tauris, 1994).

11. Approximately 80–85 percent of Valley and IJK Muslims are Sunni, 15–20 percent Shi'a.

12. Bose, *Kashmir,* 50–51.

13. Kashmir towns generally have labyrinthine old neighborhoods (*mohallas*) full of lanes and alleys, which makes the task of fighting guerrillas difficult. Srinagar, which has a population of about 1.5 million, has numerous such localities, together with more modern areas that house government buildings and residences of the more affluent.

14. India's federal government controls several hundred thousand paramilitary personnel organized in a number of different formations, the largest being the Border Security Force (BSF) and the Central Reserve Police Force (CRPF). Their "paramilitary" designation means that their structure, weaponry, and duties place them in the gray area between ordinary police and the professional military.

15. The regular army was drawn more and more into fighting insurgency as the decade progressed. Starting in 1994, some army units were formally seconded to counterinsurgency tasks on a long-term basis as the Rashtriya Rifles (RR; National Rifles). By the late 1990s, four RR formations of 10,000 men each were operating, two in the Valley and two in war zones in the Jammu region. In 2002–2003, the RR was expanded to five formations.

16. Bose, *Kashmir,* 128.

17. IJK's third region, Ladakh, covers a vast land mass but has a sparse population of 250,000 people (divided equally between Buddhists and Muslims of Tibetan ethnic stock) as it is a frozen high-altitude desert. Ladakh has remained more or less insurgency-free, although the 1999 limited war between India and Pakistan occurred on one stretch of the LOC in Ladakh, in the Kargil district, after Pakistani forces infiltrated the Indian side of the LOC and occupied a number of strategic heights. By comparison, the Kashmir Valley has more than 5 million inhabitants, and the Jammu region between 4.5 and 5 million.

18. See Strobe Talbott, *Engaging India: Diplomacy, Democracy and the Bomb* (Washington, D.C.: Brookings Institution Press, 2004).

19. On the *fidayeen* phase of insurgency in Kashmir, see Bose, *Kashmir,* 140–61.

20. *Kashmir Times,* Jammu, 23 August 2000, 1.

21. The only pro-"self-determination" elements who did participate were some members of a party called the People's Conference, based in the northern Valley district of Kupwara, whose veteran leader Abdul Ghani Lone was shot dead in Srinagar by pro-Pakistan extremists (not from JKHM but a much smaller group) in May 2002.

22. Such a framework to settle the Kashmir conflict is developed in Bose, *Kashmir,* chap. 5.

23. *Illustrated Weekly of India,* Bombay, 10–16 October 1992, 4.

24. See Bose, *Kashmir,* chap. 4.

**Chapter 8**

Epigraph: I would like to thank the organizers and participants in the SSRC-NUPI project for their constructive comments and conviviality, especially Sumantra Bose, Tore Hattrem, Brendan O'Leary, John Tirman, and particularly the late Marianne Heiberg for her inspiration and encouragement. All errors and omissions remain my own responsibility. In addition to the grant from SSRC and NUPI, a Study Abroad Fellowship from the Leverhulme Trust and a Small Research Grant from the British Academy supported some preliminary research.

1. Peter Chalk, "Liberation Tigers of Tamil Eelam's (LTTE) International Organization and Operations—A Preliminary Analysis," Commentary No. 77, Canadian Security Intelligence Service, 1999, http//:www.fas.org/irp/world/para/docs/com77e.htm, accessed 17 November 2004.

2. Radhika Coomaraswamy, *Ideology and the Constitution: Essays on Constitutional Jurisprudence* (New Delhi: Konark and International Centre for Ethnic Studies, 1997).

3. Quoted in V. S. Ganeshalingam, *Arrest and Detention Under the National Security Laws and Human Rights in Sri Lanka, 1989 Onwards* (Colombo: Bandaranaike Centre for International Studies, 1989), 46.

4. This claim can be evaluated with regard to Section 5 of the Government of Ireland Act (1920), whose minority rights protections were Jennings's model for Section 29 (2) of the Ceylon Constitution of 1947. As O'Leary and McGarry have documented, Section 5 failed to provide substantive protections against systematic anti-Catholic discrimination in both the public and private sectors in Northern Ireland, contributing directly to the outbreak of civil violence in the late 1960s and spawning the revival of militant Irish republicanism. Brendan O'Leary and John McGarry, *The Politics of Antagonism: Understanding Northern Ireland*, 2nd ed. (London: Athlone, 1996), chap 3.

5. Quoted in K. M. de Silva, *Reaping the Whirlwind: Ethnic Conflict, Ethnic Politics in Sri Lanka* (New Delhi: Penguin, 1998), 127.

6. Robert Oberst, "Youth Militancy and the Rise of Sri Lankan Tamil Nationalism," in Subrata K. Mitra and R. Alison Lewis, eds., *Subnational Movements in South Asia* (Boulder, Colo.: Westview Press, 1997), 143.

7. S. Manivasakan, "Sri Lankan Ethnic Conflict: Legal and Constitutional Aspects," in Dagmar Hellman-Rajanayagam, ed., *Peace Initiatives Towards Reconciliation and Nation Building in Sri Lanka: An International Perspective* (Kuala Lumpur: Malaysian Ceylonese Congress, 2002), 95.

8. de Silva, *Reaping the Whirlwind*, 30.

9. Official Language Act No. 33 (1956).

10. de Silva, *Reaping the Whirlwind*, 130–36; A. Jeyaratnam Wilson, *Sri Lankan Tamil Nationalism: Its Origins and Development in the 19th and 20th Centuries* (New Delhi: Penguin, 2001), chap. 6.

11. Oberst, "Youth Militancy," 149.

12. Ibid.

13. Coomaraswamy, *Ideology and the Constitution*, 23–24; de Silva, *Reaping the Whirlwind*, 61–62.

14. Manivasakan, "Sri Lankan Ethnic Conflict," 94.

15. For example, Neelan Tiruchelvam, "The Politics of Decentralisation and Devolution: Competing Conceptions of District Development Council in Sri Lanka," in Golman Wilson, ed., *Ethnic Conflict in the Third World* (London: St. Martin's Press, 1983), cited in Manivasakan, "Sri Lankan Ethnic Conflict," 95.

16. Benjamin Reilly, *Democracy in Plural Societies: Electoral Engineering for Conflict Managemen* (Cambridge: Cambridge University Press, 2001), 118–19.

17. Ibid., 119.

18. Sixth Amendment to the 1978 constitution, as quoted in Manivasakan, "Sri Lankan Ethnic Conflict," 97.

19. For an application of Michael Hechter's "internal colonialism" thesis to the Sri Lankan case, see Amita Shastri, "The Material Basis for Separatism: The Tamil Eelam Movement in Sri Lanka," *Journal of Asian Studies* 49 (1) (1990): 56–77.

20. Pon. Balasundarampillai, "Trincomalee: Geo-politics, Ethnic Dimension and Development Potential" (Thirunelvell: University of Jaffna: Sociological Society, 2002).

21. Gamini Lakshman Peiris, "Irrigation, Land Distribution and Ethnic Conflict in Sri Lanka: An Evaluation of Criticisms with Special Reference to the Mahaveli Programme," *Ethnic Studies Report* 12 (1) (1994): 43–88.

22. The eastern part of the Northern Province, including the bordering sea basin, is particularly rich in mineral sands, including ilmenite (iron titanium oxide) and rutile (titanium oxide), the two most important ores in the production of titanium.

23. Quoted in Wilson, *Sri Lankan Tamil Nationalism,* 144–45.

24. Liberation Tigers of Tamil Eelam (LTTE), "The Proposal by the Liberation Tigers of Tamil Eelam on Behalf of the Tamil People for an Agreement to Establish an Interim Self-Governing Authority for the Northeast of the Island of Sri Lanka," Colombo, October 2003.

25. Quoted in M. R. Narayan Swamy, *Prabhakaran: Inside an Elusive Mind* (Colombo: Vijitha Yapa Publications, 2003), 169.

26. Swamy, *Prabhakaran,* 220.

27. A senior defense official also believed that Prabhakaran eliminated his erstwhile colleague Mahattaya because of the latter's willingness to accept an internal federal solution. Interview with senior defense official, Colombo, 5 March 2004; these views are consistent with those held by prime minister and later president Chandrika Kumaratunga, Interview with *India Today,* 15 May 1995.

28. Interview with defence official, 5 March 2004.

29. Neelan Tiruchelvam, "Federalism and Diversity in Sri Lanka," in Yash Ghai, ed., *Autonomy and Ethnicity: Negotiating Competing Claims in Multi-Ethnic States* (Cambridge: Cambridge University Press and International Centre for Ethnic Studies, 2000), 201–2; Landon E. Hancock, "The Indo-Sri Lankan Accord: An Analysis of Conflict Termination," *Civil Wars* 2 (4) (1999): 83–105.

30. de Silva notes that under Premadasa, "bhikkhus [Buddhist leaders], both within the establishment and outside it, enjoyed greater influence with the government, in their role of articulators of Sinhalese Buddhist opinion than at any time since the mid-1950s." de Silva, *Reaping the Whirlwind,* 110.

31. Adrian Wijemanne, "Peace: From Illusion to Reality," in Jayadeva Uyangoda and Morina Perera, eds., *Sri Lanka's Peace Process 2002: Critical Perspectives* (Colombo: Social Scientists' Association, 2003), 127–30.

32. Chandrika Kumaratunga, Press Conference, New Delhi, 28 March 1995, in Avtar Singh Bhasim, ed., *India-Sri Lanka Relations and Sri Lanka's Ethnic Conflict* (New Delhi: Indian Research Publications, 2001), vol. 5, 2770–71, emphasis added.

33. Interview with S. Puleedevan, Secretary General of LTTE Peace Secretariat, Kilinochchi, 5 May 2003.

34. See the Vaddukoddai Resolution of 1976 and the Thimpu Declaration of 1985; see also Sumantra Bose, *States, Nations, Sovereignty: Sri Lanka, India and the Tamil Eelam Movement* (New Delhi: Sage, 1994).

35. Interview with Illamparithi, Jaffna LTTE political leader, Jaffna, 7 June 2003.

36. Quoted in Partha S. Ghosh, *Ethnicity Versus Nationalism: The Devolution Dis-*

*course in Sri Lanka* (Colombo: Vijitha Yapa, 2003), 428. Ghosh also notes the important qualification of the Tamil concept of territorial dimension by noting the shift in Balasingham's public conception of a "Tamil homeland" to a homeland of the Tamils and Muslims and the conception of a final settlement "amicable to our people and Sinhalese and Muslims living in the North and East" (428), quoting National Peace Council (Sri Lanka), "Situation Report," 9–20 September 2002.

37. Swamy, *Prabhakaran,* 200; see also Adele Balasingham, *The Will to Freedom: An Inside View of the Tamil Resistance,* 2nd ed. (Mitcham: Fairmax, 2003), 336.

38. And like some Irish republicans, Bose was willing to gain German assistance in the war against the British Empire. See Swamy, *Prabhakaran,* 23.

39. Interview with Sanappah Master, Kilinochchi, 1 March 2004.

40. Calculated from data compiled by South Asian Terrorism Portal, Institute for Conflict Management, Delhi, http://www.satp.org/satporgtp/countries/shrilanka/database/data_suicide_killings.htm, accessed 20 November 2004.

41. Interview with Professor S. K. Sitrampalam, Dean, Faculty of Graduate Studies, University of Jaffna, Thirunelvely, 2 March 2004.

42. Oberst, "Youth Militancy," 152–56.

43. Shastri, "The Material Basis for Separatism," 63.

44. Ibid., citing Mick Moore, *The State and Peasant Politics in Sri Lanka* (Honolulu: University of Hawaii Press, 1985), 193.

45. Shastri, "The Material Basis for Separatism," 70.

46. Ibid., 74.

47. Wilson, *Sri Lankan Tamil Nationalism,* 18–19.

48. Swamy, *Prabhakarn,* 196–97.

49. Arve Ofstad, "Countries in Violent Conflict and Aid Strategies: The Case of Sri Lanka," *World Development* 30 (2): 165–80.

50. Benedikt Korf and Kalinga Tudor Silva, "Poverty, Ethnicity, and Conflict in Sri Lanka," paper delivered at the conference Staying Poor: Chronic Poverty and Development Policy, University of Manchester, 7–9 April 2003, citing Jonathan Goodhand, David Hulme, and Nick Lewer, "Social Capital and Political Economy of Violence: A Case Study of Sri Lanka," *Disasters* 24 (4) (2001): 390–406.

51. Bose, *States, Nations, Sovereignty;* Wilson, *Sri Lankan Tamil Nationalism,* chap. 3; Bruce Kapferer, "Ethnic Nationalism and the Discourses of Violence in Sri Lanka," *Journal of Transnational & Cross-Cultural Studies* 9 (1) (2001): 33–67.

52. Personal communication with London-based LTTE supporter, originally from Velvettiturai (VVT), the same village as Prabhakaran, London, 6 March 2004.

53. K. M. de Silva, for example, claims that the basis of the territorial claim made by Tamils since the mid-1950s was based on a tendentious, partial reading of the minute prepared by British academic Hugh Cleghorn advising the colonial administration. See de Silva, *Reaping the Whirlwind,* 152–53.

54. Interview with Jenitharathy Sivasithambaram, former LTTE cadre, Kilinochchi, 4 March 2004.

55. The LTTE itself commemorates the deaths of approximately 16,000 cadres; the Sri Lankan government claimed 22,116 LTTE casualties by 1997. See Saman Kelegama, "The Economic Costs of Conflict in Sri Lanka," in Richard I. Rotberg, ed., *Creating Peace in Sri Lanka: Civil War & Reconciliation* (Washington, D.C.: Brookings Institution Press, 1997), 79.

56. Interview with V. Anandasangaree, Jaffna, 3 March 2004. Anandasangaree's outspoken criticisms of the LTTE made him a target of intimidation by LTTE supporters in Jaffna.

57. University Teachers for Human Rights (Jaffna), "The Plight of Child Conscripts, Social Degradation and Anti-Muslim Frenzy," Special Report 14, 20 July 2002.

58. Wilson, *Sri Lankan Tamil Nationalism*, 23.

59. Dennis B. McGilvray, *Tamil and Muslim Identities in the East*, A History of Ethnic Conflict in Sri Lanka: Recollection, Reinterpretation & Reconciliation 24 (Colombo: Marga Institute, 2001), 5.

60. Ibid., 23.

61. Interview with A. C. Haja Mohideen, Town President, Sri Lanka Muslim Congress, Trincomalee, 1 May, 2003.

62. Rohan Gunaratna, *Sri Lanka's Ethnic Crisis and National Security* (Colombo: South Asian Network on Conflict Research, 1998), 263.

63. Chalk, "Liberation Tigers," 3–4.

64. Oberst, "Youth Militancy," 164.

65. Chalk, "Liberation Tigers," 6.

66. Ibid., 7.

67. Oberst, "Youth Militancy," 163–64. See also "LTTE Suspect Nabbed with Rs. 6m Worth of Heroin," *Sunday Observer*, Colombo, 9 December 2004.

68. Alan Knight and Kasun Ubayasiri, "eTerror : Journalism, Terrorism and the Internet," http://www.ejournalism.au.com/ejournalist/alkas.pdf, accessed 29 November 2004.

69. Transparency International and Centre for Policy Alternatives, "Corruption in Sri Lanka" (Colombo: Centre for Policy Alternatives, 2002).

70. Interview with defense official, 5 March 2004.

71. Ibid.

72. Gunaratna, *Sri Lanka's Ethnic Crisis*, 221–32. The senior defence official interviewed for this research claimed that Gunaratna's criticisms of the army's intelligence branches were both selective and reflective of the author's contacts with (unspecified) regional intelligence agencies.

73. In October 2004 the Indian-based Eelam National Democratic Liberation Front joined with Karuna's TEPLT to form a Tamil Eelam United Liberation Front (TIVM) to "achieve the cherished rights and the reasonable aspirations of the Tamils in Sri Lanka." Quoted by Indo-Asian News Service, 21 October 2004.

74. The impact of the LTTE's ability to penetrate the Sinhalese heartland was revealed to me in May 2003 by the response of a Sinhalese shopkeeper interviewed in Galle. I asked her if she appreciated the LTTE's offer of humanitarian relief to flood victims in the Ratnapura area. She replied that the LTTE was opportunistically surveying possible future strategic bomb targets. Interview with Sinhalese shopkeeper, Galle, 12 May 2003.

75. Tertiary costs do *not* include the difficult to quantify costs of nonproductive employment such as security costs, transportation disruption, and forced outmigration. See Kelegama, "The Economic Costs of Conflict."

76. These data are based on the Lincoln Project, directed by Robert Oberst, Nebraska Wesleyan University. I am grateful for his permission to access and reproduce the data, especially since multiple requests made by the author have been ignored or refused by the Sri Lanka Ministry of Defence, Public Security, Law and Order and the Department of Census and Statistics. Also refused or ignored were requests to the LTTE on annual deaths of its cadres. According to Oberst, "The [Lincoln] project has gathered information on all casualties and arrests in Sri Lanka since 1984. Civil war casualties and arrests and ethnic riot casualties and arrests since 1970 have been included in the data set. Beginning in 1984, the project began adding information from the *Island* newspaper as well as the Federal Broadcast Information Service (FBIS). In addition, periodic reports by human rights organizations were also added to the data set. Beginning in 1988, the project began to add from several TelNet information sources. This later would be supple-

mented by internet sources. For the last 5 years, information has been added from the *Island* as well as the online editions of the *Daily Mirror* and *Daily News.* In addition, other sources include the Sri Lankan Army news site, TamilNet, TamilCanadian, EPDP news, and Colombopage."

77. Asian Development Bank, UN, and World Bank, "Humanitarian Needs Assessment in Sri Lanka," 2003, 32.

78. Norwegian Refugee Council, "Displaced Need More Help to Resettle in Safety and with Dignity," as reproduced in *Peace Monitor* 5 (4) (2003): 16–20.

79. The *Sunday Times* claimed that 30,000 Sri Lankan army soldiers had deserted as of December 2000, contributing to a significant upsurge in armed robberies and other violent crimes. *Sunday Times,* 24 December 2000.

80. Ganeshalingam, "Arrest and Detention," 86.

81. Amnesty International, *Sri Lanka: Balancing Human Rights & Security: Abuse of Arrest & Detention Powers in Colombo,* Amnesty International Index ASA 37/10/94 (London: Amnesty International, 1994), 4.

82. Amnesty International, *Sri Lanka,* 6–7.

83. See Chapter 6, Brendan O'Leary's contribution on the IRA. See also Brendan O'Duffy, "The Price of Containment: The Effect of Violence on Parliamentary Debate on Northern Ireland 1964 to 1993," in Peter Catterall and Sean McDougal, eds., *The Northern Ireland Question in British Politics* (London: Macmillan, 1996).

84. In May 2000, President Kumaratunga, acting under Public Security Ordinance No. 26 (1947, as amended) signed Emergency (Miscellaneous Provisions and Powers) Regulations No. 1.

85. J. C. Weliamuna and Dhanajaya Tilakaratna, *Emergency (Miscellaneous Provisions and Powers) Regulations No. 1 of 2000: A Review* (Colombo: INFORM, 2000), 28.

86. UN Commission on Human Rights, "Report of the Working Group on Enforced or Involuntary Disappearances," Document E/CN.4/1999/62, 28 December, 1999.

87. Kethesh Loganathan, "Reflections on the Intersection of Human Rights and Ethnic Conflict," *Peace Monitor* 5 (4) (2003): 5–6.

88. Ibid., 6.

89. Jehan Perera, "Call for Constructive Engagement," *Peace Monitor* 5 (4) (2004): 13.

90. "Smiles That Conceal the Worries," *Economist,* London, 18 July 2002.

91. See also Chalk, "Liberation Tigers," p. 4.

92. Brendan O'Duffy, *Self Determination and Conflict Regulation in Sri Lanka, Northern Ireland and Beyond,* Research Monograph (Colombo: International Centre for Ethnic Studies, 2003).

93. The Centre for Policy Alternatives (Colombo) Peace Confidence Index Topline Survey showed that the fear of federalism leading to secession declined from 41.8 percent in September 2003 to only 15.8 percent in February 2004. *Social Indicator* (Colombo: Centre for Policy Alternatives), p. 31.

94. The Norwegian-led Sri Lanka Monitoring Mission (SLMM) reported that during the 28-month truce period (from February 2002) there were a total of 4,903 complaints to the SLMM against the LTTE and 961 against the government, including 146 killings attributed (by the Sri Lankan government) to the LTTE. The LTTE attributes the majority of the killings to collusion between the Sri Lankan army and anti-LTTE Tamil groups.

95. India secured leases on extensive oil tanks in Trincomalee in 2001 in competition with U.S. interests. Free trade agreements have also led to significant acquisitions in oil service stations by the Indian Oil Corporation.

96. R. Cheran, "Diaspora Circulation and Transnationalism as Agents for

Change in Post Conflict Zones of Sri Lanka," policy paper submitted to Berghof Foundation for Conflict Management, Berlin, 2004.

97. One precedent had a significant impact on the ceasefire and negotiations in Northern Ireland: U.S. president Clinton's decision to override the advice of the State Department and grant Sinn Féin President Gerry Adams a visa to the United States in 1994, while the IRA was proscribed in Britain and Sinn Féin banned from public expression. The incident temporarily damaged U.S.-UK diplomatic relations but had a significant effect on Adams's ability to sell the ceasefire to hard-liners in the republican movement, demonstrating that a commitment to constitutional politics gave the movement access to the U.S. government and interstate recognition.

**Chapter 9**

1. Coca is the traditional Andean plant from which cocaine is produced.

2. In Peru in the1980s, well before the events of 9/11, officials, the media, civil society organizations, and most citizens—including politicians and activists on the left—routinely used the language of "terrorists" and "terrorism" when referring to Sendero. Sendero Luminoso's violence against civil society organizations, peasants, leftist political parties, journalists, academics, and others was broadly condemned and was viewed as wholly distinct from the long tradition of guerrilla struggle that spread throughout the continent following the 1959 Cuban Revolution.

3. José Carlos Mariátegui, "The Problem of the Indian," in *Seven Interpretive Essays on Peruvian Reality* (Austin: University of Texas Press, 1971).

4. There are parallels with the emergence of revolutionary groups in Colombia. Many of the founding members of the Colombian ELN, a pro-Cuban group, came out of the youth wing of a dissident Liberal faction, the Revolutionary Liberal Movement. The FARC emerged from the Liberal guerrillas of the 1940s and '50s; see Chapter 2. In Peru, a similarly named Ejército de Liberación Nacional (ELN, National Liberation Army) was founded by Héctor Béjar Rivera and largely drawn from the Aprista youth wing. After a period of training in Cuba, the ELN infiltrated combatants into southern Peru from Bolivia. In 1963, following a major military defeat in the jungles, the ELN moved operations to Ayacucho and were defeated there by early 1966. A second group, the Movimiento de la Izquierda Revolucionaria (MIR, Movement of the Revolutionary Left), was founded by Luís de la Puente Uceda with other former APRA militants in 1962 and operated mostly in the Department of Cusco bordering Ayacucho. In 1965, de la Puente was killed in action and the MIR was effectively destroyed.

5. Alfred C. Stepan, "The New Professionalism of Internal Warfare and Military Role Expansion," in Alfred C. Stepan, ed., *Authoritarian Brazil: Origins, Policies, and Future* (New Haven, Conn.: Yale University Press, 1973), 47–68.

6. Many Latin American insurgencies have justified recourse to arms as legitimate when used against the despotic caudillos that dominated much of the region's history after independence or later against the repressive, authoritarian militaries that took power across the region in the 1960s and 1970s. Che Guevara, in his classic text, *Guerrilla Warfare*, described the region's despots as "Caribbean Dictators" and asserted that these regimes were most ripe for revolution. He later claimed that the conditions for revolution were everywhere in Latin America given the region's endemic inequality, social exclusion, and poverty, even in those nations with nominal democratic governments. See Ernesto "Che" Guevara, *Guerrilla Warfare* (Lincoln: University of Nebraska Press, 1985). The Argentina guerrillas, the Montoneros, and the Uruguayan Tupumaros also emerged during a period of dem-

ocratic rule. However, the launching of a populist, Maoist war in Peru at the moment of democratic transition was unusual in comparative terms.

7. Abimael Guzmán, "Entrevista del Siglo: Presidente Gonzalo rompe el silencio," *El Diario*, Lima, 24 July 1988. *El Diario* is a Senderista newspaper that circulated freely during this period in the streets of Lima.

8. See note 4.

9. For a detailed history of the MRTA, see Comisión de la Verdad y Reconciliación Perú (Truth and Reconciliation Commission Peru), *Informe final* (*Final Report*) (Lima: Comisión de la Verdad y Reconciliación Perú, 2003), in particular, vol. 2, chap. 4 and app. 11, "Transcript of Video Broadcast to TRC of Victor Polay Campos, principal leader of MRTA, captured in May 1992." All the volumes of the TRC report are available online in Spanish at http://www.cverdad.org.pe, accessed 20 July 2005.

10. The election of APRA in 1985 was a historic achievement for the party. APRA throughout the twentieth century was Peru's largest and most institutionalized party but had been blocked from the presidency since its founding in the 1920s. In the presidential election of 1931, the party's founder, Victor Raúl Haya de la Torre, claimed that he was denied victory though fraud. In July 1932, APRA militants staged a bloody popular rebellion in Trujillo, Haya de la Torre's hometown, and executed about sixty army officers. In retaliation, the army killed more than a thousand Apristas. The events in Trujillo set up what political scientists Ruth Berins Collier and David Collier called "difficult and impossible games" between APRA and the armed forces that were to last for over half a century. Ruth Berins Collier and David Collier, *Shaping the Political Arena: Critical Junctures, the Labor Movement, and Regime Dynamics in Latin America* (Princeton, N.J.: Princeton University Press, 1991). In 1961, Haya de la Torre won a plurality of the vote but the military immediately staged a coup to prevent him from taking office. Haya de la Torre was elected president of the 1979 Constituent Assembly but died before reaching the presidency. The election of García, then, was a triumph for the party, but it carried with it the legacy of the historic distrust between the party and army that would have an impact on the conduct of the war. See Enrique Obando, "Civil-Military Relations in Peru, 1980–1996: How to Control and Coopt the Military (and the Consequences of Doing So)," in Steve Stern, ed., *Shining and Other Paths: War and Society in Peru, 1980–1995* (Durham, N.C.: Duke University Press, 1998).

11. Comisión de la Verdad y Reconciliación Perú, *Hatun Willakuy: Versión abreviada del Informe Final de la Conisión de la Verdad y Reconciliación: Peru* (Lima, 2004), 164.

12. Guzmán 1988 cited in ibid., 165; my translation.

13. Ibid., 169.

14. Some of the research for this and subsequent sections of this chapter was obtained through interviews conducted during three research trips to Ayacucho and the Rio Apurimac Valley, in July 1993, May 1994, and August 2004, the latter expressly made to research this chapter. I wish to thank my friend, guide, and mentor on Ayacucho, Huanta, and Rio Apurimac politics, the journalist Alejandro "Chan" Coronado, for arranging and accompanying me on each of these trips. During the war, Coronado was the president of the Association of Journalists of Huanta. When I met him, several of his predecessors in this post had been assassinated or disappeared. Today he continues to work as a journalist in Huanta and operates a television station there.

15. See TRC, *Final Report*, vol. 2, 23.

16. Ibid., 97.

17. Ponciano del Pino H., "Family, Culture and 'Revolution': Everyday Life with Sendero Luminoso," in Stern, *Shining and Other Paths*, 176.

18. TRC, *Final Report*, vol. 4, 32.

19. The number two leader in the PCP-SL was Osmán Moróte, son of a former rector of the University of Huamanga (UNSCH). Morote was captured in 1988 and remains in prison today. As an undergraduate at UNSCH, he wrote an anthropology thesis on feudal social relations in the province of Huanta, one of eleven provinces in the Department (State) of Ayacucho. He focused on one hacienda, Chaca, in the high altitude areas of Huanta, where he did his fieldwork while organizing and indoctrinating the campesinos in the area. I read Morote's thesis in the library of UNSCH when I first visited Ayacucho in 1992. It described a feudal agrarian structure of servile Indians exploited by *misti* (Quechua for mestizo) landowners. He likened the social system of the region to China in the 1930s, following the general interpretation of Peru by Abimael Guzmán. In July 1992 and again in August 2004, I went out to visit Chaca. In 1992, the hacienda was in ruins. Today it is the site of the small village of Chaca. In interviews conducted in 1992 in the nearby town of San José with civil patrol (*ronda campesina*) leaders, the men stated that the military government's agrarian reform was never implemented in this area of Huanta, even though formally it was decreed. The agrarian reform, including the killing of the owner of the Chaca hacienda, was implemented by Sendero Luminoso after it launched the "popular war" in 1980. Although Guzmán's analysis of a feudal society on the model of Peru in the 1930s had little basis for the whole of Peru, it held some truth when applied to the remote, high altitude areas of the Department of Ayacucho. The communities I visited in this region of Huanta first supported Sendero before turning against it in the mid-1980s.

20. del Pino, "Family, Culture and Revolution," 161.

21. Ibid., 170.

22. See, for example, the seminal text on Sendero, Gustavo Gorriti, *Sendero: Historia de la Guerra milenaria en el Perú* (Lima: Editorial Apoyo, 1990).

23. Michael Smith, "Taking the High Ground: Shining Path and the Andes," in David Scott Palmer, ed., *Shining Path of Peru* (New York: St. Martin's Press, 1992), 19.

24. TRC, *Final Report*, vol. 4, 48.

25. del Pino, "Family, Culture and Revolution," 162.

26. Truth and Reconciliation Commission, *Final Report*, vol. 4, 47.

27. Bruce H. Kay, "King Coca and Shining Path," *Journal of Interamerican Studies and World Affairs* 41 (3) (1999): 104.

28. José E. González, "Guerrillas and Coca in the Upper Huallaga Valley," in Palmer, *Shining Path of Peru*, 123.

29. Kay, "King Coca and Shining Path," 104.

30. See Paul Collier, "Economic Causes of Civil Conflict and Their Implications for Policy," World Bank Policy Research Paper, 2000.

31. Kay, "King Coca and Shining Path," 103.

32. Coca production moved to Colombia largely as a result of the U.S. "war on drugs" and the implementation in the early 1990s of its "airbridge denial strategy," a policy that shut down the air corridors between the coca fields in Peru and the processing laboratories in Colombia. Unable to transport the coca northward, drug traffickers began planting in Colombia, in areas similar to the Alto Huallaga River Valley: high jungle, limited or no state institutional presence, history of guerrilla activity in the zone that can be used to defend against national and U.S. antinarcotics programs.

33. Ronald H. Berg, "Peasant Responses to Shining Path in Andahuaylas," in Palmer, *Shining Path of Peru*, 96.

34. Steve Stern called such behavior *resistant adaptation.* See "Nueva approximación al studio de la conciencia y de las rebeliones campesinas: Las implicaciones de la experencia andina," in Steve Stern, ed., *Resistancia, rebelión y conciencia campesina en los Andes, Siglos VVIII al XX* (Lima: Instituto de Estudios Peruannos, 1990). Stern's concept was also adapted by del Pino and Carlos Iván Degregori in chapters written for Stern's excellent edited book on Sendero, *Shining and Other Paths.*

35. James Scott, *Weapons of the Weak: Everyday Forms of Peasant Resistance* (New Haven, Conn.: Yale University Press, 1985). The obvious irony here is that Scott wrote about situations of traditional exploitation between the landowners and rural laborers. In Peru in the 1980s, the resistance was not against large, semifeudal landowners but against a totalitarian revolutionary movement.

36. del Pino, "Family, Culture and Revolution," 161.

37. Interview with leader of the Antisubversive Self-Defense Committee, Comité de Autodefensa Anti-Subversiva, San Francisco, Ayacucho (Rio Apurimac Valley), July 1993.

38. See note 19.

39. Interview in San José de Secce, Huanta (Ayacucho), July 1993. Ten years after this interview, TRC interviewed thousands of victims and survivors from all regions of the country. The *Final Report* also lists three primary reasons for the rebellion against Sendero based on the Commission's extensive interviews. They summarized the reasons as follows: "The first was the intromission of Senderista groups in the community's commercial relations when they pretended to close the rural farmers markets—practically the only commercial link between the communities and the market—and to obligate the peasants to produce exclusively for their own subsistence, under the slogan 'starve the cities.' . . . The second reason was the summary executions, popular tribunals, of the village authorities. . . . The third reason was the lack of respect shown to the community's traditional authorities and the imposition of young people to govern, threatening and often assassinating elected mayors, justices of the peace, and others." Truth and Reconciliation Commission, *Final Report*, vol. 4, 64.

40. *Hatun Willakuy*, 300.

41. Guatemalan Historical Clarification Commission, *Guatemala: Memoria del Silencio, Mandato y procedimiento de trabajo*, 1999, chap. 1, at http://shr.aaas.org/guatemala/ceh/mds/spanish/, accessed 25 July 2005.

42. Marc Chernick, "Colombia: Does Injustice Cause Violence?" in Susan Eckstein and Timothy Wickham-Crowley, eds., *What Justice? Whose Justice? Fighting for Fairness in Latin America* (Berkeley: University of California Press, 2003).

43. Mauricio Romero, *Paramilitaries y autodefensas: 1982–2003* (Bogotá: Universidad Nacional de Colombia, 2003).

44. See Human Rights Watch, *Peru Under Fire: Human Rights Since the Return of Democracy* (New Haven, Conn.: Yale University Press, 1992).

45. See Carlos Iván Degregori, *Las rondas campesinas y la derrota de Sender Luminoso* (Lima: Instituto de Estudios Petuanos/Universidad Nacional San Cristóbal de Huamanga, 1996).

46. See Cynthia McClintock, *Revolutionary Movements in Latin America: El Salvador's FMLN and Peru's Shining Path* (Washington, D.C.: U.S. Institute of Peace Press, 1998).

47. The TRC received direct testimony that allowed it to specifically identify 23,969 Peruvians who were killed or disappeared as a result of the armed conflict. Of these, 18,397 were identified with complete names (first name and two last names as is customary in Peru). Yet the TRC was aware that many more people were killed than it was able to document through direct testimony. To get an accurate

account, it applied a statistical method, multiple systems estimation, developed by the Human Rights Data Analysis Group of the American Association for the Advancement of Science (AAAS). This method was used to reach the total number of fatal victims, the geographic distribution of the violence, and the final attribution of responsibilities for deaths and disappearances. The TRC's methods had a 5 percent statistical margin of error. Thus the minimum number of deaths and disappearances as a result of the armed conflict is 61,007 and the maximum number is 77,552. This statistical method had previously been applied in Guatemala by the Historical Clarification Commission and in Kosovo as part of expert testimony in the case against Slobodan Milosevic for war crimes and crimes against humanity in the International Criminal Tribunal for Crimes in the Former Yugoslavia in The Hague. See Truth and Reconciliation Commission, *Final Report*, app. 3, "¿Cuantos Peruanos Murieron?" (How Many Peruvians Died?), 4–6.

48. Guatemalan Historical Clarification Commission, *Guatemala: Memoria del Silencio*, chap. 1.

49. For a comparative discussion of Truth Commission findings, see Priscilla B. Hayner, "Fifteen Truth Commissions, 1974–1994: A Comparative Study," *Human Rights Quarterly* 1 (4) (1994): 597–655.

50. TRC, *Final Report*, 29, my translation.

51. Ibid., 123–24, my translation.

52. In an important precedent in international human rights law, the Inter-American Court of Human Rights in March 2001 found the amnesty to be invalid because it unlawfully provides impunity for crimes enumerated in the American Convention on Human Rights. *Hatun Willakuy*, 31.

**Chapter 10**

1. Compiled from figures given in the special note by the National Intelligence Organization, Prime Ministry, "PKK/KADEK/KONGRA-GEL Gelisimi (Evolution of PKK/KADEK/KONGRA-GEL), provided upon the request of the author in September 2004; and the information sheet entitled "Rakamlarla PKK Faaliyetleri ile Mucadele" (Encountering PKK Activities in Numbers), http://www.yesil.org/terror/pkkrakamlar.htm, accessed 9 April 2005.

2. Henri J. Barkey and Graham E. Fuller, *Turkey's Kurdish Question* (Lanham, Md.: Rowman and Littlefield, 1998).

3. Ibid., quoting Abdullah Öcalan's testimony in court (Document 8: Court Minutes, 3 June 1999), 389.

4. Ali Nihat Ozcan, *PKK (Kurdistan Isci Partisi), Tarihi, Ideolojisi ve Yontemi* (PKK: Kurdistan Workers' Party, Its History, Ideology and Method) (Ankara: ASAM Publications, 1999).

5. Ismet Imset, *PKK: Ayrilikci Siddetin 20 Yili* (The PKK: 20 Years of Separatist Violence) (Ankara: Turkish Daily News Publications, 1992).

6. Mahsum Hayri Pir, *Bir Yanilsamanin Sonu* (End of a Fallacy) (Istanbul: Komal, 2000), 382, 385, 388, 392. Öcalan repeated these sentences several times during his pretrial interrogation by the prosecutor on 3 April 1999 as well as at his trial on31 May, 3 June, 23 June 1999.

7. *Turkiye Buyuk Millet Meclisi Milletvekili Listesi, 21. ve 22. Donem* (List of Deputies of the 21st and 22nd Term of the Grand National Assembly of Turkey), http://www.tbmm.gov.tr/develop/owa/milletvekili_sd.liste, accessed 16 November 2004.

8. TOBB (Union of Chambers of Commerce and Industry of Turkey), *Dogu Sorunu: Teshisler, Tespitler* (The Eastern Question: Diagnosis and Findings), Special Report, 1995.

9. Abdullah Öcalan, "Document 10: Court Minutes, June 29, 1999," quoted in Pir, *Bir Yanilsamanin Sonu*, 392.

10. Interview given by Abdullah Öcalan to his lawyers, who in turn conveyed his words to *Ozgur Politika* (*Free Politics*), a Kurdish newspaper, which published it under the title, "Kurdistan Demokratik Konfederalizmi Ilan Edildi" ("The Democratic Confederalism of Kurdistan Has Been Declared)," 3 March 2005.

11. Istanbul Police Department, Counter-Terrorism Division, *KADEK (PKK)* (Istanbul: Government Publication, 2003), 1–40.

12. Ibid., 6.

13. Murat Yetkin, *Kurt Kapani: Sam'dan Imrali'ya Ocalan* (Kurdish Trap: Öcalan from Damascus to Imrali) Istanbul: Remzi Kitabevi, 2004).

14. Istanbul Police Department, *KADEK (PKK)*, 32.

15. M. Huseyin Buzoglu, *Korfez Savasi ve PKK* (Gulf War and the PKK) (Ankara: Dogus, 1997), 99–110; Ely Karmon, "The Showdown Between the PKK and Turkey—Syria's Setback," 1998, commentary ICT, Israel, http://www.ict.org.il/articles/articledet.cfm?articleid=55, accessed 17 December 2003.

16. Kemal Kirisci and Gareth M. Winrow, *The Kurdish Question and Turkey: An Example of a Trans-State Ethnic Conflict* (London: Frank Cass, 1997), 146–51; Barkey and Fuller, *Turkey's Kurdish Question*, 84–107.

17. Abdullah Öçalan's statement in prison publicized through his lawyers, quoted in Pir, *Bir Yanilsamanin Sonu*, 228–29.

18. Umit Ozdag, "The PKK and Low Intensity Conflict in Turkey," *Ankara Papers*, ASAM-Eurasian Center for Strategic Studies (London: Frank Cass, 2003).

19. This figure is an approximation derived from interviews conducted with police chiefs of southeastern Turkey in summer and fall 2004 who requested to remain anonymous.

20. "KADEK on the List of Terrorist Organizations," http:www.geocities.com/Paris/Tower/1252/11th1202.htm, accessed 15 January 2004; "Terror Organizations in Turkey," http:www.terror.gen.tr/english/turkey/separatist/pkk/aim.html, accessed 15 January 2004.

21. Abdullah Öcalan, *Bir Halki Savunmak* (Defending a People), TOBB Report (Istanbul: Cetin Publishers, 2004).

22. Dogu Ergil, "Suicide Terrorism in Turkey," *Civil Wars* 3 (1) (2000): 37–54.

23. Interview with Kemal Bulbul, an active Kurdish politician who has been a member of DEHAP and an observer of the movement, 4–8 October 2004.

24. Pir, *Bir Yanilsamanin Sonu*, 339–40, 356–57; Ozcan, *PKK*, 214–16.

25. Compiled from figures given in the special note by the National Intelligence Organization, "PKK/KADEK/KONGRA-GEL Gelisimi," and the information sheet, "Rakamlarla PKK Faaliyetleri ile Mucadele," http://www.yesil.org/terror/pkkrakamlar.htm, accessed 9 April 2005.

26. Tarik Ziya Ekinci, *Turkiye'nin Kurt Siyasetine Elestirisel Yaklasimlar* (Critical Approaches to Turkey's Kurdish Policy) (Istanbul: Cem, 2004).

27. Sabri Dilmac, *Terorizm Sorunu ve Turkiye* (*The Terrorism Problem and Turkey*) (Ankara: General Directorate of Internal Security #55, 1997), 192–200.

28. Abdullah Öcalan's testimony in court, quoted in Pir, *Bir Yanilsamanin Sonu*, 358.

29. Martin van Bruinessen, *Agha, Shaikh and State* (London: Zed Books, 1992).

30. Anadolu Ajansi (Anatolian News Agency), news release, 28 August 2003.

31. Baskin Oran, ed., *Turk dis Politikasi* (Turkish Foreign Policy), 5th ed. (Ankara: Iletisim, 2002), 230–31.

32. Tarik Ziya Ekinci, *Avrupa Birligi'nde Azinliklarin Korunmasi Sorunu ve Kurtler* (Protection of Minorities in the European Union and the Kurds) (Istanbul: Cem, 2001).

33. Turkish Human Rights Foundation, "Human Rights 2004," http://www.tihv.org.tr/basin/bas2005yilbasi.html, accessed 2 March 2005.

34. Abdullah Öcalan's testimony, Pir, *Bir Yanilsamanin Sonu*, 364–65.

35. Interview with Bulbul, 4–8 October 2004; interview with Mr. Ibrahim Guclu, Vice President of a Kurdish party called HAKPAR (Rights and Liberties), 4–6 December 2004.

36. The PUK, the Patriotic Union of Kurdistan (in Iraq), is led by Jalal Talabani. The PUK, like the PKK, included Marxists and Maoists among its founders and had been sponsored by Syria and Iran at various junctures, all of which may explain why Osman Öcalan and his supporters felt at ease resettling in the province of Sulaimania. Presently, the Kurdistan Region of Iraq is under going reunification, under a common Parliament and Cabinet, and the distinction between KDP- and PUK-administered Kurdistan is expected to disappear.

37. Anadolu Ajansi (Anatolian News Agency), news release, 18 February 2005.

38. The "Document of Mutual Understanding" is found on the TOSAM web site, www.tosam.org/english/html, accessed 20 June 2005.

39. State Institute of Statistics 2000, www.die.gov.tr/Ist Tablolar/04nf025t.xls, accessed 13 April 2005.

**Chapter 11**

1. Meena Acharya, "The Economic Foundations of the Current Socio-Political Crisis in Nepal," in D. B. Gurung, ed., *Nepal Tomorrow: Voices and Visions* (Kathmandu: Koselee Prakashan, 2003), 238.

2. Arjun Karki and Binod Bhattarai, *Whose War? Economic and Social Impacts of Nepal Maoist-Government Conflict* (Kathmandu: NGO Federation of Nepal, 2004).

3. The RPP party is divided in two factions: Thapa broke off from the mainstream RPP to form government when asked to do so by the king, but without support from his party, especially its chairman Pashupati Shamsher J. B. Rana, who subsequently participated in demonstrations against the government. Other attempts to decentralize and focus on ethnicity became evident when the armed Rural Voluntary Security Groups and Peace Committees were formed (after 4 November 2003). Many have raised objections to such groups being formed because they have little training. People who are ordered to take part in such committees may become sitting targets for the Maoists. Amnesty International. International Conflict Group (ICG), *Nepal: Dangerous Plans for Village Militias* (Brussels: ICG Asia Briefing, 17 February 2004).

4. Michael Hutt, ed., *Himalayan People's War: Nepal's Maoist Rebellion* (Bloomington: Indiana University Press, 2004), 11, app. B.

5. Amnesty International, "Disappearances Must Stop" (ASA 31/050/2003), 16 October 2003.

6. Many have raised the question of whether the army was ever under "democratic control." As the general manager for a hydropower plant in Nepal, I had many dealings with the military. In one meeting in which we sought the deployment of troops to protect our installations, participation was called with representatives from the military, the Ministry of Defense, and the Ministry of Foreign Affairs. It was canceled when the military told the ministerial representatives that they could not be deployed to protect "private industry." The army acted entirely independently of the Ministries; we were told that they would take commands only from their supreme commander, the king. Later the government and parliament were dissolved (4 October 2002), and the army expanded and created a special industrial force in 2004 that was instrumental in the royal takeover in 2005.

7. In the early 1970s a Norwegian missionary recorded sporadic attempts at guerrilla fighting and attempts on the life of the king, but there was no nationwide movement behind the incidents. Robert Bergsaker, *Gjennom Mystikkens land til Tibets Grense* (Oslo: Filadelfiaforlaget AS, 1977), chap. 9, 97–106, "Geriljan slår til."

8. I have been an election observer at all elections in Nepal after 1990 and agree that many irregularities took place—booth-capture, buying of votes, slaveowners voting in the name of their slaves, and so on. Whether these violations were sufficient wholly to discredit the election results is debatable.

9. Especially targeted was Prime Minster Koirala, who was ordered to step down because of corruption scandals involving the national airline, but within the Congress Party he has somehow managed to retain power in his and his family's hands. His case is still pending in the Supreme Court.

10. Harald O. Skar, "The Janajati, Nationalism, and the Shining Path," *Himal* 7 (3) (1994).

11. Amnesty Internationa, "Disappearances Must Stop" (ASA 31/050/2003), 16 October 2003.

12. Interview with Padma Rathna Tuladar, conflict mediator, March 2004.

13. Harald O. Skar, "The CPN (Maoist) Insurgence in Nepal: Imagined Structures and Real Power," paper presented at seminar at Macalester College, St. Paul, Minnesota, February 2004; *Himalayan Research Bulletin* forthcoming.

14. *Kathmandu Post* 1 July 2002, www.Kantipuronline.com.

15. The Maoists announced their own local elections in "liberated areas" across the villages of Achham, Kalikot, and Bajura in the Maoist-controlled heartland of midwestern Nepal. To counter the government's move to nominate village development committee members, they conduct their own elections for village and district "people's governments." Of the 75 VDCs in Achham, 62 have held elections; in 30 the Maoists won unanimously, and in 8 local representatives were appointed by the Maoist party. In Kalikot to the north, independent candidates won some positions in four village-level elections while the Maoists swept all positions in 13 of the VDCs. http://www.Nepalnews.com mbk, accessed 27 January 2004.

16. *Maoist Information Bulletin* 8, "Demand for Round Table Conference and Constituent Assembly," http://www.cpnm.org, accessed 20 January 2004.

17. In *Maoist Information Bulletin* 8 we may read:

In the . . . context of the existence of two ideologies, two armies and two states in the country, the Party is agreeable to demobilization of both the armies and carrying out of elections to the Constituent Assembly under the supervision of United Nations Organization and international human rights organizations.

• The content of the new Maoist constitution would further be:

(a) Political

Full sovereignty to the people; secular state; elected house of representatives as the highest representative body of the people; reorganization of a unified national army; provision of national and regional autonomy along with rights of self-determination; provision of constitutional changes or refinement according to the wishes of the people; guarantee of multiparty competition, periodic elections, adult franchise, rule of law and fundamental rights including freedom of speech and press; provision of special rights for women and dalits (i.e., oppressed caste); etc.

(b) Economic

Revolutionary land reforms for judicious redistribution of land on the principle of "land to the tiller"; self-reliant and national industrial policy; promotion and development of national capital; formulation of an integrated national policy for proper utilization of natural resources; etc.

(c) Social

Development of a mechanism for strict punishment to the corrupt, smugglers and profiteers; development of employment-oriented national and scientific education system; universal health service; provision of state care for the destitute, the elderly and the children; end to all forms of exploitation, discrimination and dishonor to women and dalits; guarantee of minimum wages and workers' participation in industrial management; guarantee of intellectual & academic freedom and professional rights; promotion of democratic and scientific culture in place of feudal and imperialist reactionary culture; plan of integrated national infrastructure development; guarantee of full employment to all; fulfilment of demands of class and mass organizations; etc.

(d) Foreign Policy

- Independent foreign policy of maintaining friendly relations with all on the basis of Panchasheel (i.e. five principles of peaceful coexistence) and non-alignment.
- Abrogation of all unequal treaties from the past and conclusion of new treaties and agreements on a new basis. [criticism of present relations with India, HS].
- Promotion of good neighbourly relations with neighbouring India and China with mutual cooperation in the fields of utilization of natural resources, trade and transit, etc. for mutual benefit, keeping in view the particularity of economic, political, cultural, historical and geographical relations with them.

18. Population Census 2001.

19. UNDP Human Development Report 2000.

20. Scott Gates and S. Mansoob Murshed, "Spatial-Horizontal Inequality and the Maoist Insurgency in Nepal," paper prepared for the UNU/WIDER Project Conference on Spatial Inequality in Asia (London: DIFID/PRIO, 2003).

21. The conclusion is based upon econometric analyses using UNDP 1998 districtwide data on human development indicators for 1996, the year the conflict commenced, districtwide data on landlessness as well as geographical characteristics, alongside figures for fatalities in all of the districts of Nepal, using intensity of conflict (measured by numbers of deaths) as the dependent variable, and HDI indicators and landlessness as explanatory variables. Gates and Murshed, "Spatial-Horizontal Inequality," 2.

22. Gary Leupp, "The Resumption of History, Imagining the Global Consequences of a Maoist Victory in Nepal," *CounterPunch*, New York, 21 October 2002.

23. The Maoist-affiliated All Nepal Trade Union Federation (Revolutionary), ANTUF-R called for the immediate closure of Soaltee Hotel, Surya Nepal Pvt. Ltd. (tobacco), Bottlers Nepal Ltd, Elite Oil Store, Tankeshwar Garment industry, Pashupati Spinning Mill, Shanhai Plastic industry, Norsang Carpet, Shrawan Garment, Yeti Fabric, and Makule Yatayat Pvt. Ltd., accusing the companies of exploiting the workers and spying against their party. It is estimated that 5,000 to 7,000 people will be affected. *Kathmandu Post*.

24. Ram Sharan Sedha, "Nepal Urged to Sign Mine Ban Treaty," *Kathmandu Post*, 18 September 2003: "Bangkok, Thailand, Sept 19—In the wake of renewed violence unleashed by the Maoists in Nepal, Jody Williams, the co-laureate of the 1997 Nobel Peace prize, has urged the Nepal government to sign the Mine Ban Treaty also known as the Ottawa Convention. Referring to the growing use of landmines by both the state and Maoist rebels in the seven year long Maoist insurgency, the anti-mine champion said, 'Nepal should sign the Mine Ban Treaty.'"

25. John Norris, "Hard Times in the Himalayas," *The Observer*, London, 13 April 2003.

26. Maoists killed an informer (*suraki*) in January 2005 and the incident was reported to the Bandara command, but no one came for fear of an ambush.

When the east-west highway was blocked a week later, the same command told the locals that they had to clear the road themselves as they were fed up with bombs hidden in debris. Indian dacoits again robbed some houses in 2005. No police or military arrived. The dacoits had kidnapped one Nepalese girl as they were trying to portray themselves as Maoists, who always had girls with them. Later the real Maoists killed the dacoits. In February 2005 the military did provide escorts for 30–40 vehicles to the closed off capital, and protection in the tourist center of Sauraha, where the shop owners were forced by the military to open their shops even during *bandh.* However, the state's presence is irregular, leading to doubt that help would come if one really needed it.

27. A young man from my family was threatened and bullied at gunpoint for more than two hours and told to follow a group of armed men who presented themselves as Maoists. He continued to refuse and was later told he was lucky, as they were in fact the RNA, and he would have been shot if he had agreed to go with them.

28. "Maoists Abduct over 1,300 in Eastern Nepal," 23 April 2004, http://www.nepalnews.com pd, 22 April 2004.

29. Amnesty International, "Disappearances Must Stop."

30. *Himalayan Times,* 25 February 2003.

31. The CPN-UML is led by Madav Kumar Nepal, previous minister of foreign affairs during the 1994 UML government. He was the agreed candidate for prime minister from the five parties when they jointly demonstrated against regression through peaceful demonstrations in Kathmandu and the rest of Nepal. He visited Norway in February 2002 and again in the winter of 2004 on his way to the U.S.

32. Sudheer Sharma, "The Maoist Movement, an Evolutionary Perspective," in Deepak Thapa, ed., *Understanding the Maoist Movement of Nepal,* Chautari Book Series 10 (Kathmandu: Centre for Social Research and Development, 2003).

33. Karki and Bhattarai, *Whose War,* 180.

34. The Magars are one of the lowest-ranking caste groups in Nepal, according to the Muluki Ain—the 1854 caste law, officially abolished in 1990, but still followed in most aspects of general life.

35. Meanwhile, the URPC issued a "Directory for Administration of People's Power, 2004," to bring harmony to the administration of local people's power in base areas throughout the country. There are separate chapters for the administration of autonomous regions and local bodies, general administration, public security, revolutionary land reform, forest management, industry, commerce and finance, people's cooperatives, physical infrastructure development, public health, public education, people's culture, and social welfare. Similarly a public legal code has been formulated to administer the New Democratic people's power.

36. "Previously, we had provided sufficient amount of services to the locals so that they supported "the company" rather than the Maoists, but this slowly changed and we were forced to bring in military support." Himal Power Ltd.,"Evacuation Procedures After Threats to the Power Plant" (Kathmandu: HPL, 1999).

37. In the political wing, the important Maoist leaders include "Comrade Parvati," Krishna Bahadur Mahara, Ram Bahadur Thapa alias Badal, Matrika Yadav, Deb Bahadur Gurung, Krishna Dhoj Khadka, Rekha Sharma, Rabindra Shrestha, Bamdev Chhetri and Mumaram Khanal (September 2004).

38. S. N. M. Abdi, "Power Plays," Profile 3, in Thapa, *Understanding the Maoist Movement.*

39. Baburam Bhattarai, *Asia Times,* 2000.

40. The *Asia Times* adds that Bihar police suspect one of the top ideologues of the Nepalese Maoists, Baburam Bhattarai, is hiding in Bihar. Educated at Delhi's

Jawaharlal Nehru University, Bhattarai is believed to have close links with the MCC and the People's War Group (PWG). The cooperation between these groups is not a new development. As early as December 2001, the MCC and PWG resolved to support the Maoist insurgents in Nepal.

41. Council of World Affairs, as quoted in September 2004.

42. This area is also called Naya Muluk (new land). It was given back to Nepal in 1856 (for helping to quench the revolt in India) after it had been taken away in the Sugauli Treaty with the British in 1816. Due to very strong ties with India it was neglected by the Nepalese state and the first major road was constructed only as late as in the 1980s. It is a very poor area with a large Tharu ethnic population.

43. Harald O. Skar, ed., *Nepal: Tharu and Terai Neighbours*, Bibliotheca Himalayica 3, 16 (Kathmandu: EMR, 1998).

44. Paul Collier et al. 2003. *Breaking the Conflict Trap*, World Bank Policy Research Report (Washington, D.C.: World Bank, 2003), 69, http://econ.worldbank.org/prr/CivilWarPRR/.

45. *Kathmandu Post*, 4 November 2003.

46. Quoted from http://www.nepalnews.com, 25 January 2001.

47. Ibid., 9 April 2004.

48. Participating parties and organizations of the Revolutionary Internationalist Movement include Ceylon Communist Party (Maoist), Communist Party of Afghanistan, Communist Party of Bangladesh (Marxist-Leninist) (BSD-ML), Communist Party of Nepal (Maoist), Communist Party of Peru, Communist Party of Turkey Marxist-Leninist (TKP ML), Marxist-Leninist Communist Organisation of Tunisia, Maoist Communist Party (Italy), Marxist-Leninist Communist Organisation of Tunisia, Proletarian Party of Purba Bangla (BPSP) (Bangladesh), Revolutionary Communist Group of Colombia, Revolutionary Communist, Party, USA Communist Party of Iran (Marxist-Leninist-Maoist). In addition there are candidate participants of RIM in a number of countries who are struggling to form vanguard Marxist-Leninist-Maoist parties.

49. Resolution adopted by the Second Annual Conference of the Co-ordination Committee of Maoist Parties and Organizations of South Asia, 15 September 2002.

50. For a review of the tactics and relationships between Prachanda and Guzman, see Skar, *Nepal: Thera and Terai Neighbors.*

51. Committee of the Revolutionary Internationalist Movement, "Statement on the Occasion of the 7th Anniversary of the initiation of the People's War in Nepal," 24 February 2003, distributed by A World to Win News Service.

52. *Kathmandu Post*, 19 August 2004.

53. http://www.nepalnews.com, 22 January 2004.

54. http://www.nepalnews.com, 27 August 2004. Although the source I am mostly quoting with reference to day-to-day events is Nepalnews.com, this does not indicate that it is the only source of information; see Dhruba Hari Adhikary, "Media: Press, Power, and Pressure" in Gurung, ed., *Nepal Tomorrow*, 595–607. Nepalnews.com reviews all current news in major papers, quotes other sources, and evaluates their reliability. As Kunda Dixit, one of the leading newspaper editors, said: "Up until 1 January 2005, probably no country in the world had so few restrictions on the press as Nepal, and what a difference one day makes" (Headlines Today, Indian TV Channel, 5 January 2005, 6 p.m.). Nepalnews.com is now censored with regard to actual reports from the war zone (casualties, etc.) except those provided by the government. This censorship does not affect arguments in this chapter. To verify the authenticity of the items I listened to the BBC news in Nepalese. For quotations I have preferred to use a written source rather than my memory-based review. The BBC in Nepalese has been said to have been instrumen-

tal in the 1999 revolution, and as of February 2005 is one of the few independent sources left since the king introduced total censorship and ban on Maoist news.

55. Nepalese People's Progressive Forum, Belgium, "Statement VZW 6437/ 2001" regarding asylum for those prosecuted by Royal Nepalese Army.

56. "Joint Picket Rally in Front of Brussels-Based Indian Embassy Demand: Immediate Unconditional Release of Com Guarare," *Cpmnews*, 15 November 2003. Also listed on the CPN (M) Web site.

57. "International Displacement, Pressure on Cities," *Spotlight*, Kathmandu, 23 (12), 12–18 September 2003.

58. Leupp, "The Resumption of History."

59. http://www. nepalnews.com, 16 November 2002.

60. Prakash A. Raj, *Maoists in the Land of Buddha* (Kathmandu: Nirala, 2004); Committee of the Revolutionary Internationalist Movement, "Statement by the RIM on the Occasion of the 7th Anniversary."

61. Skar, *Nepal: Tharu and Terai Neighbours.*

62. Harald O. Skar, "Myths of Origin: The Janajati Movement, Local Traditions, Nationalism and Identities in Nepal," *Contributions to Nepalese Studies* 5 (1) (1995); Skar, "Nepal, Indigenous Issues and Civil Rights, the Plight of the Rana Tharu." in R. H. Barnes, Andrew Gray, and Benedict Kingsbury, eds., *Indigenous Peoples of Asia*, Monograph 48 (Ann Arbor, Mich.: Association for Asian Studies, 1999); and Skar, "The CPN (Maoist) Insurgence in Nepal."

63. Although the Nepalese state itself had a traditional army, the Rana rulers all had military titles. They encouraged citizens to serve in foreign armies and thus the population as such had advanced experience with weapons. Gurkha soldiers had served in many tight spots with the British; by the late 1990s, a large number of retired soldiers (retirement generally occurs at age 40–45) were to be found in the majority of villages throughout Nepalese hill districts. When the war started these soldiers were coerced or forced (one such case reported in Khimti) by the guerrillas to train the cadres. The tradition of recruiting solders in the valleys also served the army, as they called out a large number of new individuals to serve. In general the lower ranks of the army had always been poor families' opportunity for extra income and a large portion of revenue still comes from soldiers serving overseas. Today, the soldiering trade has also become an employment opportunity for the poor who want to stay in Nepal. Aditya Man Shrestha, *Bleeding Mountains of Nepal* (Kathmandu: Ekta, 1999).

64. Government estimates in early 2003 that the CPN (M) movement's strength indicated approximately 5,500 combatants, 8,000 militia, 4,500 cadres, 33,000 hardcore followers, and 200,000 sympathizers. See South Asia Terrorism Portal), Nepal Terrorist Groups—Communist Party of Nepal-Maoist (Washington, D.C.: Institute for Conflict Management, 2004), http://www.satp.org/countries/nepal/terrorist outfits/index.html, accessed October 2003.

65. Skar, "The CPN (Maoist) Insurgence in Nepal."

66. Amnesty International, "Disappearances Must Stop."

67. http://www.nepalnews.com, Manoj Rijal, 4 December 2004.

68. Skar, "The CPN (Maoist) Insurgence in Nepal."

69. Baburam Bhattarai, the chief negotiator from the Maoist side of the Peace Talks, directly blames this incident for the breakdown of the talks: "The most serious and provocative incident was the massacre of nineteen unarmed political activists by the RNA in Doramba (Eastern Nepal) on the very day of start of third round of talks on August 17," *Monthly Review*, 7 September 2003.

70. http://www.nepalnews.com, 7 January 2002.

71. Interview with Padma Rathna Tuladar, conflict mediator, March 2004.

72. *Kathmandu Post*, 1 July 2002.

73. See ICG , "Nepal: Obstacles to Peace," *Asia Report* 57 (2003): note 21, p. 7 for full text.

74. *Kathmandu Post*, 30 March 2003.

75. http://www.CNN.com/2003/world/asiapcf/south/05/09/nepal.talks/index .html, 9 May 2003.

76. http://www.nepalnews.com, 6 January 2003.

77. *Time Asia*, 26 January 2004.

78. Most quoted is the British envoy Sir James Jeffrey and ICG (UK) reports.

79. All major parties except Congress joined this government, which is not elected but directly appointed by the king.

80. "Deputy Prime Minister Bharat Mohan Adhikari has said the government's position on holding peace talks with the Maoists remains unchanged. Adhikari's comments have come nearly a week after a Maoist statement that they will not hold peace negotiations with the Sher Bahadur Deuba-led government. In the statement, the Maoist supremo, Prachanda, however, said his party was ready to hold direct negotiations with HM king Gyanendra. Earlier, the rebels had said they were ready to sit for peace negotiations with the government in the presence and with support of the United Nations," htttp://www.nepalnews.com, 7 September 2004.

81. Nepal does not at this time have a credit rating. Alex Parry, *Time* Magazine, 25 April 2003.

82. "International Displacement, Pressure on Cities."

83. U.S. Department of State, "Patterns of Global Terrorism 2002," publication 11038, http//:www.state.gov/s/ct/rls/, accessed April 2003.

84. Maoists have added a fresh demand that the government should annul the Memorandum of Understanding on "terrorism" signed with the US government and "expel" all "US security advisors currently in Nepal" (*Kathmandu Post*, 28 July 2002). Bounties on the heads of senior Maoists were dropped; Interpol arrest warrants were rescinded; and the government agreed to stop calling the Maoists "terrorists."

85. Raj, *Maoists in the Land of Buddha*, 186; Committee of the RIM statement.

86. http://www.nepalnews.com, 22 September 2004.

87. Rudiger Wenk, Chargé d'Affaires of the European Commission delegation in Nepal, said that "The EC had first approached the Nepalese government offering to act as mediator on October 24, 2002." http://www.nepalnews.com, 30 September 2003.

88. Interview with ambassador Ofstad March 2004.

89. As reported in *Kathmandu Post*, 10 September 2004.

90. http://www.nepalnews.com, 16 September 2004.

91. http://www.nepalnews.com, 17 September 2004.

**Conclusion**

1. Conversation between Ernest Gellner and Brendan O'Leary, Central European University, Budapest, November 1995.

2. Monty G. Marshall and Ted Robert Gurr, *Peace and Conflict 2005* (College Park, Md.: Center for International Development and Conflict Management, 2005), 65; emphasis ours.

3. The phrase is now associated with Brigadier Frank Kitson's book, *Low Intensity Operations: Subversion, Insurgency and Counter-Insurgency* (London: Faber, 1971). Kitson is regarded by many as the eminence grise of UK counterinsurgency operations in Northern Ireland, the Middle East, and Malaysia.

4. Robert B. Asprey, *War in the Shadows: The Guerilla in History* (1975; Boston: Little, Brown 1994). Our contributors agree that terrorism, the deliberate killing of noncombatants, can be perpetrated by states as well as by guerrillas. Bruce Hoffman, *Inside Terrorism* (New York: Columbia University Press, 1998), tries to distinguish guerrillas from terrorists by size and by the fact that the former exercise "some form of sovereignty or control over a defined geographical area and its population," whereas terrorists, do not function in the open as armed units, and do not generally attempt to seize territory (41). Our group analyze matters differently: small, large, and governmental armed units can all employ terrorist methods. Small groups if they expand may move from exclusively small-scale terrorist actions to guerrilla warfare to conventional war. Small groups may well have statal ambitions—and use terrorism as their starting points.

5. Robert Taber, *The War of the Flea: Guerrilla Warfare Theory and Practice* (London: Paladin, 1965, 1977).

6. See William D'Arcy, *The Fenian Movement in the United States: 1858–1886.* (New York: Russell and Russell, 1971); Robert Kee, *The Green Flag,* vol. 2, *The Bold Fenian Men* (London: Quartet Books, 1976); Séan McConville, "The Dynamitards," in McConville, *Irish Political Prisoners 1848–1922: Theatres of War* (London: Routledge, 2003), 326–36.

7. But see inter alia Martha Crenshaw, "The Effectiveness of Terrorism in the Algerian War," in Crenshaw, ed., *Terrorism in Context* (University Park: Pennsylvania State University Press, 1995).

8. See the still very pertinent collection organized by Clark McCauley, ed., *Terrorism and Public Policy* (London: Frank Cass, 1991).

9. David Rapoport, "Terrorism," in M. E. Hawkesworth and Maurice Kogan, eds., *Routledge Encyclopedia of Government and Politics,* vol. 2 (London: Routledge, 1992).

10. For a strong argument in this vein see Alan B. Kreuger and David D. Laitin, "'Misunderestimating' Terrorism," *Foreign Affairs* 83 (5) (September/October 2004): 8ff.

11. This is a fair summation of the theses advanced in Daniel Benjamin and Steven Simon, *The Age of Sacred Terror* (New York: Random House, 2002), and which Crenshaw disputes (presentation at SSRC/NUPI and U.S.I.P. conference on terrorism, 18 September 2005, Washington, D.C.). During the Clinton administration Benjamin and Steven were respectively the National Security Council's director for counterterrorism and the first senior director of counterterrorism.

12. See, e.g., Benjamin Netanyahu, ed., *Terrorism: How the West Can Win* (London : Weidenfeld and Nicolson, 1986) or Alan M. Dershowitz, *Why Terrorism Works: Understanding the Threat, Responding to the Challenge* (New Haven, Conn.: Yale University Press, 2002); Paul Wilkinson, *Terrorism and the Liberal State,* 2nd ed. (Basingstoke: Macmillan, 1986).

13. Phil Rees, *Dining with Terrorists: Meetings with the World's Most Wanted Militants* (Basingstoke: Macmillan, 2005). Rees's publicity claims he has been the sole Western journalist to have traveled and filmed with Algeria's Islamic militants—an assertion that might warrant an interview with Robert Fisk (although the latter is not a filmmaker).

14. Marc Sageman, *Understanding Terror Networks* (Philadelphia: University of Pennsylvania Press, 2004).

15. Andrew Silke, "The Road Less Traveled: Trends in Terrorism Research," in Silke, ed., *Research on Terrorism: Trends, Achievements and Failures* (London: Frank Cass, 2004), 186–213.

16. Ariel Merari, "Academic Research and Government Policy on Terrorism," *Terrorism and Political Violence* 3 (1) (1991): 88–102, 91.

17. Andrew Silke, "The Devil You Know: Continuing Problems with Research on Terrorism," *Terrorism and Political Violence* 13 (4) (2001): 1–14.

18. C. Frankfort-Nachimas and D. Nachimas, *Research Methods in the Social Sciences*, 5th ed. (London: Arnold, 1996), 10.

19. It is remarkable how many of the research questions lucidly suggested in an excellent overview essay from fifteen years ago remain underexplored; Martha Crenshaw, "The Logic of Terrorism as the Product of Strategic Choice, and Questions to be Answered, Research to be Done, Knowledge to be Applied," in Walter Reich, ed., *Origins of Terrorism* (Cambridge: Cambridge University Press, 1990), 257–60.

20. We are skeptical of the promise of epidemiological modeling in terrorism research. The metaphor suggests that terrorism is a disease; it neglects to treat insurgents as agents; there may be no very useful analogues to pandemics, species-jumping, morphing of viruses, or inoculations and immunization. Public policy is more than public health. The speed with which infections form and travel is rather different from the initial formation and recruitment of insurgent groups. By contrast, modeling work that considers the mechanisms that may trigger "tipping points" in support or losses of support for insurgents may offer long-run value.

21. The U.S. National Science and Technology Council report, *Combating Terrorism: Research Priorities in the Social, Behavioral and Economic Sciences* (Washington, D.C., 2005) has a summary of needs and priorities. They include as "immediate priorities and capabilities": developing database infrastructures, the application of modeling methods (computational, game theoretic, and agent-based), enhancing public health capabilities, applying the decision sciences to risk communications, and applying risk, threat and vulnerability assessment and vulnerability models. These are to be supplemented by "capability development and needs": developing biometric and bio-imaging technologies, elucidating neural mechanisms (of fear, hope, vulnerability, and resilience), the development of "robust, valid models" of the psychobiological and psychosocial mechanisms of distress and resilience—and of robust (cross-cultural) models of social behaviors, social prejudice and stigmatization, the development and integration of major domestic and international databases, and developing methods that allow for the sharing of classified data. The political and legal sciences are not highlighted, no doubt because they are not regarded as sciences.

22. Martha Crenshaw, "The Causes of Terrorism," *Comparative Politics* 13 (1981): 379–99.

23. Clark R. McCauley, "The Psychology of Terrorism," essay published on the Web site of America's Social Science Research Council, http://www.ssrc.org/sept11/essays/mccauley.htm.

24. The words of Shining Path's leader, Guzmán, as cited by C. I. Degregori, "Harvesting Storms: Peasant *Rondas* and the defeat of Sendero Luminoso in Ayacucho," in Steve J. Stern, ed., *Shining and Other Paths: War and Society in Peru, 1980–1995* (Durham N.C.: Duke University Press, 1998), p. 143.

25. McCauley, "The Psychology of Terrorism."

26. See inter alia James B. Rule, *Theories of Civil Violence* (Berkeley: University of California Press, 1988), and Donatella della Porta, *Social Movements, Political Violence, and the State* (Cambridge: Cambridge University Press, 1995).

27. Economistic readings of insurgents are surprisingly unimaginative or partial when considering the multiple logics of economic incentives. For example, James Adams's 1986 book, *The Financing of Terror: Behind the PLO, IRA, Red Brigades, and M-19 Stand the Paymasters: How the Groups That Are Terrorizing the World Get the Money To Do It* (New York: Simon and Schuster, 1986), was one of the first to describe

the IRA as a mafia. Many of his stories from the 1970s and 1980s showed the IRA manipulating currency, customs. and EU livestock subsidy regulations in cross-border smuggling operations, or defrauding the Inland Revenue or unemployment bureaus. He did not treat such activities as "economic war" by the IRA. Indeed, he could not make up his mind whether the profits extracted were devoted to the cause or spent on beer (in which case the IRA would have been fairly ineffective, and he should have welcomed such a diversion from terrorism). He reported officials' skepticism about police estimates of frauds and rackets before concluding that the key to destroying the IRA was to attack its economic base. But buried in his rhetoric was an observation whose implications he had overlooked. He had observed that elections for Sinn Féin cost far more than violence for the IRA. These relative prices, if his estimates were right, should have incentivized Irish republicans toward violence and away from politics. If so, they obviously failed to do so (perhaps the relative prices shifted again?). We make these observations not because we believe in economistic explanations, but to illustrate how frequently partial they are, and how are rarely they are fully explored.

28. Gary King, Robert D. Keohane, and Sidney Verba, *Designing Social Inquiry: Scientific Research in Qualitative Research* (Princeton, N.J.: Princeton University Press, 1994), 22.

29. See John McGarry and Brendan O'Leary, *The Northern Ireland Conflict* (Oxford: Oxford University Press, 2004).

30. See, e.g., Nechemia Friedland and Ariel Merari, "The Psychological Impact of Terrorism: A Double-Edged Sword." *Political Psychology* 6 (4) (1985): 591–604.

31. Kieran McEvoy, *Paramilitary Imprisonment in Northern Ireland: Resistance, Management and Release* (New York: Oxford University Press, 2001); J. Bates-Gaston, "Terrorism and Imprisonment in Northern Ireland: A Psychological Perspective," in Silke, ed., *Terrorists, Victims and Society*, 233–55.

# Contributors

SUMANTRA BOSE, professor of comparative politics at the London School of Economics and Political Science, received his Ph.D. in political science from Columbia University. His research concentrates on conflict management and democratization in societies with protracted ethnopolitical divisions. His books include *Kashmir: Roots of Conflict, Paths of Peace, Bosnia After Dayton,* and *The Challenge in Kashmir.*

MARK CHERNICK is visiting associate professor in the Department of Government and the Center for Latin American Studies at Georgetown University and director of the Georgetown-UNDP Project on Democratic Conflict Prevention and Early Warning in Latin America. He received his Ph.D. in political science from Columbia University. He has written widely on issues in Colombia and the Andean region.

DOĞU ERGIL, professor of political science at Ankara University, received his Ph.D. from the State University of New York, Binghamton. He has written widely in both English and Turkish on the PKK and on other issues facing Turkey.

JEROEN GUNNING, deputy director of graduate studies, Department of International Politics, University of Wales, received his Ph.D. from the University of Durham. His research includes Middle Eastern politics, political Islam, the Arab-Israeli conflict, democratization, social movement theory, and terrorism.

MARIANNE HEIBERG (1945–2004) was senior researcher at the Norwegian Institute of International Affairs. She received her Ph.D. in social anthropology from the London School of Economics and Political Science in 1981. A Middle East policy expert, she served as director of UNRWA and special advisor to UNESCO's Culture for Peace Program. The Oslo Agreement was partly negotiated in her home.

BRENDAN O'DUFFY, senior lecturer in politics at Queen Mary College, University of London, received his Ph.D. from the London School of Economics and Political Science. His research is focused on nationalism and ethnic conflict regulation, especially in Northern Ireland, Sri Lanka, and Cyprus.

BRENDAN O'LEARY, Lauder professor of political science and director of the Solomon Asch Center at the University of Pennsylvania, received his Ph.D. from the London School of Economics and Political Science. His numerous publications include *Explaining Northern Ireland, The Northern Ireland Conflict* and *The Future of Kurdistan in Iraq.*

KIRSTEN E. SCHULZE, senior lecturer in international history at the London School of Economics and Political Science, received her D.Phil. from Oxford University. Her research interests include security sector reform, ethnic conflict, peace processes, and nationalism. Her books include *Tolerance on Trial, The Free Aceh Movement, The Jews of Lebanon,* and *Israel's Covert Diplomacy in Lebanon.*

ANDREW SILKE is professor in the School of Law and field leader for criminology and director of terrorism studies at the University of East London. He has published extensively on terrorists and terrorism, recently editing *Terrorists, Victims and Society* and *Research on Terrorism.*

HARALD OLAV SKAR, senior research associate at the Norwegian Institute of International Affairs, received his D.Phil. in social anthropology at Oxford University. His areas of research and publishing include development planning and environmental and social impact assessment in many parts of the world.

JOHN TIRMAN, executive director of the Center for International Studies at the Massachusetts Institute of Technology, received his Ph.D. from Boston University. He is the author of numerous books on international affairs, including *The Fallacy of Star Wars* and *Spoils of War.*

# Index